The Wiley Blackwell Companion to Human Geography

Wiley Blackwell Companions to Geography

Wiley Blackwell Companions to Geography is a blue-chip, comprehensive series covering each major subdiscipline of human geography in detail. Edited and contributed by the disciplines' leading authorities each book provides the most up to date and authoritative syntheses available in its field. The overviews provided in each *Companion* will be an indispensable introduction to the field for students of all levels, while the cutting-edge, critical direction will engage students, teachers, and practitioners alike.

Published

A Companion to Feminist Geography
Edited by Lise Nelson and Joni Seager

A Companion to Environmental Geography
Edited by Noel Castree, David Demeritt, Diana Liverman, and Bruce Rhoads

A Companion to Health and Medical Geography
Edited by Tim Brown, Sara McLafferty, and Graham Moon

A Companion to Social Geography
Edited by Vincent J. Del Casino Jr., Mary Thomas, Ruth Panelli, and Paul Cloke

The Wiley Blackwell Companion to Human Geography
Edited by John A. Agnew and James S. Duncan

The Wiley Blackwell Companion to Economic Geography
Edited by Eric Sheppard, Trevor J. Barnes, and Jamie Peck

The Wiley-Blackwell Companion to Cultural Geography
Edited by Nuala C. Johnson, Richard H. Schein, and Jamie Winders

The Wiley-Blackwell Companion to Tourism
Edited by Alan A. Lew, C. Michael Hall, and Allan M. Williams

The Wiley Blackwell Companion to Political Geography
Edited by John Agnew, Virginie Mamadouh, Anna J. Secor, and Jo Sharp

The New Blackwell Companion to the City
Edited by Gary Bridge and Sophie Watson

The Blackwell Companion to Globalization
Edited by George Ritzer

The Handbook of Geographic Information Science
Edited by John Wilson and Stewart Fotheringham

The Wiley Blackwell Companion to Human Geography

Edited by

John A. Agnew and James S. Duncan

WILEY Blackwell

This paperback edition first published 2016
© 2011 John Wiley & Sons, Ltd

Edition history: Blackwell Publishing Ltd (hardback, 2011)

Registered Office
John Wiley & Sons, Ltd, The Atrium, Southern Gate, Chichester, West Sussex, PO19 8SQ, UK

Editorial Offices
350 Main Street, Malden, MA 02148-5020, USA
9600 Garsington Road, Oxford, OX4 2DQ, UK
The Atrium, Southern Gate, Chichester, West Sussex, PO19 8SQ, UK

For details of our global editorial offices, for customer services, and for information about how to apply for permission to reuse the copyright material in this book please see our website at www.wiley.com/wiley-blackwell.

The right of John A. Agnew and James S. Duncan to be identified as the authors of the editorial material in this work has been asserted in accordance with the UK Copyright, Designs and Patents Act 1988.

All rights reserved. No part of this publication may be reproduced, stored in a retrieval system, or transmitted, in any form or by any means, electronic, mechanical, photocopying, recording or otherwise, except as permitted by the UK Copyright, Designs and Patents Act 1988, without the prior permission of the publisher.

Wiley also publishes its books in a variety of electronic formats. Some content that appears in print may not be available in electronic books.

Designations used by companies to distinguish their products are often claimed as trademarks. All brand names and product names used in this book are trade names, service marks, trademarks or registered trademarks of their respective owners. The publisher is not associated with any product or vendor mentioned in this book.

Limit of Liability/Disclaimer of Warranty: While the publisher and authors have used their best efforts in preparing this book, they make no representations or warranties with respect to the accuracy or completeness of the contents of this book and specifically disclaim any implied warranties of merchantability or fitness for a particular purpose. It is sold on the understanding that the publisher is not engaged in rendering professional services and neither the publisher nor the author shall be liable for damages arising herefrom. If professional advice or other expert assistance is required, the services of a competent professional should be sought.

Library of Congress Cataloging-in-Publication Data
The Wiley Blackwell companion to human geography / edited by John A. Agnew and James S. Duncan.
   p. cm.
  Companion v. to: Human geography. 1996.
  Includes bibliographical references and index.
  ISBN 978-1-4051-8989-7 (hardcover : alk. paper)
  ISBN 978-1-1192-5043-2 (paperback)
  1. Human geography. I. Duncan, James S. II. Human geography.
  GF41.W535 2011
  304.2–dc22
                                                         2010041033

A catalogue record for this book is available from the British Library.

Cover image: Striding Arches by Andy Goldsworthy,
Bail Hill, Moniaive, Dumfries and Galloway.
© South West Images Scotland / Alamy.

Set in 10/12.5pt Sabon by SPi Global, Pondicherry, India

Printed in Singapore by C.O.S. Printers Pte Ltd

Contents

List of Illustrations — viii

Notes on Contributors — x

1 Introduction — 1
John A. Agnew and James S. Duncan

Part I Foundations — 9

2 Where Geography Came From — 11
Peter Burke for David Lowenthal

3 Cosmographers, Explorers, Cartographers, Chorographers: Defining, Inscribing and Practicing Early Modern Geography, c.1450–1850 — 23
Robert J. Mayhew

4 Colonizing, Settling and the Origins of Academic Geography — 50
Daniel Clayton

Part II The Classics — 71

5 German Precursors and French Challengers — 73
Vincent Berdoulay

6 Creating Human Geography in the English-Speaking World — 89
Ron Johnston

7 Landscape Versus Region – Part I — 114
Nicolas Howe

	8	Landscape Versus Region – Part II *Kent Mathewson*	130
	9	From Region to Space – Part I *Trevor J. Barnes*	146
	10	From Region to Space – Part II *Anssi Paasi*	161

Part III Contemporary Approaches   177

	11	Nature – Part I *Noel Castree*	179
	12	Nature – Part II *Jamie Lorimer*	197
	13	Landscape – Part I *Don Mitchell and Carrie Breitbach*	209
	14	Landscape – Part II *Mitch Rose and John W. Wylie*	221
	15	Place – Part I *Tim Cresswell*	235
	16	Place – Part II *Steven Hoelscher*	245
	17	Territory – Part I *Stuart Elden*	260
	18	Territory – Part II *Jacques Lévy*	271
	19	Globalization – Part I *Richard Florida*	283
	20	Globalization – Part II *Emily Gilbert*	298
	21	World Cities – Part I *Carolyn Cartier*	313
	22	World Cities – Part II *Paul L. Knox*	325
	23	Governance – Part I *Wendy Larner*	336
	24	Governance – Part II *Stephen Legg*	347
	25	Mobility – Part I *David Ley*	361

26	Mobility – Part II *George Revill*	373
27	Scale and Networks – Part I *Andrew E.G. Jonas*	387
28	Scales and Networks – Part II *John Paul Jones III, Sallie A. Marston, and Keith Woodward*	404
29	Class – Part I *Andrew Herod*	415
30	Class – Part II *Clive Barnett*	426
31	Race – Part I *Kay Anderson*	440
32	Race – Part II *Arun Saldanha*	453
33	Sexuality – Part I *Natalie Oswin*	465
34	Sexuality – Part II *Mary E. Thomas*	475
35	Gender – Part I *Michael Landzelius*	486
36	Gender – Part II *Joanne P. Sharp*	501
37	Geopolitics – Part I *Phil Kelly*	512
38	Geopolitics – Part II *Merje Kuus*	523
39	Segregation – Part I *Larry S. Bourne and R. Alan Walks*	534
40	Segregation – Part II *Steve Herbert*	547
41	Development – Part I *Glyn Williams*	559
42	Development – Part II *Wendy Wolford*	575

Index   588

Illustrations

Figures

3.1	1472, Isidor T-O Map	24
3.2	Mount Chimborazo	25
10.1	The "space of keywords" in human geography and some social and Institutional background factors	164
16.1	Austin: Not Like Other Places	249
16.2	Plantation Owner. Mississippi Delta, near Clarksdale, Mississippi	253
16.3	Plantation Owner. Mississippi Delta, near Clarksdale, Mississippi. This shows the same image as cropped by Archibald MacLeish, Land of the Free (1938)	254
16.4	British air attack on Hamburg, Germany, January 1943	255
16.5	The war wrecked streets of Cologne, Germany	256
19.1	Global Distribution of Population	285
19.2	Global Distribution of Economic Activity	285
19.3	Global Distribution of Innovation	286
19.4	Global Distribution of Scientists	287
19.5	The Mega-Regions of North America	290
19.6	The Mega-Regions of Europe	291
19.7	The Mega-Regions of Asia	292
27.1	The scope of human geography as defined by hierarchical scales of analysis	389
27.2	The English city-regions as a discrete scale of analysis	391
27.3	The international geography of the credit union movement in 2004	393
27.4	The imagined territory of Padania in northern Italy	394
27.5	Multilingual restaurant sign in the Barri Gotic district of Barcelona in northeastern Spain	398
27.6	An ad campaign showing how HSBC has skillfully played on the ambiguity of scalar metaphor and branded itself as "the world's local bank"	400
41.1	North-South Divisions, according to the Brandt Line	562

Tables

18.1	An Elementary Classification of Metric	277
22.1	Alpha-level world cities in 2008	332
41.1	The Development of International Development in the late 20th Century	565

Contributors

John A. Agnew is Professor of Geography at UCLA, Los Angeles, USA. He specializes in political geography. His recent publications include *Globalization and Sovereignty* (2009), *Berlusconi's Italy* (with Michael Shin, 2008), and *Sage Handbook of Geographical Knowledge* (co-edited with David Livingstone, 2011).

Kay Anderson is Professor of Cultural Geography at the Centre for Cultural Research, University of Western Sydney. She has authored the award-winning books *Race and the Crisis of Humanism* (2007) and *Vancouver's Chinatown* (1991), plus many publications about race, historiography and Cultural Geography.

Trevor J. Barnes is a Professor and Distinguished University Scholar at the Department of Geography, University of British Columbia, where he has taught since 1983. His research interests are in economic geography and the history and philosophy of the discipline.

Clive Barnett is Reader in Human Geography at The Open University in Milton Keynes, England. He is author of *Culture and Democracy* (2003), co-author of *Globalizing Responsibility* (2011), and co-editor of *Spaces of Democracy* (2004), *Geographies of Globalisation* (2008), *Extending Hospitality* (2009), and *Rethinking the Public* (2010).

Vincent Berdoulay is Professor of Geography and Regional Planning and member of the CNRS research center on Society, Environment and Territory (SET) at the Université de Pau, France. He chaired the IGU Commission on the History of Geographical Thought from 1996 to 2004. His major publications concern the history of geography and planning, epistemology and cultural geography.

Larry S. Bourne FRSC is Professor Emeritus of Geography and Planning, and the founding director of the new Cities Centre at the University of Toronto. His research interests focus on growth and change in urban Canada and on urban form, governance and social inequalities.

Carrie Breitbach is Assistant Professor of Geography at Chicago State University. With Don Mitchell she is the co-author of *Cultural Geography: A Critical Introduction* (forthcoming from Wiley Blackwell).

Peter Burke was Professor of Cultural History, University of Cambridge until his retirement and remains a Fellow of Emmanuel College. His books include *A Social History of Knowledge from Gutenberg to Diderot* (2000) a second volume, *From the Encyclopédie to Wikipedia*, is in preparation.

Carolyn Cartier is Professor of Human Geography and China Studies at the University of Technology, Sydney. She is the author of *Globalizing South China* (2001) and the co-editor of *The Chinese Diaspora: Place, Space, Mobility and Identity* (2003) among many other publications. Her current research program includes projects on the role of the state in China's urbanization process, and debates over art and culture in the political economy of development in Chinese cities. Forthcoming books are *China's Regional Worlds* and *Sudden Culture: Urban Redevelopment in Hong Kong and a Politics of Aesthetics*.

Noel Castree is a Professor of Geography in the School of Environment and Development at Manchester University. His principal research interest is in the dynamics of capitalism-environment relations. He has also written at length about the conceptual infrastructure of human geography and the wider social sciences – notably the ideas of nature, place and space-time. He is currently managing editor of the journal *Progress in Human Geography*.

Daniel Clayton is Lecturer in Geography at the University of St Andrews. He is the author of *Islands of Truth* (2000) and numerous articles on the relations between geography and empire.

Tim Cresswell is Professor of Geography at Royal Holloway, University of London, England. He has written widely on mobilities and place.

James S. Duncan was Reader in Cultural Geography, University of Cambridge until his retirement. He is now Emeritus Fellow of Emmanuel College. His books include *Landscapes of Privilege* (2004), *The City as Text* (2005), and *In the Shadows of the Tropics* (2007).

Stuart Elden is a Professor of Political Geography at Durham University, England. He is the author of four books, including most recently, *Terror and Territory: The Spatial Extent of Sovereignty* (2009). He is currently completing a history of the concept of territory.

Richard Florida is Director of the Martin Prosperity Institute and Professor of Business and Creativity at the Rotman School of Management, University of Toronto, Canada. Previously, Florida has held professorships at George Mason University and Carnegie Mellon University and taught as a visiting professor at Harvard and MIT. He is the author of numerous books on cities and globalization including *The Rise of the Creative Class* (2003).

Emily Gilbert is Associate Professor of Geography and Director of the Canadian Studies program at the University of Toronto. She is the co-editor of *War, Citizenship, Territory* (with Deborah Cowen, 2008) and *Nation-States and Money: The Past, Present and Future of National Currencies* (with Eric Helleiner, 1999). She has published on topics such as North American integration; monetary union; borders, biometrics and citizenship; and cultural representations of national identity.

Steve Herbert is Professor of Geography and Law, Societies, and Justice at the University of Washington. His research and teaching focus on the regulation of space through law and policing. He is the author of *Policing Space: Territoriality and the Los Angeles Police Department* (1977), *Citizens, Cops and Power: Recognizing the Limits of Community* (2006), and, with Katherine Beckett, *Banished: The New Social Control in Urban America* (2010).

Andrew Herod is Professor of Geography and Adjunct Professor of International Affairs and of Anthropology, at the University of Georgia, Athens, Georgia. He is also an elected official, serving as a member of the government of Athens-Clarke County, Georgia. He has written widely on issues of labor and globalization. His recent books include: *Scale* (2010), *Handbook of Employment and Society: Working Space* (2010), *Geographies of Globalization: A Critical Introduction* (2009), and *The Dirty Work of Neoliberalism: Cleaners in the Global Economy* (2006).

Steven Hoelscher is Professor of American Studies and Geography at the University of Texas at Austin. His publications include the books *Heritage on Stage*, *Picturing Indians*, and *Textures of Place* (co-edited with Paul Adams and Karen Till) and articles in the *Annals of the Association of American Geographers*, *Ecumene*, *The Geographical Review*, *Social and Cultural Geography*, and *American Quarterly*, among others.

Nicolas Howe is a Postdoctoral Fellow in Environmental Studies at Williams College, Williamstown, Massachusetts, USA. His research interests are in environmental disputes and controversies over religious symbols in public spaces.

Ron Johnston is Professor of Geography in the School of Geographical Sciences at the University of Bristol, having previously held posts at Monash University and the Universities of Canterbury, Sheffield and Essex. Alongside his interests in the history of geography as an academic discipline he has also written widely on electoral studies and urban social geography.

John Paul Jones III and **Sallie A. Marston** are Professors of Geography at the University of Arizona, USA, and **Keith Woodward** is Assistant Professor of Geography at the University of Wisconsin, Madison, USA. They define a research collective exploring the critical fissures of and alternative paths to ontology in human geography. Following the publication of *Human Geography without Scale* (2005), they continue to write articles devoted to elucidating the theoretical, methodological and empirical dimensions of site ontology.

Andrew E.G. Jonas is Professor of Human Geography at Hull University, England. He is interested in urban and regional development in the United States and Europe and has made a number of contributions to the scale debate in human geography. He recently co-edited *Interrogating Alterity: Alternative Economic and Political Spaces* (2010).

Phil Kelly is Professor of Political Science at Emporia (Kansas) State University. A previous Fulbright Scholar in Paraguay, he has authored *Checkerboards and Shatterbelts: The Geopolitics of South America* (1997) and has edited, with Jack Child, *Geopolitics of the Southern Cone and Antarctica* (1988).

Paul L. Knox is University Distinguished Professor in the College of Architecture and Urban Affairs at Virginia Tech, Blacksburg USA. He has published widely on world cities and questions of urban design.

Merje Kuus is Associate Professor of Geography at the University of British Columbia. Her work focuses on geopolitics and contemporary Europe. Dr. Kuus is the author of *Geopolitics Reframed: Security and Identity in Europe's Eastern Enlargement* (2007) as well as numerous articles on security, identity, and intellectuals of statecraft. Her current research investigates the geopolitical discourses and policy processes that organize European Union's external relations with its eastern neighbors.

Michael Landzelius is Docent in Built Environment Preservation and is presently Research Coordinator at the Department of Sociology, University of Gothenburg, Sweden. His work on embodiment; built space and commemorative practices; dehumanization; and spatial reification has been published in journals such as Society and Space and Semiotica, as well as in companions and edited volumes

Wendy Larner is Professor of Human Geography and Sociology, and Research Director for the Faculty of Social Science and Law, at the University of Bristol, UK. She has published widely on the topics of globalisation, governance and gender. Recent contributions include a co-edited collection called *Calculating the Social: Standards and the reconfiguring of governing* (2010). She is also completing a co-authored book called *Fashioning Globalisation: New Zealand Design, Working Women and the New Economy* (Wiley Blackwell).

Stephen Legg is an Associate Professor at the School of Geography, University of Nottingham. His research focuses on the cultural and historical geographies of urban and imperial politics in interwar colonial India. His publications include *Spaces of Colonialism: Delhi's Urban Governmentalities* (2007) and the edited volume *Spatiality, Sovereignty and Carl Schmitt: Geographies of the Nomos* (2011).

Jacques Lévy is Professor at EPFL in Lausanne, Switzerland. He is best known for his work on urbanization and globalization. His most recent book is *L'invention du monde: une géographie de la mondialisation* (2008).

David Ley is Canada Research Chair of Geography at the University of British Columbia, Vancouver. He is the author of *Millionaire Migrants* (2010), *The New Middle Class and the Remaking of the Central City* (1996) and other books and articles on social and neighborhood research in the city.

Jamie Lorimer is a Lecturer in the Department of Geography at Kings College London. He was worked previously at the Universities of Bristol and Oxford. His research interests include the geographies of wildlife conservation, volunteering and citizenship and human-animal relations. Past projects have focused on the UK and South Asia. He is currently developing research relating to the concept and practice of rewilding in European conservation.

Kent Mathewson is Professor of Geography at Louisiana State University, Baton Rouge USA. A Latin Americanist, he has published widely on the history of American cultural geography.

Robert J. Mayhew is Professor of Historical Geography and Intellectual History at the University of Bristol, UK. He is the author of *Enlightenment Geography* (2000) and of numerous articles about seventeenth- and eighteenth-century geography.

Don Mitchell is Distinguished Professor of Geography in the Maxwell School at Syracuse University. With Carrie Breitbach he is the co-author of *Cultural Geography: A Critical Introduction* (forthcoming from Wiley Blackwell).

Natalie Oswin is Assistant Professor of Geography at McGill University. She has published numerous articles on queer geographies in journals such as *Progress in Human Geography, Environment and Planning D: Society and Space, Transactions of the Institute of British Geographers* and *Gender, Place and Culture*.

Anssi Paasi is Professor of Geography at the University of Oulu, currently serving as an Academy Professor (2008–2012) at the Academy of Finland. He has publications on the development of geographical ideas and concepts, on region/territory building and on the socio-cultural construction of political boundaries and spatial identities. His books include *Territories, Boundaries and Consciousness* (1996).

George Revill is Senior Lecturer in Cultural Geography at the Open University. His research interests include cultural histories of travel and transport and the study of music, landscape and national identity. His most recent book is a cultural history of railways as an icon of modernity for Reaktion Press 2010.

Mitch Rose is a Lecturer in the Department of Geography at the University of Hull, UK. He writes on questions of landscape and material culture and is currently working on a monograph on landscape and identity

Arun Saldanha is Associate Professor of Geography at the University of Minnesota. He is author of *Psychedelic White: Goa Trance and the Viscosity of Race* (2007) and many articles on race, music, embodiment and travel.

Joanne P. Sharp is a Senior Lecturer in Geography at the University of Glasgow, UK. She is the author of *Geographies of postcolonialism: spaces of power and representation* (2009) and has published on feminist, political and postcolonial geographies.

Mary E. Thomas is an Assistant Professor with a joint appointment between the Departments of Geography and Women's Studies at Ohio State University, USA. Her research examines racial segregation among US youth, particularly teenage girls

R. Alan Walks is Associate Professor of Urban Planning and Geography at the University of Toronto. His published work examines the causes and consequences of neighborhood-level social and political inequality, and place effects on social and political outcomes.

Glyn Williams is a Senior Lecturer in the Department of Town and Regional Planning, University of Sheffield. He has taught and researched in Development Geography since the early 1990s, with his primary research interests being in poverty, participatory development, and everyday state practices, areas which he has explored through extensive fieldwork in India. He has two co-authored books *Seeing the State: Governance and Governmentality in India* (with Stuart Corbridge, Manoj

Srivastava and René Véron, 2005), and *Geographies of Developing Areas: The Global South in a Changing World* (with Paula Meth and Katie Willis, 2009).

Wendy Wolford is Polson Professor of Development Sociology at Cornell University. She is the author of *To Inherit the Earth* (with Angus Wright, 2003) and *This Land is Ours Now* (2010) as well as many articles about contemporary land reform and social mobilization.

John W. Wylie is Senior Lecturer in Cultural Geography at the University of Exeter, UK. He writes on the geographies of landscape, the self and performance and is the author of *Landscape* (2007).

Chapter 1

Introduction

John A. Agnew and James S. Duncan

Contemporary human geography in the English-speaking world is amazingly pluralistic in terms of its objectives, subject matter, theories, and methods. This is judged by some as a negative: the field is "a doughnut with a hole in the middle" because there is no agreement about some central theory or method, usually that preferred by the critic in question. A tendency to laud the most recent and fashionable ideas is similarly put in a dim light. On a more positive note, it is the very absence of a disciplining orthodoxy and the openness to fresh thinking that now makes the field so interesting to a broader audience. Indeed, the flow of influence of the field on others has increased as it has developed its own heterodox ideas about landscape, environment, space, and place rather than engaged in imitating biology, economics, or whatever other field by adopting their current orthodoxies. In our view, the reason for this is not hard to fathom. What seems undeniable is that we all live in a world in which geographic space has been subject to considerable social, economic, and political reformulation and as a consequence how we think about it must also change. If Michel Lussault's (2009) adage of *De la lutte des classes à la lutte des places* (perhaps best translated as "from class struggle to the struggle of how one fits into the new global spatiality of places") probably overstates the increased importance of place-to-place differences in a globalizing world and the degree to which the basis to many old conflicts has been transcended, it nevertheless captures the sense that old theoretical frameworks are not necessarily up to the task of dealing with new "realities." This is the paramount reason for the growth of new ways of thinking in human geography that also appeal to those in fields like literary studies, sociology, economics, international relations, and cultural anthropology. But some conventional approaches are also in crisis because collectively we have become aware of the degree to which established methods of mapping the world and theorizing about it reflect political-economic and technological eras

The Wiley Blackwell Companion to Human Geography, First Edition.
Edited by John A. Agnew and James S. Duncan.
© 2011 John Wiley & Sons, Ltd. Published 2016 by John Wiley & Sons, Ltd.

that are passing away. There is much discussion, for example, of the "crisis of cartographic reason" (e.g. Harley 1987; Farinelli 2009) and the unreliability of geographical fieldwork (e.g. Gerber and Goh 2000; Driver 2000). Human Geography has gone through a veritable renaissance over the past twenty years because its pluralization signifies the advent of new ways of thinking about environment, space, and place that help us "read" and engage with the changing world around us and engage with critiques of previously dominant practice (Lévy 1999).

The purpose of this volume is to survey the history and contemporary character of the field of human geography in the English-speaking world over a fairly long time period but with a definite emphasis on the contemporary. From the outset, we make no pretense to cover physical geography or contemporary non-English language human geography, except insofar as they have had direct impacts in this world. The book is designed to supplement rather than compete with the other *Blackwell Companions* addressing such sub-fields of human geography as economic, political, and cultural geography by surveying theoretical trends and substantive emphases that have influenced and shaped all of them. Given this focus, the volume will give considerable attention to historical context as well as to contemporary themes. Much of the concentration on "key concepts," "key thinkers" and "key trends" in recent publications about the field is missing much if any sense of historical context by which to judge how the present differs from the past. Indeed, a celebratory "presentism" often prevails in which the "new" is valued independently of either how much it contributes to the collective enterprise or how it fits into longer-term trends. But we also want to avoid merely duplicating within one volume the sub-field divisions of other *Companions* and other recent surveys (e.g. Benko and Strohmayer 2004). Thus, beyond chapters that assay the historical legacies of the field, we provide chapters that have a thematic rather than a sub-field orientation.

In both nominalist and more substantive registers, present-day human geography is still worth situating in relation to past efforts at organizing a field as such. There is still such a thing as the "geographical tradition" (Livingstone 1992). Much of what goes for geographic research even now involves some situating or positioning in relation to forebears or intellectual ancestors, if only to show how much they have been "left behind." In counterpoint to the tendency to dismiss the past as irrelevant to current concerns this volume will try to situate present debates and differences in relation to past ones. Consequently, the book will be divided into three sections: *Foundations*, tracing the history of human geography (as defined today) in terms of pre-professional ideas and influences from the ancient Greeks down until the late nineteenth century; *The Classics*, surveying the significant German and French as well as British, US, and other "roots" of later human geography and then emphasizing the creation of an academic discipline in the late nineteenth and early twentieth centuries and the attempts at providing an intellectual rationale for this initiative; and *Contemporary Approaches*, highlighting the ways in which the field is subdivided and how human geography is practiced today by examining a selection of themes with two different perspectives on each, and the operations of its practitioners in education and the larger world. In this final section we do not aim to have authors confront one another but simply offer their own perspectives on the same theme. The purpose is to emphasize divergent interpretations against the tendency to offer interpretations that suggest a general consensus of opinion or a uniform account of what has been happening over the past twenty years or so. We want to show the pluralism of the field at the same time we illustrate the degree to which recent trends draw on and legitimize themselves by reference to historic precursors.

Globalization and Human Geography

Globalization is a buzzword for a world that is seen as increasingly stretched, shrunk, interwoven, integrated, and less state-centered than in the past. It thus typically involves a claim about the changing nature of the world. But it also can involve a parallel claim that this world needs new theoretical tools or modes of understanding. Approximately since the 1970s when the US government's abrogation of the 1944 Bretton Woods Agreement liberated major world currencies to float freely against one another, tariff barriers to international trade (particularly in manufactured goods) decreased dramatically, as major corporations began to the see the world as "their oyster," and cultural flows of all sorts started to undermine images of "stability" and "homogeneity" in territorialized national states, past nostrums about social and moral order (typically located at the scale of the national state) have been thrown into question. Particularly significant for a field such as human geography, long sensitive to issues of scale and geographical differentiation, this has proved to be both crisis and opportunity. Often tagged by parallel if somewhat competing terms relating more to the character of theoretical perspectives than to ontological claims about the nature of the world, "postmodernism" and "postcolonialism" are perhaps the most well known, "globalization" has evolved into a complex theoretical notion relating to a significant degree to the overarching question of how cultural and political attachments are actively mediated through space, all the way from the local to the global, and how the complexities of identity in turn affect popular and academic understandings of the world and how it works. It remains contested because of the relative emphasis placed on the source of its "power" and whether it is deployed theoretically more ontologically or epistemologically. So, if the sociologist Ulrich Beck sees globalization as a movement to a totally "new modernity," the anthropologist James Clifford sees it as an emerging world of enhanced "mobility" both geographical and psychological, and the geographer David Harvey views it as an economic process involving strategies of capital investment made possible by new space-shrinking technologies (Harvey 2006). Clearly, Beck and Clifford would be more likely to make the claim for epistemological "new times" than would Harvey.

Critical, then, has been the question of the extent to which old or well established theories and methods can be adapted to the new circumstances or should be sidelined by "completely" novel ones. Understanding the interconnection of local places, ecologies, and cultural practices in global networks of greater and lesser geographical scope has become the leitmotif of the age. This is the context in which debate over the recent past and present of human geography must be situated. As you will see in the bulk of the chapters in the *Contemporary Approaches* section of this book, this is the recurring background condition for much contemporary thinking. Many of the disputes aired out there are based in different responses to how to deal with the sense of a dramatically changing world. A field such as human geography is not at all like, say, physics, because its very subject matter is contingent on an ever-changing external world of political and economic actors and cultural forms. Arguably, therefore, theoretical frameworks and research methods must change in tandem. That this does not necessarily entail the rise of some new singular theoretical orthodoxy, however, is also an important conclusion of what we have been saying above.

Chronology versus Tradition in Human Geography

Many accounts of the history of human geography are chronological not just in the sense of sets of ideas associated with or seen as dominant in different historical eras but of new ones replacing previous ones in a rigid sequence rather like in a cladistic or tree diagram of the evolution of species (e.g. James 1972; Peet 1998). Time seems to be a causal factor with some approaches becoming more "successful" as they branch off prior ones. This can be read as akin to the notion of "paradigm shifts" developed by Thomas Kuhn to apply to the history of physics. The story of human geography does not seem to fit very well with this conception of intellectual change (Philo 2008). Rather, the field seems to exhibit much more the relative persistence of many approaches over time with different eras associated only with the invention of new ones (and adaptation of old ones) than with the total replacement of older ones. Nevertheless, there are persistent efforts if not only to "stand on the shoulders of giants" (or to cut them down to size) but to situate new approaches in relation to established ones. Thus, the "new" cultural geographies of the 1980s and 1990s explicitly situated themselves in relation to such precursors as Carl Sauer's "old" cultural geography.

Some sort of minimalist chronology, therefore, seems inevitable. In the first several chapters of this book in particular and many of the others more generally the "dating" of some key concepts and arguments is part of what they do. By and large, however, they avoid the tendency to see some kind of teleology or generic progress over time with a new "wave" or avant garde sweeping away previous ones. The focus is much more on how the common "strains" (such as determinism versus agency, conceptions of races, methodological panaceas, understandings of place or region) that crop up repeatedly as part of the arguments in favor of this or that theoretical approach or philosophical position got started and are reproduced. The first chapters do, however, attempt to offer something extra. This is a consideration of what can be called the historical "canon" on which the tradition of human geography (the basic concepts and language, the names of Big Figures, the most famous disputes, the original conceptual grounds, the institutional structures of the field) has been built and in relation to which much contemporary debate and dispute is often situated. Even when not openly acknowledged, therefore, the past of the field, its tradition, enters into subsequent practice.

Three chapters explore the *Foundations* of modern human geography. *Where Geography Came From*, chapter 2 by Peter Burke, goes back to the Greeks. Subsequent chapters focus on the roles of European exploration and colonialism as vital historical contexts for understanding the field both in the past and in the present. Contemporary debates about cartography and fieldwork, for example, have their roots in these previous epochs. But they are also important in the present day because in many respects globalization represents a challenge to what goes for classical thinking. Yet, as will become clear throughout this book, much geographical thinking about the world remains in many ways trapped in the concepts and orientations of previous eras. The past is never entirely passed. In *The Classics,* six chapters trace the professionalization of human geography in universities beginning in the nineteenth century. Arguably, it is in Germany and France that modern Anglo-American human geography has some of its most important roots. Contemporaneous British and American geographers borrowed heavily from their "continental" colleagues and subsequent generations built their careers around interpretations of seminal German and French thinkers. One thinks, for example, of the American Richard Hartshorne's heavy reliance on the writings of the German Alfred Hettner. Following the chapter on German "precursors" and French "challengers" comes one on the institutionalization and development of human geography in the English-speaking world. This is the story of how the field became a subject in higher education and how it has adapted to the increasing emphasis on "research" at the expense of the teaching (and exploration) that were long seen as its central activities. Finally, two of the great intellectual disputes in the history of the field then take center stage: the argument over whether landscape or region should be the central concept of the field (beginning in the 1920s) and the dispute over region versus space (beginning in the 1950s). With these two sets of disputes we begin our innovation of having two chapters each offering a distinctive perspective, in this case on each of the disputes in question.

Politics of Human Geography

A serious danger lies in seeing the development of the field in an entirely naturalistic light (as if it just evolved) without attending to the ways in various structured choices have always entered into decisions about different approaches. A range of influences have been proposed as critical to the origin, persistence, and relative fading of different theories, methods, and broad philosophical orientations. New ideas never arise in a politico-social vacuum. There are geopolitical, institutional, and micro-political bases to the success or failure, persistence or decline of different idea-complexes. Geopolitical hierarchies make some ideas more equal than others (e.g. Agnew 2007). It seems clear, for example, that ideas generated in US universities (particularly ones with prestigious reputations) tend these days to be more successful, other things being equal, than those generated in more "lowly" intellectual centers. Not surprisingly, then, centers of intellectual initiative in the history of human geography also have shifted, if with some lag, as geopolitical hierarchies are shuffled. Studies of influential figures in contemporary human geography using citation factors, for example, show a high positive correlation with ranking of universities. As is well known, currently most of the world's highest ranking universities are in the US and UK.

At the institutional level, some fields and theories are heavily sponsored and successful whereas others must fight for survival. What we have in mind here is the degree to which dependence of universities on external funding directs not only research but also the very academic division of labor itself. In the Cold War historical context of the US, for example, an entire intellectual division of labor arose in response to the US government's desire to fight Soviet Communism through dividing the world into zones (the so-called Three Worlds) in which different academic disciplines were to be differentially invested. Mainstream economics, political science, and sociology were designated to study the premier "modern" First World of the US and its western allies, whereas various "specialties" were trained to study the ideologized Second World of the Soviet Union and its allies and the "development" problems of the "traditional" Third World. "Special" theories and methods were needed to study the latter two Worlds, while "normal" positivist or law-like behavior being held to characterize the First, no such specialization was needed (Pletsch 1981). Human geography never fit very well into this framework. So, arguably the end of the Cold War has been a godsend for the field, if only because the "frozen" zones and national borders of that time have now once again been put in motion.

Finally, within fields themselves there are hierarchies of influentials and departmental rankings (and cultures) that affect the flows and persistence of ideas. Knowledge tends to pool up in different places and different strands become identified with them rather than easily transferred from one place to another (Meusburger 2008). "Filters" of various sorts – cultural, economic, and psychological – interfere with the ready transfer everywhere of codes of knowledge and the reputational backing that come from being associated with knowledge production in particular milieux. But different theories and methods (even schools) are closely associated with different places. Some of this tendency can be put down to a so-called intellectual "tribalism" in which scholars are inducted into specific norms that include training in particular methods and theories that they then go on to reproduce in their own careers (Campbell 1979; Johnston 2006). This can also involve defending "turf" against competitors and promoting those who conform rather than those who represent some alternative framework or approach. But the emphasis on defining and defending intellectual turf is also encouraged by institutional mechanisms of various sorts. For example, the Research Assessment Exercise in the UK has had the effect of encouraging claims to novelty in much publication because of the weighting given to so-called innovative as opposed to follow-up research. Because of the metrics used it also encourages a vast amount of self-citation and the citation of others in your particular camp publishing in your journals. One ancillary impact has been to discourage longer-term research projects and the monographs typically associated with them (Harvey 2006). Another has been to encourage the professionalization and specialization of publication at the expense of publishing for more popular audiences in more understandable language as was once apparently much more the case (Downs 2010). Geography's presumed "accessibility" to the public, written in ordinary language dealing with observable facts, has, from this point of view, been more curse than blessing.

Thematic Foci

Inevitably, selecting themes for a book such as this is fraught with difficulty. We have chosen those which have been both the subject of most debate over the past ten years from our different positions in Britain and the United States and which also have entertained some of the most sophisticated discussion from the viewpoint of theoretical differences. Obviously, two other people might have come up with themes (and labels) somewhat different from ours. We would like to believe, however, that the ones we have chosen, and the authors we have selected to write about them, give an excellent flavor of the current state of Anglo-American human geography. We have not directed authors to contest with one another nor have we tried to find authors who would provide starkly alternative views on a given theme or about how it has been engaged. In line with previous discussion about the current period as one of globalization we have selected some themes that resonate strongly with that whole broader debate but we have also included some much longer standing themes that are now being addressed in distinctive ways from how they tended to be thirty to forty years ago. Because each theme has two separate authors writing from their own perspectives we would want to emphasize the extent to which this gives a possibly richer reading of the particular themes than would either a collaborative chapter or a single one, however comprehensive.

By way of organization, we have sorted the chapters into four broad categories. The first consists of some themes (nature, landscape, place, territory) that have long been central to but that have also long bedeviled the field. The second are emergent concepts that are redolent of the current wrestling with the presumed effects of globalization (globalization, world cities, governance, mobility, networks and scale). The third grouping consists of chapters about how human geography is engaging with categories that have long loomed large in and across the social sciences and humanities but with new emphases in light of contemporary sensibilities (class, race, sexuality, gender). Finally, we have also included some older themes from the history of human geography that have gone through something of a recent revival of interest (geopolitics, segregation, development).

It is our intention that in reading through the three sections of this book you will acquire a fairly substantial understanding of the early history and institutionalization of human geography as we see it today and a detailed sense of some of the major conceptual disputes and contemporary trends in the field as a whole. Although the whole is intended as greater than the sum of the parts, a book such as this also serves to give hopefully interesting and enlightening overviews of the more specific thematic debates going on in contemporary human geography.

References

Agnew, J. (2007) Know-where: geographies of knowledge of world politics. *International Political Sociology* 1: 138–148.
Benko, G. and Strohmayer, U. (eds) (2004) *Horizons géographiques*. Bréal, Paris.
Campbell, D.T. (1979) A tribal model of the social system vehicle carrying scientific knowledge. *Knowledge*, 1: 181–201.
Downs, R.M. (2010) Popularization and geography: an inseparable relationship. *Annals of the Association of American Geographers*, 100: 444–467.
Driver, F. (2000) Field-work in geography. *Transactions of the Institute of British Geographers*, 25: 267–268.
Farinelli, F. (2009) *La crisi della ragione cartografica*. Einaudi, Turin.
Gerber, R. and Goh, K.C. (eds) (2000) *Fieldwork in Geography: Reflections, Perspectives, Actions*. Springer, Berlin.

Harley, J.B. (1987) The map and the development of cartography. In J.B. Harley and D. Woodward (eds), *The History of Cartography. Volume 1*. University of Chicago Press, Chicago, pp. 1–42.

Harvey, D. (2006) The geographies of critical geography. *Transactions of the Institute of British Geographers*, 31: 409–412.

Lévy, J. (1999) *Le tournant géographique. Penser l'espace pour lire le monde*. Belin, Paris.

Livingstone, D.N. (1992) *The Geographical Tradition*. Blackwell, Oxford.

Lussault, M. (2009). *De la lutte des classes à la lutte des places*. Bernard Grasset, Paris.

James, P.E. (1972) *All Possible Worlds: A History of Geographical Ideas*. Bobbs Merrill, Indianapolis.

Johnston, R.J. (2006) The politics of changing human geography's agenda: textbooks and the representation of increasing diversity. *Transactions of the Institute of British Geographers*, 31: 286–303.

Meusburger, P. (2008) The nexus of knowledge and space. In P. Meusburger, *et al.* (eds), *Clashes of Knowledge*. Springer, Berlin, pp. 35–90.

Peet, R. (1998) *Modern Geographic Thought*. Blackwell, Oxford.

Philo, C. (2008) Introduction. In C. Philo (ed.), *Theory and Methods: Critical Essays in Human Geography*. Ashgate, Aldershot, pp. xxiii–xlix.

Pletsch, C.E. (1981) The Three Worlds, or the division of social scientific labor, circa 1950–1975. *Comparative Studies in Society and History*, 23: 565–590.

Part I Foundations

2   Where Geography Came From   11
    Peter Burke for David Lowenthal

3   Cosmographers, Explorers, Cartographers, Chorographers: Defining,
    Inscribing and Practicing Early Modern Geography, c.1450–1850   23
    Robert J. Mayhew

4   Colonizing, Settling and the Origins of Academic Geography   50
    Daniel Clayton

The Wiley Blackwell Companion to Human Geography, First Edition.
Edited by John A. Agnew and James S. Duncan.
© 2011 John Wiley & Sons, Ltd. Published 2016 by John Wiley & Sons, Ltd.

Part I. Foundations

Chapter 2
Where Geography Came From

Peter Burke

for David Lowenthal

Introduction

Today, the phrase "I'm a geographer" has professional and academic overtones. This chapter, on the other hand, is concerned with what has sometimes been called "geography without geographers" (Miquel 1967–1980, vol.1: 191) or "geography before geography" (Staszak 1995). The topic might equally well be described as "anthropology before anthropology" (Liebersohn 2008) or "ethnography without ethnographers," or as writing at the borders of history, travel and fiction (Romm, 1992), from the *Odyssey* to the writer who claimed to be "Sir John Mandeville," offering what David Lowenthal calls "geographies of the mind." In other words, the chapter focuses on the ways in which the different peoples of the earth were perceived and imagined before the year 1500 and especially before the great division of intellectual and academic labor of the nineteenth and twentieth centuries.

It is important to avoid two opposite dangers: on one side, that of assuming that geographical thought began in the nineteenth century with the foundation of geography departments in universities, and on the other, that of looking for anticipations of later developments, the "dawn of modern geography" (Beazley 1897) for instance, rather than placing early writers in the context of their own time and asking what it was that they wanted or tried to do.

What follows discusses the history of the interest in the variety of peoples on earth, the frequent attempts to describe their manners and customs and the rarer attempts to explain this variety in terms of climate or other aspects of the environment. The period under discussion runs from the Greek Herodotus, who is generally described as a historian, to the Genoese Columbus, whom we tend to call an "explorer." To link a scholar with a man of action in this way (although Herodotus also travelled and Columbus also wrote) reminds us that knowledge of the world's peoples, like most kinds of knowledge, has developed out of collaboration or dialogue between theory and practice, between observers in the "field" (merchants, pilgrims, envoys and mariners) and scholars in their studies (Herodotus 1954).

Unfortunately, little is known today about the contributions to knowledge made in the field at this time. Indeed, little is known even about scholars who lived and worked between the relatively well-documented world of the Greeks and the Romans and that of the late Middle Ages, not to mention their Chinese and Arab colleagues. What follows necessarily involves an attempt to navigate around the many gaps in the record.

The Ancient World

Although the Greeks had a word for it, *gēographia* (writing about the earth), there was no specialized discipline called "geography," let alone "human geography," and there were no "geographers" pursuing it in the ancient world. According to Strabo, author of a 17-volume study, geography was part of philosophy. In any case, scholars did not need to specialize at this time. Today, Eratosthenes and Ptolemy are sometimes described as geographers, but Eratosthenes was a poet and an athlete as well as a writer on mathematics and astronomy, while Ptolemy studied music and optics and was best known as an astronomer.

The names of a number of ancient writers on different peoples (*ethnoi*) have come down to us, although their works have often been lost or have survived only in fragments. They include Hecateus of Miletos (lived c.530 BCE), author of *Histories* and *Journey round the World*; Ctesias of Cnidus (5th century BCE), a physician who wrote about India; Megasthenes (BCE c. 350–290), who travelled to India and wrote the *Indika*; Pytheas of Massalia, who made an expedition to the North (c.320 BCE); Posidonius of Apamea (c.135–51 BCE), who visited Gaul and wrote about it; Agatharchides of Cnidus (2nd century BCE) who wrote on Africa, and Diodorus of Sicily (first century BCE) whose world history commented on the language and customs of different peoples.

One might reasonably speak of an ancient "age of discovery," in the context of Greek colonization of what we call Italy and France, the Persian invasion of Greece and Alexander the Great's invasion of India. For the Greeks, what was discovered was the "barbarian" world, since Greeks referred to non-Greeks as *barbaroi*, people who were unable to speak properly and were therefore not fully human.

The concept was turned against the Greeks themselves by the author of the *Book of Maccabees*, a Jew writing in Greek. The Old Testament presents other Middle Eastern peoples – for instance, Philistines, Canaanites and Babylonians – in a similar way (Momigliano 1975, Gruen 2000). For their part, the Aryan invaders of India viewed the indigenous inhabitants – and later, the Greeks – as barbarian (*mleccha* in Sanskrit), in other words people incapable of speech (Thapar 1971: 418).

The foundation of the great library of Alexandria around the year 300 BCE provided a central place for scholars to study reports by travelers to different parts of the earth: one of its librarians, Eratosthenes of Cyrene, has been mentioned already (Jacob 1991: 102–104). The scholars, themselves based in the cities, generally rejected what they called barbarism; sometimes idealized it (an attitude one historian describes as "hard primitivism") or they might be ambivalent. The idea of barbaric wisdom gained acceptance among Greeks in the late classical or Hellenistic period (Momigliano 1975: 7). The Scythians and the Germans in particular were sometimes presented as noble savages, reminding the American scholars Arthur Lovejoy and George Boas (1935) of some eighteenth-century idealizations of the American Indians.

What follows concentrates on the views about different peoples (*ethnoi* in Greek, *gentes* in Latin) expressed by seven famous ancient writers, four Greeks and three Romans: Herodotus, Hippocrates, Aristotle, Strabo, Caesar, Tacitus and Ammianus Marcellinus.

Herodotus of Halicarnassus (BCE c.484–c.425), wrote a history of the conflict between the Greeks and the Persians, placing this conflict in a wider context. He described the customs of the Persians "from personal knowledge." noting, for instance, the way in which they sacrifice to their gods (without altar or fire), their fondness for wines and the importance they give to birthdays (Book One: Chapter 131). Writing about the Persian expedition to Egypt, Herodotus included a lengthy description of "the manners and customs" of the Egyptians, noting that they were often the opposite of the customs of other peoples: "for instance, women attend market and are employed in trade, while men stay at home and do the weaving … Men in Egypt carry loads on their heads, women on their shoulders; women pass water standing up, men sitting down" (Book 2: Chapter 35; cf. Hartog, 1980).

Again, before writing about the Persian attack on the Scythians, Herodotus described the customs of this barbaric people, who scalped their enemies, drank from skulls and took steam-baths (Book Four: Chapters 63–74). He quoted the King of the Scythians, who told King Darius of Persia that "we Scythians have no towns or planted lands, so that we might meet you the sooner in battle" (Book Four: Chapter 127). Herodotus described other peoples in terms of their closeness to or distance from Greek culture (Hartog 1980) and the Greeks in general tended to see themselves as civilized and the rest of the world as barbarians. Their attitude is obviously ethnocentric, but it is unlikely that any people in world history are in a very good position to criticize them for this.

Where Herodotus limited himself to description, the physician Hippocrates of Kos (c.460–c.370 BCE) – or one of his followers – attempted in the treatise *On Airs, Waters and Places* to explain the character of different peoples by their environments, hard and soft. According to this text, the Europeans, living in a cold climate, were ferocious and warlike, while the inhabitants of Asia were gentle and peaceful people, thanks to their warm climate (Glacken 1967: 80–115).

Aristotle (384–322 BCE), a polymath now best known as a philosopher, gave a political twist to the climatic theory of Hippocrates. In his *Politics* (7.6.1), Aristotle described the inhabitants of cold regions as "full of spirit but somewhat deficient in energy and skill, so that they continue comparatively free but lacking in political organization and capacity to rule their neighbors." In hot regions, on the other hand, the people are intelligent "but lack spirit, so that they are in continual subjection and slavery" (the germ of an idea that would later be developed under the name of "oriental despotism"). According to this theory, the Greeks occupied a place between the two, the golden mean.

Strabo of Pontus (c.64 BCE–c.24 CE), was a stoic philosopher and man of letters who lived for some years in Augustan Rome and travelled as far as the frontier of Ethiopia. He attempted to make a synthesis of the geographical knowledge of his time, describing his book both as a geography and as a "chorography," in other words a study of different regions. So far as customs and character are concerned, Strabo's major distinction was between people who were civilized (*politikos*), like the Greeks and Romans, and those who were barbarians, like the Massagetai, whom he calls "self-assertive, uncouth, wild and warlike" as well as "straightforward and not given to deceit," or the British, described as "more simple and barbaric" than the Celts, since there are degrees of barbarism (Strabo 4.5.2, 11.8.7: cf. Vliet 1984; Thollard 1987; Jacob 1991: 147–166). Strabo described the Scythians as nomads living in felt tents in a manner that was frugal and self-sufficient, regretting that in his day nomads and barbarians were becoming soft and corrupt. He also had something to say about the nomads of Arabia, the "tent-dwellers," living in the desert and keeping herds of camels.

Strabo explained barbarism in environmental terms. "All the mountaineers," he wrote, "lead a simple life, are water-drinkers, sleep on the ground and let their hair stream down in thick masses after the manner of women." Their wildness is the result of their remoteness. He was not a determinist, however, noting that some peoples lose their former wildness as they become Romanized (3.3.7–8). This remark may remind readers of Victorian views of savages and the civilizing influence of the Empire – an appropriate comparison, since the context in which Strabo's treatise was produced was that of Roman imperial expansion (Nicolet 1988: 90–95).

The Greeks called the Romans "barbarians" but the Romans took over the term to describe non-Romans, from the Carthaginians to the Gauls, contrasting their own "civilization" (*civilitas*) with the "savagery" (*feritas*) of the Other (Dauge 1981). The account of his conquest of Gaul given by Julius Caesar (100–144 BCE) begins with a brief description of the customs of both the Gauls and the Romans. Like Herodotus, Caesar believed that the course of the wars would not be intelligible without this account of the customs of the warriors. Caesar's description (which draws on a book by Posidonius, who had visited Gaul forty years earlier) distinguished different tribes, such as the Aedui and the Sequani, and different social groups, including the Druids. He also included remarks on the customs and character of the Britons in his narrative of his invasion of Britain. The Germanic tribes were also described by Caesar, who noted that they were warlike and pastoral peoples, and in considerably more detail by Tacitus (c.56–c.117 CE.).

Tacitus described the German manner of fighting on horseback or on foot, their religion, houses and clothes, their banquets, their way of choosing their chiefs and even their habit of washing in warm water – "Can one wonder where winter holds such sway?" He presented the Germans as noble savages – brave, warlike, frugal and temperate (in eating if not in drinking) – encouraging his readers to make comparisons with Rome in their day, already described by some critics as corrupted by luxury. In similar fashion Ammianus Marcellinus (c.330–c.378 CE), who emulated the work of Tacitus in his own history, produced a memorable description of the Huns, who burst into the Roman Empire in his time, as an "untamed race of men" (indomitum ... hominum genus), "the most terrible of warriors" who "learn from the cradle to endure cold, hunger and thirst," nomads who "are almost glued to their horses" and eat, drink and even sleep on horseback. It is difficult to resist the thought that Ammianus, a Greek writing in Latin, was recycling the description of the Scythians by Herodotus.

Summing up so far, we might distinguish the description of customs (*nomoi* or *nomaia* in Greek, *mores* in Latin) such as ways of drinking or sacrificing to the gods, from the description of traits of character (*ethos* in Greek, *natura* in Latin), such as ferocity or deceitfulness. It may also be useful to distinguish description from analysis, in other words the explanation of customs and character in terms of the environment – highlands and lowlands, rich regions and poor ones – or in terms of the local economy, agricultural or pastoral. Customs and character were often viewed as timeless, but as we have seen Strabo was aware of change in this domain.

A few words on what might be called "inhuman geography" are in order at this point, especially the idea of "monstrous races." Ctesias, for instance, described a one-legged people located in India, while Strabo mentioned dog-headed men and people with eyes in their breast. The Roman encyclopaedist Pliny the Elder described a number of these races in his *Natural History*.

The Chinese and the Arabs

Like the Greeks, the Chinese (that is, the ethnic Chinese who called themselves the "Han" or the "Hua") generally viewed other peoples as barbarians (*fan* or *sheng-fan*), and treated them as scarcely human. "Hearts of beasts" was a common description of barbarians in Tang times (618–907 CE), while comparisons of foreign peoples with wolves, dogs, tigers, dragons, wasps, mosquitoes and sharks begin to be found in the time of Confucius (Kong Fuzi, 551–479 BCE). The principal objects of these descriptions were the nomads of the steppes of Inner Asia (the Ti, Jung, Xiongnu, Xianbei, Jürchen, Khitan, Uighur, etc), with whom the "Middle Kingdom" (*Zhong-guo*), as the Chinese called their state, had frequent contacts over the centuries, including periods when the kingdom fell under the sway of nomad chiefs such as the Mongols Chinggis and Kubilai Khan (who ruled 1206–1227 and 1260–1294 CE respectively). Southern Chinese peoples, generally known as the "Lao," were also viewed as barbarians and sometimes described as "black," thanks to the fact that their skin was darker than that of northerners (Schafer 1967).

Unlike the Greeks, however, the Chinese did not show much curiosity about the customs of these barbarians and produced no equivalent of Herodotus. The closest parallel to Herodotus on the Scythians is probably a passage from the most famous Chinese historian, Sima Qian (c.145–c.87 BCE.), who wrote a few pages (1961: 129–162) on a nomadic people of his day, the Xiongnu (formerly identified with the Huns). In his own voice he condemned them, saying that: "Their only concern is self-advantage, and they know nothing of propriety or righteousness." However, Sima Qian undermined this judgment by quoting the praises of the Xiongnu by the Chinese eunuch Zhonghang Yue: "Their laws are simple and easy to carry out: the relation between ruler and subject is relaxed and intimate." Zhonghang also commented that the Chinese, unlike the Xiongnu, do not know how to fight and build too many houses. In other words, like Tacitus – but nearly two hundred years before him – Sima Qian presented nomads as both brave and frugal.

Poets too produced brief descriptions of non-Han peoples whom they encountered in China, among them nomads and forest-dwellers. Liu Yuxi (772–842 CE), for instance, described the Mak Yao people as hunters and as friends of supernatural beings: "At night they cross gorges of a thousand fathoms," while he wrote of another tribe, the Man-tzu, that: "The speech of the Man is a clucking sound/the dress of the Man is a mottled linen" (Schafer 1967: 51, 54). In Tang times painters and sculptors represented foreign peoples, especially the Persians, in a generic manner with round eyes, curly hair and large noses, as if illustrating the phrase commonly applied to them, *shenmu gaobi*, "deep eyes and high noses." During the Song dynasty (960–1279), a new genre of painting emerged, described as *fanzu*, "barbarian tribes," and representing nomads in distinctive clothes, set in a distinctive landscape and accompanied by horses and tents (Abramson 2003).

Even when Chinese pilgrims visited India in search of Buddhist texts, they sometimes took their prejudices with them. If the monk Faxian (c.337–c.422), in one of his rare recorded glances at secular society, noted with surprise that the inhabitants of Mathura "do not kill any living creature, nor drink intoxicating liquor, nor eat onions or garlic," his colleague Xuanzang (c.602–664 CE), travelling on the Silk Road, commented on the "hard and uncultivated" manners of the people of Bamiyan, the "rude and violent" manners of the people of Kapisa and the timid, deceitful and avaricious character of the Sogdians (Faxian 1886: 43; Wriggins 2004: 45–49).

A genre of literature concerned with the character and customs of different peoples emerges in the Arab world in the ninth (for Muslims, the third) century and reaches its apogee in the eleventh (fifth). An anonymous *Account of China and India* was written in Arabic around the year 850 and described different political and economic systems (including the caste system in India). Al-Jahiz (776–868 CE) had much to say about Persians and Turks and noted the influence of the environment on their health and character. Al-Muqaddasi (c.945–1000 CE), wrote a book about the regions of the Islamic world, beginning each section with the climate and moving on to describe the religion, language, economy and customs of that region (Miquel 1967–80, vol.1). Al-Biruni (c.973–1048 CE), a polymath best known as an astronomer and astrologer, wrote an account of India in which he remarked – rather like Herodotus on the Egyptians – that the Hindus "differ from us ... in all manners and usages" and disliked foreigners: "They call them *mleccha*, i.e. impure, and forbid having any connection with them" (Al-Biruni 1910: 19).

Again, in 1068, Sa'id ibn Ahmad, a judge from Toledo, wrote a book about the nations of the world, arguing that eight peoples (including Indians, Persians, Greeks, Romans, Arabs and Jews) had contributed to the advancement of knowledge, while the Chinese were worthy of respect for their craft skills and the Turks for the art of war. The rest of mankind, on the other hand, "are more like beasts than men" (quoted Lewis 1982: 68).

In the fourteenth (eleventh) century, we find two famous Arab writers, Ibn Battuta and Ibn Khaldun, interested in what we call human geography. Ibn Battuta (1304–c.1368 CE) came from Tangier. His book described the 75 000 mile journey that took him to Baghdad, Mecca, East Africa, Hormuz, Constantinople, Delhi and Beijing and had much to say about the variety of human customs (in Arabic, *adab*) that he experienced, especially in more remote regions. In Hinawr in South India, for instance, he remarked that: "The women of this town and of all these coastal districts wear no sewn garments but only unsown lengths of cloth, one end of which they gird round their waists, and drape the rest round their head and chest. They are beautiful and virtuous, and each wears a gold ring in her nose." In China, by contrast, what impressed the Ibn Battuta was a series of bureaucratic practices: recording the contents of ships and the names of travelers and circulating the portraits of foreigners (Ibn Battuta 1958–1994, vol. 4: 803, 892–893; Chelhod 1978; Euben 2006).

More analytic is the approach of Ibn Khaldun (1332–1406 CE), who came from Tunis and lived at various times in Spain, Morocco and Egypt. His most famous work, the *Muqaddimah*, is an introduction to history, organized around the opposition between two cultures, the nomadic and the sedentary. The people of the desert are described as tough, frugal and brave, while the people of the city are soft, luxurious and unable to fight. Desert civilization is inferior to urban civilization, but on the other hand the Bedouin are closer to being good than sedentary people are. Above all, the desert people possess and the city people generally (but not always) lack what Ibn Khaldun called *asabiyya* (group consciousness or solidarity). Desert people sometimes conquer cities and then they become soft and lose their solidarity and so become vulnerable to conquest themselves, so that history often takes the form of cycles. The parallels between the ideas of Ibn Khaldun and those of the Greeks, Romans and Chinese discussed earlier will be obvious enough, although his emphasis on *asabiyya* is distinctive.

The Western Middle Ages

As in the case of the ancient Greeks, the context for the rise of medieval interest in other cultures was expansion; "the medieval expansion of Europe" (Phillips 1988) and the consequent "clash of civilizations." In the early Middle Ages, the Roman Empire was invaded by the Goths, Vandals, Franks, Lombards and other peoples. In the later Middle Ages came the "expansion of Latin Christendom" (Bartlett 1993), including the invasion of Eastern Europe by the Germans (the "push eastward" or *Drang nach Osten*), and the invasion of Ireland and Wales by the Norman-English, as well as the "reconquest" of Spain from the Arabs.

The early medieval clashes produced a number of histories of the invaders – the Roman official Jordanes on the Goths, and the churchmen Gregory of Tours on the Franks and Paul the Deacon on the Lombards; but these histories have little to say about ethnic differences or particular customs (Goffart 1988). What one does find in late classical or early medieval writers – the distinction between the two is a blurred one – is little more than the expression of prejudice. The Huns in particular were perceived as ugly and ferocious, closer to beasts (especially wolves) than to humans. Such is the power of prejudice that historians still use the term "barbarian" to describe the Goths, Vandals and Huns, peoples whose names have all become pejorative.

The period after the year 1000 was richer in accounts of customs, as different peoples collided once again. The eleventh-century German chronicler Adam of Bremen, for instance, described the customs of the Scandinavians in some detail, comparing them with those of the Arabs and the Jews of Old Testament times (pastoral peoples both). A history of Norway written around the year 1200 described Sámi ritual. In the Russian *Primary Chronicle*, Nestor, a monk from Kiev, described the pagan Slavs. It was common in the Latin West to describe other peoples, such as Celts and Slavs, as ferocious and lacking in reason, thus legitimating attempts at conquering them.

At the same time, it is only fair to note that some twelfth-century writers on what we would call "other cultures" revealed an eye for significant detail, made good use of comparison, and were aware that different cultural traits fit together into a whole (Bartlett 1982: 165–167, 175). For example, Gerald of Wales, archdeacon of Brecon (c. 1146–c. 1223 CE), offered a detailed account of the customs and character of the Welsh, emphasizing their courage, frugality and hospitality and even describing their care of their teeth, "constantly cleaning them with green hazel-shoots and then rubbing them with woolen cloths until they shine like ivory." Himself partly Norman and partly Welsh, Gerald was in a good position to observe, half inside and half outside the culture he described (Bartlett 1982: 157–210).

However, it was the rise of the Mongol Empire in the thirteenth century – the rapid expansion of the "Other" into Europe – that made some Europeans most vividly aware of alien customs, as four texts reveal, three of them written by friars (Fra Giovanni di Pian di Carpine, Brother William of Rubruck, Fra Odorico da Pordenone), and one, the most famous, by a merchant, Marco Polo.

Fra Giovanni di Pian di Carpine (c.1180–1252 CE) was papal envoy to the Great Khan, whose camp he visited in 1246, writing a report on his mission that reads rather like the later reports of Venetian ambassadors and ends with advice on how to resist the Khan's attempt to conquer the world. In his Latin *History of the Mongols*, Fra Giovanni began with the land (unsuitable for agriculture) and the climate (alternating extremes of heat and cold), implying if not stating that this environment explained the manners and customs of the people, their food, clothes, housing (circular tents), religion and their way of fighting.

The Flemish friar William of Rubruck (Guillaume de Rubrouck, Willem van Ruusbroec, c.1210–c.1270 CE) visited Karakorum, the Mongol capital, in 1253. His narrative of his mission, addressed to the crusader Louis IX of France, is preceded by eight descriptive chapters, beginning with a candid admission of culture shock: "we encountered the Tartars: and when I came among them I really felt as if I was entering another world." Less analytical than Fra Giovanni's, Brother William's text is much richer in ethnographic details that range from marriage and burial customs to the manner of drinking or entering a tent (divided into male and female space). No wonder then that this description has been compared to Gerald's account of the Welsh (Phillips 1988: 73; cf. Jackson 1994). As for Fra Odorico of Pordenone (c.1265–1331 CE), who spent three years in Beijing, his *Description of the Lands of the Infidel* noted a number of local customs, from the foot-binding of women to the long fingernails of the mandarins, as well as offering detailed descriptions of the manner in which the "Tartars," as he called them, hunted and feasted.

Much better known than these three texts is the "Conversation about the World" (*Divisament dou monde*) of the Venetian merchant Marco Polo (c.1254–1324 CE), offering an account of his extensive travels in the Middle and Far East, including a description of Kubilai Khan and his palace in Beijing. This text, ghost-written in Franco-Venetian by Rustichello da Pisa, otherwise known as the author of a romance of chivalry, both is and is not a travel book. Some scholars have suggested that Marco never reached China at all, and that his account should be treated as fictional, while others point out that the book is more of a geographical encyclopedia than the story of the itinerary of an individual (Heers 1984; Larner 1999). Whether fact or fiction, it offers a fascinating account of exotic customs, not only weddings and funerals, but also tattooing, the use of paper money in China and the Indian custom "that in eating they use only the right hand; they would never touch food with their left."

Travels of this kind held considerable interest for readers who stayed at home. Although the texts of the three friars were little known until the sixteenth century, Marco Polo was widely read before 1450, especially in the Latin translation made in the author's lifetime and also in Italian, German and English. It is likely that its emphasis on the marvelous was an important reason for the appeal of the *Divisament*, witness the fact that it was overtaken in popularity by the mid-fourteenth-century *Book of Sir John Mandeville*, which purports to offer an eyewitness account of the East but is actually a compilation from earlier writers, including Odorico. About three hundred manuscripts of this text survive, written in ten different languages. "Mandeville" loves to tell stories about what he calls "marvelous things," including reversals of the readers' expectations. He explains that the Numidians, for example, think that black is beautiful and white diabolical and that in India, "the women drink wine and not the men. And women shave their beards and not the men" (Deluz 1988; Greenblatt 1991: 26–51).

In this context, the voyages of Christopher Columbus (1451–1506) in search of a new route to the East may well appear as the culmination of a process rather than (or as well as) the beginning of something new (Abulafia 2008). The newly-discovered continent was at first perceived as part of the Indies, while the monstrous races, formerly placed in Asia or Africa, would be relocated in the Americas.

Conclusion

By this time readers may well feel satiated with repetition. From ancient Greece to ancient China, people imagined the world as a set of concentric circles with themselves at the centre; a literally ethnocentric view. The more remote from them the foreigners were the less human they seemed. Barbarians were viewed as animals or at best close to animals, ferocious and greedy, though also brave and hospitable. If you have seen one of these groups, you have seen them all, so that descriptions of one (the Scythians, for instance) might be transferred to another (such as the Huns or the Mongols). Nomads in particular were perceived by farmers and townspeople with a mixture of fear, contempt and on occasion reluctant admiration.

By contrast with the centuries that will be discussed in the following chapter, we find little variation and still less development between c.450 BCE and c.1450 CE, a period that virtually spans two millennia. The situation was not static, but there is no single or simple story of change to tell.

There were continuities but there were also losses, broken traditions and independent rediscoveries. On the side of continuity, Caesar referred to Eratosthenes, the Arabs translated Hippocrates and Aristotle, fragments of Tacitus on the Germans were known to Adam of Bremen (Bartlett 1982: 174), Gerald of Wales cited Caesar on the ancient Britons and Columbus read the travels of Marco Polo.

On the other hand, the Arabs do not seem to have known the work of Strabo. Ibn Khaldun's reflections on the culture of nomads runs parallel to Strabo, Tacitus and Sima Qian but was formulated without knowledge of their writings. Gerald of Wales would doubtless have appreciated the work of Herodotus, but it was not available to him.

The interest in foreign customs and their explanation in terms of variations in climate would revive and indeed flourish as never before in the early modern period, from Bodin to Montesquieu, as the following chapter will show. Explanations by climate would be followed by explanations in terms of race, especially in the nineteenth century, and explanations in terms of culture, in the twentieth, when human geography finally became a discipline, not far removed from academic neighbors such as anthropology and history, but pursuing a course of its own.

References

Abramson, M.S. (2003) Deep Eyes and High Noses: physiognomy and the depiction of barbarians in Tang China. In N. Di Cosmo and D. J. Wyatt (eds), *Political Frontiers, Ethnic Boundaries and Human Geography in Chinese History*. Routledge Curzon, London, pp. 119–159.

Abulafia, D. (2008) *The Discovery of Mankind: Atlantic encounters in the age of Columbus*. Yale University Press, New Haven.

al-Azmeh, A. (1982) *Ibn Khaldun. An Essay in Re-Interpretation*. Third World Centre, London.

Al-Biruni. (1910) *Alberuni's India*, (trans. E. C. Sachau). Kegan Paul, London.

Ammianus Marcellinus (1935–1939), *History*, bilingual (trans. J. C. Rolfe). 3 vols. Harvard University Press, Cambridge, Mass.

Aristotle. (1932) *Politics*, bilingual (trans. H. Rackham). Harvard University Press, Cambridge, Mass.

Bartlett, R. (1982) *Gerald of Wales*. Oxford University Press, Oxford.

Bartlett, R. (1993) *The Making of Europe: conquest, colonization, and cultural change, 950–1350*. Allen Lane, London.

Beazley, C.R. (1897–1906) *The Dawn of Modern Geography: a history of exploration and geographical science*. 3 vols. Clarendon Press, Oxford.

Caesar. (1951) *The Conquest of Gaul*, (trans. S. A. Handford). Penguin, Harmondsworth.

Chelhod, J. (1978) *Ibn Battuta, Ethnologue*. Revue de l'Occident Musulman, 25, 5–24.

Dauge, Y.A. (1981) *Le barbare: recherches sur la conception romaine de la barbarie et de la civilisation*. Latomus, Brussels.

Deluz, C. (1988) *Le livre de Jehan de Mandeville*: une "géographie" au XIVe siècle. Institute d"Etudes Médiévales, Louvain-la-Neuve.

Euben, R.L. (2006) *Journeys to the Other Shore*: Muslim and Western Travellers in Search of Knowledge. Princeton University Press, Princeton.

Faxian [Fa-Hien] (1965) *Record of Buddhistic Kingdoms*, (trans. J. Legge). Dover, New York.

Gerald of Wales. (1978) *The Journey through Wales/The Description of Wales*, (trans. L. Thorpe). Penguin, Harmondsworth.

Giovanni di Piano Carpine. *Historia Mongalorum*, (trans. M. C. Lungarotti). Centro italiano di Studi sull'Alto Medioevo, Spoleto.

Glacken, C.J. (1967) *Traces on the Rhodian Shore: nature and culture in Western thought from ancient times to the end of the eighteenth century*. University of California Press, Berkeley.

Goffart, W. (1988) *The Narrators of Barbarian History* (A.D. 550–800): Jordanes, Gregory of Tours, Bede, and Paul the Deacon. Princeton University Press, Princeton.

Greenblatt, S. (1991) *Marvelous Possessions*: the Wonder of the New World. Oxford University Press, Oxford.

Gruen, E.S. (2001) Jewish Perspectives on Greek Culture and Ethnicity. In I. Malkin (ed.), *Ancient Perceptions of Greek Ethnicity*. Center for Hellenic Studies, Washington D.C., pp. 347–373.

Hartog, F.(1980) *The Mirror of Herodotus: the representation of the other in the writing of Herodotus*. (trans. 1988), University of California Press, Berkeley.

Heers, J. (1984) Der Marco Polo à Christophe Colomb: comment lire le *Devisement du Monde?" Journal of Medieval History*, 10, 125–143.

Herodotus. (1954) *Histories*, (trans. A. de Sélincourt). Harmondsworth: Penguin, Harmondsworth.

Ibn Battuta (1958–1994) *Travels*, (trans. H. A. R. Gibb), 4 Vols. Cambridge University Press and the Hakluyt Society, Cambridge and London.

Ibn Khaldun. (1958) *The Muqaddimah*: an introduction to history, (trans. F. Rosenthal), 3 Vols. Routledge, London.

Jackson, P. (1994) William of Rubruck in the Mongol Empire: perception and prejudice. In Z. von Martels (ed.), *Travel Fact and Travel Fiction*. Brill, Leiden, pp. 54–71.

Jacob, C. (1991) *Géographie et ethnographie en Grèce ancienne*. Armand Colin, Paris.

Larner, J. (1999) *Marco Polo and the Discovery of the World*. Yale University Press, New Haven.

Lewis, B. (1982) *The Muslim Discovery of Europe*. Weidenfeld and Nicolson, London.

Liebersohn, H. (2008) Anthropology before anthropology. In H. Kuklick (ed.), *A New History of Anthropology*. Blackwell, Oxford.

Lovejoy, A. O. and Boas, G. (1935) *Primitivism and related ideas in antiquity*. Johns Hopkins University Press, Baltimore.

Marco Polo (1958) *Travels* (trans. R. Latham). Penguin, Harmondsworth.

Miquel, A. (1967–1980) *La géographie humaine du monde musulman jusqu'au XIe siècle*, 4 Vols. EHESS, Paris.

Momigliano, A. (1975) *Alien Wisdom: the limits of Hellenization*. Cambridge University Press, Cambridge.

Nicolet, C. (1988) *L"inventaire du monde: géographie et politique aux origins de l"empire romain*. Fayard, Paris.

Phillips, J.R.S. (1997) *The Medieval Expansion of Europe*, 1988, 2nd edn. Oxford University Press, Oxford.

Romm, J.S. (1992) *The Edges of the Earth in Ancient Thought*: Geography, Exploration and Fiction. Princeton University Press, Princeton.

Schafer, E.H. (1967) *The Vermilion Bird*. University of California Press, Berkeley.

Sima Qian. (1961) *Records of the Grand Historian, Han Dynasty II*, trans. Burton Watson, (revised edn 1993). Columbia University Press, New York.

Staszak, J.-F. (1995) *La géographie d"avant la géographie*. Le climat chez Aristote et Hippocrate. Harmattan, Paris.

Strabo (1917) *Geography*, (bilingual edn trans. H. L. Jones). Harvard University Press, Cambridge.

Tacitus (1948) *On Britain and Germany*, (trans. H. Mattingly). Penguin, Harmondsworth.

Thapar, R. (1971) *The Image of the Barbarian in Early India*. Comparative Studies in Society and History 13, 408–436.

Thollard, P. (1987) *Barbarie et civilisation chez Strabon*. Les Belles Lettres, Paris.

Vliet, E.C.L. van der. (1984) L'ethnographie de Strabon. In F. Prontera (ed.), *Strabone: contributi allo studio della personalita` e dell'opera*. University of Perugia Press, Perugia, pp. 27–86.

William of Rubruck (1990) *The Mission of Friar William of Rubruck*, (trans. P. Jackson) Hakluyt Society, London.

Wriggins, S.H. (2004) *The Silk Road Journey with Xuanzang*. Westview, Boulder.

Guide to Further Reading

Since some of the main sources cited in this study are accessible in English and make good reading, it is probably best to begin with them; with Herodotus, for instance, Tacitus, Gerald of Wales and Marco Polo. Among works by modern scholars, the books by Hartog, Bartlett, Larner and Euben are particularly to be recommended.

Chapter 3

Cosmographers, Explorers, Cartographers, Chorographers: Defining, Inscribing and Practicing Early Modern Geography, c.1450–1850

Robert J. Mayhew

Two Visual Vignettes: Framing Early Modern Geography

In 1475, in the Southern German town of Ulm, a small and beguilingly simple-looking image of the world was printed, an image many today might hesitate to call a "map" (see Figure 3.1). It had been printed using one of the new handpresses which contemporaries and historians over the past half millennium have judged revolutionary in their impact, ushering in it is alleged the modern era (Febvre and Martin 1984; Eistenstein 2005). And yet the map in question in fact harked back in time, as did so many of the geographical products of the first age of print such as the great early editions of Ptolemy's *Geography* (c.150AD) (Gautier Dalché 2007). The map is what we now call a "T-O" map because of its key structural shapes, and its ultimate origins lie in the description of the globe provided at the outset of Book XIV of the *Etymologies*, a work by Isidore of Seville which was completed early in the 7th century AD. The *Etymologies* was one of the most oft-transcribed works in the scriptoria of medieval Europe if surviving copies are a reliable gauge, and many copyists chose to illustrate Isidore's verbal account of the globe with a map. The 1475 Ulm map was merely one of the last in this long line of visualisations of Isidore's argument some eight hundred years after its initial formulation (Barney et al. 2006: 285; Woodward 1987: 301–302).

The Wiley Blackwell Companion to Human Geography, First Edition.
Edited by John A. Agnew and James S. Duncan.
© 2011 John Wiley & Sons, Ltd. Published 2016 by John Wiley & Sons, Ltd.

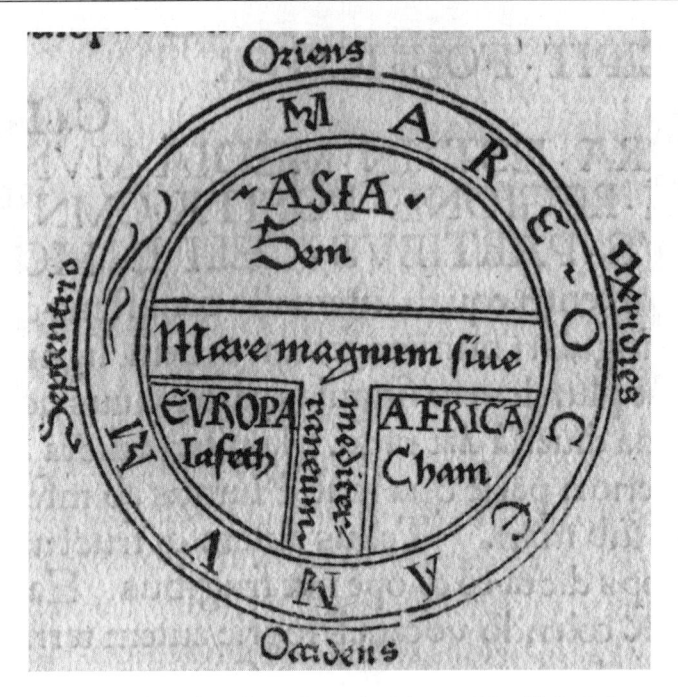

Figure 3.1 1472, An early printed version of Isidore of Seville's T-O map.

Simple as they may appear, T-O maps encapsulate a vast amount of geographical learning and lore; they amount to a distillation of Christian and classical ideas about the surface of the globe and the peopling of that surface. In short, a T-O map is a visual summary of human and physical geography as it was understood in the medieval period. Above all, and as befits the work of a Bishop of Seville, Isidore's image of the globe was dictated by Christianity. Thus Jerusalem is placed at the centre of the map (in some cases with quite startling precision) because of a prophecy in Ezekiel 5.5. Similarly, the tri-continental structuring of the map fits neatly into a schema wherein each of Noah's three sons – Shem, Ham and Japhet – were responsible for repopulating one of the continents of the earth after the Deluge described in Books 6 to 9 of *Genesis*. Likewise, T-O maps are orientated with East at the top, this being (to simplify matters) because Paradise is described in the Bible as being both in the east and atop a great hill (Scafi 2006). The basic structure of T-O maps, however, also chimes with the ways in which ancient Greek and Roman science depicted the globe, most notably in its structuring of three continents with a circumambient ocean, an image which goes back to the very earliest writings which we have inherited in the European tradition, notably Homer's depiction in his description of Achilles' shield in Book XVIII of the *Iliad* (Romm 1992). Likewise, that Isidore wrote in Latin and that his interpretive key to understanding the world and its structure was etymological speculations about that language reminds us of the complex fusion of ancient and Christian culture which denizens of the medieval age performed. Lest the modern reader feels rather haughtily superior to the world of Isidore, it is worth being aware that this schema

Figure 3.2 Alexander von Humboldt's cross-section of Mount Chimborazo from his 'Essay on the Geography of Plants' (1807). *Source*: Used courtesy of the Humboldt Digital Library (www.avhumboldt.net).

was capable of considerable empirical elaboration in the face of new information about the globe. The great European mappae mundi of the later medieval period include information flowing back from the far east from a host of characters of whom Marco Polo is only the best known, all of it effortlessly incorporated as the empirical flesh hung on the conceptual bones which Isidore had established (Edson 2007; Phillips 1998).

Scrolling forward to the end of the period covered in this essay, it is worth pausing to consider another iconic geographical image, this time gloriously colored and bursting with detail. First published in 1805, Alexander von Humboldt's cross-section of Mount Chimborazo in Ecuador from his *Essai sur la Geographie des Plantes* appears to bespeak a wholly different world of geographical understanding from that in Isidore's T-O map (Figure 3.2).

It is, of course, an image of the Americas, the continent whose discovery shortly after the printing of the 1475 Ulm map ultimately destroyed Isidore's Christian and classical tri-continental schema, even if it's immediate impact was more nuanced (Elliott 1992; Grafton 1992; Johnson 2006). Furthermore, where Isidore's geographical schema was constructed on an entirely textual basis by the study of conjectural etymologies, Humboldt's image was grounded in direct observation as he with his fellow traveller Aimé Bonpland had been the first European to ascend the mountain (then thought to be the highest in the world). If the Ulm map suggests a neat encapsulation of much information in a simple schema, the cross-section of Chimborazo bespeaks an era of proliferating knowledge and complex subdivisions, its dense tangle of botanical names showing just how complex the one topic of plant geography alone had become. Bonpland and Humboldt had been accompanied by a wagon-load of scientific instruments during their fêted expedition, science and its rigorous standards of observation and recording having replaced the Christian hermeneutics of ancient tongues on which Isidore's work had rested.

Juxtaposing the Ulm map with Humboldt's cross-section betokens some of the massive shifts through which geography as an inquiry, or more accurately as a set of inquiries, would go during the centuries covered in this chapter. Conceptions of how to collect data about the globe would change, as would accepted understandings of how to then analyze and present that data. Similarly, there would be huge changes in, and debates about, the relationships between geography, religion, science and scholarship. Where geography might fit in the "map of knowledge" was highly contested as it is today. And yet in one important respect it would be misleading to depict geography as all about change in this era, tempting as it may be to run narratives about the collapse of a benighted geography of the dark ages and its replacement with a scientific inquiry which ushered in modernity. For the 1475 Ulm map and Humboldt's plant geography share one key characteristic: in both cases the geographic image is buttressed by a cosmological understanding. In short, both approaches to inscribing geographical knowledge on the page rely on a wider sense of the way in which the universe is structured and how it functions. For just as Isidore assumed the truth of a Christian reading of the nature of our earth derived from the Bible, so Humboldt had a sense that our earth in all its complexity and profusion had underlying regularities and unities which aesthetic appreciation intimated and which scientific scrutiny could reveal. As such, for all its changes in substance, approach and intellectual location, geography remained in the thrall of broader currents in the history of ideas, those currents being the cosmologies – or framing understandings of how the universe functions and can be comprehended by mankind – within which people worked, geography reciprocally acting to further and to challenge the cosmologies on which it rested.

As such, in this chapter we canvass the range of geographical inquiries which existed in the era 1450 to 1850, doing so in the light of the framing cosmologies within which those inquiries were located. This era amounts to a coherent one in geography's history which can be labeled "early modern," albeit this phrase is normally used to pick out a shorter time period in standard historical studies (see Weisner Hanks 2006 for the standard exposition of this periodization; for its problems see Starn 2002 and Cave 2006). The early modern era was an age when discovery was at the forefront in defining geography as an empirical inquiry, this discovery not simply being the outreach associated with Columbus and his contemporaries, but also the discovery of the local through painstaking antiquarian work, for example. The key question for early modern geography in its many guises was how to fuse new information about the world garnered by first-hand experience with a suitable mode of presenting and comprehending that information. As we will see, there was a nested hierarchy of scales at which geographical description functioned from the cosmological scale of the universal down to the topographical description of specific places. Once these scales have been analyzed, we will revert to the scale at which the early modern period saw geography as functioning – that of the whole globe – before finally turning to the cosmology and the era which finally collapsed this early modern approach to the arts of geographical description in the nineteenth century.

Renaissance, Inherited Cosmography and Chaotic Empiricism

Retrospectively, it is all too easy and all too tempting to cast Christopher Columbus as a revolutionary who shattered the closed world view of the medieval era, as the visionary who turned upside down the world represented by Isidore's T-O map. This temptation has snared many, and not just in the recent past, Francis Bacon in his *Novum Organon* (1620) for example, depicting Columbus as a proto-scientist who "gave reasons why he was confident that new lands and continents, beyond those previously known, could be found" before going out and proving his hypotheses by empirical experience (Jardine 2000: 77). In truth, if Columbus's four navigations did eventually collapse the world view of Isidore of Seville, this was an unintended consequence and one which Columbus himself never cognitized. For Columbus, a man whom the contemporary chronicler Oviedo described as having "good Latin and great cosmographical knowledge," (Cohen 1969: 28), was entirely the denizen of a geographical world view molded by late medieval scholarship, both Christian and classical. Simply put, Columbus's aims as a navigator as we can reconstruct them from his own accounts of his voyages, were entirely circumscribed by understandings which would fit neatly into Isidore's schema.

Columbus's mindset, the cosmography which informed his understanding of what he was encountering, is perhaps best disclosed in his most extended set of speculations about the shape and nature of the earth which occur during his third voyage (1498–1500), for it is here that we see the complex fusion of Christian and ancient understandings which undergird Oviedo's characterization of him as possessing great cosmological knowledge. Above all, Columbus thought that his first-hand experience as a navigator disproved the ancient and medieval view that the earth was a globe (contrary to popular legend, most medieval scholars did not believe the earth was flat: see Cormack 1994; and Russell 1991). Nearing the coast of South America (as we can call it but he could not), Columbus, convinced he was off the coast of the Asia/Cathay described by Marco Polo and other medieval travelers, detected "as we passed ... the ships mounted gently nearer to the sky." As such, the earth was not shaped like a globe, instead the "uphill" section through which Columbus's crew were laboring showed, contrary to "all authorities and the recorded experiments of Ptolemy and the rest ... that it is not round as they describe it, but the shape of a pear, which is round everywhere except at the stalk, where it juts out a long way." For Columbus, this stalk lay in the southern hemisphere and "at the farthest point of the east" (Cohen 1969: 217–218). Columbus's interest in making this point was not merely to joust with ancient geographers and declare for the virtues of experience over mathematical reasoning in determining the shape of the earth, but also to suggest that his experience resolved an enduring conundrum in Christian geography. For he then goes on to suggest "that the earthly Paradise lies here," in the far east where the stalk of a pear-shaped earth protrudes, this being in concordance with "St Isidore, Bede ... St Ambrose and Scotus and all learned theologians [who] agree that the earthly Paradise is in the East" (Cohen 1969: 221). Contrary to Francis Bacon's image of the bold adventurer-scientist seeking to overturn received wisdom about the earth, Columbus was keen to locate himself in the scholarly world of late medieval geographical arguments, with their fusion of Christian and ancient ideas. If the experience of navigating the seas made a set of adjustments to an accepted understanding of the globe, it did not overturn that cosmology. In this regard, it makes sense to see Columbus as one of the set of late medieval travelers by land (such as William of Rubruck and Marco Polo) and sea (such as Diaz and Da Gama) whose experiences stretched the framework of Isidore's cosmology and added massive empirical detail of the sort to be found in Fra Mauro's late mappa mundi of 1450, but did not break that cosmology, let alone replace it with the sort of empirical science of hypothesis testing implied by Bacon's comments (Falchetta 2006).

Columbus's "human geography," his approach to the peoples he encountered, was similarly saturated in an ethnography gleaned from ancient and medieval lore. Expecting by his calculations to have reached the Cathay dotted with a thousand islands described by Marco Polo, he modeled the peoples he encountered in several ways. First, he describes them as simple, easy to convert to the true faith, and readily conquered and subjugated. He also compares the peoples of the Caribbean to another group who had come under the sway of the Spanish crown, commenting "they are not at all black, but the color of Canary Islanders, as could be expected since this is in the same latitude as the island of Hierro in the Canaries" (Cohen 1969: 56; see also Abulafia 2008). Whilst Columbus paints a sympathetic picture at many points, by suggesting the people had no religion, no organized leadership and were pliant to conversion, he placed them perilously close to falling into the category of the "natural slave" – a lower category than fully autonomous reasoning people – developed by Aristotle in his *Politics*. Just such an ascription would be deployed and rebutted in the epic debate over the rights of native inhabitants between Las Casas and Sepulveda some half century after the first landfall (Pagden 1982). Moreover, Columbus's "latitudinal" comparison of peoples separated by the Atlantic Ocean drew on both the zonal theories of antiquity and the medieval ethnography of Albertus Magnus (Gómez 2008). Finally, whilst eschewing the idea that the Americas contained "human monsters," Columbus nevertheless reported the existence of people with tails on Cuba and of an island inhabited solely by women which he calls Matinino, both of these being stories of "extraordinary or monstrous races" initially told in Pliny's *Natural History* and relayed down the centuries in medieval bestiaries (Friedman 1981; Campbell 1988).

Columbus, then, did not break apart the cosmological framework he had inherited from the late medieval world as embodied in the Ulm printing of the T-O map. And yet he was convinced that direct experience could challenge and refine the structures of geographical knowledge – human and physical – which he had inherited. The result in Columbus is a complex amalgam of ancient, Christian and empirical arguments, these last also themselves being a mixture – from the present day perspective – of claims we would support (such as large areas of new land) and of those we would dismiss as fabulous (a pear shaped earth inhabited by people with tails). In this Columbus is in fact representative of broader trends and tensions in Renaissance geographical knowledge, which in all its many forms displayed what can be called a "chaotic empiricism" which fused new claims with old learning and lore, as can be demonstrated by looking at other key components of that knowledge in the forms of cosmography, cartography and chorography in the century after Columbus's voyages.

The flood of new claims about the physical and human geography of the globe in the wake of Columbus posed a major problem to all the arts of geographical description in early modern Europe. This was perhaps most apparent in the genre of cosmography, an inquiry forged in the Renaissance age and which has aptly been described as integrating "three classical traditions: Aristotelian natural philosophy, which contributed the framework for the fundamental understanding of the natural world; Euclidean geometry and Ptolemaic geography, which provided the tools for mathematical representation of the universe; and Pomponius Mela's and Pliny's works, which served as models to incorporate the human, animal, and plant kingdoms into this universe" (Portuondo 2009: 20–21). Inspired by the classical tradition, then, cosmography aimed to update the medieval encyclopedism which Isidore represented in the light of Renaissance reverence for the ancients and the new streams of information generated by the age of discovery. The problems for cosmography as an inquiry at the largest geographical scale were the sheer quantities of information available and how to structure that information into a comprehensible argument or narrative. It is for this reason that in the Renaissance has been detected the origins of the quintessentially modern problem of "information overload" (Rosenberg, 2003).

Perhaps the greatest cosmographical projects were those sponsored by Philip II of Spain, who sought comprehensive information about his unprecedentedly large global empire. In Spain, the court, the Casa de la Contratación and the Council of the Indies all appointed cosmographers whose job was to interview those returning from the new world and incorporate new information with extant knowledge to keep maps and prose accounts of the world up-to-date. And yet these vast Spanish exploits were little known of in Europe as a whole, the works circulating in manuscript and not being printed, their contents being viewed as state secrets, as the key to wealth and power (Portuondo 2009; Barrera-Osorio, 2006; Mundy, 1996). Other cosmographies, however, were very much products of and for the public sphere of print. Perhaps the most influential such project was Sebastian Münster's *Cosmographia*, a massive and ever-expanding description of the whole globe, first published in 1544 in German and then in several other languages, notably Latin and French. By the time of Münster's death in 1552, the work stood at over 1200 folio pages long. If we look at the contents of the *Cosmographia*, an encyclopedic version of what has been termed Columbus's "chaotic empiricism" can be detected. The massive work is organized by sequential descriptions of the nations of the world, each nation in turn being described in a set of traverses along rivers. Within each place, a remarkably heterogeneous array of information is provided, starting with the geography of a place but moving out to treat history, ethnography and zoology. And as with Columbus, so Münster relies on an amalgam of things he has personally viewed and surveyed (he was a skilled cartographer and antiquarian) for areas in Switzerland and Germany, and of things others he trusts have seen and recorded for him. And yet, as the *Cosmographia* spread further afield from Europe, so Münster started to record the alleged existence of monstrous races with heads in their chests and so forth whose ultimate origin – as with Columbus tailed peoples – was Pliny's *Natural History*. Far-flung places are also depicted as having more extreme climates and animals. As Grafton has neatly summarized Münster's achievement: "new information did not modify or cancel the old, but piled up alongside it like fresh coal besides clinkers. New facts about the world – such as the existence of western continents – did not modify the old structure, which put the wild things Columbus had found where they had always been, in the East. And clear evidence that the world had changed radically with time did not modify the timeless analytic structure of most of what Münster had to say about unfamiliar peoples" (Grafton 1992: 106; for Münster see MacLean 2007; for other renaissance cosmographers, see Lestringent 1994; and Blair 1997).

The great cartographic projects of the Renaissance age show very similar contours to Münster's achievement in *Cosmographia*. And yet, the modern reception of Renaissance cartography has been very different from that for cosmographical projects, in the main because attention has focussed on the maps of Ortelius, Mercator and others, neglecting the textual apparatus which surrounded these maps and some of the ways in which the maps were constructed. Taken in the round, however, we find a form of "chaotic empiricism" which melded new information and discovery with Christian and classical frameworks drove Renaissance cartography quite as much as cosmography. This can be seen by attending to the paradigmatic work of Renaissance cartography which has lent its name to bound collections of maps ever since in the Western tradition, Gerardus Mercator's *Atlas* (1595). Mercator can easily be depicted as a "modern" cartographer, as the equivalent of Bacon's image of Columbus, by attending both to the global projection from 1569 which still bears his name and which was designed to facilitate transoceanic sailing in the "age of discovery" and to the maps of the newly discovered lands of that age which graced the *Atlas*. Yet the subtitle of the *Atlas* bespeaks a very different image of Mercator: "cosmographic meditations on the fabric of the world and the figure of the fabric" (Cosmographicae Meditationes de Fabrica Mundi et Fabricato Figura). In short, the maps which modern attention has almost exclusively attended to are part of a broader project, nothing short of a cosmography of the universe and the earth's place in that universe, this being the frame within which the cartographic subsection of the project functions. The extensive text which elaborates on this ambition is one squarely in the ambit of Christian and classical knowledge, containing as it does extensive analysis of the Biblical account of Creation in *Genesis* and references to the spheres of the universe derived from the works of Aristotle and Ptolemy. As Mercator's himself encapsulated his project:

> I have set this man Atlas, so notable for his erudition, humaneness, and wisdom as a model for my imitation ... And just as the cosmos contains the number, species, order, harmony, proportion, virtues, and effects of all things, even so, beginning from the creation, I shall enumerate all its parts and contemplate them naturally, as a methodical account demands, according to the order of their creation, so that the causes of things shall be evident. From these comes science, and from science wisdom, which directs all things to good ends. From wisdom comes prudence, which lays down an easy path for those ends. This shall be the aim of all things for me; then, in proper order, I shall treat of celestial bodies, then of astrological matters, which pertain to divination from the stars. Fourthly, I shall treat of the elements and then of geography. Thus I shall lay out the whole world as though in a mirror. (Mercator 2000: 25–26; cf. Crane 2002)

In this, Mercator stands proxy for broader currents in Renaissance cartography which continued to achieve complex mediations between inherited conceptual frameworks and new claims about the global disposition of the lands and the seas and about the physical and human geography of the world as it was being re-envisioned in the light of the age of discovery. As the recent authoritative history of Renaissance cartography summarizes this chaotic empiricism, "cartographically speaking, the Renaissance was an age that had not yet liberated itself from the authorities of its medieval and classical past, but some of the components necessary to achieve that liberation were already in place" (Woodward 2007: 5).

After the grandeurs of Mercator and Münster with their dizzying ambitions to realize global and universal descriptions in maps and prose, and in the wake of Columbus's death-defying navigations into the unknown, the following may appear somewhat bathetic:

> Malmesbury stands right on the top of a large, slate-like crag, in a marvelous naturally defended position. The Newnton Water flows to the town from two miles to the north, and the Avon Water from Luckington village four miles to the west, and they meet near a bridge on the south-east side of the town. Here, as the Avon, they flow south for a while, and then turn directly west towards Bristol. (Chandler 1993: 487)

This is how the pioneering English antiquarian, John Leland, described a Wiltshire town on his way to Cornwall in 1542. Leland was part of a Europe-wide drive to describe local, regional and national geographies, an intellectual pursuit categorized as "chorography" in the early modern era. As with cosmography and cartography, classical precedents were easy to find for this descriptive practice, most notably in Pausanias's description of Greece. Moreover, if describing Malmesbury seems to modern eyes "parochial" in the sense of "small minded," in its own era it was seen in more noble terms as ensuring that local knowledge, lore and geography were preserved for posterity. As such, Leland's practice was every bit as much the exploration and recording of the unfamiliar as was Columbus's in the eyes of his contemporaries. As John Bale put it of Leland:

> marke herin his laborious and fruteful doings, and ye shal fynde him no lesse profitable unto us, in the descrypcion of this particular nacyon, than were Strabo, Pliny, Ptholome, and other Geographers to their perusers, in the pycturinge out of the universall world. (Chandler 1993: 10).

Bale was not alone in tying chorography to the larger labors of geographical description, Sebastian Münster's aforementioned *Cosmographia* being grounded in the chorographical works of both Münster himself and a whole generation of German antiquarian and topographical writers in the circle of Conrad Celtis (MacLean 2007; Strauss 1959). By the time Münster and Lelend were writing, chorography had been in existence for at least a century since the pioneering efforts of Biondo Flavio's *Italia Illustrata* (1453), the work which best shows that describing the local and the national was quite as integral to the newfound world of Renaissance geographical scholarship as the more oft-remembered navigational, cartographical and cosmographic exploits discussed thus far. For Flavio, with the collapse of the Roman Empire, "the barbarians confounded everything," and, "as a result [we] are in great part ignorant of the very location of the regions of Italy, of the cities, towns, lakes and mountains, whose names appear so frequently in the ancient authors." Yet Flavio saw his own era, that which both we and they labeled the "renaissance," as one where "times have changed for the better" and the knowledge lost in the middle ages could be recovered. This was the task Flavio set himself, travelling around Italy both in person and through textual analysis to correlate the modern geography of fifteenth-century Italy to the provinces and towns recorded in ancient histories and early Christian chronicles. As such, *Italia Illustrata* begins with a survey of the geography of Italy as a whole before conducting a province-by-province survey of towns in ancient and modern Italy, following a sequence determined by Pliny's *Natural History*. If Flavio was not finding new worlds as Columbus was, to Renaissance geographical contemporaries his practice, that of recovering lost local worlds from antiquity, was every bit as important, something his prefatory comments modeled in suitably navigational terms as "having hauled ashore some planks from so vast a shipwreck, planks that were floating on the surface of the water or nearly lost to view" (Flavio 2005: 3–5). The results of these chorographic labors by antiquarians such as Flavio and Leland appear heterogeneous to the modern eye, local lore and sound early archaeology being juxtaposed in endless arrays of detail, much of it lacking interest. If one reverts to Leland's description of Malmesbury, for example, we are told that it was named after a certain Scot called "Maildulphus," that there is a fair on the feast of St Aldhelm, and that the Abbey buildings are "now the property of a man named Stumpe." And yet this mixture of facts and local traditions was a variant of precisely the same chaotic empiricism which drove the geographical cultures of cosmography, cartography and travel writing in this era.

If Flavio recovered lost worlds and Columbus discovered new worlds, both processing their information through inherited cosmologies, another major activity in this era that is worth mentioning briefly is the imagining of new or lost worlds. For the geographical culture of the Renaissance was also interested in places which were unknown or unreal, with how the very radical uncertainties about what is in the world might lead us to reflect on our own world. This was a category which transcended a "fact-fiction" divide. Thus Mercator and Ortelius confidently placed "terra nondum cognita" on various lands they depicted on their otherwise empirical maps. Likewise, Thomas More's *Utopia* (1516) was placed somewhere in the clutch of Caribbean Islands which twenty years of exploration after Columbus had uncovered and amounted to a profound thought experiment about those most basic of political questions, what is a good society and how will it be organized. And a century after More, Joseph Hall's dazzling *Mundus Alter et Idem* (1605) was a spoof set of travels to the lands of the Southern Continent which Mercator had placed on his maps, their aim being to show that human manners and vices are the same everywhere, making travel itself superfluous to the sort of moral project Mercator's own preface (quoted above) had outlined (Hiatt, 2008; Fausett, 1993).

Putting these strands of geographical work together, we can detect a coherent pattern to them. In each arena, geographical description witnessed a complex balancing act between on the one hand inherited conceptual frameworks, mainly those from ancient – essentially Aristotelian – science and from the Bible and its scholastic interpretation, and on the other hand a proliferation of new knowledge claims, both about new worlds such as those disclosed by Columbus, Da Gama and other luminaries of the "age of discovery" and about lost worlds swallowed by the passage of time and turmoil, as in the chorographical labors of Biondo Flavio and John Leland. In a culture of chaotic empiricism, there was a proliferation of claims about the world, its human and physical geography, and there was also an increasing tension between inherited frameworks of understanding and the new insights which new and lost worlds provoked. But it would only be when a shared new cosmology, a new frame for understanding, emerged that vast accumulations of geographical data would be surpassed or at least modified by a more restrictive sense of the empirical, of what counts as knowledge about the globe and its peoples. This would be the achievement of the mechanical philosophy of the seventeenth and eighteenth centuries.

Enlightenment, Mechanical Cosmography and Mathematical Empiricism

During the course of the seventeenth century, there arose an increasing call for a way of verifying knowledge claims which would build a new understanding of the globe, allowing the chaotic accumulation of information in the age of discovery to be disciplined in the light of a simple set of principles. One of the first and most eloquent to articulate this need and try to realize it was Francis Bacon, whose *Novum Organon*, quoted earlier, was one component of a larger project, The Great Instauration, whose aim was to build a new way of collecting information – empirically through the direct evidence of the senses – as a prolegomena to developing clear and indubitable laws about how nature functions. For Bacon, this would allow us to look to things rather than relying lamely on intellectual edifices from the past, notably those of Aristotelian science (Webster 1975). Bacon's grand designs were never realized, his treatises being an array of fragments themselves redolent of the chaotic empiricism he wanted to transcend. And yet the Baconian project, to strip away inherited myth and thereby improve our understanding of the world, was an inspiration to the systematizing efforts of the generation who followed in the later seventeenth century. Thus René Descartes penned several treatises in the 1630s and 1640s whose aim was to show how the simple principle of gravity between atoms could "supply causes for all natural objects" (Cottingham, Stoothoof and Murdoch 1985: 267). But it was Descartes's successor in this project, Isaac Newton, whose work was to finally satisfy the Baconian demand for a new image of the earth, one which would move the arts of geographical description and analysis away from the chaotic empiricism of the Renaissance and develop a new approach which can be labeled as "Enlightened." Whilst the details of Newtonian science and its cosmological underpinnings are beyond our scope here, some key points are worth making as they explain eighteenth-century approaches to analyzing the world. First, where providence and the active intervention of a Christian God as described in the Bible had been key to Renaissance geography, the Newtonian cosmology argued that God was the Creator of all things and their prime mover, but that the earth functioned by natural laws whose operation was discernible by the senses of mankind. Second, these laws – of which gravity or attraction at a distance was the most readily discernible – could be comprehended or captured by mathematical reasoning. Third, once natural laws had been modeled in mathematical terms, their accuracy could be tested by empirically confirming that the real-world ramifications of mathematical laws were in fact manifested on our globe. Taken together, the Newtonian image of the world can be said to be one encouraging a mechanical and mathematical empiricism, this being the cosmology which replaced the chaotic empiricism of the Renaissance. Newtonian or Enlightenment empiricism was mechanical in that it modeled the physical and human world in terms of a series of cause-effect structures, and it was mathematical in that it prioritized number as the way to turn sensory experience into a set of testable hypotheses about the earth, its peoples and their mutual interaction (Frängsmyr, Heilbron and Rider 1990).

The Newtonian impact on the arts of geographical description in the eighteenth and early nineteenth centuries can be discerned at two levels. First, many projects in geography and in the geographically-sensitive understanding of the physical and human worlds were directly inspired by queries arising from Newton's work and by his model of inquiry, just as his work itself had drawn heavily on geographically disparate sources (Schaffer 2009). Second, and akin to the aether which for Newton must connect objects for action at a distance to occur, Newton's cosmology imperceptibly impacted upon the working assumptions of generations of scholars practicing geographical description (for a full exposition of the sheer range of these projects, see Withers 2007).

Taking Newton's direct impact briefly first, some of the great geographical projects of global mapping and data collection in the age of Enlightenment were inspired by Newton. Most notable here was the attempt in the 1730s and 1740s to test Newton's proposition that the earth is an oblate spheroid, and therefore bulges at the equator and is flattened at the Poles. This suggestion had been queried in the light of another great Newtonian project of mathematical and cartographical enumeration, the Cassini survey of France, which had suggested that the earth was a prolate spheroid, thus being flattened at the Equator. To address this conundrum, the French Academy of Sciences sent two voyages, one to Lapland under Maupertius, and the other to the Amazon under La Condamine, to measure a degree of latitude accurately. That the findings of these two voyages showed Newton to be "right" is less important for our purposes than the fact that the solution was seen to rest with rigorous mathematical determination of the true nature of the world. Newton's mathematical and mechanical cosmology drove the quest to test his own hypothesis about the shape of the globe (Greenberg 1995; Terrall 2002; Safier 2008). This cosmology also undergirds many of the great intellectual projects of the "long" eighteenth century which sought to advance our understanding of the physical and human world. Charles Lyell's massively influential *Principles of Geology* (1830-1833) for example, was explicitly modeled on Newton's achievement in the *Principia* (1687), its aim being to reduce the complex realities of earth science to simple principles which explained empirical outcomes, in this case Lyell positing that simple, small processes could explain massive changes in the earth when aggregated over a long enough timeframe (Rudwick 2008: part 3). Equally important, Newton's impact underlay great Enlightenment projects to understand mankind, notably David Hume's philosophical masterpiece, *A Treatise of Human Nature* (1739–1740), whose Newtonian inspiration is revealed in its subtitle: 'an attempt to introduce the experimental method of reasoning into moral subjects'. And many of these

Newtonian forays into what became known as "the science of mankind" were strongly geographical in their orientation, using data about global cultural geographies to seek and test lawlike regularities about human behavior (Porter and Wokler 1995). This, for example, can be seen both in Montesquieu's *Spirit of the Laws* (1748), where climatic variations are hypothesized as key to why different political systems suit different nations, and half a century later in Malthus's *Essay on the Principle of Population* (1798), where the early chapters survey civilizations across the globe at different levels of advancement to suggest that they all have to respond to the tendency for population growth to outstrip increases in food production.

More generally, however, the Newtonian understanding of the way the world functions and can be described and understood undergirded the distinctive ways in which geographical description functioned across a range of spatial scales. At the broadest scale, the cosmographic tradition of universal and encyclopedic description and analysis which we have seen encouraged by Phillip II of Spain and practiced by Sebastian Münster all but disappeared. In part this is because the Newtonian approach, whilst framed by a belief in God, saw God as in all but unmoved by it; it also saw matter in motion as made by and moving by God's hand, but in ways which could be modeled mathematically as if God were not involved. As such, there was no need for geographical description to concern itself with cosmology as it did not alter what was described nor impact on how it should be analyzed. If for Newton God's universe was a mechanical entity functioning according to mathematical regularities, God could be dropped from the descriptive and analytic project.

What the Newtonian cosmology meant for the arts of geographical description can be seen by looking at exploration, cartography and chorography in the age of Enlightenment. In terms of Enlightenment exploration, the three voyages of James Cook can be taken as representative. For a start, each voyage had clear scientific hypotheses about the physical geography of the globe which it was charged with investigating, the first for instance testing the validity of the Newtonian system itself by observing the "Transit of Venus," the time it took for Venus to pass directly between the sun and the earth. Furthermore, the collection of data about the physical and human geography of the globe was no longer to be a haphazard activity; on the contrary, specific instructions about what to observe were tendered, a project with its roots in Robert Boyle's early paper for the Royal Society which enumerated the headings under which travelers should collect information in order to make it readily digestible and useful to scientists back in Europe (Boyle 1692). True to the demand for direct sensory evidence, several men aboard Cook's voyages were charged with keeping journals, scientists were on board as well, and artists ensured that the geographies encountered were recorded visually as well as verbally (Smith 1985). It is for this reason that Cook's vessels and those of other enlightenment navigations have been depicted as floating laboratories (Sorrenson 1996). What this meant to the quotidian mentality of an explorer in the Newtonian age of mechanical and mathematical empiricism can be seen by glimpsing any page from Cook's logbook, where a precise, mathematically-determined longitude and latitude measurement prefaces a detailed account of the day's sailing and precise pen portraits of the phenomena in the physical and human world which Cook encounters. In terms of human geography, Cook was keen to assess the assemblage of language, agriculture, customs, religion and political structure of the peoples he encountered to develop a sense of their civilization, this being rather different from Columbus's imperial and providential approach to human geography and part of an emergent anthropological approach in the Enlightenment (Wolff and Cippolini 2007). If Cook's journals were paradigmatic they were by no means exceptional, the journals of Meriwether Lewis and William Clarke's pioneering expedition across the continental interior of America (1804–1806) and those of Alejandro Malaspina's Spanish-funded traverses of the Pacific Ocean (1789–1794), for example, being every bit as Newtonian in their ambition to record quantitatively and empirically the functioning of the world (Stafford 1984).

If we remember James Cook as a navigator, he was equally proud of his skills as a cartographer. Indeed, when Cook commented on his second voyage's impact that "the Sciences will receive some improvement there from especially ... Geography" he was using the term geography as synonymous with cartography (Edwards 1999: 333). For Cook was skilled in the navigational art of sailing close to the shore in order to allow for a precise chart of the shoreline and offshore depths to be constructed, scores of these contributions to the science of geography (or, more accurately in the terms of the era, hydrography) being deposited with the Admiralty at the conclusion of each voyage (David, Joppien and Smith 1988–1997). Again, Cook exemplifies how the Newtonian cosmology altered the geographical art of cartography, in that his charts were based on precise quantification *in situ*. This is a far cry from the world of Mercator we outlined earlier, for Mercator relied on a complex amalgam of textual and empirical evidence, and further was happy to take theoretical constructs – notably the idea of a large southern continent whose mass was supposed to counterbalance the overabundance of land in the northern hemisphere – and turn them into cartographic realities. Cook and Enlightenment cartography more generally gradually removed such myths from their maps (Cook's second voyage in particular scotching the notion of a habitable southern continent), preferring increasingly to acknowledge areas where direct evidence was lacking in the form of blanks on the map (Belyea 1992) (yet we should not underestimate the persistence of geographical myths in the age of Enlightenment as Polk's 1995 study of the idea of California being an island shows). And yet, the Enlightenment's thirst for direct knowledge about the globe led to massive, government-sponsored cartographic projects by a host of European nations to mathematically survey and cartographically delineate both unknown spaces such as the Pacific and the burgeoning imperial spaces under their command; the empirical attitude which led to the acknowledgement of blanks on the map also demanded their elimination. The first such projects were spawned in seventeenth-century France in the form of the Cassini surveys, successors to which would continue to be funded by the French state well into the nineteenth century (Konvitz 1987; Petto 2007). Further massive projects were embarked upon by the empire Britain lost in the eighteenth century, the gargantuan task of surveying, dividing and apportioning land in the US leading to the Rectangular Survey in the early nineteenth century, and in the empire Britain retained, in the form of the Great Trigonometrical Survey of India (Hubbard 2009; Edney 1990). In each of these cases and others such as Napoleon's demand to survey Egypt (Godlewska 1995), a mathematically accurate map at a high scale of resolution was demanded, the aim being to produce maps of use to the state in planning resource use and the appropriation of lands.

Chorography was the art of geographical description least affected by Newtonian cosmology. It was for this reason that this art and its practitioners were increasingly subject to gentle ridicule as irrelevant antiquarians preserving little fragments from the past regardless of their lack of any real worth, a view encapsulated in Sir Walter Scott's *The Antiquary* (1816), but also prefigured over a century earlier in Thomas Shadwell's play *The Virtuoso* (1676). And yet if one looks to chorographical works rather than their literary reception, there were in fact important moves to make the art of local description more precise and to move away from the chaotic empiricism of a Flavio or a Leland. If one looks at later editions of the greatest work of English chorography, *Britannia* by Leland's successor William Camden, for example, the massive annotations by Edmund Gibson (1695 and 1722) and then by Richard Gough (1789 and 1806) show an increasing desire both to visit sites and then to reproduce what is found in the form of inscriptions and fragments in illustrations. Clearly, there was some drive to make chorography a practice predicated on direct sensory impressions of places (Sweet 2004; Hanson 2009). This trend became still stronger in the early nineteenth century when chorography began to mutate into archaeology, the scientific excavation of sites to determine past lifestyles and human geographies, something which is evidenced in the more empirical approach to chorography in pioneering texts such as Richard Colt Hoare's *Ancient History of Wiltshire* (1812–1821) for which work he excavated over three hundred sites (Levine 1986).

Putting all this together, it was not Columbus and the age of discovery which overthrew a Christian and classical understanding of the world. It took the accumulation of data over generations in the sixteenth century before an Aristotelian and Biblical approach to the arts of geographical description came to be seen as outmoded and inadequate. Seventeenth century projects to develop new cosmology reached fruition in the Newtonian image of a mechanical world, which, whilst created and maintained by a God, functioned via laws which were amenable to mechanical and mathematical scrutiny. This image of the world led to profound changes in the arts of early modern European geographical description, particularly in the arenas of exploration accounts and of cartography, where quantification, precision and witnessing for oneself came to be the guarantors of the scholarly and scientific worth of geographical work.

Early Modern Geography: Chaotic and Mathematical Empiricism

Thus far, discussion has ranged from Mercator's vision of cosmography as a "total" inquiry into the description and causes of all things in the universe down to Leland's description of Malmesbury. Yet discussion of the scale of description and analysis which early modern scholars normally called "geography" has deliberately been postponed until now.

Above all, geography was the description of the whole earth; it was distinctive not so much for what it described nor for how it analyzed information as for the spatial scale at which that description and analysis functioned. Early modern scholars essentially reproduced the division of spatial knowledge into a nested hierarchy which Ptolemy had set out in the opening book of his *Geography*, with chorography and topography attending to scales smaller than the globe and cosmography linking global descriptions to explanatory structures accounting for the universe as a whole. Pitched in between these scales, geography's task was to describe the whole globe. As perhaps the most celebrated dictionary of the era put it, "geography ... in a strict sense ... [is] the knowledge of the earthly globe, and the situation of the various parts of the earth. When it is taken in a little larger sense, it includes the knowledge of the seas also; and in the largest sense of all, it extends to the various customs, habits and governments of nations" (Johnson 1755, sub "geography"). To see just how ancient the inspiration behind this definition is, it can be compared with Ptolemy's original from circa 150AD, where he argued that 'the essence of *geōgraphia* is to show the known world as a simple and continuous entity, its nature and how it is situated, [taking account] only of the things that are associated with it in its broader, general outlines (such as gulfs, great cities, the more notable peoples and rivers, and the more noteworthy things of each kind)' (Berggren and Jones 2000: 57).[1] And yet, the Ptolemaic scalar definition of geography should not be seen as a rigid one; on the contrary, those who practiced the art of topographical description were routinely labeled as geographers as we have already seen Bale do in respect of Leland, and equally many writings at the spatial scale of the globe were also described and titled as cosmographies, as in Peter Heylyn's global geographical description, *Cosmographie in Foure Bookes* (1652) (on the multiple meanings of geography in this era, see Withers 2006).

To categorize geography as description of the globe immediately demands three qualifications. First, "description" did not have the almost exclusively prosaic meaning we assume today; on the contrary, and as best exemplified by Ptolemy himself, description could mean a factual visual account, notably in the form of a map. As such, where there were many for whom geography was a textual practice of collating information about the globe, the term could just as easily be used to mean the construction of global maps, a cartographic understanding of "geography" we have already seen exemplified by James Cook. As the eighteenth century progressed, moreover, geography books increasingly included quantitative data in the form of statistical digests about the nations of the world. This was pioneered in geography by the German Anton Büsching in the 1750s and suggested the ways in which the mathematical cosmology of Newtonian science could be incorporated into the otherwise ancient delimitation of the art of geographical description, something only previously realized in Bernhard Varenius's exceptional *Geographia Generalis* (1650). Second, Ptolemy in fact spoke of geography as describing the known world or ecumene, where that was in fact far smaller than the entirety of the globe. Obviously, the European exploration of the globe in the early modern era increasingly brought the known world into line with the entire globe, but geographers in general did try to include descriptions of lands not yet fully known, something which attracted the satirical ire of Jonathan Swift and others who continued the line of imaginary geographies which More's *Utopia* had originated. As such, early modern geography by and large attempted to describe the globe, not simply the known world, this leading it to include fictitious material in a manner akin to that we have already seen in Columbus and Mercator. Third, if geographical writing was predominantly descriptive in the early-modern era, this does not mean that it lacked an interest in explaining the nature and distribution of phenomena, but rather that this was ultimately less significant than description. As Clarence

Glacken showed in his classic work on the history of geographical thought, religious ideas of a creator of the earth, ideas that physical and climatic geography determine human character, and an awareness of human impacts on the natural environment all acted as explanatory structures in early modern geographical writing (Glacken 1967).

As a mode of writing early modern geography was normally encompassed in two forms, either gazetteers, alphabetically-organized descriptions of the world, or what the English language tradition called "grammars," global descriptions structured by continent and then by nation. The gazetteer had no obvious precedents in antiquity, but the geographical grammar was a variant on the structured descriptive tour around the world by which Strabo's *Geography* and Pomponius Mela's *De Situ Orbis* organized a prose account of the known world. In the terms of the era, either mode of organization justified deeming geography a "science" where this term, from its Latin root "scientia," merely meant organized knowledge. Such works were hugely popular and were the main printed form through which geography could be learned in the early modern era (Bowen 1981; Mayhew 2000).

Burrowing a little deeper, what sorts of descriptive information did such global summaries contain? In truth, throughout the era geography books – akin in this to the chorographical tradition – were remarkably diverse in their contents. To exemplify this, we can focus on the most oft-reprinted geographical grammar in the English language tradition, a text constantly in print from 1770 to 1842, William Guthrie's *New Geographical, Historical and Commercial Grammar* (for the print history of which, see Sitwell 1993 and Sher 2006: 487–493 and 573–582). For each nation in this global survey, the author deploys the same set of headings to organize his material. Descriptions start with the boundaries of the nation in question and then move on to address matters we would deem to be physical geographical: "Soil Air and Water," the "face" or landscape of the country, rivers, forests, metals and minerals, and finally, vegetables and animals. Guthrie then shifts his attention to the human world, wherein he routinely treats the population of a country, manners and customs, religion, languages, scholarly culture, cities and towns, commerce and manufactures, the constitution, laws and taxes, the armed forces, and, finally, the history of the nation. Most of this information was conveyed in prose, but geography books increasingly included mathematically determined information in the eighteenth century, starting with longitudes and latitudes and later extending to statistical digests. But lest this makes Guthrie's work and other grammars of the same ilk sound rather "modern," it needs to be made clear that the eclecticism of the age of chaotic empiricism remained in geographical texts right through into the nineteenth century all but untouched by the Newtonian drive to strip out such elements (as we will see in the next section, this would be one reason for the collapse of early modern geography). Thus geography books routinely included information concerning topics such as heraldry and how to correctly address a monarch which would seem to be wholly irrelevant to the subject of geography as it was understood then and now. Such material remained as the main aim of geographical texts seems to have been inclusiveness rather than thematic focus. Also, geography books were happy to retell "myths" about the world even where few credited them; Guthrie, for example, was still in his Scandinavian section discussing the mythic sea-creature known as the Kracken as well as mermaids, this despite the complete lack of evidence for their existence outside mariners' tales (Guthrie 1771: 74–75). Geography, then, had a vexed relationship with the scientific idea of hypothesis testing by the collection of direct sensory data which Bacon, Boyle and Newton had enshrined. In summary, geography as an inquiry continued to do what we have seen Münster do in the *Cosmographia*; it simply juxtaposed old and new claims about the world, being as a discourse an amalgam of the tenets of chaotic and mechanical empiricism.

Geography was a clearly defined mode of inquiry albeit one whose realization sprawled into every conceivable arena. It also had readily identifiable audiences, as the prefaces to geography books themselves pointed out. First, students were deemed to need a working knowledge of the geography of the globe; in particular it was argued in an essentially humanist conception of the curriculum that to understand Christian and classical texts, one needed to understand their geography first. An oft-rehearsed commonplace posited geography as "the eye of history," the means by which the historian could see their subject matter aright. This commonplace, which had ancient origins, was coined by Mercator's great cartographic contemporary, Abraham Ortelius, but was rehearsed with regularity into the nineteenth century. And yet the age of Enlightenment in fact saw a considerable expansion in geography's audience: works of geographical instruction were penned especially for children, John Newbury specializing in such publications in the British context, whilst specialist academies for merchants and naval officers also routinely included geography in their curriculums. Furthermore, a number of books aimed at popularizing Newtonian natural philosophy which included geographical instruction were targeted at a female as well as a male audience, this amounting to the first time geography had been explicitly deemed a subject suitable for both genders. Second, geography was deemed vital to statesmen and politicians; this was an ancient canard which Strabo, for example, had rehearsed around the time of the birth of Christ, but it continued to be deemed relevant. Maps and geographical descriptions were needed to plan military campaigns and to apportion territories in an age of imperial aggrandizement by the European powers across the face of the globe. It was this which led to Phillip II's previously-discussed demand for cosmographical work at the beginning of the period and was still driving George III to amass a massive map collection at the end of the period. Third, geography was always seen as providing useful information to business men, notably as the globalization of trading networks ran alongside global empire building. Geography books routinely included details about tariffs and resources around the world, and it was this which led to the interest of the business academies which mushroomed in the early eighteenth century (Mayhew 1998).

And yet, if geography as an inquiry was fairly precisely defined and had a clear audience, it was most definitely not a "discipline" in the modern sense of the term. Schooling and university education were directed towards a general education in the arts, the outcome of which would be familiarity with the classics, sacred and secular. There was no specialist qualification to be had in geography (or, indeed, in our other modern disciplines) until the nineteenth century at schools or universities. Geography was seen to be a body of descriptive knowledge, one acquired as an adjunct to historical studies, and moreover, it was argued – most influentially by John Locke – that this acquisition being primary through the eyes by the close perusal of maps, geography could be picked up when one was very young (Locke 1989: 235, argued a six year old could acquire as much geography as anyone would need). Obviously, there were "specialist" geographers, in the sense that governments appointed cartographers and identifiable individuals were charged with teaching geography in the university curriculum, but most had no credentials beyond a general education which justified their appointment (see Withers and Mayhew 2002 in the UK context and Smith and Vining 2003 in the US context). This brings us to the final key point, that in a sense there was no such thing as a "geographer" in early modern Europe, rather, there were people who wrote geography or inscribed it in maps, most of whom were also engaged in other activities to make ends meet. For example, if posterity remembers Mercator for his *Atlas* and Münster for his *Cosmographia*, the former was also a mathematical instrument maker and the latter's income was predicated on being a professor of Hebrew, not a geographer. Similar comments apply to geography in the age of Enlightenment; those we memorialize as "geographers" tended to be authors in a wide range of genres, earning their living in a cutthroat commercial world of print. William Guthrie, for example, wrote his geographical grammar in the last year of a vastly productive writer's life which had seen him write for newspapers and periodicals as well as being a prolific writer of histories. As such, if in the modern era we see a "geographer" as one who writes a series of works to contribute to a discipline called geography, in the early modern era there was no such discipline and therefore geography books were very rarely the sole preoccupation of any writer, the arts of history, theology and mathematical demonstration often being twinned with geography in authorial oeuvres. Relatedly, there was certainly no clear distinction between "physical" and "human" geography, these terms and the division they bespeak only gaining currency in the nineteenth century. Geographical descriptions, as we have seen for Guthrie, did tend to group "physical" then "human" matters in each description, and they were clearly aware of a distinction between these two arenas as was Johnson's dictionary definition of geography, but the task of geography was precisely to provide a description which encompassed both arenas. Moreover, geography compiled information about the globe, it did not to go out and collect it at first hand; no one could be expected to know about the entire globe from direct experience and geography, therefore, was an art of collation and construction, of the adjudication and reconciliation of sources to create a synthesis both in prose as in Guthrie's *Grammar* and in maps such as those of the great French cartographer Jean Baptiste D'Anville. If a Baconian and Newtonian approach demanded direct sensory empiricism, geography as a global description could only rely on the direct impressions of others, not global fieldwork by the geographer, hence its continuing foothold in the mental world of chaotic empiricism right into the nineteenth century.

Putting all this together, geography was a clearly defined area of inquiry in early modern Europe, albeit its boundaries with other inquiries such as cosmography and chorography were porous. Geography described in prose, maps and (increasingly) numbers the physical and human nature of the entire globe. Such a task was performed through structured accounts which juxtaposed the copiousness of chaotic empiricism with an emergent rigor redolent of mathematical empiricism. There were well defined audiences for geography which were catered for by a burgeoning print culture, but the subject was not taught as a discrete or disciplinary type of inquiry, but in the main as an adjunct to history in a humanist curriculum. This marginal role was one of the reasons why there were not "geographers" as such (let alone physical and human geographers), but rather individuals who as part of a broader portfolio produced geographical descriptions.

Vitalism, Connectivity and the Disciplinary Imagination: the Decline of Early Modern Geography

By the late eighteenth century geography as sketched in the previous section started to appear woefully archaic to many. As geography had been founded on a platform bringing together elements from the chaotic empiricism of the age of discovery and the mechanical empiricism of the age of enlightenment, it is unsurprising that the critique of this form of geographical inquiry came as part of a broader questioning of the tenets of Newtonian cosmology and of empiricism more generally. In the course of the nineteenth and early twentieth centuries geography would be reworked in a thoroughgoing fashion, and the early modern platforms of and frameworks for geography would be replaced with forms and features far more familiar to those who practice geography in the present day.

Newtonian mechanics was, of course, never accepted without demur, being attacked by Leibniz when first proposed and then being criticized variously on scientific and religious grounds. Core to its replacement as the cosmological bedrock of geographical inquiry, however, were the ideas of vitalism which were far more powerful in eighteenth-century Europe than was previously supposed and which flowered into nineteenth century romanticism (Reill 2005). Vitalism suggested a dynamic spirit flowed through the world which mere mechanical and empirical analysis could not capture. As such, the Newtonian project could model superficially the way the universe functioned, but could not explain why nor see the unity of the whole. One of the great early exponents of this view was the poet William Blake, who railed against Newton throughout his life:

> You don't believe – I won't attempt to make ye:
> You are asleep – I won't attempt to wake ye.
> Sleep on, Sleep on! while in your pleasant dreams
> Of Reason you may drink of Lifes clear streams
> Reason and Newton they are quite two things
> For so the Swallow & the Sparrow sings
> Reason says "Miracle": Newton says "Doubt."
> Aye! that's the way to make all Nature out.
> "Doubt, Doubt, & don't believe without experiment":
> That is the very thing that Jesus meant,
> When he said, "Only Believe! Believe & try!
> "Try, Try, & never mind the Reason why."
> (Blake, 1966: 536)

Blake was a lonely prophet in the English context, but this element of his project came to be far more generally held in the romantic conception of nature (Richards 2002). It was in Germany that vitalism and the reinvigorated spiritual conception of nature first ushered in a critique of early modern geography and a new conception of geography in the early years of the nineteenth century, this movement being spearheaded by Alexander von Humboldt and Carl Ritter (Tang 2008). In the summa of his life's work, *Cosmos*, Humboldt made his criticism of early modern geography transparent: 'it is desirable to deviate as widely as possible from the imperfect compilations designated, till the close of the eighteenth century, by the inappropriate term of *popular knowledge*' (Humboldt 1997: 51–52). A true knowledge of the universe came not from collecting together discrete facts in ever-more unwieldy compendia, but instead from seeing the connections between categories, the interconnection of laws, the ways in which the awesome beauties of nature could be understood as interconnected and therefore found more beautiful still: "in considering the study of physical phenomena ... we find its noblest and most important result to be a knowledge of the chain of connection, by which all natural forces are linked together, and made mutually dependent upon each other ... [The universe is] a Cosmos, or harmoniously ordered whole" (Humboldt 1997: 23–24). In this context, Humboldt found the geographical writings of the past dry and irrelevant, but saw in the "delineation of comparative geography, drawn in its full extent, and in all its relations with the history of man, by the skilled hand of Carl Ritter," a model of how geography should work in the cosmology he sketched in *Cosmos* (Humboldt 1997: 67). As its name suggests, the project of comparative geography was precisely not to simply amass facts about the globe, but instead to interrogate the similarities and differences between the physical and human geography (and the interconnections thereof) of selected places. The idea of comparative geography, true to Humboldt, was to find the general connections between geographical categories, thereby moving beyond empirical particularities to the underlying interconnections making the seamless web of our world.

Humboldt, then, developed a new cosmology which in turn encouraged a different mode of geographical inquiry, one which remodelled the empiricism of its early modern predecessor. Humboldt was hugely influential in the early nineteenth century, to the extent that some historians discern a distinctively "Humboldtian" style of scientific inquiry (Cannon 1978). Whatever the truth of this, there certainly were parallel moves elsewhere in Europe to develop a more holistic and less atomistic conception of the natural world, this having important ramifications for the character of geographical inquiry. To simply instance the British context, for example, Darwin – a keen admirer of Humboldt – in his *Origin of Species* (1859) engaged in a project to show the underlying processes which created the complex diversities and adjustments seen in the plant and animal worlds, ending in Humboldtian vein: "there is grandeur in this view of life, with its several powers, having been originally breathed into a few forms or into one; and that, whilst this planet has gone cycling on according to the fixed law of gravity, from so simple a beginning endless forms most beautiful and most wonderful have, and are being, evolved" (Endersby 2009: 376). The generation after these words were penned witnessed a series of British geographers seeking to change the nature of the subject to accord with a Humboldtian and Darwinian project of tracing the connections and unities behind the empirical multiplicity which early modern geography had done so much to catalogue and so little to analyze (Stoddart 1987). Perhaps the most influential of these reformers was Halford Mackinder, who in 1887 announced a project for a "new" geography which would be a bridge between the arts and the sciences, looking to unravel the complex mutual interrelations between human beings and their physical environment (Mackinder 1887). Similar projects to remold geography away from its purely empirical leanings were also announced by figures as diverse as Paul Vidal de la Blache in France, Élisée Reclus in Belgium, and Friedrich Ratzel in Germany. These European models, most notably the Germanic ones, would also have a huge impact on the redefinition of North American geography under the aegis of figures such as Carl Sauer and Richard Hartshorne.

These various projects to develop a new, unified and connected geography demanded seismic shifts in the character of the subject, shifts which to a considerable extent made the intellectual terrain on which we still stand. First, looking to the complex mutual interrelations of the human and physical worlds led to a focus on scales smaller than the global. There was still work done at the global scale – notably Mackinder's own geopolitical work on the "pivot of history" for example (Mackinder 1904) – but increasingly geography jettisoned this Ptolemaic definition, preferring to attend to national and regional work, scales at which complex mutual determinations between the physical and the human were more readily detected. Related to this, there was an increasing sense that, as well as looking to smaller areas, it was legitimate for geographers to specialize in parts of the subject, the result being the emergence of different communities of practice in physical and human geography where, as previously stated, there had been no clear demarcation of these realms before. Obviously, the project of a connective "new" geography suggested the need for geographers to work across the divide between the physical and human worlds, but they could do so with human emphases – as in the political geography of Mackinder – or with a predominant interest in the physical world – as in the fluvial work of William Morris Davis. Second, looking at interrelations led into an image of geography as a "causal" inquiry, as a practice whose quarry was not a sprawling catalogue of facts, but an explanation of the interrelation of facts. Relatedly, geography's self-definition moved away from being "scientia," the organization of knowledge, towards being science, the creation and testing of hypotheses. Furthermore, geography was alleged to have its own particular set of causal interests which were different from those of other scientists, these resting in the interrelationship between the physical and human spheres. Here we see the emergence of the modern "disciplinary" sense of geography as a distinct subject and the resultant demand that there be specialist training in geography at all levels from elementary schooling right through to research professors. This "disciplinary imagination" led to the panoply of institutions and apparatuses we are now familiar with: school qualifications, university departments, and societies to promote and promulgate geography were all, by and large, the progeny of the late nineteenth century, the educational landscape of early modern European geography having none of these features (for a wide ranging survey, see Dunbar 2001). For all the battles which geography has witnessed since the nineteenth century, many of which are chronicled and indeed rejoined in other chapters in this volume, none has been anyway near as profound or thoroughgoing as that which destroyed the empirical descriptive geography of the early modern age and replaced it with the connective causal discipline of modern geography. Modern geographers are all, to ape A.N. Whitehead on Plato, merely a series of footnotes to that moment.

Note

1 I have replaced the translator's term, "world cartography," with the original word "geōgraphia" to facilitate comparison with Johnson's definition.

References

Abulafia, D. (2008) *The Discovery of Mankind: Atlantic Encounters in the Age of Columbus.* Yale University Press, New Haven.
Barney, S.A., Lewis, W.J., Beach, J.A. and Berghof, O. (trans and eds) (2006) *The Etymologies of Isidore of Seville.* Cambridge University Press, Cambridge.
Barrera-Osorio, A. (2006) *Experiencing Nature: The Spanish American Empire and the early Scientific Revolution.* University of Texas Press, Austin.
Belyea, B. (1992) Images of Power: Derrida/Foucault/Harley. *Cartographica* 29, pp. 1–9.
Berggren, J.L. and Jones, A. (trans and eds).(2000) *Ptolemy's Geography: An Annotated Translation of the Theoretical Chapters.* Princeton University Press, Princetown.
Blair, A.(1997) *The Theater of Nature: Jean Bodin and Renaissance Science.* Princeton University Press, Princeton.
Blake, W.(1966) *Complete Writings.* Oxford University Press, Oxford.
Bowen, M.(1981) *Empiricism and Geographical Thought: from Francis Bacon to Alexander von Humboldt.* Cambridge University Press, Cambridge.
Boyle, R. (1962) *General heads for the natural history of a country, great or small: drawn out for the use of travellers and navigators.* John Taylor, London.
Campbell, M. (1988) *The Witness and the Other World: Exotic European Travel Writing, 400–1600.* Cornell University Press, Ithaca, NY.
Cannon, S. (1978) *Science in Culture: the Early Victorian Period.* Dawson, New York.
Cave, T. (2006) Locating the Early Modern. *Paragraph* 29, 12–26.
Chandler, J. (ed.) (1993) *John Leland's Itinerary: Travels in Tudor England.* Allan Sutton, Stroud.
Cohen, J.M. (ed.) (1969) *Christopher Columbus: The Four Voyages.* Penguin, Harmonsworth.
Cormack, L. (1994) Flat earth or round sphere: misconceptions of the shape of the earth and the fifteenth century transformation of the world. *Ecumene* 1, 363–385.
Cottingham, J., Stoothoff, R., and Murdoch, D. (trans and eds) (1985) *The Philosophical Writings of Descartes, Volume I.* Cambridge University Press, Cambridge.
Crane, N.(2002) *Mercator: The Man who Mapped the Planet.* Weidenfeld and Nicolson, London.
David, A., Joppien, R., and Smith, B. (eds) (1988–1997) *The Charts and Coastal Views of Cook's Voyages, 3 volumes.* Hakluyt Society, London.
Dunbar, G. (ed.) (2001) *Geography: Discipline, Profession and Subject since 1870: An International Survey.* Kluwer, Dordrecht.
Edney, M.(1990) *Mapping an Empire: The Geographical Construction of British India, 1765–1843.* University of Chicago Press, Chicago.
Edson, E. (2007) *The World Map 1300–1492: The Persistence of Tradition and Transformation.* Johns Hopkins University Press, Baltimore.
Edwards, P. (ed.) (1999) *James Cook: The Journals.* Penguin, Harmonsworth.
Eisenstein, E. (2005) *The Printing Revolution in Early Modern Europe*, 2nd edn. Cambridge University Press, Cambridge.
Elliott, J.H. (1992) *The Old World and the New: 1492–1650.* Cambridge University Press, Cambridge.

Endersby, J. (2009) *Charles Darwin: On the Origin of the Species*. Cambridge University Press, Cambridge.
Falchetta, P. (2006) *Fra Mauro's World Map*. Turnhout, Brepols.
Fausett, D.(1993) *Writing the New World: Imaginary Voyages and Utopias of the Great Southern Land*. Syracuse University Press, Syracuse.
Febvre, L. and Martin, H.-J. (1984) *The Coming of the Book: The Impact of Printing, 1450-1800*. Verso, London.
Frängsmyr, T., Heilbron, J.L., and Rider, R.E. (eds) (1990) *The Quantifying Spirit in the Eighteenth Century*. University of California Press, Berkeley.
Friedman, J.B. (1981) *The Monstrous Races in Medieval Thought and Art*. Harvard University Press, Cambridge, MA.
Gautier Dalché, P. (2007) The reception of Ptolemy's Geography (end of the fourteenth to beginning of the sixteenth century). In Woodward, D. (ed.), *The History of Cartography: Volume 3: The European Renaissance*. University of Chicago Press, Chicago, pp. 285–364.
Glacken, C. (1967) *Traces on the Rhodian Shore: Nature and Culture in Western Thought from Ancient Times to the End of the Eighteenth Century*. University of California Press, Berkeley.
Godlewska, A. (1995) Map, Text and Image. The Mentality of Enlightened Conquerors: A New Look at the Description de l'Egypte. *Transactions of the Institute of British Geographers, New Series* 20, 5–28.
Gómez, N.W. (2008) *The Tropics of Empire: Why Columbus sailed South to the Indies*. MIT Press, Cambridge.
Grafton, A. (1992) *New Worlds, Ancient Texts: The Power of Tradition and the Shock of Discovery*. Harvard University Press, Cambridge.
Greenberg, J.L. (1995) *The Problem of the Earth's Shape from Newton to Clairaut: The Rise of Mathematical Science in Eighteenth-Century Science and the "Fall" of Normal Science*. Cambridge University Press, Cambridge.
Guthrie, W.(1771) *A New Geographical, Historical and Commercial Grammar*, 3rd ed. J. Knox, London.
Hanson, A. (2009) *The English Virtuoso: Art, Medicine and Antiquarianism in the Age of Empiricism*. University of Chicago Press, Chicago.
Hiatt, A. (2008) *Terra Incognita: Mapping the Antipodes before 1600*. British Library, London.
Hubbard, B. (2009) *American Boundaries: The Nation, the States, The Rectangular Survey*. University of Chicago Press, Chicago.
Humboldt, A. (1997) *Cosmos: a Sketch of the Physical Description of the Universe*. Johns Hopkins University Press, Baltimore.
Jardine, L. and Silverthorne, M. (eds) (2000) *Bacon, F. The New Organon*. Cambridge University Press, Cambridge.
Johnson, C. (2006) Renaissance German Cartographers and the Naming of America. *Past and Present* 191, 3–43.
Johnson, S. (1755) *A Dictionary of the English Language*. J & P Knapton, London.
Konvitz, J.(1987) *Cartography in France, 1660–1848: Science, Engineering and Statecraft*. University of Chicago Press, Chicago.
Lestringent, F. (1994) *Mapping the Renaissance World: The Geographical Imagination in the Age of Discovery*. Polity Press, Cambridge.
Levine, P. (1986) *The Amateur and the Professional: Antiquarians, Historians and Archaeologists in Victorian England, 1838–1886*. Cambridge University Press, Cambridge.
Locke J. (1989) Yolton J and Yolton J. (eds) *Some Thoughts Concerning Education*. Clarendon Press, Oxford.

Mackinder, H.J. (1887) On the Scope and Methods of Geography. *Proceedings of the Royal Geographical Society, NS* 9, pp. 141–174.

Mackinder, H.J. (1904) The Geographical Pivot of History, *Geographical Journal* 23, 421–444.

MacLean, M. (2007) *The Cosmographia of Sebastian Münster: Describing the World in the Reformation*. Ashgate, Aldershot.

Mayhew, R. (2000) *Enlightenment Geography: the Political Languages of British Geography, c.1650–1850*. Macmillan, London.

Mayhew, R.(1998) Geography in Eighteenth Century British Education, *Paedagogica Historica* 34, 731–769.

Mercator, G. (1595) Atlas sive Cosmographicae Meditationes de Fabrica Mundi et Fabricati Figura. Octavo (2000) CD Rom, Oakland.

Mundy, B. (1996) *The Mapping of New Spain: Indigenous Cartography and the Maps of the Relacíones Geográficas*. University of Chicago Press, Chicago.

Pagden, A. (1982) *The Fall of Natural Man: The American Indian and the Origins of Comparative Ethnography*. Cambridge University Press, Cambridge.

Petto, C.M. (2007) *When France was King of Cartography: The Patronage and Production of Maps in Early Modern France*. Rowman and Littlefield, Lanham.

Phillips, J.R.S. (1998) *The Medieval Expansion of Europe*, 2nd edn. Clarendon Press, London.

Polk, D. (1995) *The Island of California: A History of the Myth*. University of Nebraska Press, Lincoln.

Porter, R. and Wokler, R. (eds) (1995) *Inventing Human Science: Eighteenth-Century Domains*. University of California Press, Berkeley.

Portuondo, M. (2009) *Secret Science: Spanish Cosmography and the New World*. University of Chicago Press, Chicago.

Rosenberg D. (2003) Special Section on Early Modern Information Overload. *Journal of the History of Ideas* 64, 1–72.

Reill, P. (2005) *Vitalizing Nature in the Enlightenment*. University of California Press, Berkeley.

Richards, R. (2002) *The Romantic Conception of Life: Science and Philosophy in the Age of Goethe*. University of Chicago Press, Chicago.

Romm, J. (1992) *The Edges of the Earth in Ancient Thought: Geography, Exploration, and Fiction*. Princeton University Press, Princeton.

Rudwick, M.J.S. (2008) *Worlds Before Adam: The Reconstruction of Geohistory in the Age of Reform*. University of Chicago Press, Chicago.

Russell, J.B. (1991) *Inventing Flat Earth: Columbus and Modern Historians*. Praeger Press, Westport.

Safier, N. (2008) *Measuring the New World: Enlightenment Science and South America*. University of Chicago Press, Chicago.

Scafi, A. (2006) *Mapping Paradise: A History of Heaven on Earth*. British Library, London.

Schaffer, S. (2009) Newton on the Beach: the Information Order of the *Principia Mathematica*. *History of Science* 47, 243–276.

Sher, R.B. (2006) *The Enlightenment & the Book: Scottish Authors & their Publishers in Eighteenth Century Britain, Ireland and America*. University of Chicago Press, Chicago.

Sitwell, O.F.G. (1993) *Four Centuries of Special Geography*. UBC Press, Vancouver.

Smith, B. (1985) *European Vision and the South Pacific*, 2nd edn. Yale University Press, New Haven, Yale.

Smith, B. and Vining, J. (2003) *American Geographers, 1784–1812: A Bio-bibliographical guide*. Praeger Press, Westport.

Sorrenson, R. (1996) The ship as a scientific instrument in the eighteenth century. *Osiris, 2nd series.* 110, 221–236.

Stafford, B.M. (1984) *Voyage into Substance: Art, Science, Nature and the Illustrated Travel Account, 1760–1840*. MIT Press, Cambridge.

Starn, R. (2002) The Early Modern Muddle, *Journal of Early Modern History* 6, 296–307.

Stoddart, D. (1987) *On Geography: and its History*. Blackwell, Oxford.

Strauss, G. (1959) *Sixteenth-Century Germany: Its Topography and Topographers*. University of Wisconsin Press, Madison.

Sweet, R. (2004) *Antiquaries: The Discovery of the Past in Eighteenth-Century Britain* Hambledon, London.

Tang, C. (2008) *The Geographic Imagination of Modernity: Geography, Literature and Philosophy in German Romanticism*. Stanford University Press, Stanford.

Terrall, M. (2002) *The Man who Flattened the Earth: Maupertius and the Sciences in the Enlightenment*. University of Chicago Press, Chicago.

Webster, C. (1975) *The Great Instauration: Science, Medicine and Reform, 1626–1660*. Duckworth, London.

Weisner Hanks, M. (2006) *Early Modern Europe, 1450–1789*. Cambridge University Press, Cambridge.

White, J.A. (ed. and trans) (2005) *Biondo Flavio Italy Illuminated: Volume 1*. Harvard University Press, Cambridge.

Withers, C.W.J and Mayhew, R. (2002) Rethinking 'disciplinary' history: geography in British universities, c.1580-1887. *Transactions of the Institute of British Geographers* NS 27, 1–19.

Withers, C.W.J. (2006) Eighteenth-century geography: texts, practices, sites. *Progress in Human Geography* 30, 711–729.

Withers, C.W.J. (2007) *Placing the Enlightenment: Thinking Geographically about the Age of Reason*. University of Chicago Press, Chicago.

Wolff, L. and Cipolloni, M. (eds) (2007) *The Anthropology of the Enlightenment*. Stanford University Press, Stanford.

Woodward, D. (1987) Medieval *Mappaemundi*. In J.B. Harley and D. Woodward (eds), *The history of cartography, volume 1: Cartography in prehistoric, ancient and medieval Europe and the Mediterranean*. University of Chicago Press, Chicago. pp. 286–370.

Woodward, D. (2007) Cartography and the Renaissance: Continuity and change. In D. Woodward (ed.), *The history of cartography: volume 3: The European Renaissance*. University of Chicago Press, Chicago, pp. 3–24.

Further Reading

For the social and economic context of the early modern era, see, M. Weisner Hanks, *Early Modern Europe, 1450–1789* (Cambridge, Cambridge University Press, 2006). The context of scientific inquiry is well set out in Peter Bowler and Iwan Rhys Morus, *Making Modern Science: A Historical Survey* (Chicago, University of Chicago Press, 2005). For the history of exploration see in general Felipe Fernández-Armesto, *Pathfinders: A Global History of Exploration* (Oxford, Oxford University Press, 2006), and, for more detail, J.H. Parry, *The Age of Reconnaissance: Discovery, Exploration and Settlement 1450–1650* (Berkeley, University of California Press, 1963) and Jeremy Black, *Europe and the World, 1650–1830* (London, Routledge, 2002). For European conceptualisations of their widening knowledge of the world, see, in addition to Parry and Black, J.H. Elliott, *The Old World and the New,1492–1650* (Cambridge, Cambridge University Press, 1970), P.J. Marshall and Glyndwr Williams, *The Great Map of Mankind: Perceptions of New Worlds in the Age of Enlightenment* (Cambridge, Ma, Harvard University Press), and Charles Withers, *Placing the Enlightenment:*

Thinking Geographically about the Age of Reason (Chicago, University of Chicago Press, 2007). For the history of geography, see in general David Livingstone, *The Geographical Tradition: Essays in the History of a Contested Enterprise* (Oxford, Blackwell, 1992) and, for more detail, see Lesley Cormack, *Charting an Empire: Geography at the English Universities* (Chicago, University of Chicago Press, 1997) for the Renaissance and Margarita Bowen, *Empiricism and Geographical Thought: From Francis Bacon to Alexander von Humboldt* (Cambridge, Cambridge University Press, 1981) for the seventeenth and eighteenth centuries. On the breakdown of early modern geography and the emergence of new forms, see Anne Godlewska, *Geography Unbound: French Geographic Science from Cassini to Humboldt* (Chicago, University of Chicago Press, 1999) and Chenxi Tang, *The Geographic Imagination of Modernity: Geography, Literature and Philosophy in German Romanticism* (Stanford, Stanford University Press, 2008).

Chapter 4

Colonizing, Settling and the Origins of Academic Geography

Daniel Clayton

Surveying Geography and Empire

In September 1908 Major E.H. Hills C.M.G., R.E., the Head of the Geographical Section of the General Staff, which produced and collated maps for the British War Office and worked closely with the Royal Geographical Society of London (RGS), travelled to Dublin to deliver his Presidential Address to Section E (Geography) of the British Association for the Advancement of Science (BA). Entitled "The Survey of the British Empire," and published in the October 1908 issue of the *The Scottish Geographical Magazine (SGM)*, Hills began by noting how great changes had occurred in the "science and character of geography" since the BA had last met in Dublin, in 1878. "Then large parts of the earth's surface still remained un-trodden by the feet of a white man; large areas were open to the enterprise and intrepidity of the explorer; large spaces were blank paper upon our maps. Now there is little of the earth's surface absolutely unknown." Furthermore, the "scientific traveler" of yesteryear, with "his rough map-making equipment" had "yielded his place to the scientifically equipped survey-party."

The British Empire provided as fulsome a testing ground as any surveyor could hope for, Hills continued, but Britain was badly in need of a "central department" overseeing territorial mapping and the work of international boundary commissions. The quality of both varied considerably, he opined, partly because the primary "trigonometrical connection of Greenwich and Paris" remained incomplete, and particularly in Africa, which had been the focus of European imperial rivalries since the 1880s; and such variation also pointed to a troubling distance between metropole and colony – the resurfacing of an age-old problem of "imperial overstretch." Science and politics had conspired to dent Hills's dream of a global trigonometrical survey, just as they had to forestall German geomorphologist Albrecht Penck's

---

The Wiley Blackwell Companion to Human Geography, First Edition.
Edited by John A. Agnew and James S. Duncan.
© 2011 John Wiley & Sons, Ltd. Published 2016 by John Wiley & Sons, Ltd.

equally ambitious idea of producing a 1:1 million scale International Map of the World, which, he hoped, would foster international cooperation.

Admittedly, Hills continued, "the substitution of the surveyor for the explorer has necessarily destroyed much of the old romance" associated with the word "geography." "The feelings born when any fraction of the earth's surface was for the first time opened to our ken can never be revived," he lamented, and the "idea of geographical advance" will no longer be so closely connected to the "perilous traversing of virgin lands ... navigation of unknown waters ... [and] penetration of forests or deserts." Many viewed the *Challenger* expedition (1872–1876) to the Southern Hemisphere as the apogee of oceanic scientific travel. Hills's priority was the mapping of colonial space, including small scale cadastral mapping, which was fundamental to the planning of settlement, allocation of property, inventorying of resources, and administration of Britain's far-flung possessions.

Global imperial geographies – of exploration, trade, warfare, migration, settlement, resource extraction, technological change (the advent of steam power, the railway and telegraph, and large irrigation projects), agricultural modernization and industrial production, and the (often abrupt and destructive) environmental changes wrought by this suite of colonizing projects – were built and supported by geographical discourses and practices. Since the fifteenth century, exploration had played a pivotal role in the development of Eurocentrism (the West's estimation of itself as the hearth and pinnacle of civilization) – chiefly through the fashioning of a series of binaries between "us" and "them," between the West (Occident) and East (Orient), the Old World and the New, the temperate and tropical world, civilization and savagery, modernity and tradition, and so on (Heffernan 2007: 17–40; Lewis and Wigen 1997; Driver and Martins 2005). Framed and fuelled by this "colonizer's model of the world" (Blaut 1993), the West arrogated to itself the right to decide on what counted as right, normal and true (and what did not). The West's presumptive right to colonize, and dispossess and exterminate indigenous peoples, was the outer face of this will to power, and it was spurred by the West's confidence in its ability to encircle the globe and penetrate its interiors physically and intellectually (Cosgrove 2001: 205–234).

The public still consumed factual and fantastical travel narratives and maps avidly in Hill's day. By 1900, however, albeit with exploration momentarily being given a last romantic fillip by the international race to reach to Arctic and Antarctic poles, the concerns of Hills and a wider scientific community were practical and political through and through. What forms of knowledge and kinds of practice, it was widely asked, would exemplify Western superiority and facilitate imperial mastery? What would Western civilization do without any large "unknown spaces" to expand into? Mapping and surveying, environment determinism (an eclectic and profoundly ideological body of ideas about how variations in the physical environment, and especially climate, condition human progress, racial character, and national strength), and behind both the ideal of science as the quest for truth, formed the cornerstones of geography's search for answers. Wherever the surveyor worked, Hills suggested, "he was a shining example of the power of that spirit of adventure and thirst for information" and that "unselfish devotion to duty which has carried our race so far in the past," and a figure who was still "pushing his way through jungles" and "braving the attacks of savage animals, of treacherous natives ... [and]

the far more insidious assaults of the germs of some deadly disease" (Hills 1908: 505, 507, 518, 523).

Hills guides us to a world and period in the configuration of geography – broadly conceived here as both the study and human use of the earth – that I seek to take up (all too briefly) in this chapter: a modernizing world at its imperial zenith, with over 80 percent of earth's surface under the imperial aegis of a select number of older and newer imperial powers (Britain and France had long been pre-eminent, but by 1908 their supremacy was being challenged by Germany, Japan and the USA); an age of empire, stretching from the 1870s to the 1920s, that was instrumental in the emergence of geography as an academic, university-based discipline; a combative and promethean age in which the West had a strong faith in its civilizational superiority, imperial prowess, technological mastery, and license to label far-flung peoples and places as it saw fit (in Hills's words, as "unknown," "virgin," "savage," "perilous"); yet an age that was also marked by flux and disorientation, and not least, as Hills intimates, in perceptions of space and time, stemming from what Halford Mackinder (appointed to the first academic position in geography in Britain, at Oxford University, in 1887), in 1904, described as the end of "the Columbian epoch" of exploration stretching back 400 years and formation of a new era of "closed" space, a "new world," as his American counterpart, Isaiah Bowman (President of the American Geographical Society [AGS] from 1915 to 1935), described it, in which states were "absorbed" by their "mutual relations … and mutually antagonistic political systems and doctrines" (Mackinder [1904] 2004: 422; Bowman 1921: 732).

Geographical Impressionism

I start with this vignette for three reasons. Ostensibly, because it points both to the confidence of a period that was characterized by what Edward Said (1993: 62 and *passim*) has called a "consolidated vision of empire" (a broadly held and masculinist set of ideas and assumptions within "the West" about progress, its rightful dominance of much of the world, and the more or less insuperable backwardness of non-Western lands and peoples), and to some of the travails that accompanied the state-centered ethos of territorial expansion – dubbed "imperialism" by contemporaries – through which this vision was expedited. But I also alight on Hills's disquisition in order to flag the importance of an undertaking that is inadequately represented in what follows: of delving into the relations between geography and empire by venturing beyond geography's leading practitioners, texts and institutions, treating the subject "as a heterogeneous field rather than a tightly defined enclave," as Felix Driver (2001: 217) puts it, and, as David Livingstone (1992: 220) urges, considering the "anonymous geographical practitioners – cartographers, surveyors and the like – whose skills actually constructed the empire." Lastly, the crosshatched – self-assured yet tremulous, and past- and future-oriented – qualities of Hills's survey elicit a mode of reading and analysis that Patrick Brantlinger (1996: 279), with reference to Joseph Conrad's famous 1901 novella *Heart of Darkness*, calls "impressionism."

Brantlinger (1996: 287) adapts this term from modernist art to describe the "fragile skein of discourse" in Conrad's writing: the way it simultaneously reveals and obscures imperialism's mix of fantasy and fear, idealism and ruthlessness, moralizing and sensationalizing, belief and doubt, and thus draws the reader to the complex and often equivocal braiding of text and context in the making of imperial and colonial projects, lives and texts; and how, in Conrad, "Europe" itself becomes the "dark continent" (the label that Victorian explorers conferred on Africa), the bastion of civilization that struggles to eschew the charge that it stands for the very barbarism and idolatry that it saw in the "savage" and colonial other. The passage from what Conrad (cited in Driver 2001: 1–24) elsewhere termed "geography militant" (the romantic image of the explorer/geographer) to "geography triumphant" (exploration now "condemned to ... beaten tracks" and sullied by brute ambition and self-interest) was a vivid illustration of this "dark truth" about Europe's imperial achievement. By 1900, annexed, mapped, sequestrated and bureaucratized spaces of empire (its frontier outposts, forts, plantations, mines, ports, cities, cantonments, native reserves, medinas, schools and missions) spawned banalities of power that outlived the age of colonial empires and became founding predicaments of a post-war post-colonial age promising freedom and autonomy – routine onslaughts on land, life and human dignity that made colonialism's inherent cruelty, corruption, racism, and veneration of hierarchy seem part of a natural and eternal order; everyday forms of power that are captured in Conrad's haunting refrain "the horror, the horror" (Mbembe 2001).

This imperial mix animates the origins of academic geography and we might adopt the term "geographical impressionism" to express a concern with the diverse and shifting ground on which geography's imbroglio with empire should be arraigned. Over the last twenty years geographers have dwelt critically and ever more elaborately on the long shadow that empire has cast over their discipline, and on how imperialism operated as what Said (1993: 7) influentially described as a multi-faceted "struggle over geography." Late nineteenth-century geography has been seen as a pivotal "instrument" and practical and ideological "midwife" of imperialism, and as bequeathing future generations of geographers an imperial skein of discourse that they have found difficult to negotiate and reconcile (Livingstone 1992: 352; Bell, Butlin and Heffernan 1995: 6; Bonnett 2008).

From the 1870s, Brian Hudson (1977: 13) argued in a Marxian vein, the "new geography" – so named by academic pioneers such as Mackinder and Andrew Herbertson in Britain, Paul Vidal de la Blache and Jean Brunhes in France, Alfred Hettner and Friedrich Ratzel in Germany, and Bowman and William Morris Davis in the USA (to name only the most influential) – "was vigorously promoted ... largely, if not mainly, to serve the interests of imperialism in its various aspects including territorial acquisition, economic exploitation, militarism and the practice of class and race domination." And Driver (1992: 26) suggests, in more postcolonial vein (with a sensitivity to the collusion of power, knowledge and geography) that "the writings of our predecessors were so saturated with colonial and imperial themes that to problematize their role is to challenge the very status of the modern discipline."

Both in terms of its conceptual concern with process (bio-physical and social variation and change) inherited from the Enlightenment, and its methodological quest to provide a "systematic" (global and integrated) account of workings and interactions of nature and culture on the earth's surface, academic geography was intricately bound up with the nineteenth-century pursuit and pressures of empire. Cartography is often deemed to be of special significance. Long central to the idea and practice of geography, the map was a tool for colonization and national propaganda *par excellence*, and cartography has been treated as a root metaphor for western culture and the proprietorial logic of colonialism (Gregory 1994; Olsson 2007). As Matthew Edney (1993: 63–67) writes of Britain's mapping of India, "Surveyors were the point men of British imperialism," and the ideal of systematic mapping creating two images of empire that reinforced British hegemony; a "conceptual image [founded on science] that consciously set the Europeans apart from the Indians they ruled ... [and a] cartographic image of the empire as a single territorial and political entity, that is, an imperial space."

Yet geography was neither a unitary nor an uncontested instrument of power, and (like Conrad's writing) was not imperialist or racist in any straightforward way. Patrons of geography and professional geographers adopted a wide variety of stances on imperial and colonial issues, were exercised by domestic problems (of industrialization, rapid social and regional change) as well as foreign-imperial affairs, and the nature and intensity of connections between geography and empire varied between countries and geographical traditions (Bell 1998; Godlewska and Smith 1994).

We thus need to ask: What is gained and what is lost when empire's grip on the discipline is viewed in different lights; as potent, exaggerated, embarrassing, damaging, or still unexamined? The following two sections touch on just two ways of pursuing such questions. The next section traces the bearing that geography's relationship with exploration had on how the subject became positioned as an academic discipline. This is followed by a short foray into how the value of geographical knowledge as a university discipline was gauged in terms of its national and imperial worth. I proceed with very broad strokes, chiefly with American, British and French examples (and a selection of primary and secondary references that I hope are instructive), and with an emphasis on intellectual and disciplinary arguments and arrangements, and less account of the more heterogeneous and anonymous practices alluded to above.

Positioning Geography: Science Contra Exploration

Geography had been taught in schools, military academies and universities across Europe, as well as in colonial territories, in different forms for centuries, and often as a branch of other subjects (Withers and Mayhew 2002). It did not gain a firm foothold in universities until the nineteenth century, and then only tentatively – initially in Prussia (see Mayhew chapter), Austria and Switzerland, then from the 1870s in France and a unified Germany, the 1880s in Britain and Russia, and the 1890s in other parts of Europe, the USA and Japan (Claval 2001; Livingstone 1992; Martin and James 1993). From the outset, the configuration of geography as an academic discipline was an agonistic process that gave the fledgling discipline a fractured identity. This was due, in part, to geographers' need to position their subject in wider, and combative, intellectual spaces.

The idea of "science" (of how a field of inquiry was to be delimited in terms of the uniqueness of its objects of study, the exactitude of its methods, and the systematic nature and universal reach of its theories and findings) was commonly used as a rhetorical tool in early debates about the nature of academic geography, and metaphors (largely biological, organic and mechanistic metaphors) were important vehicles of disciplinary discrimination (see Blouet 1981; Hartshorne 1939: 366–86; Livingstone 1992: 19–28, 151–54, 181–86). This scientific framing of geography's identity had deep roots in the search for meaning and order in the natural world, which had been part of geography's etymology for over 100 years and was integral to nineteenth-century intellectual endeavor more generally – an undertaking forged and made credible in particular "spaces of science" (the field, study, laboratory, museum and garden; learned societies, international congresses) (Livingstone 2003; Withers 2007: 112-135). The question of how geography was a science was posed from within and outside the discipline, and in two main ways; as a spatial issue of the subject's contiguity to other disciplines (especially geology and history), and as a developmental issue of how geography had emerged from older modes of knowledge production (especially exploration) and how it should engage with evolutionary thought, which by the end of the century was deeply encrusted in the idea of science as such (Bowler 1989).

Geography's vexed disciplinary merger with imperialism was rooted in the view (now pronounced in postcolonial thought) that "science" was as much an exclusive mark of Western superiority as it was a yardstick for measuring the utility and acceptability of the West's own disciplinary grids of knowledge. Western reason and science led duplicitous lives as putatively universal paths to objective understanding and human betterment. Fields of knowledge and study like geography were imbued with what Gyan Prakash (1999: 55) terms an "arrogant rationalism" that buoyed colonialism and empire by claiming that however much the "savage" and "superstitious" colonial subject was educated in the ways of reason, s/he would always lag behind the West and never quite be ready for self-government.

The leading and contending Western worldviews of the day – of struggle and cooperation, competition and federation, hierarchy and equality, and progress and decay – were imbued with the relations between science, imperialism and this arrogant rationalism. Climate became a powerful "hermeneutical expedient facilitating the projection of moral designations [between 'inquisitive' and 'indolent' peoples and races, and 'favorable' and 'debilitating' environments] onto global space" – a "moral cartography," Livingstone (2002: 50) calls it, which was couched in the language of science and was applied to a range of imperial (commercial, geopolitical, military and scientific) questions. The question of acclimatization – of how and whether Europeans could survive in alien environments, and especially tropical climes – had a high profile in Said's "consolidated vision" (Duncan 2007; Livingstone 1991). However, this vision itself was fractured and fleeting, and was turned on its head by the Great War of 1914–1918. The French geographer Pierre Gourou, born in 1900, spoke for a generation of early twentieth century geographers who thought that the world and their discipline needed to be built anew in the wake of a war that had crippled "the very idea of Europe" as a civilizational achievement, the pinnacle of modernity (Gourou 1982: 7).

In fact, debate about this 'idea' had been part of geographical discourse for a longer time, and around the turn of the twentieth century dissident (anarchist and utopian) visions of geography – such as those of Elisée Reclus, Peter Kropotkin and Patrick Geddes – jostled with more dominant forms of "imperial consciousness" (Bell 1998; Dunbar 1996). Still further back, the Scottish explorer David Livingstone's *Missionary Travels and Researches in Southern Africa* (published in 1857, two years before Charles Darwin's *The Origin of Species*) was a best seller, and a volume that was read as much for its proselytizing criticism of slavery and Europe's violent imperial record as for the way it cemented the image of the explorer as a heroic figure engaged in an impartial quest for truth and spreading the blessings of Western civilization to "primitive" peoples who beseeched colonial rule (Driver 2001: 68–89). In short, geography and empire were not always or necessarily in sync. Rather, geographers expressed and disavowed the mix of imperial drives we can find in Conrad.

While public enthusiasm for geography in Britain was augmented during the mid-nineteenth century by Livingstone and African exploration, and under the auspices of the RGS and it's charismatic figurehead Roderick Murchison, public and political interest in empire waxed and waned during this period, and was only reinvigorated in Britain and across western Europe from the 1870s onwards, culminating in the so-called "scramble for Africa" and "Great Game" in Central Asia (Porter 2004). The factors behind this end of century imperial acceleration were complex and lay beyond our purview. For the French, however, the disasters of the Franco-Prussian War of 1870–1871 played a key role in the rejuvenation of imperialism as a political priority and focus of nationalism, and geographers and geographical societies, acutely aware of the great strategic advantage the Prussian army had gained from its use of maps during this war, gave France's imperial drive overseas (primarily into North and West Africa, and Southeast Asia) much of its military and technical momentum (Deprest 2009; Heffernan 1994).

By contrast, Mackinder (1902: 341–352) and George Chisholm (1902: 119) – lecturer at Edinburgh University, exponent of "economic geography," and author of the widely used *Handbook of Commercial Geography*, which was updated numerous times from 1889 – charted as well as any economist or historian how a return to empire in Britain was a response to economic depression and an adverse balance of trade, and how it involved an industrial re-girding of older maritime and continental geographies of empire that revolved around how the mother country sought raw materials and foodstuffs (especially cotton, wheat, sugar, tea and timber) from foreign markets and overseas possessions (fuelling industry and feeding and clothing the country's fast-growing urban-industrial populace); how it sought to cultivate colonial markets for its manufactures (especially textiles and iron and steel goods); and how it viewed its empire as a vital outlet and safety valve for surplus British capital and labor.

However, this utilitarian liaison between geography and empire did not deflect attention from what the Scottish geographer Hugh Robert Mill (librarian at the RGS, and confidant of the British polar explorers Scott, Shackleton and Bruce) in 1905 saw as the "chief problem" facing the nascent discipline: "the definition of geography" itself, its lack of "a central theory" (Mill 1905: 7). Similar conclusions about geography's precariously plural existence had been reached three years before in a debate in the SGM about the teaching of "university geography," and the sentiment was not uniquely British (Herbertson 1902). A poll of professional geographers in the USA conducted by the AGS in 1914 revealed that there was still "little or no agreement" among them "as to what geography was" (Schulten 2001: 90).

In a mid-1920s survey of academic geography over the previous fifty years, Lucien Febvre (1924: 316) observed that "Young sciences [like geography] which become conscious of their own individuality and vindicate their right to a free and independent existence never grow on a soil which is free and void of obstacles." A key concern was how and why academic geography should extricate itself from the subject's strong association with the geographical societies – such as the RGS (founded in 1830), the AGS (1854), the Washington-based National Geographic Society (NGS, 1888), and the Société de Géographie de Paris (1821) – and from exploration.

By the 1890s there were over 100 geographical societies around the world, with three quarters of them in Europe, and a growing number in overseas colonies such as French North Africa and ex-colonies such as the USA (Butlin 2009: 281 and *passim*). Membership of the RGS, for instance, which totaled over 4000 by 1900, was drawn from a broad cross-section of Britain's social elite and middle classes, and the Army and Navy were well represented (women were not admitted as fellows until 1913, and only after protracted debate; Bell and McEwan 1996). Indeed, there was a military sea change in RGS membership in just a few decades, with the preponderance of army officers over naval officers nearly doubling between 1870 and 1900, from around two-to-one to over four-to-one, reflecting the switch in imperial attention from coasts to continents identified by Hills, and with over 20 percent of the RGS's total membership coming from the ranks of the military by 1900 (Collier and Inkpen 2003; Stoddart 1986: 60).

The geographical societies of Europe had a panoply of educational, research and commercial aims, and societies based in imperial centers such as London, Paris, Berlin and New York sometimes had fractious relations with provincial geographical societies (such as those in Manchester and Newcastle in Britain, and Bordeaux and Le Havre in France), which tended to trumpet commerce and regional interests over national or scientific ones, and with newer professional bodies, such as the Geographical Association in Britain (established by Mackinder in 1893), the Association of American Geographers (established by Davis in 1904), and the International Geographical Congresses (the first held in Antwerp in 1871), which were set up to represent the interests of, and facilitate communication between, geography academics and school teachers (MacKenzie 1995). Much that the European public knew about the imperial world came through the geographical societies – their meetings, lecture series, publications, patronage networks and links with allied societies such as the BA – and the way their knowledge and expertise filtered into the public domain through atlases, school textbooks and newspapers (Ploszajska 1999; Withers, Finnegan and Higgitt 2006). They were powerful information exchanges in the global traffic of empire, and key patrons of science, commerce and national interest in an era of limited direct state sponsorship of education and research.

As part of its educational mission, the RGS, housed in South Kensington, the architectural and institutional hub of imperial London, spent around £20 000 over a 35 year period on the promotion of geography teaching at the universities of Cambridge and Oxford (Driver and Gilbert 1999: 1–17; Stoddart 1986: 83–127).

But such investment placed academic geography in a bind, in Britain at least. While it was pivotal to the establishment and survival of the academic subject – the number of degree-awarding departments of geography in Britain rose steadily from 2 in 1903 to over 20 by the 1940s (Stoddart 1986: 46–54) – it also fuelled skepticism in neighboring disciplines over geography's intellectual wherewithal. Such skepticism was rehearsed in a lengthy report on the state of geographical education commissioned by the RGS and compiled by the Scottish geographer James Scott Keltie in 1884. Keltie (who later became the RGS's Secretary) reported that the subject was poorly taught in schools, as "mere memory work" (especially in comparison with Germany, where there were 12 university chairs in geography by 1884) because it was very weakly developed at university level, where, he added, British academics regarded the subject as "both uninteresting and unprofitable," generating a "descriptive catalogue" of undigested facts rather than "scientific knowledge" (Keltie 1885: 501–503; Stoddart 1975: 5).

Such lambasting came from American as well British university quarters, and in both countries came most vigorously from geologists, who went to great lengths to represent geography as an amateur and populist pursuit that lacked scientific rigour and was parasitical on other disciplines (Lapworth 1893; Livingstone 1992: 206–215; Stoddart 1986: 63–76). As an emerging group of professional geographers jockeyed for position in this combative environment – with one ardent British promoter of academic geography, Douglas Freshfield (1886: 704), setting out to show how the "science" of geology "leaves off where ours begins" – two strategies emerged. The first was to make academic geography appear more "scientific" by distancing it (intellectually and symbolically) from the explorer tradition. The second was to argue that geography's strength lay in what Mackinder, in a wide-ranging 1887 address to the RGS, "On the Scope and Methods of Geography" (which was prompted by Keltie's report) described as its "inherent breadth and manysidedness" – its systematic (evolutionary) concern with environment and society (Mackinder [1887] 1996: 172).

In Britain and the USA, where the main pressure on geography to define itself came from geology, human geography (or what Davis termed "ontography") was worn as a badge of identity, albeit one that by the 1910s was already veering into what Neil Smith (2003: 215) describes as "the scientific *cul de sac*" of environmental determinism – with doctrines about what one of American geography's leading exponents of this "science," Ellen Churchill Semple (1903), termed "geographic influences" on human behavior and aptitude. Livingstone (1984; 1992: 186–89) has shown that this species of environmental determinism was hewn more directly from the evolutionary thought of Jean Baptiste de Lamarck than from Darwin's theory of natural selection, and was geared to the justification of colonization within and beyond the borders of Europe and America. Environmental determinists re-worked Lamarck's "doctrine of the inheritance of acquired characteristics," Livingstone (1992: 188) explains, with characteristics acquired through human adaptation to environmental conditions during a life cycle, and the adaptive know-how accumulated in the process, being passed on to future generations; and with "the directive force of organic variation [attributed] to will, habit or environment."

In this skein of discourse, debate centered on the relative importance accorded to human agency, cultural tradition and environmental controls. The hypothesis that climate determined race was a persistent refrain, albeit one promulgated in a range of ways and with differing degrees of vigor and complexity. In early twentieth-century America, for example, human progress was explained not solely by recourse to climate, but in terms of the imbrications of climate, commerce and resource endowment. As Susan Schulten (2001: 117) observes, American strength was seen as a function of both natural abundance and American ingenuity, and it was by "holding out the possibility of altering one's physical constitution through behavioral modification and environmental adjustment, [that] geographers justified imperial intervention, in both the abstract and the concrete."

In France, Vidal de la Blache, who began to form a "school of geography" that championed "human geography" at the École Normale Supérieure during the 1870s, also emphasized the physical dimensions of "milieu" and "genres de vie," the former signifying long-term human adaptation to varying environmental conditions, and producing the latter, distinct "lifestyles." But he invoked "environmental conditions" for a different reason: in order to distinguish his "science of geography" from the imposing French academic territory of history and emerging human sciences of sociology and ethnology, and also to eschew German influence on French geography, and particularly Ratzel's influential arguments about the organic nature of states, their evolutionary struggle for survival through their quest for adequate living space (*lebensraum*) which necessitated territorial competition and expansion (Bassin 1987; Berdoulay 1981).

The representation by an emerging academic discourse within geography of exploration as an immature and bygone project of collecting and description was crucial to this positioning process. Mill (1903: 11), for instance, argued that the business of collecting new geographical knowledge was essentially over, and that an academic geography needed to focus its energies on ordering and classifying that knowledge. For Mill, Darwin had "done more than any geographer" to provide an appropriate theoretical framework. In the USA, Davis (who had been trained by the renowned geologist Nathaniel Southgate Shaler, and was appointed Assistant Professor of Physical Geography at Harvard University in 1885) distanced his academic efforts (at the center of which lay his theory of landform evolution, the "cycle of erosion") from the NGS's populist *National Geographic Magazine*, which, he thought, cast geography in a disabling light, as a pioneer and genteel pursuit that was prone to sensationalism and ideological manipulation, the latter borne out by the *Magazine*'s widely read coverage of the Spanish–American War of 1898 (Davis 1904; 1924).

Back in France, Vidal de la Blache ([1926] 1996: 182) saw the separation of what was called "colonial geography" from the work of the geographical societies as essential to the advancement of "geographical science." Marcel Dubois was appointed to the first named chair of Colonial Geography at the Sorbonne in 1893, and by 1914 a high proportion of the 20 university chairs in geography in France were held by specialists in this field. In 1891 Vidal joined forces with Dubois in the first issue of the academically-oriented *Annales de Géographie* to criticize what they described as an older "descriptive" and "sensationalist" geography of exploration, which had been indulged for too long by newspapers and populist geographical journals and reviews such as the *Bulletin de la Societé de Géographie* and *Revue de Géographie*. Such accounts could still form part of colonial geography, they argued, but only if they rested on a new "precision" in geographical reasoning and a new "freedom of critical spirit" (cited in Singaravélou 2011).

Davis hinted at what a later generation of critical human geographers has now probed in great detail: how exploration and its representational artifices shaped and naturalized Western dominance. As Clive Barnett (1998: 240–248) observes in connection with "the Africanist discourse of the RGS" (a racial discourse) how explorers' journals and maps asserted that "knowledge is the monopoly of only one party, and this in turn is taken to confer rights of possession over territory. Yet the texture of the written discourse shows this to be a retrospective rewriting of an encounter in which communication between different knowledge formations [the African and the European] took place, the evidence of which survives despite attempts to erase it." Considerable efforts have now been made to unearth the way nineteenth-century exploration worked as a project of othering (rendering non-European peoples and places as backward and inferior to a superordinate Europe – a project with gendered and sexualized as well as racial contours), and to restore hitherto excluded and denigrated "native" voices to stories of exploration, frontier expansion and colonization (Fabian 2000; Phillips 1997; McEwan 1999). On both counts, the "manly" project of scientific exploration has been deemed pivotal to the way the European subject was fashioned as the fount of knowledge and avatar of universal reason, and "local"/non-European knowledge and practices were deemed "the confusion and noise against which European science takes shape and secures its authority" (Barnett 1998: 48).

This critical enterprise, which some see as having the salutary – distancing and 'hand wringing' – effect of allowing geographers to say that "they now do things differently" has been important in forging a postcolonial geography that "reposition[s] European systems of thought so as to demonstrate the long history of their operation as the effect of the colonial other" (Young 1990: 119; Gregory 1994: 166–196; Sharp 2009). However, this venture runs the risk of flattening understanding of the mediated and inter-subjective nature of cultural and colonial encounters at the margins of empire, which provides much of this work with its critical bearings; its attempt to recover native agency and resistance, and make Western power seem less self-assured. Understanding, it is argued from such "margins," is not repositioned enough in this kind of postcolonialism. Critical attention remains focused on the imperial center and its epistemological ruses, and runs roughshod over the detailed arrangement and subversion of colonialism in far-off localities (Harris 2004).

But this does not end matters, for it is by no means clear that such a "postcolonial rewriting" of exploration is the most appropriate way of handling the record of exploration and the involvement of geographical societies. Recent scholarship reveals that the RGS's guardianship of the explorer tradition was subject to contestation and fostered what some see as a liberal attitude to debate about imperial issues rather than a straightforwardly arrogant rationalism or chauvinism (Kearns 2004). Robert Stafford (1999: 318) observes that "Victorian British culture was pervaded by geographical knowledge and metaphors" and that exploration "exemplified the cultural importance of geography more clearly than any other contemporary activity." But as Driver (2001: 56) cautions, the publication by the RGS of a manual, *Hints to Travellers*, in 1854 points to confusion surrounding how exploration was to be done, and suggests that the RGS was seeking to "exert authority on a field of knowledge that was already too large and diverse to be mastered."

Geography, Practical Use and Power

Environmental determinism was viewed as a means of shoring up geography's identity problems, lending it an air of scientific respectability founded on a clear model of causality that did not spring from other disciplines. As part of what Livingstone (1992) has described as geography's grand nineteenth-century "experiment" in keeping nature and culture in a unitary analytical (evolutionary) frame, ideas of environmental influence and control, and the seeming ubiquitousness of their impact on regional character and national history, helped academic geography to buck the nineteenth-century political-intellectual trend (at least in Britain and the USA) of defining a discipline by delimiting the uniqueness of its subject matter. Ellsworth Huntington, for instance, constructed "maps of climatic energy" showing how climatic conditions exerted "powers of selection," which, in turn, explained (in his mind) how the "idea of liberty" developed in the white-temperate-north of the USA but not in the black-south, and how Europe came to dominate the world because its people resided in the most "stimulating climatic area" in the world (Huntington 1928: 221–236). As this example suggests, there was little that environmental determinism did not take on, and it was in good measure due to its specious universality that the likes of Bowman and Vidal de la Blache saw this body of ideas as a more arrogant and worrying facet of modern geographical reason than the explorer tradition.

Yet geography's route to disciplinary definition was not solely via questions of environmental influence. As Mackinder (1911: 79–80) told geography teachers in 1911, students of geography needed to be trained to serve their country on the "world stage." Viewing geography "from the British point of view" was perhaps "to deviate from the cold and impartial ways of science," he observed, yet "we are not training scientific investigators … [but] practical and surviving citizens of an Empire." He concluded his 1887 address with an even more ambitious call to arms: that geography needed "to satisfy at once the practical requirements of the statesman and the merchant, the theoretical requirements of the historian and the scientist, and the intellectual requirements of the teacher" (Mackinder [1887] 1996: 172). This was his "manysidedness" at full stretch. And Mill (1905: 7) added, "The world is not yet so fully dominated by the highest civilization, not so completely settled, as to deprive geographers of an opportunity of showing how the settlement and development of new lands can best be carried out in the light of the permanent relationships between land and people" discovered by the geographer.

The issue at stake was geography's imperial and national worth. Mackinder and Bowman seized upon the idea of "closed space" in order to make political and commercial geography, and the geo-politics of domestic and foreign affairs, relevant to the worlds of the statesman and planner. What Bowman, in the most widely read geography book of the inter-war years, *The New World* (1921), described as a new age of international competition and state struggle helped to gain him a place on the powerful American Council of Foreign Relations, and his interest in "the geography of internal affairs" helped to make him a key domestic policy advisor to President Franklin Roosevelt (Smith 2003). While less immediately influential, Mackinder's global geo-political theorizing in "The Geographical Pivot of History" (a 1904 paper read at the RGS that was turned into a book in 1919), namely that land power (and the prospect of continental empire) in the Eurasian "heartland" (Russia and Eastern Europe) had eclipsed sea power and maritime empire as the fulcrum of global power relations, deployed the same mix of "geo-strategic" musing and "geo-economic calculation" that exercised Bowman (O'Hara and Heffernan 2006, 67; Blouet 2005).

In the case of Mackinder and Bowman (and Karl Haushofer and *Geopolitik* in Nazi Germany), there was a direct correlation between the explanatory quality of their ideas, the attractiveness of their work as possible instruments of statecraft, and their eagerness to serve as policy advisors. Mackinder advised the British Colonial Office's Visual Instruction Committee before entering politics himself and sitting on various imperial committees (Blouet 2005; Ryan 1995). Bowman (1953: 248–251) had a more enduring connection with the American political establishment, and saw his research on "pioneer problems" in the USA and Canada "a priceless laboratory for the study of [environment and society] cause-and-effect" and of "frontier assemblages" (American individualism and market-oriented spatial behavior).

Their geographical visions traded (as did those of Semple and Huntington) on the power of abstraction: on their ability to manipulate understanding of the earth and its peoples, to lock it in western grids of meaning. From the end of the nineteenth century French geographers venturing overseas raised a slightly different question. How motile were Western geographical models and concepts? Olivier Soubeyran (1989: 88) has explored how, in creating "a Vidalian geography of colonized spaces," French geographers (such as Gourou in Indochina and E-F. Gautier and Augustin Bernard in the Maghreb) thought carefully about what would happen to metropolitan-geographical hypotheses and generalizations when they were deployed overseas. For example, what light might the experience of French colonialism throw on Vidal de la Blache's (1902) and Jean Bruhnes' (1910) global classification of "lifestyles" (*genres de vie*)? Answers to this question pivoted on how one dealt with Vidal's (1911, 304, 289 *my translation*) central claim that "genres de vie" were "highly evolved" and "permanent forms" that stemmed from "a series of accumulated efforts cemented over time". If this observation, based on an understanding of the French countryside, held, then how would one explain or justify colonialism's status as a rapid process of material (lifestyle) transformation? And if adaptation was an inherently incremental process, what would happen when "evolved" Europeans were suddenly lifted out of their age-old lifestyles and landscapes and transposed to radically alien environments?

One important response was to equate the "permanence" of "native" lifestyles with "traditionalism," cultural inertia and backwardness, thus justifying colonial intrusion. Another was to see colonialism as injurious to the intricately textured nature of "native" adaptation to environmental circumstances (Bowd and Clayton 2003; Singaravélou 2008). And native resistance to French colonialism politicized the issue of acclimatization. In short, Vidal's concept of permanence was amenable to Orientalist manipulation (with geographical research cementing Western ideas about the innate difference between "dynamic" and "progressive" Western, and "static" and "despotic" Oriental lifestyles), but also nurtured what Yves Lacoste (2006) terms "anti-colonial colonial geographies" that were variously paternalist, humanitarian and primitivist, and that (in Gourou's case, for instance) clung to the idea of empire while being critical of particular colonial policies (Deprest 2009).

Within Europe, the connection between geography, practical use and state power found its most direct and consummate expression immediately after the Great War, when the allied politicians who met at Versailles to re-draw the map of Europe and dissolve the Ottoman Empire (turning it into mandated territories under the jurisdiction of Britain and France) turned to geographers to help them assess the maze of competing national-territorial claims. Bowman led the large American delegation of geographers that assisted President Woodrow Wilson. There were also geographers in the Czech and Polish delegations, and two of France's leading geographers, Albert Demangeon and Emmanuel de Martonne, who came with the French team, played an important role in reconfiguring the borders of Central Europe and the Balkans (Crampton 2006; Heffernan 2007; Smith 2003).

The British delegation at Versailles was comprised not of the notable geographers of the day, like Mackinder, but of cartographers and surveyors attached to the War Office. That it was their expertise which was called upon, rather than that of "academics," gives us further insight into furtive development of geography as a discipline in Britain, and why Hills saw the surveyor and the geographer as different beings. In an 1899 paper entitled "The Use of Practical Geography Illustrated by Recent Frontier Operations," one of the military stalwarts of the RGS (and one of Hills associates), Colonel Sir Thomas Holdich drew a sharp distinction between an "academic" and "practical" geography when he proclaimed:

> [J]ust as the Providence of battles usually favors' the biggest battalions, ... so it is likely that the widest geographical knowledge will prove the best safeguard against misunderstanding, and will at once dispose of such false estimates of the value of portions of the world's surface which we gain by surveying. (Holdich 1899: 466, 477)

Geography, for Holdich, meant knowledge of those "natural laws" that explain the configuration of mountains and the course of rivers, and the "dangers of inaccurate geographical knowledge" to imperial defense and frontier operations meant that the creation of such knowledge was too important to be left to geographers. It is "our soldiers and our sailors who know how to make geography and how to make use of it," he declared.

Mackinder (1899: 480) beseeched Holdich "to soften a little the frontier ... between the academic and the practical," but the colonel had hit a nerve. For many members of the RGS, academic geography was an arcane, ivory tower pursuit that veered towards the bloodless and disconnected treatment of regions, countries and commerce. That one of the first geography lecturers at Cambridge, Francis Guillemard, was a specialist in birds of paradise did not help matters in this regard (Stoddart 1975).

Holdich and Hills helped to establish the British Colonial Survey Committee in 1905, which would train colonial personnel (native and British) to survey new imperial frontiers, and they impressed on the RGS the need to make instruction in surveying a more formal part of the Society's remit (Collier 2006; Collier and Inkpen 2003). The first course in surveying organized by the RGS was not introduced until 1879, and by 1900 many of the naval surveying practices that the RGS had long touted as 'best practice' appeared increasingly ill-equipped to deal with the demands of land surveying in Africa and Central Asia. An increasingly vocal army lobby within the RGS (not least Holdich) looked to India and its system of trigonometrical surveying as a better model, and began to win the debate in 1896, when it was agreed that the RGS should provide training in surveying that resulted in an accredited diploma.

The intelligence unit headed by Hills was created in response to vigorous complaints that British troops had struggled needlessly during the Boer War (and that the British public had struggled to comprehend the conflict) due to a paucity of accurate maps (Stoddart 1994; Heffernan 2009). The staff and equipment that the RGS lay at the disposal of the War Office was vital in subsequent efforts to redress the problem, and the President of the RGS during the Great War, Douglas Freshfield, was convinced that the Society's expertise would be decisive in the war effort in Europe and the Middle East.

Debating Geography and Empire

In sum, we cannot think about the origins of academic geography without thinking about the impress of colonialism and Western dominance. But should we describe geography during this period as the marionette of empire? Much, I think, depends on the kind of geography and kind of empire that one is talking about. As I have sought to outline, there was not a unitary understanding of what geography was, or how it was to be used for imperial ends. Evolutionism proved to be a strong philosophical current in the make-up of academic geography through to the 1920s, when geographers started to beat a retreat from it's more racist and chauvinist forms in American and German geography (Sauer 1941). The practical nature of geography was also a consistent theme. But these twin trajectories led a convoluted existence in an avowedly academic geography that was seeking to find itself an intellectual and institutional niche. Exploration, cartography, environmental determinism, and their practical applications, were contested enterprises and gave geography a plural identity. I have adopted the term "geographical impressionism" to describe the mix of imperial drives and impulses that helped to give this geography a "many-sided" existence and opened up what proved to be an enduring set of questions and distinctions between "theoretical" and "practical," "pure" and "applied," and "academic" and "popular" understandings of geography.

The Great War was a tipping point in all of this, and the short story told here should now be placed against the backdrop of a resurgent (American-led and British-backed) imperialism promulgated in response to the catastrophe of the 9/11 attacks, and against what this "new imperialism" has wrought: a much greater range of opinion about the pros and cons of empire – including burly reaffirmations of its modernizing, democratizing and stabilizing benefits that are laced with imperial nostalgia – than there was fifty (or even twenty) years ago, when there was more of a politico-intellectual consensus over the exploitative and dehumanizing nature of imperialism and its binaries of civilization and savagery, colonizer and colonized, and white and black (Cooper 2005: 33–58). Among other things, our current imperial *mise en scène* – especially for us the recognition that geography is still being pressed into imperial service – is serving to heighten awareness of the importance of thinking historically about the relations between geography and empire, and rekindling discussion of how and from where the critique of imperialism and colonialism should be undertaken.

Should the historical study, teaching and critique of geography and empire be conceived as an ameliorative and therapeutic exercise that helps the discipline to exorcize its imperial ghosts (as much work in this vein implies) and produce geography graduates who are critically minded citizens of the world rather than ones who are encouraged to look at the world from a national (British, American, and so on) point of view? Or should we heed the complaint that this cosmopolitan line of inquiry is itself biased: that it still frequently ends up fixating on the imperial centre, the needs and foibles of a metropolitan-based discipline of geography, and obscures the diverse and complex ways in which colonial power was (and continues to be) grounded and localized in far-flung peripheries?

In these ways (and many more) there is no single or simple aim to work that grapples with the imperial/colonial collusion of geographical knowledge and power. To be sure, empire has been an important historical and theoretical crucible in which the allegory of geography as a march towards objectivity and truth, and story of progress and refinement, has been questioned. At the same time, the critical use of empire to expose the situated and power-laden qualities of past modes of geographical inquiry in order to put the past "behind us" is a moot point given the current imperial work being done by an emboldened GIS-fuelled military geography and the "violent geographies" that spiral around it (Gregory and Pred 2006). Recovery of signs of plurality, ambivalence and contestation in the archive of what Driver (1992) aptly termed "geography's empire," in an attempt to democratize understanding and leave room for "hidden" histories and geographies to enter the fray, has become a routine critical tactic (and one exemplified in much of the above). But this may not be what is needed today. A more principled moral critique of imperialism's inherently divisive and exploitative logic may be what is required; a critique that does not lose sight of empire's omniscience within the West during the period we have reviewed, and the public's acquiescence to it, and that emphasizes that scientific choices of the day (to map, explore, order, classify) also involved moral choices (to rank, divide, conquer and demean other peoples and places).

Empire was not the only political pressure point around which the question of geography's disciplinary status was initially raised. But it was a seminal one, and with new and old imperial wars raging in Central Asia and the Middle East remains a vital cog in geography's critical wheel (in British and North American geography particularly). Our "colonial present" (Gregory 2004) is revamping historical interest in geographies and spaces of war and destruction, and in what Trevor Barnes (2008) has dubbed geography's imperial "underworld." In fine, it is impossible to draw a clear or straight line between a geography that was once complicit in empire and one that is now not. Geographical practice today, as in Hills's day, still involves the drawing of moral and epistemological as well as terrestrial and technical lines across the surface of the earth – lines of empire that indubitably shape what human geography and its history mean.

References

Barnes, T. (2008) Geography's Underworld: The Military-Industrial Complex, Mathematical Modelling, and the Quantitative Revolution. *Geoforum* 39, 3–16.

Barnett, C. (1998) Impure and Worldly Geography: The Africanist Discourse of the Royal Geographical Society, 1831–73. *Transactions of the Institute of British Geographer* 23, 2, 239–252.

Bassin, M. (1987) Imperialism and the Nation State in Freidrich Ratzel's Political Geography. *Progress in Human Geography* 11, 473–495.

Bell, M. (1998) Reshaping Boundaries: International Ethics and Environmental Consciousness in the Early Twentieth Century. *Transactions of the Institute of British Geographers* 23, 151–176.

Bell, M. and McEwan, C. (1996) The Admission of Women Fellows to the Royal Geographical Society, 1892-1914; the Controversy and Outcome. *Geographical Journal* 162, 295–312.

Bell, M., Butlin, R., and Heffernan, M. (eds) (1995) *Geography and Imperialism, 1820–1940*. Manchester University Press, Manchester.

Blaut, J. (1993) *The Coloniser's Model of the World: Geographical Diffusionism and Eurocentric History*. Guildford Press, London and New York.

Blouet, B. (2005) *Global Geostrategy: Mackinder and the Defence of the West*. Frank Cass, London and New York.

Blouet, B. (ed.) (1981) *Origins of Academic Geography in the United States*. Archon Books, Hamden, Conn.

Bonnett, A. (2008) *What is Geography?* Sage, London.

Bourdelay, V. (1981) *La formation de l'école française de géographie*. CTHS, Paris.

Bowd, G. and Clayton, D. (2003) Fieldwork and Tropicality in French Indo-China: Reflections on Pierre Gourou's *Les paysans du delta tonkinois (1936)*. *Singapore Journal of Tropical Geography* 24, 147–168.

Bowler, P. (1989) *Evolution: The History of an Idea, Revised Edition*. University of California Press, Berkeley.

Bowman, I. (1921) *The New World: Problems in Political Geography*. The World Book Company, New York.

Bowman, I. (1953) Settlement by the Modern Pioneer. In G. Taylor (ed.) *Geography in the Twentieth Century: A Study of Growth, Field, Techniques, Aims and Trends*, 2nd edn. Metheun, London.

Brantlinger, P. (1996) Heart of Darkness: Anti-imperialism, Racism, or Impressionism? In R.C. Murfin (ed.) *Heart of Darkness: Complete, Authoritative Text with Biographical and Historical Contexts, Critical History and Essays*. St. Martin's Press, New York, pp. 277–298.

Bruneau, M. and Dory, M. (eds) (1994) *Géographies des Colonisations XV–XX Siècles*. L'Hartmattan, Paris.

Brunhes, J. (1910) *La Géographie Humaine: Essai de Classification Positive, Principes et exemples*. Felix Alcan, Paris.

Burnett, G. (2000) *Masters of all They Surveyed: Exploration, Geography and a British El Dorado*. University of Chicago Press, Chicago.

Butlin, R. (2009) *Geographies of Empire: European Empires and Colonies c.1880–1960*. Cambridge University Press, Cambridge.

Chisholm, G. (1902) Economic Geography. *Scottish Geographical Magazine* 14, 113–132.

Claval, P. (2001) *Histoire de la Géographie*, Presses Universitaires de France, Paris.

Clayton, D. (2004) Imperial Geographies, In J. Duncan, N. Johnson, and R. Schein (eds), *A Companion to Cultural Geography*. Blackwell, Oxford UK and Malden USA, pp. 449–468.

Clayton, D. (2009) Colonialism. In D. Gregory, R. Johnston, G. Pratt, G., M. Watts, and S. Whatmore (eds), *The Dictionary of Human Geography*, 5th edn. Blackwell, Oxford UK and Malden USA, pp. 94–98.

Collier, P. (2006) The Colonial Survey Committee and the Mapping of Africa. International Symposium on the History of Colonial Cartography, Utrecht, NL.

Collier, P. and Inkpen, R. (2003) The Royal Geographical Society and the Development of Surveying 1870-1914. *Journal of Historical Geography* 29, 93–108.

Cooper, F. (2005) *Colonialism in Question: Theory, Knowledge, History*. University of California Press, Berkeley.

Cosgrove, D. (2001) *Apollo's Eye: A Cartographic Genealogy of the Earth in the Western Imagination*. University of Chicago Press, Chicago.

Crampton, J. (2006) The Cartographic Calculation of Space: Race mapping and the Balkans at the Paris Peace Conference. *Social and Cultural Geography* 7, 731–752.

Davis, W.M. (1904) Geography in the United States. *Science* 19, 120–132.

Davis, W.M. (1924) The Progress of Geography in the United States. *Annals of the Association of American Geographers* 14, 158–215.

Deprest, F. (2009) *Géographes en Algérie: Savoirs univeristaires en situation coloniale (1880–1950)*. Belin, Paris.

Driver, F. (1992) Geography's Empire: Histories of Geographical Knowledge. *Environment and Planning D: Society and Space* 10, 23–40.

Driver, F. (2001) *Geography Militant: Cultures of Exploration and Empire*. Blackwell, Oxford UK and Cambridge, USA.

Driver, F. and Gilbert, D. (eds) (1999) *Imperial Cities: Landscape, Display and Identity*. Manchester University Press, Manchester.

Driver, F. and Martins, L. (eds) (2005) *Tropical Visions in an Age of Empire*. University of Chicago Press, Chicago.

Dunbar, G. (1996) *The History of Geography: Collected Essays*. Dodge-Graphic Press, New York.

Duncan, J. (2007) *In the Shadows of the Tropics: Climate, Race and Biopower in Nineteenth Century Ceylon*. Ashgate, Aldershot.

Edney, M. (1993) The Patronage of Science and the Creation of Imperial Space. *Cartographica* 30, 61–67.

Fabian, J. (2000) *Out of Their Minds: Reason and Madness in the Exploration of Central Africa*. University of California Press, Berkeley.

Febvre, L. (1924) *A Geographical Introduction to History*, (trans E. Mountford and J. Paxton). Routledge & Kegan Paul, London.

Freshfield, D. (1886) *The Place of Geography in Education*. Proceedings of the Royal Geographical Society, New Series, pp. 698–714.

Godlewska, A. and Smith, N. (eds) (1994) *Geography and Empire*. Blackwell Publishers, Oxford UK and Cambridge USA.

Gourou, P. (1982) *Terre de Bonne Esperance – Le Monde Tropical*. Pion, Paris.

Gregory, D. (1994) *Geographical Imaginations*. Blackwell Publishers, Oxford.

Gregory, D. (2004) *The Colonial Present*, Blackwell, Oxford UK and Cambridge USA.

Gregory, D. and Pred, A. (eds) (2006) *Violent Geographies: Fear, Terror and Political Violence*. Routledge, London and New York.

Harris, C. (2004) How Did Colonialism Dispossess? Comments from an Edge of Empire. *Annals of the Association of American Geographers* 94, 165–182.

Hartshorne, R. (1939) *The Nature of Geography: A Critical Survey of Current Thought in the Light of the Past*. Association of American Geographers, Lancaster.

Heffernan, M. (1994) The Science of Empire: The French Geographical Movement and the Forms of Imperialism, 1870–1920. In A. Godlewska and N. Smith (eds), *Geography and Empire*. Blackwell, Oxford, pp. 92–114.

Heffernan, M. (1996) Geography, Cartography and Military Intelligence: The Royal Geographical Society and the First World War. *Transactions of the Institute of British Geographers* 21 (3), 504–533.

Heffernan, M. (2007) The European Geographical Imagination. Hettner-Lecture 10. Franz Steiner, Stuttgart.

Heffernan, M. (2009) The Cartography of the Fourth Estate: Mapping the New Imperialism in British and French newspapers, 1975–1925. In J. Ackerman (ed.) *The Imperial Map: Cartography and the Mastery of Empire*. University of Chicago Press, Chicago, pp. 261–299.

Herbertson, A. (1902) Geography in the University. *Scottish Geographical Magazine* 18, 124–132.

Hills, E. (1908) The Survey of the British Empire. *Scottish Geographical Magazine* 14, 505–523.

Holdich, T. (1899) The Use of Practical Geography Illustrated by Recent Frontier Operations. *Geographical Journal* 12, 465–480.

Hudson, B. (1977) The New Geography and the New Imperialism, 1870–1918. *Antipode* 9, 12–19.

Huntington, E. (1928) *The Human Habitat*. Chapman and Hall, London.

Kearns, G. (2004) The Political Pivot of Geography. *Geographical Journal* 170, 337–346.

Keltie, J. (1885) Geographical Education. *Scottish Geographical Journal* 1, 497–505.

Lacoste, Y. (2006) La *question postcoloniale*. *Hérodote* 120, http://www.herodote.org/ (accessed 15th October 2010).

Lapworth, C. (1893) The Limits Between Geology and Physical Geography. *Geographical Journal* 2, 518–534.

Lewis, M. and Wigen, K. (1997) *The Myth of Continents: A Critique of Metageography*. University of California Press, Berkeley.

Livingstone, D. (1984) Natural Theology and Neo-Lamarckism: The Changing Context of Nineteenth-Century Geography in the United States and Great Britain. *Annals of the Association of American Geography* 74, 9–28.

Livingstone, D. (1991) The Moral Discourse of Climate: Historical Considerations on Race, Place and Virtue. *Journal of Historical Geography* 17, 413–434.

Livingstone, D. (1992) *The Geographical Tradition: Episodes in the History of a Contested Enterprise*. Blackwell, Oxford.

Livingstone, D. (2002) *Science, Space and Hermeneutics*. Hettner-Lectures 5. Franz Steiner, Stuttgart.

Livingstone, D. (2003) *Putting Science in its Place: Geographies of Scientific Knowledge*. University of Chicago Press, Chicago.

MacKenzie, J. (1995) The Provincial Geographical Societies in Britain, 1884–1914. In M. Bell, R. Butlin and M. Heffernan, (eds), *Geography and Imperialism, 1820–1940*. Manchester University Press, Manchester, pp. 93–124.

Mackinder, H. (1899) Discussion. *Geographical Journal* 13, 477–480.

Mackinder, H. (1902) *Britain and the British Seas*. Heinemann, London.

Mackinder, H. (1911) The Teaching of Geography from an Imperial Point of View, and the Use Which Should be Made of Visual Instruction. *Geographical Teacher* 6, 79–86.

Mackinder, H. [1887] (1996) On the Scope and Methods of Geography. In J. Agnew, D. Livingstone, and A. Rogers (eds), *Human Geography: An Essential Anthology*. Blackwell, Oxford, pp. 155–172.

Mackinder, H. [1904] (2004) The Geographical Pivot of History. Reprinted in *Geographical Journal* 170 (4), 298–321.
Martin, G. and James, P. (1993) *All Possible Worlds: A History of Geographical Ideas*, 3rd edn. John Wiley & Sons, New York.
Mbembe, A. (2001) *On the Postcolony*. University of California Press, Berkeley.
McEwan, C. (2000) *Gender, Geography and Empire: Victorian Women Travellers in West Africa*. Ashgate, London.
Mill, H. (1903) Geography: Principles and Progress. In H Mill (ed.) *The International Geography*, 3rd edn. George Newnes, London, pp. 1–13.
Mill, H. (1905) The Present Problems of Geography. *Geographical Journal* 1, 1–17.
O'Hara, S. and Heffernan, M. (2006) From Geo-Strategy to Geo-Economics: The "Heartland" and British Imperialism Before and After MacKinder. *Geopolitics* 11, 54–73.
Olsson, G. (2007) *Abysmal: A Critique of Cartographic Reason*. University of Chicago Press, Chicago.
Phillips, R. (1997) *Mapping Men and Empire: A Geography of Adventure*. Routledge, London and New York.
Ploszajska, T. (1999) *Geographical Education, Empire and Citizenship: Geographical Teaching in English Schools, 1870–1944*. IBG-Historical Geography Research Series 35, London.
Porter, B. (2004) *The Absent Minded Imperialists: Empire, Society and Culture in Britain*. Oxford University Press, Oxford.
Prakash, G. (1999) *Another Reason: Science and the Imagination of Modern India*. Princeton University Press, Princeton.
Ratzel, F. [1896] (1996) The Territorial Growth of States. In J. Agnew, D. Livingstone, and A. Rogers (eds), *Human Geography: An Essential Anthology*. Blackwell, Oxford, pp. 525–535.
Ryan, J. (1995) Visualizing Imperial Geography: Halford Mackinder and the Colonial Office Visual Instruction Committee, 1902–11. *Ecumene* 1, 157–176.
Said, E. (1993) *Culture and Imperialism*. Alfred A. Knopf, New York.
Sauer, C. (1941) Foreword to Historical Geography. In J Leighly (ed.) *Land and Life: A Selection From the Writings of Carl Ortwin Sauer*. University of California Press, Berkeley, pp. 351–379.
Schulten, S. (2001) *The Geographical Imagination in America, 1880–1950*. University of Chicago Press, Chicago.
Semple, E. (1903) *American History and its Geographic Conditions*. Houghton Mifflin, Boston.
Sharp, J. (2009) *Geographies of Postcolonialism*. Sage, London.
Singaravélou, P. (2011) The Institutionalisation of 'Colonial Geography' in France (1880–1940). *Journal of Historical Geography*, in press.
Singaravélou, P. (ed.) (2008) *L'Empire des Géographie: Géographie, Exploration et Colonisation, Xixe-Xxe Siècle*. Belin, Paris.
Smith, N. (2003) *American Empire: Roosevelt's Geographer and the Prelude to Globalization*. University of California Press, Berkeley.
Soubeyran, O. (1997) *Imaginaire, Science et discipline*. L'Harmattan, Paris.
Stafford, R. (1999) Scientific Exploration and Empire. In A. Porter (ed.) *The Oxford History of the British Empire, Volume III: The Nineteenth Century*. Oxford University Press, Oxford, pp. 294–319.
Stoddart, D. (1975) The RGS and the Foundations of Geography at Cambridge. *Geographical Journal* 141, 1–24.
Stoddart, D. (1986) *On Geography and Its History*. Blackwell, Oxford.
Stoddart, D. (1994) Geography and War: The "New Geography" and the "New Army" in England, 1899-1914. *Political Geography* 11, 87–99.

Vidal de la Blache [1926] (1996) Meaning and Aim of Human Geography. In J. Agnew, D. Livingstone, and A. Rogers (eds), *Human Geography: An Essential Anthology*. Blackwell, Oxford, pp. 181–191.

Vidal de la Blache, P. (1902) Les conditions géographique des faits sociaux. *Annales de Géographie* 6, 13–23.

Vidal de la Blache, P. (1911) Les genres de vie dans la géographie humaine. *Annales de Géographie* 20, 289–304.

Withers, C. (2007) *Placing the Enlightenment: Thinking Geographically About the Age of Reason*. University of Chicago Press, Chicago.

Withers, C. and Mayhew, R. (2002) Rethinking 'Disciplinary' History: Geography in British Universities, c.1580–1887. *Transactions of the Institute of British Geographers* 27, 1–19.

Withers, C. Finnegan, D., and Higgit, R. (2006) Geography's Other Histories: Geography and Science in the British Association for the Advancement of Science, 1831–c.1933. *Transactions of the Institute of British Geographers* 31, 433–451.

Young, R. (1990) *White Mythologies: Writing History and the West*. Routledge, London and New York.

Part II The Classics

5	German Precursors and French Challengers *Vincent Berdoulay*	73
6	Creating Human Geography in the English-Speaking World *Ron Johnston*	89
7	Landscape Versus Region – Part I *Nicolas Howe*	114
8	Landscape Versus Region – Part II *Kent Mathewson*	130
9	From Region to Space – Part I *Trevor J. Barnes*	146
10	From Region to Space – Part II *Anssi Paasi*	161

The Wiley Blackwell Companion to Human Geography, First Edition.
Edited by John A. Agnew and James S. Duncan.
© 2011 John Wiley & Sons, Ltd. Published 2016 by John Wiley & Sons, Ltd.

Part II The Classics

Chapter 5

German Precursors and French Challengers

Vincent Berdoulay

Introduction

German and French geographic thought and achievements played a foundational role in the development of geography as a discipline in European and American academic institutions during the late nineteenth century and the first decades of the twentieth. Although the German contribution was quite early, creative and important, a full-fledged French school emerged slightly later, taking inspiration from it while challenging it significantly. Together, they formed the standard against which scholars in other countries came to compare themselves. This is why human geography in the English-speaking world cannot be adequately understood without some reference to its German and French forebears. Obviously, many factors played a role in the development of geography in specific countries, be they political, economic or cultural. Nevertheless, the circulation of ideas has always had an international dimension. This was the case during the period at hand, especially because of the models set by the early German contributions and the inflections and alternatives brought to the field by French geographers.

In order to figure out what human geography in the English-speaking world owed to German and French foundational work, it is necessary to first clarify how such transfer of ideas has to be approached. Then, the German and French contributions will be summarized in turn, in order to be able to assess the transfer of ideas into the English-speaking world. Finally, in order to conclude, issues and perspectives on the flow of ideas will be raised in light of today's geographic research.

Text and Context

The study of the history of science has repeatedly shown that it is impossible to confine the explanation of the evolution of scientific ideas to the influence that some individuals may have had on others. Rather, the issue is to know why some ideas and not others are taken advantage of by scientists who are working in various time and place settings. A contextual approach is thus in order for analyzing the conjunction of the inner logic and content of science with the context in which the scientist is placed (Berdoulay 1981). This approach insists on the intermingling of text and context, or, in other words, on the co-construction of each other. By varying the scales of study – a methodology familiar to geographers – it is possible to perceive the complex interactions of ideas, which take place between the individual and aspects of her/his context, from daily social and material constraints and satisfactions to more or less imperative societal issues. Significant mediations have been shown in various studies and they include the institutional setting within which scientific work is achieved.

As the late nineteenth century and the beginning of the twentieth form a period when the institutionalization of scientific research and teaching occurred in universities via a deep institutional transformation, the establishment of geography as a new academic discipline was profoundly affected by this mediation (Dunbar 2001). Much institutional innovation took place in Germany and served as an inspiration in other countries, making its scientific practices an almost international norm. This early model of institutionalization reinforced the foundational role of German geographic thought in the Western world of the time.

German institutional innovation dates back to the Prussian initiative in the first half of the nineteenth century when the university was developed as a major basis on which a modern powerful country could be built. The reform was handled by the linguist Wilhem von Humboldt, brother of the well-known geographer and botanist Alexander. The idea was to provide advanced education for a large number of young people and to associate them with scientific research through small-scale classrooms, tutorials, seminars, and well equipped laboratories, and through a close interaction between the students and their professors. By developing scientific research in the universities, it was hoped that science would give impetus to intellectual, economic and industrial activities. This association of scientific progress with the modernization of the country made the German institutional initiatives valued among other Western countries. Its prestige grew and became so well established that it provided the model on which other university systems were to be reformed. A significant number of academicians and students in various fields arranged for visits and study periods in German universities up until the 1930s. Combined with theoretical and empirical breakthroughs, all this provided international standards for scholarship in many disciplines, geography included.

Visits, training periods, international congresses amplified the impact of another aspect of the institutionalization of science, which was the establishment of high quality scientific journals and other specific publications. With the help of private publishers, German scientists excelled at this. In the field of geography, journals such as the *Petermanns Mitteilungen* or publications and atlases by private publishers such as the Justus Perthes Geographic Institute defined international standards for scientific achievement. The German language was then widely appreciated among scientists in both French- and English-speaking countries to gain immediate access to these achievements.

The international circulation of ideas was also facilitated by the fact that several Western (or "Westernized") countries shared similar political, economic and social challenges, as well as a common intellectual and cultural background. In addition to the overall process of modernization in which German scientific institutions played a significant role, there were important issues to be tackled which directly concerned geography: nation-building or strengthening; territorial expansion and colonization, including empire-building; and the inculcation of moral values to be spread through the education of the whole population. In addition, scientists and other intellectuals shared a concern for evolutionism. In many cases, the evolutionist common ground combined with philosophical issues where the importance of the Kantian contribution was inescapable. As the "thinker of modernity," Kant provided much of the epistemological and ethical groundwork in relation to which later intellectuals had to take a position. In fact, the late nineteenth and early twentieth centuries were characterized by a "return to Kant" in most countries and this familiarity conditioned the international transfer of ideas (Willey 1978; Blais 2000).

These contextual issues combined together with scientific work not only through higher education and research institutions but also by means of other mediations. These particularly involved "circles of affinity" (Berdoulay 1981) whereby scientists would significantly interact with various individuals who ranged from some colleagues in the same or another discipline to philosophers, writers, artists, or politicians. By cutting across institutional networks, such circles of affinity allowed for the transfer of new ideas emerging from the interaction of scientific and societal challenges. As this creative activity took place, it had to come to terms with the stabilizing force which discourse imposes on the formulation of new ideas. This is another important mediation linking text and context, which has to be taken into account for understanding the structuring and subsequent diffusion of thought (Berdoulay 1988).

This is a way of approaching the contributions made by "great" individuals, who should not be discarded simply because of the attention given to context nor regarded as simple "gatekeepers" when contested by younger scientists. Through their respective circles of affinity, those well-known or remembered individuals responded most promptly to societal challenges but, most significantly, they also epitomized the universally significant contribution that particular text/context interactions may produce. From the point of view of the international transfer of ideas, they can be considered as *passeurs*, that is, dedicated individuals who dare to transgress an established order for making ideas, goods or people pass from one national context to another where they can blossom. In the history of human geography, Ratzel, Vidal de la Blache, Semple, Bowman, Hartshorne, and Sauer are among them.

The German Academic Grounding of Human Geography

Since the European Renaissance, German-speaking lands have had a long tradition of geographic activities, especially in cartography and in the archivistic reconstitution of past territories. Geographic thought was also sustained by religious and philosophical (metaphysical and moral) concerns about the fate of Man on the Earth. In addition, at the beginning of the nineteenth century, the definition of Geography as a major scientific discipline was owed greatly to three impressive authors: Immanuel Kant, who had never ceased to underline the epistemological significance of geography as a preliminary to all other types of empirical knowledge; Alexander von Humboldt, who proved very innovative in the empirical study of the complexity of physical environments and in the human appreciation of them; and Karl Ritter, who brought long-term, historical depth to the explanation of human interaction with the various aspects of the earth. It is on the grounds laid by such figures that geography progressively grew as an academic discipline.

At the time of the Franco-Prussian war (1870–1871) which gave birth to a politically unified Germany under the leadership of the Kaiser and his minister Bismarck, geography was taught in institutions of higher education of Prussia and soon after it finished spreading to all major academic centers of the new Reich, while strengthening its institutionalization thanks to the establishment of a greater number of chairs in well-known universities throughout the 1880s (van Valkenburg 1951; Brogiato 1995). With the high reputation acquired by its journals, books and atlases, the international prestige of German geography probably then reached its apex. However, this prestige can be laid mostly to contributions in cartography, physical geography, fieldwork, and scientific explorations abroad. Geographers such as Oskar Peschel or later Ferdinand von Richthofen well represented this orientation towards natural sciences. Human aspects of geography came as a complement to these advanced investigations and did not structure geographic theory. This is why Friedrich Ratzel's proposal of an "anthropogeography" in the 1880s gained immediate attention – if not equally shared fascination – in Germany and abroad (Bassin 1987a).

Basically, Ratzel's breakthrough consisted in setting geography within a scientific-evolutionary discourse (Ratzel 1882, 1891). There already existed theories about physical, especially geomorphological, evolution (e.g., Lyell) or about historical and social evolution (e.g. Comte, Spencer), but their unilinear evolutionism did not provide a larger picture of how human cultural diversity could emerge from environmental conditions. Building first on the Darwinian paradigm as interpreted by Ernst Haeckel and Moritz Wagner, Ratzel conceived geography as an ecology of human populations, in a broad analogy between Darwin's focus on species and his own focus on cultures and states. His evolutionism was grounded in biology and this contribution fitted in well with the German, and international, wish for a sound anchoring of geography in the natural sciences. Although partially accepted and at times distorted by other German geographers, his contribution brought a significant turn in the geographic study of environmental conditions and territorial political organization.

With Ratzel, geography became an indispensable science for explaining the diversity of human societies or cultures, which was seen as echoing the environmental diversity of the earth. The key for human geographical explanation rested on physical geography, or, more specifically, on a biogeographical outlook. De facto, actual work depended more on analogy than on the detailed study of processes, and many geographers, including Ratzel himself, often indulged in leaping quickly from the overall view of geography as ecology to biological, organismic interpretations of regions and states. His stress on the necessity of a *Lebensraum* (vital space) for the development of a society led to its indiscriminate and excessive use by later promoters of political geography in the form of a *Geopolitik* which ended up being absorbed within Nazi ideology. However, Ratzel himself vigorously opposed any idea of racial determinism (Bassin 1987b).

Thus, mixed together in Ratzel's essential contribution, several aspects of German geography gained audiences abroad. They can be referred to in terms of three interrelated characteristics. Although quite pervasive in German geographic conceptions and practices, they seem ill-defined for foreigners because they have deep roots in the German cultural context. The first one rests on the fundamentally spatial view of the discipline. This is not as simple as it may seem. The spatial view can equally concern an interest in geometry or distance measures and a focus on local complex interrelationships. German geography was first of all a chorology (Marthe 1877; Richthofen 1883); its basic focus was on spatial differentiation, on the finding of principles of regionalization, on what makes an area different from another through the understanding of general, universal processes at work. In contemporary English terms, the German geographers' concern for *Raum* was as much about place as it was about space (Olwig 2002). This is quite evident in the *Länderkunde* studies they wrote until World War I (Wardenga 1996). To some extent, a similar spatial conception may be found in the quite theoretically innovative, but still inductive modeling of central places published by Walter Christaller in the early 1930s (Christaller 1933).

The same type of issue is present in a second, important characteristic of German geography, that is, its concern for landscape. Here again, the notion of *Landschaft* became increasingly used to refer not only to what is seen (a landscape) but also to what local interrelationships it encompasses (a region or area). What could be perceived today as an ambiguity served the German geographers to freely mix investigations on spatial and ecological relationships with the study of what is perceived by visual observation (Hard 1970). Initially used for pedagogical purposes, this *Landschaft* idea became the subject of research (Schultz 1980, 1989). This evolution owed greatly to the contribution of Otto Schlüter, who showed how the human transformation of nature leads to a *Kulturlandschaft* (Schlüter 1903). Advocated as a central concept of the discipline in the 1920's, *Landschaft* helped in giving more importance to human geography. However, with the revanchist and later increasingly Nazi leanings of some geographers, it led to a focus on spatial entities viewed as organisms. These individual wholes were then approached in large part through the researcher's intuition at the expense of causal analysis. In spite of the Nazi collapse with the end of the Second World War, the idea of *Landschaft* kept its appeal in German geography, especially because of its significance for regional geography (Bobek and Schmithüsen 1949). And this lasted at least until the major self-examination and paradigmatic changes within German geography, which occurred in the late 1960s and 1970s.

These characteristics of German geographic thought and practice can be related, although not necessarily, to the third characteristic, which proceeds from the foundational Kantian concern for epistemology and from the strength of historical and cultural studies in nineteenth century Germany. Many German geographers explicitly discussed the foundations, concepts, and compass of geography. They were concerned with the issue of the unity of the discipline. In addition, the German geographers' interest in epistemological issues was reinforced by the larger debates on the overall status of the historical and cultural sciences. Although empirical, positivistic science attracted most of them in the beginning, some argued later in favor of methodologies which should be different from the natural sciences. In this respect, philosophers of the Southwestern German (or Heidelberg, or Baden) school of neo-Kantianism such as Wilhelm Windelband and Heinrich Rickert served to give epistemological legitimacy to focusing on particular phenomena. In spite of initial hesitations, the issue was not to distinguish sciences according to their object of study, but rather to characterize distinct methodologies for understanding the world (Strohmayer 1997). Alfred Hettner is best known for echoing these debates in his writings on the aims and methods of geography, through his use of the nomothetic/idiographic distinction (Hettner 1927). It served him to characterize two distinct methodologies that allow geographers to explain phenomena either according to the point of view of their generality or to the point of view of their individuality. His main point was that geography depended on the use of both methodologies (Wardenga 1995).

While the institutionalization of the discipline grew at the turn of the century in other countries, the international prestige of German geography was tarnished by the political turmoil linked to the two World Wars. Particularly damaging was the revanchist, and later racist nationalism that swept across Germany and Austria. Many German geographers worked in contesting the new European state boundaries erected after the First World War. For many, however, the rising tide of National Socialism in the 1930s provoked a retreat to traditional themes. At the same time, the success of *Geopolitik* in the hands of the Nazis brought a lasting discredit on political geography in Western Europe. The same type of reaction contributed to delay in the recognition of the significance of Walter Christaller's central place theory. It was only with the late 1960s that the conservative imposition of older themes became strongly contested; consequently, German geography is now paradoxically faced with the need to innovate when the potential breakthroughs laid by some of its forerunners have already come to fruition in the hands of foreign geographers.

Innovations by the "French School"

When historian-trained Paul Vidal de la Blache started his professional career in geography in 1872 and began his life-long dedication to the formulation and institutionalization of what came to be called the French school of geography, he did not work in a geographic-thought vacuum (Berdoulay 2008). As in Germany, geographic activity was a multi-century story, and the nineteenth century had begun with significant advances, including the foundation of the world's first geographical society in Paris in 1821 (Godlewska 1999). However, the humiliating defeat by Prussia in 1870–1871 created such a shock to French society that the growing Republican Party turned toward Germany as a source of inspiration for reforming the university system. The institutionalization of geography, under the wing of Vidal de la Blache, grew at the same time as the university developed, giving the "French school" its exceptional, albeit relative, coherence which in turn facilitated its international visibility. The creation in 1891 of the *Annales de géographie* and of its adjunct, fully international *Bibliographie géographique* marked the beginning of this recognition: French geography could meet the standards set up by German scholarship and yet bring its own distinctive scientific contribution. Thus, German academic achievements strongly infused the incipient French school of geography, but the latter developed on epistemological and theoretical bases which proved different. Following German geographers, Vidal and his disciples spent a lot of time studying the natural sciences, mostly geology and botany, in order to get a better grasp of the ecological functioning of the environment. Clearly, they were strongly attracted by the ideas of Ratzel, whom they visited, and they took care to comment on his major publications. In their own writings, the term *anthropogéographie* shifted to *géographie humaine*, an expression made popular by Vidal's disciple Jean Brunhes (1910), which acquired a world wide diffusion once adopted in other languages (Vidal 1922). Ratzelian foundations are still recognizable: human life on earth is viewed in an ecological and evolutionary perspective; great attention is devoted to the analysis of complex milieus; movements in space of goods, ideas and population are scrutinized; the colonial and territorial extension of states as well as regional organization are key themes focused upon (Mercier 1995). But Vidalian human geography had more to offer.

It brought a distinctive perspective on geography. In epistemological terms, it rested on neo-Kantian foundations that the "return to Kant" had strengthened. In France, it took orientations, which proved different from those taken elsewhere. Interested in the dilemma of determinism versus free will, it insisted on the value of science at the same time as it tried to demonstrate the power of the human mind to conceptualize the world. The emphasis which was put on the cognitive capacities of the mind, served to justify human freedom and autonomy without deprecating science. This led to "conventionalism," a philosophy of science advocated by authors such as Henri Poincaré or Pierre Duhem, whereby theories and laws are viewed as categories imposed by the mind on reality and whose validity depends on their convenient simplicity to explain the world. Vidal repeatedly made it clear that he and other scientists were working with "notions," "theories," "principles," "ideas," and not with the reality of, say, "regions," "migrations," or "terrestrial unity." Geography as a science is a point of view, not exclusive of others. Somehow extending this neo-Kantian perspective from the scientist's to any inhabitant of the earth, Vidal considered that human interaction with milieu depended in part on representations and gave birth to relatively stable forms of compromise, be they areas, landscapes or *genres de vie* (ways of life). This constructivist approach was at the root of what was termed later "possibilism," that is, Vidal's theoretical approach to the study of human relationship to the environment whereby human initiative is recognized as significant (Berdoulay 2009).

Drawing also from neo-Kantian discussions of explanation, Vidal explicitly rejected the positivist model. Rather than looking for universal laws in order to explain particular cases, Vidal argued for the identification of series of cause-and-effect phenomena, speaking of *enchaînement* as a synonym of Ritter's idea of *Entwicklung* (development). What came out of this was a geographic discourse where a narrative overtone was grounded in scientific observation and causal explanation. This is why it may be impossible to encapsulate his way of doing regional geography. Spatial differentiation cannot be its major goal or means. What interests Vidal is the identification of series of causes and effects, which may produce various types of compromise between humans and the earth. Vidal had some of his students work on regional monographs for scientifically demonstrating that human populations have significantly interacted with the local milieu (de Martonne, Demangeon). Their detailed and polished presentations impressed other geographers in France and abroad, so that many geographers imitated them at the expense of other types of research. At any rate, in his studies, Vidal kept changing the scale of observation, not systematically selecting elements in the environment, and providing multifaceted geographic narratives. It cannot be said that a definite regional geography characterized his work; rather, it was a geography of places. In addition, he was attentive to the human geographical restructuring of the earth's surface, which could have potential for the future; consequently, Vidal and many within the French school did not shy away from getting involved in planning. They actively participated in the establishment of urban and regional planning in France, making use of the possibilist framework for identifying what possibilities should be tapped for the future (Berdoulay and Soubeyran 2002). The neo-Lamarckian view of evolution helped Vidal and his disciples to insist on the mutual transformation of human society and milieu and to give possibilist geography a legitimate role in the urban and regional planning process (Berdoulay *et* Soubeyran 1991; Berdoulay 2009).

In tune with French Republican ideology, which turned toward Kant's philosophy for providing moral (and not religious nor positivist) foundations to their policies, the possibilist approach gave room within geography for the autonomy of the individual as member of society. This enhanced the role of geography in the education of citizens in a modern democracy, whereby their moral behavior partly comes from the experience of interacting with the natural and human milieu. This is why a significant divergence could emerge in relation to German geography. In France, the emphasis was leaning more toward a social-geographic "Kantian" subject than on collective identification with a predefined culture. It is revealing that French geographers were reluctant for a long time to adopt the notion of culture, preferring to speak of *genres de vie* or occasionally of (large scale) civilizations. Similarly, they diverged in the way to approach political geography, insisting more on civic nation-building or reinforcement than on ethnic or linguistic data in the territorial definition of a nation as the German geographers did.

Beyond the uninspired reproduction of aspects of the Vidalian foundations by later generations of French geographers, and in relation to the growing weaknesses of German geography following World War I, Vidal and his disciples have left an image of a school of thought in which a humanistic concern was at the core of a coherent human geography. It benefited from the contribution of scholars in other countries, such as Belgium or Spain, who built their own national networks around some key features of the French school. However, the Marxist militancy of many French geographers after World War II increased the already difficult challenge of renovating the Vidalian school of thought, which had restricted itself to only a part of the Vidalian heritage (Claval 1998; Berdoulay 2001). Francophone and French geographers who worked in other countries, such as Jean Gottmann (1961, 1972) who brought new insights in political and urban geography (e.g., in his analysis and naming of the North-Eastern megalopolis), helped in the transfer of ideas from abroad, which have contributed to rejuvenating the rich heritage of the French school.

Transforming Transfers

Working at the center of a growing, impressive empire in competition with the (re)emergent German and French hearths, British geographers were less keen to borrow ready-made paradigms from abroad than geographers in the United Sates, which still had to consolidate its national fabric. The reciprocal long lasting interest between British and Anglo-American cultured classes and the French ones favored flows of ideas (e.g., William M. Davis had great success in teaching at the Sorbonne in 1911–1912), which partly counter-balanced those stemming from the closer economic and folk ties with German-speaking lands (especially because of German migration to the United States). Sometimes, German achievements were received in their "filtered" form through the reading of the work of Vidal and of his first disciples. Transfers involve complex, direct and indirect, and often reciprocal, flows.

What made the transfer of ideas have unexpected outcomes was the epistemological background which immersed geographers in the English-speaking world. Broadly speaking, whereas neo-Kantian thought brought some balance to positivism in continental Europe, empiricist and positivist philosophies were dominant in English-speaking countries. However excessive this generalization may be when related to actual individual intellectual production, it should be kept in mind in order to understand the challenge of borrowing ideas which have emerged in another epistemological context. If the borrower does not succeed in adapting it to its new context, it can hardly bear fruit for further research. A good example of this is how early urban studies in Chicago benefited from German achievements. In a context marked by pragmatism (a philosophy sharing some aspects of neo-Kantianism), sociologist Robert Park took better advantage of German geographic contributions than his fellow geographers did, for founding a distinctive, world famous approach to the human ecology of cities (Entrikin 1980). Mentioning the University of Chicago, it is interesting to pinpoint here that it was the seedbed of the major institutional innovation which transformed the German model through the creation of graduate studies programs, including geography as early as 1903, and provided the new standard for higher education and research which kept spreading throughout the twentieth century in the United States and abroad. Starting in the late 1880s, the progressive institutionalization of geography in universities of Britain and the United States was geared to meet the scientific standards set by their continental European predecessors; consequently, they took partial inspiration from them, notably through the participation in international congresses, invited lectures, study journeys abroad (especially in Germany). Among the diverse flows and exchanges of ideas, one can distinguish five areas of debate which were important for British and Anglo-American geographers and in which German and French contributions were heavily used for purposes of argumentation.

The first nexus concerns environmental determinism. To what extent should human geography be explained by environmental determinism? Two reasons concurred for the significance of this question. Physical geography had quite early gained a heavy weight in geographic teaching and research and de facto created a potential dependence for a weaker and theoretically deficient human geography. And most of all, in the United States, the first stage of the institutionalization of geography occurred under the tutelage of W.M. Davis, so that, until World War I, the discipline primarily focused on "physiography," confining human geography to the study of the "response" (or "influence," or "adjustments") to natural environments. This environmentalist definition, or reduction, of the scope and aim of geography induced a search for natural-environmental causation of human societies. This was at the root of the complex and confusing entanglement of arguments for or against environmental determinism, which distinctively characterized geographic thought in the English-speaking world up to the 1950s (Platt 1948; Tatham 1952; Lewthwaite 1966). Positivist thought helped in this respect, because of its search for general, universal laws. Of course, American geographers realized that there were other types of determination (especially economic) on human action and they became increasingly dissatisfied with this approach. This is why they turned toward German and French geographic production for giving more depth or balance to their own research. Even Ellen Semple's deterministic account of Ratzel's search for environmental influences on human activities should not be stereotyped, because her analyses proved less systematic (Semple 1903, 1931). In fact, this is where the more balanced and coherent views of the French school became useful. Several geographers trained under Davis's wings cited German as well as French works as they distanced themselves from the deterministic bias of their initial research. For instance, Albert P. Brigham used Ratzel as well as Jean Brunhes in warning against unverified generalization about environmental influences. Another example is Isaiah Bowman who was enthused by his reading of Brunhes' *La géographie humaine* and had it translated into English (Martin 2000). Understandably, after World War I, younger geographers tried to reject the whole Davisian program of geographic influences, by looking for alternate foci, which they greatly borrowed from German or French geography. Citing Vidal and Brunhes, they adopted possibilism as their philosophy regarding human-land relationships, and they could appreciate again American precursors such J.P. Marsh who had insisted many years previously on "man as a geographic agent." However, by reducing possibilism to the opposite of environmental determinism, these authors tended to miss its epistemological and theoretical significance, especially its non anti-deterministic stance. The overall idea was transformed for other purposes. Nevertheless, *la géographie humaine* kept providing English-speaking geographers with a cautious look at environmental deterministic interpretations as well as with a model for resisting the frequent hegemony of physical geography and the divide between the latter and human geography (Glacken 1956; Berdoulay and Chapman 1987). The French school legitimated the aspiration for a more integrated discipline. For many geographers, especially with the onset of the sweeping "quantitative revolution" in the 1960s, it also embodied the possibility of a humanistic practice of the discipline (Buttimer 1971).

A second nexus concerns regional geography. Here again, there is much confusion in the English-speaking world about the use and the research implications of the terms (Whittlesey 1954; Gilbert 1960; Dickinson 1976; Entrikin 1981). It may refer to the study of a particular region or to the task of dividing a vast area, or the earth, into different regions. Early British geographers such as Marion Newbigin or

Herbert Fleure took inspiration from French ideas, including the identification of a *genre de vie* as a basis for defining a region, and the goal of integrating various types of phenomena. However, the transfer was hampered by the empiricist belief in the objective reality of the region. In the United States, there already was a technical tradition of regionalization through the mapping of the land and resources, to which British regional geography introduced some academic standards of its own; but most significant was the overall regional upsurge, which followed the waning of the Davisian paradigm in the 1920s. Carl Sauer's leadership in this intellectual turn used mostly German sources for giving weight to his arguments (Sauer 1925). In so doing, he leaned toward a chorological point of view, giving a lot of attention to whatever can explain the differentiation of the earth surface at whatever scale of observation. This became an important focus for Anglo-American geography. At the same time, several English-speaking regional geographers were fascinated by the challenge of expressing the individual, singular aspect of a region. Calling forth the Vidalian model, they tried to grasp the personality of various areas (Dunbar 1974). Thus mixed with this reference to Vidal and the French school, the chorological view taken from German scholarship persisted, feeding numerous debates on the nature and validity of the regional method. In other words, in the complex, if not confusing, debates, which dealt with regional geography in the English-speaking world, German and French ideas were intertwined in an inextricable manner, very far away from their respective epistemological homes.

The third and related nexus concerns the notion of landscape, which attracted many American geographers and which became central to cultural geography. Here again, Sauer played a major role in orienting the idea when transferred from its German context. Although he was aware of the Vidalian contribution on the "physiognomy" of the land and its close relationship with *genres de vie*, Sauer preferred the German geographers' focus on the *Kulturlandschaft*. He wanted to break away from environmental determinism and, although he cited several French or Belgian authors in support of this (e.g., Michotte, Febvre, Brunhes), the German approach in the footsteps of Schlüter offered him a convenient family of ideas to do so (Sauer 1931, 1941). It drew attention to human agency in the transformation of the natural environment and it gave form and content to Sauer's chorological concern. By deliberately stressing the visible aspects of the landscape and the spatial diffusion of its key features, he progressively shifted the idea away from its German kernel where the notion referred as much to scenery as to the specific material features of a region. This relative removal of the ambiguity of the concept by Sauer prevented him from following the drift of the *Landschaft*-oriented German geographers who held a strongly organicist view of culture areas. It is significant that Anglo-American landscape studies evolved by following directions which were different from those they took in Germany. On the other hand, by so doing, Sauer and his so-called Berkeley school left relatively unexamined the notion of culture. Although understandable from their human geographic point of view and with their focus on visible, material artefacts, the implied reference to the notion of culture when referring to a cultural landscape begs the question of how values, traditions and innovations emerge and evolve through their interaction with the social as well as natural environment. In this respect, American cultural geography did not take inspiration from the social-geographic views of Vidal and from the French caution about adopting an ethnographic view of culture. The possibilist content of the Berkeley school did not extend to the formal discussion of the issue of the multiple determination of human action, although it served to keep a humanistic concern alive in American geography.

A fourth important nexus concerns methodology, and more specifically the idiographic-nomothetic distinction, which pervaded Anglo-American geography for many years. Richard Hartshorne was at the crux of the debates, because he was responsible for the way they were transferred from German geography, specifically from the work of Hettner (Hartshorne 1939, 1959). The issue of attributing scientific interest and validity to the study of a particular phenomenon was not new. As mentioned above, in line with neo-Kantianism, Vidal adopted the solution of focusing on a series of causes and effects, and thus on rejecting the dichotomy between regional and systematic geography. Hettner turned in part toward the same solution, that is, the search for *Ursachenreihe* (chains of causes), but he placed it, as idiographic, in contradistinction to the other, nomothetic approach, which the German Southwestern school of neo-Kantianism had distinguished. In order to clarify the articulation of the regional method and of systematic sub-disciplines within geography, Hartshorne used Hettner's presentation. It has been shown that, despite widespread belief to the contrary and despite his own claim to the contrary, Hartshorne's argumentation differs greatly from Hettner's (Entrikin 1989; Harvey and Wardenga, 2006). A major reason for this divergence is the transfer of the idea from its German neo-Kantian context of significance into an Anglo-American epistemology where positivism is dominant. The paradox was not perceived by later critics of Hartshorne who were the logical-positivist leaders of the quantitative revolution and who thus brought even more confusion into the debate (Schaeffer 1953).

Finally, another nexus, very conflictual, should be raised here. It concerns the issue of the geographic approach to politics and geopolitics. With Britain's imperial successes and challenges, British political geography was basically concerned with global geopolitical issues, as illustrated by Halford Mackinder's famous essays on the pivot of history (Mackinder 1904). Enhancing Ratzel's concept of the state as a territorial organism as well as Mackinder's global view, the emerging German *Geopolitik* in the 1920's and 30's and its enrolment in Nazi ideology called for intensive criticism at the time of World War II. Now, transfer gave way to conflict, and interesting discussions emerged. French geographers insisted on the voluntary, civic nation rather than on linguistic or ethnic principles of political aggregation (Ancel 1936). Through equally informed critiques and through their reading of German and French works, Anglo-American geographers' response focused on the relationship of power and democracy, explicitly introducing the moral issue into political geography (Kiss 1942; Bowman 1942). The post-war equation between political geography and *Geopolitik* obscured the reading of Ratzel's contribution in France and Germany for several decades (Schöller 1957; Parker 2000). French geographer Jean Gottmann became one of the few scholars who could connect ideas among the German, French, British and Anglo-American worlds in political geography (Gottmann 1972). Nevertheless, what remained untapped in the English-speaking world were French conceptions of culture, which could have induced greater reflection on citizenship and the relative autonomy of the individual subject in contemporary political society.

Perspective

At the end of this brief and necessarily sketchy survey of the flow of geographic ideas from the early German and French hearths to the English-speaking world, one gets a mixed impression about their importance and significance. On the one hand, they did exist, they concerned deep intellectual issues, they truly bridged very different cultural and linguistic traditions, and (although this could not be dealt with here) they included a great deal of reciprocity. On the other hand, we have seen that little was truly transferred as such: what took place was basically a process of transformation, which both distorted the original ideas and gave them a new, or renewed, significance. These remarks point to the legitimacy of conceiving a history of geography that would rest on the point of view of the transfer *and* transformation of ideas.

In a globalization perspective, which is often advocated nowadays for the advancement of science, does it mean that local contexts should be contested as having any significance whatsoever for the "larger" enterprise? Past experience in geography shows that there is no need for it, as far as innovation is concerned. On the contrary, we have seen that high standards of scholarship could be developed in the past century while preserving both international flows and local conditions for creativity. At least, this was the case for close to a century. But the last few decades evidence a new pattern. There is a growing flow of geographic ideas and paradigms from the English-speaking world to other countries, which cannot be viewed as symmetrical as to what occurred in the past. This flow is unidirectional with either quasi- or no reciprocity, and depends on the power of imperialistic structures of the so-called internationalization of scientific activity. Contrary to what was the case not long ago, the voluntary ignorance by many leading geographers in the English-speaking world of contributions written in other languages prevents deep intellectual exchange. It is only the vast extension of the English-speaking scientific empire that gives the illusion of a significant internationalization of geographic thought. Interestingly enough, the enrichment from abroad is still felt to be necessary; but it is searched for increasingly from outside the discipline. For instance, the recent interest in "French theory" (Barthes, Foucault, Derrida, Mouffe, Lefebvre, etc.) shown by English-speaking geographers is evidence of this process of intellectual advancement, which we saw above occurring within geography (that is, by disconnecting ideas from their intellectual ecology) and which is at work in other places (e.g., the current French geographers' interest in the ideas of Hannah Arendt or American pragmatist philosophers).

It should be mentioned in closing that other German and French to Anglo-American flows could not be dealt with here and may have been quite significant in the long run. These range from non-academically institutionalized ideas such as those of Elisée Reclus or Frédéric Le Play (whose reception was better in the English-speaking world than in their home country of France) to detours by way of another discipline (e.g., the roles of the German anthropologist Boas or the French historian Braudel in Anglo-American human geography), and – much more importantly – to the complex set of techniques, skills, and practices which have come to make up the profession of "geographer" (Berdoulay and van Ginkel 1996). The world history of geography depends as much on these largely shared aspects of a common savoir-faire, which are directly connected to the human experience on earth, as well as to the intellectually difficult and culturally loaded process of transferring ideas from some national settings to others.

References

Ancel, J. (1936) *Géopolitique*. Delagrave, Paris.
Bassin, M. (1987a) Friedrich Ratzel 1844–1904. *Geographers: Biobibliographical Studies* 11, 123–132.
Bassin, M. (1987b) Space contra race: the conflict between German Geopolitik and National Socialism. *Political Geography Quarlerly* 6, 1151–1134.
Berdoulay, V. (1981) In D.R. Stoddart (ed.) *The contextual approach: Geography, Ideology, and Social Concern*. Basil Blackwell, Oxford, pp. 8–16.
Berdoulay, V. (1988) *Des mots et des lieux. La dynamique du discours géographique*. Paris, Editions du CNRS, Paris.
Berdoulay, V. (2001) Geography in France: Context, practice, and text. In G.S. Dunbar (ed.), *Geography: Discipline, Profession and Subject since 1870. An International Survey*. Kluwer Academic Publishers, Dordrecht, pp. 45-78.
Berdoulay, V. (2008) *La formation de l'école française de géographie (1870–1914)*, 3rd edn. with a Postscript. Editions du CTHS, Paris.
Berdoulay, V. (2009) Possibilism. In R. Kitchin and N. Thrift (eds), *International Encyclopedia of Human Geography*. Elsevier, Oxford, pp. 312–320.
Berdoulay, V. and Chapman, L. (1987) Le possibilisme de Harold Innis, *Canadian Geographer/ Géographe canadien* 31, 2–11.
Berdoulay, V. and van Ginkel J.A. (eds) (1996) *Geography and Professional Practice*. N.G.S, Utrecht.
Berdoulay, V. and Soubeyran, O. (1991) Lamarck, Darwin et Vidal: aux sources naturalistes de la géographie humaine. *Annales de géographie* 617–634.
Berdoulay, V. and Soubeyran, O. (eds) (2002) *L'écologie urbaine et l'urbanisme. Aux fondements des enjeux actuels*. La Découverte, Paris.
Blais, M.-C. (2000) *Au principe de la République. Le cas Renouvier*. Gallimard, Paris.
Bobek, H. and Schmithüsen, J. (1949) Die Landschaftsbegriff in logischen System der Geographie. *Erdkunde* 2–3, 112–120.
Bowman, I. (1942) Geography vs. Geopolitics. *Geographical Review* 32, 646–658.
Brogiato, H.P. (1995) Schwerem Kampfe um die Geltung der Geographie. Die Schulgeographie im Spiegel der Deutschen Geographentage 1881–1948. In U. Wardenga and I. Hönsch (eds), *Kontinuität und Diskontinuität der deutschen Geographie in Umbruchphasen*. Institut für Geographie der Westfälischen, Wilhelms-Universität, Münster, pp. 51–81.
Brunhes, J. (1910) *La géographie humaine*. Félix Alcan, Paris. Translated as: *Human Geography (1920)*. Rand MacNally, New York.
Buttimer, A. (1971) *Society and Milieu in the French Geographic Tradition*. Rand McNally, Chicago.
Christaller, W. (1933) *Die zentralen Orte in Süddeutschland*. Jena, G. Fischer, Jena. Translated: *Central Places in Southern Germany* (1966). Englewood Cliffs, NJ, Prentice Hall, Englewood Cliffs.
Claval, P. (1998) *Histoire de la géographie française de 1870 à nos jours*. Nathan, Paris.
Dickinson, R.E. (1976) *Regional Concept: The Anglo-American Leaders*. Routledge and Kegan Paul, London.

Dunbar, G.S. (1974) Geographical Personality. *Geoscience and Man*, vol. V. Louisiana State University, Baton Rouge, pp. 25–33.

Dunbar, G.S. (ed.) (2001) *Geography: Discipline, Profession and Subject since 1870. An International Survey.* Kluwer Academic Publishers, Dordrecht.

Entrikin, J.N. (1980) Robert Park's human ecology and human geography. *Annals of the Association of American Geographers* 70, 43–58.

Entrikin, J.N. (1981) Philosophical issues in the scientific study of regions. In D.T. Herbert and R.J. Johnston (eds), *Geography and the Urban Environment, vol. 4.* John Wiley, Chichester, England, pp. 12–17.

Entrikin, J.N. (1989) Introduction: *The Nature of Geography* in Perspective. In J.N. Entrikin and S.D. Brunn (eds), *Reflections on Richard Hartshorne's The Nature of Geography.* Association of American Geographers, Washington, D.C, pp. 11–15.

Gilbert, E.W. (1960) The Idea of the Region. *Geography* 45, pp. 157–175.

Glacken, C.J. (1956) Changing ideas of the habitable world. In W.L. Thomas Jr. (ed.), *Man's Role in Changing the Face of the Earth.* University of Chicago Press, Chicago, pp. 70–92.

Gottmann, J. (1961) *Megalopolis. The Urbanized Seaboard of North-Eastern United States.* MIT Press, Cambridge.

Gottmann, J. (1972) *The Significance of Territory.* University Press of Virginia, Charlottesville.

Godlewska, A. (1999) *Geography Unbound. French Geographic Science from Cassini to Humboldt.* University of Chicago Press, Chicago.

Hard, G. (1970) *Die 'Landschaft' der Sprache und die 'Landschaft' der Geographen.* Colloquium Geographicum, Bonn.

Hartshorne, R. (1939) The nature of geography. A critical survey of current thought in light of the past. *Annals of the Association of American Geographers* 29, pp. 171–658, Reprinted as: *The Nature of Geography* (1939). Association of American Geographers, Lancaster.

Hartshorne, R. (1959) *Perspective on the Nature of Geography.* Rand McNally, Chicago.

Harvey, F. and Wardenga, U. (2006) Richard Hartshorne's adaptation of Alfred Hettner's system of geography. *Journal of Historical Geography* 32, pp. 422–440.

Hettner, A. (1927) *Die Geographie. Ihre Geschichte, ihr Wesen und ihre Methoden.* Ferdinand Hirt, Breslau.

Kiss, G. (1942) Political geography into geopolitics. Recent trends in Germany. *Geographical Review* 32, pp. 632–645.

Lewthwaite, G. (1966) Environmentalism and determinism: A search for clarification. *Annals of the Association of American Geographers* 56, pp. 1–23.

Mackinder, H.J. (1904) The geographical pivot of history. *Geographical Journal* 23, pp. 421–437.

Marthe, F. (1877) Begriff, Ziel und Methode der Geographie und v. Richthofens China. Bd. I. *Zeitschrift der Gesellschaft für Erdkunde zu Berlin* 12, 422–478.

Martin, G.J. (1977) Isaiah Bowman 1878–1950. *Geographers: Bibliographical Studies* 1, 9–18.

Mercier, G. (1995) La région et l'état selon Friedrich Ratzel et Paul Vidal de la Blache. *Annales de géographie* 104, 211–235.

Olwig, K.R. (2002) The duplicity of space: Germanic 'Raum' and Swedish 'rum' in English language geographical discourse. *Geografiska Annaler* 84 B, 1–17.

Parker, G. (2000) Ratzel, the French School and the birth of alternative geopolitics. *Political Geography* 19, 957–969.

Platt, R.S. (1948) Determinism in geography. *Annals of the Association of American Geographers* 38, 126–132.

Ratzel, F. (1882) *Anthropo-Geographie oder Grundzüge der Anwendung der Erdkunde auf die Geschichte*, vol. 1. Engelhorn, Stuttgart.

Ratzel, F. (1891) *Anthropogeographie. Die geographische Verbreitung des Menschen*, vol. 2. Engelhorn, Stuttgart.

Richthofen, F. von (1883) *Aufgaben und Methoden der heutigen Geographie. Akademische Anstrittrede*. Veit, Leipzig.

Sauer, C.O. (1925) The morphology of landscape, *University of California Publications in Geography*, 2, pp. 19–53. Reprinted in (1967). In J. Leighly (ed.), *Land and Life*. University of California Press, Berkeley and Los Angeles, pp. 315–350.

Sauer, C.O. (1931) Cultural geography. *Encyclopedia of the Social Sciences* 6, 621–623.

Sauer, C.O. (1941) Foreword to historical geography. *Annals of the Association of American Geographers* 31, pp. 1–24. Reprinted in (1967). In J. Leighly (ed.), *Land and Life*. University of California Press, Berkeley and Los Angeles, pp. 351–379.

Schaefer, F. (1953) Exceptionalism in geography. A methodological examination. *Annals of the Association of American Geograhers* 43, 226–249.

Schultz, H.-D. (1980) *Die deutschsprachige Geographie von 1800 bis 1970. Ein Beitrag zur Geschichte ihrer Methodologie*. Geographisches Institut der Freien Universität, Berlin.

Schultz, H.-D. (1989) *Die Geographie als Bildungsfach im Kaiserreich*. Osnabrück, Osnabrücker Studien zur Geographie 10.

Schlüter, O. (1903) *Die Siedlungen im nordöstlichenThüringen*. H. Costenoble, Jena and Berlin.

Schöller, P. (1957) Wege und Irrwege der Politischen Geographie und Geopolitik. *Erdkunde* 11, 1–20.

Semple, E. (1903) *American History and its Geographic Conditions*. Houghton Mifflin, Boston.

Semple, E. (1931) *The Geography of the Mediterranean Region. Its Relation to Ancient History*. Henry Holt, New York.

Strohmayer, U. (1997) The displaced, the deferred or was it abandoned middle. Another look at the idiographic-nomothetic distinction in the German social sciences. *Review – A Journal of the Fernand Braudel Center for the Study of Economics, Historical Systems, and Civilizations* 20, 279–344.

Van Valkenburg, S. (1951) The German school of geography. *Geography in the Twentieth Century*. (ed. G. Taylor). Philosophical Library, New York, pp. 91–115.

Vidal de la Blache, P. (1922) *Principes de géographie humaine*. Armand Colin, Paris. Translated as (1926): *Principles of Human Geography*. Henry Holt, New York.

Wardenga, U. (1995) *Geographie als Chorologie. Zur Genese und Struktur von Alfred Hettners Konstrukt der Geographie*. Steiner, Stuttgart.

Wardenga, U. (2006) Geographical thought and the development of Länderkunde. *Inforgeo* 18/19, 127–147.

Willey, T. (1978) *Back to Kant. The Revival of Kantianism in German Social and Historical Thought, 1860–1914*. Wayne State University, Detroit.

Whittelsey, D. (1954) The regional concept and regional method. In P.E. James and C.F. Jones (eds), *American geography: Inventory and Prospect*. Syracuse University Press, Syracuse. NY, pp. 19–69.

Chapter 6

Creating Human Geography in the English-Speaking World[1]

Ron Johnston

> ... we English geographers require, above all things, a tradition. We vary so widely in our views, and our examiners examine so differently, that teachers are at a loss whether to keep the old methods or venture on the new. ... German geography, despite its modern growth, has a tradition, for Germans are all sons in geography of the ancestral group – Humboldt, Ritter, Berhaus and Perthes.
>
> (Mackinder 1895, 377–378)

Introduction

Human geography is a major – in some places dominant – component of the geographical discipline in the English-speaking world. Many geographers identify themselves with the adjective "human," but such is the breadth of work now undertaken that they also adopt a more specialized term to define themselves, especially among their peers. So we get urban geographers, medical geographers, population geographers and so forth. Yet a century ago when geography was establishing its place as a discipline within academic institutions the term "human geography" was rarely deployed. Practitioners were just, or simply, geographers. What has stimulated the emergence, first, of a separate sub-discipline of human geography and then of sub-sub-disciplines within it? This essay addresses this question with a reconstruction – necessarily personal: one cannot write "the history" only "a history" – of the sociology and politics of the emergence of human geography in a particular set of places.

The Wiley Blackwell Companion to Human Geography, First Edition.
Edited by John A. Agnew and James S. Duncan.
© 2011 John Wiley & Sons, Ltd. Published 2016 by John Wiley & Sons, Ltd.

The Foundations

Geography has been practiced as a subject since the Greeks invented the name – and probably before that. Its task was to depict and "make sense of nature" by recording information about the earth's diversity cartographically and in descriptive texts. Skills in navigation and map-making were key to the information-gathering component of that enterprise, underpinning the explorations and expeditions that provided raw material for texts, maps and atlases. Two main types of geography were recognized: *general geography* was concerned with the earth as a whole, including cartography's mathematical foundations (which included links to astronomy, fundamental to navigation and map-making); and *special geography* (later termed chorology or chorography) involved the description of particular segments of the globe (Cormack 1997; Livingstone 1992). Within this general framework, particular national conceptions emerged, especially as an academic discipline emerged from the late nineteenth century on (as illustrated in Johnston and Claval 1984; Dunbar 2001: see also the special issue of the *Journal of Geography in Education*, Volume 31, 2007). There are contrasts between these – some stronger than others – but each has followed its own trajectory, as illustrated here for the English-speaking world – within which there have also been inter-national (as well as intra-national) differences in geographical practices (Johnston and Sidaway 2004b).

Like most academic subjects, until the nineteenth century geography was very much a minority interest for small, educated elite and merchant classes. The growth of world trade stimulated wider interest, which in the United Kingdom was associated with the zenith of British imperialism. The Royal Geographical Society (RGS) was founded in 1830 with a mission to "promote the advancement of geographical science" (Freeman 1980), linking geography as a subject with geography as a practice. It stimulated and supported expeditions and their findings were transmitted to commercial interests as well as those involved in the statecraft and military aspects of imperial expansion and control.[2] It accumulated an extensive library and map collection, promoted the technical skills of surveying, mapmaking and navigation, and published its much-used and -revised *Hints to Travellers*:[3] its regular lectures provided upper and middle class audiences with "intellectual entertainment" about the explorers' and adventurers' exploits and the characteristics of the far-off places and peoples they visited, providing reassurance of the superiority of "British civilisation" (Driver 2001; Livingstone 2003).

Other geographical societies, many with a strong commercial orientation, were founded in major British cities as well as imperial centers in Australia and Canada, for example (Lochhead 1984; MacKenzie 1995; on other such societies, see Butlin, 2009). In the United States, the American Geographical Society (AGS) performed a similar function – without the strong imperial overtones. It became a repository for geographical knowledge, widely used by commercial interests and in statecraft. Isaiah Bowman, its Director in the early twentieth century, for example, played a key role in putting the Society's resources at the state's disposal during World War I and then as a member of Woodrow Wilson's delegation to the peace talks at Versailles (Smith 2003). As Wright (1952: 189) shows, Bowman's two decades as the Society's Director saw it establish a broad program of work "oriented to shed the light of scientific understanding on contemporary world and national issues" while never losing sight "of values that spring from man's thirst for knowledge irrespective of its immediate applications to questions of the day." The advancement of knowledge was the Society's main focus:

> To maintain a library and map collection and to publish works of geographical value have been the cornerstones of its policy from the outset. It has never accepted the doctrine that a sharp line should be drawn between geography and what is not geography or that its interests should be confined within an academic definition of the subject. ... On the other hand, it has limited the range of its chief activities to enterprises designed to advance geography along scientific, scholarly, professional and educational lines and, except in its lecture courses, has in general avoided attempts to popularize the field. ... With the funds, personnel, and facilities at its disposal, the Society has felt it preferable to concentrate on what it could do well, rather than to spread its effort too thinly. (Wright 1952: 386)

This was undertaken within its general appreciation of geography's nature. Wright preferred not to offer a definition noting that geography:

> ... assumes different shapes and natures, which have something in common. It appears as a Science, to be developed through accurate observation and logical reasoning; and also as an Educational Discipline. It takes the form of an Instrument of practical use to sailor and soldier, merchant, philanthropist, or statesman, and from this it emerges as a Guide pointing the way towards action. (Wright 1952: 381–382)

From the 1960s, this mission became increasingly divorced from that of the academic discipline, however, as reflected by the declining status of its academic journal – *The Geographical Review*. Associated financial difficulties, together with the changing nature of academic geography at the time (Schulten 2001), saw the Society decline in importance and activity, with its library and map collection being moved from New York to Milwaukee in 1978.[4] This was not the fate of the AGS alone. The RGS became increasingly estranged from academic geography – especially human geography – in the period between the two World Wars, leading to the formation of the Institute of British Geographers (IBG) in 1933 (Steel 1983). For much of the twentieth century, therefore, the various sectors of British geography were represented by separate institutions: academic research by the IBG; education, especially school education, by the Geographical Association (GA), founded in 1893; and exploration, mapping and empire by the RGS. In 1995, however, the RGS and the IBG merged to form a single professional and "quasi-popular" society, working alongside and with the GA which continues to promote geographical education.

In the United States, there was even greater division: the academic sector was represented by the Association of American Geographers from 1904, but this had strict, research-based entry criteria and there was a parallel body for other practitioners – the Association of Professional Geographers – with which it merged in 1949 (James and Martin 1978). The AGS continued to represent the traditional view of the subject, which was also popularized by the National Geographic Society;[5] and a National Council for Geographical Education was founded in 1915 to promote geographical teaching. In both countries, therefore, a small discipline was disadvantaged by the existence of these separate bodies. The International Geographical Union (founded in 1922) provided the foundation for a growing global community, but its quadrennial International Geographical Congresses (first held in 1871) provided only rare opportunities for international discussions (see Pinchemel 1972).[6]

Interest in geography expanded through the nineteenth century, influencing its further development in two main ways. The first was educational. In the UK, the RGS argued that geography should be included in school curricula so as to develop "world citizens" aware of not only the earth's diversity but also their position within it. Its campaigns focused on the grammar and public (i.e. private) schools (Unstead 1949; Wise 1986),[7] but limited success suggested that the subject would not flourish there unless it had the standing of an academic discipline, which could only be gained if geographical study was established at the country's premier universities – Cambridge and Oxford. Offers of financial support to employ staff there eventually triumphed (Stoddart 1986), and geography teaching was introduced (though full degree schemes were not established for some decades, subsequent to their introduction at other universities: Slater 1988). Much early effort was spent training school teachers and the GA's continued promotional efforts ensured that geography was a core discipline throughout the country's school system, including inclusion in the national curriculum established in the late twentieth century (Balchin 1993; Walford 2001). School and university geography enjoyed a symbiosis; the schools produced students who wanted to study the subject further at university, and the universities educated them, and for several decades the majority of their graduates became school teachers (on which see Mackinder, 1921; on the institutionalization of academic geography in the UK, see Johnston, 2003a.)

The American situation was different. The need for rudimentary knowledge of geography was appreciated in most states, and basic education of a factual nature – what is where – was provided at the early educational stages. But high school provision was reduced in the early twentieth century as a broad-based social studies curriculum was preferred to one focused on separate disciplines (Schulten 2001). Some geography was taught but there was little demand for specialist teachers, hence no need for training courses in the normal schools and universities. There was some call for geography instruction at individual universities to complement that in other disciplines (commerce and geology, for example); as was also the case in the UK. In some US universities this led to the creation of small geography departments, some of which later developed graduate schools. (On the history of geography in the United States, see Martin, 2005.[8])

Geography was thus slowly institutionalized as a small academic discipline in both countries.[9] As a University subject, geography was concerned not only with the transmission of knowledge (the educational element) but also its creation (through research and scholarship).[10] Most academic disciplines have emerged during the last 150 years or so because they have a distinct research mission, with the teaching element following. Geography is one of the few that followed a different route – a research tradition had to be "invented." Its subject matter was clear, describing the diversity of the earth's landscapes; its new research goal was to account for that diversity. The raw materials were at hand, from exploration and later fieldwork; from ethnographic inquiry; and from narrative descriptions of places. These had to be welded together into a set of academic practices that characterized a separate and viable discipline.

A Parallel Stream

The institutionalization of academic geography and creation of its distinctive research practices occurred alongside a parallel stream in popular geography, building on the RGS, AGS and similar societies' work propagating geographical knowledge. In the late nineteenth century the National Geographic Society, founded to support and promote scientific research, introduced a new mode of popularizing geography through its magazine, *National Geographic*. Initially not very successful its mission was restructured, involving a break with the academic community and a new focus on high quality journalism about the earth's diversity – especially places few readers could expect to visit. The magazine was at the forefront of developments in using photography, especially color, and its editor for 55 years, Gilbert Grosvenor, drew on lines from Tennyson's *Ulysses* (Grosvenor 1957: 1) to define its mission:

> The key phrase, which suggests a theme for this history of the National Geographic Society, is simply "roaming with a hungry heart." The world teems with people who long to visit faraway places, to travel adventurously, to see strange customs and races, to explore mysteries of the sea and air. Not many persons can do these things in the physical sense, but they can venture far and wide through the pages of the NATIONAL GEOGRAPHIC MAGAZINE.

The Society also supported explorations and expeditions, such as becoming involved in the conflict over who was first to reach the North Pole; it continues to provide grants for a wide range of exploratory scientific research, little of it by academic geographers.

National Geographic is a major commercial success. Its high-quality cartography, photography and journalism has informed millions monthly about many aspects of the changing world. Grosvenor (1957: 4–5) included among the magazine's underpinning principles that it should employ an "abundance of beautiful, instructive and artistic illustrations," should avoid all personalities and trivia, include nothing of a partisan or controversial character and "Only what is of a kindly nature is printed about any country or people, everything unpleasant or unduly critical being avoided;" some areas were largely ignored – such as the Soviet Union for much of its existence. *National Geographic* is now published in 27 different language editions, and the Society runs its own TV Channel ("Discovery").

A British counterpart – *The Geographical Magazine* – was launched by Sir Clements Markham (explorer, geographer to the Indian Office, RGS Secretary, 1863–1888 and President for the next 12 years) in 1874, but lasted for only five years, to be replaced by the *Proceedings of the Royal Geographical Society* (which ceased publication in 1892).[11] A new *Geographical Magazine* (now *Geographical*) was launched in 1935, with a similar orientation and format, although it carried material by academic geographers – a much weaker practice now, despite the RGS owning the title. *African Geographic, Australian Geographic, Canadian Geographic*, and *New Zealand Geographic* have joined it in recent decades. all of them operating not only independent of but with very little reference to academic geography. In recent years they – alongside, but without any links to, *National Geographic* – have highlighted issues relating to environmental (especially wildlife) conservation, identifying with a major theme within academic geography without associating themselves with the discipline. There is a parallel family of *Géo* magazines, initiated in Germany in 1976 and now appearing in 20 other countries (including an Indian edition, launched in 2008); they, according to their editorial credo, focus on "a liking for the unusual; an openness for the future; a curiosity in what's worth knowing; and an awareness for the endangered." (On these magazines, see Johnston 2009a, 2009b.)

These popular magazines and related media sustain a focus on geography as it was understood in the nineteenth century – a subject which illustrated the earth's diversity to a wide audience by pictures, words and maps (until TV and video came along); intriguingly, they rarely use the terms "physical geography" and "human geography," even today. Alongside it was the emerging academic discipline, also dedicated to studying that diversity.

The Region is the Thing

A division into physical and human geography is fundamental to the contemporary discipline, but it emerged only slowly. Geography was presented by many of its protagonists from the outset as a holistic, synthetic discipline: the earth and its inhabitants are inter-dependent and should be studied as such. In a small enterprise, the views of a few leaders were very significant in establishing research and teaching directions. Thus, for example, American geographers such as William Morris Davis (trained as a geologist and a very influential early US geographer, he used physiography and ontography to refer to physical and human geography respectively, with the latter subservient to the former: Chorley *et al.* 1973), Ellsworth Huntington and Ellen Churchill Semple all followed the lead of German Karl Ratzel's *anthropogeographie* which explored the links between humans and nature. His disciples developed this into a determinist stance in which human uses of the earth's surface were largely determined by environmental conditions. Others gave greater prominence to human free will in determining how they responded to, and made their impress upon, the environment. Carl Sauer, for example, promoted geography as a field-based discipline, based on ideas from cultural anthropology; he identified the cultural characteristics of societies through their changing impress on the landscape (Speth 1999; on determinism and possibilism, see Tatham 1957).

These separate developments became strands of the new discipline but another achieved dominance in the 1920–1930s, in large part reflecting a rejection of determinism's extremes – which probably meant that the anthropogeographic tradition, identified with determinism by many of its critics, was less influential than might have been the case. Geography's focus, it was argued, should be on the areal differentiation that characterizes the earth by identifying, portraying, and offering accounts for the characteristics of regions, areas of relative homogeneity in their nature, both physical and human-made. This orientation had French and German roots. In France, Paul Vidal de la Blache pioneered geographical descriptions of *pays*, regions characterized by both their landscape characteristics and their ways of life (*genres de vie*); many of his students and followers established their geographical credentials by producing regional monographs describing such unique areas (Clout 2009).

The views of a German geographer, Alfred Hettner, underpinned American Richard Hartshorne's *The nature of geography* which provided a widely-adopted statement of the discipline's rationale at the time – "concerned to provide accurate, orderly and rational descriptions of the variable character of the earth's surface" (Hartshorne 1939: 21) by interpreting the "realities of areal differentiation of the world as they are found, not only in terms of differences in certain things from place to place, but also in terms of the total combination of phenomena in each place, different from those at every other place" (Hartshorne 1939: 462; see, however, Harvey and Wardenga 2006, on Hartshorne's partial representation of Hettner's work). The first of these tasks involved studies in *systematic geography*, presenting areal differentiation of a particular characteristic (agricultural practices, perhaps); the other was *regional geography*, establishing relationships between the subject matter of separate systematic studies and identifying the combination of features that gave each region its unique characteristics. Regional geography was widely accepted as the discipline's defining feature in the 1930–1950s, synthesizing the scientific findings in systematic geography and related studies into depictions of the uniqueness of individual places. It dominated American geography for several decades – with its major cores at Chicago and Clark Universities; its methodology was addressed at geographic field conferences held in parts of the Midwest between 1915 and 1940 – with Hartshorne a regular attendee (James and Mather 1977; Rugg 1981; Koelsch 2001). By mid-century it was under considerable attack, however, notably in Kimble's denunciation of what he perceived as an obsolete concept:

> From the air it is the *links* in the landscapes, the rivers, roads, railways, canals, pipelines, electric cables, rather than the *breaks* that impress the aviator … regional geographers may be trying to put boundaries that do not exist around areas that do not matter. (Kimble 1951: 159)

This view was widely adopted from the mid-1950s on, as illustrated below.

In the UK, although as in the USA a number of separate threads characterized geography's development, reflecting the backgrounds (necessarily outwith geography) and interests of its initial leaders, the region also became the central focus of the discipline's claimed niche within the sciences (the social sciences, apart from anthropology and economics, were very much a post-1945 development there). Thus, the founding professor at Aberystwyth, H.J. Fleure, whose background was in zoology and anthropology, inaugurated a particular style of "cultural geography" that was continued by his successors there. George Chisholm at Edinburgh, Halford Mackinder at Oxford, Clifford Darby at Cambridge, and Dudley Stamp at the London School of Economics, promoted other specialisms (commercial geography, political geography, historical geography, and land use patterns respectively). Each – as with their contemporaries elsewhere – based his work firmly in the physical landscape and an appreciation of land-forming processes and other aspects of physical geography. Mackinder (1895: 368), head of the first British geography school, at Oxford, identified the three stages of geographical work as "observation, cartography, and scholarship," although he also wrote of the "three correlated arts (all concerned chiefly with maps) which may be said to characterize geography; observation, cartography, and teaching" (Mackinder 1895: 374; the importance of the first two of these is illustrated in the archaeological career of one of the school's early graduates and temporary staff-members: Crawford 1955; Hauser 2008).

Many British geographers, like their American counterparts, emphasized the importance of regions and regional geography as the discipline's leitmotif. According to Wooldridge and East's (1951) influential British book on *The spirit and purpose of geography*, "General Geography, involves a number of distinct and systematic studies. These find their application in the description and interpretation of actual areas or regions, large and small" (p. 38).[12] Nevertheless, although they argued that: "The serious study of the subject cannot begin without the findings of physical geography" (p. 29), separate aspects of human geography got substantial attention. (Their chapter on physical geography occupies 25 pages; those on historical, economic, and political occupy 23, 18, and 19 respectively. There was neither a separate social geography – although they later used the term as a portmanteau incorporating "economic, political, demographic etc." (p. 141) – nor cultural geography.[13]) Human geography, unlike physical geography, does not generate "formal categories and universal principles and processes" (p. 30) but this does not imply "inferiority; it is rather to admit that it is infinitely more complex, subtler, more flexible and manifold." Because of that, however, there can be "no generalized human geography. The nature of man and of human evolution ensures that each region which we study is in large measure unique" (p. 32) – hence their adherence to the same argument as Hartshorne's that regional geography is the discipline's core, although by discussing "urban regions" at the end of their chapter on regional geography they divorced some types of regional definition from the firm environmental foundation that many others deployed (p. 160).[14] The study of regions within British geography was also influenced by the work of the polymath Patrick Geddes (Meller 1993) and the activities of the le Play Society, in which geographers interacted with sociologists in, for example, 71 major field surveys (mainly overseas) between 1931 and 1960 (Beaver 1962; Herbertson 1950). and which was the model for the later Geographical Field Group based at the University of Nottingham.[15]

The importance of environmental influences – if not determinants – permeated much geographical writing during the first half of the twentieth century, perhaps retarding movement towards a separate sub-discipline of human geography. Chisholm's famous *Handbook of commercial geography* exemplified this. The preface to its first edition (Chisholm 1889) makes clear that its discussion of the "facts of commercial geography" – i.e. gazetteer-like material on what is produced where and traded with where – are set within an explanatory framework comprising material on the physical features of the earth's surface: the first chapter is on climate. American authors took a similar approach: Huntington, Williams and van Valkenburg introduced (1933: v) their *Economic and social geography* with the statement that:

> A continuous thread of geographic reasoning runs through the whole of this book. It begins with a section on the major factors of geographic environment and the principles

which govern their relation to plants, animals and men. Climate naturally comes first because it is the most widespread, pervasive and variable of the factors. ... Climate, relief, and soil are the main determinants of the geographic regions into which the earth's surface is naturally divided.

They identified two basic sets of facts: "the purely physical ... and ... the facts of economics." The former predominated, although "Other factors of a political, racial and social nature also play a part and introduce all sorts of complications" (p. 1) – an argument illustrated with the example of rubber production. They included much material relating to the "all sorts of complications" that influence what is produced where – such as maps of the costs of producing corn and the prices received for it in the USA – but these are seen as deviations from a "geographic norm." After describing some of the social, cultural and political factors influencing the geography of wheat production, they concluded that (Huntington *et al.* 1933: 229):

> ... the geographer does not lose faith, but keeps on dreaming of a future in which the economic development of the world will conform to geographical factors, unhampered by political interference.

At the global scale, regional definition was based almost entirely on physical features – notably climatic zones, as in Herbertson's (1905) classic early work. At more local scales, such as the exercises associated with the Midwest geographic field conferences (Platt 1959), field investigations identified patterns of human occupancy, linked to features of the physical landscape, which created areas with separate characteristics, such as settlement patterns and agricultural land use. Much of this work had a strong implicit deterministic thrust, notably in the many regional textbooks which portrayed the physical environment first before mapping human patterns on to it.

Creating Human Geography

As the quotations from Wooldridge and East indicate, the holistic approach to areal differentiation and a regional focus on the human impress on the landscape suggested the need for a "human geography" as a major element in the systematic parts of the discipline which serviced and nurtured the regional definitions and descriptions. But it was slow to emerge – certainly slower than its counterpart physical geography which, especially in the UK and in line with the underlying determinist basis of empirical inquiries, developed earlier and more rapidly as a sub-discipline with specialisms focused on, for example, landforms and their genesis (geomorphology), climate, biogeography, and soils. In the USA, there was a strong feeling, advanced by Hartshorne (1939), that geographers need not study physical processes, only their outcomes; they needed a "geography of landforms" rather than geomorphology (Peltier 1954). One stimulus for Hartshorne writing *Nature* was an argument against regional geography from the "Berkeley School of cultural geography" associated with Carl Sauer, one of whose members claimed that "The elements of the landscape that have a cultural origin ... can not be understood rationally, but only historically" (Leighley 1937: 141).

According to Gilbert (1972: 198), the term "human geography" was first used in the UK by Mackinder,[16] but it was Herbertson, Mackinder's colleague and then successor at Oxford, who first gave it a full usage – in the subtitle of a school textbook written with his wife (Herbertson and Herbertson 1899) which was introduced as "so far as we know, ... the first attempt to present in popular form the principles of human geography." No such principles were explicitly adduced; they are, however, readily inferred from the introductory chapter's closing paragraph which shows (p. 6–1931 edition):

> ... how the occupation of very different groups of mankind depends on their geographical surroundings, and how these occupations in their turn affect not only the material life, the houses, food, clothing etc., but also family life, notions of property, progress in trade and manufactures, power of expansion, and ideals of government. All these are classified, not according to race, which is often an accident, but according to those permanent influences by which all races are affected.

Such an environmental determinist approach permeates the book. (Mackinder was only slightly less implicitly determinist. In his 1895 paper he suggested that although at times "human genius seems to set geographical limitations at defiance" over long time periods "the significance even of the most vigorous initiative is seen to diminish," p. 379. On the strong Darwinian and racist-imperialist influences on Mackinder's conception of human geography, see Kearns 2009 and Taylor 1957.)

In part the absence of any reference to "human geography" was semantic only. In his classic paper "On the scope and methods of geography," presented to the RGS before he had been offered appointment as the first geographer at the University of Oxford, Mackinder (1887: 142) used the term "political geography" for that part of the discipline whose function was to "trace the interaction between man and his environment" – asking whether it should be any more than an "appendix" to history just as physical geography might be seen as merely an appendix to "geology" unless a separate discipline of geography could be fashioned.[17] Geography was defined as "the science whose main function is to trace the interaction of man in society and so much of his environment as varies locally," "no *rational* political geography can exist which is not built upon and subsequent to physical geography" (his emphasis); and "At the present moment we are suffering under the main effects of an irrational political geography, one, that is, whose main function is not to trace causal relations, and which must therefore remain a body of isolated data to be committed to memory" (p. 143).[18]

Several attempts were made to define human geography at this time. British geographers, for example, were concerned to establish their scientific credentials within the British Association for the Advancement of Science (BA) – a leading scientific society whose annual meeting was widely attended and (as now) publicized in the media. (For geographers, it and the GA provided the only national forums for meeting to discuss academic issues. The RGS was not seen as a welcoming institution by human geographers, and the IBG was only founded as an academic learned society in 1933 (Steel 1983). Geographers feared that their position within the BA, and their status within academia and society more generally, would be undermined unless their scientific status was established and recognized (Withers

2010). But did geographers do more than observe, map and teach, as Mackinder (1895) had suggested? Newbigin in her Presidential Address to the BA's Section E (Geography) claimed that:

> ... the main interest of geography is not in its facts as such – for if geography ceased to exist the geologists, meteorologists, botanists, zoologists and so forth would continue to collect most of these. Rather does it lie in the way in which the geographer studies these facts in their relations to each other and to the life of man. (Newbigin 1922: 210)

Human geography focused on responses to environmental conditions:

> ... it is necessary to distinguish between human geography and animal geography. ... when we turn to look at man, two facts are at once apparent. In the first place, at the present time, he does not appear to respond to environmental influences by adaptive modifications of bodily form. Secondly, there was certainly a time, before he had come fully to his heritage, when he did so respond. ... In other words, there was a time when there was no human geography, when men reacted to the sum-total of the conditions as an animal does; but that time appears to have largely passed. (Newbigin 1922: 211–212)

Humans have responded collectively to environmental conditions, developing civilizations with a "vast power of modifying" their environments; those modifications are human geography's subject matter (Sack 2001).

This strong emphasis on the human-nature inter-relationship established by Mackinder permeated early British human geography textbooks. Lebon (1951) identified three basic concepts of "modern" geography: correlation of physical features with human occupancy; areal diversity and regions; and terrestrial unity. Within this overall conception, human geography could either follow Ratzel's *anthropogeographie*, linking physical with human regions, or that of the "French school" which contended, according to Brunhes and following the Vidalian tradition that was the foundation of French academic geography (Buttimer 1971)[19], that "much of the stuff of geography – the city, the village, the people, the country – is the product of group effort" (Lebon 1951: 38). For the latter, whom British geographers – along with contemporaries in eastern Europe and Japan – tended to follow rather than the German model, "human geography is barren unless social and political institutions, as well as the technical attainments, of groups, tribes and nations, are comprehended" (Lebon 1951: 41). The physical environment provides a major constraint, but alongside ecological concepts human geographers also need recourse to those from sociology and economics. According to Brunhes:

> The forces of physical nature are bound to each other in their consequences, in their relations, and in the consequences of these relations. Man does not escape the common law; his activity is included in the network of terrestrial phenomena. But if human activity is thus circumscribed, it does not follow that it is fatally determined. ... That is why we must add to the group of material forces, whose incessant interplay we have seen, this new force – human activity – which is not only a material thing but which also expresses itself through material effects. That is why, as geographers, we are led

to study man's part in nature – without ever separating it from the study of physical geography. (Brunhes 1920: 27)

The emergence of a separate human geography along these lines – although, as with Lebon, paying greater attention to sociological than economic concepts – is exemplified by a textbook from the following decade. Emrys Jones was educated at Aberystwyth, where geography (building on Fleure's legacy) was closely allied with anthropology, and developed a geographical philosophy clearly reflecting that background (Johnston 2008). For him the physical environment provides a "geographical circumstance" within which human activities are shaped and expressed in the landscape. The key element in that shaping, and continual reshaping, is culture – specifically group culture as defined by family, religion, language, ethnicity and class. Jones was later one of the pioneers of a new sub-discipline of social geography (Jones and Eyles 1977). For him, cultural-historical circumstances dominate the "geographical" (or physical), so his introductory text – *Human geography* (Jones 1965) – began not with the physical environment but with the distribution of population because "We are faced not only with an immensely diversified society, but with an environment much of which has long since ceased to be "natural," which bears the heavy imprint of man" (Hooson 1960: 17).

The increasing importance given to the human imprint on the landscape, increasingly in towns rather than in rural areas, stimulated an expanding portfolio of material considered within the general ambit of human geography, as illustrated by some of the chapter titles in a book designed as a "progress report on the present content of geography as at January, 1954" (James and Jones 1954, p. viii) in the USA.

Historical geography	The geographic study of population
Settlement geography	Urban geography
Political geography	The geography of resources
The fields of economic geography	Marketing geography
	Recreational geography
Agricultural geography	The geography of mineral production
The geography of manufacturing	Transportation geography

(Note the absence of social geography, heralded in a parallel book: Watson 1951.)

But this systematic material was subsidiary to the discipline's main purpose (Johnston 2005):

> The various kinds of duality which have been popular in the past, such as regional as opposed to topical [or systematic] geography, or physical as opposed to human geography, seem to have obscured the true nature of the discipline. The separation [between physical and human] … is intolerable for geographers, for they must deal with man as well as that which is not man (now commonly defined as nature), and the two are intimately intermixed wherever man has been on the earth. Geography, which has to do with places on the earth, simply cannot be made to fit into so arbitrary a classification of knowledge. Actually, there is just one kind of geography. (James 1954: 15)

That is regional geography (p. 7):

> Persons who undertake to carry on geographic studies must specialize in order to develop competence in a portion of the field. Nevertheless, whether they specialize on the physical, biotic or cultural aspects of geography, the analysis of the meaning of likenesses and differences among places involves the use of certain common concepts and methods: basic to the whole field is the regional concept; fundamental to the effective study of geographic phenomena is the method of precise cartographic analysis.[20]

Geographers with developed specialisms within human geography were few at the time and the scope of their work not wide. Most of their studies were heavily descriptive and drew little inspiration from the theories and methods of the other social sciences. (A major exception was the innovative work in urban and transport geography by Harris and Ullman 1945: see also Ullman 1941, 1956.) Hartshorne had proclaimed that geography, like history, was an exceptional discipline, relying on others for much of its source material.

Whereas the James and Jones volume sustained the argument that regional study is at the core of geography, a volume published at the same time (*Geography in the twentieth century*) significantly downplayed this – while not making any strong case for an alternative. Although in the introductory chapter Griffith Taylor sustained his widely-promoted case that the environment provides clear limits to human activity (what he termed "nature's plan," Taylor 1957), nevertheless after a group of chapters on the history and philosophy of geography his volume also included a chapter by his Toronto colleague on "environmentalism and possibilism" (Tatham 1957) and two further sections – one on "The environment as a factor" and the other on "Special fields of geography" – without linking the two. The latter section included chapters on racial geography, the sociological aspects of geography, urban geography, and two on aspects of political geography ("Geography and empire" and "Geopolitics and geopacifics"). Geography is presented as "the discussion of the *causes of patterns of distribution*" (Taylor 1951: v; his emphasis) – at least implicitly accepting that human geography can be studied largely apart from either physical or regional although all of Taylor's own work focused on environmental influences (Taylor 1958; Sanderson 1988; Strange and Bashford 2008).

The Human Geography Boom

Major change followed soon after the end of the Second World War. Alongside the expanding specialisms within physical geography new sub-disciplines within human geography were recognized as separate research activities with their particular agenda and courses within degree curricula – reflecting the growing number of scholars establishing niches within institutions where research activity and publication became both a dominant focus and the major criterion on which a career trajectory was based. The argument underpinning this shift in emphasis within human geography was the realization that although the "vertical" inter-relationships between people and their environments were key to human well-being and life chances, the "horizontal" links between "places" were much more important. ("Place" increasingly replaced "region" as a core geographical concept, alongside space, environment and scale.) As Cox (1976: 192) expressed it, whereas the main links in less-developed societies are between relatively isolated groups and their physical environments, creating a "spatially differentiated nature," as societies develop so their interactions over space change the focus to "spatially differentiated societies." Through the 1960s and 1970s, therefore, human geography was increasingly presented as a social science discipline focusing on spatial patterns of the human impress upon, and behavior within, the environment – the non-physical geographical circumstances stressed by Emrys Jones. Human geography's focus became "order in space," the identifying characteristic of a "discipline in distance" (Johnston 2003b). This involved geographers exploring the other social sciences for sources of inspiration regarding what and how to study these areas. An early pioneer was Dickinson, whose 1947 book *City region and regionalism* was based on wide reading of American and German material and stimulated him to promote geographers' participation in post-war urban and regional planning (Johnston 2002), but it was texts like Haggett's (1965; see also Abler, Adams and Gould 1971; Morrill 1970) which introduced that literature to wide audiences within the discipline.

This search for new stimuli had foundations in geographers' wartime experiences, notably in the USA where they worked alongside scholars from other disciplines in the intelligence services (Barnes 2006; Barnes and Farish 2006). Some became acutely aware of geography's scientific shortcomings, realizing that if it was to play a prominent role in an increasingly evidence-based, planned and regulated society, the discipline needed to change. They led the way through their writings and ability to attract disciples who adopted and promoted new ways of working – stimulated by other disciplinary literatures, notably economics in the early years. They rejected regional geography's descriptive accounts (forcibly in some cases: Gould 1979), offering as a replacement a scientifically-based discipline that explained spatial patterns, and for which the physical landscape was a relatively unimportant foundation only. Some essayed scientific approaches to human-environment interactions (Curry 1962; Gould 1963) but they were few and their example not followed at the time. Physical and human geographers found some common ground in technical issues regarding data analysis, but the two sub-disciplines rapidly moved apart during this period.

This search for the new occurred when there was an expanded demand for geographers. Universities grew very rapidly, with geography participating. There was a small geography department in virtually every UK University by 1950, for example, and most subsequently expanded dramatically in student and staff numbers. More universities were established; not all offered geography degrees but many did and the subject flourished with a rapid increase in its, increasingly research-active, practitioners. The student population grew even more in the USA. Unlike the situation in the UK and the English-speaking dominions (Australia, Canada, New Zealand, South Africa) plus some colonies (notably in east and west Africa, plus Singapore and Hong Kong), in all of which geography was firmly established in the schools and universities, geography wasn't central to American high school curricula, so few students there went to university intending to study geography. Departments had to attract them to undergraduate courses by their quality and perceived interest and relevance. Their products fed the graduate schools, which also attracted non-geographers by their course and research offerings (and for a time in the 1950–

1970s students with undergraduate degrees from the UK and other English-speaking countries, where establishment of graduate programs occurred later than in North America); geography boomed in both (as described by Murphy 2007; Sidaway and Johnston 2007).

This was also a time when the social sciences came of age (Backhouse and Fontaine 2010). Apart from economics the others, like geography, had been relatively small and (especially in the UK) of little perceived relevance to national goals. The growth of welfare states, the macro-management of the economy, the planning of urban and the regulation of rural environments; these and other aspects of the new societies created demand for social science graduates and research. As geographers adopted and adapted other disciplines' practices they were eventually accepted as social scientists (if somewhat grudgingly, and also reluctantly in the case of some geographers: Johnston 2004) and their potential was realized in a widening range of applied agenda.

Increased size was crucial – without it links to the other social sciences may not have been developed and the discipline's relevance not realized. A few individuals could dominate a small discipline and prescribe its directions. In 1949, for example, Clifford Darby was appointed professor and head of the department of geography at University College London. Within four years all of the staff there when he was appointed had left, and he erected a new structure based on his conception of the discipline, centered on historical geography (Clout 2003). A few individuals did explore new ideas and ways of working but many were frustrated – much of their time being spent teaching a wide range of courses. As the discipline expanded, opportunities widened, specialism became more feasible, and increased resources (time, libraries, travel, equipment etc.) became available. The power of senior figures to direct the discipline's trajectory – often benignly exercised but constraining nevertheless – weakened and human geographers now explore a myriad of characteristics of the human condition and its areal differentiation.

Dividing and Sub-Dividing

Human geography was a relatively small part of the disciplinary enterprise in the first decade after World War II, therefore specialist divisions were either practiced by no more than a few – such as urban and economic geography – or were still to be invented, even though the term may have been occasionally used – such as social and rural geography. (The first text in the former was Jones and Eyles 1977, and in the latter Clout 1972.)

The first evidence of a major shift emanated in the mid- and late-1950s from a number of centers, of which the most important initially was the University of Washington, Seattle. A group of graduate students, attracted to work with one mentor, Edward Ullman (Eyre 1977; Boyce 1980), but soon to cluster around another – William Garrison – was stimulated by work in economics on location theory and the testing of hypotheses regarding spatial patterns and spatial behavior using mathematical and statistical modeling. They vigorously promoted their alternative view of the discipline as a spatial science and soon attracted adherents elsewhere, in some cases where one or two individuals were developing similar ideas. A few British geographers – initially though not solely focused on the University of

Cambridge – were similarly exploring those literatures and developing an approach based on theories, models and statistical hypothesis-testing, in which there was for a short while a unity of purpose among human and physical geographers (Johnston and Sidaway 2004a; Chapters 3–4; Johnston *et al.* 2008).

These developments – given a variety of names such as the "quantitative and theoretical revolutions," locational analysis, spatial analysis, spatial science – had an uneven impact across human geography: students of economic geography, especially of urban areas, were more likely to adopt the new approach than those in, say, historical or cultural geography. But the "new geography" was in tune with the spirit of the times, seeking theoretical and empirical justification for general statements about human behavior to underpin programs of (spatial) planning and regulation. Geography could be both scientific and useful. Cultural and historical geographers stood largely aloof from this (though they were much involved in the later "revolutions"); political, social, population, medical and rural geography were as yet under-developed; and the main loser was regional geography, despite some stout defenses. Teaching regional courses and writing regional texts rapidly declined. Human geography was changing, and fast.

It soon changed even more. The spatial science paradigm remained well-established within the discipline, expanding its range of interests and increasing the sophistication of its methodologies, while shedding some of the more deterministic early elements which emphasized the search for "laws." It received a significant boost from the late 1980s on with the development of geographic information systems (GIS) – combined computing hardware and software which enables the collection, collation, storage, display and analysis of spatially-referenced data (Longley *et al.* 2005). Not only did this technological advance facilitate more sophisticated analyses of geographical data than before, it also had a wide range of public and private sector applications. A quasi-separate discipline of geographic information science emerged with geographers occupying key central roles alongside statisticians, computer scientists, engineers and a wide range of science and social science scholars interested in spatial analyses and their application. Geographers had found a new niche within society.

That niche did not suit everybody. Spatial analysis was being critiqued from two directions, both of which stimulated alternative approaches. The first – which eventually morphed into a "cultural turn" – criticized what it saw as an overly- economic-deterministic approach in which human culture and free will had little place. The other, a "radical turn," saw spatial science as deeply implicated in the capitalist system and all of its associated inequalities, without any ability to appreciate the underlying forces which make such inequalities a necessary component of capitalism; its "applied" contributions were thus largely oriented towards reproducing that society (Harvey 1973, 1974). Both critiques were strongly influenced by events and arguments in wider society as well as in their own and other disciplines. The promise of a planned, regulated society increasing prosperity for all was for many failing to deliver; Marxist arguments were attractive to some seeking an alternative while others focused on the lived experiences of individuals and communities – subjects that were not susceptible to study within the spatial analysis paradigm's emphasis on data and objectivity. (For overviews of these changes see Johnston and Sidaway 2004a; Johnston 2010.)

Other new ways of thinking also entered human geography at this time. Among the most influential was feminism, which not only identified inequalities within the discipline, that were (slowly at first) tackled (Rose 1993), but also the importance of positionality and identity within society: too much human geography – and other social science – treated society as a homogeneous unit (Women and Geography Study Group 1997). An alternative approach emphasized difference – community as well as individual – and its importance in appreciating the areal differentiation that remained at the core of much geography. In this, place was important – as context, but a socially-engineered construct, not something externally given. In much geography it had previously been treated as a backdrop only, but now it became part of the argument; places are the locales in which people interact, reproducing and re-creating their cultures. A dualism between structure and agency was identified: places provide the contexts within which people learn and behave, and as they do so, they change the places in which further learning occurs. Thus the human condition, as made, re-made and experienced in a great variety of places and at a wide range of spatial scales, became a central geographical concern – and in its exploration geographers established links with a wider range of other disciplines and sub-disciplines, as illustrated elsewhere in this volume.

These new approaches didn't replace the old. After the general demise of regional geography nothing has since disappeared, although relative and sometimes absolute importance of approach within the discipline may have changed (Jackson *et al.* 2006; Philo 2009). Human geography became a wider, more diverse, in one sense more divided, discipline. The introduction of new ways of looking at and studying the world went alongside new things to study, as the world itself changed – geography itself was involved in a structure-agency dualism. It became increasingly clear, for example, that capitalism was not dominated by profit-maximizing firms making optimal decisions on the basis of perfect information, so economic geographers developed new ways of analyzing the increasingly complex landscapes of contemporary capitalism (Thrift 2005). Furthermore, since the 1970s environmental issues came into increasing public and political prominence and human geographers (in some cases working with their physical colleagues) have focused attention on these in a variety of ways and at scales from the local to the global. Issues of social justice and responsibility are central to much of this work, as illustrated by the development of a critical human geography (Blunt and Wills 2000). This increasingly wide spread of interests was reflected in the creation from the 1960s on of sub-disciplinary groups operating within the major learned societies – arranging sessions at the annual meetings as well as their own specialist conferences and publications (including journals in some cases); in 2009, for example, the RGS (IBG) had 27 separate Research Groups and the AAG had 62 Speciality Groups – all promoting diversity within a, perhaps fragile, unity.

Summary

A discipline concerned to appreciate the earth's diversity requires a pragmatic approach, responding to changes in its subject matter both substantively and methodologically. Human geography has done this in recent decades in part because of its size – which reflects its success as an academic enterprise. Student demand sustains a substantial disciplinary presence in many universities, and the scholars appointed to teach them have developed a wide range of research and teaching expertise, based on a plethora of multi- and inter-disciplinary interactions.

A variety of publishing ventures chart the emergence and expansion of this disciplinary phenomenon. In 1979, the first edition of *Geography and geographers: Anglo-American human geography since 1945* comprised a book of 223 pages (with a bibliography of some 650 items) outlining the discipline's contemporary history, focusing on how it was practiced rather than on what it studied (Johnston 1979). Twenty-five years later, a sixth edition (Johnston and Sidaway 2004a) contained 527 pages and its bibliography had over 2500 entries. A parallel set of volumes of a similar vintage tells the same story: the 1981 first edition of the *Dictionary of human geography* (Johnston et al. 1981) contained 411 pages, with some 620 separate entries by 18 different authors: the 2009 fifth edition drew on 111 authors who produced c.1100 separate items for a volume of 1052 pages (Gregory et al. 2009). In the United States, a pair of overview volumes drawing on the various specialist groups within the Association of American Geographers demonstrates the discipline's expansion and change over only 15 years (Gaile and Willmott 1989, 2004). And in July 2009, a 12-volume, 7662-page *International Encyclopedia of human geography* (Kitchin and Thrift 2009) was launched, with over 1000 separate essays.

In little over a century, therefore, a very substantial discipline has been established based on people's interest in the great diversity of the earth and their desire to understand, exploit and change it. We cannot accept reality as it is, and so we change it to fit our ideas of how reality should be. We take landscapes and places, and from them create new ones (Sack 2001); we are forever changing geography – and so making more geographical material. Academic geographers have responded by changing their discipline. And yet what they do and how they do it has relatively little impact outwith the universities and schools where it is taught. Academic geography is not the same as popular geography, as promoted through magazines such as *National Geographic*. Although they often stray well beyond what might generally be considered geography in the coverage of their articles, those magazines continue to present geography – they very rarely use the adjectives physical and human – in the way that many nineteenth century enthusiasts saw it, as the presentation of the earth, especially the less accessible areas, in its great diversity. Human geographers in universities seek to appreciate that diversity too, but in very different ways and with very different practices. There remains a hunger to know and appreciate the world, but that appetite is assuaged very differently according to the audience.

Notes

1 My thanks to David Livingstone and Charles Withers for valuable comments on a draft of this chapter.
2 Geography is taught in most military schools and academies, and political geography was at the core of the discipline's development in some South American countries (Hepple, 1992). It is one of the 31 academic programs at the US Military Academy, West Point, with majors offered within its degree structure in "environmental geogra-

phy," "geospatial information science," and "human geography." (see http://admissions.usma.edu/moreInfo/wp_catalog_08-09.pdf.)

3   These first appeared in 1854 in the *Journal of the Royal Geographical Society of London* (Raper and Fitzroy, 1854; see also Driver 2001).

4   This can readily be inferred by reading the section of the Society's history at http://www.amergeog.org/history.htm. However, the Society still funds scientific expeditions (as discussed in http://www.amergeog.org/bowman-expeditions.htm) as well as educational trips for the general public (http://www.amergeog.org/travel_program.htm).

5   Foundation of the AAG, in which William Morris Davis played a major role, was stimulated by the National Geographic Society's (NGS) role in lobbying for the 1903 IGC to be held in Washington DC (the AGS had been pressing for New York), the NGS having presented itself as the country's major learned society for geography (James and Martin,1978; 29).

6   There were other occasional opportunities, such as the eight-week American Transcontinental Excursion of 1912, in which 43 European geographers participated (Clout 2004).

7   Mackinder (1895: 372–3) criticized the then current situation with regard to geography teaching in English schools with the example of one where "Separate hours are set apart for "physical geography" and for "geography." The one is studied with a text-book written from a geological standpoint, the other is a manual of mere names, lit up occasionally with a few ideas drawn from Ritter or Strabo." Human geography did not exist, it seemed! Mackinder was one of the group who established the Geographical Association in 1893 to counter this problem.

8   A series of university departmental histories can be accessed at http://www.geog.psu.edu/hog/dept_histories.html.

9   Its status was often in doubt, however (Johnston 2003a), Mackinder (1935: 10–11) noting wryly that "The Professor of Geography is at times conscious that beneath the friendly comradeship of the Common Room there is a covert denial of his real equality of status. This would not so much matter did it not affect the estimate of their own subject held by geographers. Too often do they try to appease the critic by differentiating between Physical and Human Geography."

10 For parallel developments in other countries see the essays in Johnston and Claval (1984) and Dunbar (2001).

11 On Markham, see http://en.wikipedia.org/wiki/Clements_Markham and http://www.oxforddnb.com/ view/article/34880?docPos=5.

12 Mackinder (1935: 8) had earlier written that "The object of the geographer is to understand the concrete complexity, not to abstract and reduce to simplicity. Both geographer and scientist proceed no doubt by analysis with a view to subsequent synthesis, but the synthesis of the strict scientist is of like with like, whereas that of the geographer is of unlikes."

13 Sauer gets but one mention, albeit positive (p. 28)

14 Wooldridge and East were very much following the lead set in British geography by Mackinder, who wrote that "... Geography is admirably fitted as a correlating medium. It may very easily be made the pivot on which the other subjects may hang, and hang together" (Mackinder 1921: 382).

15 See http://www.geographicalfieldgroup.co.uk/index.html.

16 Mackinder (1895; 375) referred to the "facts of human geography," but does not specify what they are. However, elsewhere in that paper he used the German term, noting that "The anthropogeographer is in some sense the most typical and complete of geographers" (p. 375). Geography "culminates in the human element" and the "ideal geographer," among other skills, can "picture the movements of communities driven by

their past history, stopped and diverted by the solid forms, conditioned in a thousand ways by the fluid circulations, acting and reacting on the communities around; he can even visualise the movement of ideas and of words as they are carried along the lines of least resistance" and "In his cartographic art he possesses an instrument of thought of no mean power" (p. 376).

17 Unstead (1949, 47) wrote that "Political, or as it was sometimes called General, Geography consisted of facts about countries and capitals, peoples and productions with little relation to one another and practically none to the physical conditions of the earth's surface."

18 Such a geography, he contends, "can never be a discipline, can never, therefore, be honoured by the teacher, and must always fail to attract minds of an amplitude fitting them to be rulers of men" (p. 143) because "the political portion of such a work even at best rises no higher than to the rank of a good system of mnemonics" (p. 148) – one of the first criticisms of what became known as "capes and bays" geography (he referred to "capes and inlets").

19 The Vidalian tradition was extremely influential through much of the world – though less so in the English-speaking world than elsewhere.

20 In an earlier attempt to refashion geography, Barrows (1923) entitled his Presidential address to the AAG "Geography as human ecology," stressing "the relationships existing between natural environments and the distribution and activities of man. Geographers will, I think, be wise to view this problem in general from the standpoint of man's adjustment to environment, rather from that of environmental influence" (Koelsch 1969: 3; Chappell 1971).

References

Abler, R.F., Adams, J.S., and Gould, P.R. (1971) *Spatial organization: the geographer's view of the world*. Prentice-Hall, Englewood Cliffs.

Backhouse, R. and Fontaine, P. (eds) (2009) *The history of postwar social science*. Cambridge University Press, Cambridge.

Balchin, W.G.V. (1993) *The Geographical Association: the first hundred years*. The Geographical Association, Sheffield.

Barnes, T.J. (2006) Geographical intelligence: American geographers and research and analysis in the Office of Strategic Services, 1941–1945. *Journal of Historical Geography* 32, 149–168.

Barnes, T.J., Farish, M. (2006) Between regions: science, militarism, and American geography from World War to Cold War. *Annals of the Association of American Geographers* 97, 807–826.

Barrows, H.H. (1923) Geography as human ecology. *Annals of the Association of American Geographers* 13, 1–14.

Beaver, S.H. (1962) The Le Play Society and fieldwork. *Geography* 40, 25–240.

Blunt, A. and Wills, J (eds) (2000) *Dissident geographies: an introduction to radical ideas and practices*. Prentice-Hall, London.

Boyce, R.R. (ed.) (1980) *Geography as spatial interaction: Edward L. Ullman*. University of Washington Press, Seattle.

Brunhes, J. (1920) *Human geography: an attempt at a positive classification principles and examples*. George G. Harrap & Co, London.

Butlin, R.A. (2009) *Geographies of empire: European empires and colonies c. 1880–1960*. Cambridge University Press, Cambridge.

Buttimer, A. (1971) *Society and milieu in the French geographic tradition*. Rand McNally, Chicago.

Chappell, J.E. Jr. (1971) Harlan Barrows and environmentalism. *Annals of the Association of American Geographers* 61, 198–201.

Chorley, R.J., Beckinsale, R.P. and Dunn, A.J. (1973) *The history of the study of landforms, volume 2: the life and work of William Morris Davis*. Methuen, London.

Chisholm, G.G. (1989) *Handbook of economic geography*. Longmans Green, London.

Clout, H.M. (1972) *Rural geography: an introductory survey*. Pergamon Press, Oxford.

Clout, H.D. (2003) *Geography at University College London: a brief history*. University College London, Department of Geography, London.

Clout, H.D. (2004) Lessons from experience: French geographers and the transcontinental excursion of 1912. *Progress in Human Geography* 28, 597–618.

Clout, H.D. (2009) *Patronage and the production of geographical knowledge in France: the testimony of the first hundred regional monographs, 1905-1966*. Historical Geography Research Series, Historical Geography research group of the RGS (with IBG), London.

Cormack, L. (1997) *Charting an empire: geography at English universities, 1580–1620*. University of Chicago Press, Chicago.

Cox, K.R. (1976) American geography: social science emergent. *Social Science Quarterly* 57, 182–207.

Crawford, O.G.S. (1955) *Said and done: the autobiography of an archaeologist*. Phoenix House, London.

Curry, L. (1962) The climatic resources of intensive grassland farming: the Waikato, New Zealand. *The Geographical Review* 52, 174–194.

Dickinson, R.E. (1947) *City region and regionalism*. Routledge & Kegan Paul, London.

Driver, F. (2001) *Geography militant: cultures of exploration and empire*. Blackwell, Oxford.

Dunbar, G.S. (ed.) (2001) *Geography: discipline, profession and subject since 1870. An international survey*. Kluwer, Dordrecht.

Eyre, J.D. (ed.) (1977) *A man for all regions: the contributions of Edward L. Ullman to geography*. University of North Carolina, Department of Geography, Chapel Hill, NC.

Freeman, T.W. (1980) The Royal Geographical Society and the development of geography. In E.H. Brown (ed.), *Geography, yesterday and tomorrow*. Oxford University Press, Oxford, pp. 1–99.

Gaile, G. and Willmott, C.J. (eds) (1989) *Geography in America*. Merrill Publishing, Columbus, OH.

Gaile, G. and Willmott, C.J. (eds) (2004) *Geography in America at the dawn of the 21st century*. Oxford University Press, New York.

Gilbert, E.W. (1972) *British pioneers in geography*. David & Charles, Newton Abbott.

Gould, P.R. (1963) Man against his environment: a game theoretic framework. *Annals of the Association of American Geographers* 53, 290–297.

Gould, P.R. (1979) Geography 1957–1977: the Augean period. *Annals of the Association of American Geographers* 69, 139–151.

Gregory, D., Johnston, R.J., Pratt, G. Watts, M.J., and Whatmore, S. (2009) (eds) *The dictionary of human geography*, 5th edn. Wiley-Blackwell, Oxford.

Grosvenor, G. (1957) *The national geographic Society and its magazine: a history*. National Geographic Society, Washington, DC.

Haggett, P. (1965) *Locational analysis in human geography*. Edward Arnold, London.

Harris, C.D. and Ullman, E.L. (1945) The nature of cities. *Annals of the American Academy of Political and Social Science* 242, 7–17.

Hartshorne, R. (1939) *The nature of geography*. Association of American Geographers, Lancaster, Penn.

Harvey, D. (1973) *Social justice and the city*. Edward Arnold, London.

Harvey, D. (1974) What kind of geography for what kind of public policy? *Transactions, Institute of British Geographers* 63, 18–24.

Harvey, F. and Wardenga, U. (2006) Richard Hartshorne's adaptation of Alfred Hettner's system of geography. *Journal of Historical Geography* 32, 442–440.

Hauser, K. (2008) *Bloody old Britain: O.G.S. Crawford and the archaeology of modern life*. Granta, Cambridge.

Hepple, L.W. (1992) Metaphora, discurso geopolitico, y los militares en America el Sur. *Geopolitica (Buenos Aires)* 45, 45–50.

Herbertson, A.J. (1905) The major natural regions. *The Geographical Journal* 25, 300–301.

Herbertson, A.J. and Herbertson, F.D. (1899) *Man and his work: an introduction to human geography*. A. & C. Black, London.

Herbertson, D. (1950) *The life of Fréderic le Play*. le Play House Press, Ledbury.

Hooson, D.J.M. (1960) The distribution of population as the essential geographical expression. *The Canadian Geographer* 17, 10–20.

Huntington, E., Williams, F.E., and van Valkenburg, S. (1933) *Economic and social geography*. John Wiley & Sons, New York.

Jackson, A., Harris, R., Hepple, L.W., Hoare, A.G., Johnston, R.J., Jones, K., and Plummer, P.S. (2006) Geography's changing lexicon: measuring disciplinary change in Anglophone human geography though journal content analysis. *Geoforum* 37, 447–454.

James, P.E. and Mather, E.C. (1977) The role of periodic field conferences in the development of geographic ideas in the United States. *The Geographical Review* 67, 446–461.

James, P.E. and Martin, G.J. (1978) *The Association of American Geographers. The First seventy-five years*. Association of American Geographers, Washington DC.

Johnston, R.J. (1979) *Geography and geographers: Anglo-American human geography since 1945*, 1st edn. Edward Arnold, London.

Johnston, R.J. (2002) Robert E. Dickinson and the growth of urban geography: an evaluation. *Urban Geography* 22, 702–736.

Johnston, R.J. (2003a) The institutionalisation of geography as an academic discipline. In R.J. Johnston and M. Williams (eds), *A century of British geography*. Oxford University Press for the British Academy, Oxford, pp. 45–92.

Johnston, R. J. (2003b) Order in space: geography as a discipline in distance. In R.J. Johnston and M. Williams (eds), *A century of British geography*. Oxford University Press for the British Academy, Oxford, pp. 303–346.

Johnston, R.J. (2004) Institutions and disciplinary fortunes: two moments in the history of UK geography in the 1960s – II: human geography and the Social Science Research Council. *Progress in Human Geography* 28, 204–226.

Johnston, R.J. (2005) Geography – coming apart at the seams. In N. Castree, A. Rogers, and D. Sherman (eds), *Questioning geography: fundamental debates*. Blackwell, Oxford, pp. 9–25.

Johnston, R.J. (2008) Emrys Jones. *Proceedings of the British Academy* 153, 243–290.

Johnston, R.J. (2009a) Popular geographies and geographical imaginations: contemporary English-language geographical magazines. *GeoJournal* 74, 347–362.

Johnston, R.J. (2009b) On geography, Geography, and geographical magazines. *Geography* 94, 207–214.

Johnston, R.J. (2010) Sixty years of change in human geography. In R. Backhouse and P. Fontaine (eds) (2009), *The history of postwar social science*. Cambridge University Press, Cambridge.

Johnston, R.J. and Claval, P. (eds) (1984) *Geography since the Second World War: an international survey*. Croom Helm, London.

Johnston, R.J., Fairbrother, M., Hayes, D., Hoare, A., and Jones, K. (2008) The Cold War and geography's quantitative revolution: some messy reflections on Barnes' geographical underworld. *Geoforum* 39, 180–186.

Johnston, R.J., Gregory, D., Haggett, P., Smith, D.M., and Stoddart, D.R. (eds) (1981) *The dictionary of human geography*, 1st edn. Blackwell, Oxford.

Johnston, R.J. and Sidaway, J.D. (2004a) *Geography and geographers: Anglo-American human geography since 1945*, 6th edn. Edward Arnold, London.

Johnston, R.J. and Sidaway, J.D. (2004b) The trans-Atlantic connection: "Anglo-American" geography reconsidered. *GeoJournal* 59, 15–22.

Jones, E. (1965) *Human geography*. Chatto & Windus, London.

Jones, E. and Eyles, J. (1977) *An introduction to social geography*. Oxford University Press, Oxford.

Kearns, G. (2009) *Geopolitics and empire: the legacy of Halford Mackinder*. Oxford University Press, Oxford.

Kimble, G.H.T. (1951) The inadequacy of the regional concept. In L.D. Stamp and S.W. Wooldridge (eds), *London essays in geography: Rodwell Jones memorial volume*. Longmans Green, London, pp. 151–174.

Kitchin, R.M. and Thrift, N.J. (eds) (2009) *International encyclopedia of human geography*. Elsevier, Oxford.

Koelsch, W.A. (1969) The historical geography of Harlan H. Barrows. *Annals of the Association of American Geographers* 59, 632–651.

Koelsch, W.A. (2001) East and Midwest in American academic geography: two prosopographic notes. *The Professional Geographer* 53, 97–105.

Lebon, J.H.G. (1951) *An introduction to human geography*. Hutchinson, London.

Leighley, J. (1937) Some comments on contemporary geographic method. *Annals of the Association of American Geographers* 27, 125–141.

Livingstone, D.N. (1992) *The geographical tradition: essays in the history of a contested enterprise*. Blackwell, Oxford.

Livingstone, D.N. (2003) British geography, 1500–1900: an imprecise review. In R.J. Johnston and M. Williams (eds), *A century of British geography*. Oxford University Press for the British Academy, Oxford, pp. 11–44.

Lochhead, E. (1984) The Royal Scottish Geographical Society: the setting and sources of its success. *Scottish Geographical Magazine* 100, 69–80.

Longley, P.A., Goodchild, M.F., Maguire, D.J., and Rhind, D.W. (eds) (2005) *Geographical information systems: principles, techniques, management and applications*, 2nd edn, abridged. John Wiley, New York.

Mackenzie, J.M. (1995) The provincial geographical societies in Britain, 1884–1914. In M. Bell, M., R. A. Butlin, and M. Heffernan (eds), *Geography and imperialism: 1820-1940*. Manchester University Press, Manchester, pp. 93–124.

Mackinder, H.J. (1887) On the scope and methods of geography. *Proceedings of the Royal Geographical Society and Monthly Record of Geography* 9 (3), 141–174.

Mackinder, H.J. (1895) Modern geography: German and English. *The Geographical Journal*. 6, 367–379.

Mackinder, H.J. (1921) Geography as a pivotal subject in education. *The Geographical Journal* 57, 376–384.

Mackinder, H.J. (1935) Progress of geography in the field and in the study during the reign of His Majesty King George the Fifth. *The Geographical Journal* 86, 1–12.

Martin, G.J. (2005) *All possible worlds; a history of geographical ideas*, 4th edn. Oxford University Press, New York.

Meller, H. (1993) *Patrick Geddes: social evolutionist and city planner*. Routledge, London.

Morrill, R.L. (1970) *The spatial organization of society*. Wadworth, Belmont, CA.

Murphy, A.B. (2007) Geography's place in higher education in the United States. *Journal of Geography in Higher Education* 31, 121–141.

Newbigin, M. (1922) Human geography: first principles and some applications. *Scottish Geographical Magazine* 38, 209–221.

Peltier, L.C. (1954) Geomorphology. In P.E. James and C.F. Jones (eds). *American geography: inventory and prospect*. Syracuse University Press, Syracuse, pp. 362–381.

Philo, C. (2009) Introduction. In C. Philo (ed.), *Theory and methods: critical essays in human geography*. Ashgate, xiii–xlix, Aldershot.

Pinchemel, P. (ed.) (1972) *La géographie à travers un siècle de congrès internationaux*. International Geographical Union, Paris.

Platt, R.S. (1959) *Field study in American geography: the development of theory and method exemplified by selections*. Research Paper 61. Department of Geography, University of Chicago, Chicago.

Raper, H. and FitzRoy, R. (1854) Hints to travellers. *Journal of the Royal Geographical Society of London* 24, 328–358.

Rose, G. (1993) *Feminism and geography*. Polity Press, Cambridge.

Rugg, D.S. (1981) The Midwest as a hearth area in American academic geography. In B.S. Blouet, (ed.), *The origins of academic geography in the United States*. Archon Books, Hamden, pp.175–191.

Sack, R.D. (2001) The geographic problematic: moral issues. *Norsk Geografisk Tiddskrift* 55, 117–125.

Sanderson, M. (1988) *Griffith Taylor: Antarctic scientist and pioneer geographer*. Carleton University Press, Ottawa.

Schulten, S. (2001) *The geographical imagination in America, 1800–1950*. University of Chicago Press, Chicago.

Slater, T.R. (1988) Redbrick academic geography. *The Geographical Journal* 154, 169–180.

Sidaway, J.D. and Johnston, R.J. (2007) Geography in higher education in the UK. *Journal of Geography in Higher Education* 31, 57–80.

Smith, N. (2003) *American Empire: Roosevelt's geographer and the prelude to globalization*. University of California Press, Berkeley.

Speth, W.W. (1999) *How it came to be: Carl O. Sauer, Franz Boas and the meaning of anthropogeography*. Ephemera Press, Ellensburg.

Steel, R.W. (1983) *The Institute of British Geographers: the first fifty years*. Institute of British Geographers, London.

Stoddart, D.R. (1986) *On geography and its history*. Blackwell, Oxford.

Strange, C. and Bashford, A. (2008) *Griffith Taylor: visionary environmentalist explorer*. University of Toronto Press, Toronto.

Tatham, G. (1957) Determinism and possibilism. In G. Taylor (ed), *Geography in the twentieth century: a study of growth, fields, techniques, aims and trends*, 2nd edn. Methuen, London, pp. 128–163.

Taylor, G. (ed.) (1951) *Geography in the twentieth century: a study of growth, fields, techniques, aims and trends*. Methuen, London.

Taylor, G. (1957) Introduction: the scope of the volume. In G. Taylor (ed.), *Geography in the twentieth century: a study of growth, fields, techniques, aims and trends*, 2nd edn. Methuen, London, pp. 3–27.

Taylor, G. (1958) *Journeyman Taylor: the education of a scientist*. Robert Hale, London.

Thrift, N.J. (2005) *Knowing capitalism*. Sage, London.

Ullman, E.L. (1941) A theory of location for cities. *American Journal of Sociology* 46, 853–864.

Ullman, E.L. (1956) the role of transportation and the bases for interaction. In W. L. Thomas Jr., (ed.), *Man's role in changing the face of the earth*. University of Chicago Press, Chicago, pp. 862–880.

Unstead, J.F. (1949) H. J. Mackinder and the "New Geography." *The Geographical Journal* 113, 47–57.

Walford, R. (2001) *Geography in British schools 1850–2000*. Woburn Press, London.

Watson, J.W. (1951) The sociological aspects of geography. In G. Taylor (ed.), *Geography in the twentieth century*. Methuen, London, pp. 453–499.

Wise, M.J. (1986) The Scott Keltie Report 1885 and the teaching of geography in Great Britain. *The Geographical Journal* 152, 367–382.

Withers, C W.J. (2010) *Geography and science in Britain, 1831–1939: a study of the British Association for the Advancement of Science*. Manchester University Press, Manchester.

Women and Geography Study Group (1997) *Feminist geographies: explorations in diversity and difference*. Longman, Harlow.

Wooldridge, S.W. and East, W.G. (1951) *The spirit and purpose of geography*. London: Hutchinson.

Wright, J.K. (1952) *Geography in the making: the American Geographical Society 1851–1951*. American Geographical Society, New York.

Chapter 7

Landscape Versus Region
Part I

Nicolas Howe

An Odd Antagonism

In ordinary English, "landscape" and "region" are disparate things, neither complementary nor conflicting. But in the lexicon of mid-century Anglo-American geography, they clashed. To outsiders, this conflict might have seemed odd. How much could such mundane terms matter? But to insiders, it called the very nature of the field into question. In America, it also helped spawn the sub-field of cultural geography, which grew in part by challenging what it saw as the crass anti-culturalism of the dominant regional approach. How this happened is the subject of this chapter.

Tensions between landscape and region appeared in the 1920s, when *Landschaftskunde*, or landscape science, was imported from Germany as a rival to regional geography, which was rapidly becoming "the common denominator of what was considered geographic" (Martin 2009: 112). Soon the terms turned totemic. By the 1940s, they marked a sharp divide within the field, especially in the United States, where geography had split into rival camps: the so-called Midwestern and Berkeley Schools. Led by two utterly unlike intellects, Richard Hartshorne and Carl Sauer, these groups used region and landscape as their respective shibboleths in a series of hostile exchanges in journals and professional conferences. I focus on these exchanges, starting with Sauer's seminal 1925 essay, "The Morphology of Landscape" (1963) and ending with his presidential address to the Association of American Geographers in 1941; a speech in which he symbolically severed ties with his Midwestern colleagues.

To speak of landscape or region in particular ways, in particular professional contexts, was to announce that one was a particular *kind* of geographer. Yet the terms themselves were not thought inimical. Indeed, in a 1943 letter to his Berkeley colleague John Leighly, Sauer wrote:

The Wiley Blackwell Companion to Human Geography, First Edition.
Edited by John A. Agnew and James S. Duncan.
© 2011 John Wiley & Sons, Ltd. Published 2016 by John Wiley & Sons, Ltd.

I think we may consider that for the duration geographers will be considered as people who know something about regions. As you know, I don't disagree with this view at all, and have objected to the regionalists only because they have been too often short on knowledge and curiosity. (quoted in Martin 2009: 113)

Sauer, like Hartshorne, saw geography as chorology, or the study of regional differentiation. But he also thought the regional concept had been co-opted by positivist social science. To the geographer Preston James, Sauer complained that the field had "taken refuge in a regionalism that is descriptive without being analytic, because we refuse to face the analysis of cultural processes ... we've shied away from the dynamics of cultural origins and cultural change." From Sauer's perspective, Hartshorne and the Midwestern school did not err by studying regions. Their cardinal sin was a lack of "curiosity." Curiosity, for Sauer, was a term that embodied all the virtues of cultural geography: interest in history and nature, disregard for disciplinary borders, and a pluralistic fascination with traditional lifeways. To be "curious" was to take culture seriously.

The root of the problem, then, was neither landscape nor region, but culture. Rarely discussed in the self-consciously scientific world of early and mid-century human geography (Claval and Entrikin 2004), cultural theory was the proverbial elephant in the room, looming behind the landscape-region debate. The disagreement ran deep. Put simply, Sauer saw geography as a way to understand culture; Hartshorne saw culture as a way to understand geography. In an obituary for Sauer, Leighly (1976: 340) called culture a "liberating concept." For the Berkeley School, it seemed to possess an almost magical quality. For the Midwesterners, it held little allure. In fact, they saw the Berkeley School's fascination with culture as a dangerous distraction from geography's true calling. Culture was but one dependent variable among many, and not a very interesting one at that.

Since the early 1980s, there has been a whiggish tendency to portray this era of disciplinary infighting as the Dark Ages of human geography, a period of ignorance before the field "discovered" theory in the 1960s and 1970s. Usually Hartshorne is cast as the arch-villain and Sauer as a rather misguided anti-hero, someone who produced valuable empirical work and raised ecological consciousness but kept cultural geography mired in the anti-modern, Romantic nostalgia of Boasian ethnology (e.g. Mitchell 2000). According to the critical geographer Neil Smith (1989: 107–109), Hartshorne "assassinated" the landscape idea in his magnum opus, *The Nature of Geography* (1939), leaving it in "narrowly descriptive, aesthetic, and idealist confines" until the efflorescence of critical landscape studies in the early 1980s. The quantitative geographer Peter Gould (1991: 331–332), citing the mid-century closure of geography departments at Harvard, Yale, Stanford, and Northwestern, claims that early-twentieth-century geography, under Hartshorne's influence, was stricken with a "boundary-marking syndrome" that produced "tragic consequences for the discipline."

This picture is flawed. First, it ignores that geographers in the twenties, thirties, and forties wrestled with many of the same theoretical issues that geographers still wrestle with now: the construction of geographic knowledge, the materiality of place, and the visuality of landscape, to name just a few. Second, and more important, it ignores that geography's internal conflicts provided a fertile milieu for intellectual innovation. By divorcing landscape from region and thus excluding it from what Smith (1989: 107) calls "serious theoretical discourse," Hartshorne made it even more appealing to the Berkeley School. Regionalist dogma fueled a desire for an autonomous, self-consciously culturalist branch of geography, a branch that would treat culture itself as an autonomous domain of social life, requiring its own ethos of investigation. By attempting to "assassinate" landscape, Hartshorne gave it reason to live. Regionalist dogma gave cultural geographers an ideal Other against which to define themselves.

The birth of American cultural geography was, in other words, a cultural process like any other. As the sociologists Isaac Reed and Jeffrey Alexander (2009: 30) write, "social science, in its production and pursuit of truth, is a performance, consisting of speech acts that are symbolic and connotative as much as they are constative and denotative." "Stabilized via circulating networks of symbolic exchange," these speech-acts become the rituals through which "schools of thought" are constructed and maintained. Thus, to invoke the Hartshornian region or the Sauerian landscape was to signal one's loyalty to "the good guys" in the struggle for geography's soul. Like most theoretical shibboleths (today we might speak of "power," "network," "affect," or "materiality") landscape and region were shifting signifiers, rhetorical tools for constructing domains of inquiry and building communities of feeling.

It would be a mistake, however, to view this as simply a struggle for disciplinary dominance and symbolic authority, *à la* Bourdieu (1988). It also had a moral dimension. For Sauer, geography could help preserve, at least in memory, ways of life endangered by industrial capitalism. By contributing to the broader project of what he called "culture history," it could paint a picture of the good life as expressed in the cultural landscape, of "humanity living in some sort of state of grace" – which, above all, meant living "ecologically in balance" (Sauer 2009a: 391). With its utilitarian, economistic, and universalizing tendencies, regional geography was not just dull. It was destructive.

Regional Geography and its Discontents

In many ways, the story of the Sauer/Hartshorne rivalry is a story of cultural diffusion. Each seemed to see himself as *the* American interpreter of European geographic thought. Each studied the French masters of regional synthesis, and each was steeped in German methodological debate. Like most evangelists of Old World innovation, they both displayed a distinctively American zeal for intellectual reform (indeed, Sauer repeatedly and only half-jokingly referred to his methodological interventions as "sermons"). From where they both stood, American geography was in trouble. Yet despite reading from the same scriptures, they saw very different sins.

In this respect, Sauer and Hartshorne were arguably the first Americans simply to toe well-established methodological lines. As David Livingstone (1992: 265) remarks, *fin de siècle* German geography was embroiled in an "intramural fracas" between the positivist chorology of Alfred Hettner and the upstart *Landschaftskunde* of figures such as Otto Schlüter and Siegfried Passarge (see Martin 2005: 171–177; Livingstone 1992: 262–265; Elkins 1989; Harvey and Wardenga 2006). The debate between these two schools – the former "causal scientific-genetic" and the latter "aesthetic-artistic" (Fahlbusch *et al.* 1989: 358–359) – helped push Sauer and Hartshorne in very different directions. Sauer, as Denis Cosgrove (2004: 65) notes, shared a "commitment to examining and explaining supposedly deep, organic connections between premodern cultures and the land." Hartshorne, on the other hand, inherited Hettner's fear that the aesthetic bias of *Landschaftskunde* would exclude the chorological study of immaterial phenomena, which, among other things, would exclude most of political and economic geography (Livingstone 1992: 264). For Hartshorne, who wrote *The Nature* while on research leave in Germany during 1938–1939, *Landschaftskunde* too easily veered into *völkisch* mysticism.

Yet neither Sauer nor Hartshorne were purely parasitic thinkers. Sauer may have been attracted to certain aspects of the aesthetic program in German geography, even to its cultural conservatism, but attempts to portray him as a misty-eyed romantic are strained at best. In fact, he liked landscape in part because it seemed more scientific than region. Landscape invited inquiry into the origins and dispersals of cultural practices – into cultural *process*, not just cultural pattern. As regional synthesis caught on in the 1920s and 1930s, Sauer was among a number of geographers who worried that historical depth and scientific integrity were being lost to a clerical obsession with data collection and a scholastic fascination with social and economic theory.

Social scientists today, having thoroughly internalized the post-Kuhnian critique of scientism, might be confused by this dual accusation of presentism and scientific laxity. Yet for Sauer and his allies, the second failing flowed directly from the first. In his classic paper on "Sequent Occupance," for example, Derwent Whittlesey (1929: 165) claimed that investigating historical patterns of landscape modification "holds the hope of a system of classification despaired of so long as chorology remains merely the multiplication of observations and their presentation." Sauer and others saw regional geography "as compilation and not investigation" (Martin 2009: 112). Without including the dimension of time, inquiry into regional differentiation produced a static, sterile picture of the earth.

By the late 1930s, anxiety about the scientific legitimacy of regional geography had reached something of a climax (see, for example, Finch 1939; James 1934; Hall 1935; Platt 1935; Renner 1935). Leighly (1937: 125–132) published a controversial broadside in the *Annals of the Association of American Geographers*, in which he wrote with undisguised disdain for regional analysis, portraying it as vapid, unscholarly, and most of all, unscientific. Presaging later complaints by Sauer, he saved special scorn for the regionalists' narrow-minded fascination with economic data ("a sop to a commercial Cerberus"), and he wrote of the "appalling" and "mind-sickening" effect of regional classification. Most provocatively, Leighly claimed. "There is no prospect of our finding a theory so penetrating that it will bring into rational order all or a large fraction of the heterogeneous elements of the landscape. There is no prospect of our finding such a theory, that is to say, unless it is of a mystical kind, and so outside the pale of science." True regional synthesis belonged to "literary art," and "the regionalist admits as much when he resorts to the colorful adjective and the startling juxtaposition of phrase in order to enliven the drab objectivity of map and numerical table."

As a more salutary alternative to regional description, Leighly called for redefining cultural geography as the "topography of art," or what Sauer would later refer to as "material culture in areal massiveness" (Sauer 1929; quoted in Entrikin 1984: 405). He argued that by seeing the "art region" as a "geographic expression of a cultural process rather than the cultural expression of a geographic process," and the settlement as "a local and locally conditioned embodiment of esthetic values," geographers could break free from their unseemly obsession with "rationalism" as *both* a principle of inquiry *and* a model of human behavior. They could, in other words, participate in the study of culture history, an enterprise that looked beyond "rational, utilitarian motives," to the irrational, "often violent, subjugation of nature to cultural uses." Culture – especially urban, capitalistic culture – was often highly maladaptive, and "from any rational point of view many of its products are monstrosities." With "no basic equations of social psychodynamics on which a science of the cultural landscape can be built," Leighly concluded, "we must be content with the historical rather than the rational type of understanding." Historicism, as Leighly (and Sauer) understood it, was incompatible with the liberal positivism of mainstream geography.

But what did they mean by "culture"? Unlike anthropologists, who had already begun to struggle in earnest over the term, geographers seemed to hope it would speak for itself. The result was a cacophony of implied definitions. For many regional geographers, culture was simply all that was not nature. Regions contained both "cultural elements" and "natural elements" in varying proportion, both easily catalogued. For the Berkeley School, however, culture was an independent variable, a transformational force. Landscape, with its inherent emphasis on processes of cultural transformation, seemed to offer an escape from the "rationalist" confines of regionalism.

Many saw this attack on regional geography as gross materialism. As the geographer Vernor Finch (1939: 6) remarked in an AAG presidential address, Leighly's critique limited the geographer to studying "the physical aspects of the field; physical earth in some one or all of its manifold features, or to the physical features of human culture, if perchance he can stake out there a claim not already preempted." This "multiplication of scientific minutiae" was inadequate precisely because it seemed to exclude so much cultural data from the regional picture: language, ideas, all that was intangible.

Hartshorne's *Nature* began as a brief response to Leighly's 1937 article, which had irked him greatly (Lukermann 1989: 54). It quickly became a full-blown codification of chorology, a regionalist scripture. By the early forties, battle lines had been clearly drawn, and evidence of what James Duncan (1994) much later identified as cultural geography's "heterotopic" tendencies was already clear. As Sauer complained in his 1941 AAG presidential address, his one direct response to Hartshorne's attack on landscape geography, geographers were starting to speak in mutually incomprehensible tongues.

Landscape against Region

This impasse had been a long time brewing. In his 1915 doctoral dissertation, Sauer (2009b: 99) had called regional geography "the most urgent field of geographic inquiry." Ten years later, in his seminal essay "The Morphology of Landscape" (1963), he took a decisive step toward a renegade landscape science (for a careful reading of this exegetically exhausted text, see Penn and Lukermann 2003; on its reception within the field, see Martin 2003). From that point on, three closely related themes became the most persistent points of contention between the then-nascent Berkeley School and its Midwestern rival: historicism, naturalism, and common-sense empiricism (on the philosophical origins of these themes, see Entrikin 1984; for a contrasting view, see Speth 1999).

In "The Morphology," Sauer asserts that landscape, area, and region are, "in a sense," equivalent terms, but that area is too colloquial for scientific usage and that region had "come to imply, to some geographers at least, an order of magnitude." Region, in other words, implied synchronic spatial analysis. It was a scalar concept. Landscape, on the other hand, was "a land shape, in which the process of shaping is by no means thought of as simply physical." "Process," for Sauer, was always the essential term. "We cannot form an idea of landscape except in terms of its time relations as well as of its space relations," he wrote. "It is in continuous process of development or of dissolution and replacement." Later, Leighly (1937: 135) would go farther and urge geographers to focus on "the essential time-bond of culture [*rather*] than its looser place-bond." Hartshorne (1939: 179) was so annoyed by this prescription that he wondered if it was not "the antithesis of geography."

If historicism was the primary bone of contention, then naturalism was a close second. The Sauerians bemoaned the regionalists' neglect of physical geography, which they saw as inseparable from its human counterpart. Sauer, much like Vidal, believed in a "dialectical unity" of nature and culture (Cosgrove 1983: 2–3). He was intensely interested in the natural sciences, especially biology and geology. Indeed, "the guiding ideas and controlling metaphors" of his work were drawn from these fields (Entrikin 1991: 37). For Sauer, regional geography's presentism was closely related to its indifference to nature. Both were symptoms of a progressive rationalism increasingly endemic to all social sciences (save anthropology). Although he professed an aversion to social theory in general, theories of humans as rational, self-interested, and benefit-maximizing repelled Sauer most of all. Culture, he thought, provided the human group with a "functionally valid *and* aesthetically satisfying solution for living in the environment at [its] disposal" (Sauer 1944: 529; my italics). Neither environmental determinism nor liberal socio-economics could account for the power of "aesthetic satisfaction," for what Sauer called the "purely cultural" attachment to local lifeways (2009c: 171). Nor could it account for the "monstrosities" of capitalist modernity, or what he often called its need for "destructive exploitation" (Speth 1977).

The third bone of contention, common-sense empiricism, was more important than most commentators recognize. In "The Morphology," Sauer wrote that "area or landscape is the field of geography, because it is a naïvely given, important section of reality, not a sophisticated thesis" (1963: 316), and "Geography assumes the responsibility for the study of areas because there exists a common curiosity about that subject." Elsewhere he (1927: 178) wrote, "The interest that sustains geography is the same in general that at a popular level results in books of travel." Curiosity about places, satisfied by observation, was the essence of geography. Yet in a speech he prepared for (but never delivered to) a joint meeting of the Pacific Coast Economic Association and the Pacific Sociological Society, he complained that the rationalization of social science devalued both (Sauer 2009c). The "shamans" (social and economic theorists) were "growing in power and wealth," whereas "the workers" (field researchers) – "those who fetch things and work goods" – were "poorly regarded." Worse, he implies, in their search for universal laws of social life the "shamans" have in fact hastened the death of regional lifeways. They had become accomplices to ecological and cultural destruction.

Recognizing this fact required no "sophisticated thesis." One simply needed to get outside and look around. Calling "this curious world" "unendingly fascinating," Sauer chided social scientists for trying to make it "conform to our reason." "We can do without economic man," he declares. "We do not need to define society." Indeed, such theoretical pursuits are merely "constructions of a given civilization that is dated and localized, the expressions of an 'intellectual climate,' " which, like physical climate, "is a quality of place and subject in course of time to change." Cultural geography demanded that social scientists parochialize their own perspective. Conversely, it demanded that they examine their own regional cultures with the same curiosity and wonder that they reserve for the exotic.

Sauer was no progressive. In a 1960 letter to the journal *Landscape*, for example, he (2009a: 391) gasped at the "appalling distribution" of the "more strident and dissonant forms of American night club music" and the "sensational, violent, stupid, and sybaritic" nature of popular cinema. His anti-modernism and valorization of rural and indigenous peoples has struck many critics as politically unacceptable (for a summary, see Mathewson 2009). But it is not hard to see why an anti-imperialist radical like James Blaut – a geographer best known for his devastating critique of Eurocentric "diffusionism" (e.g. Blaut 1993) – would be attracted to Sauer's pluralist, processual, and polycentric view of culture (Sluyter 2005). Nor is it hard to see why Sauer identified so strongly with the field of cultural anthropology, a field he praised for its "encyclopedic curiosity" and "joy of inquiry" the two qualities he saw most lacking in mainstream geography.

It is not surprising, then, that Sauer's commitment to landscape morphology was gradually replaced by the synoptic, inter-disciplinary pursuit of culture history. Allergic to causal and reductionist methodologies, even landscape became too narrow for him. In his address to the AAG in 1941 – the same year he published "The Personality of Mexico," an essay that invokes a key trope of European regionalism (Dunbar 1974) – Sauer actually seems to distance himself from the landscape idea. He speaks of the cultural landscape as simply a "useful restriction" on geographic inquiry, a tool that allows the geographer to focus systematically on the more comprehensive *genre de vie* or "personality" of place (1941: 7). "The whole task of human geography," he wrote, "is nothing less than comparative study of areally localized cultures, whether or not we call the descriptive content the cultural landscape." Geographers, he said, "all know that this is what gives meaning to our work, that our one general problem is in the differentiating qualities of terrestrial space ... We are not concerned with universalized economic man, family, society, or economy, but with the comparison of localized patterns, or areal differentiations." That Sauer used the plural form of Hartshorne's favored term, areal differentiation, was telling. There was no singular law or principle of differentiation. Hence, "We deal not with Culture, but with cultures, except in so far as we delude ourselves into thinking the world made over in our own image."

Region against Landscape

Hartshorne did not like landscape. An obscure blend of "scene" and "area," it muddied geography's methodological waters. Having become "perhaps the single most important word in geographic language," it had sown "confusion" throughout the discipline (1939: 149). Those responsible had played a "shell game" and "a conjurer's trick." He chided his German contemporaries for using *Landschaft* to mean both "the appearance of a land as we perceive it" and "simply a restricted piece of land" (1939: 150), and he felt that this ambiguity had infected Anglo-American geography (on this seminal tension in geographic thought, see Olwig 2002a). Region, however, offered conceptual precision and scientific elegance. Stripped to its epistemic core, region was crisp and economical – so economical that many have since wondered that Hartshorne put so much effort and erudition into establishing so very little. It was, as he put it, a "mental construction" that provided "some sort of intelligent basis for organizing our knowledge of reality" (1939: 275). But this parsimoniousness was precisely his point. Geography, he sensed, seemed capable of colonizing any field. It needed to be reigned in.

Hartshorne's case against landscape was stronger than most critics have allowed. It is true he could not tolerate the ambiguity of a term that meant both the appearance of a place and the place itself. It is also true that he dismissed the psychological and aesthetic experience of landscape as beyond (or beneath) the geographer's interest. Still, he had serious concerns about materialist myopia. For Hartshorne, the landscape idea excluded ideas. "Material things, and particularly visible objects, are the sort of phenomena that students trained in physical sciences know how to deal with," he wrote, clearly thinking of Sauer. "Geographers with that background, which includes most geographers today, would naturally prefer to have to study only such definitely tangible *things*." At the same time, he wrote, "Only from the point of view of aesthetics or of visual sensations can we regard the external form of a forest as more important than its contents, the surface buildings of a coal mine as more important in the area than the underground workings, or the contour of the land as more important than the precipitation that falls upon it." Put simply, by focusing so intensely on the material surface of the region the "landscape purists" (a label he enthusiastically borrowed from Crowe [1938]) had succumbed to both simple-minded empiricism *and* fuzzy-minded aestheticism.

Smith (1989: 108–109) speculates that Hartshorne could not stand the "muddling" of space and society implied by the landscape idea because it threatened geography's ideological commitment to "spatial absolutism." Yet Hartshorne was worried about two more immediate problems: the marginalization of political geography and the narrowing of cultural geography into a kind of ecological antiquarianism. As Mischa Penn and Fred Lukermann (2003: 255, n.2; see, also, Lukermann 1989) note, Hartshorne's almost obsessive need to refute the "visible phenomenon" thesis stemmed in part from his fear that the landscape purists did not take political geography seriously. In an essay for a broad social scientific audience, Sauer (1927: 207–210) had panned the sub-field as "the wayward child of the geographic family" and "certainly the least scientific." "The subject is mixed up especially with nationalist aspirations," he wrote, "in which case it may serve as a 'scientific' reason for violating the Tenth Commandment." Sauer saved special scorn for the study of political boundaries, Hartshorne's area of expertise, and he patronizingly suggested that "as a very modest field" political geography may be someday integrated into cultural landscape studies.

Hartshorne (1935a, 1935b) hit back in a series of articles for *The American Political Science Review*. Although he commended Sauer for his "vigorous efforts" to introduce German geographic thought to America – in particular for his Hettnerian declaration that "The task of geography is to grasp the content, individuality, and relation of areas" (Sauer 1927: 186) – Hartshorne accused him of going astray (after Schlüter and Brunhes) by limiting geographic study to "observable features" of the landscape. Followed to its logical conclusion, Sauer's ocularcentrism would limit political geography to the study of "boundary stones," and it would force human geography as a whole to ignore "one of the major cultural fact[s]" of an area, the division into states (1935a: 803–804). Had he taken a more ecumenical and politicized view of culture – and had he read Hettner and Passarge more carefully – Sauer would presumably have held boundaries in higher esteem, or so Hartshorne suggested.

Landscape, for Hartshorne, was little more than the "face" or "picture" of the region (1939: 167). It was the "the surface which the area presents us under its atmosphere." By confusing this "picture" with area itself, the landscape purists had restricted geography to examining a small slice of reality. "In itself the landscape is literally a superficial phenomenon," Hartshorne complained, "and a field of science that concentrated on it alone would be superficial." Geography must concern itself with the full dimensionality of area, which includes functional relations between things and ideas:

> To be sure, the moment the study passes beyond bare description the student must leave the landscape itself, must go beneath it, even to state what its form represents – to translate the outer foliage of a forest into the forest, the outer surface of buildings into different kinds of buildings, etc … Our interest in houses, factories, and forests cannot be confined to their surface form; only in the limited field of aesthetic geography could such a restriction be justified. Our very use of such words as house, barn, factory, office building, etc., indicates that we are primarily concerned with the internal functions within these structures; the external form is a secondary aspect which we use simply as a handy means to detect the internal functions – and should use only insofar as it is a reliable means for that purpose." (Hartshorne 1939)

Hartshorne posits the existence of a firmer foundation beneath the aesthetic surface of place, a level of reality that enjoys what the literary theorist Barbara Herrnstein Smith (2010) calls "underneath-it-all status." Landscape is "merely an outward manifestation of most of the factors at work in the area" (Hartshorne 1939: 217), factors mostly related to political and economic relations. Indeed, Hartshorne explicitly claims that most geographically relevant cultural features are *actually* economic features; "Consequently geographers are justified in regarding human, or cultural geography very largely in terms of economic geography." Much has been made of Hartshorne's idealist definition of the region, but in many ways he had more in common with latter-day materialists, especially orthodox Marxists. For him, what the Sauerians called "culture" was superstructural froth.

Conclusion: Culture against Itself

The geographer Fred Lukermann (1989) argued that the dispute over landscape turned on basic assumptions about the nature of social science, not methodological questions about field observation or material culture. "The crux of the matter," wrote Lukermann, "... was the failure of Hartshorne to understand that landscape(s) were not observable, they were constructs, they were conceptual; based on the areal *experience* of human beings. Landscapes were *expressions* of the value systems of the culture groups occupying specific areas/regions." With his positivist faith in "objective science" and "the empirical," Hartshorne simply failed to grasp the role of "subjective values" and "the experiential" in Sauerian cultural geography. Others have told much the same story, with Hartshorne paving the way for quantitative spatial science (Sack 1974; Entrikin 1981; Gregory 1978; Olwig 2002b) and Sauer opening the door to hermeneutic and humanistic approaches (Relph 1970; Olwig 2003).

A slightly more complicated story might also be told. In this story, their dispute had less to do with clear-cut philosophical differences and more with conflicting sensibilities. In other words, their conflict over culture was itself cultural, as Sauer suggested. After all, both men clearly saw geography as an objective science (Cosgrove 1998:32). And while it is true that Sauer rejected the "rationalism" of mainstream regional geography, he did not show much interest in exploring the psychological, moral, or aesthetic dimensions of landscape interpretation. Sauer's interest in culture was decidedly naturalistic (Entrikin 1984). He may have opened the door to work that challenged the nature/culture binary (Olwig 2008), but he certainly did not step through it. Indeed, he once described himself as "an earth scientist with a slant toward biogeography, of which man is a part" (Leighly 1976: 342), and there is no reason to doubt the accuracy of this description.

Hartshorne, on the other hand, was deeply suspicious of this fusion of nature and culture. He was also much more interested in the kinds of epistemological questions that have since exercised humanistic and critical geographers. Foreshadowing future concerns about reification and essentialism, he worried that the Berkeley School had simply replaced environmental determinism with its culturalist opposite. Discussing their interest in house types and settlement forms, he wrote, "Whether they claim that they study these simply because they are visible features in the landscape or recognize that they are actually attempting to study the geography of culture, their readers will not be deceived, it is culture they are pursuing."

Yet culture, for Hartshorne, could not *explain* anything. The forces that changed regions over time, "both the will and energy of the individual inhabitants and the changes in individual natural elements," had no inner logic; they did not form "a unit force, but merely a summation of more or less independent, often conflicting forces." Though aimed specifically at Sauer's claim that landscapes could be treated as holistic, quasi-organic entities, these comments go far beyond a critique of cultural evolutionism. They call the very notion of cultural agency into question. "The natural landscape is not converted into a cultural landscape as an artist applies extraneous materials to a canvas to 'develop' a unit picture," Hartshorne wrote, "for the changes are not the work of one artist, or of an organized group of artists, but merely a collection of somewhat independent natural and human forces." Cultures were not historical or geographical agents; *people* were.

Whether Sauer actually subscribed to a "superorganic" theory of culture is, I think, an open question (for a précis of the many challenges to and defenses of Duncan's [1980] classic paper on this subject, see Penn and Lukermann [2003: 255, n.1]). One thing is for sure: Hartshorne took Sauer's organismic analogy far too literally. True, Sauer (1927: 190) regarded the region as "a corporeal thing." But he explicitly emphasized the "as" in this formulation. "One may be ever so conscious of the fictive character of the region as an organism," he wrote, "[but] its study under such a view-point yields significant results, if its specific identity is not taken with too much seriousness." Similarly, Preston James (1934: 79) wrote of landscape as a "pseudo-organic unity." Although they lacked the theoretical language (and probably the desire) to say so explicitly, both James and Sauer were addressing the problem of reification by arguing for the analytical autonomy of cultural landscape from the concrete reality of terrestrial space (on the difference between concrete and analytical autonomy in cultural analysis, see Kane 1991). Indeed, two years after "The Morphology" was published, Sauer (1927: 190) made a crucial but rarely quoted revision to his now-notorious dictum on cultural agency, writing that "The group [not culture] is the active force, the natural area the medium (milieu) in which the group works, the cultural landscape is the result." Although Sauer (2009c: 170) defined culture traits as "communicated and applied ideas" that form "the pattern of life of a group," he was hardly a cultural determinist, at least not in practice.

Sauer hoped his work would speak for itself. He was not about to mount a systematic theoretical defense of culture history. Indeed, for Sauer, the whole point of cultural geography was to *show* how cultural values were expressed in the land. In this sense, geography could play a heroic, even redemptive role by documenting areal diversity in the face of a leveling, homogenizing modernity (Entrikin 1991: 37). Condemned as "imperialist nostalgia" by contemporary critical theory (Rosaldo 1989), this declensionist view of culture stood at the heart of Sauer's intellectual program.

It was also at the heart of his opposition to Midwestern regional geography. When Sauer was finally invited to deliver the presidential address to the AAG in 1941, he accused his rivals of abetting the rise of a bureaucratic and rationalistic worldview, a worldview rooted in Midwestern commercial triumphalism and assimilationist ideology. Regional geographers had dispensed with "serious consideration of cultural or histori[c]al processes" (1941: 3) because their culture and history *made* them. Thus, he wrote:

> ... in the simple dynamism of the Mid-West of the early Twentieth Century, the complex calculus of historical growth or loss did not seem particularly real or important. Was it, in view of such "rational" adjustment of activity and resource, being very realistic to say that any economic system was nothing but the temporarily equilibrated set of choices and customs of a particular group? In this brief moment of fulfillment and ease, it seemed that there must be a strict logic of the relationship of site and satisfaction, something approaching the validity of natural order. (Sauer 1941)

Sympathetic scholars have sometimes lamented that Sauer did not defend himself in a more systematic, forceful way against the charges leveled by Hartshorne, that he "retreated" from theoretical debate. But he did not see the need to defend himself. His whole corpus was directed against a worldview that he saw embodied in positivist regional geography. *The Nature*, he remarked to the AAG, is simply "the latest and, I think, best statement of what is in fact, if not by avowal, a pretty general view-point in this country." With that accusation, his break with regional geography was essentially complete. Over the next two decades, North American geography departments read either Sauer or Hartshorne, rarely both (Butzer 1989: 36).

Yet Sauer never turned the provincializing lens of cultural analysis on himself. As Nicholas Entrikin (1984: 407) writes, his "culture historian was a curiously transcendental figure ... seemingly unaffected by the social context that so contaminated the research of the collectivist academics of twentieth-century social science." Neither activist nor bureaucrat, this figure was able to simply reject "the universal and normative" and embrace "a pluralistic world" (Sauer 2009: 170). This posture was not problematized until a second generation of cultural geographers brought Sauer's ecumenical historicism to bear on the kinds of theoretical questions that fascinated Hartshorne. Led by figures such as David Lowenthal (a student of both Sauer and Hartshorne) and Yi-Fu Tuan, these inheritors of Sauer's culturalism rejected his empiricism, his macho insistence on exploration, and his disdain for epistemology. They practiced "armchair geography" with both philosophical rigor and historical awareness. By the time *their* students became involved in building a "new" cultural geography in the late seventies and early eighties, the ideological biases of Sauerian landscape science had been thoroughly exposed. Yet Sauer himself set this train in motion.

So, in sense, the Berkeley School won the fight, at least in cultural geography. Landscape is the subject of a vibrant and contentious literature (for the latest overview, see Wylie 2007). And although in political and economic geography the region is still "possibly the most entrenched of all geographical concepts" (Harvey 2005: 245), in cultural geography it is effectively dead. Nobody reads Hartshorne any more. Yet to chalk this result up to some Manichean struggle within geographic thought between "materialism" and "idealism" is to place far too much stock in philosophy. Over the past three decades, the history of geographic thought has suffered from attempts to impose philosophical coherence on often incoherent structures of feeling. As Mischa Penn and Fred Lukermann (2003) argue, Sauer (and, by extension, Hartshorne) were, first and foremost, university professors who sought to steer their field in particular directions in response to immediate institutional and personal pressures. They undoubtedly *used* philosophy to intervene in methodological debates. But they did so in often *ad hoc* and internally contradictory ways. Sometimes Sauer was a hard-nosed empiricist, other times a starry-eyed romantic. In this sense, cultural geography has changed very little over the past nine decades. Geographers that succeed at depicting an "architectonic vision of reality," as Penn and Lukermann put it, are few and far between. Most are philosophical dabblers. They consume their ideas buffet-style, with salad and pudding on the same plate. Sometimes the result is a startlingly original juxtaposition of flavors; often it is a mess. This, perhaps, is the most important legacy of the landscape tradition: geography's stubborn disregard for intellectual boundaries.

References

Blaut, J.M. (1993) *The Colonizer's Model of the World: Geographical Diffusionism and Eurocentric History*. The Guilford Press, New York.

Bourdieu, P. (1988) *Homo Academicus*. Stanford University Press, Palo Alto.

Butzer, K.W. (1989) Hartshorne, Hettner, and *The Nature of Geography*. In J.N. Entrikin and S.D. Brunn (eds), *Reflections on Richard Hartshorne's: The Nature of Geography*. Association of American Geographers, Washington D.C., pp. 32–52.

Claval, P. and Entrikin J.N. (2004) Cultural geography: place and landscape between continuity and change. In G. Benko and U. Strohmeyer, (eds), *Human Geography*: A History for the 21st Century. Arnold, London, pp. 25–46.

Cosgrove, D.E. (2004) Landscape and Landschaft. *German Historical Institute Bulletin* 35, 57–71.

Cosgrove, D.E. 1998 [1984] *Social Formation and Symbolic Landscape*. University of Wisconsin Press, Wisconsin.

Cosgrove, D.E. (1983) Towards a radical cultural geography: problems of theory. *Antipode* 15, 1–11.

Crowe, P.R. (1938) On progress in geography. *Scottish Geographical Journal* 54, 1–19.

Dunbar, G.S. (1974) Geographical Personality. *Geoscience and Man* 5, 25–33.

Duncan, J.S. (1994) After the civil war: reconstructing cultural geography as heterotopias. In K. Foote, et al. (eds), *Re-reading Cultural Geography*. University of Texas Press, Austin, pp. 401–411.

Duncan, J.S. (1980) The superorganic in American cultural geography. *Annals of the Association of American Geographers* 70, 181–198.

Elkins, T.H. (1989) Human and regional geography in the German-speaking lands in the first forty years of the twentieth century. In J.N. Entrikin and S.D. Brunn (eds), *Reflections on Richard Hartshorne's: The Nature of Geography*. Association of American Geographers, Washington D.C., pp. 17–34.

Entrikin, J.N. (1981) Philosophical issues in the scientific study of regions. In D.T. Herbert and R.J. Johnston (eds), *Geography and the Urban Environment*. John Wiley, Chichester, pp. 1–27.

Entrikin, J.N. (1991) *The Betweenness of Place*. The Johns Hopkins University Press, Baltimore.

Entrikin, J.N. (ed.) (2008) *Regions*. Ashgate, Farnham.

Entrikin, J.N. (1984) Carl O Sauer, Philosopher in Spite of Himself. *Geographical Review* 74, 387–408.

Fahlbusch, M., Rössler. M., and Siegrist, D. (1989) Conservatism, ideology and geography in Germany 1920–1950. *Political Geography Quarterly* 8, 353–367.

Finch, V.C. (1939) Geographical science and social philosophy. *Annals of the Association of American Geographers* 29, 1–28.

Gould, P. (1991) On Reflections on Richard Hartshorne's. *The Nature of Geography. Annals of the Association of American Geographers* 81, 328–334.

Gregory, D. (1978) *Ideology, Science and Human Geography*. Hutchinson, London.

Hall, R.B. (1935) The geographic region: a resume. *Annals of the Association of American Geographers* 25, 122–136.

Hartshorne, R. (1935a) Recent developments in political geography, I. *The American Political Science Review* 29, 785–804.

Hartshorne, R. (1935a) Recent developments in political geography, II. *The American Political Science Review* 29, 943–966.

Hartshorne, R. (1939) *The Nature of Geography; a Critical Survey of Current Thought in the Light of the Past*. The Association of American Geographers, Lancaster.

Hartshorne, R. (1959) *Perspective on the Nature of Geography*. Rand McNally, Chicago.

Harvey, D. (2005) The sociological and geographical imaginations. *International Journal of Politics, Culture, and Society* 18, 211–255.

Harvey, F. and Wardenga, U. (2006) Richard Hartshorne's adaptation of Alfred Hettner's system of geography. *Journal of Historical Geography* 32, 422–440.

James, P.E. (1934) The terminology of regional description. *Annals of the Association of American Geographers* 24, 78–92.

Kane, A. (1991) Cultural analysis in historical sociology: the analytic and concrete forms of the autonomy of culture. *Sociological Theory* 9, 53–69.

Leighly, J. (1976) Carl Ortwin Sauer, 1889–1975. *Annals of the Association of American Geographers* 66, 337–348.

Leighly, J. (1938) Methodologic controversy in nineteenth century German geography. *Annals of the Association of American Geographers* 28, 238–258.

Leighly, J. (1937) Some comments on contemporary geographic method. *Annals of the Association of American Geographers* 27, 125–141.

Livingstone, D.N. (1992) *The Geographical Tradition: Episodes in the History of a Contested Enterprise*. Oxford University Press, Oxford.

Lukermann, F. (1989) Post hoc, ergo propter hoc? In J.N. Entrikin and S.D. Brunn (eds), *Reflections on Richard Hartshorne's The Nature of Geography*. Association of American Geographers, Washington, D.C., pp. 53–68.

Martin, G.J. (2005) [1972] *All Possible Worlds: A History of Geographical Ideas*. Oxford University Press, New York.

Martin, G.J. (2003) From the cycle of erosion to "The morphology of landscape": or some thought concerning geography as it was in the early years of Carl Sauer. In K. Mathewson and M.S. Kenzer (eds), *Carl Sauer, Culture, Land, and Legacy: Perspectives on Carl O. Sauer and Berkeley School Geography*. Geoscience Publications, Dept. of Geography and Anthropology, Louisiana State University, Baton Rouge, pp. 19–53.

Martin, G.J. (2009) Introduction. In W.M. Denevan and K. Mathewson (eds). *Carl Sauer on Culture and Landscape: Readings and Commentaries*. Louisiana State University Press, Baton Rouge, pp. 111–118.

Mathewson, K. (2009). Carl Sauer and his critics. In W.M. Denevan and K. Mathewson (eds), *Carl Sauer on Culture and Landscape: Readings and Commentaries*. Louisiana State University Press, Baton Rouge, pp. 9–28.

Meinig, D.W., (ed.) (1979) *The Interpretation of Ordinary Landscapes: Geographical Essays*. Oxford University Press, New York.

Mitchell, D. (2000) *Cultural Geography: A Critical Introduction*. Blackwell Publishers, Oxford.

Olwig, K.R. (2008) Has "geography" always been modern?: choros, (non)representation, performance, and the landscape. *Environment and Planning* A40, 1843–1861.

Olwig, K.R. (2003) Landscape: the Lowenthal legacy. *Annals of the Association of American Geographers* 93. 871–877.

Olwig, K.R. (2002a) *Landscape, Nature, and the Body Politic: From Britain's Renaissance to America's New World*. University of Wisconsin Press, Madison.

Olwig, K.R. (2002b) The duplicity of space: Germanic "raum" and Swedish "rum" in English language geographical discourse. *Geografiska Annaler, Series B, Human Geography* 84, 1–17.

Penn, M. and F. Lukermann (2003) Chorology and landscape: an internalist reading of "The morphology of landscape." In K. Mathewson and M.S. Kenzer (eds) *Culture, Land, and*

Legacy: Perspectives on Carl O. Sauer and Berkeley School Geography. Geoscience and manv. 37. Geoscience Publications, Dept. of Geography and Anthropology, Louisiana State University, Baton Rouge, pp. 233–260.

Platt, R.S. (1935) Field Approach to Regions. *Annals of the Association of American Geographers* 25, 153–174.

Reed, I. and J. Alexander (2009) Social science as reading and performance: a cultural-sociological understanding of epistemology. *European Journal of Social Theory* 12, 21–41.

Relph, E. (1970) An inquiry into the relations between phenomenology and geography. *The Canadian Geographer* 14, 193–201.

Renner, G.T. (1935) The statistical approach to regions. *Annals of the Association of American Geographers* 25, 137–152.

Rosaldo, R. (1989) Imperialist nostalgia. *Representations* 26, 107–22.

Sack, R.D. (1974) Chorology and spatial analysis. *Annals of the Association of American Geographers* 65, 439–452.

Sauer, C.O. (1927) Recent developments in cultural geography. In E.C. Hayes (ed.) *Recent Developments in the Social Sciences*. J.B. Lippincott Company, Philadelphia, pp. 154–212.

Sauer, C.O. (1944) A geographic sketch of early man in America. *Geographical Review* 34, 529–573.

Sauer, C.O. (1963)[1925] The Morphology of Landscape. In J. Leighly (ed.), *Land and Life: A Selection from the Writings of Carl Ortwin Sauer*. University of California, Berkeley, pp. 315–350.

Sauer, C.O. (2009a) Letter to Landscape [on past and present American culture]. In W.M. Denevan and K. Mathewson (eds), *Carl Sauer on Culture and Landscape: Readings and Commentaries*. Louisiana State University Press, Baton Rouge, pp. 390–391.

Sauer, C.O. (2009b) Preface to The Geography of the Ozark Highland of Missouri. In W.M. Denevan and K. Mathewson (eds), *Carl Sauer on Culture and Landscape: Readings and Commentaries*. Louisiana State University Press, Baton Rouge, pp. 99–102.

Sauer, C.O. (1927) Recent developments in cultural geography. In E.C. Hayes (ed.), *Recent Developments in the Social Sciences*. J.B. Lippincott Company, Philadelphia, pp. 154–212.

Sauer, C.O. (2009c) Regional reality in economy. In W.M. Denevan and K. Mathewson (eds), *Carl Sauer on Culture and Landscape: Readings and Commentaries*. Louisiana State University Press, Baton Rouge, pp. 162–172.

Sluyter, A. (2005) Blaut's early natural/social theorization, cultural ecology, and political ecology. *Antipode* 37, 963–980.

Smith, B.H. (2010) *Natural Reflections: Human Cognition at the Nexus of Science and Religion*. Yale University Press, New Haven.

Smith, N. (1989) Geography as museum: private history and conservative idealism. In J.N. Entrikin and S.D. Brunn (eds), *The Nature of Geography*, Reflections on Richard Hartshorne's The Nature of Geography. Association of American Geographers, Washington D.C., pp. 91–120.

Speth, W.W. (1977) Carl Ortwin Sauer on destructive exploitation. *Biological Conservation* 11, 145–160.

Speth, W.W. (1999) *How it came to be: Carl O. Sauer, Franz Boas, and the Meanings of Anthropogeography*. Ephemera Press, Ellensburg.

Wagner, P.L. and Mikesell, M.W., (eds). *Readings in Cultural Geography*. University of Chicago Press, Chicago.

Whittlesey, D. (1929) Sequent occupance. *Annals of the Association of American Geographers* 19, 162–165.

Wylie, J. (2007) *Landscape*. Routledge, New York.

Further Reading

Landscape and region are the subjects of very large literatures in human geography. However, most of what has been written since the 1970s deals only in passing with how these terms were used and debated during the first half of the twentieth century. Hartshorne's The Nature of Geography (1939) and Perspective on the Nature of Geography (1959) are still the most comprehensive and penetrating discussions of the region in late-nineteenth and early twentieth-century geography. For more recent discussions of the philosophical and political issues surrounding regional geography in the early twentieth century, see Entrikin and Brunn (1989). For a broad selection of influential papers on the region written during the past three decades, see Entrikin (2008). The two most widely read histories of modern geographical thought, Martin's (2005) All Possible Worlds and Livingstone's (1992) The Geographical Tradition, both provide excellent overviews of the landscape/region debate. Two recent edited collections provide excellent introductions to the work of Carl Sauer: Denevan and Mathewson (2009) and Mathewson and Kenzer (2003). Wagner and Mikesell's (1962) edited collection is still the best introduction to the Berkeley School of cultural geography. In recent decades, classic texts on the landscape idea in human geography are Cosgrove (1998[1984]), Duncan (1990), and Meinig (1979). For a far-reaching history of the Landschaft idea and its relation to Anglophone landscape geography, see Olwig (2002). Wylie (2007) provides a succinct overview of landscape geography since the 1970s.

Chapter 8

Landscape Versus Region Part II

Kent Mathewson

Landscape and Region at Mid-Century

Preston E. James (1952) opened his presidential address to the Association of American Geographers in 1951, with the assertion: "The regional concept constitutes the core of geography." Yet the talk's title: "Toward a Further Understanding of the Regional Concept" bespeaks more of tentativeness than certitude, and less of confident consolidations than diffident extensions. James was by no means alone in whistling into the increasingly dim and turgid conceptual space that chorology had come to occupy. Across the Atlantic, Wooldridge and East's (1951) *The Spirit and Purpose of Geography* called on the authority of figures such as Hettner, Vidal, Sauer and Hartshorne in echoing James' conviction that regional study was the geographer's main métier. At the same time, Oxford geographer E.W. Gilbert (1951: 346) pitched a similar, if oddly phrased note: "The study of regionalism and the region has awakened geography from the deep slumber into which it had fallen. It is through the region that new life has been given to the dead bones of geography." His forensic remarks appeared in the chapter on "Geography and Regionalism" in *Geography in the 20th Century* edited by Griffith Taylor (1951). This was the first of two major "state of the art" volumes assessing anglophone geography at mid-century. It is unclear what antecedent condition Gilbert refers to; the reader is left to speculate. Perhaps it was the confident cause-and-effect determinisms of the previous generation? Or less plausibly, it might have been the landscape/*Landschaft* tradition that some anglophone figures fingered as a deviation, like German *Geopolitik*, but not quite as deviant in geography's development. Whatever had been superseded, within a very few years, a loud and growing chorus of spatial analytical geographers would decry chorology on similar grounds and call for a new scientific certitude based on locational analysis rather than the study and understanding of region and place.

The Wiley Blackwell Companion to Human Geography, First Edition.
Edited by John A. Agnew and James S. Duncan.
© 2011 John Wiley & Sons, Ltd. Published 2016 by John Wiley & Sons, Ltd.

It was left to Derwent Whittlesey, chorologist and senior geographer at Harvard, to contribute the lead chapter, "The Regional Concept and the Regional Method," in *American Geography: Inventory & Prospect* (James and Jones 1954), the second benchmark volume. While certainly not the last word on regional geography and its methodology, it stands out as one of those symbolic sentinels or minor monuments representing the *status quo ante* just before they are deflated or toppled in the wake of sudden historical change. It was something of a swan song for both Whittlesey (he died two years later from heart failure) and chorology as then conceptualized and practiced. The poignancy of the piece is magnified by Whittlesey's unwitting and unwilling role in the dismantling of Harvard's geography program a few years before, in part because of chorology's alleged lack of scientific rigor. Chemist and Harvard president James B. Conant held Whittlesey's small program, together with academic geography's larger claims to disciplinary coherence and value, to be suspect if not fraudulent (Smith 1987). The ax fell at Harvard in 1948. Institutionally, it was a turning point in the fortunes of academic geography at elite US private universities and a few public ones – the opening discord in a decades-long recessional. Disciplinarily, it was one of many signs that regional geography and regionalism had entered a new phase that elicited strong critique, but generated weak rebuttals. More generally, the late 1940s and early 1950s saw one of the most profound and abrupt cultural shifts in modern history. Regionalism and allied realist/synthesis-seeking sentiments were challenged and largely displaced by an abstract, analytical international style and sensibility. Academic geography during this period offers a microcosm of these manifestations.

Curiously, landscape-as-concept, the often entangled and sometimes estranged twin of the regional method and construct, was little in evidence during the contentious transition from chorology to its immediate successors (primarily locational analysis). Landscape as a geographical concept and research perspective appears to have its origins in Alexander von Humboldt's complex embrace of both Enlightenment science and Romantic aesthetic concerns (Minca 2007). Although perhaps not as precipitous as the post-WWII cultural shift from regionalism to abstract internationalism, the Enlightenment/Romantic reversal invites comparison with this latter shift. Both pairs share parallels, especially epistemological. The nature of these similarities is examined in more detail in the genealogical treatment of landscape and region as concepts and constructs in geographic history. Conventionally, the regional concept is thought to have much deeper roots in geography's formal history than the relative newcomer, landscape. As it turns out, however, landscape has an informal history of considerable depth and import that has only recently been uncovered (see Olwig 1996; 2002). Whereas region as a "concrete object" of study or more broadly as a chorologic construct has been a staple of geographical art and science since Classical Antiquity, landscape's appearances have been both more recent, and more elusive of definition and elaboration. Viewed over the past two millennia or so: one, a fixture, the other often only an ephemeral presence and even more an absence. But viewed over the past two centuries, they have formed something of a dyad, sometimes in contention, at other times complementary, and most recently enjoying somewhat separate rejuvenations.

If the early 1950s marked regional geography's maturity, though some might say senescence, it also saw the emergence of a new development in landscape studies.

In 1951, the same year as Preston James' regional address, John Brinckerhoff "J.B." Jackson launched the inimitable journal *Landscape* from his ranch in Cline's Corners, New Mexico. It was a flare that soon attracted followers. Jackson wrote many of the early articles under a suite of pseudonyms. In 1956 Jackson was introduced to Carl Sauer and his encampment of Berkeley cultural-historical geographers, both students and colleagues. From there mutual appreciation diffused throughout the Berkeley network and well beyond. As biographer Helen Horowitz (1997: xxvii) suggests, meeting Sauer led to a wider circle of contributors including Lewis Mumford, Jean Gottmann, Kevin Lynch, Paul Sheppard and others who made their own original contributions to both landscape and regional studies. Jackson's initial inspiration had been a series of monographs on human geography authored by French geographers, read in France after serving in WWII. He had also been exposed to French human geography in undergraduate courses with Whittlesey at Harvard in the 1930s. Although the dominant French form at the time was the regional monograph, Jackson favored the studies focused on human use of the land. Landscape rather than region became his lodestar. For the next four decades *Landscape* served as quasi-underground enterprise, but one with top talent and a clear, if implicit, critique of mainstream geographic currents. Jackson (1984) can also be credited with pioneering a distinctive approach to landscape studies. By championing the quotidian dimensions of place and landscape, he opened up an inexhaustible field of exploration and interpretation of the everyday or ordinary landscape experience (Meinig 1979; Wilson and Groth 2003). This trajectory has continued to the present, and represents one of the most legible and readable approaches to landscape studies in geography and related fields.

Mid-century American academic geography then, harbored a chorologic or regional approach that had largely run its most recent course. Landscape was making one of its periodic (re)appearances, joining the ongoing and equally distinctive approach tended by Sauer at Berkeley, which in turn, he had partially fashioned from late 19th and early 20th century German and French sources. Although disciplinary geography may have been closer to the margins than the center of American academia, and Sauer's landscape school in academic geography's left field (far West on the map), with Jackson's creations on or beyond the periphery, region-as-concept and regionalism as a movement, had been forcefully and effectively challenged and displaced in the larger societal and cultural arena. This history, and its impacts on geography, has not been fully written. World War II and its aftermath brought change of a magnitude similar to that experienced by the eclipse of the Enlightenment and the rise of Romanticism after the Napoleonic Wars, only with the epistemological poles reversed. The roll call of regionalist percepts and perspectives abandoned in different fields after WWII is remarkable in its conformity and finality. Equally impressive is the sudden ascendance of opposite tastes and tendencies. Barnes and Farish (2006) have ably excavated and elucidated the impact of WWII and the Cold War on American chorology. Drawing on historians of science Andy Pickering's (1995) "World War II regime" and Donna Haraway's (1997) "millenarian technoscience" depictions of WWII as producing an epochal rupture in the nature of scientific organization and formation, they contextualize the history of the transition from chorology to spatial analysis and regional science in American geography. Yet Geography hardly had a monopoly on regionalism in academic disciplines. As the collection of essays *Regionalism in America* (yet another artifact from 1951) attests, the regional concept and method had widespread currency in the social sciences as well as the humanities (Jensen 1951; Odum and Moore 1938). Though its main precincts aside from geography were in anthropology, history, literature, political science, and sociology, examples could be found elsewhere, including linguistics, economics, ecology, and soil science to name a few. Following Barnes and Farrish's lead, the larger history of WWII's impact not only on academia, but also on global-scale cultural production, awaits elaboration.

Regionalism Writ Large

Outside of academia the transfer from realist/regional to abstract/international aesthetics could literally be seen taking place in the landscape. Although this shift was a global phenomenon, and examples abound in many cultural and national contexts, it was in the US that the examples are perhaps most striking and the changes most abrupt. The various schools of realist-regional painting (most often depicting rural landscapes or public murals with populist content), were rendered obsolete almost overnight by the abstract expressionists. The heartland canvases of Thomas Hart Benton, John Steuart Curry, and Grant Wood became instant icons in the 1930s – isomorphic to the mood and manner of a nation focused by material crisis, on the here and the now. But they became passé just as quickly with the Depression and regional chic in recession. In contradistinction, the painters of abstract art and their partisans were concentrated in New York City, not only the hub of the dominant US Northeast region, but also the new international capital of art, business, and the rapidly consolidating American empire. Jackson Pollock, Mark Rothko, Willem de Kooning and scores of lesser-known artists with their startling abstractions burst onto the national and international scene. Photography also followed form here. The Depression Era photographers Walker Evans, Dorothea Lange, and Ben Shahn were among the most graphic and effective transmitters of the realist/regionalist aesthetic. Avant garde practices in photography resurfaced in the post-WWII period. With architecture the shift was even more dramatic. The regional style of Frank Lloyd Wright and other practitioners of telluric and localist themes were overshadowed by the modernist international style, in part diffused from Europe, in part celebratory of the newly won American hegemony. This was post-WWII American triumphalism expressed in a corporate-sponsored glass and steel verticality and aggressively taking and remaking urban central business district's (CBD's).

Aural space was also soundly punctuated in the late 1940s. Large ensemble jazz bands of the Dixieland and Big Band traditions playing generally melodic, arranged, and danceable music dissolved, and were replaced by smaller combos devoted to Bebop (East Coast and Mid-West) and Cool Jazz (West Coast) stressing speed, improvisation, asymmetrical phrasing, and individual virtuosity. Instead of being America's dominant popular music as swing jazz had become by the 1940s, in the 1950s jazz became its cerebral, abstract, and urban sequestered opposite. A parallel development occurred with modern classical or art music. The major composers of the 1930s and 1940s such as Charles Ives, Aaron Copland, and Vigil Thomson all celebrated American places and landscapes in their works. They might be considered "modernist regionalists" in that they were innovative and cosmopolitan, but did not pursue avant garde and experimentalist forms in the manner of their younger contemporary John Cage or his early atonal mentor Arnold Schonberg. By the 1960s Cage's music came to symbolize in retrospect the rupture that had occurred between realism and abstraction in the arts a decade or so before.

In the literary arts, especially fiction and drama, realist/regionalist themes and techniques helped set the standards in the 1930s and '40s. As a genre, regionalism, especially in its "local color" variant had been a vibrant part of American literary production since the Civil War, but during the 1930s its realist tendencies were turned to social issues and causes. John Steinbeck's *The Grapes of Wrath* (1939) is perhaps the most enduring example. Much of the literary production during the 1930s had an explicit regionalist bent. The South might claim the most obvious adherents along with some latitude in perspectives – from the antimodernist Vanderbilt Agrarians to Zora Neal Hurston's ethnographically grounded fiction focused on the African-American experience (both "conservative" in differing ways) to the progressive populist prose of many minor, and some major authors. The nation's other regions each had a number of expositors of land and life in their own precincts, many sponsored by the New Deal W.P.A. (Works Project Administration). By the 1950s a less realist/regionalist and a more abstract, cosmopolitan and urban-oriented aesthetic was being experimented with and practiced in both fiction and poetry.

Central Sites

Not surprisingly, the larger economic and political currents that moved and molded cultural production at global, national, and regional levels, also spawned stunning change in geographical theory and practice, at least initially at select sites, with subsequent if uneven diffusions globally over the next several decades. Although one can find prefiguring of the future shapes of things to come in disparate pronouncements or publications from the 1940s or earlier, geography's spatial analytical moment or what has been called its "quantitative revolution," was launched from several US university sites beginning in the 1950s (Barnes 2004). The key site and perhaps date – 1951 yet again – was William Garrison's arrival at the University of Washington. Garrison was to become the "godfather" of the new movement, though not without aid from other like-minded faculty at Washington and a few other campuses. By 1957 he had attracted a squadron of graduate students who became the vanguard the "revolution," and they in turn moved out to graduate geography departments, mostly in the US Midwest. Their principle adversaries and targets were the "descriptive" chorologists and area specialists that may have served marginal utility in the war effort, or fit well with the regionalist climate of the '30s, but confronted a rapidly modernizing, and (sub) urbanizing America with much less to offer or to command. The spatial analysts' principle allies (outside geography) were apt to be statisticians, economists, and other quantitatively-minded social scientists. Unlike Carl Sauer and the Berkeley school adherents who had long since moved beyond simple chorology, seeking their extra-disciplinary inspiration from, and fellowship with, anthropologists, historians, botanists, and other practitioners of landscape studies, the spatial analysts sought "spatial laws" and a new scientific respectability for their discipline.

Perhaps the gulf between landscape studies and spatial science was too broad to permit much engagement, even of an adversarial sort. Or, it might have been a question of numbers. Geographers with a landscape orientation were in the minority. Sauer and his cultural-historical followers comprised the largest and most cohesive group in North America. German geographers such as Carl Troll, emerging from the rigidities of Nazi orthodoxy and wartime chaos, helped to revitalize and redirect one wing of landscape studies toward bio-physical groundings in ecology and geology (Tilley 1984). Elsewhere at this time, landscape as concept or method was not much in the mix, though British historical geographer Clifford Darby and his associates did put landscape change at the center of their concerns (Williams 1989), and the "Celtic fringe" figures Herbert J. Fleure and E. Estyn Evans studied elements of cultural landscapes in ways that were parallel to Sauer's and his students such as Fred B. Kniffen (Graham 1994). French geographers' artful depiction of *pays* could be seen as a genre of landscape study, but chorologic concerns were usually in the foreground (Buttimer 1971). Moreover, in the post-WWII period French geography was moving toward a more state-centric outlook with regional planning and urban questions at the fore. Like the Germans, the Russian geographers had long-standing a tradition of landscape studies, but under Stalinist constraints and the ascendancy of economic geography at the expense of other less "practical" sub-fields, landscape study was muted. The situation with regional geography was quite different. Most if not all geography departments in all countries and colonies had one or more regional specialists. Although most of the chorologists also had topical or "systematic" proficiencies along side of their regional expertise, their professional identities were often tied most closely to their regional callings. The spatial analysts on the other hand, were primarily men (very few of the few women geographers were attracted to spatial science in the early stages) without strong regional associations. The point, of course, of spatial science was that it sought "placeless" and universal laws of spatial behavior, thus the idiographic particularities of places and regions were to be eschewed and had little or no place in the coming reformation of geography.

As with most upheavals, whether physical or societal, preliminary indicators are evident, but often read as such only after the fact. By 1950 regionalism in geography was not without critics, but published critiques were sparse. Edward Ackerman's 1945 article in the *Annals of the Association of American Geographers* on the role of geography and geographers in the war effort stood out for both its pointed criticism and broad prescriptions. He (Ackerman 1945: 122) felt that geography's wartime area specialists demonstrated an "inability to handle foreign language sources, and a lack of competence in topical or systematic subjects." As a corrective, he called for more research and training in the systematic fields. He also castigated geographers for maintaining a "dualistic" division between chorology and the systematic sub-fields. While generally deferring to the authority of Richard Hartshorne's (1939) *Nature of Geography*, and acknowledging a continued place for regional geography, he clearly felt the future lay in developing geography's systematic pursuits. If Ackermann, a junior recruit to Whittlesey's Harvard group, no doubt felt somewhat constrained in his critique, George H.T. Kimble (1951) on the other side of the Atlantic felt less inhibited. In 1951 he authored "The Inadequacy of the Regional Concept." In what was intended as a broadside on British regionalists, presumably to sink the regional concept, was less than a total critique. His main complaint was that no one individual could ever perform regional syntheses adequately, thus teams of topical specialists should be deployed, echoing aspects of Ackerman's way forward. Up to this point, contention over regional geography's efficacy had involved mostly methodological issues.

Spatial Science in Command

In 1952, German émigré economist turned geographer, Fred K. Schaefer (1953) authored a polemical critique of Richard Hartshorne's *The Nature of Geography* specifically, and the regional approach in general. Entitled "Exceptionalism in Geography: A Methodological Examination," it was published in the *Annals of the Association of American Geographers* at the end of 1953. Members of the *Annals* editorial board had reservations about the tenor of article and Schaefer's failure to substantiate many of his allegations, especially characterizing Hartshorne's work as strictly derivative of Hettner's, who in turn was depicted as following Kant's putative relegation of geography to idiographic studies and mere description (Martin 1989). Schaefer used the term "exceptionalism" to characterize Kant's view that geography, like history, dealt with particular or unique cases, and did not seek generic principles or general laws as did the natural or physical sciences. In Schaefer's view, Hartshorne's methodological focus on areal differentiation was utterly idiographic, and not amenable to nomothetic, or law-seeking methods. Somewhat ironically, Schaefer himself prescribed an exceptionalist, if nomothetic, course for geography in arguing that the laws it sought were morphological, and that geography was not capable of deriving principles or laws on a par with the mature sciences. Compounding the irony, Schaefer died in June, 1953 while the paper was still in review. *Annals* editor Henry Kendall decided to publish it despite the board's reservations, and invited Gustav Bergmann, Schaefer's University of Iowa friend and colleague, and former Vienna Circle logical positivist to oversee the submission. It appeared in the September 1953 number of the *Annals*, and drew strenuous response from Hartshorne. He requested space to rebut Schaefer's overall critique and to correct both errors of commission and omission line by line. This was granted. Hartshorne (1954) first published a brief comment on Schaefer's article informing readers that a comprehensive critique would follow. This he (Hartshorne 1955) published the following year, and followed this up with a broader article (1958) on the "Concept of Geography as a Science of Space, from Kant and Humboldt to Hettner." The next year, Hartshorne (1959) published a monograph *Perspective on the Nature of Geography* in which he responded not only to issues that the Schaefer affair had raised, but also ones that Sauer and others had raised during the two decades since the publication of *The Nature*. He devoted a chapter each to ten key questions or topics. The first set dealt with the persistent questions of areal differentiation or chorology as geography's core concern, the second with the question of the human versus natural factors in geographic research. The third considered geography's relation to time, or the temporal dimension. The fourth topic was the regional/systematic split. The fifth topic was geography's nomothetic versus idiographic debate, and the final question was: What was geography's place in the classification of the sciences? Although Hartshorne had adjusted his views somewhat in the intervening two decades, most notably in regard to the genetic or historical perspective and dimension in geographic studies, he still maintained that geography's fortunes were tied to regional studies with allowances for methodological advances in step with the discipline as whole.

In the six years since Schaefer's polemic and Hartshorne's programmatic (re)appraisal of geography's nature, change on the level of a paradigmatic shift was underway, or so it seemed to the main actors. Over the following decade, partisans of geography's spatial or quantitative revolution would move from their originating hearth in Seattle to a number of departments, particularly in the Midwest. By the end of the 1960s Iowa, Northwestern, Ohio State, and Chicago had all become secondary centers of innovation and diffusion, though each had established preconditions by the 1950s that allowed rapid adoption of new ideas and techniques that anticipated the Seattle coalescence. In addition, many of the top geography graduate programs had hired one or more theorists and practitioners of the new wave. Minnesota, Wisconsin, Michigan, and Penn State among others, all made room, though not without contention, for expansion in the new directions. Regional studies were not bypassed entirely, but the new emphasis was clearly on groundings in systematic approaches directed by theoretical concerns. Collectively, the spatial analysts' work was characterized by: 1) scientific methodology, 2) theory building 3) systematic skill sets, 4) multidisciplinarity, 5) applied orientation. For the most part, and clearly in combination, these five markers set the spatial science far apart from both traditional chorology and the landscape tradition. Applied regional geography, as mentioned previously, had not met the test in WWII, and seemed even less applicable in a post-WWII de-colonizing world. The landscape tradition maintained a healthy cross-disciplinary bent, but its main strain – the Sauerian Berkeley School – crossed boundaries with diachronic/synthetic rather than synchronic/analytic goals in mind.

Although Schaefer did not live to see his charges answered, or the changes his critique called for, with time it was seen as something of a manifesto for the spatial analytical movement. William Bunge, one of "Garrison's Raiders" as he dubbed them, was the most energetic in apotheosizing Schaefer and his ideas. Bunge's Washington dissertation was published in 1962 in Lund, Sweden as *Theoretical Geography*. He extended Schaefer's critique of Hartshorne, and defined geography as the science of spatial relations, with geometry as its logical language. Bunge went on to a checkered career in academia through the 1960s before withdrawing to pursue personal campaigns against racism, imperialism, and capitalism. These efforts, plus publications in both scholarly outlets and through his own agency, established him as one of the prime instigators of a radical emergence within geography following the 1960s. Although his mid-century critiques of establishment geography did not focus on either chorology or landscape studies as such, one might credit him in oblique ways with helping to clear the way for critical approaches to both regional and landscape studies by century's end. In less oblique ways he kept aspects of the Schaefer-Hartshorne affair alive, long after it had simply become an episode in geographic history, by maintaining that Schaefer's fatal heart attack had been brought on by McCarthyite repression. Schaefer had been a socialist in Germany and Bunge maintained that OSS-CIA (Office of Strategic Services – Central Intelligence Agency), elements within the geographic establishment, principally Hartshorne, were implicated in the harassment. While proof is lacking to support these allegations, Neil Smith (1989), on the other hand, has charged Hartshorne with a less elusive, but no less lethal crime, and provided plausible evidence. It is an interpretation that takes us to the heart of the region versus landscape rivalry.

Hartshorne and "The Assassination of Landscape"

Fifty years after the publication of *The Nature of Geography*, the Association of American Geographers published a collection of papers aimed at putting Hartshorne's opus and its place in geography in historical perspective (Entrikin and Brunn 1989). The essays also provide insightful commentary on region and landscape as concepts, along with some of the debates they generated. Smith's (1989) essay stands out for its critical vigor and acumen, and crediting Hartshorne with a major role in keeping landscape at bay – both as a concept and as a central organizing principle – in anglophone geography. In the section titled "The Assassination of Landscape" Smith argues that:

> If his discussion of regions [in *The Nature*] is an effort to construct a useable category, Hartshorne's approach to landscape is wholly destructive. The argument was sufficiently successful in convincing succeeding generations of English language geographers that the notion of landscape has 'little or no value as a technical scientific term' (p. 158), that as a result this 'single most important word in geographic language' (p. 149) has been largely excluded from serious theoretical discourse almost to the present day. (Smith 1989: 107)

In the two decades since Smith wrote this, there has been an energetic discovery and recovery of the landscape category, but he is accurate in depicting the previous five decades as ones of relative quiescence. The degree, to which Hartshorne's disapproval actually served to sublate, or at least sidetrack landscape, is a topic that deserves further exhumation. Smith (1989: 107) suggests a number of reasons for this antagonism: first, landscape, and especially its German cognate *Landschaft*, is "inherently confusing." Its two primary meanings are: the general aspect or appearance of land, and as distinct area. On these grounds alone, Hartshorne felt it a poor candidate for geography's core concept. Second, in its meaning as a distinct area, it competed with the term region, a well established concept in geography. Third, landscape being concerned only with land surface, literally would be a "superficial" scientific or scholarly pursuit. Fourth, Hartshorne objected to Sauer's (and prior German geographers') emphasis on material features and morphology. Fifth, he contended that "the natural landscape" (central to Sauer's method) was a faulty theoretical concept and a fictitious entity in reality. Sixth, Hartshorne's Kantian idealism demanded categorical separation of space and time, of geography and history. All but the most sterile exercises in landscape studies opened the door to commingling categories – space and society, time and culture, land and life, violating the norms of Hartshorne's ahistorical chorology. Finally, he most likely was wary of the turn that *Landschaftskunde* had taken under the direction of the Nazis. *The Nature* was largely written in Vienna during 1938–1939, immediately after the *Anschluss*. In sum, Hartshorne saw no future in landscape as a method or central concept for geography, and in his view, its past represented one of the main "deviations" from the discipline's correct trajectory. Instead, Hartshorne argued that chorology held a privileged place in geography's historical development, and that it offered the best prospects for its future.

Origins of the Landscape Perspective

Thus far the focus has been on the decades immediately following WWII, but Hartshorne's *The Nature* and the issues that precipitated it belong to the years just before. The quarrel between region and landscape was not so much an antinomy between concepts and principles as an antagonism among principals. Juxtaposed to Hartshorne and chorology were Carl Sauer and landscape. Although Hartshorne had begun to take issue with landscape studies in the early 1930s after returning from political geographic field work in Germany, largely because they stressed observable materiality's (Penn and Lukermann 1989: 60), his magnum opus was set in motion by a pair of papers by John Leighly (1937, 1938) on methodology. Leighly was Sauer's erstwhile student and close associate at Berkeley. In the first paper, he argued that there could not be a scientific chorology, only artistic endeavors aimed at regional description. In the second he traced developments in 19th century German geography, particularly regionalism's roots in Ritter's chorology. The papers unsettled Hartshorne and he made his objections known. Derwent Whittlesey, editor of the *Annals of the AAG*, invited him to respond in print. What began as a brief grew into 600 page manuscript over the course of a year. The AAG published it in two numbers of the *Annals*, and then as a monograph. The main thrust was to defend and legitimize regional geography and the logic and methods of areal differentiation, but the delegitimization of landscape studies was an important secondary objective.

Since publishing his "Morphology of landscape" in 1925, Carl Sauer was considered the leading anglophone advocate of landscape studies, and his Berkeley school confreres the main practitioners. In turn, Sauer's initial inspiration for his cultural landscape approach came from Continental geography, particularly Vidal de la Blache's *paysage* and Otto Schlüter's *Kulturlandschaft*. Over time, Sauer and his Berkeley students crafted a distinctive style of landscape studies. Emphasis was often on the morphology of landscape as expressed in visible material attributes, but the processes of landscape modification were also the quarry. Accordingly, plant and animal origins and dispersals, aboriginal depopulation, primitive and traditional agriculture, cultural diffusions, and colonial destructive exploitation were all pursued. As Sauer's interests moved farther from modernity, both spatially and temporally, the historical dimension of his studies deepened. In 1940 he delivered his presidential address "Foreword to Historical Geography," to the AAG annual meeting in Baton Rouge (Sauer 1941). The Louisiana State University Department of Geography and Anthropology was becoming "Berkeley South" under the lead of Sauerites Richard Russell and Fred Kniffen, and a propitious place and time to answer Hartshorne (Livingstone 1992: 260–262; Mathewson and Shoemaker 2004). Sauer took swipes at Hartshorne's dictates, but refused to engage in protracted debate or "dialectics." He called out Hartshorne for demoting physical geography to a chorographic backdrop, and exiling historical geography to "the outer fringes of the subject." He added that the two decades leading up to "Hartshorne's recent résumé" might be remembered as the "Great Retreat," and only when disciplinary boundary tending abated would there be recovery from "the pernicious anemia of the 'but-is-it-geography?' state" (Sauer 1941: 2, 4).

The Sauer-Hartshorne non-debate probably brings the tendencies and tensions of region-versus-landscape framing into clearest relief. But it doesn't shed much historical light on the basic proposition. As it turns out, a generation earlier Hettner and Schlüter enacted a similar choreography (Livingstone 1992: 264) but with charges of exclusion reversed. Hettner attacked Schlüter for allegedly restricting the phenomena of landscape study to the material and visible, but the real tension came from Hettner's perception that *Landschaftskunde* posed a threat to chorology's assumed dominance. As Livingstone (1992: 265) points out, this was more an "intramural fracas between devotees of the regional model" than a fundamental epistemological divide. As with much in traditional cultural geography, Friedrich Ratzel (1898) has been credited with originating the term *Kulturlandschaft,* but a decade earlier Joseph Wimmer (1885) had used it extensively in his *Historische Landschaftkunde*. Even earlier Carl Ritter (1822–1859) used the term in in *Die Erdkunde* in its variant spelling "*Culturlandschaft*." Suffice it to say, that by the late 19th Century, German geographers had begun to see landscape studies as an alternative to von Richtofen's (1883) call for chorography (areal inventory) and chorology (areal synthesis) to be the new organizing framework for descriptive or Special Geography, the counterpart of General Geography and its systematic, analytic pursuit of generalization. It was left to others, principally Otto Schülter (1906) in Germany, and Sauer (1925) in North America, to elaborate the concept of cultural landscape and inspire others to pursue these kinds of studies.

Disentangling, or at least tracing, the roots of region-landscape dualism prior to the advent of modern disciplinary geography (starting in Germany post 1870) requires a less lineal descent. Space here does not allow even a partial excavation, but the next node down, and perhaps the most foundational, is intellectual terrain created and occupied by the twin progenitors of modern geography – Carl Ritter and Alexander von Humboldt. Ritter has routinely been seen as a major way-station (first half of the 19th Century) in chorology's passage from Classical Antiquity to the late Renaissance codification of geography into Special (regional/descriptive) and General (global/systematic) divisions, and so on to modern times. He did serve as a stationmaster, directing geography's main branch along regional lines, but also pointed it to other destinations – some dead-end such as teleology. Humboldt on the other hand, was "all over the place." A polymath and genius, he founded and cultivated so many topics and even fields, that it is obtuse to assign primacy to any single accomplishment. Although he appreciated both the enjoyment and utility of regional research and writing, it is his physical systematic work that is best remembered. His watchwords were "unity in diversity" and his mission was the discovery and uncovering of the processes and relationships that constituted these unities in nature. Humboldt is often cited as commending landscape painting as a mode for apprehending nature's physiognomy and morphology (Bunksé 1981). But his appreciation of landscape study extended well beyond aesthetic considerations. As

Godlewska (1999: 248–249) has pointed out, Humboldt's "favorite scale of analysis" was at the landscape level. To borrow Olwig's (1996) term, Humboldt's conception of landscape and its application to geographic study was a "substantive" one, not just a pictoral/perspective usage, or alternatively an areal/territorial category. Similar to Sauer's conception of landscape, the Humboldtian landscape was morphological, a construct grounded in human areal experience. And as with Sauer, the dualisms of cosmologic/nomothetic versus the chorologic/idiographic (or as Penn and Lukermann (2003) term them, the "Galilean" and "Goethian") are largely resolved, if not dissolved, in the morphological approach to landscape studies. Minca (2007) partially agrees, but following Farinelli (2003) sees Humboldt's resolution as a critical political/ epistemological "compromise" or transitional moment between Feudal/aristocratic and fully Modern/bourgeoise control (after 1848) of the landscape concept.

Prospecting and Projecting

One might take the excavations of the region and landscape concepts, with their various discordances, beyond Humboldt and Ritter's articulations. But within the narrow canonical bounds that historians of geography have generally performed, landscape's genealogy would become hardly traceable, whereas region's lineaments would enjoy a clear trail, if in places disjunctive, back to the chorographers and chorologists of Classical Antiquity. This project awaits future historians of geography, working with more contextual license and critical imagination than has been the convention to date. With regard to landscape, the deepest findings so far have been made by Kenneth Olwig (1996, 2002, 2009), working in a northern European context. Following philological leads, he has shown that the cognates of landscape/*Landschaft* in the older Germanic languages derive from an original term meaning a local polity and the customary laws that constitute it. Over time the meaning shifted from commonplaces to scenic spaces and on to its modern meanings, both ordinary and academic (Olwig 2002: 214). Prior plotting by Denis Cosgrove (1984, 1985) had fixed landscape's origins in "ways of seeing," most notably among Italian Renaissance elites' patronage of new forms of perspective painting, particularly normative landscapes. Cosgrove's leads led to a range of studies on landscape "as text" and its representational significance (Cosgrove and Daniels 1988; Barnes and Duncan 1992; Duncan and Ley 1993). This body of work did vanguard duty in the emergence of the "new cultural geography" and was a key pivot point in geography's "cultural turn." The landscape concept continues to offer a stage on which new perspectives can be charted and performed. Don Mitchell (1996, 2003) has called for radical rematerialization of the concept through a focus (using Marxist lenses) on the human labor that produces landscape, and in turn the work (ideological) that landscape does. Another direction that the call for rematerialization has taken, is toward phenomenological foci, especially on the materiality and performativity of "embodied practices." Non-representational theory developed by Nigel Thrift (1996) and others is often cited as a major influence on this approach. By comparison, over the past few decades chorology's revitalizations or reinterpretations have not been as notable in their theoretical or conceptual ambitions. Regional geography has enjoyed a common-sense appeal and rejuvenation of sorts with the advent of globalization's globalizing forces (Hönninghausen *et al.* 2005). And openings have been suggested for a critical chorology (Pudup 1988), but the regional concept remains as it has for much of geography's history, familiar grounds and a common location for both contestation and accommodation. Landscape, on the other hand, both in its ghostly traces and material appearances, is likely continue to provide one of geography's most complex and compelling arenas of theory and practice.

References

Ackerman, E.A. (1945) Geographic training, wartime research, and immediate professional objectives. *Annals of the Association of American Geographers* 35 (4), 121–143.

Agnew, J. (1989) Sameness and difference: Hartshorne's The Nature of Geography and geography as areal differentiation. In J.N. Entrikin and S.D. Brunn (eds) *Reflections on Richard Hartshorne's; The Nature of Geography*. Association of American Geographers, Washington, DC, pp. 121–140.

Barnes, T. and Farrish, M. (2006). Between Regions: Science, Militarism, and American Geography from World War to Cold War. *Annals of the Association of American Geographers* 96 (4), 807–826.

Barnes, T.J. (2004) Placing ideas: genius loci, heterotopia and geography's quantitative revolution. *Progress in Human Geography* 28 (5), 565–595.

Barnes, T.J. and Duncan, J.S. (eds) (1992) *Writing Worlds*. Routledge, London.

Bender, B. (1994) The politics of vision and the archaeologies of landscape. *Landscape: Politics and Perspectives*. Routledge, London.

Billinge, M., Gregory, D., and Martin, R. (eds) (1984) *Recollections of a Revolution: Geography as Spatial Science*. Macmillan Press, London.

Bowen, M. (1981) *Empiricism and Geographical Thought: From Francis Bacon to Alexander von Humboldt*. Cambridge University Press, Cambridge.

Bunge, William. (1962) *Theoretical Geography*. Lund Studies in Geography, Series C1. C.W.K. Gleerup, Lund.

Bunksé, E.V. (1981) Humboldt and an aesthetic tradition in geography. *Geographical Review* 71 (2), 127–146.

Buttimer, A. (1971) *Society and Milieu in the French Geographical Tradition*. Rand McNally, Chicago.

Claval, P. (1998) *An Introduction to Regional Geography*. Blackwell, Oxford.

Cosgrove, D. (1984) *Social Formation and Symbolic Landscape*. Croom Helm, London.

Cosgrove, D. (1985) Prospect, perspective, and the evolution of the landscape idea. *Transactions of the British Institute of Geographers*. NS 10 (1), 45–62.

Cosgrove, D. and Daniels, S. (eds) (1988) *The Iconography of Landscape*. Cambridge University Press, Cambridge.

Daniels, S. (1987) Marxism, culture and the duplicity of landscape. In R. Peet and N. Thrift (eds), *New Models in Geography*, Vol. 2. Unwin Hyman, London.

Denevan, W.M. and Mathewson, K. (eds) (2009) *Carl Sauer on Culture and Landscape: Readings and Commentaries*. Louisiana State University Press, Baton Rouge, Louisiana.

Dickinson, R.E. (1976) *Regional Concept: The Anglo-American Leaders*. Routledge, Kegan, Paul, London.

Duncan, J. and Ley, D. (eds) (1993) *Place/Culture/Representation*. Routledge, London.

Duncan, J.S. (1990) *The City as Text: The Politics of Landscape Interpretation in the Kandyan Kingdom*. Cambridge University Press, Cambridge.

Entrikin, J.N. (1991) *The Betweenness of Place: Towards a Geography of Modernity*. Johns Hopkins University Press, Baltimore.

Entrikin, J.N. and Brunns, S.D. (eds) (1989) *Reflections on Richard Hartshorne's*. The Nature of Geography. Association of American Geographers, Washington D.C.

Farinelli, F. (2003) *Geografia. Un'introduzione ai modelli del mondo*. Einaudii, Turin.

Gilbert, E.W. (1951) Geography and regionalism. In G. Taylor (ed.), *Geography in the 20th Century*. Methuen, London, pp. 345–371.

Godlewska, A.M.C. (1999) *Geography Unbound: French Geographic Science from Cassini to Humboldt*. University of Chicago Press, Chicago.

Graham, B.J. (1994) The search for common ground: Estyn Evan's Ireland. *Transactions of the Institute of British Geographers*. NS 19 (2), 183–201.

Harraway, D.J. (1997) *Modest_witness@second millenium. femaleman_ meets_ oncomouse: Feminism and technoscience*. Routledge, London.

Hart, J.F. (1982) The highest form of the geographer's art. *Annals of the Association of American Geographers* 72 (1), 1–19.

Hartshorne, R. (1939) *The Nature of Geography: A Critical Survey of Current Thought in the Light of the Past*. Association of American Geographers, Lancaster.

Hartshorne, R. (1954) Comment on Exceptionalism in geography. *Annals of the Association of American Geographers* 44 (1), 108–109.

Hartshorne, R. (1955) *Exceptionalism in geography* re-examined. *Annals of the Association of American Geographers* 45 (3), 205–244.

Hartshorne, R. (1958) The concept of geography as a science of space, from Kant and Humboldt to Hettner. *Annals of the Association of American Geographers* 48 (2), 97–108.

Hartshorne, R. (1959) *Perspective on the Nature of Geography*. Rand McNally, Chicago.

Head, L. (2004) Landscape and culture. In J.A. Matthews and D.T. Herbert (eds), *Unifying Geography: Common Heritage, Shared Future*. Routledge, London, pp. 240–255.

Hönnighausen, L., Frey, M., Peacock, J., and Steiner, N. (eds) (2005) *Regionalism in the Age of Globalism. Vol. 1 Concepts of Regionalism*. University of Wisconsin Press, Madison.

Horowitz, H.L. (1971) J.B. Jackson and the discovery of the American landscape. In Horowitz, H.L. (ed.) *Landscape in Sight: Looking at America/John Brinckerhoff Jackson*. Yale University Press, New Haven, pp. ix–xxxi.

Jackson, J.B. (1984). *Discovering the Vernacular Landscape*. Yale University Press, New Haven.

James, P.E. (1951) Toward a further understanding of the regional concept, *Annals of the Association of American Geographers* 41 (3), 195–222.

James, P.E. and Jones, C.F. (1954) *American Geography: Inventory & Prospect*. Syracuse University Press, Syracuse, New York.

Jensen, M. (ed.) (1951) *Regionalism in America*. University of Wisconsin Press, Madison.

Kimble, G.H.T. (1951) The inadequacy of the regional approach. In. L.D. Stamp and S.W. Woolridge (eds) *London Essays in Geography: Rodwell Jones Memorial Volume*. Longmans Green, London, pp. 151–174.

Leighly, J.B. (1937) Some comments on contemporary geographic method. *Annals of the Association of American Geographers* 27 (3), 125–141.

Leighly, J.B. (1938) Methodologic controversies in nineteenth-century German geography. *Annals of the Association of American Geographers* 28 (4), 238–258.

Livingstone, D. (1992) *The Geographical Tradition: Episodes in the History of a Contested Enterprise*. Blackwell, Oxford.

Martin, G.J. (1989) *The Nature of Geography and the Schaefer-Hartshorne debate*. In J.N. Entrikin and S.D. Brunn (eds), *Reflections on Richard Hartshorne's* The Nature of Geography. Association of American Geographers, Washington D.C, pp. 69–90.

Mathewson, K. and Shoemaker, V. (2004) Louisiana State University geography at seventy-five: "Berkeley on the Bayou" and beyond. In J.O. Wheeler and S.D. Brunn (eds), *The Role of the South in the Making of American Geography: Centennial of the AAG, 2004*. Bellwether, Columbia, pp. 245–267.

Meinig, D.W. (1979) *The Interpretation of Ordinary Landscapes*. Oxford University Press, Oxford.

Minca, C. (2007) Humboldt's compromise, or the forgotten geographies of landscape. *Progress in Human Geography* 31 (2), 179–193.

Mitchell, D. (1996). *The Lie of the Land: Migrant Workers, and the California Landscape*. University of Minnesota Press, Minneapolis.

Mitchell, D. (2003) Cultural landscapes: Just landscapes or landscapes of justice? *Progress in Human Geography* 27 (6), 787–796.

Mitchell, W.J.T. (1994) Introduction. In W.J.T. Mitchell (ed.), *Landscape and Power*. University of Chicago Press, Chicago, pp. 1–4.

Murphy, A.B. (1991) Regions as social constructs: The gap between theory and practice. *Progress in Human Geography* 15 (1), 22–35.

Norton, W. (1989) *Explorations in the Understanding of Landscape*. Greenwood Press, Westport, CT.

Odum, H.W. and Moore H.E. (1938) *American Regionalism: A Cultural-Historical Approach to National Integration*. Holt, New York.

Olwig, K.R. (1996) Recovering the substantive nature of landscape. *Annals of the Association of American Geographers* 86 (4), 630–653.

Olwig, K.R. (2002) *Landscape, Nature and the Body Politic: From Britain's Renaissance to America's*. University of Wisconsin Press, New World, Madison.

Olwig, K.R. (2009) Landscape, culture and regional studies: connecting the dots. In N. Castree et al. (eds) *A Companion to Environmental Geography*. Wiley-Blackwell, Chichester, pp. 239–252.

Penn, M. and Lukermann, F.(2003) Chorology and landscape: An internalist reading of "The Morphology of Landscape," In K. Mathewson and M.S. Kenzer (eds), *Culture, Land, and Legacy: Carl O. Sauer and the Berkeley School of Geography*. Geoscience Publications, Baton Rouge, pp. 233–259.

Pickering, A. (1995) Cyborg history and the World War II regime. *Perspectives in Science* 3 (1), 1–49.

Price, M. and Lewis, M. (1993) The reinvention of cultural geography. *Annals of the Association of American Geographers* 83 (1), 1–17.

Pudup, M.B. (1988) Arguments within regional geography. *Progress in Human Geography* 12 (3), 369–390.

Ritter, C. (1822–1859) *Die Erdkunde, im Verhältniss zur Natur und zur Geschichte des Menschen*, 19 vols. G. Reimer, Berlin.

Richthofen, F. von (1883). *Aufgaben und Methoden der heutigen Geographie*. Veit, Leipzig.

Sack, R.D. (1974) Chorology and Spatial Analysis. *Annals of the Association of American Geographers* 64 (3), 439–452.

Sauer, C.O. (1925) The morphology of landscape. *University of California Publications in Geography*, University of California Press, Berkeley, 2 (2), 19–54.

Sauer, C.O. (1941) Foreword to historical geography. *Annals of the Association of American Geographe* 31 (1), 1–24.

Schaefer, F.K. (1953) Exceptionalism in geography: A methodological examination. *Annals of the Association of American Geographers* 43 (3), 226–249.

Schein, R. (1997) The place of landscape: a conceptual framework for interpreting an American scene. *Annals of the Association of American Geographers* 87 (4), 660–680.

Schlüter, O. (1906) *Die Ziele der Geographie des Menschen*. R. Oldenburg, Munich.

Shaw, D.J.B. and Oldfield, J.D. (2007) Landscape science: A Russian geographical tradition. *Annals of the Association of American Geographers* 97 (1), 111–126.

Smith, N. (1987) Academic war over the field of geography: The elimination of geography at Harvard, 1947–1951. *Annals of the Association of American Geographers* 77 (2), 155–172.

Smith, N. (1989) Geography as museum: Private history and conservative idealism in The Nature of Geography, In J.N. Entrikin and S.D. Brunns (eds), *Reflections on Richard Hartshorne's*. The Nature of Geography. Association of American Geographers, Washington D.C., pp. 91–120.

Steinbeck, J. (1939) *The Grapes of Wrath*. Viking Press, New York.

Taylor, G. (1951) *Geography in the 20th Century*. Methuen, London.

Thrift, N. (1994) Taking Aim at the Heart of the Region. In D. Gregory, R. Martin and G. Smith (eds), *Human Geography: Society, Space and Social Science*, Macmillan, London, pp. 200–231.

Thrift, N. (1996) *Spatial Formations*. Sage, London.

Tilley, P.D. (1984) Carl Troll 1899-1975. *Geographers: Biobibliographical Studies*, Vol. 8. Mansell, London, pp. 111–124.

Whittlesey, D. (1954) The regional concept and the regional method, In P.E. James and C.F. Jones (eds), *American Geography: Inventory & Prospect*. Syracuse University Press, Syracuse, NY, pp. 21–68.

Williams, M. (1989) Historical geography and the concept of landscape. *Journal of Historical Geography* 15 (1), 92–104.

Wilson, C. and Groth, P. (eds) (2003) *Everyday America: Cultural Landscape Studies after J.B. Jackson*. University of California Press, Berkeley.

Wimmer, J. (1885) *Historische Landschaftskunde*. Verlag der Wagner'schen Univeritaet, Innsbruck.

Wooldridge, S.W. and East, W.G. (eds) (1951) *The Spirit and Purpose of Geography*. Hutchinson, London.

Wylie, J. (2007) *Landscape*. Routledge, London.

Chapter 9

From Region to Space
Part I

Trevor J. Barnes

> The region, it seems, is an idea that just won't go away.
>
> MacKinnon (2009: 229)

Introduction

In 1935, the American geographer Clarence Fielden Jones published a textbook, *Economic Geography*, based on a class he taught at Clark University, Worcester, Massachusetts. The volume was subsequently used "as the standard introductory text on the subject for thousands of college students" (Hudson 1993: 167). It begins:

> **The work of different regions.** Whether young men and women do the things they would like to do when they grow up depends on many things, but especially the kind of country that they live in and the number of neighbors nearby. Eskimos spend much of their time hunting and fishing to obtain food and clothing. Indians on the Amazon gather food from the forest and streams: they don't have to work as hard as the Eskimos. Not many people live in Eskimo land or in the Amazon forest: but their youths have to learn to do the things their parents did. (Jones 1935: 3)

In 1965, the British geographer Peter Haggett published a textbook, *Locational Analysis in Human Geography*, also based on a class that he taught, this one held at 9am Saturday morning given to third year students at Cambridge University. The first paragraph of his first substantive chapter, "Movement," begins:

> One of the difficulties we face in trying to analyse integrated regional systems is that there is no obvious or single point of entry. Indeed the more integrated the system, the harder it is to crack. Thus in the case of nodal regions, it is just as logical to

---

The Wiley Blackwell Companion to Human Geography, First Edition.
Edited by John A. Agnew and James S. Duncan.
© 2011 John Wiley & Sons, Ltd. Published 2016 by John Wiley & Sons, Ltd.

begin with the study of settlement as with the study of routes. As Isard comments: "the maze of interdependencies in reality is indeed formidable, its tale unending, its circularity unquestionable. Yet, its dissection is imperative. ... At some point we must cut into its circumference." We chose to make that cut with movement. (Haggett 1965: 31)

And in 1984, the British geographer Doreen Massey published *Spatial Divisions of Labor*. This book was not written as a textbook, but *de facto* became one, with economic geographers subsequently talking about the discipline as "before" *Spatial Divisions* and "after." Massey ends her book this way:

The geographical organisation of society is integral to its social reproduction and to politics in the widest sense. For decades now the battle over labourism, and to some extent trade union power itself, has been fought in and over particular regions. ... "Thinking geographically" is part of thinking about society more generally, and recognition and understanding of geographical variation is essential for any strategy of national political change. (Massey 1984: 305)

In each of these quotations, the word "region" appears, but the surrounding intellectual frame is vastly different. Region for Clarence Jones is defined as a geographically circumscribed container of natural conditions that makes life for the people who live there easier or harder. List those conditions in the appropriate classification scheme and you understand the "work of the region." The ante is upped in Peter Haggett's text where the region is now part of a larger system, but also an integrative problem to be solved. Analytical "dissection is imperative," revealing *the* logic of regional spaces. And for Doreen Massey the region is about politics. The regional question is inseparable from social reproduction, and for her sodden in political conflicts between labor and capital.

These intellectual differences about the region, of course, are conjoined with historical ones. Jones's paragraph is shaped in part by when he is writing in the early 1930s, a period when formal empires were still a going concern, when most people in the world lived in the countryside pre-occupied with resource production, and when, despite the beginning of time-space compression, places like the Amazon and "Eskimo land" appeared impossibly far-off and exotic to most Western readers (certainly for American Freshman undergraduates). When Haggett published his book thirty years later, the Anglo-American world was quite different. The Second World War, followed by the Cold War, fostered a scientific instrumentalism that was taken up by the state, and subsequently seeping into various academic disciplines including human geography. Consequently, the region was redefined, conceived by Haggett as explanatory, theoretical, and instrumental, a tool to achieve functional objectives like "integrated regional systems." Moreover, the state itself changed, becoming interventionist, rationally managing economic and social life, ensuring that people "never had it so good," as one of the British Prime Ministers of the time, Harold Macmillan, expressed it. But when Doreen Massey published *Spatial Divisions* in 1984 just shy of twenty years after Haggett's book, it seemed that many people had never had it so bad. State rational planning by the late 1970s was clearly failing. The economy was hemorrhaging jobs and investment as deindustrialization and industrial restructuring convulsed Western countries. Amidst this trauma, the region was a principle political battle ground where social reproduction was undone, redone and done up.

The purpose of this chapter is to review the changing definitions and purposes of the region found in Anglo-American human geography over the course of the twentieth century. The philosopher Ludwig Wittgenstein once likened different equations that looked alike to bones separated from their bodily integuments. Outside of the body, the bones appeared similar. But re-attached to the "surrounding manifold context of the organism," the bones could hardly be more different (Wittgenstein quoted in Bloor 1983: 103). I will make the same point about the region. While different versions of the region when taken out of context might look alike, once re-inserted into the sinews and gristle of the academic and historical context in which they were originally set, they take on inimitable identities.

The Region in Geography and the Geography of the Region

David Livingstone (1992) provides an elegant historical account of the "regionalizing ritual" practiced by the first academic geographers in Western Europe and the United States from the late nineteenth century until roughly the mid-twentieth century (Paasi 2009: 217–220). Regional geography didn't come in just one version, but was itself regionally variegated. Initially there were three entangled national traditions – German, French and British – that folded into a fourth, American.

Germany was perhaps the most important because it was there that the twin foundations of the institutionalized form of the discipline were laid down by Alexander von Humboldt (1769–1859), principally a physical scientist (the *Kosmos*, 1845), and Carl Ritter (1779–1859), principally an anthropologist (the *Erdkunde*, 1817–1859). Consequently, from the get-go geography was a hybrid discipline: natural science and human science: "the study of earth and the study of life on earth" (Pudup 2001: 12905). And where could this interaction best be studied? The region. The region was the laboratory where the two different disciplinary ends were investigated, fitted together, unified. As Pudup (2001: 12905) puts it: "the region fell into the discipline's lap as the obvious focus of its pursuits."

But that still left the question of how to conceive the region. The Heidelberg geographer Alfred Hettner (1859–1941) at the turn of the century revived Greek "chorology" as the basis. For the Ancient Greeks, *choros* was the study of particular regions by telling stories about them. It contrasted with *geos*, the examination of the entire face of the earth, involving the use of general analytical principles, often mathematical (Lukermann 1961; Curry 2005). Hettner's definition and use of chorology was complex (Elkins 1989; Harvey and Wardenga 2006), but two points were straightforward. First, the region was to be geography's primary epistemological object. The geographical world could be known only by organizing facts regionally. To fail to reference the region was to fail to do geography. Second, regions were to be studied by the scrupulous collection of geographical facts (a geographical fact by definition was one that was different from one region to another). Each unique geographical fact was to be sorted by its region into a set of pre-determined typological boxes (Hettner's *Länderkundliche Schema*) such as relief, settlement, population, biogeography, and resources. By then running your eye along the rows of the *Schema* the distinctiveness of each region was immediately apparent. Chorology stared you in the face.

Such a stern Germanic regimen was relaxed under the French regional school of Paul Vidal de la Blache (1845–1918). While still believing in a science of the region, Vidal shunned the encyclopaedic recitation generated by Hettner's *Schema* (a "machine" for producing geographical facts), as well as some of his lingering environmental determinism that stemmed from Ritter's influence. Sorting out the relationship between nature and culture was always going to be difficult in a discipline that made them its twin starting points. While the Germans inclined to the primacy of the environment, Vidal stressed culture as the moving force. Culture modified nature, creating distinctive integrated assemblages of people and environment, unique ways of life (*genres de vie*), and which were, and this was the point, organized and set regionally. The region (*pay*) was the unit in which people and their environment gelled. They became one, even taking on a single distinctive character or personality. As Vidal wrote in *The Personality of France*:

> It is man [sic] who reveals a country's individuality by molding it to his own use. ... In establishing a connection between unrelated features ... a country acquires a specific character differentiating it from others, till at length it becomes, as it were, a medal struck in the likeness of its people. (Vidal 1928: 14)

In the UK, the elements of regional geography were mixed in yet a different combination. There was certainly an inclination towards the encyclopedic as in George Chisholm's *Handbook of Commercial Geography* published in 1889 (its flavor perfectly captured by Chisholm's statement that "if ... there is some drudgery in the learning of geography, I see no harm in it," quoted in MacLean 1988: 25). A.J. Herbertson, the second geographer ever at Oxford University (Halford Mackinder's replacement), provided the first British theorization of the region combining elements of environmentalism with Vidal's *jolie géographie*. On the one hand, Herbertson believed that the boundaries of the region were literally carved in stone, inscribed by and into the natural environment. Climate, Herbertson thought, was especially important, delimiting "natural regions" (Herbertson 1905; also see Paasi 2009: 215). But on the other hand, regions by their very constitution were vitally human, possessing a distinctive cultural, aesthetic and metaphysical content, a "consciousness" (Herbertson 1916). They acquired "a *genius loci* as well as a *Zeitgeist* – a spirit of place as well as of time" (Herbertson 1916: 153).

There wasn't much sense of a *jolie géographie* or *genius loci* in the American conception of the region surfacing in the late nineteenth century especially in courses in economic geography offered in economics departments and business schools (the dismal science strikes again; Fellman 1986). An example is the work of J. Russell Smith (1913) who taught at the Wharton Business School, University of Pennsylvania. His nine-hundred-and-fourteen page *Industrial and Commercial Geography* (it reads longer) is as much an extended geographical shopping list as a textbook. If there was a theory of the region it was bound to an ethically suspect environmental determinism. Ellen Churchill Semple (1911: 1) had provided an early statement: "Man is a product of the earth's surface" was her blunt first sentence. It was later systematized by Harvard's Professor of Geography, Ellsworth Huntington, who attempted to enlist both Chisholm and Smith into one of his environmental determinist ventures to define and rank all regions in the world according to their "level of civilization," correlating them with their respective levels of "climatic energy." The principled Chisholm declined to participate, but J. Russell Smith did, gleefully agreeing to "take a half day off to sit in judgment upon the world" (quoted in Livingstone 1994: 143).

Critiques of environmental determinism as bigoted and unscientific led to its demise. But the result for American geography was its replacement by an anodyne version of the Germanic regional regimen (Porter 1978): regional facts collected in thematically marked boxes. Of course, that's what Clarence Jones was doing in 1935. He had eight boxes, and into them he sorted the regional facts of the world. For British Columbia, put the Fraser under rivers, Coastal Mountains under relief, Vancouver under settlement, cedar and hemlock under forestry, coal and gold under mining, and salmon and halibut under fishing. The eight-fold typology used by Jones to organize facts collected in part from his world travels was more finely variegated than some others (Ray Whitbeck and Vernon Finch 1924, for example, used only a parsimonious four boxes in their textbook). But they all performed the same role: a typological grid for classifying observations that could then be photographed, mapped, tabulated, or most likely, merely listed under the appropriate classificatory heading. By comparing the facts of the different regions by using the same typological grid, regional differences were immediately seen, and the distinctiveness of each region shone by its own light.

But still there was no explicit intellectual rationale in English for this conception of the region. That was provided by Richard Hartshorne (1939) in his *The Nature of Geography*. The volume was in effect a reply that got out of hand. It started life as a response to the Berkeley geographer John Leighly's (1937) paper published in the *Annals of the Association of American Geographers*. Although the editor, Derwent Whittlesey, told Hartshorne that his rejoinder "could be brief," Hartshorne just kept on writing, taking the piece with him on sabbatical to Vienna in 1938 (Hartshorne 1979: 63). Because of the Nazi Anschluss in Austria that same year, Hartshorne ended up spending most of his leave at the University of Vienna library working on the reply rather than investigating political boundaries of the mid-Danube (his original plan). *Nature* finally weighed in at 600 manuscript pages.

The book was an elaboration of the Germanic regional regimen. It drew especially on Hettner, making "chorology" key. In fact, Hartshorne wrote to Hettner after he arrived in Vienna to tell him that *Nature* was "primarily an exposition – in considerable part a literal translation – of your studies in this field" (Hartshorne quoted in Harvey and Wardenga 2006: 423). In the end it wasn't quite that (Harvey and Wardenga 2006), but Hartshorne, like Hettner, made the region the disciplinary epistemological bedrock. Here the region was an assemblage of elements – an "element complex" – composed of unique combinations of objective geographical entities.

But defining the region as a unique combination of elements meant that traditional natural scientific explanations based on physical laws could not apply. Scientific laws pertain only to classes of phenomena that are homogenous. Because one atom of hydrogen gas is like every other, applying pressure to any sub-set of atoms that form the larger class "hydrogen gas" necessarily produces the same effect. But regions are not like hydrogen atoms. The mixture of constitutive elements forming them is always different from one case to another, producing heterogeneous responses to common causative factors. No law-like generalization is possible. As Hartshorne (1939: 446) summarized, "We arrive, therefore, at a conclusion similar to that which Kroeber has stated for history: 'the uniqueness of all historical phenomena. ... No laws or near laws are discovered.' The same conclusion applies to the particular combination of phenomena at a particular place." Geographers, therefore, cannot do any of the things that natural science is able to accomplish because of its recourse to physical laws; that is, to explain, to predict, and knowingly to intervene. In the Hartshornian conception of the region, geographers only describe. "Regional geography, we conclude, is literally what its title expresses: ... It is essentially a descriptive science concerned with the description and interpretation of unique cases. ..." (Hartshorne 1939: 449).

In retrospect, however, the timing of Hartshorne's argument for a science of geography based on the descriptive study of unique regions could not have been worse. 1939 was at the very threshold of a fundamental transformation in US social sciences and humanities to general explanation, prediction, and policy intervention. Doubly ironic, within two years of writing *The Nature*, Hartshorne was playing a central role in the organization that helped shift American geography away from "mere description" of unique regions to precisely general explanation, prediction and intervention. It was a move from an old regional geography to what was later called "the new geography" in which regions were still present, but conceived utterly differently, not as unique places but as abstract spaces to be rearranged, manipulated, formally represented, and used as a tool to achieve instrumental planning objectives.

As the Regional World Turns

The American geographer Kirk Stone said:

> World War II was the best thing that has happened to geography since the birth of Strabo. (Kirk Stone 1979: 89)

For the purposes here, the Second World War produced two main effects that transformed the conception of the region, culminating from the late 1950s and early 1960s in the development of a "new" geography of regional space.

The first, at least in the United States, was setting geography within the social sciences, and increasingly infused by what Carl Schorske (1997) called "the new rigorism." An early site where geographers encountered both social sciences and "the new rigorism" was at the wartime Research & Analysis (R&A) Branch of the US Office of Strategic Services (OSS). The OSS (the forerunner of the Central Intelligence Agency) was inaugurated in 1941, charged with gathering, analyzing and disseminating information in matters relating to national security.[1] Its "heart and soul" was R&A (Winks 1987: 114), in effect a social scientific research institute that assembled, dissected, interpreted, manipulated, and instrumentally deployed knowledge (Katz 1989). Richard Hartshorne occupied a central administrative role, responsible for overseeing the assignment, production, vetting and distribution of all research reports. In researching and writing those reports, geographers at OSS (there were more geographers at OSS than at any other branch of the US government) interacted closely with other social scientists (Barnes 2006). That's where the trouble began. Especially younger geographers felt ill-equipped and poorly served by their disciplinary training, and more broadly by geography's older regional imperative (Ackerman 1945; Committee 1946). Geographers could catalogue geographical information, insert it within classification schemes, and describe it, but that was it. They lacked systematic methods to collect information, theories and models to interpret and explain what they had collected, and a vocabulary and set of tools to realize instrumental ends.

After the war was over, some of those younger geographers began to practice a different kind of geography, aligning it with a post-war social science that emphasized analysis, quantitative methods, model-building, and theory. In the process, the very meaning of the region changed. Stressed was not a region's uniqueness, its bill-of-laden list of singular features, but its formal spatial character, its functional similarities, its pragmatic potential to realize policy ends. Such a shift was given further momentum during the Cold War (Barnes 2008). The US "military-industrial complex" and concomitant "Cold War University" prized scientific, applied knowledge above all else. Moreover, it could get exactly what it wanted by the judicious disbursement of research funds from its financial wing, primarily the Office of Naval Research. The only mystery was just how long it took American geographers to get with this new agenda given its overwhelming impress.

Second, the World War II also helped produce a different conception of the region by its emphasis on state planning. The seed of that idea had already been planted by the English economist John Maynard Keynes in his *The General Theory of Employment* published just before the War began. *The General Theory* was a how-to manual for government intervention, for planning the economy, for saving it from itself. Subsequent war-time experience amply demonstrated the effectiveness of the state as a planner, and later taken up by the military-industrial complex during "peace" time. In this brave new world of Keynesian military-industrial planning, economists devised an ever burgeoning array of models, measuring techniques, theoretical precepts and predictive tools to accomplish state intervention and control like activity analysis, cost-benefit analysis, and game theory (Mirowski 2002). They were inventing (Mitchell 2002 would say "performing") a new economy.

Not that most economists were interested in the regional character of the economy. But there were some, and, of course, geographers had a longstanding interest. But the Hartshornian Germanic regional regimen wasn't going to cut ice in this new conversation. A different conception of the region was necessary involving both a new vocabulary and set of analytical instruments for achieving practical ends. An economist at Harvard, Walter Isard, saw the possibilities of what he called "regional science," later inaugurating a Department of that same name at the University of Pennsylvania in 1955 (Barnes 2004). It was concerned with providing exactly that new vocabulary and set of analytical instruments, conceiving the region as an abstract theoretical object, and providing a manual of formal techniques capable of realizing Keynesian state planning objectives. By the mid-1950s, several American geographers beyond those who were at OSS began to re-conceive the region along similar lines. But given geography's internal disciplinary power structure and history they kept close to Isard and regional science (not that Isard was especially sympathetic given his view of geographers as only hewers and drawers of data for regional science theorists; Isard 1990: 304–305).

Among these geographers, especially notable were "the space cadets" at the University of Washington, Seattle. They were a group of talented, energetic and ambitious graduate students who serendipitously arrived at "U Dubb" Geography Department around the same time, *annus mirabilis* 1955, to work with either one of the former OSSers, Edward Ullman, or a young Assistant Professor from North Western University, William Garrison. As a graduate student in the late 1940s Garrison had been a Teaching Assistant for Clarence Jones's economic geography class that used his textbook. But it was not a happy experience, with Garrison later saying about Jones's lectures: "they led me to keep asking: 'What's the theory? What's the theory? What's the theory'" (Garrison 1998). Specifically, "... a systematic approach was in order. ..." (Garrison 1979: 119). It was a systematic approach to the region that Garrison pioneered with the cadets in the late 1950s. With money from the Office of Naval Research and the Federal Highways Commission, courses in statistics and social physics, use of the newly installed IBM 650 computer in the attic of the Chemistry Building, Garrison and his students produced what Richard Morrill (1984: 61), one of the co-authors, called a "revolutionary book," *Studies of Highway Development and Geographic Change* (Garrison et al. 1959). It remains a remarkable volume, crammed with calculations, data matrices, statistical techniques, costs curves and demand schedules, and conventional maps overlaid with numbers, arrows, starburst lines, and balancing equations. Its real revolution was the changed conception of the region as a theoretical spatial object: now generalizable, mathematical, explainable, abstract, rigorous, and bearing upon "significant, theoretical, policy and/or practical questions" (Garrison 1959: 232).

Although I made Peter Haggett the exemplar of this new conception of the region in my introduction, in the scheme of things he was a latecomer. While his book *Locational Analysis* (1965) was a brilliant summary and synthesis, it was a review of work that had been mainly already carried out in North America. As Haggett reflected later, "there was very little of my own research reported [in *Locational Analysis*] ... It is rather like a kind of Alistair Cooke commenting on the American scene" (Browning 1982: 47). More generally, British geography was slower to move towards the new conception of the region, even though compared to the United States regional planning was more entrenched in the UK, and the state more interventionist. Isard tried to bring regional science to the UK in 1964, giving a pep talk at the London School of Economics (LSE). But there was resistance from traditionalists like then President of the Institute of British Geographers, William Kirk, who wrote to the *Guardian* where the story of Isard's LSE appearance appeared: "I am at a loss to differentiate between what Professor Isard calls a regional scientist and what I would call a regional geographer" he said tartly.[2] But there was resistance also from a group of younger British geographers who while seemingly sympathetic to Isard's intellectual project thought it smacked too much of Americanism. It needed Europeanizing. The Regional Studies Association (RSA) was born the following year at LSE, and attempted to stake out a middle ground somewhere between traditional regional geography and Isardian regional science. Peter Self, one of the original RSA members, said at the meeting that led to the new organization's formation, it would offer "a more distinctive approach [than regional science]," one that "would follow its own line," and would be "more modest," concerned with representing at best "Europe rather than the world"[3].

But this did not stop Isard. Plan B involved sending Allen Scott, a faculty member at Regional Science at Penn, to the UK as a roving European ambassador for the movement (and based at the Bartlett School, University College London; Barnes 2004). This brought converts, and was especially successful in publication, netting an alliance with the publisher Pion Ltd. that agreed to put out the London Papers in Regional Science (under Scott's editorship) and also in effect a British regional science journal (at least initially), *Environment and Planning* (edited by Alan Wilson). All this resonated with Haggett's *Locational Analysis*.

Specifically, *Locational Analysis* was divided into two main parts. The first ("models of locational structure") was about theoretical forms and explanations of abstract regional space. There were no boxes labeled "relief," "rivers," "settlement." Instead, Haggett's regional space was divided into "nodes," "hierarchies," "surfaces," "networks," and a category that admittedly does not fit the geometrical designation but remains spatial, "movement." Further, those categories were not stuffed with the brute facts of the region (in spite of the book's separate "Locational Index;" Haggett 1965: 329–332. Instead, they were crammed with theories, models, equations, and above all graphs, maps, schematic illustrations, bar charts, and polygons of various forms (there were 162 numbered diagrams in 310 pages of text). Regions were turned on the page into a series of miniature diagrammatic abstract spaces that could be controlled, dominated, rearranged and manipulated. In comparison, Clarence Jones' regional descriptions of "Eskimo land" and the "Amazon forest" appeared as if they were from a different planet. The second part ("Methods in locational analysis") was the toolbox. It was about showing how you got things done, how you intervened, how you improved reality. It was full of formal techniques, procedures, algorithms, and flow charts for realizing specific spatial ends. They read as the epitome of rationality and expertise. How could they go wrong?

Regional Worlds

But they did. Charles Jencks (1989: 9), the architectural historian, dates the end of modernist architecture that like Haggett's locational analysis was all about rationality, efficiency, purified space, and technical expertise with the dynamiting of the infamous Igoe Pruitt public housing project in St. Louis on July 15th, 1972. The prize-winning building opened in 1955, and was the very model of modernist architecture. But it went horribly awry with the building afflicted by crime, poverty, social segregation, vandalism, decay, and mechanical breakdown. It was best just to blow it up and start all over again.

It wasn't quite so dramatic for spatial science and its conception of the region (although Isard's Regional Science Department at Penn was closed in 1993). But throughout the 1970s Haggett's conception of the region began to fail, to stop working, to be dismantled and abandoned. Partly it was too singular an approach in a discipline that historically was open-ended and pluralist. Partly it was the force of an internal critique that revealed assorted contradictions, inconsistencies and *aporias* within a supposedly impregnable regional logic, and made often by those who were proponents of that logic only a short time before (Gunnar Olsson 1975 was perhaps the best example). But mainly it was because the times no longer seemed to fit. A former colleague of Haggett's at Bristol University, David Harvey, and also formerly Secretary to the British section of the Regional Science Association, expressed it well as early as 1972 (but by then he had moved to America):

> There is a clear disparity between the sophisticated theoretical and methodological framework we are using and our ability to say anything really meaningful about events as they unfold around us. There are too many anomalies between what we purport to explain and manipulate and what actually happens. There is an ecological problem, an urban problem, an international trade problem, and yet we seem incapable of saying anything of any depth or profundity about any of them. When we do say something it appears trite and rather ludicrous. In short, our paradigm is not coping well. It is ripe for overthrow. (Harvey 1972: 6)

Harvey's litany of problems misses out one, but it was to prove crucial in the reconstruction of the region as a conceptual idea and a relevant unit of analysis: the economy. The late 1970s and much of the 1980s in North America and Western Europe saw a profound economic restructuring as traditional Fordist manufacturing was variously cast off, radically rejigged, or replaced by something completely different. Moreover, once the dust settled, it was a different world. Globalization had taken hold, but rather than eradicating space (as some economists suggested), it left sub-national regions more important than ever. It was now a "regional world" as Michael Storper (1997) described it.

The whirlwind destruction that ripped through North America and Western economies as deindustrialization and economic restructuring was geographically uneven, distributed in distinctive regional patterns. In some cases, capital upped and left the region leaving workers bereft; in other regions one sort of capital departed, but another sort arrived, sometimes employing former workers, other times hiring a brand new set; and yet in other cases, new capital arrived but fundamentally changed the working conditions of existing workers. In all of this change, the region was the arena in which new relations between capital and labor were worked out. Understanding this regional process could not mean returning to Hartshorne's and Hettner's chorology, however. Regional specificity and unique outcomes were important. But arranging such specificities and outcomes in seriatim rows of a common classification scheme was not the answer. The intent was not regional description for regional description's sake. People were traumatized, suffering, old patterns of social reproduction turned inside out, with whole communities unraveling. There needed to be analysis, theoretical scrutiny, explanation, a calling to account. But analysis could not be based on Haggett's regional science either. That was too purified, antiseptic, and removed; too rational for the resulting irrational outcome, too politically neutral for events saturated in politics. It needed to be theory that was muddied, politicized, passionate, grounded in the thick of things. It needed to be social theory.

David Harvey (1982) early on drew on social theory, Marx's, making the relation of capital and labor central. But the regions that emerged were reduced only to capital and labor, with geography lost in the shuffle. In contrast, Doreen Massey

(1984) also drew on social theory, never losing sight of the pressing political obligations around the capital-labor relation, but at the same time she kept the geographical composition and particularity of the region in tact.

Her brilliant achievement was to combine regional particularity and general principles. It was both/and rather than either/or (in terms of the Ancient Greeks, both *choros* and *geos*). Central was the idea of spatial divisions of labor, that is, a changing geography of industrial specialization and always organized regionally (Massey 1984). On the one hand, she theorized the general dynamics of industrial capitalism. This wasn't Haggett-style theory written in Greek letters, however. Nonetheless, it identified necessary features of the geographical reproduction of capitalism, for example, continued investment. They were necessary in the sense that without them capitalism would cease to exist. On the other hand, the abstract necessary conditions of capitalist reproduction always came down to earth in specific material and social forms, and when they did, geography mattered, regions mattered. It was not investment in the abstract, say, in South Wales, but concrete investment in coal mines and iron and steel mills, and producing a specific geographical region, a region with a distinctive character. Massey's critical point, making her work a "new regional geography" (Pudup 1988: 376), was the contention that the unique geographical character of the region recursively interacted with general principles, rearranging both regions and principles. One must always be alive to both geographical specificity and general principles. The two were entangled, each changing and changed by the other.

Massey's approach that combined both specific regional and general theoretical sensitivities prompted the UK "localities project" in which the region was central (Cook 1989). While the localities approach was later criticized, even by Massey, the region as topic went from strength-to-strength. As capitalism shed its old skin of national mass production, becoming increasingly global and high tech, the region was ever more important as an object both theoretically and substantively. There were learning regions, creative regions, new industrial regions, high-tech regions, and Global-city regions. The region wasn't merely background atmospherics, to add color to the story. It was the story. The region was the very basis for the generation of national and global wealth, innovation, and trade and investment. Exactly how the region did all this varied by specific site and specific theory. But again that was the point: the need for theory and regional specificity.

Of course, this was in only economic geography. But versions of Massey were happening in other parts of geography. Derek Gregory's (1978: 171) important early review of social theory finished with a call for a new regional geography (not that he actually provided it). And in the first half of the 1980s Allan Pred (1984) and Nigel Thrift (1983) drew upon the Swedish geographer Torsten Hägerstrand, and the British sociologist Anthony Giddens to outline, and in Pred's case later empirically fill in, a socially theoretical informed notion of the region that drew on ideas of recursiveness. Since then there have been other specific theorizations of the region (Gilbert's 1988; Paasi's 1986, 2002, 2009; and Pudup's 1988, are the most important.) The important point has been to bring together theory (no more description for description's sake) *and* regional detail (no more equations for equations' sake). This is the new geographical world for regions and the discipline.

Conclusion

Danny MacKinnon (2009: 229) is surely right: the region as an idea just won't go away. What do go away are larger external historical and internal academic contexts that shape and torque particular definitions of the region. As those contexts change, so do the usefulness, applicability, and plausibility of concomitant regional definitions. That is why there have been such varied reactions to specific definitions of the region, from applause and commendation, to embarrassment and shame, to incomprehension and anger, to a political compulsion to do something different. As Paasi says:

> ... the contested understanding of what the "region" is has been part and parcel of ... struggles [around] ... entangled societal and academic power relations. (Paasi 2009: 214)

Knowing that doesn't make it any easier. As geographers it seems we can't help ourselves but talk about regions. It is part of the furniture of our discipline. But if as this review has suggested the region is fundamentally a pluralist object, an assemblage of many different things, with "the word 'and' trail[ing] along after every sentence" (James 1912: 321), it is important to be pluralist about its very definition. This means the task is less one of finding the perfect definition of the region (impossible), but being open-minded and modest in our talk and aims while adhering to our geographical tradition.

Notes

1 The Office of Strategic Services was renamed in 1942. Before that date it was called the Office of the Co-ordinator of Information and founded in July 1941. After just over a year gap following the closure of OSS, the CIA was set up 1947.
2 Letter to the Guardian, 20th July, 1964, File "Newspaper clippings," Box 22, Archive of the Regional Studies Association, London School of Economics.
3 RSA Research Meeting, no date, Folder: Annual General Meeting and Conferences 1965, Box 15, Archive of the Regional Studies Association, London School of Economics.

References

Ackerman, E.A. (1945) Geographic training, wartime research, and immediate professional objectives. *Annals of the Association of American Geographers* 35, 121–143.
Barnes, T.J. (2004) The rise (and decline) of American regional science: lessons for the new economic geography? *Journal of Economic Geography* 4, 107–129.
Barnes, T.J. (2006) Geographical intelligence: American geographers and Research and Analysis in the Office of Strategic Services 1941–1945. *Journal of Historical Geography* 32, 149–168.
Barnes, T.J. (2008) Geography's *Underworld*: The military-industrial complex, mathematical modelling and the quantitative revolution. *Geoforum* 39, 3–16.

Bloor, D. (1983) *Wittgenstein: A Social Theory of Knowledge.* MacMillan, London.

Browning, C. (ed.) (1982) *Conversations with Geographers: Career Pathways and Research Styles, Department of Geography occasional paper 16.* University of North Carolina, Chapel Hill, North Carolina.

Committee on Training and Standards in the Geographic Profession, National Research Council. 1946. Lessons from the war-time experience for improving graduate training for geographic research. *Annals of the Association of American Geographers* 36, 195–214.

Cook, P.N. (ed.) (1989) *Localities: The Changing Face of Urban Britain.* Unwin Hyman, London.

Curry, M.R. (2005) Toward a geography of a world without maps: Lessons from Ptolemy and postal codes. *Annals of the Association of American Geographers* 95, 680–691.

Elkins, T.H. (1989) Human and regional geography in the German-speaking lands in the first forty years of the twentieth century. In S. Brunn and N. Entrikin (eds), *Reflections on Richard Hartshorne's The Nature of Geography.* Occasional publications of the *Association of American Geographers* 1, pp.17-34.

Fellmann, J.D. (1986) Myth and reality in the origin of American economic geography. *Annals, Association of American Geographers* 76, 313–330.

Garrison, W.L. (1979) Playing with ideas. *Annals, Association of American Geographers* 69, 118–120

Garrison, W.L. (1959) Spatial structure of the economy, I. *Annals of the Association of American Geographers* 49, 232–239.

Garrison, W.L., Berry, B.J.L., Marble, D.F., Nystuen, J.D., and Morrill, R.L. (1959) *Studies in Highway Development and Geographic Change.* University of Washington Press, Seattle.

Garrison, W.L. (1998) *Interview with the author; March 1998.* Berkeley, California.

Gilbert, A. (1988) The new regional geography in English and French-speaking countries. *Progress in Human Geography* 12, 208–228.

Gregory, D. (1978) *Ideology, Science and Human Geography.* Hutchinson, London.

Gregory, D. (2009) Regional geography. In D. Gregory, R. Johnston, G. Pratt, M. Watts, and S, Whatmore (eds), *The Dictionary of Human Geography.* Wiley-Blackwell, Chichester, pp. 632–636.

Haggett P. (1965) *Locational Analysis in Human Geography.* Edward Arnold, London.

Hartshorne, R. (1939) *The Nature of Geography: A Critical Survey of Current Thought in the Light of the Past.* Association of American Geographers, Lancaster.

Hartshorne, R. (1979) Notes towards a bibliography of *The Nature of Geography. Annals of the Association of American Geographers* 69, 63–76.

Harvey, D. (1972) Revolutionary and counter-revolutionary theory in geography and the problem of ghetto formation. *Antipode* 4 (2), 1–13.

Harvey, D. (1982) *Limits to Capital.* University of Chicago Press, Chicago.

Harvey, F. and Wardenga, U. (2006) Richard Hartshorne's adaptation of Alfred Hettner's system of geography. *Journal of Historical Geography* 32, 422-440.

Herbertson, A.J. (1905) The major natural regions of the world: An essay in systematic geography. *Geographical Journal* 25, 300–312.

Herbertson, A.J. (1916) Regional environment, heredity and consciousness. *Geographical Teacher* 8, 147–153.

Hudson, J.C. (1993) In memoriam: Clarence Fielden Jones 1893–1991. *Annals of the Association of American Geographers* 83, 167–172.

Isard. W. (1990) Location Analysis and General Theory: Economic, Political, Regional and Dynamic. In C. Smith (ed.), *Selected Papers of Walter Isard, Volume 1.* NYU Press, New York.

James, W. (1912) *A Pluralistic Universe. Hibbert Lectures at Manchester College on the Present Situation in Philosophy.* Green, Longmans, New York.

Jencks, C. (1989) *What is Postmodernism?* St. Martin's Press, London and New York.
Jones, C.F. (1935) *Economic Geography* Henry Holt and Company, New York.
Katz, B.M. 1989. *Foreign Intelligence: Research and Analysis in the Office of Strategic Services, 1942–1945*. Harvard University Press, Cambridge.
Leighly, J.B. (1937) Some comments on contemporary geographic methods. *Annals of the Association of American Geographers* 27, 125–141.
Livingstone, D.N. (1992) *The Geographical Tradition: Episodes in the History of a Contested Enterprise*. Blackwell, Oxford.
Livingstone, D.N. (1994) Climate's moral economy. Science, race and place in post-Darwinian British and American geography. In A. Godlewska and N. Smith (eds) *Geography and Empire*. Blackwell, Oxford, pp. 132–154.
Lukermann, F.E. (1961) The concept of location in classical geography. *Annals of the Association of American Geographers* 51, 194–210.
MacLean, K. (1988) George Goudie Chisholm 1850–1930. In T.W. Freeman (ed.) *Geographers Bibliographical Studies*, Vol. 12. Mansell, London, pp. 21–33.
Massey, D. (1984) *Spatial Divisions of Labour: Social Structures and the Geography of Production*. MacMillan, Basingstoke and London.
MacKinnon, D. (2009) Regional geography II. *International Encyclopaedia*. In R. Kitchin and N.J. Thrift (eds), *Human Geography*. Elsevier, Amsterdam, pp. 228–235.
Mirowski, P. 2002. *Machine Dreams: Economics Becomes Cyborg Science*. Cambridge University Press, Cambridge.
Mitchell, T. (2002) *Rule of Experts: Egypt, Techno-Politics, Modernity*. University of California Press, Berkeley and Los Angeles.
Morrill, R.L. (1984) Recollections of the 'quantitative revolution's' early years: the University of Washington, 1955–1965. In M. Billinge, D. Gregory, and R. Martin (eds), *Recollections of a Revolution: Geography as Spatial Science*. Macmillan, London, pp. 57–72.
Olsson, G. (1975) *Birds in Egg*. Michigan Geographical Publications, Number 15. Department of Geography, University of Michigan, Ann Arbor.
Paasi, A. (1986) The institutionalization of regions: A theoretical framework for understanding the emergence of regions and the constitution of regional identity. *Fennia* 164, 10–46.
Paasi, A. (2002) Region and place: regional worlds and words. *Progress in Human Geography* 26, 802–811.
Paasi, A. (2009) Regional geography I. *International Encyclopaedia*. In R. Kitchin and N.J. Thrift (eds), *Human Geography*. Elsevier, Amsterdam, pp. 214–227.
Porter, P.W. (1978) Geography as human ecology: a decade of progress in a quarter century. *American Behavioral Scientist* 22, 15–39.
Pred, A. (1984) Place as historically contingent process: structuration and the time-geography of becoming places. *Annals of the Association of American Geographers* 74, 279–297.
Pudup, M.B. (1988) Arguments within regional geography. *Progress in Human Geography* 12, 369–390.
Pudup, M.B. (2001) Region geographical. In N.J. Smelser and P.B. Baltes (eds) *International Encyclopaedia of the Social and Behavioral Sciences*. Elsevier, Amsterdam, pp.12905–12908.
Schorske, C.E. (1997) The new rigorism in the human sciences, 1940–1960. *Daedalus* 126, 289–309.
Semple, E.C. (1911) *Influences of Geographic Environment*. Henry Holt and Co., New York.
Smith, J. Russell. (1913) *Industrial and Commercial Geography* Henry Holt and Co., New York.
Stone, K.H. (1979) Geography's wartime service. *Annals of the Association of American Geographers* 69, 89–96.

Storper, M. (1997) *Regional World: Territorial Development in a Global* World. Guildford Press, New York.
Thrift, N.J. (1983) On the determination of social action in space and time. *Environment and Planning D: Society and Space* 1, 23–57.
Vidal de la Blache, P. (1928) *The Personality of France*. Alfred A. Knopf, New York.
Whitbeck, R.H. and Finch, V.C. (1924) *Economic Geography*. McGraw-Hill, New York.
Winks, R.W. (1987) *Cloak and Gown: Scholars in the Secret War*. William Morrow, New York.

Chapter 10

From Region to Space
Part II

Anssi Paasi

Settled places and regions, however arbitrarily delimited, are the essence of human geographic inquiry … Place … always involves an appropriation and transformation of space and nature that is inseparable from the reproduction and transformation of society in time and space.

(Pred 1984: 279)

… the worst thing one can do with words is to surrender to them.

(Orwell 1953: 169–170)

Introduction

Raymond Williams (1976: 17) showed in his *Keywords* how words that are crucial for understanding society and culture ceaselessly take on new meanings that mirror the transformation of society: "We find a history and complexity of meanings; conscious changes, or consciously different uses; innovation, obsolescence, specialization, extension, overlap, transfer; or changes which are masked by a nominal continuity so that words which seem to have been there for centuries, with continuous general meanings, have come in fact to express radically different or radically variable, yet sometimes hardly noticed, meanings and implications of meaning."

Academic fields also depend on keywords, which are crucial for the (re)shaping of a field, its public image, its scholarly identities and the theoretical-methodological approaches adopted in it. Keywords express diverse levels of abstraction and wider socio-historical connections; they motivate and even oblige scholars not to "surrender to them" but rather to defy them and to develop new ones. The debate on keywords is common in social sciences that study open systems, contrary to the

The Wiley Blackwell Companion to Human Geography, First Edition.
Edited by John A. Agnew and James S. Duncan.
© 2011 John Wiley & Sons, Ltd. Published 2016 by John Wiley & Sons, Ltd.

closed systems of natural science. Openness means that we can interpret the same material conditions and statements in different ways and learn new ways of responding (Sayer 1992). Keywords inspire debate, since they are not just words or even fixed concepts, but dynamic, context-dependent categories that often bring together efforts to advance such concepts and the power related to social practices such as governance and social control. Keywords hence inform us of how science is constituted spatially, cognitively, institutionally and socially. Even though new ideas may emerge piecemeal in a few locations, be created by a limited group of people and be distributed to a limited number of others, such ideas can ultimately become symbols of a whole era in a certain field (Barnes 2004).

This article will examine the shaping of geographical thinking and research practice through two keywords, region and space. Region has been the most important keyword that denoted for a long time to distinct, bounded units. Contemporary relational ideas of region challenge such boundedness and accentuate power relations, networks and hybrid identities. Space is a more recent keyword in English-speaking geography that has been related e.g. to abstract spatial relations or to the production/ reproduction of social life. While words like region or space may remain the same, the concepts behind them denote different ideas in different times and places. Therefore the roles of these keywords have to be traced historically and contextually, in relation to wider social practices. If we take them as given we run a risk of anachronism, i.e. projecting current concepts to the past, without reflecting upon them historically. Also, new keywords may have a past that is sometimes omitted because it is not known or, even worse, because of "theoretical amnesia" (Jessop *et al.* 2008).

This article will look first at the contested histories of geography and will then trace on a general level the rise and meanings of region and space as keywords. The level has to be "general," because it is practically impossible to detail the place (and person) specificity of keywords in a brief article. The roles of region and space will be evaluated through three strata, each characterized by partly overlapping meanings associated with these keywords and their "derivatives." The formation of such strata will be related to social practices, institutions and theoretical discourses. The paper will then analyze how the idea of region has found expression in research practice. Finally some conclusions will be drawn.

Contested Histories of Geography

The question of how the ideas of region and space are related to the history of geography is a tricky one, since there is *no* single history of geography but a bewildering variety of different, often competing versions of the past (Heffernan 2003). For some scholars this history extends to ancient times and justifies the present. They often recognize *Strabo* as a forefather of *chorography*, "writing about place." The origin of the idea of areal differentiation, a key justification for traditional regional geography, is similarly located "before the dawn of written history" (Martin and James 1993: v). Another view of history accentuates the importance of the institutionalization of academic geography at the end of the 19th century and of the social forces lying behind this: the interests of governments and the nationalist European bourgeois class. This geography served power from the very beginning

(Taylor 1985). Geography appeared in such practices as exploration, imperialism and the interpretation of human-nature relations.

Space, time and the history of the creation of spatial abstractions are crucial for understanding words like place, territory or region (Harvey 2009). Even before the institutionalization of geography, region was already important to rulers who sought to manage territories, to plan their development, to control their populations or to conceive military operations (Claval 2007). Region was originally a fiscal, administrative and military notion, whereas territory was a juridico-political category, an area controlled by power (Foucault 1980). Region became significant during the 19th century. Particularly important background figures in this were the German scholars Alexander von Humboldt and Carl Ritter. Humboldt worked in the spirit of the natural sciences, collecting data and making generalizations, while Ritter was committed to a historical approach and the finding of "unity in diversity" by identifying separate regions. In spite of such ideas, region became a *problem* only in the context of the institutionalized field, as it was now needed for methodological thinking and for creating a past, present and future for the emerging field, i.e. for outlining an identity, task and purpose for geography.

How did this happen? The diagram in Figure 10.1 has been compiled as a background for scrutinizing this. This heuristic device brings together what can be labeled as the "space of keywords" and may be seen as a modification of Williams' (1976) idea that culture exists in three forms: ideas that are *dominant* in cultural discourse and practice, others that have dominated earlier and may still have some impact as *residual* elements, and new, *emergent* meanings, values, practices and relations that are perpetually being created. Thus the space of keywords contains residual, dominant (core) and emerging categories, i.e. it is dominated by keywords/concepts that are perpetually being challenged, are replaced by emergent ones at times and become residual at times. Keywords characterize geographical discourse and research practice, often with compelling force. They are not "free-floating" but are created by researchers in the context of national and local institutions that both shape such ideas and render them possible (Barnes 2004).

It is useful to make an analytical distinction between three *strata*: "regional geographies," "spatial analysis/systematic geographies" and "space, region and social practice." "Strata" is an apt wording here because it implies social stratification/status, materiality and partly overlapping historical social series. Thus, instead of searching for the break where the idea of region is simply replaced by space, I will look at how such strata have emerged and suggest that a selective accumulation and fusion of keywords/concepts is perpetually occurring. Besides region and space, Figure 10.1 also contains other related concepts; some of which are discussed here, while others are merely noted in the figure as examples. In addition, the diverging roles of region in research practice are also distinguished and will be analyzed below.

The three strata are related to philosophical-methodological backgrounds, concepts of space, social practices, interests of knowledge and institutions/events (Figure 10.1). The space of keywords hence reflects a fusion of the practical needs of states (e.g. education, regional planning, and military interests) with academic motives. States and academic institutions set practical and ideological goals for scholars, whereas inside the disciplines "academic tribes" (Becher and Trowler 2001: 75) ceaselessly develop new conceptual "totems" and methodologies to signify and

	1900	1920	1940	1960	1980	2000
Space of keywords						
Residual			Vernacular region/Regionalism/ Cultural region	Chorology		
Dominant (Core)		**R e g i o n a l g e o g r a p h i e s**		Landscape		Locality
				Spatial analysis/ systematic geographies		**Space, region & social practice**
	Pays	Chorological approach		Spatial Geometry Locational analysis	TimeSpace Territory Identity Scale	Virtual space
	Raum	Landscape		Models Distance Networks	Region Locality Space of Flows	
	Landschaft	Functional region		Diffusion Movement Sense of Place	Landscape Network City-region	
		Language of unity		Nodal region	Place	
Emergent	Circulation	Functional organization of regions		Place	Production of space Scale	ThirdSpace Mobility
	Space-Politics	Location Space economy		Territory	Time Geography	Site TPSN
				Site-situation		
Philosophy-methodology	Neo-Kantianism Empiricism		Positivism		Marxism Phenomenology Post-modernism Post-structuralism	
					Behavioralism Realism Structuration theory	
					Feminism Social constructionism	
Concept of space	Absolute space Coexisting order/Container		Relative-Functional Space		Social space	Relational-topological space
					Relational space	
Regions						
Pre-scientific				"Region as Given" Statistical regions	Administrative regions	Regions as settings for economic activity
Discipline-centred	Natural region	Human/Geographic region		Functional region	Cultural region Perceptual region	
		Formal/homogeneous region				
Critical					Regions as Result of capital accumulation Unbounded relational	
					social constructs: Part of Life-world entity	
					Historically contingent process	
					Institutionalization process	
'Boundedness' of the region		Distinct 'real' unit or mental category or a unit with no precise limits		Instrument for classifying phenomena in space	Region as social practice and discourse: 'boundedness' is context bound	
Key social practice	Colonialism	Nationalism/national identity Regionalism	Geopolitics	National/regional planning and policy	New spatial divisions of labour Globalization Rescaling	
					Uneven development New regionalism of the state	
Interest of knowledge		Practical-instrumental		Technical	Emancipatory	
Events, think-tanks, institutions		World War I	World War II	Marshall Plan Citation indexes		EU/ European Research Area
				OEEC OECD		Research Assesment

Figure 10.1 The "space of keywords" in human geography and some social and institutional background factors.

legitimate new perspectives. Science studies demonstrate that the motives for research are both institutional and personal. Institutional interests appreciate novelty and innovation – especially today, when research is being subjected to continuous assessment. Individual scholars are primarily moved by factors intrinsic to their disciplines, especially the desire to contribute to a certain field and to build up a reputation in it.

Stratum I: Regional Geographies

Region, place and space are widely recognized as keywords in English-speaking geography. Together with landscape, region was the category on which the identity of the new field was largely built up. The first geographers in the US, UK, Germany and France shared a fervent search for such an identity. Different regional worlds gave rise to different but overlapping keywords related to space, region or landscape. Fitting examples are the German *Raum*, which is often translated into English as space but actually combines elements of both abstract, void space and historically rooted place, and *Landschaft*, which brings together (visual) landscape and region. The "encounter" between these and their respective English terms was a complicated process and sometimes reflected personal aspirations, such as efforts to push the idea of landscape aside (Olwig 2002). The keywords studied here emerged in a specific order in Anglo-American geography. At first only the region was theorized intensively – space became a theoretical issue much later.

The first decades of the 20th century were crucial for the shaping of the concepts of region. Although geographical discourse relied on different ideas of how regions "exist," the practical aim was to distinguish regions on various grounds. Many geographers were searching for "natural regions" on various scales, after which they moved on to identify human or geographic regions. Some influential books were also published on this subject. Alfred Hettner introduced the principles of chorological thought in Germany, and Richard Hartshorne relied on the same continental European tradition in his work carried out in the US in the 1930s. Both drew on the idea of the philosopher Kant of geography as a chorological field characterized by its approach rather than any specific object of research. If history examined the world in relation to time, geography studied phenomena in relation to space, in their regional association. Many ideas that emerged in English-speaking geography thus originated from German and French traditions. Hartshorne (1939) admitted this intellectual debt, and much of his discussion on the concept of region consisted of comments on the works of European scholars. Likewise, the major inspiration for regional geography in the UK came until the 1950s from the ideas of the French classics (Clout 1989).

Since the word region carried different meanings in different countries to some extent, a search for coherence became crucial. A "language of unity" emerged including such expressions as synthesis, uniqueness, holism, total composition/complexity, whole, *Zusammenhang*, *Ganzheit*, individual, totality, organism or personality. In this way geographers tried to convince themselves and others of the value of region as a unity or organizing principle that would bring nature and culture together. This led to a stereotypic idea of region as a unique, "bounded" unit, an idea that is still being criticized even today when geographers challenge "bounded regions" (Allen *et al.* 1998). Not all scholars accepted such boundedness, however. For Hartshorne (1939) the problem of establishing the boundaries of a "geographic region" presented a dilemma for which we have no reason to even hope for an "objective" solution (Gauthier and Taaffe 2002). Kimble (1951) noted that regional geographers may perhaps be trying to put "boundaries that do not exist around areas that do not matter." Neither were geographers unanimous on what a "region" is, and there were almost as many concepts of region in the 1930s as there were regional geographers (Paasi 2009a). There was no agreement on whether the region is a "really existing unit" or a "mental category," a creation of the student's mind and thoughts (Minshull 1967). As Agnew (1999) has shown, this old dualism still lurks behind current geographical thinking and practice.

Stratum II: Spatial Analysis and Systematic Geographies

Scholars may be motivated to develop new concepts by social and institutional pressures, the struggle for academic prestige, or a lack of relevant categories, regardless of whether these concepts become new keywords or not. Pre-World War II regional geography was largely a non-theoretical, empirical enterprise that – guided by a practical-instrumental interest of knowledge – collected information and prepared regional descriptions. At times the search for new ideas leads scholars to look at other fields. This occurred in human geography when "space" gradually emerged as a keyword. This was part of the slow rise of the second stratum that was related to the emerging criticism of regional geography, to the strengthening of systematic approaches and to the rise of a technical interest of knowledge that manifested the need to control society and nature more effectively and accurately.

World War II and the transformation of capitalist societies were important watersheds. Demands for a more scientific geography had emerged in the US during the war, where a number of geographers were enlisted in the service of the military-industrial complex. The contrast between the old regional geography and a new form of scientific analysis – yet to be developed – actualized when scholars from various fields cooperated (Barnes and Farish 2006). The war economy established in many countries increased the power of governance and gave rise to the control, management and planning of regional systems. Capitalist urbanization and industrialization and the related concentration of population and the economy created uneven development and urban problems. Systematic approaches to economic, urban and transport issues accentuated functional/nodal regions, relative location and interaction: an idea that had been emergent in geography before the war. Positivism became a major philosophy and a guide to understanding what theory means. This stressed the need for mathematical and statistical methods for the purposes of generalization and explanation.

Even so, it took 10–15 years after the war before a "toolbox" of keywords and methods was created and the new stratum was strengthened, beginning in the US and UK, where people with such skills were recruited into geography departments (Barnes 2004). The language of geography also became diversified. Space, a word associated with cosmology, mathematics and philosophy, began to resonate in many people's minds with a new modern, scientific aura. The set of potential ideas on space was wide, varying from the ideas of Greek philosophers to the Newtonian notion of absolute space; from the Kantian view of space as an intuition to Leibniz's relational space and the time-spaces of relativity theory. This literature emphasized that absolute space refers to "a space itself," with an independent existence, while relative space(-time) is the relation between objects, and is typically linked to astrophysics, whereas relational space concerns the order of coexisting phenomena.

Before the war Lundberg (1939), a sociologist, followed the positivist *Zeitgeist* and used the term social space "... as a mathematical (geometric) construct defined as a manifold in which positional relationships of *any kind* may be expressed." He suggested that "Topology, as the geometry of such spaces, may therefore be of great importance to sociology as a solution of the controversy over quantitative *versus* qualitative methods" (Lundberg 1939: 131). It was this positivist lead that geographers were to follow, although there would also have been other ways to proceed. At the same time, existential philosophers regarded spatiality as a mode of human existence. The sociologists Durkheim and Simmel had discussed the role of space in social life much earlier, and urban sociologists had looked at "natural areas" and values and symbolic environments in cities. The idea of social space in geography had to wait, however.

If German scholars had their Chorologische Geographie und *Raum*, their English-speaking colleagues still had chorological geography and the *region*. Many German geographers had referred decades earlier to geometrical-physical-philosophical spaces (e.g. Kantian and Leibnizian ideas) when discussing *Raum*, but had often made a distinction between "geographical space" and mathematical-physical spaces (Paasi 1983). New words also emerged in English-speaking geography, however. Hartshorne (1939: 284) suggested that the integrating factor in geography is "space," "the association of phenomena ... related to each other in spatial terms, i.e. in terms of relative location," but he did not theorize upon the idea of space. Platt (1948: 355) asked, "What space is studied in geography?" but the answer was traditional, "Not mathematical space, including concepts of a fourth dimension ... not absolute space, of all conceivable aspects of relevance. The space of geography is that of the earth's surface, the home of man."

The works by two Germans, Walter Christaller (1893–1969) and August Lösch (1906–1945), and their translations into English in the 1950–60s provided an important background for new ideas in English-speaking geography. Their *Raum* was not related to concrete, unique regions on the terrestrial earth's surface but to abstract space in models, an isotropic plain where processes operating/interaction between centers and hinterlands created certain patterns. Such models were highly influential among the rising generation of US scholars and provided a strong promise of a new, more scientific geography.

Harvey (1973: 13) has suggested that space is "neither absolute, relative or relational *in itself*, but it can become one or all simultaneously depending on circumstances." Thus the concepts of space in Figure 10.1 also have to be seen as "relational" and overlapping rather than neatly successive elements separating the three strata from each other. Some confusion occurred in the early use of such ideas, perhaps also indicating linguistic differences between the concepts of *Raum* and space in the context of chorology. Absolute, relative and relational views on space were discussed in English-speaking geography by Blaut (1961), who looked through this conceptual prism into the past of geographical thinking. It later became typical to regard the views of chorologists as examples of absolute space and container thinking (Harvey 1969), but the list given by Blaut (1961) was different and included not chorologists but Lösch, many geopolicians and "social physicists" who analyzed human interaction by means of physical models. For Aay (1972), chorological views included "far more than a commitment to absolute space," as they "conceived of space as coexistence of phenomena." Even so, he labeled this approach as an example of geometrical "absolute space" and also linked social physicists with this category.

Bunge, in his *Theoretical Geography* (1962), regarded geography as a science of spatial relations and interaction: since geometry is the mathematics of space, it is the "language of geography." Space, spatial relations and change in space were important for Morrill (cited in Aay 1972), whereas distance, direction/orientation and connection/relative position were the key concepts for Nystuen (1963). Broek (1965:6) emphasized both the internal nature of the area (the site) and its external relations (the situation), while Haggett's (1965) theorization of nodal regions reminds us of the language of current relational thinking. For him functional/nodal regions are open systems and any analysis of the build-up of such systems requires an analysis of movement, the channels along which this occurs, networks, nodes and their organization in a hierarchy.

All in all, a number of social and academic-institutional events thus gave rise to the second strata. This was also a march of the new *generation* of geographers (Johnston 1991: 283–285). Peter Gould (1985) saw the rise of new language as a *revolution* and found evidence for this precisely in ways that geographical keywords developed from the 1950s to the 1960s. He analyzed the titles of geographical journals and described how the words "regional," "spatial" and "model" exploded onto the scene. Gould discussed why the word "spatial" diffused so rapidly and suggested that "the word itself obviously plucked a deep chord in many of the people forming a new generation of geographers" and that "spatial" became an expression of identity, a keyword that "gave a generation a sense of breaking away and doing something different." Compared with "geographic," "spatial was new, sounded much more scientific, and people were so impressed they did not usually ask what it meant" (Gould 1985: 24). While scholars like Hartshorne (1939: 284) had used "spatial" and discussed the role of relative location in geography, Gould (1999: 86) made a distinction from the traditionalists: "with the exception of one or two works of scholarship in historical geography, it was practically impossible to find a book in the field that one could put in the hands of a scholar in another discipline without feeling ashamed."

The translation of Torsten Hägerstrand's *Innovations förloppet ur korologisk synpunkt* (The development of innovations from a chorological point of view, 1953) is a good example of the power of new keywords. The English title "*Innovation diffusion as a spatial process*" (1967) was modified from the Swedish by Allan Pred to reflect the *Zeitgeist*; hence "diffusion," "spatial" and "process" in the title. *Hägerstrand* commented later that "I did not express my wording "korologisk synpunkt" as "spatial process" but had to accept it because I had no proper alternative" (Olwig 2002: 15).

In spite of its visibility, Barnes (2004) observes, the quantitative revolution was not universal but "punctuated, spotty and peculiar to particular sites," and the first proponents were in trouble when trying to publish in existing forums. They were ultimately forced to establish new journals, and it took time for the new approaches, many of them originally initiated in continental Europe, to spread back there from the English-speaking world.

The role of regional geography varied after World War II. The new theoretical approaches and quantitative methods soon dominated the new intellectual stratum in the US and UK, which led to a decline in *regional geography* as a research field. The *region* was still important, but the new concept was abstract, instrumental and had a bearing on significant theoretical and practical questions (Barnes and Farish 2006). Regionalization became a matter of classification and the construction of taxonomies (Grigg 1967). A region was now a "data-bound cell" that could be analyzed by statistical methods. This idea of region has remained important with the advent of digital geographical information systems and the related science (Montello 2003).

The new theoretical approaches did not mark the end of regional geography. This was based on the simple fact that regional knowledge is crucial for the reproduction of the state and for *spatial socialization*, i.e. for the making of citizens and the shaping of their world-views. The ideas of region and regional geography were also discussed in journals during the heyday of spatial analysis and pleas even appeared for a balance between regional geography and the spatial approach (Paasi 2009a). Region continued to inspire also traditional scholars, so that e.g. Gilbert (1960) still regarded geography as the art of recognizing, describing and interpreting the personalities of regions. Perhaps the last visible plea was put forward by Hart (1982: 2, 22). For him the task of regional geography was to make "evocative descriptions that facilitate an understanding and appreciation of places, areas and regions" and regions were "subjective artistic devices, and they must be shaped to fit the hand of the individual user." Also, although representing residual thinking, regional geography still existed in the US in the form of studies of cultural/vernacular regions. New approaches emerged when behavioral geographers began to study *perceptual regions*. Many of these people were leading spatial analysts inspired by quantitative methods (like Peter Gould), whereas others relied on qualitative approaches.

Stratum III: Space, Region and Social Practice

David Harvey's *Social Justice and the City* (1973) was a major manifesto for the need to reflect space as a *social* category. The author of *Explanation in Geography* (1969) was now looking at the world through Marxist categories, and a number of scholars followed suit. Harvey (1973: 13) suggested that "the problem of the proper conceptualization of space is resolved through human practice with respect to it." This was the idea that scholars interested in regional research were to follow from the late 1970s onwards. The emphasis on the relations between social and spatial was crucial for re-thinking the region and other spatial categories. Amidst the dominant positivist and emerging humanist and Marxist perspectives, Gregory (1978) suggested that it was vital to revive regional geography. More specific societal backgrounds were the problems of uneven capitalist development and changing spatial divisions of labor. Massey (1978) took up a Marxist position and saw regions as results of uneven economic development and of successive, overlying rounds of *capital accumulation* expressed spatially. Another extreme way of looking at human practice was through humanistic approaches, often based on phenomenological perspectives, which put emphasis on *human experience*. Place was their keyword rather than region (Tuan 1977).

Studies based on structuration theory, emphasizing structure-agency relations, gave rise to the new or reconstructed regional geography (Thrift 1983). Region again became an important keyword for human geographers, now as a deeply contextual category: "... regional geography is central to the practice of doing human geography ... the contextual cannot be swept under the carpet by grand social theories, for it remains where we actually live. It is the margin that constitutes the centre" (Thrift 1994: 226–227). The strata of space, region and social practice were thus characterized by a new interest of knowledge. The practical and technical interests represented by regional geography and spatial analysis were paralleled by an emancipatory one. New regional geographers tried to understand social and cultural practices and discourses and to reveal the power relations embedded in region-building processes and in the construction of boundedness and identities.

The idea of region was also re-conceptualized. Where traditional regional geographers pondered over whether regions are "real" or mental categories and spatial analysts gave them an analytical-instrumental role, the questions/answers regarding the "being" and "becoming" of regions or space for the new regional geographers was based on *social practice*. Regions were conceptualized as processes that are perpetually "becoming" (Pred 1984) or "institutionalize" (Paasi 1986), rather than "being" stable. Also, as historically contingent social processes, they could come to an end, i.e. deinstitutionalize. What mattered were power relations and daily activities in which individuals, social groupings and classes produced, reproduced and gave meanings to regions. This occurred in wider practices such as politics, governance, economics, education, the media and communication. Where regional geographers studied regions as a complex horizontal mosaic of spatial units, the new regional geographers scrutinized regions as parts of the rescaling of the state in the face of globalizing capitalism. Regions and region-building processes are materially embedded and constituted. Also crucial are issues such as identity, a sense of belonging, loyalties and the mobilization of memory. Re-thinking the "objectivity" of regions led to their conceptualization as processes that are performed, limited, symbolized and institutionalized through practices, discourses and power relations that are not inevitably bound to a specific scale but may be networked in both time and space (Paasi 2009a, 2009b).

New related keywords also appeared. Locality studies emerged in the UK in the 1980s, and scholars reflected on how wider social processes can manifest themselves in local contexts. Thrift (1994) showed how such studies were soon labeled as empiricist, as avoiding Marxist metanarratives, as conservative in their textual strategies and as unable to produce evidence of autonomous spatial effects. It may have been such a harsh criticism that soon swept the locality concept as residual, leading to an exceptionally short life-cycle for this keyword.

The concept of place pursued a different track. It became important in the 1960s and was a keyword in humanistic geography from the 1970s onwards. While a humanistic view remained important, in the 1990s place was adopted and re-defined by critical scholars such as Massey (1995). It was the socially constructed, hybrid and relational character of place and the power geometries involved in this construction that were now accentuated. Relational space also soon emerged as a keyword in geography, having been promoted above all by the post-structuralists who accentuate the relational-topological character of space and the networked, unbounded nature of spatiality (Murdoch 2006). Relational thinkers try to "replace topography and structure-agency dichotomies with a topological theory of space, place and politics as encountered, performed and fluid" (Jones 2009). Relational views may be purely ontological, stressing the hybrid and networked character of the world, but they may also be normative-political, promoting the progressive character of such ideas compared with "territorial" views, which are regarded as politically regressive.

Such relational thinking is supported by the fact that most (con)temporary regions stretch in space and their social contents are networked across borders. These networks modify, reconstitute and at times remove regions: regional boundaries and identities do *not* need to be exclusive or permanent (Paasi 2009b). Yet we should not be one-eyed with such generalizations but should recognize the contextuality of boundedness and the inherent relations of power. Although regional or state boundaries can sometimes be insignificant, they are sometimes more persistent and can certainly not be erased by making pure ontological claims. The recent resurgence of the region and the rise of the so-called "new regionalism" have indicated this once again. Many regions are *territories* deployed within processes of governance, and hence are made socially meaningful entities. Territories show how absolute, relative and relational aspects of space became fused in material practices (boundary-making), representations (mapping) and lived meanings (affective loyalties to territorial units) (Harvey 2009: 174). Boundaries may also have a constitutive role in the governance and control of social action. The significance of regions and even boundaries as catalysts for regionalist movements, ethno-territorial groups and planning strategies is also evident (Agnew 2001). Similarly, the identity narratives created by regional activists and advocates, the media and governmental bodies force us to study such politics of distinction rather than denying their existence.

Geographical Keywords and Research Practice

As shown in Figure 10.1, the three strata are related differently to research practice, and three perspectives on region emerge: pre-scientific, discipline-centered and critical (Paasi 2002, 2009a). *Pre-scientific* implies that researchers do not problematize the region but take it for granted. This is typical in applied research, where the planning/regional authorities present scholars with the relevant "regions" (e.g. statistical or administrative units). *Discipline-centered regions* are constructed by researchers using criteria such as homogeneity of content, uniformity of features, functional coherence or perceptual qualities. Regions are thus seen as objects or results of research activity. Such views were typically used to legitimize a specific "geographical perspective" during the emergence of the first stratum.

Region was not taken as given when the "making" or "finding" of regions was the major task. Traditional regional geographers continuously generated new interpretations of regional categories that were products of research processes. Similarly, it is easy to understand how "regions as given" became typical when applied research emerged after World War II. The first applied scholars operated with the functional regions needed in planning; actually adopting discipline-centric views (e.g. those based on central place hierarchies). The increasing use of statistical information and the acceptance of given administrative units as "regions," made them particularly significant (Cliff et al. 1975). This is also common in current economic geography, where "regions" are identified as being crucial to regional development but are then taken largely as given as settings for economic development (Paasi 2002). It is obvious that modern GIS techniques will again add a category that implies the "making" of regions for various purposes.

In critical interpretations regions are manifestations of contested individual and social practices and discourses. It is, of course, still the (critical) geographer who abstracts and conceptualizes the ideas of the region and their construction, but such abstractions are developed to reveal the power relations, mechanisms and processes characterizing social, political, economic and cultural worlds on all spatial scales. A region is hence not just a given setting in which such processes occur nor a mechanical instrument that can be used for analyzing such elements.

Discussion

In tracing the ideas of region/space within the framework of knowledge production and societal power, this paper displays not a neat cumulative logic or a successive replacement of such keywords but rather a multilayered montage of overlapping categories that are ceaselessly on the move as scholars react to academic and social challenges by re-conceptualizing spatial categories. New keywords do not always replace old ones but become a new "layer" in academic discourse and practice. The fact that the space of keywords has become "thicker" indicates the fragmentation of geography. It was partly this that led Jessop et al. (2008), for instance, to suggest that instead of the currently popular "churning around" of separate categories, it would be useful to bring them together. Their "TPSN framework" (Territory, Place, Space, Network) is one example of this.

Spatial categories are increasingly being combined with other ideas. Olwig (2002) speaks of a "hocus-pocus" or "abracadabra" effect that can be associated with fetishized debates on spatiality. While the current keywords are probably no worse examples of this effect than the old ones (Peter Gould's comments on the word "spatial" above!), yet we can ask why such an accelerating "pumping" of new keywords into the "discursive market" has occurred? As we have seen, social contexts and events may lead to a re-thinking of keywords: nationalism, war or uneven developments, for example, have shaped conceptual thinking. Nowadays the tendency for increasing academic management, research assessment, or evaluation based on citation data and the related claims to be productive and novel probably motivate scholars to search for new conceptualizations. Such international pressures show the power of state and institutions/think-tanks such as the EU and OECD, in standardizing research practice and creating a competitive academic environment in which internationalization is the new mantra.

Ackerman (1945: 122) identified two major problems in the postwar US geography: the inability to handle foreign language sources, and the lack of competence in topical/systematic subjects. After the war the US authorities tried actively to reconfigure also the European scientific landscape, especially in the "hard" sciences

(Krieger 2006). International science became a vehicle for promoting American values and interests in the new ideologically divided world. Ironically, previous international institutions seem to have provided a solution to Ackerman's language skill problem in the English speaking world, a solution that is definitely not what Ackerman was calling for. In current geography "internationalization" does not mean an increase in linguistic skills and interaction between geographers from different language backgrounds as much as the rise of English as an academic *lingua franca*.

We saw how the first two strata in the space of keywords were largely products of an exchange of ideas, whereas stratum III is an increasingly monolingual one. English language provides today the widest medium for international communication. Institutional claims for "internationalism" have made geographers outside the English-speaking world increasingly dependent on anglophone publication forums and on the corresponding conceptual discourses used in this context. The theoretical dialogue between English-speaking geographers and scholars working elsewhere over key spatial categories has largely disappeared. A major simultaneous paradox is that since the 1990s the overwhelming majority of international theoretical influences on spatial thinking in English-speaking geography have come from *outside* geography itself, especially from German, French, or Italian philosophy and sociology, typically through English translations of original texts (see Crang and Thrift 2000). This issue is not new: almost 30 years ago Agnew and Duncan (1981) wrote that there is a need for geographers to display more critical acuity in borrowing ideas from the outside of the field. While such borrowing provides an opportunity for the increasingly rapid – mostly unidirectional – adoption of new ideas, it is far removed from an exchange of conceptual ideas in truly international science of geography.

References

Aay, H. (1972) Re-examination: geography – the science of space. *Monadnock* 46, 20–31.
Ackerman, E.A. (1945) Geographic training, wartime research, and immediate professional objectives. *Annals of the Association of American Geographers* 35, 121–143.
Agnew, J. (1999) Regions in mind does not equal regions of the mind. *Progress in Human Geography* 23 (1) 91–96.
Agnew, J. (2001) Regions in revolt. *Progress in Human Geography* 25, 103–110.
Agnew, J.A. and Duncan, J.S. (1981) The transfer of ideas into Anglo-American human geography. *Progress in Human Geography* 5, 42–57.
Allen, J., Cochrane, A., and Massey D. (1998) *Rethinking the Region*. Routledge, London.
Barnes, T.J. (2004) Placing ideas: genius loci, heterotopia and geography's quantitative revolution. *Progress in Human Geography* 28, 565–595.
Barnes, T.J. and Farnish, M. (2006) Between regions: Science, militarism, and American geography from World War to Cold War. *Annals of the Association of American Geographers* 96, 807–826.
Becher, T. and Trowler, P.R. (2001) *Academic Tribes and Territories*. The Open University Press, Suffolk.
Blaut, J.M. (1961) Space and process. *Professional Geographer* 13, 1–7.
Broek, J.O.M. (1965) *Geography: Its scope and spirit*. Charles E. Merrill, Columbus, Ohio.

Bunge, W. (1962) *Theoretical Geography*. Gleerup, Lund.
Christaller, W. (1966) [1933] *Central Places in Southern Germany*. Prentice Hall, Englewoods Cliffs.
Claval, P. (2007) Regional geography: past and present. *Geographica Polonica* 80, 25–42.
Cliff, A., Haggett, P., Ord, J.K., Bassett, K., and Davies, R. (1975) *Elements of Spatial Structure*. Cambridge University Press, Cambridge.
Clout, H. (1989) Regional Geography in the United Kingdom: a trend report. In L.J. Paul (ed.), *Post-War Development of Regional Geography*. Utrecht, Nederlandsche Geografische Studies 86, Utrecht, Nederlansche, pp. 25–41.
Crang, M. and Thrift, N. (eds) (2001) *Thinking Space*. Routledge, London.
Foucault, M. (1980) Questions on geography. In C. Gordon (ed.), *Michel Foucault, Selected Writings 1972–1977*. Pantheon Books, New York, pp. 63–77.
Gauthier, H.L. and Taaffe, E.J. (2002) Three 20th century "revolutions" in American Geography. *Urban Geography* 23, 503–527.
Gilbert E.W. (1960) The idea of the region, *Geography* 45, 157–175.
Gould, P. (1985) *A Geographer at Work*. Routledge, London.
Gould, P. (1999) *Becoming a Geographer*. Syracuse University Press, Syracuse, New York.
Gregory, D.(1978) *Ideology, Science and Human Geography*. Hutchinson, London.
Grigg, D. (1967) Regions, models and classes. In R. Chorley and P. Haggett (eds), *Models in Geography*. Methuen, London, pp. 461–509.
Haggett, P. (1965) *Locational Analysis in Human Geography*. Edward Arnold, London.
Hart, J.F. (1982) The highest form of geographer's art. *Annals of the Association of American Geographers* 72, 1–29.
Hartshorne, R. (1939) *The Nature of Geography*. The Association of American Geographers, Lancaster.
Harvey, D. (1969) *Explanation in Geography*. Edward Arnold, London.
Harvey, D. (1973) *Social Justice and the City*. Blackwell, Oxford.
Harvey, D. (2009) *Cosmopolitanism and the geographies of Freedom*. Columbia University Press, New York.
Heffernan, M. (2003) Histories in geography. In S.L. Holloway, S.P. Rice, and G. Valentine (eds), *Key Concepts in Geography*. Sage, London, pp. 3–22.
Hettner, A. (1927) *Die Geographie, ihre Geschichte, ihr Wesen*. Ferdinand Hirt, Breslau.
Jessop, B, Brenner, N, and Jones M., (2008) Theorizing socio-spatial relations. *Environment and Planning D: Society and Space* 26, 389–401.
Johnston, R.J. (1991) *Geography and Geographers*. Edward Arnold, London.
Jones, M. (2009) Phase space: geography, relational thinking, and beyond. *Progress in Human Geography* 33, 487–506.
Kimble, G.H.T. (1951) The inadequacy of the regional concept. In L.D. Stamp and S.W. Woolridge (eds), *London Essays in Geography*. Green, Longmans, London, pp.151–174
Krieger, J. (2006) *American Hegemony and the Post-War Reconstruction of Science in Europe*. MIT Press, Cambridge, MA.
Lefebvre, H. (1991) [1974] *The Production of Space*. Blackwell, Oxford.
Lösch, A. (1954) [1940] *The Economics of Location*. Yale University Press, New Haven.
Lundberg, G.A. (1939) *Foundations of Sociology*. The Macmillan Company, New York.
Martin, G.J. and James P.E. (1993) *All Possible Worlds: a History of Geographical Ideas*. Wiley, Chichester.
Massey, D. (1978) Regionalism: some current issues. *Capital and Class* 6, 106–126.
Massey, D. (1995) The conceptualization of place. In P. Jess and D. Massey (eds), *A Place in the World*. Oxford University Press, Oxford, pp. 45–77.
Minshull, R. (1967) *Regional Geography: Theory and Practice*. Hutchinson, London.

Montello, D.R. (2003) Regions in geography: process and content. In M. Duckham, M.F. Goodchlid, and M.F. Worboys (eds), *Foundations of Geographic Information Science*. Taylor & Francis, London, pp. 173–189.

Murdoch, J. (2006) *Post-Structuralist Geography*. Sage, London.

Nystuen, J.D. (1963) *Identification of some fundamental spatial concepts*. Michigan Academy of Science, Arts, and Letters 48, pp. 373–384.

Olwig, K.R. (2002) The Duplicity of space: Germanic 'Raum,' and Swedish 'rum' in English language geographical discourse. *Geografiska Annaler* 84B, pp. 1–17.

Orwell, G. (1953) *Politics and English language. A collection of Essays*. Harcourt Brace, New York.

Paasi, A. (1983) *The subject of geography? The road to modern themes of humanistic and behavioural geography* (in Finnish with a summary in English). University of Joensuu, Publications of Social and Regional Sciences no. 34.

Paasi, A. (1986) The institutionalization of regions: a theoretical framework for understanding the emergence of regions and the constitution of regional identity. *Fennia* 164, 105–146.

Paasi, A. (2002) Region and Place: regional worlds and words. *Progress in Human Geography* 26, 802–811.

Paasi, A. (2009a) Regional geography I. In R. Kitchin and N. Thrift (eds), *International Encyclopaedia of Human Geography* Vol. 8. Elsevier, London, pp. 217–227.

Paasi, A. (2009b) The resurgence of the "region" and "regional identity": theoretical perspectives and empirical observations on the regional dynamics in Europe. *Review of International Studies* 35; S1, 121–146.

Platt, R.S. (1948) Environmentalism versus geography. *American Journal of Sociology* 53, 351–358.

Pred, A. (1984) Place as historically contingent process: structuration and the time-geography of becoming places. *Annals of the Association of American Geographers* 74, 279–297.

Sayer, A. (1992) *Method in Social Science*. Routledge, London.

Taylor, P.J. (1985) The value of a geographical perspective. In R.J. Johnston (ed.), *The Future of Geography*. Methuen, London, pp. 92–110.

Thrift, N. (1983) On the determination of social action in space and time. *Environment and Planning D: Society and Space* 1, 23–57.

Thrift, N. (1994) Taking aim at the heart of the region. In D. Gregory, R. Martin, and G. Smith (eds), *Human Geography*. Macmillan, London, pp. 200–231

Tuan, Y-F. (1977) *Space and Place: The Perspective of Experience*. University of Minnesota Press, Minneapolis.

Williams, R. (1976) *Keywords*. Fontana, London.

Williams, R. (1987) *Marxismi, kulttuuri ja kirjallisuus (orig. Marxism and Literature, 1977)*. Vastapaino, Jyväskylä.

Part III Contemporary Approaches

11	Nature – Part I *Noel Castree*	179
12	Nature – Part II *Jamie Lorimer*	197
13	Landscape – Part I *Don Mitchell and Carrie Breitbach*	209
14	Landscape – Part II *Mitch Rose and John W. Wylie*	221
15	Place – Part I *Tim Cresswell*	235
16	Place – Part II *Steven Hoelscher*	245
17	Territory – Part I *Stuart Elden*	260
18	Territory – Part II *Jacques Lévy*	271
19	Globalization – Part I *Richard Florida*	283
20	Globalization – Part II *Emily Gilbert*	298
21	World Cities – Part I *Carolyn Cartier*	313
22	World Cities – Part II *Paul L. Knox*	325
23	Governance – Part I *Wendy Larner*	336

The Wiley Blackwell Companion to Human Geography, First Edition.
Edited by John A. Agnew and James S. Duncan.
© 2011 John Wiley & Sons, Ltd. Published 2016 by John Wiley & Sons, Ltd.

24	Governance – Part II *Stephen Legg*	347
25	Mobility – Part I *David Ley*	361
26	Mobility – Part II *George Revill*	373
27	Scale and Networks – Part I *Andrew E.G. Jonas*	387
28	Scales and Networks – Part II *John Paul Jones III, Sallie A. Marston, and Keith Woodward*	404
29	Class – Part I *Andrew Herod*	415
30	Class – Part II *Clive Barnett*	426
31	Race – Part I *Kay Anderson*	440
32	Race – Part II *Arun Saldanha*	453
33	Sexuality – Part I *Natalie Oswin*	465
34	Sexuality – Part II *Mary E. Thomas*	475
35	Gender – Part I *Michael Landzelius*	486
36	Gender – Part II *Joanne P. Sharp*	501
37	Geopolitics – Part I *Phil Kelly*	512
38	Geopolitics – Part II *Merje Kuus*	523
39	Segregation – Part I *Larry S. Bourne and R. Alan Walks*	534
40	Segregation – Part II *Steve Herbert*	547
41	Development – Part I *Glyn Williams*	559
42	Development – Part II *Wendy Wolford*	575

Chapter 11

Nature
Part I

Noel Castree

Introduction

In this chapter I want to demonstrate that "nature" is not what it seems to be – at least for the many human geographers who have been writing on the matter since the late 1980s. I put the term in scare-quotes because these geographers – an increasingly prominent and influential group within the discipline – have in different ways sought to question nature's apparent naturalness. Their writings have endeavored to "de-naturalize" our understandings of those myriad things – birds and bees, genes and glaciers, hippos and hurricanes – to which we routinely attach the label "natural" in one or other sense of this polysemic and polyreferential word. I will explain how and why in the pages that follow.

It may seem strange to include a chapter on nature in a book about *human* geography. Indeed, as recently as twenty years ago, a volume like this would probably not have contained such a chapter. But in the wake of Margaret Fitzsimmon's (1989) germinal essay "The matter of nature" – in which she reprimanded human geographers for ignoring biophysical entities and processes in their research and teaching – things changed. Through the nineties and noughties a growing number of human geographers rectified their predecessors' habit of leaving the topic of nature to the physical geographers and so-called environmental geographers (who examine human-environment interactions). The division of intellectual labor shifted, but with the benefit of hindsight it shifted in rather surprising ways. Why surprising?

After the Second World War, the incipient schism between the human and physical sides of the subject became progressively wider and deeper in anglophone geography. The former became a social science and humanities subject concerned with

The Wiley Blackwell Companion to Human Geography, First Edition.
Edited by John A. Agnew and James S. Duncan.
© 2011 John Wiley & Sons, Ltd. Published 2016 by John Wiley & Sons, Ltd.

the thoughts, actions and institutions of people, while physical geography became an environmental science with several sub-branches (the largest being geomorphology). Environmental geographers spanned the divide, but were increasingly few in number as their colleagues flocked to one or other of the discipline's two major branches and their myriad subfields. This being so, one might have expected human geographers' "rediscovery" of nature to have involved either a closer dialogue with physical geographers or at least a focused engagement with environmental geography. After all, the former were and are professionally preoccupied with understanding natural processes and events in the atmosphere, cryosphere, pedosphere, biosphere and hydrosphere; and the latter were and are interested in how different societies utilize, and are shaped by, the non-human world. But recent history tells another story. As we'll see in this chapter, the "renaturalization" of human geography has done little, if anything, to bridge the much discussed "divide" between contemporary geography's two major branches.

Whether this is seen as a lost opportunity is very much a matter of perspective. By refusing to "import" knowledge about nature from their physical geography counterparts, and by often remaining quite aloof from their environmental geography colleagues, those on the human side of the discipline have delivered new and valuable insights into a topic of central concern to global humanity. This does not make a closer engagement between human and physical geographers impossible, nor a future expansion of environmental geography improbable; but it does alter the terms on which any future *rapprochement* involving geography's small "centre" and large "flanks" will be achieved.

The chapter is organized as follows. I begin by setting human geographers' recent attention to nature in its longer-term disciplinary and societal context. I then explore the principal meanings of the term "nature" as a necessary prelude to describing and explaining the varied ways in which human geographers have recently sought to "denaturalize" our understanding of it. I highlight three approaches, which are the focus of sections four, five and six of this essay. The penultimate section then seeks to evaluate these approaches in a range of ways, leading to a short conclusion.

The "Nature" of Contemporary Human Geography: Intellectual and Social Contexts

Nature, as an object of research and a focus of teaching, was central to academic geography's early identity. When, in the late nineteenth century, it became a recognized school and university subject it was on the basis of two central ideas, both of which strongly accented the realm of nature. The first was the idea of human-environment relations – the varied interactions between people and their biophysical milieu – as geography's defining focus. This idea positioned the nascent discipline as "bridging" subject, one able to span the gap between the social sciences and humanities on the one side, and the biophysical sciences on the other. It was a conception of geography put forward by Halford Mackinder in Britain, William Morris Davis in the USA and Karl Ritter in Germany (among others). The second idea was of geography as an idiographic subject, one whose unique focus was on what American geographer Richard Hartshorne (1939) later called "areal differentiation." In France Paul Vidal de la Blache accented this idea, so too Andrew Herbertson in Britain and Ellen Semple (1911) in the US. In each case the suggestion was that every place and region on the earth's surface has a distinctive biophysical character that forms the material basis for specific forms of human settlement.

What the two conceptions of academic geography shared was a commitment to producing *synthetic* knowledge: that is, to understanding reality as a totality of interconnected parts. In respect of this chapter's focus, the key point is that the natural world and the world of people were seen as intimately related rather than existing as discrete domains of reality. The "nature" of interest to the early geographers was not one abstracted from people, their activities and their creations. This meant that geography occupied a fairly distinctive niche within the wider academic division of labor at both school and university levels. Unlike the "natural sciences" it was not interested in interrogating the natural world for its own sake; and unlike the social sciences and humanities it did not leave the study of nature to the natural scientists and them alone.

Clearly, the early professional geographers had grand ambitions and with hindsight we can see that was it far from easy to build a credible discipline on the basis of the two above-mentioned ideas. The problem was a practical one. Many other research and teaching subjects were relatively specialized and focused on discrete domains of reality. In many cases, this enabled them to offer deep and precise insights into the nature of these domains. For instance, around the turn of the 20th century, physicist Ernest Rutherford was making fundamental discoveries about the nature of atoms, while Alfred Marshall's *Principles of economics* (1890) presented a new approach to understanding and managing the economy. Geography could boast no equivalent achievements. Its two defining ideas committed practitioners to the study of pretty much *everything*, whether at a local, national or global scale. It was no surprise that many of the books and essays authored by the early professional geographers were characteristically descriptive and lacked any convincing explanation of the concrete interactions between people and their environment. The explanations that were offered were frequently broad-brush and speculative, lacking the sort of detailed and comprehensive evidence-base that underpinned some of the notable scientific theories of the Victorian and Edwardian eras – such as Charles Darwin's theory of species evolution (1859). The fact that many of the early geographers sought after an explanatory framework as grand as Darwin's was not helpful. His path-breaking book *Origin of species* focused on species differentiation and development (itself a huge topic), while geographers' determination to examine the interrelations between plants, soils, water, atmosphere, economy, politics and so on made the search for a unifying theory a search, in effect, for the impossible.

In short, however laudable its aims were, geography in the late nineteenth and early twentieth centuries was intellectually weak and at times embarrassingly so with the benefit of hindsight. By the late 1930s many geographers felt the understandable need to "raise their game" intellectually. Continued breakthroughs in other disciplines, like physics, placed geography's shortcomings in ever starker relief. Moreover, during the Second World War (1939–1945) many who would subsequently gain positions in university geography departments served in the military and intelligence services. The experience was formative for most, instilling a belief that precision and rationality were virtues to be aspired to. In addition, many outside geography (such as the philosophers Wilhelm Dilthey and Edmund Husserl) had successfully argued that the physical sciences and the social sciences (with the humanities) had to be different by virtue of their subject matter. There could be no overarching theory or analysis of people and nature, it was argued, because the former possessed ontological properties quite different from rocks, rivers or ravines. For instance, humans are self-reflexive, linguistic, tool making beings able to make their own history and geography. This argument drove a wedge between the two spheres – society and nature – that the original geographers had sought to bring together in a single intellectual frame.

After 1945 academic geography progressively splintered into two major halves (human and physical), with each fragmenting into relatively discrete "systematic" sub-disciplines. The turn to specialization was undertaken in the hope that human and physical geography could become "spatial sciences." They would discover – through careful measurement, hypothesis testing and use of statistics – laws explaining spatial patterns (such as the common tendency of rivers to meander or migration flows to be inversely proportional to the size of destination cities). This necessitated a shift in the ways that geographers tackled nature as a topic. First, this topic increasingly became the preserve of a progressively sub-divided physical geography. Second, human geography increasingly abstracted the study of political, economic and cultural practices from their biophysical integument. The pre-war fondness of some geographers for discussing "human nature" (in the biological sense) was also quickly abandoned. Third, physical geographers produced increasingly "scientific" descriptions, explanations and even predictions of earth surface phenomena. Specialization, new databases, new remote sensing capabilities and new computer technologies made this possible, but the price paid was intellectual disunity: physical geographers divided nature into the five areas that comprise the field to this day (geomorphology, biogeography, climatology, hydrology and Quaternary environmental change). Finally, all of the above meant that the study of human-environment relations became something of a minority pursuit, with "spatial analysis" and the search for general laws and theories the new *modus operandi* of geography's two growing halves.

These changes together bolstered geographers' intellectual self-esteem and improved their external image within the world of higher learning. Ironically, though, geography was effectively abandoning the study of society-nature relations at the very moment when the title of William Thomas's 1956 edited book, *Man's role in changing the face of the earth,* was assuming a literal and serious importance. British scholar C.P. Snow's famous complaint about the estrangement of "the two cultures" – one literary-humanistic, the other scientific-rational – was (ironically) applicable to post-war geography, the one subject that had made intellectual synthesis its *raison d"etre*. Some efforts to maintain the "unity of geography" were made, with "systems theory" and conceptual "models" two of the suggested ways in which human and physical geographers might make common-cause. But these efforts could not prevent a growing schism between human and physical geography, with nature effectively erased from the former's intellectual preoccupations. This occurred despite a spike in social concern about human impacts on the environment from the late 1960s onwards. The era of the first Earth Day, when Greenpeace and

Friends of the Earth were founded, did not inspire a notable revival of human-environment study in geography.

The situation as described above prevailed for the best part of thirty five years. However, as I intimated in my introduction, things changed from the early 1990s onwards. Since that time human geographers have brought nature back-in to their half of academic geography. This has not, as might be assumed, involved some rapprochement with physical geography. On the contrary, many human geographers have taken issue with something that most physical geographers still take for granted: namely, that nature is – by definition – natural. Before I explain how and why, it is necessary to be explicit about something that has so far remained implicit. The next section examines the meanings of the word "nature." As we will see, these meanings are themselves anything but "natural."

What Is Nature?

Nature is a very old world in the English language, and its meanings have varied through time. It refers to a wide range of phenomena in a plurality of different ways – this is why it is an unusually complicated word, some would argue the most complex of all. As a linguistic philosopher might say, it is a "signifier" (word or sound) that has more than one "signified" (a specific meaning) and these signified's attach themselves to an astonishing number and range of material things ("referents"). Today, the term has four principal meanings. First, the non-human world, especially those parts untouched or barely affected by humans ("the natural environment"); second, the entire physical world, including humans as biological entities and products of evolutionary history; third, the power or force governing some or all living things (such as gravity or the conservation of energy); finally, the essential quality or defining property of something (e.g. it is natural for birds to fly and fish to swim). As a shorthand, we can (respectively) call these meanings "external nature," "universal nature," "super ordinate nature" and "intrinsic nature."

Clearly, depending on the context of usage, the idea of nature can function as a noun, a verb, an adverb or an adjective; it can also be characterized as object or subject, passive or active. For instance, we can talk of a "nature reserve," "natural beauty," a "naturally destructive" hurricane or the "natural order" being restored. "Nature" is both an ordinary word used in everyday discourse, and also part of the lexicon of scientists and other credentialized "experts." Equally clearly, several meanings of the term nature can be in play simultaneously. For example, consider the sentence "You can only understand the nature of academic Geography by understanding the different ways that geographers have studied nature." Here the fourth meaning of "nature" is used to describe the quality of an academic subject, only then to mean an object of study (in potentially all four senses of the term) in the second part of the sentence. What is more, the term can be used in evaluative as well as non-evaluative ways. Consider the best-selling books *The end of nature* (McKibben 2003, 2nd edition) and *Enough: staying human in an engineered age* (McKibben 2003), in which the American writer suggests that both non-human nature and human nature are together progressively disappearing. This, he argues, is because modern societies (with their colossal ecological footprints and powerful technologies) are destroying that which evolution bequeathed us – by both design and accident. On the basis of this non-evaluative observation, McKibben then criticizes the modern way of life: for him, "nature" is that which we should seek to protect, nurture and sustain. Like many others, he espouses a nature-centric morality implying that nature equals good, therefore less nature equals bad. This overlaps with a widespread assumption that what is natural is "normal" and what is unnatural is "abnormal," "artificial," "fake" or in some other way unsuitable.

In summary, the term nature and its multiple meanings are promiscuous in the English language. This becomes even more evident if we consider its "collateral concepts." These are terms whose meanings are closely related, and sometimes synonymous with, the meanings of "nature." For instance, widely used words like "biology," "sex," "genes," and "race" are often proxies for the term nature. If, to take one example, one says that Tay Sachs disease is "natural" among certain unlucky people, it's because it is a genetic illness inherited at birth. In other words, it is part of the biological hardware of those affected by it. Likewise, when two evolutionary biologists published a highly controversial book entitled *A natural history of rape* (Thornhill and Palmer, 2000), they argued that sexual assault of women by men is a "natural" reproductive strategy programmed into the latter's biological repertoire.

In light of all this, it is easy to get lost in the complexity of meaning and the range of contexts in which the term "nature" and its collateral concepts get used. However, I would argue that there are some signals in the noise. It seems to me that when we use the word nature and its proxy terms, we typically think we are making *ontological* statements of a cognitive, moral or aesthetic kind. That is to say, we believe we are making statements about a biophysical reality that exists independently of the words, concepts and terms we use to make linguistic sense of it. In this respect, we are apt to assume that "nature" is a "mimetic concept" whose meanings capture in words actually existing phenomena that exist "out there" (or "in here" if we are discussing our own physiology and neurology).

However, this assumption is questionable. Why so? Comparative anthropology provides an answer. In his study of several aboriginal societies, Tim Ingold (1996: 120) came to the following conclusion. "Hunter-gatherers," he suggested, "do *not*, as a rule, approach their environment as an external world of nature that has to be grasped conceptually and appropriated symbolically within the terms of an imposed cultural design ...; indeed, the separation of mind and nature has no place in their thought and practice." Ingold's conclusion chimes with that of cultural critic Raymond Williams, whose famous book *Keywords* (1976) inquired not into the "proper" meanings of words – as if physical reality somehow dictates this – but their social history of invention and usage. According to Williams, the meanings of "nature" are as much a reflection of those societies in which the term has currency, as they are the properties of the phenomena to which the term by convention refers. When we talk about "nature," Williams famously opined, we are talking about ourselves without necessarily knowing it or admitting it.

This is why I have devoted this section to discussing the *concept* of "nature," rather than assuming that it is secondary to the material world it is intended to depict. In anglophone cultures, we apprehend reality using a meshwork of concepts that compartmentalize the world into dualisms, including nature-society, organic-artificial, civilized-wild, urban-rural, city-country, raw-cooked, irrationality-reason, fact-fiction, material-immaterial, and so on. These dualisms form a cognitive template for us, and it is easy to forget the cultural specificity and historical contingency of this template – hence Ingold's and Williams' reminders.

Am I suggesting that "nature" does not exist, only the concept and its proxy terms? In one sense, yes I am. This is not the same as arguing that the material things to which the concept refers do not exist: they assuredly do. But it is purely a matter of convention to call them "natural" in the various ways and contexts that we choose to; indeed, it is arguably a matter of convention to divide the world into words and things, symbols and reality, mind and matter. For many (perhaps including some readers of this chapter), this is no doubt a difficult argument to accept. It accords a lot of importance to language, its social origins and its practical effects; and it challenges the conventional idea that many or most concepts are semantic "mirrors" that faithfully represent the material world. Nature, *by definition*, seems to be that which lies outside and is irreducible to linguistic conventions. But appearances are deceptive. In the end, there is nothing "natural" about our habit of designating certain things as belonging to "nature," nor about using those things as a reference-point to anchor our ethical or aesthetic beliefs (as McKibben and others do). As historical geographer William Cronon (1995) once said, we cannot fall into the trap which the word lays for us.

These arguments, as we will see in the next three sections, are highly germane to human geographers' efforts to "re-naturalize" their research and teaching since the late 1980s. I will briefly explore a trio of influential contributions that, in different ways, *take nature seriously by way of a seemingly paradoxical insistence on questioning its naturalness*. They have renaturalized human geography by denaturalizing "nature." The first emphasizes economic activity, the second cultural norms, while the third challenges the nature-society dualism that is seen to underpin the other two. In different ways, they all take what philosopher Kate Soper (1995) has called a "nature skeptical" stance.

The Production of Nature

For reasons I cannot detail here, Karl Marx's theory of capitalism made a major impact on anglophone human geography from the mid-1970s onwards. Initially, Marxist geographers expressed little interest in questions pertaining to nature, but that changed with the publication of Neil Smith's book *Uneven development* in 1984. This landmark publication argued that capitalism – the dominant system by which goods and services are today produced – generates geographically uneven development as a constitutive feature, not as a random occurrence or accident. This is because capitalism is inherently contradictory: its compulsion to increase wealth incessantly leads it to scour the earth for new investment opportunities, new markets, new raw materials, and new labor forces. According to Smith, the generation of profits and their deployment on a vast scale not only explains the rise and fall of cities, regions and whole countries; it also underpins what he called "the production of nature." This, as Smith himself observed, is a counter-intuitive idea: "We are used to conceiving of nature as external to society … or else as a grand universal in which human beings are but small and simple cogs. But … our concepts have not caught up with reality. ... Capitalism ... ardently defies the ... separation between nature and society, and with pride rather than shame" (Smith 1984: xiv).

What did Smith mean by "production"? Capitalism, Marx argued, is an historically specific mode of commodity production that began life in Europe during the early 18th century. What makes it distinctive, he argued, is that commodities are produced not for their use value (i.e. their practical utility) but their exchange value (i.e. how much money they can command upon sale). Capitalists are thus fixated on "accumulation for accumulation's sake," employing workers to do their bidding and facing competitive pressures from rival capitalists. These pressures, Marx argued; necessarily force all capitalists to innovate and to seek a competitive-edge by making new products, hiring more-or-less workers, employing "smart machines," relocating factories, and so on.

What has this got to do with "nature"? A great deal. According to Smith, capitalism has remade nature head-to-toe over the last two centuries, meaning that such things as genetically modified crops are only the latest in a very long line of material transformations of the non-human world. Nature has become a mere means to the end of profit-realization, and in the process it has been physically reconstituted into an anthropogenic "second nature." Though not formally referenced to his book, a brilliant 1991 monograph by William Cronon illustrated Smith's arguments in bracing detail. *Nature's metropolis* tells the epic story of how the rise of Chicago during the 19th century was umbilically connected to the formation of entirely new agricultural landscapes throughout the mid-West of the US. For instance, in a superb chapter on grain production Cronon shows how money invested in new railways, new storage facilities and new farm equipment created a vast new geography of fields and fences that replaced the natural grasslands created by evolution and the actions of indigenous/native peoples. Capitalism, in both metaphorical and literal terms, revolutionized Chicago's hinterland in a few short decades.

Smith's arguments may seem somewhat overstated, even in an era where the genetic composition of species is being altered by science and technology. After all, even the "produced" landscapes of modern, commercial farms are "natural" in the sense that the animals, seeds and crops have not been created by people from scratch. So why did Smith not favor the use of "softer" verbs (like "modification" or "alteration") when describing the capitalism-nature relationship? The answer is two-fold. First, he wanted to challenge those who continued to reference a non-social, supposedly pure, external "nature" when advancing their own cognitive, moral or aesthetic arguments. His PhD supervisor, David Harvey, had already set a precedent here back in 1974. Harvey strenuously resisted then-popular arguments claiming that the world was increasingly "overpopulated," because there were more people alive than the earth's natural resource could sustain. He argued that advocates of policies to limit birth-rates justified them by talking of "natural limits to growth" that were supposedly fixed. This, Harvey argued, was an "ideological" move because it neglected the fact that "optimum" population numbers can only ever be defined *relative to* culturally specific assessments of what a "suitable" standard of living is. Those neo-Malthusians arguing for population control, Harvey argued, were typically developed world inhabitants using spurious claims about "natural resource scarcity" to imply that developing world poverty was caused by reckless procreation. To repeat Raymond Williams, when we talk about "nature" we are usually talking about ourselves (whoever we are) – even though we don't usually acknowledge the fact.

Secondly, Smith arguably favored the metaphor of "production" because he believed that in a capitalist world "nature" and "society" was no longer discrete domains of reality. In other words, they comprise an ontological unity not two ontological spheres. Terms like "alteration" and "modification" suggest some residuum of "natural nature" untouched by capital. But Smith's point was that those aspects of what we call "nature" that are germane to our everyday lives are increasingly defined in relation to the needs and actions of capitalists. It is not so much that all of nature is produced "all the way down" physically – the earth's molten core, for instance, is hardly "produced" by capital – it's more that so much of what we consider to be "modified" or even "pristine" nature is, as it is because it serves the material and discursive demands of capitalist enterprises, as they vary in time and space. And where it does not – as in the case of global warming, which is caused unintentionally by atmospheric pollution – this nature is the indirect result of the intentional production of other aspects of nature.

This said, Smith said precious little about the material properties and causal efficacy of those things we by convention call "natural," be they consciously "produced" or not. His was a one-sided analysis that accorded considerable power to capitalism. It was left to others to fill this intellectual vacuum. There were two aspects to this. One the one side some showed how capitalism was able to physically mould some parts of nature in the interests of profitability. Examples include environmental sociologist Jack Kloppenburg's *First the seed* (1988) and David Goodman et al.'s *From farming to biotechnology* (1987). Both books focused, like Cronon's, on farming. They showed how science was used by agro-foods companies to breakdown the physical "barriers" posed by crops and farm animals to enhanced profits – barriers such as crops" vulnerability to certain pests or a chicken's inability to grow to adult size in a few weeks rather than months. In both books, the physical malleability of certain components of "nature" was made plain in a way Smith only made theoretical mention of.

On the other side, other Marxist researchers interrogated cases where capital (or, rather, certain capitalists) is *unable* to impose its will entirely and where the agency of "nature" becomes important. Two examples will suffice. Karen Bakker's (2003) *An uncooperative commodity* shows how the physical properties of water made a huge difference to the way that privatizing British water services unfolded post-1989. Its weight and bulkiness give it certain intransigence, to which the new water market had to adjust. Likewise, Scott Prudham's book *Knock on wood* (2005) shows how the Pacific coast forestry industry has, in key respects, had to adapt to the material challenges posed by softwood trees growing in mountainous environments. Bakker and Prudham are not reintroducing a concept of non-social "nature," of which Smith would surely disapprove. Their point is that what we call "nature" possesses a degree of agency and influence, but this is always defined *relative to* the needs and wants of capitalist firms not *sui generis*. It is thus never absolute and is thoroughly contingent and conditional.

The Marxian work on capitalism and nature prioritizes economic processes and motivations. As we have seen, the suggestion is that the conventional idea of "nature" has been rendered obsolete (in some or all of its four meanings) because biophysical entities can no longer be understood in abstraction from the influences of capitalist enterprises. As Smith and Harvey also argued, this idea can be used for ideological purposes even as it has outlived its usefulness. This implies a gap between "discourse" and "reality," wherein the concept of "nature" is used as a smokescreen by those with power or influence. I want now to summarize a second strand of "nature skeptical" research in human geography, one that also gained momentum from the late 1980s onwards. As we will see, this strand largely brackets economic concerns and focuses more on the influence of cultural norms and beliefs writ-large – which are deemed to be of equal importance.

The Cultural Construction of Nature

Starting twenty years ago, the social sciences and humanities – including human geography – experienced a so-called "cultural, interpretive and linguistic turn." To simplify, this entailed a major focus on how different societies and social groups make the world *meaningful* to themselves and others. Theoretically, the inspiration for this turn was a motley collection of European intellectuals including Antonio Gramsci, Stuart Hall, Roland Barthes, Jacques Lacan, Jacques Derrida and Michel Foucault (among several others). For all their intellectual differences, these thinkers shared a common aversion to "vulgar Marxism" – the sort of Marxism that fixated on economic processes and which relegated other aspects of life (such as culture and politics) to some "superstructure" supposedly governed by the stern demands of the "economic base." More positively, each of these thinkers argued that "culture" is a crucial medium through which power, politics, identity and resistance are expressed and negotiated. Culture does not here mean (only) things such as classical music, great literature or fine art. Instead, in different ways Gramsci *et al.* suggested that "culture is ordinary": it comprises the various media through which people construct and communicate meaning day-in, day-out. Accordingly, the "turn" to culture, interpretation and language entailed a focus on everything from the symbolism of clothing and hairstyles through the way the mass media frame reality for consumers to advertising, pop music and spoken dialects.

In human geography, this turn involved a reformulation, revival and expansion of the sub-field of cultural geography. In Carl Sauer's classic 1925 formulation, different cultural groups modify nature, so creating distinctive cultural landscapes that are literal embodiments of those groups' habits and norms. Sauer's agenda inspired numerous studies of various cultural landscapes worldwide. However, not only did it simplify "culture," by positing it as a coherent "way of life" shared in common by discrete communities; it also presumed that "nature" existed outside of "culture," waiting to be physically altered in the latter's image. What is more, Sauer paid relatively little mind to questions of social power and resistance.

So-called "new cultural geographers" set about challenging Sauer's legacy some twenty years ago. The new emphasis was on "representations:" their origins, their content, their contexts of use, the ways they are interpreted, and their material effects. Representations are all those media (and their messages) which "speak to" us in some way; be they spoken, or written, seen or heard, factual or fictional. They convey meaning. The presumption was that these representations express relations of inequality common to most societies worldwide; that they reflect and constitute specific social identities (of class, "race," sexuality, gender etc.); that they are thus plural and often contested; and that they are influential, not secondary to the "realities" they re-present. The new catch-cry was that all sorts of representations have a "cultural politics" to them and a certain "materiality" as well.

How did this translate into new research into nature by human geographers? The true answer is complicated, so I will simply summarize a broadly indicative example. Some took inspiration from Jacques Derrida's linguistic philosophy known as "deconstruction." In his detailed examinations of Western philosophical discourse, Derrida argued that representations do not, contrary to common belief, capture in spoken or visual form "realities" existing "out there." Instead, he argued, all meanings are generated *within* linguistic systems such that – as Derrida (in) famously put it – "there is nothing beyond the text." For Derrida, representations form the grid through which the world becomes intelligible, and he insisted that all representation is purely conventional-cum-arbitrary, and in no way "anchored" in something solid outside itself. In a now classic essay and related book, Canadian geographer Bruce Braun (1997; 2002) applied Derrida's ideas to the topic of nature and wedded them to "post-colonial theory."

His empirical focus was the early-1990s clash between environmentalists and a commercial logging company over whether to fell an area of temperate rainforest in British Columbia called Clayoquot Sound. The former saw Clayoquot as one of the last remaining spaces of "pristine nature," while the latter regarded it as a valuable economic resource that should be logged in a responsible way for the good of the Canadian economy and those communities dependent on forestry jobs. In a detailed analysis of both sides' representations of Clayoquot, Braun shows how the region's "realities" were made to appear quite different depending whose side you were on. There was a clash between representations that made Clayoquot appear wild, intricate, threatened and special on the one side, and those (on the other side) that made it appear as one more "resource zone" to be rationally harvested by hi-tech logging firms. In both cases, the authors of the representations claimed to be depicting Clayoquot as it actually was. But Braun's point was that these representations – which comprised books, pamphlets and newsletters – reflected the specific agendas of those promoting them. In other words, one could not adjudicate between them by testing their veracity against the non-representational actualities of Clayoquot's old growth trees.

Arresting though this insight was, Braun's research contained a further surprise. Notwithstanding the *differences* in content and message between the environmentalists' and forest company's representations, Braun argued that they ultimately shared the *same* symbolic universe: a specifically Anglo-North American one that reflects the linguistic conventions and cultural suppositions of those colonists who spread through the US and Canada from the 17th century onwards. He makes this point with reference to Clayoquot Sound's small groups of remaining "native" or indigenous peoples. These groups had, historically, lived a peripatetic existence and had used the forest for generations to meet their material and symbolic needs. Yet both the environmentalists and the logging company fighting over Clayoquot's future assumed that the region was largely empty. This, Braun argued, constituted a geographical expression of a specifically Western belief that nature and society are two separate things. Clayoquot's indigenous peoples, he concluded, were thus victims of symbolic violence, even in the supposedly *post*-colonial conditions of modern Canada. Their history and present day claims to control of Clayoquot simply did not register in the unthinking assumptions made by the descendents of the original European colonizers.

Braun's research was among the first contributions to a now large, theoretically diverse and political plural body of geographical work that examines how representations of what we call "nature" commonly get conflated with the material things those representations refer to. Today, almost every issue of journals such as *Cultural Geographies* or *Geoforum* will contain an essay in this tradition. This work has uncovered the hidden values and agendas contained in everything from wildlife films to domestic gardens to adventure tourism guidebooks to discussions of supposed "racial differences" between people. It has demonstrated that representations of "nature" are rarely innocent, and frequently become the surreptitious vehicle for the exercise of power and acts of social resistance. And it has challenged Sauer's legacy, by showing "culture" to be a field of conflict and "nature" to be an effect of representation (not something existing outside it waiting to be modified by culture).

These virtues notwithstanding, concerns about this approach to "nature" were expressed almost from the get-go. If "nature" does not exist outside representation then, critics suggested, this leads to three key problems. First, researchers like Braun get snarled-up in ontological contradictions since they become anti-realists about a world beyond representation, but realists about representations. This is inconsistent and illogical, so the argument goes. A second charge is that researchers like Braun have no means of registering the fact that nature acts in certain ways regardless of how we represent it (for this and the previous criticism see Sayer 1993). For instance, it might be said that human's biological need for water is no discursive construction! Finally, a third criticism issued from environmentalists who argued that if one concedes that all understandings of nature reflect contingent cultural belief systems, then we have no way of valuing nature in its own right. We become trapped in a hall of mirrors, unable to appreciate the "otherness" of that existing beyond culturally specific representations (Soule and Lease 1995).

In fairness to Braun and subsequent fellow-travelers, none of these criticisms are entirely valid or compelling. Their aim was not (and is not) to suggest that representations, images or discourses are everything, nor to pull the rug from under "ecocentric" (or pro-nature) thinkers and activists. A more reasonable interpretation of their project is this: they wish to uncover the processes by which certain representations of "nature" get made and deployed and to show that these representations can be every bit as material as the things they depict. In a political sense, their objective is to get those constructing and using these representations to take responsibility for them – rather than pretend that they are nature's faithful representatives. In the latter respect, the "cultural construction of nature" approach shares the Marxist geographers' determination reveals the social underbelly of apparently factual claims about natural phenomena.

Beyond the Society-Nature Dualism: Hybrid and Non-Representational Geographies

Notwithstanding their differences, the two approaches discussed so far arguably have one cardinal commonality – at least according to the third approach that I will discuss. This third perspective, that of human geography's so-called "new materialists" (Braun 2009: 27), challenges the society-nature dualism that animates the other two. It favors a non-dualistic ontology in which the world is envisaged as comprising entities and relationships that have no discrete, *a priori* identities. This means that "society" and "nature" are simply the terms we have invented to pigeon-hole certain things that cannot, in fact, be so cleanly separated. As Donna Haraway (2003: 6, 20) has put it; "Beings do not pre-exist their relatings," which means that "the relation" is the smallest possible unit of analysis." As I will now describe briefly, the new materialists fall into two related camps.

The first we might call "hybrid geographers," who take intellectual inspiration from so-called "actor network theory" (ANT) and the "process philosophy" of Gilles Deleuze (among others). The term "hybrid" here refers to these geographers' insistence that, when we look at the world, we often exaggerate qualitative differences between things (bodies, machines, institutions etc.) and so fail to see how co-constituted and interdependent things really are. This insight extends to geographers themselves: as both researchers and teachers they are seen as being thoroughly *immersed* in the world they ostensibly "study" at one remove. As a corollary, scholarship and pedagogy are both regarded as particular sorts of *engagements* with reality. These ideas have been most comprehensively articulated by Oxford University geographer Sarah Whatmore (2002), in her influential book *Hybrid Geographies* (and more recently by Steve Hinchliffe (2007), in *Geographies of Nature*). Following ANT, Whatmore eschews the nature-society binary in favor of a focus on different actor-networks: that is, specific, more-or-less durable, more-or-less important, more-or-less lengthy entanglements of what we call "social" and "natural" things. After process philosophy, Whatmore also emphasizes the "commotion" of the world: it is constantly "becoming," never entirely "fixed," stable or predictable.

On this basis, she shows that the world cannot be carved up into two ontological zones that are qualitatively distinct, albeit "connected" in practice. Instead, her numerous case studies – of wildlife conservation, of property rights in plants and of genetically modified foods – demonstrate that life is more complicated, lively, and surprising that our usual analytical and moral categories can reveal. As part of this, Whatmore reveals that we humans are not the only (significant) "agents" in the world: other entities constantly make a difference too, albeit in relation to other actors in particular networks. As a geographer, she argues that our conventional spatial taxonomy is deeply impoverished, supposing as we do that some areas (e.g. nature reserves or cities) are qualitative or quantitative incarnations-cum-concentrations of nature or society (but not both). What follows from all this is not simply a plea to *see* the world differently, but to *engage* with it differently in moral terms? Traditionally, ethical beliefs and arguments have rested on solid ontological foundations based, in turn, on qualitative distinctions (e.g. between animals and humans or endangered and common species). However, Whatmore's work suggests the need for a less certain, more open and "generous" ethics that is alive to the world's vitality and less keen to rush to judgment about what matters most. With Hinchliffe (Hinchliffe and Whatmore 2009)), she has called for a more "careful political ecology," where "careful" means both analytically attentive and morally sensitive.

So-called "non-representational geographers" share the broad sensibility expressed by Whatmore and her fellow-travelers. However, inspired by Nigel Thrift's (2007), *Non-representational theory*, non-representational geography (NRG) focuses more on the human actors in actor-networks does not take inspiration from ANT alone (or principally). This has involved an exploration of what is called "affect." According to Thrift, human geography's "cultural turn" during the 1990s led to a fixation on the power of "cultural beliefs" and led to an obsession with the analysis of "representations" (e.g. paintings, television adverts, magazines) and "discourses" (e.g. newspaper reports). This, Thrift argues, tended to render the world *lifeless*. It made it appear as if we engage with each other and our surroundings in purely visual, cognitive and/or linguistic terms; and it made the world appear as a *tabula rasa* onto which we project our ideas, ideals, hopes, prejudices and fears. By contrast, NRG emphasizes human embodiment and focuses on multi-sensory forms of human practice involving emotion, sound, touch, and bodily motion. "Affect" describes the myriad pre- and unconscious ways in which we both influence and are influenced by the world, and it goes beyond the registers of cognition, reason and signification. Non-representational geographers, typically, focus in great detail on the myriad different ways in which people "perform" their lives, and they have paid attention to things previously consider "unsuitable" topics for research; such as dance and experiences of boredom. Geographically, attention is usually paid to the micro-spaces and micro-environments in which "affect" takes shape – such as a coastal pathway in John Wylie's (2005) case. The normative implications of NRG are similar to those of "hybrid geography." Because life is seen as a sequence of "events" and "happenings" there is always, it is argued, the possibility for ethical novelty and political surprise. The recent reviews of the field authored by Hayden Lorimer (Lorimer 2005) indicate that NRG is now a maturing field of research – albeit once largely based in Britain.

Together, hybrid geography and NRG seek to reveal a world more complex and "lively" than that seen through either Marxian or culturalist optics. Politically and ethically they are also more "hopeful." Where many Marxian and culturalist analyses of "nature" regard it as a medium through which power operates, the likes of Whatmore and Thrift attend to the way in which life frequently escapes the imperatives of either economic production or cultural representation. However, the new materialists' work can be criticized for a number of reasons. First, it is arguably naïve in its celebration of change, surprise and "becoming," betraying a degree of romanticism among its authors. Second, and relatedly, it arguably down-plays the role of overarching social relations and social structures in governing patterns of human activity. Third, it arguably also fails to differentiate people in class, ethnic, gender and other terms since these social distinctions make a big difference to the nature of "affect." Finally, it arguably creates a dualism between itself and those approaches to nature it rejects, in the process contradicting its own commitment to a relational epistemology.

Evaluations

The previous three sections I summarized the leading approaches to understanding "nature" developed by present-day human geographers. In different ways, each of them is "nature skeptical." For heuristic reasons I have deliberately overdrawn the differences between them; in practice, they bleed into each other to various degrees. What are we to make of these approaches? This question can be answered from two different perspectives. The classic attitude to academic research is that it's in the business of revealing the "truth" – if not in an absolute sense, then at least in a provisional sense. After all, professors do not simply "make things up" (or at least not consciously!) and an ethic of rigor and "objectivity" is commonplace in the academic world. As sociologist of knowledge Tim Dant (1991: 1) once put it, "… we tend to live as if knowledge could be settled, as if there is only one true knowledge which we are striving for. …" From this perspective, each of the three approaches summarized needs to be assessed according to how truthful it is. However, the problem with this is plain to see: the trio does not share a common criterion by which their relative "truthfulness" can be defined. For instance, the second approach regards the representation-reality dualism upon which the post-Enlightenment concept of truth is founded to be a convention rather than an ontological given. Meanwhile, the third approach rejects dualistic thinking and any belief that the knower is separate from the object of their curiosity, desire or interest such that objects can ultimately "speak for themselves" if one only uses the "right method." This third approach favors a fluid, dynamic ontology in which "truth" is simply the name we give to those things and relations we can render stable enough to "re-present" them in knowledge until we find a reason to alter our representations.

A second perspective on the question posed above – and to my mind a preferable one – is to see all three approaches as epistemic *interventions*: as attempts to *alter* or *affect* the world they purport merely to *describe*. This is consistent with a long line of philosophical thinking, illustrated well by the "pragmatist" epistemology developed by John Dewey and William James a century ago and revived by the recently deceased American philosopher Richard Rorty. My earlier discussion of the concept of "nature" was animated by a pragmatist sensibility. Pragmatists do not concern themselves with whether any given body of knowledge is intrinsically "true" or "false," "factual" or "fictional," "objective" or "subjective." Instead, they inquire into the goals of knowledge-producers and the actual effects of their discourses. In its different forms and genres, knowledge is thus seen as "performative" in a range of ways and to varying degrees. For instance, pragmatists would argue that "scientific" knowledge is not inherently more "objective" than science fiction writing. Instead, they would argue that – for historically contingent reasons – "objectivity" is the attribute that self-declared "scientists" have given to the knowledge they produce. This kind of knowledge is especially good at enabling us to manipulate our material environment (and our own bodies) for certain socially-defined ends. It temporarily congeals our beliefs about certain things so that we can use or alter them for whatever our purposes happen to be. The labels "objective" and "truthful" allow this knowledge to gain an often far-reaching degree of societal credibility, and therefore considerable power.

Seen from this second perspective on knowledge, the three approaches considered in this chapter are epistemically equal attempts to shape our understanding of the world – equal in the sense that there is nothing intrinsically "better" about any one of them because the very criteria for judging their persuasiveness or utility are themselves a matter for debate and thus conventions (not givens). This does not mean that we should *accept* their insights equally and together. We can still make choices about which of them seem to us the most insightful, persuasive or useful. Or we can hope for greater dialogue between these approaches than there has so far been, in the hope of seeing their mutual enrichment over time. The point, simply, is that we can neither step outside these approaches to find some neutral site from which to judge their relative merits, and nor can we presume to fairly judge any two from the perspective of the other (since this immediately presupposes that they conform to the latter's precepts).

Conclusion

As we have seen, human geographers these days have a lot to say about "nature," but in a rather subversive, "denaturalizing" way. For the most part, their recent rediscovery of nature has not brought them closer to their physical geography counterparts, or to those environmental geographers who try to combine social and physical science perspectives on society-nature interactions. For many in the discipline this is a lost opportunity, indeed, little less than a tragedy. After all, ours is the era of genetically modified foods, "designer babies," artificial life (AI), cloned mammals, accelerating species extinctions, global climate change, the deforestation of the Amazon Basin, oil and water scarcity, and much more besides. Such is modern humanity's capacity to transform natural processes and phenomena that the Nobel Laureate Paul Crutzen calls our time "the anthropocene." In his view, it is akin to a new geological era and a distinct phase of earth history. Surely, some argue, this is the moment to reunite human and physical geographers so as to address all manner of problems caused by the "human impact." Why fiddle while Rome burns?

Persuasive as such arguments might appear, they rather imply that the three approaches summarized here are not strictly relevant to this agenda, and therefore of little value. But as I suggested in the previous section, the value of academic knowledge must always be defined in relative and contextual terms: a supposedly objective "reality" existing "out there" does not dictate how we could or should seek to understand it. Responding to the challenges of the "anthropocene" is simply one of several options we have, even though it might seem like a "no-brainer" to some. Once we appreciate this fact, we can start to discuss – in an open and mature fashion – which sorts of knowledge we want to value, believe in and foster, and to what ends. That discussion needs to be democratic and inclusive, and we should not be cowed by the seeming "imperatives" dictated if we are to avoid "catastrophic" environmental change this century. We are certainly not there yet. Talking of human geography as a whole, Eric Sheppard and Paul Plummer (2007) argue that there is currently far too little dialogue and shared respect between the discipline's various "epistemic communities" and sub-fields. In microcosm, that argument applies to the trio of approaches considered here: we need a more "engaged pluralism" that will break-down some of the barriers to mutual criticism and understanding. If this can be achieved, then shared intellectual enrichment will follow through constructive debate and the transfer of ideas. It may even lead to a greater rapprochement between human geographers and their physical and environmental geography counterparts – not in the name of some forced "unity of geography," but in the interests of greater unity-in-difference across the whole subject.

References

Bakker, K. (2003) *An uncooperative commodity?* Oxford University Press, Oxford.
Braun, B. (1997) Buried epistemologies: the politics of nature in (post)colonial British Columbia. *Annals of the Association of American Geographers* 87 (1), 3–32.
Braun, B. (2002) *The intemperate rainforest*. Minnesota University Press, Minnesota.
Braun, B. (2009a) Theorizing the nature-culture divide. In K. Cox, M. Low, and J. Robinson (eds), *Handbook of political geography*. Sage, London.
Cronon, W. (1991) *Nature's metropolis*. W.W. Norton, New York.
Cronon, W. (1995) In W. Cronon (ed.), *Common ground*. W.W. Norton, New York.
Dant, T. (1991) *Knowledge, ideology and discourse*. Routledge, London.
Darwin, C. (1859) *The origin of species*. John Murray, London.
Fitzsimmons, M. (1989) The matter of nature. *Antipode* 21 (2), 106–120.
Goodman, D., Sorj, B. and Wilkinson, J. (1987) *From farming to biotechnology*. Blackwell, London.
Haraway, D. (2003) *The companion species manifesto*. Prickly Paradigm Press, Chicago.
Harvey, D. (1974) Population, resources and the ideology of science. *Economic Geography* 50 (2), 256–277.
Hinchliffe, S. (2007) *Geographies of nature*. Sage, London.
Hinchliffe S. and Whatmore, S. (2009) Living Cities: Towards a politics of conviviality. In D.F. White and C. Wilbert (eds), *Technonatures: environments, Technologies, Spaces and Places in the Twenty-first Century*. Wilfred Laurier University Press, Canada, pp.105–124.
Ingold, T. (1996) Hunting and gathering as ways of perceiving the environment. In R. Ellen and K. Fukui (eds), *Redefining nature*. Berg, Oxford, pp. 117–155.
Kloppenburg, J. (1988) *First the seed*. Cambridge University Press, Cambridge.
Lorimer, H. (2005) Cultural geography: the busyness of being more-than-representational. *Progress in Human Geography* 29 (1), 83–94.
Marshall, A. (1890) *Principles of economics*. Macmillan and Co., London.
McKibben, R. (2003) *The end of nature*, 2nd edn. Bloomsbury, London.
McKibben, R. (2003) *Enough: staying human in an engineered age*. Henry Holt, New York.
Prudham, S. (2005) *Knock on wood*. Routledge, New York.
Sauer, C. (1925/1963) The morphology of landscape. Reprinted in J. Leighley (ed.) *Land and life*. University of California Press, Berkeley, pp. 315–350.
Sayer, A. (1993) Postmodernist thought in geography: a realist view. *Antipode* 25; 4, 320–344.
Semple, E. (1911) *Influences of geographic environment*. Henry Holt, New York.
Sheppard, E. and Plummer, P. (2007) Towards engaged pluralism in geography. *Environment and Planning A*. 39 (12), 2545–2548.
Smith, N. (1984) *Uneven development*. Blackwell, Oxford.
Soper, K. (1995) *What is nature?* Blackwell, Oxford.
Soule, M and Lease, G. (eds) (1995) *Reinventing nature?* Island Press, Washington.

Thomas, W. L. (ed.) (1956) *Man's role in changing the face of the earth*. Chicago University Press, Chicago.
Thornhill, R. and Palmer, C. (2000) *A natural history of rape*. MIT Press, Cambridge, Massachusetts.
Thrift, N. (2007) *Non-representational theory*. Routledge, London.
Whatmore, S. (2002) *Hybrid geographies*. Sage, London.
Williams, R. (1976) *Keywords*. Fontana, London.
Wylie, J. (2005) A single day's walking. *Transactions of the Institute of British Geographers* 30 (3), 234–247.

Further Reading

For the story of how geographers as a whole have dealt with the question of "nature" see my chapter in *The Handbook of Geographical Knowledge* (Agnew and Livingstone, 2011) and chapter 2 of my book *Nature* (Castree 2005). For more on each of the three approaches discussed here see (respectively) the chapters by myself, by Braun and Wainwright, and by Castree & Macmillan in the book *Social nature* (2001, Castree and Braun). The contents of this chapter find an echo in essays by my sometime co-editor Bruce Braun (see Braun 2009a, 2009b). Finally, those interested in the complexities of the idea of "nature" should see the excellent books by Habgood (2002) and Soper (1995).

Braun, B. (2009b) Nature. In N. Castree *et al.* (eds) *A companion to environmental geography*. Wiley-Blackwell, Oxford, pp. 19–36.
Castree, N. (forthcoming, 2011) Society and nature. In J. Agnew and D. Livingstone (eds), *The handbook of geographical knowledge*. Sage, London
Castree, N. (2005) *Nature*. Routledge, London and New York.
Castree, N. and Braun, B. (eds) (2001) *Social nature*. Blackwell, London.
Habgood, J. (2002) *The concept of nature*. Darton, Longman and Todd, London.

Chapter 12

Nature
Part II

Jamie Lorimer

Things are a little different now. Nature … seems to have stopped working so well. It no longer offers a stable category to which objects can be intuitively allocated … It is neither a source of smooth facts which seem to speak for themselves … nor an unchanging ground on which one might rely. Nature does not form a rallying site where an agreeable collective might be formed … or serve as an external arbiter which could speed matters along past due process.

(Bingham and Hinchliffe 2008: 83)

Introduction

The idea of a singular Nature – as essential essence or pure realm of objects removed from Society and revealed by Science – is facing extinction. It is imperiled on many fronts, fatally wounded by regular public failures and multidisciplinary sorties. From the natural sciences these include the epochal diagnosis of the anthropocene, biotechnologies for genetic modification and the growing appreciation of animal sentience. Philosophers and social scientists have made sustained assaults upon the dualistic ontology and objective epistemology of modern Science (Latour 2004a) and the exclusive and disembodied cartographies of the Humanist Subject (Thrift 2007). Opinions are divided about this 'end of Nature' and the post-natural and post-human futures it offers. For some it heralds a crisis or even an apocalypse (Fukuyama 2002; McKibben 1990). For others it opens opportunities for cautious or even hyperbolic optimism (see Wolfe 2010). Geographers have been in the vanguard of these developments and have been swift to reflect upon their disciplinary implications. There are familiar tales, often told, of the deficiencies of stable and dualistic ontologies and the political and ethical geographies they engender and sustain (Castree 2005; Whatmore 2002).

The Wiley Blackwell Companion to Human Geography, First Edition.
Edited by John A. Agnew and James S. Duncan.
© 2011 John Wiley & Sons, Ltd. Published 2016 by John Wiley & Sons, Ltd.

In this chapter I will assume that these tales have been followed and that the case has been made for unstable and relational ontologies, new geographies and alternative relationships between science and politics. This is perhaps presumptuous, but space is limited. Instead of recovering this terrain I will look at what happens next, aware that the identification of hybridity, relationality and instability is but the beginning of any project for surviving humanism. Pressing intellectual and political challenges are presented by the need to map the forms, temporalities and modalities of existing relations, to acknowledge pluralistic claims to natural knowledge and to affirm convivial posthuman alternatives that need not recourse to a singular Nature. The end of Nature has provided fertile ground for a diverse range of relational approaches to the politics of nature/the environment (for a flavor of this diversity see Castree and Braun 2001; Cronon 1996; Giffney and Hird 2008; Peet and Watts 2004). This chapter will develop one strand of this work and should be read in conversation with its companion essay. Here I focus on recent developments in "more-than-human geography" (Whatmore 2006), which has sought to take up the challenge of a world without a singular Nature. It has done so in conversation with developments in science studies and geo/biophilosophy and through detailed empirical and conceptual investigations across an array of geographical arenas. The central imperative has been to develop modes of "multinaturalism" (Latour 2004a) that can articulate plural natures and deliberate between multiple forms of natural knowledge to recast the spaces of and relations between science, natures and politics (Bingham and Hinchliffe 2008).

Multinatural Geographies

Multiple modalities of multinaturalism now animate more-than-human geography. Although relational theorists are wary of typologies, these modalities can be distinguished by the forms that they interrelate and the character of the "biopolitics" (Braun 2007) that frames their relations. Hot topics include: biosecurity and the challenges of living well with zoonotic viruses (Braun 2007; Donaldson 2008; Hinchliffe and Bingham 2008), bacteria (Enticott 2008) and invasive (Clark 2002) and dangerous (Buller 2008) species; eating well in an era of transgenic organisms (Roe 2006) and infectious prions (Hinchliffe 2001; Stassart and Whatmore 2003); coping with fluvial (Clark 2007) and pyric (Franklin 2006) hazards; and companionship and the welfare of plants, animals and microbes (Bingham 2006; Hinchliffe et al. 2005; Hird 2009). In this short intervention I will identify three themes that distinguish, connect and differentiate this work; namely materiality/life, affect and experimentation and cosmopolitics. The chapter will conclude by outlining future challenges and opportunities for multinatural geographies.

Materiality/Life

More-than-human geography nurtures and extends the interest in materialities that is well established across the social sciences (Anderson and Wylie 2009). At its inception this approach was strongly influenced by the relational materialism of actor-network theory (Latour 2005) which emphasized the role of assemblages of technologies, texts and other ordering devices in establishing what comes to be understood as Nature and the spatial formations through which this is achieved (Murdoch 2006; Thrift 1996). Ongoing work in this vein has explored the role of such assemblages in performing geographies of power (Legg 2009), the topological forms that these comprise (Law and Mol 2001) and the 'ontological politics' of their operation (Mol 2002). Rich and heated debates continue concerning the implications of this materialism for core geographical questions of scale, agency and history (see Marston *et al.* [2005] and subsequent responses). Political matter, or the "stuff of politics," has emerged as an important concern at the interface of geography, science studies and political theory (see Latour and Weibel 2005; Whatmore and Braun 2010).

These interdisciplinary conversations connect to ongoing efforts to reanimate geography; bringing life back in to the discipline, in all its diverse forms and temporalities. There are three strands to this revitalization that are most relevant to discussions of multinaturalism. The first is work employing non-representational theories that seek to acknowledge the vital roles played by embodiment, affect and emotion in the practice everyday life (Thrift 2007). This approach challenges the mind-body dualism at the heart of modern theories of the subject and the preoccupations with textual representations that characterized much cultural geography after the cultural turn (Thrift and Dewsbury 2000). This intervention has been strongly expressed in work on landscape, which situates human bodies as lively co-inhabitants of a world replete with multiple other animate beings (H. Lorimer 2006; Wylie 2006). It discloses a plurality of ways of being affected by the world and thus a multiplicity of natural knowledges (Urry and Macnaghten 2001). It also draws attention to the '"corporeal generosity" (Diprose 2002) of porous bodies and the material connections and exchanges that are both necessary for and risky to continued existence.

The animation of subjectivity and the recognition of co-inhabitation have been embraced in recent work in animal studies (Flynn 2008) and animal geography (Wolch *et al.* 2003). Here the aim is open up the lumpen category "animal" to explore the diverse and specific forms of nonhuman difference that it subsumes (Derrida and Mallet 2008). Rich empirical work has documented complex and sophisticated modes of nonhuman life, with a growing interest in the long histories and geographies of human-animal "companionship" (Haraway 2008) – or "anthropo-zoo-genesis" (Despret 2004) – that characterize the anthropocene. This intervention unsettles simplistic divisions between humans and other animals and maps a menagerie of "companion species" that confound simple wild-domestic binaries (Anderson 2006; Whatmore 2002). These lively forms emerge from diverse imbrications between human and animal lives where nonhuman difference plays a vital role. Here water voles (Hinchliffe *et al.* 2005), mushrooms (Tsing forthcoming), microbes (Hird 2009), butterflies (Bingham 2006), elephants (Lorimer and Whatmore 2009), bison (Lulka 2004) and dogs (Haraway 2008) have been shown to differ markedly in the claims they make for posthumanist geographies of responsibility.

A third animation is provided by recent engagements with geo- and bio-philosophy – particularly the work of Bergson, Deleuze and Whitehead – to develop modes of vital materialism (Bennett 2010; Braun 2008). Here the earth moves and life is a seething and promiscuous collection of forces and tendencies. Stable fixed beings following linear and equilibrium temporalities give way to turbulence and uncertain becomings. Form is secondary to morphogenesis. The virtuality of life is paramount in this approach, where the virtual "refers not to a nonexistent or immaterial entity, as in popular usage, but to a potentiality that is immanent in every object and in every situation" (Braun, 2007: 17).

For Braun, Hinchliffe and Bingham, the virtual potentials of zoonoses or the indeterminable and infectious natures of the prions implicated in the disease CJD, coupled with the corporeal generosities of human and animal bodies, pose great challenges to modern regimes of biosecurity. In a different vein, this concern for immanence connects to the growing interest in nonequilibrium ecologies in the life sciences (Botkin 1990), including biogeography (Lorimer 2008b; Manning *et al.* 2009). Here the trajectory of an ecological assemblage is not necessary linear or predictable; events and disturbance regimes play an important role in determining future natures.

Experimental Epistemologies

As the opening quotation makes clear, the end of Nature and its associated crises of objectivity have posed fundamental challenges to the "political epistemology" (Latour 2004a) of a singular Natural Science. If natures are multiple, dynamic, uncertain and discordant, than many futures and many natural sciences are possible. Recourse to a singular Nature is problematic if its sole aim is to provide and police smooth "matters of fact" around which one can build political consensus. For Latour, Stengers and others, making natures singular is anti-political. Here Science short-cuts politics and due process. Instead, they argue that we should attend to the practices through which "matters of concern" become "matters of fact" and look to develop multinatural alternatives that are pluralist and deliberative. I will attend to the political implications of this intervention below, but first it is important to identify the multinatural epistemologies that currently orientate the more-than-human geographies that draw on this work.

Those working at the interface of non-representational theory and animal studies have sought to develop approaches that conjoin ethology and ethnography in an effort to witness practical interactions between technologically assisted humans and lively animals in dynamic environments (Laurier *et al.* 2006; H. Lorimer 2006; J. Lorimer 2007). The concern here is less for what is said; more for what is done – attending to gesture, comportment, affect and behavior – to witness multispecies becomings. Models of knowledge and perception tied to rationality and visual cognition have been rethought to acknowledge the multisensory processes through which bodies "learn to be affected" (Latour 2004b) by their environment. For example, in work on the vernacular ecologies of wildlife conservation, Steve Hinchliffe and others have traced the processes through which diverse naturalists learn to be affected by the animals and environments they study (Hinchliffe *et al.* 2005; J. Lorimer 2008a). These investigations map natural knowledge as skilful, embodied and affective field craft that requires corporeal calibration and time deepened familiarity. Recent work in this vein has begun to explore the potential of moving imagery for witnessing such entanglements (J Lorimer 2010). Connected explorations amongst captive animals have attended to the embodied experiences of nonhuman subjects through modes of "critical anthropomorphism" (Morton *et al.* 1990). Skilled critical anthropomorphists eschew the humanist tendency to assimilate animals' experiences to our own and instead look to enhance animal welfare through their detailed understandings of individual histories and species ethologies and ecologies. Here researchers invoke "somatic sensibilities" that cut across species divides (see Acampora 2006; Franklin *et al.* 2007).

Recent work concerned with immanence and vital materialism has documented the methodological and epistemological problems associated with attending to the virtual in an effort to predict, prevent or nurture future emergence. Here contingency and uncertainty are ascendant; multiple trajectories possible and speculation perhaps the best that can be hoped for (Braun 2008). Such conditions have spawned experimental epistemologies that are open to the virtual and seek, in their own humble ways to be "future-invocative" (Cooper in Braun 2007; see also Anderson 2007). For example, in her work on companion species Donna Haraway (2008) cites favorably the experiments performed by the ethologist Theresa Rowell. Rowell creates experimental spaces that ask questions of her feral sheep, allowing them to respond with unexpected behavior (Despret 2005). This openness to the virtual and to emergent events chimes with Stengers' (2007) appeal for experimental knowledge practices that are able to "slow things down" and put accepted knowledges "at risk."

This ethos of epistemological experimentation characterizes a growing interest amongst more-than-human geographers in developing novel techniques for interdisciplinary collaboration, public engagement and the redistribution of expertise, especially in relation to scientific knowledge controversies characterized by multiple and incommensurable understandings. For example, Gail Davies reports on recent work developing innovative deliberative mapping processes for debating xenotransplantation and stem-cell research (Davies 2006a; 2006b). These techniques have some similarities with the 'experimental methodological apparatus' of the "competency group," currently being developed by Sarah Whatmore and co-researchers in their on-going work developing deliberative approaches to flood-risk modeling. Whatmore explains that this methodology puts Stengers' principles to the test allowing natural and social scientists to collaborate with affected local residents "to interrogate the expert knowledge claims and practices associated with the science and management of flood risk" (Whatmore 2009: 8).

Cosmopolitics

A diverse range of philosophers and social scientists have recently outlined posthumanist political-ethical frameworks that address how best to organize the relations that characterize our multinatural world in the light of the uncertainties and instabilities detailed above. One of the most comprehensive of these frameworks, that is currently receiving a great deal of attention in geography and across the social sciences, is the model of cosmopolitics outlined by Isabelle Stengers (2007) and refined by Bruno Latour (2004a). Cosmopolitics outlines a pluralistic model of the relationships between nature, science and politics in which all the actors are not human and all the expertise is not exclusive to a singular Science. It focuses on the entanglements of science and politics and looks to redistribute expertise both within and beyond species boundaries (see Bingham 2008; Hinchliffe *et al.* 2005; Hinchliffe and Whatmore 2006).

Haraway employs Stengers' cosmopolitics in her recent efforts to outline flourishing modes of human-animal companionship (Haraway 2008). In so doing she seeks to challenge the modern/humanist/romantic trinity that confines animals to the three identities of resource/sub-human/wild. Drawing on critical anthropomorphism she develops what can be understood (after Latour 2004a) as an ethologized politics that takes nonhuman difference and thus multinaturalism seriously. Haraway's primary concern is for the affective and genetic health of domesticated animal breeds; contemporary forms that inherit fraught past-presents and concomitant human responsibilities. Her model of flourishing is configured – not unproblematically (Lulka 2009) – around the maintenance of these identities in the face of political and ecological change. Parallel work in geography and science studies has sought to develop frameworks for flourishing ethics/politics with a wider range of alternative companion species, subject to less coercive biopolitics. For example, recent work on nature conservation in the context of urbanization and biotechnology has outlined convivial modes of relating, grounded in friendship and an agonistic respect for nonhuman difference (Bingham 2006; 2008; Hinchliffe and Whatmore 2006). These are explored through "careful" modes of political ecology that aim to shelter emergent nonhuman forms (Hinchliffe 2008). Myra Hird (2008) has developed a microbial ethics for convivial encounters with organisms that are not 'big like us'. Here she draws on Margulis' (2002) theory of symbiogenesis to flag the importance of living well with the microbial stuff of life. Similarly Braun (2007) argues for flourishing in the context of debates over biosecurity, demanding modes of biopolitics in sharp contrast to those dedicated to the prevention and elimination of difference. Multiple, sometimes conflicting biopolitics for flourishing emerge from this work (Buller 2008); the challenge is to develop spaces and procedures through which these can be deliberated.

Further examples of cosmopolitics in action can be found in the outcomes of the deliberative engagements reported by Davies and Whatmore. For example, Davies identifies the prevalence of "corporeal reasoning" in public responses to xenotransplantation and stem cell therapy. This takes differing forms, including "profane" knowledge's and a recourse to the sacred that trouble modernist (rationalist) modes of scientific reasoning and their associated political institutions (Davies 2006b). Similarly, Whatmore explains how competency groups reveal important uncertainties in flood risk mapping and develop "new collective competences ... that redistribute expertise across the 'scientific'/'vernacular' divide" (2009: 9). These experiments help materialize new political practices, discussed in earlier work on urban ecologies which:

> ... require that we treat our subjects, the people that we work with, as colleagues, in a similar vein to the ways in which some science practitioners manage to treat their nonhuman subjects. This is a collective, experimental politics not a critical endeavour intent on positioning others as representative of a peculiar or particular species, interest, belief, or practice ... Thus, cosmopolitics ... involves a double injunction: to take risks (in other words, to engage in ontological politics rather than in perfect epistemological eyepieces) and to allow others, of all shapes, sizes, and trajectories, to object to the stories we tell about them, to intervene in our processes as much as we intervene in theirs. Only by doing this can we hope to learn how things matter to humans and nonhumans.' (Hinchliffe *et al.* 2005, 655)

The redistribution of expertise associated with a turn to cosmopolitics significantly expands the scope of natural knowledge that matters for politics, ranging far beyond the disembodied dispassionate subject. There is a growing awareness of the importance of affect or passion and the ways in which these registers help constitute complex political-ethical landscapes in which rationality is but one of many affective logics that guide multinatural encounters (Connolly 2005; Protevi 2009). In mapping these landscapes theorists have drawn attention to enchantment (Bennett 2001), hope (Anderson 2006), hatred (Thrift 2005), comedy (Davies 2007) and disgust (Stassart and Whatmore 2003) as just a few of the visceral registers that catalyze political-ethical engagement. Attending to affect offers up models of "affirmative critique"[1] that can nurture new modes of engaging with the world. These approaches help avoid the "denunciatory" or "prophetic" tone of much political ecology (Latour 2004a) and the apocalypticism, dogmatism and certain closure of traditional modes of left critique (Gibson-Graham 2006).

Implications for Geographies and Geographers

The end of Nature and the rise of multinaturalism represent both a radical break from much modern natural science and a return to modes of analysis with a long intellectual tradition in geography and cognate disciplines (Braun 2003; Whatmore 2006). In conclusion I will attend to some of the possibilities offered by multinatural geographies for addressing ongoing disciplinary debates about intra-disciplinarity and relevancy. As a discipline with long-standing concerns for and diverse approaches towards exploring human-nonhuman relations, geography should be especially well placed to address the hot topics of 21st Century environmental knowledge controversies. Geographers have at their disposal a powerful array of tools and concepts for sensing, visualizing and comprehending human and nonhuman forms and processes. Used in conjunction these could offer valuable means for apprehending our multinatural condition and intervening to secure convivial futures. However, and in spite of concerted efforts to establish conversations across intra-disciplinary divides (Harrison *et al.* 2008, 2004), human and physical geographers still rarely share more than a building, while differing strands of relational human geography proceed incommunicado. This situation is unfortunate but the conditions are now favorable for renewed attempts at intra-disciplinary rapprochement.

For example, there is a widely shared interest in the human and physical strands of the discipline in the distribution and dynamics of life and the importance of difference and diversity. These bio-geographers (Spencer and Whatmore 2001) share concerns for hybridity, nonequilibrium dynamics and the challenges of human-nonhuman conviviality or reconciliation. Although these interests appear to have developed in parallel and employ different techniques and epistemologies, they offer great potential to forge new biogeographies better placed to address the political materialities of multinaturalism. This is clearly illustrated in relation to the long standing disciplinary concern for wildlife conservation. Here, at the interface of human and physical biogeographies, there are shared but differentiated concerns for hybrid, fluid and networked ecologies, experimental epistemologies and cosmopolitan forms of deliberative governance (Lorimer 2008b, 2010; Zimmerer 2000).

Disciplinary divisions also characterize the work of the growing collection of human geographers concerned with human-nonhuman relations after the end of nature. While there is a widespread agreement about the paucity of dualistic approaches that fix nature and essentialize natural science, there is limited consensus as to the character and dynamics of the relational ontologies that animate our multinatural present, which relations matter most and what the best means are for intervention. Multiple and sometimes conflicting modes of materialism now characterize the discipline (Anderson and Wylie 2009). This diversity is not well conveyed by (albeit heuristic) attempts to establish, divide and police disciplinary factions. A diversity of geographical materialisms is a healthy state of affairs, but it requires a pluralistic culture of academic endeavor that can foster this diversity and its productive tensions. This will require the continued ecologizing and ethologizing of the political (rather than the politicizing of ecology) (Latour 2004a) to attune to the specificities of the relations under consideration. It will also require a continued attention to both the persistence of relations and connections and the lively and uncertain potential of any assemblage to become-otherwise. Undoubtedly patterns and consistencies exist in the emergence and endurance of human-nonhuman relations but we should be cautious about the closure and certainties of universal theory – we still do not know what a multinatural world will do. Nonetheless it might be useful to think about typologies, not of forms, but of relations. Here exploitation and enchantment might be considered in conjunction in a sincere intellectual climate.

It is important to bear in mind that an interest in multinaturalism has been spurred by crises in the relationship between science and politics and the proliferation of matters of concern. The uncertainty inherent to multinaturalism opens a space for intervention and experimentation. Cracks are appearing in the modern constitutions that offer opportunities for geographers to get involved. The theories and methodologies outlined above make geography immensely relevant to the contemporary condition. This will not be achieved through the disciplinary practice of shoring up Natural Knowledge through the foreclosures associated with much work on Public Engagement in Science and Technology (PEST) (Demeritt 2009). Instead, geography and geographers are well placed to disentangle matters of fact, raising concerns that put knowledge at risk. Such interventions require a new approach to theory, where the role of theory is not about representing the world but as an active and practical mechanics for intervention (Whatmore 2006). Such theories require active methodologies for collaboration and the gathering of collectives. This may well be awkward, uncomfortable and time-consuming for those of us used to the security of academic judgment and such endeavors may not be well served by the time-poor, target-led culture of contemporary academic institutions. Nonetheless, opportunities persist for experimentation.

Note

1 *Affirmative critique* was the title of a workshop organized by Ben Anderson and Andrea Noble at Durham in 2009 to explore this theme.

References

Acampora, R.R. (2006) *Corporal compassion*: animal ethics and philosophy of body. University of Pittsburgh Press, Pittsburgh.

Anderson, B. (2006) Becoming and being hopeful: towards a theory of affect. *Environment and Planning D-Society & Space* 24, 733–752.

Anderson, B. (2007) Hope for nanotechnology: anticipatory knowledge and the governance of affect. *Area* 39, 156–165.

Anderson, B. and Wylie, J. (2009) On geography and materiality. *Environment and Planning A* 41, 318–335.

Anderson, K. (2006) *Race and the crisis of humanism*. Routledge, London.

Bennett, J. (2001) *The enchantment of modern life: attachments, crossings, and ethics*. Princeton University Press, Princeton.

Bennett, J. (2010) *Vital materiality*: the political life of things. Duke University Press, Durham.

Bingham, N. (2006) Bees, butterflies, and bacteria: Biotechnology and the politics of nonhuman friendship *Environment and Planning A* 38, 483–498.

Bingham, N. (2008) Slowing things down: Lessons from the GM controversy. *Geoforum* 39, 111–122.

Bingham, N. and Hinchliffe, S. (2008) Reconstituting natures: Articulating other modes of living together. *Geoforum* 39, 83–87.

Botkin, D. (1990) *Discordant harmonies: a new ecology for the twenty-first century*. Oxford University Press, New York.

Braun, B. (2003) *Nature and Culture*: On the Career of a False Problem. In J. Duncan and N. Johnson (eds), *A Companion to Cultural Geography*. Blackwell, Oxford, pp.151–179.

Braun, B. (2007) Biopolitics and the molecularization of life. *Cultural Geographies* 14, 6–28.

Braun, B. (2008) Environmental issues: inventive life. *Progress in Human Geography* 32, 667–679.

Buller, H. (2008) Safe from the wolf: Biosecurity, biodiversity, and competing philosophies of nature. *Environment and Planning A* 40, 1583–1597.

Castree, N. (2005) *Nature*. Routledge, London.

Castree, N. and Braun, B. (2001) *Social nature: theory, practice, and politics*. Blackwell, Oxford.

Clark, N. (2002) The demon-seed: bio-invasion as the unsettling of environmental cosmopolitanism. *Theory, Culture & Society* 19, 101–125.

Clark, N. (2007) Living through the tsunami: Vulnerability and generosity on a volatile earth. *Geoforum* 38, 1127–1139.

Connolly, W.E. (2005) *Pluralism*. Duke University Press, Durham.

Cronon, W. (1996) Uncommon ground: rethinking the human place in nature. W.W. Norton, New York.

Davies, G. (2006a) Mapping deliberation: Calculation, articulation and intervention in the politics of organ transplantation. *Economy and Society* 35, 232–258.

Davies, G. (2006b) The sacred and the profane: Biotechnology, rationality, and public debate. *Environment and Planning A* 38, 423–443.

Davies, G. (2007) The funny business of biotechnology: Better living through chemistry comedy. *Geoforum* 38, 221–223.

Demeritt, D. (2009) Geography and the promise of integrative environmental research. *Geoforum* 40, 127–129.

Derrida, J. and Mallet, M-L. (2008) *The animal that therefore I am*. Fordham University Press, New York.

Despret, V. (2004) The Body We Care For: Figures of Anthropo-Zoo-Genesis. *Body and Society* 10, 111–134.

Despret, V. (2005) Sheep do have opinions. In B. Latour and P. Weibel (eds), *Making things public: atmospheres of democracy*. MIT Press, Harvard, pp. 360–369.

Diprose, R. (2002) *Corporeal generosity: on giving with Nietzsche, Merleau-Ponty, and Levinas*. State University Press, Albany, New York.

Donaldson, A. (2008) Bio security after event: Risk politics and animal disease. *Environment and Planning A* 40, 1552–1567.

Enticott, G. (2008) The spaces of biosecurity: prescribing and negotiating solutions to bovine tuberculosis. *Environment and Planning A* 40, 1568–1582.

Flynn, C.P. (2008) *Social creatures: a human and animal studies reader*. Lantern Books, New York.

Franklin, A. (2006) Burning cities: A posthumanist account of Australians and eucalypts. *Environment and Planning D: Society and Space* 24, 555–576.

Franklin, A., Emmision, M., Haraway, D. and Travers, M. (2007) Investigating the therapeutic benefits of companion animals: problems and challenges. *Qualitative Sociology Review* III 42–58.

Fukuyama, F. (2002) *Our posthuman future: consequences of the biotechnology revolution*. Farrar, Straus and Giroux, New York.

Gibson-Graham, J.K. (2006) *A post capitalist politics*. University of Minnesota Press, Minneapolis.

Giffney, N. and Hird, M.J. (2008) *Queering the non/human*. Ashgate Aldershot, Hampshire.

Haraway, D.J. (2008) *When species meet*. University of Minnesota Press, Minneapolis.

Harrison, S. Massey, D. and Richards, K. (2008) Conversations across the divide. *Geoforum* 39, 549–551.

Harrison, S., Massey, D., Richards, K., Magilligan, F.J., Thrift, N., and Bender, B. (2004) Thinking across the divide: perspectives on the conversations between physical and human geography. *Area* 36, 435–442.

Hinchliffe, S. (2001) Indeterminacy in-decisions – science, policy and politics in the BSE (Bovine Spongiform Encephalopathy) crisis. *Transactions of the Institute of British Geographers* 26, 182–204.

Hinchliffe, S. (2008) Reconstituting nature conservation: Towards a careful political ecology. *Geoforum* 39, 88–97.

Hinchliffe, S., and Bingham, N. (2008) Securing life: the emerging practices of biosecurity. *Environment and Planning A* 40, 1534–1551.

Hinchliffe, S., Kearnes, M.B., Degen, M. and Whatmore, S. (2005) Urban wild things: a cosmopolitical experiment. *Environment and Planning D-Society & Space* 23, 643–658.

Hinchliffe, S., and Whatmore, S. (2006) Living cities: towards a politics of conviviality. *Science as Culture* 15, 123–138.

Hird, M. (2009) *The Origins of Sociable Life: Evolution After Science Studies*. Palgrave Macmillan, Basingstoke.

Latour, B. (2004a) *Politics of nature: how to bring the sciences into democracy*. Harvard University Press Cambridge, Massachusetts.

Latour, B. (2004b) How to Talk About the Body? The Normative Dimension of Science Studies. *Body and Society* 10, 205–229.

Latour, B. (2005) *Reassembling the social: an introduction to actor-network-theory*. Oxford University Press, Oxford.

Latour, B., and Weibel, P. (2005) *Making things public: atmospheres of democracy*. MIT Press Cambridge, Massachusetts.

Laurier, E., Maze, R., and Lundin, J. (2006) Putting the dog back in the park: Animal and human mind-in-action. *Mind, Culture, and Activity* 13, 2–24.

Law, J. and Mol, A. (2001) Situating technoscience: an inquiry into spatialities. *Environment and Planning D-Society & Space* 19, 609–621.

Legg, S. (2009) Of scales, networks and assemblages: the League of Nations apparatus and the scalar sovereignty of the Government of India. *Transactions of the Institute of British Geographers* 34, 234–253.

Lorimer, H. (2006) Herding memories of humans and animals. *Environment and Planning D-Society & Space* 24, 497–518.

Lorimer, J. (2007) Nonhuman charisma. *Environment and Planning D-Society & Space* 25, 911–932.

Lorimer, J. (2008a) Counting corncrakes: The affective science of the UK corncrake census Social. *Studies of Science* 38, 377–405.

Lorimer, J. (2008b) Living roofs and brownfield wildlife: towards a fluid biogeography of UK nature conservation. *Environment and Planning A* 40, 2042–2060.

Lorimer, J. (2010) Elephants as companion species: the lively biogeographies of elephant conservation in Sri Lanka. *Transactions of the Institute of British Geographers* 35, 491–506.

Lorimer, J. (2010) Moving image methodologies for more-than-human geographies. *Cultural Geographies* 17, 237–258.

Lorimer, J. and Whatmore, S. (2009) After "the king of beasts": Samuel Baker and the embodied historical geographies of his elephant hunting in mid-19th century Ceylon. *Journal of Historical Geography* 35, 668–689.

Lulka, D. (2004) Stabilizing the herd: fixing the identity of nonhumans. *Environment and Planning D-Society & Space* 22, 439–463.

Lulka, D. (2009) Form and formlessness: The spatiocorporeal politics of the American Kennel Club. *Environment and Planning D-Society & Space* 27, 531–553.

Manning, A.D., Fischer, J., Felton, A., Newell, B., Steffen, W., and Lindenmayer, D.B. (2009) Landscape fluidity - A unifying perspective for understanding and adapting to global change. *Journal of Biogeography* 36, 193–199.

Margulis, L. and Sagan, D. (2002) *Acquiring genomes: a theory of the origins of species*. Basic Books, New York.

Marston, S.A., Jones, J.P., and Woodward, K. (2005) Human geography without scale. *Transactions of the Institute of British Geographers* 30, 416–432.

McKibben, B. (1990) *The end of nature*. Anchor Books New York.

Mol, A. (2002) *The body multiple: ontology in medical practice*. Duke University Press, Durham.

Morton, D., Burghardt, G., and Smith, J. (1990) Critical Anthropomorphism, Animal Suffering, and the Ecological Context. *The Hastings Centre Report* 20, 13–19.

Murdoch, J. (2006) *Post-structuralist geography: a guide to relational space*. Sage, London.

Peet, R. and Watts, M. (2004) *Liberation ecologies: environment, development, social movements*. Routledge, London.

Protevi, J. (2009) *Political affect: connecting the social and the somatic*. University of Minnesota Press, Minneapolis.

Roe, E.J. (2006) Material connectivity, the immaterial and the aesthetic of eating practices: an argument for how genetically modified foodstuff becomes inedible. *Environment and Planning A* 38, 465–481.

Spencer, T. and Whatmore, S. (2001) Editorial: Bio-geographies: putting life back into the discipline. *Transactions of the Institute of British Geographers* 26, 139–141.

Stassart, P. and Whatmore, S.J. (2003) Metabolising risk: food scares and the un/re-making of Belgian beef. *Environment and Planning A* 35, 449–462.

Thrift, N. (1996) *Spatial formations*. Sage, London.
Thrift, N. (2005) But malice aforethought: Cities and the natural history of hatred. *Transactions of the Institute of British Geographers* 30, 133–150.
Thrift, N. (2007) *Non-representational theory: space, politics, affect*. Routledge, London.
Thrift, N. and Dewsbury, J.D. (2000) Dead geographies – and how to make them live. *Environment and Planning D-Society & Space* 18, 411–432.
Tsing, A. (In Press) Unruly Edges: Mushrooms as Companion Species. In S. Ghamari-Tabrizi (ed.), *Thinking with Donna Haraway*. MIT Press, Harvard.
Urry, J. and Macnaghten, P. (2001) *Bodies of nature*. Sage, London.
Whatmore, S. (2002) *Hybrid geographies: natures, cultures, spaces*. Sage, London.
Whatmore, S. (2006) Materialist returns: practising cultural geography in and for a more-than-human world. *Cultural Geographies* 13, 600–609.
Whatmore, S. (2009) Mapping knowledge controversies: science, democracy and the redistribution of expertise. *Progress in Human Geography* 33, 587–598.
Whatmore, S. and Braun, B. (2010) *Political matter: technoscience, democracy and public life*. Oxford University Press, Oxford.
Wolch, J., Emel, J., and Wilbert, C. (2003) Reanimating Cultural Geography. In K. Anderson (ed.), *Handbook of Cultural Geography*. Sage, London, pp.184–206.
Wolfe, C. (2010) *What is posthumanism?* University of Minnesota Press, Minneapolis.
Wylie, J. (2006) Depths and folds: on landscape and the gazing subject. *Environment and Planning D-Society & Space* 24, 519–535.
Zimmerer, K.S. (2000) The reworking of conservation geographies: Nonequilibrium landscapes and nature-society hybrids. *Annals of the Association of American Geographers* 90, 356–369.

Further Reading

There is an extensive and growing body of writing in geography and cognate disciplines exploring the problem and politics of nature. Recent books by Noel Castree (2005), Sarah Whatmore (2002) and Steve Hinchliffe (2007) provide useful introductions to this work. Outwith geography, the writings of Bruno Latour (2004; 2005) and Donna Haraway (2008) have made very influential contributions from science studies. Key works in biophilosophy include recent books by Cary Wolfe (2010) and Jane Bennett (2010). Animal studies and animal philosophy is in good health. Important starting points would include Flynn (2008) and Calcaro (2008). Those interested in developments in biogeography which offer hope for reconciliation with social science might explore Botkin (1990) and Rosenzweig (2003).

Calarco, M. (2008) *Zoographies: the question of the animal from Heidegger to Derrida*. Columbia University Press, New York.
Rosenzweig, M. (2003) *Win-win ecology: how the earth's species can survive in the midst of human*. Oxford University Press, New York.

Chapter 13

Landscape
Part I

Don Mitchell and Carrie Breitbach

> Landscape is everyone's fundamental heritage. It is all embracing and unavoidable. It inspires and shapes much of what we learn and do. Landscape is where we all make our homes, do our work, live our lives, dream our dreams.
>
> (David Lowenthal, 2009: 256)

Learning Landscape

Long ago, the geographer Peirce Lewis (1983) implored scholars of the "American Scene" to *learn by looking*. He argued that if we went out into the landscape, and if we learned to really look, we could learn a lot about what that landscape meant. The landscape could be, *and ought to be*, read (Lewis 1979; see also Pugh 1990). This is an enormously attractive idea, in part because it democratizes landscape study. Anyone driven by curiosity could, with just a little guidance, learn to find meaning in landscape using primarily common sense. At the root of Lewis's argument is the assumption that cultural forms "encode" cultural meaning, meaning which later could be decoded. Landscape is, as Lewis (1975) pungently put it, "cultural spoor."[1] By following and by analyzing the spoor that is landscape, a lot can be learned about the worlds we live in: their construction, the cultural values at their root, the possibilities for living that they open up and close down. Like Don Meinig (1979a, 1979b) and especially like J.B. Jackson (1984), Lewis wanted us to understand the landscape in its very *ordinariness*. For many of us such imploring was utterly welcome. It helped, as Rich Schein (2003) put it in an acknowledgement of Lewis's formative role, cause the scales to fall from our eyes. Being asked to *look* and to *learn* from looking was seductive,[2] not least because it was such a familiar imploration. This is what *our parents* were always asking us to do as we became alive to the world around us. "What's that?" we might ask; "You tell me," was the

---

The Wiley Blackwell Companion to Human Geography, First Edition.
Edited by John A. Agnew and James S. Duncan.
© 2011 John Wiley & Sons, Ltd. Published 2016 by John Wiley & Sons, Ltd.

inevitable answer. "Why's it look like that?" was equally inevitably followed by, "You figure it out." Such direction is empowering, as it is meant to be. It endows each of us with our own set of built-in field equipment, and encourages us to trust our individual abilities.

And we've tried to figure it out. But where do we start? *What part* of the landscape – which is, after all, a "totality" – should be looked at first? What kinds of "clues to culture" (as Lewis called the landscape) should we focus our attention on? Our professors – Peirce Lewis, Larry Ford, and others – pointed us towards J.B. Jackson's journal *Landscape* which published brilliant essay after brilliant essay "about generic archetypal landscape elements, such as the house, the yard, or the suburb" (Groth and Wilson 2003: 9). For Larry Ford (2000) it was frequently the overlooked spaces – the waste spaces between buildings, the back alleys, the service entries and weird landscaping in strip malls – that needed our attention.[3] These spaces were no less archetypal, no less generic, no less crucial for understanding the culture that gave rise to them. Landscape is ordinary, and landscape is everywhere (cf. Cosgrove 1989). But if it is everywhere (and everything), then just what *is* it? Carl Sauer (1963 [1925]: 321), in his seminal statement upon which much thinking in American cultural geography rested, and to which our attention was early directed, called it "the unit concept of geography" that denoted "the peculiarly geographic association of facts. Equivalent terms in a sense are 'area' and 'region,'" but it was more specific than these because, as its derivation from the German *landschaft* indicated, it was "a land shape, in which the process of shaping is by no means thought of as simply physical. It may be defined, therefore, as an area made up of a distinct association of forms, both physical and cultural." A *distinct association* of forms: that's the key term. But that just rephrases the issue: How do we know what to count as part of the *association*, and how do we know it is *distinct*? Can we, most particularly, figure this out by looking? If we are going to learn from looking then we have to know, somehow and in advance, just what we are looking at. If that's the case then it is simply impossible to learn *from* looking, as important as it may be to learn *to* look.

This is a realization that landscape reading is not simply an exercise of individual, innate endowment or common sense. From its conceptualization as a term, to its representation in art or advertisement, to its very appearance on the ground, landscape is infused with layers of historical and social meaning that help to comprise its distinction and associations. In order to begin making sense of landscape, we must work to understand these meanings. Does this then relocate landscape reading from an exciting excursion in the field open to anyone willing, to trawl through fusty archives limited to those with the institutional resources and background who can make the esoteric legible? Yes and no, is really the answer.

One of the problems with the assumption that landscape is a simple mark of culture is that it does not take into account the complexity of culture itself (cf. Williams 1958, 1976, 1977, 1980; Eagleton 2000). Neither does the assumption recognize that any particular "reader" of the landscape will inevitably be herself positioned somewhere in the complexity of social relations and history that produce both landscape and culture, that make the vast and infinite set of facts and features into comprehensible forms. But exposing these assumptions and redefining landscape study as a pursuit of the complexity of the social world is actually more empowering than conceiving of landscape study as a knack or talent to be honed. Positioning the tools needed to understand landscape in the archive (or in other narratives of social process), rather than in one person's version of common sense, actually opens up the pursuit, instead of closing it down (Holdsworth 1997).

Part of the historical evidence that needs to be gathered in order to learn from landscape is the history of the term and its usage. We came of age as geographers in a particular milieu, and it was not one defined only by Jackson, Lewis, Ford, or Meinig (as important as they were and are). It was also defined by the intellectual and theoretical excitement surrounding the proclamation of a "new cultural geography" (Cosgrove and Jackson 1987; Jackson 1989) and its thorough reconsideration of the whole landscape idea.[4] Cosgrove (1984, 1985) strove with particular force to historicize the concept of landscape, to deny in particular one of Sauer's (1963 [1925]: 316, 349) central arguments: that landscape was a "naïvely given section of reality." Rather, the very *idea* of landscape had a history and it was not at all an innocent one. Instead, it was a quite specific "way of seeing" (Berger 1972) the land wrapped up in the transition from feudalism to capitalism and rooted in specific locales, such as Venice and its hinterland and Flanders (Cosgrove 1984, 1985). It was tied up with an expropriation of land and its reorganization into estates designed, often, for the viewing pleasure of their owners.[5] If "landscape" was (as in common definitions) not just "nearly everything we see when we go outdoors" (Lewis 1979: 12), but a "(a view presented by) an expanse of terrain or district which is visible from a particular place and direction; an expanse of (country) scenery" (*Shorter Oxford English Dictionary*, "Landscape," 3a), then the view, the expanse itself, *and* the viewing all had a history. None were "naïvely given." If it had a history, then it required a theory, an analysis, to understand it and to reveal the processes driving those historical shifts in meaning. Learning could not be accomplished by looking alone. If the landscape encoded meaning, then that meaning was not one of a "culture" that could somehow be "read off" it, but rather of social practices and social histories, driven by real people and their efforts. And if, finally, one of the very functions of landscape, both as built form and as mode of representation, was precisely to mask or hide or obscure the social practices and social histories that went into its making (see, e.g. Barrell 1980; Bermingham 1987; Cosgrove and Daniels 1988; Daniels 1989; W. Mitchell 1995), then how could we possibly properly *see* the landscape that Lewis (and our parents) wanted us to both see and understand? Obviously understanding landscape required not only learning how to look, but also learning the theories that explain *why* we see (or don't see) what and as we do (cf. Gregory 1994, Part I).

Landscape

This was a tough, but exciting, lesson to learn. It made the whole concept of landscape difficult to get our heads around, since it clearly required some grasp of the basic relationships of social processes and, more importantly, the priority of those social processes in determining landscape's "distinct associations." *Which* social relations make landscape's forms? Was landscape best understood as an insider's affective relation to place, as much of J.B. Jackson's work averred, and much phenomenological research seemed to show (e.g. Relph 1976, 1981, 1987)?[6] If so, the key to knowing landscape was in understanding experience and the sense of belonging or fit humans experienced in places. Or was landscape best thought of as the built form, the morphology, of the world within which we lived and worked (Sauer 1963 [1925])? If so, our focus should be on the function of material features. Could it be, instead, the quintessential outsider's view, discernible through intricate knowledge of regional histories and struggles (Cosgrove 1985; Williams 1973)? Or was it some combination of these, and if so, what kind of combination? Both Cosgrove (1984) and Daniels (1989) had shown the vital importance of a certain strain of economic and cultural Marxism for the development of answers to these questions, placing priority on the relationships of labor and production that serve as a foundation for human societies. But this presented its own problems. Raymond Williams (1973: 120) famously maintained that "a working country is hardly ever a landscape," suggesting that landscape somehow becomes distinct from those foundational relations. If that is the case, how can what is essentially a *labor theory* of social production and reproduction explain landscape's making? How can something be worked and not worked at the same time? How can landscape rely on the basic processes of social production at the same time that it transcends those processes? The answers to these questions lie in understanding landscape as an *alienated commodity* that is also at the same time more than a commodity. Or, rather, it is what David Harvey (1982: 233) called "a geographically ordered, complex, composite commodity," and like all commodities it is highly fetishized, and largely alienated from precisely those who have made it (D. Mitchell 2009; Olwig 2005). This answer helps explain the character of landscape, as both a product of the basic historical relationships through which human society builds itself, and as a fundamental feature in composing each of our life experiences. But this answer about the way landscape interacts in society still returns us right back to that old question: just what *is* the landscape? And even more, just why does it *matter*, not only intellectually or theoretically, but especially socially? The particularity of landscape within fundamental, historical social processes suggests it is something especially important to understand – but what is it, and why does it matter?

Landscapes, according to James Duncan and Nancy Duncan (2004: 37), are "the visible surface of places." They "are ensembles of physical elements and economic infrastructure – hills, fields, streams, dirt roads, barns, mansions and cottages, railroads, offices, stores and village scapes, as well as images, views, and individual and collective memories. They are media molded into grand compositions that are enacted within a framework of culturally and historically particular discourses." This is right, but the invocation of "discourse" is overly limiting, for landscapes are not only molded discursively, but also and especially they are given form through social processes and practices (for example, the alienation of labor and the accumulation of capital) that may be only partially, or unimportantly, "discursive." The "framework" of landscape is not just discursive; it is solid. As built form (and the geographical landscape is first and foremost built form – the "ensemble of physical and economic infrastructure"); landscape is a produced *thing*, which is to say that it is the condensation of the social relations that have gone into its making (D. Mitchell 1996); landscape *is* in this sense and in capitalist societies, "dead labor" – the work of its makers concretized (D. Mitchell 2003, 2009). And like other dead labor, like other commodities, it can come to have a phantasmagorical power over its makers (Marx 1987: 294).[7] What it is – the realization and concretization of human labor organized within particular social relations – gives landscape its power, since so much of that organization of human labor is specifically intended to control and direct the goods of society for the benefit of the powerful. While the priority of this intent is essential to understanding landscape's form and function, as an alienated commodity landscape does not adhere to any singular intent. Still, landscape is both the realization and the medium of every human purpose, as the next paragraphs attest.

Much of the landscape is built, first, precisely as (complex) *instruments of production*, and in that sense serves as a form of *fixed capital* ("various instruments of labor … produced as commodities, exchanged as commodities, productively consumed within a work process given over to surplus value production, and at the end of their useful life, replaced by new commodities …" [Harvey 1982: 205]). It functions as fixed capital to the extent that it is "actually used to facilitate the production of surplus value" (Harvey 1982: 205), but as is obvious even landscape items built *especially* for surplus value production (a factory, a farm, a rail line leading to a coal mine, a nuclear power station), are not used *only* for surplus value production, and even when they are used primarily for that, they may, after a time, be converted to other uses, and no longer count as fixed capital. This is to say that the reasons why landscapes are built are crucial but not totally determinant; uses are multifarious and susceptible to change, even as the built form "locks in" (Harvey 1982: 220) a set of limits to what can be done in the landscape (it is impossible, for example, to use a farm field *as such* for swim meets or the production of iPods; though it can be used for music a festival).

Other parts of the landscape are built, second, so as to facilitate the circulation of capital (roads, railroads, canals, transmission lines, computer server farms), or to serve as the foundation of economic production. Marx (1973: 686–687) calls this *"fixed capital of an independent kind"* and it is vital to the *realization* of the value and surplus value wrapped up in commodities (Harvey 1982: 226–227; Henderson 1999). Malls, stores, airports, and all manner of other landscape forms may be built to take on this function. But again, as with the other kind of fixed capital, the potential uses (and meanings) of fixed capital of an independent kind may easily exceed the immediate reasons for its production, even as the specific built forms once again significantly limit these other uses and meanings – as any teenager hanging out in a mall will readily attest.

Still other parts of the landscape are produced, third, as *instruments of consumption* (houses and neighborhoods, apartments blocks, "and the various means of collective consumption such as parks and walkways" [Harvey 1982: 229]). Here landscape is constructed as part of systems less of production and more of *social reproduction*, and landscape produced for this reason thus includes also schools, churches, community and union halls, parks (again) and other recreation facilities, and so forth, none of which are entirely divorced from systems and practices of commodity production and exchange; even as they are not reducible to it and may in fact *encompass* it (Breitbach 2009, 155; K. Mitchell *et al* 2003). If social reproduction is taken to mean the forms, institutions, practices (and even discourses) that make *physical reproduction* (life itself) possible, then it is obvious that a primary *function* of the landscape, not only in addition, but prior, to facilitating the circulation and accumulation of capital (and the forms of consumption that realize the value built into it), is establishing the *conditions* of social reproduction, conditions which might be, from the perspective of any normative sense of justice, completely *dys*functional (Breitbach 2009; Henderson 2003).

Finally, fourth, some of the landscape is not produced, clearly at least, for any of these functions. A median strip planted with flowers by neighbors; the Watts Towers or Carhenge; a swimming hole with a rope hung from a tree: such forms have no easily identifiable or generally theorizable purpose, but are instead constitutive of, and result from, basic human ingenuity, a love for cleverness and fun, a drive to flourish, to live fully and well, and to leave a mark.[8] They may, of course, *take on* other functions, just as landscapes of production and reproduction can. Carhenge and the Watts Towers have become tourist sites and are marketed as such; neighbors getting together and beautifying the roads that run past their homes might also be increasing property values (and "helping save the environment"); swimming holes are great places for courting (a prelude to reproduction, or attempts to avoid it).[9]

In these terms, the notion that landscape is a "distinct association of forms" has some purchase, for we can begin to specify the *nature* of those forms as well as their *purpose*. Even more importantly, we can begin to understand how their *distinctiveness* is constructed through identifiable, and quite often identical, processes. Even taking into account the fourth reason for landscape production, it is obvious that the landscape is produced *in relation to* the circulation and accumulation of capital, and thus the struggle to produce, manage, and distribute surpluses (cf. Gilmore 2007).[10] The working out of this *general* process in *specific* locales gives rise to distinctiveness: the retained expanses of open space in the San Francisco Bay Area, for example, are a function of *how* the post-war economic expansion "set the trip wires that turned the guerilla skirmishes of the Bay Area conservationists into a full-scale insurgency against the forces of urban expansion and property capital," as Richard Walker (2007: 82) put it in his thorough account of the politics of the "greening of the San Francisco Bay Area." The expansive regional parks, all the hiking and biking trails, even, sometimes, the oases of green in the vast suburban and urban wastes of the "flatlands" are all a function of the struggle over just how capital is going to circulate and accumulate, where production will take place, and the specific processes and relations through which the working and middle classes will reproduce themselves. While the specific ways, for example, white insecurity over economic prospects and a rapidly changing region might be expressed politically and legally in the landscapes of racially homogenous or partially integrated neighborhoods in the Bay Area (Self 2003) will vary as compared, say, to Detroit (Sugrue 1998; Darden 1982; Darden *et al.* 1990), nonetheless both are structured through the relations of production, circulation, and consumption (complicated and made interesting by desire and ingenuity) as they are *built into* the ground.

Of course, what gets "built into the ground" must contend with what is *already* built into the ground. There is no *tabula rasa*. Past, even dead, "associations of forms" channel and direct new investment, new struggles, and crucially limit not just what is socially, politically, or economically possible, but what is *physically* possible. History (and environment) matters (Lewis 1979; D. Mitchell 2007); even more it *determines* – in exactly that sense Raymond Williams (1977: 87) notes as the "setting of limits" and "exertion of pressures." The physical, built landscape has hegemonic power over social relations, even as it is itself the product of hegemonic practices (and struggles against them). Past landscapes can thus very much be a fetter on current productive, distributive, and consumptive practices (Harvey 2001: 242–249; Marx 1987), even as they are a fetter on the creation of new forms of social life, new ways of living. They must be destroyed (Jakle and Wilson 1992). Or they must be revalorized in some way, preserved from the wrecking ball and infused with new value and values: a contentious and not always very just process (Duncan and Duncan 2004). This is a competitive process. Landscape is a fetter for capital and for living to the degree that it is a fetter in comparison to other places subject to congruent pressures and limits, especially congruent pressures to reproduce the socio-spatial relations that allow for continued accumulation and thus continued reproduction. These fetters are defined precisely by limits on the ability to destroy existing forms. The solidity of the landscape, its deadness, its relative permanence, matters. "Creative destruction," in relation to the built landscape, is only ever a tendency; it can never be a reality, for it is within the built landscape that we *live* (Breitbach 2009).[11]

Teaching Landscape

The quotation from Lowenthal that opens the chapter suggests both the promise and the prison that is landscape; Lowenthal's words also hint at the attraction of landscape as an approach for both learning and teaching about social justice. Often students are attracted to landscape study because a good explication of landscape usually includes a narrative of human life and identity formation; such explanations are incredibly important for students learning to be geographers, to situate their lives and themselves within the wider world.[12] Yet, because landscape is both reflective and constitutive of hegemonic social powers, working class students often discover the solidity and historical rootedness of their own life experiences (and their own oppression) as they study landscape. This can be far from the democratizing and scales-lifting pursuit that we claimed for landscape study, since it is difficult to see how landscape can be both the hard-and-fast embodiment of uneven social power as well as being the key to empowering, emancipatory change.

But a thorough understanding of just how landscape works, and how it has worked in place after place, shows that it really *is* both a means of social control and one of resistance, and a necessary one at that. Time and time again we have observed this process in our classes, a process not unlike the kind of theoretical-political awakening we went through as we came to terms with landscape theory and the landscapes around us: at some point – often in the midst of a discussion about social reproduction, and in the wake of days and weeks of landscape analysis and discussion – things click. Students – *we* – begin to see more clearly that focusing on how and why landscape is produced opens up a dual horizon. In one direction we can begin to see what a landscape *does*, and thus why it is crucial to understand its structured "thingness." In the other direction, we can begin to see what it *means* – not at some clue to an amorphous culture, but in the everyday lives of the people who live and work in it, as well as in the eyes of those who have the most power to produce it. In this sense landscape *can* be read, but now only because we are possessed of the proper tools to read, tools fashioned out of an analytical orientation that requires a keen focus on production and reproduction and a political orientation that asks us to understand the landscape normatively in terms of what a just landscape possibly (and literally) could *be*.

Here lies the important task in landscape research, and in landscape teaching: recognizing (and organizing) the power that ordinary people do have (and have had) in producing landscape. This requires understanding the purposes for which particular landscapes are formed, and the social relations that allow their creation. It requires learning about the way power is organized, controlled and taken, and it also requires looking at the landscape as a person engaged in the pursuit of social justice.

Notes

1. This naturalistic metaphor is important. It makes clear an underlying assumption about the "culture" that makes the landscape; for Lewis, culture is part of its natural landscape even as it is a transformative agent in this landscape. This ecological understanding of "culture" has its roots in the founding document of landscape study in American geography, Sauer's "The Morphology of Landscape" (1963 [1925]). It also sets Lewis's notion of decoding the landscape apart from theories of "reading" culture concomitantly developed in the field of cultural studies (see e.g. Hall 1980) and more deconstructionist theories of reading developed in the "new cultural geography" of the 1980s (e.g. Duncan and Duncan 1988).
2. Maybe literally so: see Rose (1992, 1993); Nash (1996).
3. The brief obituary of Larry Ford, who died way too young, in the November 2009, *Newsletter* of the Association of American Geographers, gives an excellent sense of how he approached the question of urban landscapes.
4. In addition to the works cited directly, the special issue of *Environment and Planning D: Society and Space* 6 (2) (1988) was central to this reconceptualization, as were Barnes and Duncan (1992); Duncan and Ley (1993); and Daniels (1993).
5. Cosgrove's reevaluation of the idea of landscape, his tracing of its origins as a particular way of seeing, was prefigured (if without his Marxian emphasis) in an J.B. Jackson (1984: 1–8); and Mikesell (1968); it has been significantly critiqued and deepened in recent years by Ken Olwig (1996, 2003, 2005).
6. The essays collected in Wilson and Groth (2003) develop a suite of arguments about this aspect of landscape (among other things). The landscape as affective insideness has been recently revived in the so-called "new phenomenology" in cultural geography. For a concise review, see Wylie (2007), chapter 5.
7. In his essay on "Determination" in *Marxism and Literature*, Williams (1977: 87) makes an important argument about "society" that with minimal adjustment holds also for "landscape." "'Society' is … never *only* the 'dead husk' which limits social and individual fulfillment. It is always *also* a constitutive process with very powerful pressures which are both expressed in political, economic and cultural formations and, to take the full weight of 'constitutive,' are internalized and become individual wills." We have emphasized "only" and "also" because the weight in this argument must be on those terms, a point often lost on cultural theorists overly concerned with the emergent and fluid at the expense of a close analysis of the historic forms – the "dead husks" – out of which the emergent arises and through which the fluid must stream.
8. In this sense, then, can there be anything more thoroughly depressing than a new concert hall built *because* it will be an engine of economic development?

9   In this sense, aspects of landscape are, as Sauer (1963 [1925]: 344) put it, "beyond science:" "The best of geography has never disregarded the esthetic qualities of landscape, to which we know no other approach than the subjective."
10 We are talking, of course, specifically of landscapes in capitalism (which is to say, most of the world); however, it is also obvious that *any* human society will have to have instruments of production, circulation, and consumption. The question is the specific social and institutional relations through which these are produced. In capitalism, the circulation and accumulation of capital is a dominant social fact.
11 In these terms the inadequacy of the "new phenomenology" in landscape studies becomes readily apparent. It is simply not enough to assert the vital importance of the "materiality" of landscape (and our bodily interactions with it) *at the expense* of the landscape's *historical* materiality (as in Wylie 2007).
12 James Duncan and Nancy Duncan's (2004, 2006) work on landscape and identity in and around Bedford, New York, is an excellent example of landscape writing that works well in the classroom.

References

Barrell, J. (1980) *The Dark Side of Landscape: The Rural Poor in English Landscape Painting, 1730–1840*. Cambridge University Press, Cambridge.
Barnes, T. and Duncan, J. (eds) (1992) *Writing Worlds: Discourse, Text, And Metaphor in the Representation of Landscape*. Routledge, New York.
Berger, D. (1972) *Ways of Seeing*. Penguin, London.
Bermingham, A. (1987) *Landscape and Ideology: The English Rustic Tradition*. Thames and Hudson, London.
Breitbach, C. (2009) The geographies of a more just food system: building landscapes for social reproduction. In K. Olwig and D. Mitchell (eds), *Justice, Power and the Political Landscape*. Routledge, London, pp. 153–175.
Cosgrove, D. (1984) *Social Formation and Symbolic Landscape*. Croom Helm, London.
Cosgrove, D. (1985) Prospect, perspective and the evolution of the landscape idea. *Transactions of the Institute of British Geographers* 10, 45–62.
Cosgrove, D. (1989) Geography is everywhere: culture and symbolism in human landscapes. In D. Gregory, and R. Walford (eds), *Horizons in Human Geography*. N.J: Barnes and Noble Books, Totowa, pp. 118–135.
Cosgrove, D. and Daniels, S. (eds) (1988) *The Iconography of Landscape*. Cambridge University Press, Cambridge.
Cosgrove, D. and Jackson, P. (1987) New directions in cultural geography. *Area* 19, 95–101.
Daniels, S. (1989) Marxism, culture, and the duplicity of landscape. In R. Peet and N. Thrift (eds), *New Models in Geography, Volume 2*. Unwin Hyman, London, pp. 196–220.
Daniels, S. (1993) *Fields of Vision: Landscape Imagery and National Identity in England and the United States*. Princeton University Press, Princeton.
Darden, J. (1982) Black residential segregation: impact of state licensing laws. *Journal of Black Studies* 12, pp. 415–426.
Darden, J., Hill, R., Thomas, J., and Thomas, R. (1990) *Detroit. Race and Uneven Development*. Temple University Press, Philadelphia.
Duncan, J. and Duncan, N. (2004) *Landscape of Privilege: The politics of the Aesthetic in an American Suburb*. Routledge, New York.
Duncan, J. and Ley, D. (eds) (1993) *Place, Culture, Representation*. Routledge, London.

Duncan, J. and Duncan, N. (2006) Aesthetics, abjection, and white privilege in suburban New York. In R. Shein (ed.), *Landscape and Race in the United States*. Routledge, London, pp. 157–176.

Duncan, J. and Duncan, N. (1988) (Re)reading the landscape. *Environment and Planning D: Society and Space* 6, 117–126.

Eagleton, T. (2000) *The Idea of Culture*. Blackwell, Oxford.

Ford, L. (2000) *The Space Between Buildings*. Johns Hopkins University Press, Baltimore.

Gilmore, R. (2007) *Golden Gulag: Prisons, Surplus, Crisis, and Opposition in Globalizing California*. University of California Press, Berkeley.

Gregory, D. (1994) *Geographical Imaginations*. Blackwell, Oxford.

Groth, P. and Wilson, C. (2003) The polyphony of cultural landscape study: an introduction. In C. Wilson and P. Groth (eds), *Everyday America: Cultural Landscape Studies after J.B. Jackson*. University of California Press, Berkeley, pp. 1–22.

Hall, S. (1980) Encoding/decoding. In S. Hall, D. Hobson, A. Lowe, and P. Willis (eds), *Culture, Media, Language*. Hutchinson, London, pp. 128–140.

Harvey, D. (1982) *The Limits to Capital*. University of Chicago Press, Chicago.

Harvey, D. (2001) *Spaces of Capital*. Routledge, New York.

Henderson, G. (1999) *California and the Fictions of Capital*. Oxford University Press, Oxford.

Henderson, G. (2003) What (else) we talk about when we talk about landscape: for a return of the social imagination. In C. Wilson and P. Groth (eds), *Everyday America: Cultural Landscape Studies After J.B. Jackson*. University of California Press, Berkeley, pp. 178–198.

Holdsworth, D. (1997) Landscape and archives and texts. In P. Groth and T. Bressi (eds), *Understanding Ordinary Landscapes*. Yale University Press, New Haven, pp. 44–55.

Jackson, J.B. (1984) *Discovering the Vernacular Landscape*. Yale University Press, New Haven.

Jackson, P. (1989) *Maps of Meaning: An Introduction to Cultural Geography*. Unwin Hyman, London.

Jakle, J. and Wilson, D. (1992) *Derelict Landscapes: The Wasting of America's Built Environment*. Rowman and Littlefield, Lanham.

Lewis, P. (1975) Common houses, cultural spoor. *Landscape* 19, 1–2.

Lewis, P. (1979) Axioms for reading the landscape: some guides to the American scene. In D. Meinig (ed.), *The Interpretation of Ordinary Landscape: Geographical Essays*. Oxford University Press, New York, pp. 11–32.

Lewis, P. (1983) Learning from looking: geographical and other writing about the American cultural landscape. *American Quarterly* 35, 242–261.

Lowenthal, D. (2009) Living with and looking at landscape. In K. Olwig and D. Mitchell (eds), *Justice, Power and the Political Landscape*. Routledge, London, pp. 253–274.

Marx, K. (1973) *Grundrisse*. Penguin, Hammondsworth.

Marx, K. (1987) *Capital, Vol. 1*. International Publishers, New York.

Meinig, D. (1979a) The beholding eye: ten versions of the same scene. In D. Meinig (ed.), *The Interpretation of Ordinary Landscape: Geographical Essays*. Oxford University Press, New York, pp. 33–50.

Meinig, D. (1979b) Reading the landscape: an appreciation of W.G. Hoskins and J.B. Jackson. In D. Meinig (ed.), *The Interpretation of Ordinary Landscape: Geographical Essays*. Oxford University Press, New York, pp. 195–244.

Mikesell, M. (1968) Landscape. In D. Sills (ed.), *International Encyclopedia of the Social Sciences*. Crowell, Collier and Macmillan, New York, pp. 575–580.

Mitchell, D. (1996) *The Lie of the Land: Migrant Workers and the California Landscape*. University of Minnesota Press, Minneapolis.

Mitchell, D. (2003) California living, California dying: dead labor and the political economy of landscape. In K. Anderson, S. Pile, and N. Thrift (eds), *Handbook of Cultural Geography*. Sage, London, pp. 233–248.

Mitchell, D. (2007) New Axioms for Reading the Landscape: Paying Attention to Political Economy and Social Justice. In J. Wescoat and D. Johnson (eds), *Political Economies of Landscape Change: Places of Integrative Power*. Springer, Dordrecht, pp. 29–50.

Mitchell, D. (2003) Work, struggle, death, and the geographies of justice: the transformation of landscape in and beyond California's Imperial Valley. In K. Olwig and D. Mitchell (eds), *Justice, Power, and the Political Landscape*. Routledge, London, pp. 178–195.

Mitchell, D. (2009) Work, Struggle, Death, and Geographies of Justice: The Transformation of Landscape in and beyond California's Imperial Valley. In K. Olwig and D. Mitchell (eds.), *Justice, Power and the Political Landscape*. Routledge, London, 178–195.

Mitchell, K., Marston, S., and Katz, C. (2003) (eds) *Life's Work*: Geographies of Social Reproduction. Blackwell, Malden.

Mitchell, W.J.T. (ed.) (1995) *Landscape and Power*. University of Chicago Press, Chicago.

Nash, C. (1996) Reclaiming vision: looking at landscape and the body. *Gender, Place, and Culture* 3, 149–169.

Olwig, K. (1996) Recovering the substantive nature of landscape. *Annals of the Association of American Geographers* 86, 630–653.

Olwig, K. (2003) *Landscape, Nature, and the Body Politic*. University of Wisconsin Press, Madison.

Olwig, K. (2005) Representation and alienation in the political land-scape. *Cultural Geographies* 12, 19–40.

Olwig, K and Mitchell, D.(2009) *Justice, Power and Political Landscape*. Routledge, London.

Pugh, S. (ed.) (1990) *Reading the Landscape: Country – City – Capital*. Manchester University Press, Manchester.

Relph, T. (1976) *Place and Placelessness*. Routledge and Keegan Paul, London.

Relph, T. (1981) *Rational Landscape and Humanistic Geography*. Rowman and Littlefield, Lanham.

Relph, T. (1987) *The Modern Urban Landscape*. Johns Hopkins University Press, Baltimore.

Rose, G. (1992) Geography as science of observation: the landscape, the gaze, and masculinity. In F. Driver and G. Rose (eds), *Nature and Science: Essays in the History of Knowledge*. RHBNC and QMWC, University of London, London.

Rose, G. (1993) *Feminism and Geography: The Limits of Geographical Knowledge*. University of Minnesota Press, Minneapolis.

Sauer, C. (1963) [1925] The morphology of landscape and Life. In J. Leighly (ed.), *A Selection from the Writings of Carl Ortwin Sauer*. University of California Press, Berkeley, pp. 315–350.

Schein, R. (2003) The normative dimensions of landscape. In C. Wilson and P. Groth (eds), *Everyday America: Cultural Landscape Studies after J.B. Jackson*. University of California Press, Berkeley, pp. 199–218.

Self, R. (2003) *American Babylon: Race and the Struggle for Postwar Oakland*. Princeton University Press, Princeton.

Sugrue, T. (1998) *The Origins of the Urban Crisis: Race and Inequality in Postwar Detroit*. Princeton University Press, Princeton.

Walker, R. (2007) *The Country in the City*. University of Washington Press, Seattle.

Williams, R. (1958) *Culture and Society*. Chatto and Windus, London.

Williams, R. (1973) *The Country and the City*. Oxford University Press, New York.

Williams, R. (1976) *Keywords*. Fontana, London.

Williams, R. (1977) *Marxism and Literature*. Oxford University Press, Oxford.

Williams, R. (1980) *Problems in Materialism and Culture*. Verso, London.

Wylie, J. (2007) *Landscape*. Routledge, Abingdon.

Further Reading

Key starting places for learning to *see* the landscape are Jackson (1984) and Meinig (1979). Wilson and Groth (2003) bring together a wide-ranging set of essays of the importance of this tradition in landscape studies. Cosgrove's (1984) account of landscape within transforming social relations is the vital text for understanding the rise of landscape as a mode of knowing and transforming the earth in early-modern Europe. Olwig (2003) presents a vital counterbalance in his wide-ranging examination of the "substantive" landscape in the same period. Mitchell (1996) attempts a labor theory of landscape, but there is no better source for understanding the role of capital in the landscape than Harvey (1982). Olwig and Mitchell (2009) bring together a suite of essays questioning the relationship between landscape and justice, a topic examined in rich theoretical and empirical detail by Duncan and Duncan (2004). Wylie (2007) usefully summarizes and synthesizes the whole field, and Mitchell and Breitbach (forthcoming) seek to ground all this wide-ranging landscape theory by examining the range of practices that construct iconic landscapes from the suburb to the beach, and from the retirement community to the national park.

Chapter 14

Landscape
Part II

Mitch Rose and John W. Wylie

Introduction

Over the last ten to fifteen years, geographers – and others – have been developing a series of novel approaches to the analysis and writing of landscape. Inspired by the philosophical work of Heidegger (1971, 1996) and Merleau-Ponty (1962, 1968), this body of landscape research has come to be loosely described as "phenomenological," an approach broadly characterized by an interest in how landscape appears in and through human experience. The question of human experience, however, is by no means a straight-forward matter and the notion that phenomenological approaches condone an uncritical or romantic subjectivism is a powerful misreading of contemporary phenomenological work. Indeed, the question of "experience" is at the heart of phenomenological work. It is the problem presented by the seemingly simple phenomenon of a person viewing a landscape. For traditional approaches this scene is taken as axiomatic, that is: it is the situation from which all further analysis can justifiably proceed. A viewer standing apart from the landscape views the environment from a distance and uses that distance to see, interpret and judge the scene with some matter of perspective. While contemporary approaches recognize that the landscape being viewed is indicative of a culture community to which the viewer also belongs (i.e. the viewer is himself embedded in the same cultural milieu), the landscape is nonetheless understood as something viewed across a space separating seer and seen, subject and object, human and world.

Phenomenological approaches, however, take their start by questioning this pre-existing distance and the project it sets in motion. This means that they do not conceptualize landscape first and foremost as an image – a scene viewed at a distance. The landscape is not simply a catalyst of deeper social/cultural meanings; it is not something produced for reading and interpretation. Rather, landscape is a

The Wiley Blackwell Companion to Human Geography, First Edition.
Edited by John A. Agnew and James S. Duncan.
© 2011 John Wiley & Sons, Ltd. Published 2016 by John Wiley & Sons, Ltd.

mode of engagement. It is something we live in and through; not a distant scene but our day to day geography. In this rendering, the landscape reveals itself through intimate and practical engagement, rather than distanced reading. While there are many kinds of phenomenological approaches and projects, they can be broadly characterized by a desire to think about landscape in terms other than the cognitive and the visual. In Tilley's (2004) work on embodiment; Dubow (2010) and Wylie's (2002, 2005) work on movement and in Cloke and Jones' (2001, 2004) work on dwelling, there is a sustained interest in how practices (like walking), emotions (like wonder) or sensations (like light and distance), engender a certain kind of engagement that transcends the observational and/or cognitive. Phenomenological approaches to landscape are generally interested in the relationship between seer and seen itself; a relationship that is understood as involved, practical and engaged.

The aim of this chapter is to elucidate what we mean by a phenomenological approach to landscape by doing two things: First, explaining the basic philosophical stance of existential phenomenology (the branch of phenomenology that has most influenced this work) and second, illustrating how this perspective enables a variety of different landscape projects to take shape. In addition, to these two primary goals there is a third aim, which is to illustrate how phenomenology, has always been part of landscape research (indeed, has always already been part of landscape research). Indeed, since the founding of the Sauer school of landscape interpretation in the early 1930s, there has been an ongoing ambition among landscape scholars to, if not dissolve, then at least mitigate the distance between seer and seen; to understand the landscape as something that is both intimate and estranging, powerful and compelling, violent and seductive. This is what Daniels (1989) has called the duplicity of landscape: the intertwining of landscape's meaningful and exploitative roles. Similarly we have suggested that landscape can be understood as a tension: "the tension of regarding at a distance that which enables one to see – the tension of what Wylie (pace Deleuze) calls folding, of engendering synthetic forces from a disassociative depth" (Rose and Wylie, 2006: 478). This tension of landscape, the tension between being intimate and distant, distinct from and yet embedded in, is not one that is resolved by phenomenological approaches (it is a tension inherent to all landscape research). But what is unique about this approach, is the way it allows us to explore this tension more fully. While this chapter does not propose a specific theory of landscape – though phenomenologically influenced theories have certainly been made (Rose 2006; Wylie 2006) – nor determine a set of methods or even relevant questions (very "traditional" landscape questions about power, politics, exploitation and economy appear in much of phenomenological work – albeit in a different key), it does offer a certain perspective – a way of thinking about landscape that broadens our horizon for experiencing, researching and writing about the tension of being in, of and on the world all at the same time.

Principles of Phenomenology

In order to understand the basic concepts of existential phenomenology, we need to explain something of the context it was operating both in and against. So, we begin with Rene Descartes, whose long shadow hangs over philosophy, geometry, mathematics and the sciences as a whole. It is Descartes (1968) who is often accredited with establishing the basic parameters of modern scientific method; primarily by promoting the idea that rational thought could provide a firm foundation for discovering truth (scientific rationalism). The problem with this foundation is that it, like any foundation, comes with baggage – baggage that the social sciences are, in many ways, still struggling with. In brief, Descartes' argument began with a series of meditations designed to illustrate the elusive and illusory nature of the senses. By doubting the validity of personal experience (doubting that he is awake rather than dreaming, that his experience is real rather than an illusion), Descartes quickly comes to the conclusion that the only thing he cannot doubt is the fact that he is doubting. In other words, the first truth to emerge from Descartes' meditation is the certainty of his own self-consciousness as a thinking being; the fact that he knows it is he himself that is thinking and doubting, that he hears himself speak to himself in his own voice inside his head. The fact that Descartes can determine to himself that he is a thinking being is, for him, enough to prove that he exists and exists as a rational, self-aware subject: "I am thinking" Descartes proclaims "therefore I exist" (*cogito ergo sum*).

The relevance of this moment is it establishes the subject's existence on the basis that he is what is often termed "self-present:" he is present to himself by the fact that he can hear himself thinking and knows that the thinking voice he hears belongs to himself. Thus, the subject does not need anything outside himself – no external sense of himself or his world – to know, clearly and distinctly, that he exists. The fact that he is self-conscious is enough to justify his existence. Descartes, it is often thought, establishes a justification for self-hood that does not need external validation. The promise of this position is that it establishes the subject's rational mind as having the capacity for attaining objective truth. While our senses may deceive us, our rational self-thinking mind has the ability to see through such deception. Thus, the mind is not reliant on the world "out there" for what it knows. The subject, rather, harbors its own self-knowing that is more primordial to what he secondarily senses. The problem of this position, however, is it establishes a powerful separation between the subject and the world. The subject is effectively rendered as someone (or something) distinct from the world, as the rational mind always has the capacity to see through all worldly mystifications.

It is precisely this anxiety about the separation between self and world that phenomenology will seek to address. Yet, it paradoxically begins this process through a re-affirmation of Cartesian thought. Edmund Husserl is often thought of as the founder of modern phenomenology. Husserl's aim, however, was not to discredit Descartes, but on the contrary, to take up Descartes' project of providing a secure philosophical foundation for the scientific process. In his *Cartesian Meditations*, Husserl (1973) thus similarly begins his enquiry by suggesting that the world we perceive cannot be assumed to be the world as it truly is. Indeed, knowledge of the world can only be trusted if it is what Husserl termed *apodictic*, meaning beyond all doubt. However, rather than relying on a *Cogito* to prove the existence of a disconnected rational mind, Husserl arrives at a similar point *via* the concept of intentionality; an idea with its origin in the philosophy of mind. For Husserl all mental perceptions and states (whether they are perceptions of an object, idea, emotion, etc.) have their origin in some external property or source. Thus, there is always "something out there" that is the cause of our mental intentions (our perceptions, our judgments', our hopes, our fears). This is not to say that we have certainty about what that source is. All we know is that there is something *there*. The question Husserl raises is how to gather certain (apodictic) knowledge about those objects that cause our intentions. And his solution is not dissimilar to that of Descartes, that is; Husserl establishes the pre-existing presence of a knowing "I" that transcends the content of its own experience. This "I" does not immediately know the truth of its perception but it does know that it perceives and can work from there to work out what is true and untrue about its perception. Husserl calls this "I" the Transcendental Ego and while there are many similarities between it and the "I" discovered via the Cogito, there are also some critical differences. Primarily, for Husserl, the Transcendental Ego is intimately connected to the object it perceives. *In other words, the perceiving consciousness cannot be separated from the object of its perception*. Thus, unlike Descartes' rational subject, the Transcendental Ego is tethered to the world, entwined with it. Indeed, it only knows itself because it knows itself as a being that perceives. It is not simply conscious of itself as a self-questioning voice speaking only to itself. It is conscious of itself as a perceiving self, as a self who encounters phenomenon, even if it does not perceive those phenomenon in truth.

The reason why this maneuver is so critical is because it opens the door for Husserl's student, Martin Heidegger, to begin asking a slightly different question about the relationship between the perceiving subject and the world that she perceives. For Heidegger, the question raised by Husserl by-passes a more fundamental issue, an issue that has been by-passed by philosophers since the Greeks. Understanding this issue can be begun by considering the following question: to what extent can the relationship between the perceiving subject and the perceived object be understood not by conceptualizing the structures of human perception itself but by considering the structure of the everyday situation in which both perceiver and perceived are caught-up in? In other words, what is the structure of existence itself? What is it about everyday existence (or more accurately the situation that everyday existence establishes) that makes the subject's understanding of the world seem to precede their ability to accurately or truthfully "sense" or "know" it? Another way of putting the question is "what is the nature of being itself" – what does it mean to be a being existing *in* the world and in particular what does it mean to be the unique kind of being that is self-conscious and questioning of its own being – the being that we typically refer to as "human being"? It is Heidegger's turning of the question away from a question about the nature of the subject or indeed, the nature of the subject's transcendental character that makes this philosophy "existential" that is, concerned with everyday existence. This phenomenology does not seek to delve into the essence of the world's discreet phenomenon nor the structure of the "I" as a distinctive mechanism for knowing. Rather, it explores the essence of being and existing itself. What is the nature of our existing situation? What does it mean to be?

To outline the details of how Heidegger addresses these questions would be a book unto itself, so in the remainder of this section we will sketch out some of the central concepts in Heidegger that have had particular influence on cultural geographers and landscape theorists. First and foremost is the concept of *Dasein*, Heidegger's term for the subject. Why doesn't Heidegger simply use the term "the subject"? Because Heidegger's intention is to disassociate his ideas from all received notions, particularly the Cartesian notion of subjectivity. *Dasein* literally translates as "being there," meaning the being who finds herself in a specific situation (a "there" situation, a situation she is *in*). The situation that *Dasein* finds itself in is her bequeathed cultural historical world. For Heidegger, this world does not simply establish certain taken-for-granted interpretations, but situates a whole way of life; the kinds of projects one can engage (to build, to teach or to marry), the kind of ambitions and roles those projects provide (to be working class, an intellectual or a homemaker) and the kinds of equipment and tools that can be brought to bear (a hammer, a degree, a home). Heidegger's project, it should be stressed, is to try and understand the fundamental structure of *Dasein* by exploring how it operates in its normal existence, that is, how it exists "in-the-world." For Heidegger, *Dasein* is a being who practically and unquestioningly pursues those projects that *Dasein's* world establishes as possible. It is not simply that *Dasein* is influenced by her culture or her bequeathed cultural historical world – she exists as a modulation of that world; her being is given definition as it comports itself to a pre-existing "way of life."

The second key concept that has been of relevance for geographers is the concept of dwelling, which we will discuss further in the next section of the chapter. The discussion above implies that *Dasein* exists in the world through "doing" rather than through "thinking." Indeed, being-in-the-world is not about how a subject intends (perceives and or contemplates the world they sense) but about how they exist in it, that is; how they go about their everyday "being." The term that Dreyfus (1990) uses to explain dwelling is "involvement." *Dasein* is involved in the world; she is engaged in the activities, projects and equipment that the world provides and engaged in a non-contemplative fashion. This is not to say that *Dasein* doesn't think or intellectualize. Rather it is to suggest that what she thinks about are the tasks at hand, the issues that are practically in front of her and need negotiating on a regular basis. This is a radically different subject than that which appears in Descartes. For Descartes the subject is first and foremost a contemplative subject. This subject decides it needs shelter to escape from the elements so it considers the possibilities for building some kind of cover; possibilities that the subject secondarily translates into action (finding a cave, building a home, etc.). For Heidegger, however, *Dasein* does not consider her need for shelter. Rather she engages with the demands and protocols of her world; a world where we presume that shelter is an issue and an issue that needs to be addressed in a particular manner. Thus, *Dasein* does not contemplate an idea of her home, build it and dwell there. Rather, she is already dwelling in a world were certain ideas of home and homeliness are already present and waiting to be found. Dwelling thus precedes building. We do not build in order to dwell, rather we are always already dwelling and build in accordance to how we dwell (Heidegger, 1971).

A further theme within existential phenomenology picked up by geographers is the concept of embodiment. Here, however, it is the work of Maurice Merleau-Ponty that is most relevant; a philosopher working in the phenomenological tradition of Heidegger, but interested more squarely in questions of perception. For Merleau-Ponty, practical and involved being-in-the-world is not simply a matter of projects and equipment. There is also sensory involvement; the lived experience of seeing and sensing in and through the world. Existence, for Merleau-Ponty is sensory existence, we abide in the visible, the tactile, the tasty, the sonic and so on – we are anchored within these sensory worlds by virtue of being subjects who exist in and through a sensing body. Thus, for Merleau-Ponty, the subject is first and fore-most an embodied subject whose senses are definitively intertwined with the fabric of the world. The world touches the subject, embedding her in sensual experience, plunging her into the world *as a world* of texture, color and sound. In addition, it is through this embedding of the subject that the subject comes to perceive herself as a sensing being (a visible, touchable and audible subject). Again, in response to Descartes, it is not that a self-conscious cognitive subject finds himself in the world through his senses. Rather an embodied subject perceives herself first and foremost as a sensing subject in a sensible world. The world affords the subject the capacity to sense herself within the worldly fabric to which she intimately (and corporeally) belongs.

The aim of the next section is to illustrate how these conceptual themes have filtered into landscape studies in geography and beyond, and how in doing so they have given rise to new projects and approaches. Throughout, we will see how work has consistently aimed to overcome the Cartesian separation of subject and world, and to think landscape as something we are attached to and constituted through.

Current Research in Landscape Phenomenology

It must be noted here at the outset that phenomenological currents have long been present within cultural geography. Carl Sauer (1963 [1925]: 25) himself, for example, describes his morphological analysis as attentive to "a phenomenology of landscape." Equally, J.B. Jackson (1984), and subsequently humanistic geographers' (Tuan 1971, Buttimer 1976, Pickles 1985), drew strongly on variants of phenomenology in their studies of place, landscape and experience. And insofar as it sought to advance a hermeneutic interpretative sensibility, elements of new cultural geography (Duncan and Ley 1993) also inherit a distinctively phenomenological legacy.

However, landscape phenomenology *can* claim a measure of novelty as an approach. This is because, over the past ten to fifteen years, a range of new landscape research adopting and deploying phenomenological approaches has appeared, both in geography and also in cognate disciplines including anthropology, cultural studies, archaeology and performance studies. Having outlined some of the epistemological and ontological principles underpinning existential phenomenology, the task of this section is thus to map out some of the key thematics and arguments of recent work in this vein from geography and beyond.

Landscape and Dwelling: Landscape as Dwelling

The work of the cultural anthropologist Tim Ingold is a cardinal reference-point for recent landscape phenomenologies. In particular, his 1993 essay '*The Temporality of the Landscape*' (reprinted; Ingold 2000), may be credited with helping to inaugurate and specify a distinctively phenomenological understanding of landscape, in terms of dwelling-in-the-world. This essay provides an especially useful route into phenomenology for human geographers, because Ingold here explicitly opposes "landscape as dwelling" to the understanding of landscape as a "way of seeing" or representing the world which were, and still are, common currency in cultural geography. Ingold argues that, despite its critical intentions, a definition of landscape as way of seeing divisively enshrines and perpetuates a series of dualities – between subject and object, mind and body and, especially, between culture and nature. For example, in their introduction to the influential collection, *The Iconography of Landscape*, Stephen Daniels and Denis Cosgrove (Daniels and Cosgrove 1988: 1) define landscape as "a cultural image, a pictorial way of representing or symbolizing surroundings." But, citing this definition, Ingold declares:

> I do not share this view. To the contrary, I reject the division between inner and outer words – respectively of mind and matter, meaning and substance – upon which such distinction rests. The landscape, I hold, is not a picture in the imagination, surveyed by the mind's eye, nor however is it an alien and formless substrate awaiting the imposition of human order. (Ingold 2000: 19)

Therefore, for Ingold, the definition of landscape as a "cultural image," as first and foremost a symbolic representation is schismatic. This is because it involves positing on the one hand a set of disembodied cultural meanings – a symbolic landscape – and on the other a "physical" landscape onto which such cultural meaning is projected. In other words the definition of landscape as a cultural image, or as a "way of seeing," assumes and reproduces a fundamental distinction between the *ideas of culture* and the *matter of nature*. As a prime consequence of this division, Ingold writes, conceptualization of landscape has persistently been bedeviled by a, "sterile opposition between the naturalistic view of the landscape as a neutral, external backdrop to human activities, and the culturalistic view that every landscape is a particular cognitive or symbolic ordering of space." The often-implicit presence of this "sterile opposition" is, for Ingold, at the heart of a series of intellectual dilemmas facing human geography, anthropology and archaeology. As a consequence, Ingold argues, for much Western thought, "meaning does not lie in the relational contexts of the perceiver's involvement in the world, but is rather laid over the world by the mind," thus perpetuating an understanding of human being previously referred to in this chapter – the subject as disengaged and distanced spectator.

Ingold's solution to this problem involves a turn towards phenomenology, and the elaboration of what he terms "the dwelling perspective." As previously suggested, the notion of dwelling concerns how subjects practically inhabit their world. Colloquially, the word dwelling suggests ideas of home and inhabitation, and Heidegger's understanding is also rooted in these understandings. Yet, for Heidegger (and Ingold), being-at-home is a *practical activity*: it is a matter of putting to work the materials one finds in one's world. In this framing, we can no longer think of landscape as a mental substrate placed on a material world. It is not primarily a way of seeing a "natural" environment. Rather, landscape is the effect of practically engaging and being involved in one's world: "the forms people build, whether in the imagination or on the ground, arise within the current of their involved activity" (Ingold 2000: 187). Constructing or producing the landscape cannot, therefore, "be understood as a simple process of transcription of a pre-existing design of the final product onto a raw material substrate," it is not an importation of mental images into a physical plane. As Ingold suggests, we are first and foremost *inhabited* by the world we are always already within; and "it is through being inhabited...that the world becomes a meaningful environment" (2000: 173). To be clear, Ingold is not drawing a distinction here between the landscape "as meaningful" and the landscape "as practical." On the contrary, the landscape is meaningful *by* being practical. As a milieu of involvement, landscape is the world in which meaningful human activity takes place; it is the world we are within and the world we create by existing within it. In this fashion, Ingold presents a conception of landscape that is neither a cultural framing (a "way of seeing") nor a physical surface (an inert terrain). Landscape instead is the ongoing practice and process of dwelling:

> The landscape, in short, is not a totality that you or anyone else can look *at*, it is rather the world *in* which we stand in taking up a point of view on our surroundings. And it is within the context of this attentive involvement in the landscape that the human imagination gets to work in fashioning ideas about it. For the landscape, to borrow a phrase from Merleau-Ponty, is not so much the object as "the homeland of our thoughts." (Ingold 2000: 207, emphasis in original)

Moving Bodies, Sensing Bodies

Embodiment, inhabitation, participation and movement are characteristic substantive themes of much recent geographical research deploying phenomenological concepts and approaches. To put this another way, the focus of such work falls upon what Hayden Lorimer (2005: 85) usefully phrases as "embodied acts of landscaping," in other words, everyday practices *via* which senses of self, body and landscape emerge. The turn towards phenomenological approaches must thus be understood in terms of a wider recent geographical interest in issues of *practice* and *performance*, often associated with the advent of "non-representational theory" (see Thrift and Dewsbury 2000; Dewsbury *et al.* 2002; Thrift 2008; Anderson and Harrison 2010). What we see in the turn to phenomenology and performance, therefore, is both a topical shift – from landscape considered as a representational and signifying strategy to landscape conceived in terms of material practices and "doings" – and a concomitant methodological shift – from the interpretative ethos of new cultural geography to an approach which emphasizes auto-ethnographic and performative *participation* in landscape practices.

Within these contexts, geographers and others have sought to engage with a wide range of contemporary "landscape practices," and in a relatively short space of time a substantial literature has taken shape. Here, given space constraints, we can only indicate some of this work, and encourage the reader to further pursue studies of landscape practices, such as walking (Michael 2000; Wylie 2002, 2005; Lorimer and Lund 2003; Lund 2005; Sidaway 2009), writing (Brace and Johns-Putra 2010; Romanillos 2008), planning (Buscher 2006) climbing (Lewis 2000), cycling (Spinney 2006), urban *parkour* (Saville 2008), dance and movement therapy (McCormack 2004), gardening (Cloke and Jones 2001; Crouch 2003), and train travel (Bissell 2009; Watts 2008). Consistent across this wide topical variety is a stress upon the body as it moves and senses the world around – the body as sensually embedded in landscape *via* the sonorous, the visual and the tactile – and, reciprocally, a sense of landscape as composed of material elements and "affective atmospheres" within and *with* which senses of self and world are composed and fragmented (see Wylie 2005, on landscape and affect). In this there may be glimpsed at least partial connections to previous geographical articulations of landscape, place and mobility, for example, J.B. Jackson's (1984) well-known work on American landscape and mobility and David Seamon's (1979) pioneering accounts of rhythm and "place ballets." More widely, perhaps, we can also sense connections and continuities between humanistic geography's focus on mythopoetic conceptions of landscape (Tuan 1974), and recent, phenomenologically-oriented work on spiritual landscapes and subjectivities (Holloway 2003; Dewsbury and Cloke 2009).

Landscape, Memory and Performance

As the above brief audit of recent landscape phenomenology in geography demonstrates, the accent of much of this work is upon the *materialities* of landscape : the fleshy materialities of moving, sensing bodies and the vital materialities afforded by the world's varied elements, surfaces and textures. This perhaps reflects a concern that a prior "new cultural" dispensation had overlooked such materialities in its focus upon landscape's discursive and significatory roles. It also segues with work seeking to re-theorize materiality beyond materialist and culturalist readings (Whatmore 2006; Anderson and Wylie 2009). It is important to stress, however, that landscape phenomenology is not limited, as it were, to what might be understood as "concrete" contexts of practice. As was noted in our introduction and second section, phenomenology involves a first-order re-thinking of the nature of selfhood and worldhood, and in this regard it opens up possibilities for new work on landscape in relation to, for example, identity, memory and imagination.

This is most clearly evident in recent geographical work offering biographical and auto-biographical accounts of life, landscape and memory. For example Caitlin De Silvey (2007a, 2007b), Owain Jones (2007, 2008) and Hayden Lorimer (2003, 2006) set out to amplify the lived affinities and affectivities at work in particular landscapes (for DeSilvey Montana, for Jones, the Severn estuary on the England-Wales border, for Lorimer, the Scottish Highlands) *via* creative and performative interventions in life histories which have, as it were, seeped into the landscape as haunting memories, and thus require deft textual re-animation and framing. Here therefore we see the possibilities for phenomenologically and materially-oriented geographies to supply evocative, historiographically-nuanced accounts of life, love and loss. Outside geography narrowly defined, performance scholar and practitioner Mike Pearson has recently explored similar terrain in *"In Comes I": performance, memory, landscape* (2007), a book-length study excavating layers of memory and local place-lore *via* a mixture of narrative re-enactment and *in situ* performative encounter.

Mention of Pearson's work here leads onto the wider interdisciplinary uptake of landscape phenomenologies. *Theatre/Archaeology* (Shanks and Pearson 2001) was an early pioneer text in this respect, arguing for a performative and phenomenological approach to the study of archaeological and heritage sites. Equally, British archaeologist Chris Tilley (2004) advocates what might be termed a "purist" phenomenology, grounded in Merleau-Ponty's account of embodiment and perception, as an alternate means of apprehending and understanding prehistoric landscapes. The merits of these sorts of approaches have been hotly debated within archaeology (Brück 2005; Barrett and Ko 2009). More generally however, there has been, in the UK in particular, a generous embrace of performative and phenomenological approaches stressing embodied encounters between self and landscape, by both scholars and practitioners in performance studies, and this represents one possible future avenue for cultural geographical work in this area (Wylie 2010, for a fuller discussion). Work in this vein, encompassing site-specific, sonic and installation art, visual essays, walking narratives and oral histories, was extensively showcased in the UK at a recent conference on *Living Landscapes* (2009). Emphasis here most often falls upon relations between bodies, landscapes and memories (Smith, Lavery, and Heddon 2009), and the intervention of artists, performers and writers has also fore grounded what might be called the expressive and creative elements of phenomenological research. Landscape phenomenology, it can be argued, is in part concerned with both *expressing* and *elucidating* our grounded experiences of self and memory – experiences, that is, in which there occurs an apparent enlacing together of perceiving self and perceived landscape, to a point where self and landscape, inner and outer worlds, are intertwined in a "perception-with-the-world." It is concerned with *elucidating* such experiences because they are testimony of a sort to the central argument that human being is, fundamentally, embodied, involved being, "caught in the fabric of the world" (Merleau-Ponty 1962: 256). And it is concerned with *expressing* such experiences because the insight that we are caught in this fabric seems to be most aptly and powerfully articulated *via* literary, poetic or artistic registers, rather than by any perhaps more strictly critical or analytical language

Post-phenomenologies?

The aim of this section of the chapter has been to spotlight recent research adopting phenomenological perspectives to investigate landscape. We would argue that this is a rich and diverse field that demands significant inclusion within human geography's landscape legacies and possible futures. Lest our account seem too celebratory, however, we will conclude this section by noting some emergent queries regarding the limits and limitations of current phenomenological work. "Post-phenomenology" is an unwieldy phrase, but it does help to capture the sense of a movement from *within* phenomenologically-inspired geographies that seeks, in various ways, to move beyond what could be understood as "classically" phenomenological precepts and principles. At the heart of this is an unease with the central place accorded to the *perceiving subject* in the work of both Heidegger and Merleau-Ponty, and latter-day standard-bearers such as Tim Ingold. The risk, as we see it, is not that of lapsing into a voluntarist and agent-centered account of landscape, nor is it that landscape phenomenology might somehow overlook the role of power in shaping landscapes – these charges can, we feel, be straightforwardly countered by pointing to the fact that virtually all recent landscape phenomenology is alive to such risks. Rather it is the risk of overlooking, (a) the varied non-human agential forces and affectivities through which perception and sensation are emergent *per se*, and (b) the indelibly post-structural status of both subjects and landscapes as incomplete, incoherent, in actuality never-present-as-such – as, in truth, haunted and aporetic materialities.

Recent geographical research on, for instance, questions of affect, hybridity, relationality and vitality can be termed "post-phenomenological," insofar as it pictures a world of circulating affective forces and atmospheres in which notions of individual agency have little purchase. Our concern, however, is more focused on the need to develop accounts of self and landscape which is sensitive to the post-structural displacement and distancing of a subject whose unexamined presence would act to inadvertently center and cohere landscape. Our own recent work, for example, has sought to query the phenomenological subject *via* accounts of culture as a "dream of presence" (Rose 2006) and examinations of landscape in terms of absence (Wylie 2009). We would also, in this vein, point to Dubow's (2010) elaboration of W.G Sebald's "negative phenomenology," to Romanillos' (2008) account of the non-perspectival landscapes of Alain Robbe-Grillet, and to Harrison's (2009) critical examination of the "active" suppositions of Ingold's (2000 [1993]) conception of self and landscape, as indicative of how phenomenologically-inspired research might develop thematically in the years ahead.

Conclusion

The central task of this chapter has been to elucidate "landscape phenomenology," firstly by outlining the philosophical arguments which underpin this approach, and secondly by describing the main substantive agendas and concerns of current landscape phenomenologies in geography and cognate disciplines. In doing so, our tone has, for the most part, been explicatory, that is; we have been driven primarily by a concern to open up this field for readers and students who may be relatively or largely unfamiliar with the materials and arguments. Hopefully the chapter supplies both a context and a platform for further reading and study, and highlights the ambit and scope of phenomenological research within landscape studies. We will conclude, therefore, with a stronger claim – landscape phenomenology is a rich, diverse and substantial field of practice, one which has yielded, and will continue to yield, important and innovative insights regarding relationships between self and world, culture and nature, place and memory.

References

Anderson, B. and Harrison, P. (eds) (2010) *Taking-Place: Geography and Non-Representational Theory*, Aldershot, Ashgate.
Anderson, B. and Wylie, J. (2009) On Geography and Materiality. *Environment and Planning A* 41 (2), 318–335.
Barrett, J. and Ko, I. (2009) A phenomenology of landscape. A crisis in British landscape archaeology? *Journal of Social Archaeology* 9 (3), 275–294.
Bissell, D. (2009) Visualising everyday geographies: practices of vision through travel-time. *Transactions of the Institute of British Geographers* 34 (1), 42–60.
Brace, C. and Johns-Putra, A. (2010) Recovering inspiration in the Spaces of Creative Writing. *Transactions of the Institute of British Geographers* 35 (3), 399–413.
Brück, J. (2005) Experiencing the past? The development of a phenomenological archaeology in British prehistory. *Archaeological Dialogues* 12, 45–72.
Büscher, M. (2006) Vision in motion. *Environment and Planning A* 38 (2), 281–299.

Buttimer, A. (1976) Grasping the Dynamism of Lifeworld. *Annals of the Association of American Geographers* 66, 277–292.

Cloke, P., and Jones, O. (2001) Dwelling, place and landscape: an orchard in Somerset. *Environment & Planning A* 33, 649–666.

Cloke, P. and Jones, O. (2004) Turning in the graveyard: trees and the hybrid geographies of dwelling, monitoring and resistance in a Bristol cemetery. *Cultural Geographies* 11, 313–341.

Crouch, D (2003) Spacing, performing and becoming: tangles in the mundane. *Environment and Planning A* 35, 1945–1960.

Daniels, S. and Cosgrove, D. (1988) Introduction. In S. Daniels and D. Cosgrove (eds), *The Iconography of Landscape*. Cambridge University Press, Cambridge.

Daniels, S. (1989) Marxism, culture and the duplicity of landscape. In R. Peet and N. Thrift (eds), *New models in geography: the political economy perspective*. Routledge, London

Descartes, R. (1968) *Discourse on method, and other writings*. Penguin Classics, Harmondsworth.

DeSilvey, C. (2007a) Art and Archive: Memory-work on a Montana Homestead. *Journal of Historical Geography* 33 (4), 878–900.

DeSilvey, C. (2007b) Salvage Memory: Constellating Material Histories on a Hardscrabble Homestead. *Cultural Geographies* 14, 401–424.

Dewsbury, J.D. and Cloke, P. (2009) Spiritual landscapes: existence, performance and immanence. *Social & Cultural Geography* 10(6), 695–711.

Dewsbury, J.D., Harrison, P., Rose, M., and Wylie, J (2002) Enacting Geographies. *Geoforum* 32, 437–441.

Dreyfus, H.L. (1990) *Being-in-the-world: a commentary on Heidegger's being and time, division I*. MIT Press, Cambridge.

Dubow, J. (2010) Still-Life, After-Life, Nature Morte: W.G. Sebald and the Demands of Landscape. In S. Daniels, D. Richardson, and D. DeLyser (eds), *Geography and the Humanities*. Routledge, London.

Duncan, J. and Ley, D. (1993) Introduction: Representing the place of culture. In J. Duncan and D. Ley (eds), *Place/Culture/Representation*. Routledge, London.

Harrison, P. (2009) In the absence of practice. *Environment and Planning D: Society and Space* 27(6) 987–1009.

Heidegger, M. (1996) *Being and time: a translation of Sein und Zeit*. SUNY series in contemporary continental philosophy. State University of New York Press, Albany.

Heidegger, M. (1971) Building Dwelling Thinking. In D. Krell (ed.), *Basic Writings*. University of Manchester Press, Manchester.

Holloway, J. (2003) Make-Believe: Spiritual Practice, Embodiment and Sacred Space. *Environment and Planning A*, 35(11), 1961–1974.

Husserl, E. (1973) *Cartesian meditations: an introduction to phenomenology*. Nijhoff, The Hague.

Ingold, T. (2000) [1993] *The Perception of the Environment: Essays in Livelihood, Dwelling and Skill*. Routledge. London.

Jackson, J.B. (1984) *Discovering the vernacular landscape*. Yale University Press, New Haven.

Jones, O. (2007) *Dark Matter: Memory, Writing and Landscape*. Writing Landscape: An Interdisciplinary Symposium for Scholars Supported by the Arts and Humanities Research Council. University College, London.

Jones, O. (2008) *Emptiness and presence in photographed and (un)remembered landscapes of the Severn Estuary*. Perfomativity and Emptiness Closing, Symposium, AHRC Landscape and Environment Network, June 2008. Avonmouth.

Lewis, N. (2000) The climbing body: nature and the experience of modernity. *Body and Society* 6, 58–81.

Living Lanscapes (2009) University of Aberystwyth, June 2009, see http://www.landscape.ac.uk/2009conference.html (accessed 24th October 2010)
Lorimer, H (2003) Telling small stories: spaces of knowledge and the practice of geography. *Transactions of the Institute of British Geographers* 28, 197–218.
Lorimer, H. (2006) Herding memories of humans and animals. *Environment and Planning D: Society and Space* 24, 497–518.
Lorimer, H. (2005) Cultural geography: the busyness of being "more-than- representational". *Progress in Human Geography* 29 (1), 83–94.
Lorimer, H. and Lund, K. (2003) Performing facts: finding a way through Scotland's mountains. In B. Szerszynski, W. Heim, and C. Waterton (eds), *Nature performed: environment, culture and performance*. Blackwell, London.
Lund, K. (2005) Seeing in motion and the touching eye: walking over Scotland's mountains. *Etnofoor* 18 (1), 27–42.
McCormack, D.P. (2004) Drawing out the lines of the event. *Cultural Geographies* 11 (2), 211–220.
Merleau-Ponty, M. (1962) *The Phenomenology of Perception*. Routledge & Kegan Paul, London.
Michael, M. (2000) These boots are made for walking: mundane technology, the body and human – environment relations. *Body and Society* 6 (3/4), 107–126.
Pearson, M. (2007) *In Comes I: performance, memory and landscape*. University of Exeter Press, Exeter.
Pickles, J. (1985) *Phenomenology, science and geography: spatiality and the human Sciences*. Cambridge University Press, Cambridge.
Romanillos, J.L. (2008) Outside, it is snowing: experience and finitude in the nonrepresentational landscapes of Alain Robbe-Grillet. *Environment and Planning D: Society and Space* 26 (5), 795–822.
Rose, M. (2006) Gathering "dreams of presence": a project for the cultural landscape. *Environment and Planning D: Society and Space* 24, 537–554.
Rose, M. and Wylie, J. (2006) Animating landscape. *Environment and Planning D: Society and Space* 24, 475–479.
Sauer, C. (1963) [1925] The morphology of landscape and Life. In J. Leighly (ed.), *A Selection from the Writings of Carl Ortwin Sauer*. University of California Press, Berkeley, pp.25.
Saville, S.J. (2008) Playing with fear: parkour and the mobility of emotion. *Social and Cultural Geography* 9 (8), 891–914.
Seamon, D. (1979) *A Geography of the Lifeworld*. Croom Helm, London.
Shanks, M and Pearson, M. (2001) *Theatre/Archaeology*. Routledge, London.
Sidaway, J.D. (2009) Shadows on the path: negotiating geopolitics on an urban section of Britain's South West Coast Path. *Environment and Planning D: Society and Space* 27 (6), 1091–1116.
Smith, P., Lavery, C., and Heddon, D. (2009) *Walking, Writing and Performance: Autobiographical Texts*, Roberta Mock (ed.). Intellect, Bristol.
Spinney, J. (2006) A Place of sense: an ethnography of the kinaesthetic sensuous experiences of cyclists on Mt Ventoux. *Environment and Planning D: Society and Space* 24, 709–732.
Thrift, N. and Dewsbury, J-D. (2000) Dead Geographies – and how to make them live. *Environment and Planning D. Society and Space*, 18, 411–432.
Thrift, N. (2008) *Non-Representational Theory: space, politics, affect*. Routledge, London.
Tilley, C. (2004) *The Materiality of Stone: explorations in landscape phenomenology*. Berg, Oxford.
Tuan, Yi-Fu. (1971) Geography, Phenomenology and the Study of Human Nature. *The Canadian Geographer* 15, 181–192.

Tuan, Yi-Fu. (1974) *Topophilia*. Prentice Hall, Englewood Cliffs.

Watts, L. (2008) The art and craft of train travel. *Social & Cultural Geography* 9 (6), 711–726.

Whatmore, S. (2006) Materialist returns: practising cultural geography in and for a more-than-human world. *Cultural Geographies* 13, 600–609.

Wylie, J. (2005) A Single Day's Walking: narrating self and landscape on the South West Coast Path. *Transactions of the Institute of British Geographers* NS 30, 234–247.

Wylie, J. (2006) Depths and folds: on landscape and the gazing subject. *Environment and Planning D: Society and Space* 24, 519–535.

Wylie, J. (2009) Landscape, absence and the geographies of love. *Transactions of the Institute of British Geographers* 34, 275–290.

Wylie, J. (2010) Cultural Geographies of the Future, or looking rosy and feeling blue. *Cultural Geographies* 17 (2), 211–217.

Wylie, J. (2002) An essay on ascending Glastonbury Tor. *Geoforum* 33, 441–454.

Chapter 15

Place
Part I

Tim Cresswell

Review

There seems little doubt that place is one of the two or three most important concepts in the theory and practice of human geography. It has frequently featured in the titles of books on the notion of geography itself (Johnston 1991; Unwin 1992) or books on particular approaches to geography such as feminism (Johnson *et al.* 2000; Domosh and Seager 2001). The historical and ongoing importance of place points to the fact that it is fundamental to human existence, or, indeed, existence itself (Sack 1997; Casey 1997). Despite this self-evident importance place is a necessarily fuzzy concept. It is often used alongside or instead of a host of other related concepts including location, locale, region, space, territory and landscape. For most of the history of geography it has been more of a taken-for-granted concept than a carefully considered one. The word "place," for instance, is there in the idea of central place theory but there is little to tell us about what place is within that theory. It is simply assumed to mean location (relative to other locations) (Christaller 1966).

This is, perhaps, place at its most elemental – *location*. Place refers to the where of something. This is a common usage in everyday speech. "What is the correct place for x?" is a question about where something belongs. Location is the first of Agnew's three part definition of place that has stood the test of time: location, locale and sense of place (Agnew 1987). Location, as we have seen, refers to the where of something, either in an absolute sense according to some agreed measure such as longitude and latitude, or in a relative sense (35 miles east of Y). It was this kind of place that was invoked by Aristotle who argued that place "takes precedence over all other things" (Casey 1997: 51). The geographical question of "where" is key to Aristotle for everything that exists must be somewhere "because what is not

The Wiley Blackwell Companion to Human Geography, First Edition.
Edited by John A. Agnew and James S. Duncan.
© 2011 John Wiley & Sons, Ltd. Published 2016 by John Wiley & Sons, Ltd.

is nowhere – where for instance is a goat-stag or a sphinx?" (Aristotle in Casey 1997: 51). Place comes first, to Aristotle because everything that exists has to have a place - has to be located. Thus "that without which nothing else can exist, while it can exist without the others, must needs be first" (Casey 1997: 52). This argument is that things have to be *located*. Location often seems like the most trivial aspect of Agnew's tripartite definition of place. A place is somewhere. But here, in Aristotle, we see that this aspect of place is possibly its most philosophically crucial characteristic. Place (as location) comes first. It is the bedrock of the possibility of existence.

The second of Agnew's aspect of place is *locale*. Locale refers to the material context for social and cultural life – the fact that we live in a world of buildings, roads, parks, fields, etc. When we think of a place we tend not to think of an abstract location but of a particular collection of material things. If I say, "think of a place" you are not going to describe it to me as a set of co-ordinates. You might name it – Solsbury Hill, The Grand Canyon, Islington, Vancouver Island, Melbourne – and you might describe it in terms of its observable, tangible features. If I say I like the place Oxford, I do not mean its location (although it is convenient to reach it from West London where I live and from my parents' home in West Oxfordshire) but I mean its High Street, the University Parks, the Colleges, the pub in Summertown where I used to drink at lunchtimes, the labyrinth of Blackwell's bookshop, even the arcane desks of the Bodleian Library. I mean place as locale – a material world in which things happened during my life.

The third of Agnew's place characteristics is *sense of place*. Sense of place refers the way in which places are given meaning. When I wrote about Oxford (above) many of you probably felt some immediate connection regardless of whether you have been there or not. Oxford has a strong sense of place in an academic environment, amongst tourists and all watchers of *Inspector Morse*. Oxford's sense of place to me results (mostly) from the fact that I grew up nearby for much of my childhood and early adulthood. I worked there in the summers. I fell in love there. I had picnics in the parks, I went on pub-crawls, I spent a good deal of time conducting research for my PhD there. These memories (and the fact that I still visit from time to time) mean that it has an intensely personal set of meanings for me – meanings that make it distinct from places I have never been – such as Sydney. This is the first way we attach meanings to place – through personal experience. But some places, such as Oxford, have heavily mediated senses of place too. We see them on television, read about them in novels, hear them in the cds we listen to, see them in films. Senses of place are mediated and shared. Oxford and its universities are constantly represented in particular ways that make it appealing to tourists for instance, who visit in the summer from around the world. I have never been to Sydney but it still has a sense of place for me – one that would be likely to change if and when I visit.

Place became a central object of geographical theorization in the 1970s with the advent of humanistic geography. It was this final aspect of place, its meaning, that lay at the centre of this line of enquiry. Geographers such as Yi-Fu Tuan, Anne Buttimer, Edward Relph and David Seamon, demoralized by the abstraction of spatial science (including the descendants of central place theory) began to insist on the necessity of figuring out what place was in all its richness (Tuan 1974; Buttimer and Seamon 1980; Relph 1976). To them place was far more than location and philosophically distinct from space. Place denoted a centre of meaning and field of care. It was a meaningful segment of space – somewhere we were experientially invested in and could develop attachments to. It needn't be a place in the conventional sense of a settlement like Oxford. It could be, as Tuan has argued, as small as a favorite chair in the corner of a room or as large as the whole earth as seen from the moon by homesick astronauts. A place could even move. A ship, inhabited for months on end by a crew, becomes a moving place. Even a particular chair and table space on an intercity train is momentarily made place-like as we read a book, listen to music, stretch out and eat a snack. To the humanist the term "place" named a particular relation between people and the world – a sense of "being in the world" borrowed from the phenomenology of Martin Heidegger and Maurice Merleau-Ponty (Tuan 1971; Seamon 1979; Heidegger 1971; Merleau-Ponty 1962).

Humanists put place at the centre of a human geography agenda. They made something that had always been there more explicit. Since the late 1970s place has remained a central concern of the discipline. In the 1980s and 90s critical geographers of different theoretical and political persuasions (Marxists, feminists, poststructuralists, etc) continued to use place but insisted on the role of power and politics in both the ways in which places are made and the role places play in the constitution of society. These were themes that had never been central to humanists. One of the ways we use the word place in everyday speech is in phrases such as "he was put in his place" or "she should know her place." These suggest more than location in any strict sense, and more than a straightforward engagement with meaning. They suggest a notion of the proper or appropriate that is laden with power. Place in this sense combines the spatial with the social. Certain kinds of people (with particular genders, ethnicities, sexualities, ages, levels of [dis]ability and so on) are said to "belong" in different places and this notion of belonging is often defined by people with the power to define people according to place (Cresswell 1996; Sibley 1995). We are familiar with seemingly outdated notions such as "the woman's place in the home." There are many, often unstated, varieties of this kind of logic concerning children (who should be seen and not heard), black people, gay people, the disabled and others. Place structures society by being used to define who and what belongs where and when. The meaning of place is rarely neutral or innocent. The 1990s saw a proliferation of studies of the role of place in processes of domination and resistance – in the practice of power. These included work on children (Valentine 1997), sexuality (Valentine 1993; Hubbard 2000; Bell *et al.* 1994), disability (Imrie 2000; Kitchin 1998), homelessness (Cloke *et al.* 2000; May 2000; Veness 1992), race (Delaney 1998; Keith and Pile 1993; Domosh 1998) and youth culture (Skelton and Valentine 1998).

By the end of the 1990s it was clear that places are saturated with notions of power. Place is not simply the result of individual or collective processes of meaning making but part of the process by which society is produced, reproduced and (occasionally) transformed. It was also in the 1990s that the notion of a "progressive" or "global" sense of place emerged from the work of Doreen Massey. Massey was responding (in part) to a suggestion by David Harvey that the "militant particularism" of some kinds of place politics could be very dangerous. He was referring to the urge some people (on both the right and left of the political spectrum) have to withdraw and cut themselves off from the globalised and connected world in which we live. This is a tendency shared by some kinds of commune on the one hand, and some kinds of gated community on the other. These are practices that tend to withdraw into some notions of a purified place that can be defined against and defended from the rest of the world. Such a move, as Harvey suggests, is reactionary and dangerous (Harvey 1993). Massey responded to Harvey's suggestion that place based politics were likely to be reactionary by outlining an alternative "progressive" sense of place that was not defined by tightly drawn boundaries, an exclusive sense of identity (this is where "we" belong) or a singular notion of roots and history.

In Massey's account of a progressive (or global) sense of place she draws on her experience of Kilburn High Road in north London. In a colorful evocation of a place of constant mixing she reflects on the range of identities at play as she wanders down the street encountering a Moslem paper seller, passing a sari shop and an Irish pub with Irish Republican posters. This, she tells us, is a place made through its connections with the rest of the world. It is not a place defined by strict boundaries or any easy sense of a singular identity. Its histories are very much the histories of the connections (to Ireland, the empire, the Commonwealth, the global capitalist economy) that come together in a unique way in Kilburn (Massey 1993). To Massey this provides a model for thinking of place in general. All places are made in horizontal space by their connections, their role in networks that spread across the globe. Her essay marked a transformation from thinking of place vertically – as rooted in time immemorial – to thinking of it horizontally, as produced relationally through its connections. Such a notion of place, rather than being introverted and reactionary, is extrovert and politically hopeful.

Prospect

How might the concept of place be developed? We have inherited notions of place as meaningful space, as a sometimes reactionary form of insularity and as a progressive and open coming together of flows and connections. There have been suggestions of the demise of place for a while now with the advent of hyper-mobility, the internet, the mobile phone and global flows of capital and information (Augé 1995; Relph 1976; Castells 1996; Thrift 1994). But such predictions seem to have little purchase in a world where people still appear to inhabit their homes, do the garden, decorate the walls, sit in parks and go on holidays to sites they find interesting. No doubt our experience of place has qualitatively changed and has, in many ways, been augmented, but place is still quite clearly there. At least in Aristotle's sense, things still have to be somewhere.

A number of ideas in recent social theory have the potential to inform research on place in the coming years. Places are complex and dynamic collages of things (material culture, objects), representations (places as representations and representations of place) and practices (the things people do, often habitually). All of these aspects of place have been open to theoretical development in recent years (Cresswell and Hoskins 2008). The turn (back) to materiality in cultural theory has made its mark on geography (Miller 1997, 2008; Bennett 2001; Kopytoff 1986; Jacobs 2006; Jackson 2000). While the "new cultural geography" of the late 1980s and 1990s has been accused of turning its back on the solid, concrete materiality of place and landscape in favor of more ethereal notions of text, performance and representation, more recent work has sought to examine the specific roles played by "things" in the ongoing geography of everyday life. This has involved a much closer attention to the physical properties of the "stuff" that surrounds us and forms the micro and macro level topographies and textures of place and landscape. Places continue to be implicated in the work and play of representation. Places, themselves, are representational. They continue to be marketed and sold for businesses and tourism. They continue to project power and authority, whether private and corporate or public and political. Exactly how they do this and how the material properties of place are enrolled in this is an important ongoing question that can be informed by both new work on material culture but also by work that inhabits the blurred borderlands between the brutal solidity of things and the hazy world of (for instance), enchantment and the spectral (Pile 2005; Adey and Maddern 2008).

Places are also stages for, and made through, the loosely allied notions of practice, performance and the performative. This, of course, was the insight of David Seamon's work on body routines and place ballets from the 1980s (Seamon 1980). It was also at the centre of approaches to place and time-geography influences by structuration theory (Pred 1984). Places are made by the sometimes repeated, sometimes surprising things that people do in them. The daily commute, the school run, the opening and closing of shops, museums, service providers – all of these produce a kind of drama in place that helps to make the place what it is. Work on the embodied doing of place has been influenced by theorists of practice, performance and embodiment (Butler 1996; Bourdieu 1990; de Certeau 1984) as well as my vitalist, phenomenological and non-representational philosophies (Merleau-Ponty 1962; Shotter 1993; Serres 1995; Massumi 2002). This has led to a flowering of work on qualities, emotions, affects and affordances in place that has revived some aspects of humanistic engagements with place under a new guise and informed by new thinking (McCormack 2003; Dewsbury 2000; Kraftl and Adey 2008; Latham and McCormack 2004).

Places as Assemblages

Places are increasingly thought of as the interplay of these realms of the material, the immaterial and representational. One key approach that might allow us to examine this interplay creatively is "assemblage theory." Assemblage theory is derived from the work of Delueze and Guattari (Deleuze and Guattari 1987) and is developed most fully by Manuel De Landa (De Landa 2006). De Landa is seeking to develop a new theory of society that avoids the pitfalls of theoretical and methodological individualism – an approach that breaks everything down to its smallest essential parts – and forms of holism or structuralism that insist on the overpowering efficacy of overarching systems – such as capitalism or "society." In De Landa's work he insists on an ontology derived from the connections between people and things (De Landa 2006). His outline of assemblages includes everything from face to face meetings to the constitution of nation-states:

> This is because assemblages, being wholes whose properties emerge from the interactions between parts, can be used to model any of these intermediate entities: interpersonal networks and institutional organizations are assemblages of people; social justice

movements are assemblages of several networked communities; central governments are assemblages of several organizations; cities are assemblages of people, networks, organizations, as well as of a variety of infrastructural components, from buildings and streets to conduits for matter and energy flows; nation-states are assemblages of cities, the geographical regions organized by cities, and the provinces that several regions form. (De Landa 2006: 5–6)

De Landa defines the concept of assemblage along two dimensions. One dimension connects the *material* to the *expressive*. The other connects *territorialization* to *deterritorialization*. Let us consider each in turn. A material role is played by the physical properties of things. De Landa gives the following example: "Community networks and institutional organizations are assemblages of bodies, but they also possess a variety of other components, from food and physical labor, to simple tools and complex machines, to the buildings and neighborhoods serving as their physical locales" (De Landa 2006: 12). Expressive roles refer to such obviously symbolic capacities inherent in language and symbols but also to the capacities of non-linguistic social expressions (such as 'body-language' or meaningful actions of obeying or disobeying commands for instance). Processes of territorialization are processes that tend to add coherence to an assemblage while processes of deterritorialization are ones which are destabilizing and tend to dilute an assemblage. In the first instance this is a spatial process where spatial boundaries are either sharpened or blurred. But these processes also refer to forces which increase homogeneity (territorializing) or heterogeneity (deterritorializing).

> The concept of territorialization must be first of all understood literally. Face-to-face conversations always occur in a particular place (a street-corner, a pub, a church), and once the participants have ratified one another a conversation acquires well-defined spatial boundaries. Similarly, many interpersonal networks define communities inhabiting spatial territories, whether ethnic neighborhoods or small towns, with well defined borders. (De Landa 2006: 13)

To De Landa the breaking down of an assemblage into parts that play both material and expressive roles is an analytical exercise while the focus on territorialization is synthetic "since it is in part through the more of less permanent articulations produced by this process that a whole emerges from its parts and maintains its identity once it has emerged" (De Landa 2006: 14).

Let's consider place as an assemblage. As we have seen, place clearly has a *material* aspect as evidenced by all the things (both solid and more ethereal) that go into making up the topography and textures of place. The buildings, 'natural' topography, open spaces, junk, commodity goods, conduits, roadways and the whole multitude of objects that combine in a particular location. Places also have *expressive* capacity. Most obviously, perhaps, there are *territorializing* functions at play in place. Political boundaries, labeling, mapping, place promotion, forms of representation, naming and all the individual and group practices that are characteristic of a place all act to hold the assemblage of a particular place together. Similarly there are *deterritorializing* forces at play in place that erode, replace or dissipate elements in the place assemblage. The flight of capital, forms of communication technology, movement in and out of place all operate in extroverted and centrifugal ways.

Any process which either destabilizes spatial boundaries or increases internal heterogeneity is considered deterritorializing. A good example is communication technology, ranging from writing and a reliable postal service, to telegraphs, telephones and computers, all of which blur the spatial boundaries of social entities by eliminating the need for co-presence: they enable conversations to take place at a distance, allow interpersonal networks to form via regular correspondence, phone calls or computer communications, and give organizations the means to operate in different countries at the same time. (De Landa 2006: 13)

These deterritorializing processes are not supposed to be morally or ideologically negative. Assemblages may still be strong but simply more spread out and heterogeneous. Massey's global sense of place clearly includes very strong deterritorializing processes.

Thinking of places as assemblages focuses attention on the fact that places, as instances of the particular, are always neither essentialist entities (they could always be otherwise and the particular way that they are is a product of history) not are they overarching totalizing systems. The notion of assemblage resonates with efforts within geography to conceptualize place as a particular instance of a combination of things that are often held apart. We have already seen how Massey has conceptualized place as a site produced through relations with an outside – as an extroverted site of connections where things (people, ideas) from elsewhere merge in a particular kind of way (Massey 1993, 2005). We might also think of the work of Sack who has long argued for a vision of place as an entangled weave of strands from the realms of nature, social relations and meaning. He has argued that theorists have tended to approach the geographical world from one or the other of these realms – as an expression of nature, society or culture. If we start from place, instead of thinking of it as an expression of something else, he suggests, then we can see the way that place interweaves all three realms and cannot be reduced to any of them (Sack 1997, 1992).

Conclusion

Future work on place needs to theorize and exemplify the assemblage qualities of place. This will involve both itemizing the material and expressive qualities of place and accounting for the processes that hold place together and those that are more centrifugal (Jones 2009). Massey's account of a global sense of place has had a powerful hold on theorization of place over the last decade. Clearly places are made through their connections to the world beyond. Precise accounting for this process has been notably absent. Why do flows combine in the way they do, exactly where they do? Answering such questions involves re-focusing on the vertical aspects of place – the "thereness" of a particular location and locale that is both the product of horizontal flows and a reason for those flows combining precisely there.

Think of Schiphol airport, a major international hub just outside Amsterdam. It is the fourth busiest airport in Europe. Airports are frequently thought of as archetypes for non-place or the space of flows (Augé 1995; Castells 1996). If any place is defined by its connections it is an international 'hub' airport. I once spent three weeks in this airport conducting research on mobility (see chapter 9 in Cresswell 2006). While I was there I shared lunch with a homeless man who lived in the airport during the day.

He traveled daily on trains while the airport was closed during the night. He knew the place well. He knew where to sleep undisturbed, where to get food and reading material, where to watch the planes. He remembered arriving at this airport with his ex-wife with hopes of a new life in a new place. He came from Curacao in the Dutch Antilles. This man was in the airport for the affordances it offered him; the shelter, warmth, food, reading materials. He was also there because of its direct connection to the Dutch empire. And Schiphol is where it is because of the available land on the old polder where an agricultural way of life was fading. It is there because of its connections to Amsterdam and because, on the North West coast of Europe if provides a good location for making connections between flights to different parts of Europe and other continents. Schiphol, in other words, is a place (like any other but more exaggerated than most) that combines material and expressive qualities and territorializing and deterritorializing processes. It is a place that forms and reforms daily through the connections and flows that partly constitute it. But those connections connect precisely there because of where and what Schiphol is. Its vertical and horizontal qualities combine to make it what it is. One direction for the future theorization of place is to think of place as an assemblage that combines material, expressive and practical components in particular ways that reflect the constant recombination of vertical roots and horizontal routes.

References

Adey, P. and Maddern, J. (2008) Editorial: spectro-geographies. *Cultural geographies* 15, 291–295.

Agnew, J.A. (1987) *Place and politics: the geographical mediation of state and society*. Allen and Unwin, Boston.

Augé, M. (1995) *Non-places: introduction to an anthropology of supermodernity*. Verso, New York, London.

Bell, D., Binnie, J., Cream, J., and Valentine, G. (1994) All hyped up and no place to go. *Gender, Place and Culture* 1 (1), 31–47.

Bennett, J. (2001) *The enchantment of modern life: attachments, crossings, and ethics*. Princeton University Press, Princeton.

Bourdieu, P. (1990) *The Logic of Practice*. Stanford University Press, Stanford.

Butler, J. (1996) Performativity's Social Magic. In T. Schatzki and W. Natter (eds), *The Social and Political Body*. Guilford, New York.

Buttimer, A. and Seamon, D. (1980) *The Human experience of space and place*. St. Martin's Press, New York.

Casey, E.S. (1997) *The fate of place: a philosophical history*. University of California Press, Berkeley.

Castells, M. (1996) *The rise of the network society*. Blackwell Publishers, Cambridge, Massachusetts.

Christaller, W. (1966) *Central places in Southern Germany*. Prentice-Hall, New Jersey.

Cloke, P., Milbourne, P., and Widdowfield, R. (2000) Homelessness and Rurality: "out-of-place" in purified space? *Environment and Planning D: Society and Space* 18, 715–735.

Cresswell, T. (1996) *In Place/Out of Place: Geography, Ideology and Transgression*. University of Minnesota Press, Minneapolis.

Cresswell, T. (2006) *On the move: mobility in the modern Western world*. Routledge, New York.

Cresswell, T. and Hoskins, G. (2008) Place, Persistence and Practice: Evaluating Historical Significance at Angel Island, San Francisco and Maxwell Street, Chicago. *Annals of the Association of American Geographers* 98 (2), 392–413.

de Certeau, M. (1984) *The Practice of Everyday Life*. University of California Press, Berkeley.

De Landa, M. (2006) *A new philosophy of society: assemblage theory and social complexity*. Continuum, London, New York.

Delaney, D. (1998) *Race, Place and the Law*. University of Texas Press, Austin.

Deleuze, G. and Guattari, F. (1987) *A thousand plateaus: capitalism and schizophrenia*. University of Minnesota Press, Minneapolis.

Dewsbury, J.D. (2000) Performativity and the event: enacting a philosophy of difference. *Environment and Planning D: Society and Space* 18, 473–496.

Domosh, M. (1998) Those "Gorgeous Incongruities": Polite Politics and Public Space on the Streets of Nineteenth-Century New York City. *Annals of the Association of American Geographers* 88 (2), 209–226.

Domosh, M. and Seager, J. (2001) *Putting women in place: feminist geographers make sense of the world*. Guilford Press, New York.

Harvey, D. (1993) From Space to Place and Back Again. In J. Bird, B. Curtis, T. Putnam, G. Robertson, G., and L. Tickner (eds), *Mappiing the Futures*. Routledge, London.

Heidegger, M. (1971) *Poetry, language, thought*. Harper and Row, New York.

Hubbard, P. (2000) Desire/disgust: mapping the moral contours of heterosexuality. *Progress in Human Geography* 24 (2) 191–217.

Imrie, R. (2000) Disability and Discourses of Mobility and Movement. *Environment and Planning A* 32 (9), 1641–1656.

Jackson, P. (2000) Rematerializing social and cultural geography. *Social and Cultural Geography* 1 (1), 9–14.

Jacobs, J.M. (2006) A geography of big things. *Cultural geographies* 13 (1), 1–27.

Johnson, L.C., Huggins, J., and Jacobs, J.M. (2000) *Placebound: Australian feminist geographies*. Oxford University Press, Oxford, Victoria.

Johnston, R.J. (1991) *A question of place: exploring the practice of human geography*. Blackwell, Oxford, Cambridge.

Jones, M. (2009) Phase space: geography, relational thinking, and beyond. *Progress in Human Geography* 33 (4), 487–506.

Keith, M. and Pile, S. (eds) (1993) *Place and the Politics of Identity*. Routledge, London.

Kitchin, R. (1998) "Out of Place", "Knowing One's Place": Space, Power and the Exclusion of Disabled People. *Disability and Society* 13 (3), 343–356.

Kopytoff, I. (1986) The cultural biogrpahy of things: commodotization as process. In A. Appadurai (ed.), *The social life of things: commodities in cultural perspective*. Cambridge University Press, Cambridge.

Kraftl, P. and Adey, P. (2008) Architecture/Affect/Inhabitation: Geographies of Being-In-Buidings. *Annals of the Association of American Geographers* 98 (1), 213–231.

Latham, A. and McCormack, D. (2004) Moving cities: rethinking the materialities of urban geographies. *Progress in Human Geography* 28 (6), 701–724.

Massey, D. (1993) Power-Geometry and Progressive Sense of Place. In J. Bird, B. Curtis, T. Putnam, G. Robertson, and L. Tickner (eds), *Mapping the Futures: Local Cultures, Global Change*. Routledge, London.

Massey, D.B. (2005) *For space*. Sage, London.

Massumi, B. (2002) *Parables for the virtual: movement, affect, sensation*. Duke University Press, Durham.

May, J. (2000) Of nomads and vagrants: single homelessness and narratives of home as place. *Environment and Planning D: Society and Space* 18 (6), 737–759.

McCormack, D.P. (2003) The event of geographical ethics in spaces of affect. *Transactions of the Institute of British Geographers* 28, 488–507.

Merleau-Ponty, M. (1962) *The Phenomenology of Perception*. Routledge and Kegan Paul, London.

Miller, D. (1997) *Material cultures: why some things matter*. UCL Press, London.

Miller, D. (2008) *The comfort of things*. Polity, Cambridge.

Pile, S. (2005) *Real cities: modernity, space and the phantasmagorias of city life*. Sage, London.

Pred, A.R. (1984) Place as Historically Contingent Process: Structuration and the Time-Geography of Becoming Places. *Annals of the Association of American Geographers* 74 (2), 279–297.

Relph, E. (1976) *Place and Placelessness*. Pion, London.

Sack, R.D. (1997) *Homo Geographicus*. Johns Hopkins University Press, Baltimore.

Sack, R.D. (1992) *Place, modernity, and the consumer's world: a relational framework for geographical analysis*. Johns Hopkins University Press, Baltimore.

Seamon, D. (1979) *A geography of the lifeworld: movement, rest, and encounter*. St. Martin's Press, New York.

Seamon, D. (1980) Body-Subject, Time-Space Routines, and Place-Ballets. In A. Buttimer and D. Seamon (eds), *The Human Experience of Space and Place*. Croom Helm, London.

Serres, M. (1995) *Angels, a modern myth*. Flammarion, Paris.

Shotter, J. (1993) *Cultural politics of everyday life: social constructionism, rhetoric and knowing of the third kind*. University of Toronto Press, Toronto, Buffalo.

Sibley, D. (1995) *Geographies of Exclusion: Society and Difference in the West*. Routledge, London.

Skelton, T. and Valentine, G. (1998) *Cool places: geographies of youth cultures*. Routledge, New York; London.

Thrift, N. (1994) Inhuman Geographies: Landscapes of Speed, Light and Power. In P. Cloke (ed.), *Writing the Rural: Five Cultural Geographies*. Paul Chapman, London.

Tuan, Y.-f. (1971) Geography, phenomenology, and the study of human nature. *Canadian Geographer* 15, 181–192.

Tuan, Y.-f. (1974) Space and Place: Humanistic Perspective. *Progress in Human Geography* 6, 211–252.

Unwin, P.T.H. (1992) *The place of geography*. Longman Scientific and Technical, Harlow.

Valentine, G. (1993) (Hetero)sexing space: lesbian perspectives and experiences of everyday spaces. *Environment and Planning D: Society and Space* 11, 395–413.

Valentine, G. (1997) Angels and Devils: Moral Landscapes of Childhood. *Environment and Planning D: Society and Space* 14 (5), 581–599.

Veness, A. (1992) Home and Homelessness in the United States; Changing Ideals and Realities. *Environment and Planning D: Society and Space* 10, 445–468.

Chapter 16

Place
Part II

Steven Hoelscher

The question, what is Place? presents many difficulties for analysis.
(Aristotle, Physics, Book 4, Part 1)

Place is latitudinal and longitudinal within the map of a person's life. It is temporal and spatial, personal and political. A layered location replete with human histories and memories, a place has width as well as depth. It is about connections, what surrounds it, what formed it, what happened there, what will happen there.
(Lippard 1997:7, The Lure of the Local)

I am mainly ignorant what place this is.
(King Lear, Act 4, Scene 7)

Introduction

A central concept in human geography, "place" is both commonsensical and a technical keyword. It is used in everyday speech, as a noun to describe a location – "Austin is a place in Texas" – and as a verb to assign a position – "she placed a pencil on her desk." Within human geography, place is that and more as it is frequently considered one of the discipline's defining ideas. Together with landscape, area, region, environment, and territory, place is essential to the geographer's craft.

Place is also one of those concepts that is simple enough until you begin to think about how people create, perceive, and transform actual places; only then does its commonsensical nature begin to melt away. Very little about place, as ordinary a word as it is, seems fully obvious or unambiguous. Like its conceptual twin, "culture" – famously described by Raymond Williams (1983; Tuan 1992) as one

---

The Wiley Blackwell Companion to Human Geography, First Edition.
Edited by John A. Agnew and James S. Duncan.
© 2011 John Wiley & Sons, Ltd. Published 2016 by John Wiley & Sons, Ltd.

of the two or three most complicated words in the English language – the complexity of place derives mainly from its competing meanings in several distinct intellectual disciplines. Anthropologists Low and Lawrence-Zúñiga (2003: 18) seek to "describe the intricacies of mutually constituting social relations with place through ritual and metaphor;" for sociologist Roger Friedland (1992), place is "a cultural artifact of social conflict and cohesion;" for neuroscientist John Zeisel (2006), sense of place is something that can be located in a brain with the assistance of an MRI; for historian Philip J. Ethington (2007: 466) places are the "topi of human action"; and for philosopher Edward Casey (1997: 24), our own lived body is the specific medium for experiencing the "place-world."

If that's not enough, geographers, the human scientists who have devoted most scholarly attention to the concept of place, seem equally at odds when defining this keyword. For David Harvey (1996: 293), "place, in whatever guise, is like space and time, a social construct;" while for Yi-Fu Tuan (1977) place is a space that has been humanized and made meaningful. Robert Sack (1997) understands place to be something deeper than a social construct, and a fundamental element to creating "the social;" Tim Cresswell (1996) prioritizes the ideological use of places by those with greater power as well as the transgressive resistance to that power; while Gillian Rose (1993) takes a more skeptical view, and is at pains to describe the highly patriarchal and oppressive nature of places associated with home. Such conceptual fuzziness has even led some, like Edward Soja (1996: 40), to dismiss "place" as an obfuscating term without analytical value.

This last point misses the mark and, in this chapter, I present a contrasting viewpoint. While I acknowledge the broad-ranging meanings attached to "place," it's my central argument that place – as it's experienced, created, and destroyed by a multitude of different people, and interpreted by a range of scholars – is too important to send packing. On the contrary, evidence abounds that, as paradoxical as it may seem, place is becoming ever more important in an increasingly globalized world of instantaneous communication, time-space compression, worldwide flows of capital. Making sense of this paradox helps prepare for the discussion of place to follow.

Place and the Paradox of Globalization

On New Year's Eve of 2009, the Harvard psychologist, public television host, and best-selling author of *Stumbling on Happiness*, David Gilbert, offered a series of gloomy thoughts to readers of the *New York Times* editorial page. Bemoaning the "homogenization" and the "industrial smoothing of our nation's once-variegated" places, Gilbert (2009) nostalgically recalled a day when "downtowns were once collections of local businesses that lured us with claims to uniqueness." Today, by contrast:

> Americans can drive from one ocean to the other, stopping every day for the same hamburger and every evening at the same hotel. ... When they remember the Starbucks where they met the one they married or the Gap where they lost the one they didn't, they will be marinating in memories that happened everywhere but not somewhere, reliving experiences that are located in time but dislocated in space. (Gilbert, 2009)

Much like the confused King Lear, blindly lost in the wilderness, Americans have become ignorant of the places they find themselves in, unthinkingly trading an Old Navy for Abercrombie, TGI Fridays for an Olive Garden. Most unhappy of all is the prospect of the end to nostalgia itself, which Gilbert defines as the longing for the places of one's past: "Ours may be the last generation of Americans to suffer for return – to remember events that took place when place still mattered."

If David Gilbert's lament for a time when place still mattered sounds familiar, it's because this is a story that's been told repeatedly for the better part of two centuries. Every generation, it seems, discovers what the historian William Leach (1999: 6) calls "the destruction of place in American life," or the "weakening of place as a centering presence in the lives of ordinary people." Writing in the 1970s, journalist Peter Schrag (1970: 12), in *Out of Place in America*, bemoaned the "bulldozers of modernization [that] invade the neighborhood like tanks," rendering Americans "fugitives in our own country." Fifty years earlier, Lewis Mumford (1926: 80–81) warned of America's emerging crisis of modernity, of an ever more "abstract and fragmentary" landscape that left American places with "a blankness, a sterility, a boredom, a despair." The literary critic Rebecca Solnit (2003: 22) pushed the moment of decline back further still, as she identified the late nineteenth century as the time when "places were homogenized, where a network of machines and the corporations behind them were dispelling the independence of wilderness, remoteness, of local culture." And, as early as 1835, Alexis de Tocqueville noted the absence of long-lasting attachment to place as a foundational element of American life, finding that "an American changes his residence ceaselessly" (quoted in Rybczynski 1995: 109).

It's not only a familiar story, but an appealing one as well, infused with nostalgia and the apparent logic of self-evidence: Americans, and increasingly Europeans, *do* move a lot; the forces of globalization that have long animated political economies *are* reshaping cities and regions today at warp speed; and, because of major advances in technology and global communication, to put it in the contemporary idiom, the earth *does* seem to be flattening (Friedman 2005; cf. DeBlij 2009).

What's more, the destruction of place is seen to be occurring not only in the United States, but also throughout much of the Western world. "The remark I here apply to America may indeed be addressed to almost all our contemporaries," Tocqueville (2004 [1840]: 723) wrote: "Variety is disappearing … the same ways of acting, thinking, and feeling are to be met with all over the world." Writing from the vantage point of Paris more than a century later, the French social theorist Henri Lefebvre (1991 [1974]: 74–75) concurred: for many places "the moment of creation is past; indeed, the city's disappearance is already imminent." At one time, places such as Venice were "unique, original … highly expressive and significant." However, due to unrelenting ability of capital to transform cities into mere commodifiable products, Lefebvre lamented:

> It is obvious, sad to say, that repetition has everywhere defeated uniqueness, that the artificial and contrived have driven all spontaneity and naturalness from the [the city] … Repetitive spaces are the outcome of repetitive gestures (those of workers) associated with instruments which are both duplicatable and designed to duplicate: machines, bulldozers, concrete-mixers, cranes, pneumatic drills, and so on. Are these spaces

interchangeable because they are homologous? Or are they homogenous so that they can be exchanged, bought and sold, with the only difference between them being those assessable in money – i.e. quantifiable – terms? ... At all events, repetition reigns supreme. (Lefebvre (1991 [1974])

Lefebvre's rhetorical questions have been answered repeatedly. For some, such as French anthropologist Marc Augé (1995), such serial spaces of repetition – the freeways, big box stores, airports of our world today – are best considered "non-places;" for Canadian geographer Edward Relph (1976) they define the very essence of "placelessness;" and for American cultural critic James Howard Kunstler (1993) they exemplify a "geography of nowhere." For each of these authors, and many more, spaces of contemporary circulation, consumption, and communication is evidence of the declining importance of place (Augé 1995: 110; Meyrowitz 1985).

But are they really? The notion of the perpetual recession into the distant past – back to a time "when place still mattered" – should make us suspicious that such a Golden Age ever existed (Williams 1973: 12). But so, too, should the response of ordinary people to forces of globalization. Certainly many people in the place I currently call home would disagree – and strongly so. Austin, Texas, known nationally and internationally for its citizens' efforts to keep the city "weird," epitomizes cultural resistance to forces of homogenization and the deleterious effects of globalization. In their attempts to preserve the city's unique personality, defined for many as "a liberal Mecca in a desert of conservativism," Austinites go to great lengths: "if they have to paint their house fuchsia, erect a tinfoil T-Rex statue, or wallpaper the outside of their VW bus so that there's no mistaking Austin with the likes of Dallas or Houston, then by God, they'll do it" (Long 2010: 2). At bottom, small efforts such as these and larger ones like enacting stringent zoning ordinances or protesting certain kinds of development are intended to demonstrate that, indeed, Austin is "not like other places" (Figure 16.1).

"Keep Austin Weird" is not just a slogan to help support local business, although it is that, too; rather, it is a civic motto embraced by those residents who are involved in the fight against global corporate hegemony and its destructive effects on place. While detractors (including those with substantial political and economic power) see Austin's eccentric reputation as an impediment to progress, many more celebrate its famed nonconformity. It's certainly a major factor, along with the city's booming high-tech industry, in Austin's position at the top of Richard Florida's (2004) oft-cited "Creativity Index." No doubt the promise of a tolerant, creatively expressive, and educated population with a vibrant nightlife has helped attract businesses that enjoy the flexibility to locate nearly anywhere. Such perceived uniqueness is an increasingly important factor for civic and business leaders to "sell" the city (Kearns and Philo 1993). But, for those who celebrate Austin's "weirdness," this is not about marketable urban imagery: it's about saving the "soul" of a place under siege.

Envisioning Place

At once an expression of deep emotional connection, a tool for local business promotion, and a critical space in the ongoing history of capitalism and globalization, the celebration of place in Austin, Texas, confounds simplistic assessments of its

Figure 16.1 Austin: Not Like Other Places … 8½ inch by 11 inch postcard. Political advertisement by "I'm 4 PAC," a ballot measure supporting the issuance of $31.5 million general obligation bonds for the construction and renovation of various city community and cultural facilities, 2006.

demise. Indeed, in their efforts to maintain the city's distinctive qualities – to save its "soul" – Austinites are hardly alone. Across the world, neighborhood organizers, organic farmers, community artists, consumer advocacy groups, and environmental activists are striving to create their own, unique environments for living and working. Such resistances to the forces of place homogenization, which David Harvey (2001: 172) calls "militant particularism," are occurring in the long shadow of global capitalism, sometimes flying below the radar, sometimes coming in direct opposition. The paradox, of course, is that at exactly the same time that the very political-economic processes that would seem to homogenize place – to render the globe "placeless" – in fact increase its importance. "Place-bound identities," Harvey (1993: 4) argues, "become more rather than less important in a world of diminishing spatial barriers to exchange, movement, and communication." Thus, spatial flows of capital and information – seen by many as the primary forces of globalization – not only bring the world together, but they tear it apart, giving rise to militant particularism of Austin and its celebration of "weirdness."

David Harvey is hardly the only commentator on the unexpected resurgence of place in locations like Austin and beyond. Indeed, beginning in the 1970s and continuing today, scholars from across the humanities and social sciences have given sufficient attention to this classic geographic concept so that we now speak of a "spatial turn" in the human sciences (Withers 2009). After decades of devaluation in orthodox social science – including human geography itself – place has reemerged with an intellectual vigor that few would have predicted several decades ago (Agnew

1989). The signs of such a revival of place, as the philosopher Edward S. Casey (1997: 286) puts it, are widespread: "in France, Bachelard, Braudel, Foucault, Deleuze and Guattari; in Germany, Benjamin and Arendt; and in North America, Relph, Tuan, Entrikin, Soja, Sack, Berry, Snyder, Stegner, Eisenman, Tschumi, and Walter. Each of these figures has succeeded in fashioning a fresh face for place."

The interdisciplinary, transnational nature of place's scholarly renaissance is critical, for it suggests something much more expansive and vital than merely an updating of traditional regional geography or simply an extension of humanistic geography (Adams, et al. 2003). With its conception of place as an "element complex" – a country-by-country, or continent-by-continent, inventory of natural resources, population, economic sectors, and the like – the chorological method confined regional geography to museum-like status, marginalized from both social sciences and the humanities. In this view, place, as a collection of objective facts that could be analyzed scientifically, contained little room for the people who inhabit places and their subjective experiences. The humanistic tradition, by contrast, emphasized a concept of place dramatically at odds with this positivistic version. Humanistic geographers recoiled from the abstract theorizing of space as an objective entity and emphasized the subjective qualities of place. As Relph (1976: 43) put it: "the essence of places lies in the largely unselfconscious intentionality that defines places as profound centers of human existence."

Recognizing the moral, aesthetic, and affective qualities of place was fundamental to invigorating the concept, but the limitations of humanistic geography also became apparent. In particular, fewer scholars today seek to describe the "essence of place," but instead interpret its multiplicity of meanings; rather than focusing on "human existence," they try to unearth the many ways that place impinges on identities surrounding race, ethnicity, class, gender, and sexuality; and more than focusing on "unselfconscious intentionality," many investigations of place today explore how human creativity is structured by large-scale social, political, and economic processes. Contemporary notions of place, in short, are less focused on community and coherence than on power, politics, and the struggled over nature of place-making. Thinking of places in this way, "implies that they are not so much bounded areas as open and porous networks of social relations," notes Doreen Massey (1994: 121). "It reinforces the idea, moreover, that [place] identities will be multiple ... and this in turn implies that what is to be the dominant image of any place will be a matter of contestation and change over time." Thus, while a tremendous diversity of approaches to place are evident, so too is at least one shared thread: "Common to all these rediscoverers of the importance of place is a conviction that place itself is no fixed thing: it has no steadfast essence" (Casey 1997: 286).

And so, where – without a "steadfast essence" – does place reside? What can be said about place that will give it both conceptual precision and the flexibility to encompass the multiple readings and interpretations that also define it? Two general points stand out.

First, it's helpful to consider something of the genealogy of place and to recall that competing definitions are as old as Classical Antiquity. Even then, Aristotle declared that "the question, what is Place? Presents many difficulties for analysis." His answer to this question, to which he devoted a section of his *Physics*, envisioned place as an empty container, as the precise dimensions of the space that contains something. Plato, by contrast, understood place as one of the great modes of being in the universe, "as it were, the nurse of all becoming," and the receptacle of forms, powers, and feelings (Walter 1988: 120–126; Casey 1997). These competing definitions of place – as a detachable container of location and thus more akin to "space" or as a realm of experience and meaning remain with us and are at the root of concept's utility, and ambiguity.

Among contemporary geographers who have sought to define "place" with greater precision, John Agnew's (1987: 28) multi-prong classification stands out for both its clarity and range. First, he defines *place as locale*, or the setting for social relations, either material or institutional. Locale here bears considerable resemblance to Massey's (2000: 58, 1994) idea of place as "a meeting-place," the nodal point of "intersections of particular bundles of activity spaces, of connections and interrelations, or influences and movements." Second, Agnew defines *place as location* – the longitudinal and latitudinal coordinates of the earth's surface, which can be objectively measured. In many ways, this is the most common usage of the term, as it refers to simple or absolute location. Third, Agnew calls attention to *sense of place*, which he understands to encompass the affective bond that people have to place. To these three components, I would add a fourth: *place as social construction*, whereby such structural conditions as neoliberal capitalism or imperialism take a dominant role in shaping both the material environment and our understanding of it.

Taken cumulatively, each of these four ways of envisioning place – as locale, as location, as sense of place, as social construction – are useful in helping clarify an inherently slippery concept. Thus, when the art critic Lucy Lippard (1997: 7) writes that "place is latitudinal and longitudinal within the map of a person's life," that it "has width as well as depth," and that it is "about connections," she is incorporating each element into her own definition of place. Such a concept does not fit into standard methodological and epistemological categories. As Nicholas Entrikin (1991) argues, place is best viewed with regard to the objective characteristics of location, in terms of subject experiences, and from the vista of multiple vantage points. This quality of "betweenness" defines what matters most about place.

A second general point centers on the relationship of place with its theoretical partner in the geographical lexicon: space. The signal contribution of Yi-Fu Tuan's *Space and Place* (1977) – a book at once foundational to contemporary human geography and yet, as Peter Taylor (1999:10) notes, "generally undervalued" – was to highlight the manifold ways that these two concepts are *intrinsically* interrelated. "The ideas 'space' and 'place' require each other for definition," Tuan (1977: 6) wrote. In an oft-cited passage, he presents his brief with great care:

> Space is more abstract than "place." What begins as undifferentiated space becomes place as we get to know it better and endow it with value... From the security and stability of place we are aware of the openness, freedom, and threat of space, and vice versa. Furthermore, if we think of space as that which allows movement, then place is pause; each pause in movement makes it possible for location to be transformed into place. (Tuan 1977: 6)

In Tuan's view, place refers to the process by which everyday life is inscribed in space and given meaning for specific groups of people and their organizations. Place is thus created from space when people care about it, either positively or negatively – when they invest it with their time, money, fear, anxiety, love, and antagonism. This is what Tuan means when he describes place as a "field of care" and distinguishes it from the more impersonalized arena of space (1977: 164). Although places are typically perceived as local, due primarily to the sense of familiarity that we associate with them, there is no inherent reason to limit our thinking to this scale. "Place exists at different scales," Tuan (1977: 149) writes. "At one extreme a favorite armchair is a place, at the other extreme the whole earth."

This distinction between the abstract realm of space and the affective, experiential world of place remains a powerful conceptual model for human geography. Tuan's model does have its detractors – in particular those who favor the terminology of Lefebvre (1991), in which different kinds of abstract space (absolute space) are distinguished from various forms of lived and meaningful space (social space). But upon close inspection, it's clear that social space bears a very close resemblance to Tuan's definition of place (Cresswell 2004: 10, 12; Sack 1997: 33). Beyond the linguistic clarity of Tuan's model, another advantage follows from its multiple-scale nature and one that is perfectly synchronized with much of critical theory's emphasis on a decentered subject: the same location can be both space or place depending one's perspective. This insight has significant theoretical and practical repercussions, especially when we consider how places are made and unmade.

Making and Destroying Place

Among the implications that follow from the place-space tension, arguably the most important is its dynamism. Places are never static; they are constantly being made and remade. Attentive researchers examine the social forces, individual agency, and political-economic structures that both encourage and constrict the transformation of space into place. David Harvey (1996: 261) describes a similar process of "place formation," which he explains as "a process of carving out 'permanence's' [places] from the flow of processes creating spaces." This is most easily seen in the cultural landscape, when processes like deforestation, urbanization, or highway construction alter the built environment. Certainly, those scholars committed to a descriptive approach to place have taught us a great deal about, say, the "geography of the American South" by examining its unique and particular landscape (Aiken 1998).

But there's more to making places than merely cultivating the cotton or building the plantation homes that comprise the southern landscape. The work of postcolonial theorists such as Said (1978) has been instrumental in considering the means by which the rhetorical constructions and notions of place serve various political agendas. Notably, this occurs at all geographic scales, from naming and telling stories about a small patch of soil by invading colonists in Australia or the dividing of continents into political entities called states (Agnew and Smith 2002). As Paul Carter (2010: xxiv) writes of the Australian case, "by the act of place-naming, space is transformed symbolically into place, that is, space with a history."

Language, in other words, is essential to the place-making dynamic. Speech alone cannot mold nature, but it can "make things formerly overlooked – and hence invisible and nonexistent – visible and real" (Tuan 1991: 685). Thus, the seemingly simple act of naming a street after Martin Luther King, Jr., in a southern city, has the potential of transforming an entire neighborhood with the charged memories of the slain Civil Rights leader and with the flow (of lack thereof) of investment capital (Hoelscher and Alderman 2004). In this context, naming the place – here, a street in locations like Birmingham, Alabama, or Memphis, Tennessee – can trigger a series of emotions and actions that change lives and connect this place to others throughout the region (Dwyer and Alderman 2008). And in the case of the American South, what is especially clear is that control over the making of place – the ability to make place in particular ways – also gives powerful groups the ability to create race (Mitchell 2000: 258). Modern American segregation, or the geographical separation of people as a way of making and fixing absolute racial difference, offers a preeminent example of the interdependence between race and place. What is especially fascinating for historical geographers is the shifting balance of power, and its ongoing struggle, between black and white in their efforts to create race and place.

I hasten to add that other components of communication, such as performance, film, and visual images, do the same work as language in making place (Adams 2009). Creating images of place can play an important role in remaking the places being represented. For instance, segregationists in the post-Civil War South relied on staged performances of whiteness, backed legal codes and an ever-present threat of violence, to create the place known as the Jim Crow South (Hoelscher 2003). But just as senses of place can vary across social groups, and even within an individual, so too can place images be open to multiple readings. Take, for example, Dorothea Lange's famous 1936 photograph titled *Plantation Owner, Mississippi Delta, Near Clarksdale, Mississippi* (Figure 16.2). The photograph, taken by a

Figure 16.2 Plantation Owner. Mississippi Delta, near Clarksdale, Mississippi. Photograph by Dorothea Lange, June 1936. Source: Library of Congress, Prints and Photographs Division, FSA/OWI Collection, LC-USF34-T01-009599-C.

Figure 16.3 Plantation Owner. Mississippi Delta, near Clarksdale, Mississippi. Photograph by Dorothea Lange, June 1936. This shows the same image as cropped by Archibald MacLeish, *Land of the Free* (1938). Source: Library of Congress, Prints and Photographs Division, FSA/OWI Collection, LC-USZ62-103367 (b&w film copy neg. of illus. in E169.M16, P&P Ref).

socially committed photographer who consciously and consistently opposed American racism at every turn, constructs a place, by way of social critique, where the social-economic structure of Jim Crow racism endures. Some 70 years after the end of slavery, this photograph seems to suggest, the relations of power and deference between whites and blacks on the southern plantation persist. And yet, two years later, when the poet Archibald MacLeish reproduced the photograph in his book, *Land of the Free* (1938), he severely cropped it leaving only the white overseer as its subject (Figure 16.3). Here, the state of Mississippi is constructed not as the continuing site of racial oppression, but as the ground producing a sort of salt-of-the-earth pioneer Americanism (Gordon 2009). One photograph, two very different places.

Just as people make places, they can destroy them as well. Here, my argument comes full circle. But, unlike those critics like David Gilbert and William Leach, who bemoan the "weakening of place as a centering presence in the lives of ordinary people," I wish to make a rather different point: namely, that how we view a given location – whether we see it as a place or a space – makes all the difference. E.V.

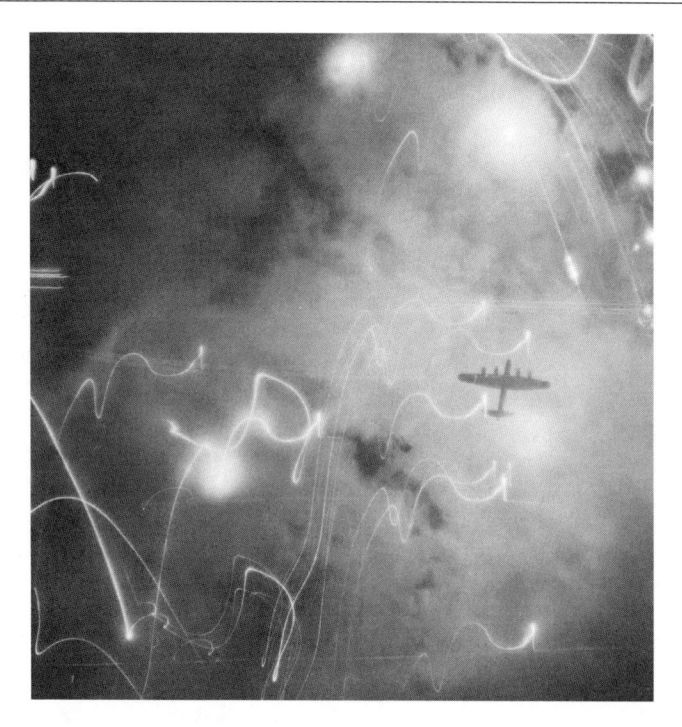

Figure 16.4 British air attack on Hamburg, Germany, January 1943. Source: Imperial War Museum, photo number C3371.

Walter (1988) makes the interesting argument that the Aristotelian view of place as a detachable container – as empty space – provides a philosophical foundation for destructive policies of dislocation and uprooting, such as post-war American "urban renewal." One of its arch proponents, Robert Moses, certainly believed so. On his way to "modernizing" New York with a half dozen major expressways, his "renewal" projects evicted between a quarter- and a half-million people. In response to the devastated neighborhoods left in his wake, Moses commented that "you have to hack your way with a meat ax" when building a modern metropolis (Short 2006: 38).

More extreme is war, "the most thorough-going or consciously prosecuted occasion of collective violence that destroys places" (Hewitt 1983: 258). Indeed, modern war, especially air war that targets civilian cities, *relies* on the conversion of place into space – at least for those initiating its destruction. Cities with people become sites of enemy forces through a process of increasing abstraction. The extraordinary destruction of German cities during the Second World War provides a striking example (Figure 16.4).

Between 1939 and 1945, Allied forces bombed 131 German towns and cities, and killed somewhere between 350,000 and 600,000 civilians (Friedrich 2006; Gregory 2011). In Dresden alone, a place spared the ravages of war until its bitter end in 1945, British and American aircraft armed with 4,500 tones of high explosive and incendiary bombs devastated the entire central city, killing an estimated 25,000 people, most of whom were civilians and refugees (Taylor 2004). Destruction on

Figure 16.5 The war wrecked streets of Cologne, Germany, photograph by Werner Bishof, 1946. Source: Magnum Photos.

such a massive and one-sided scale can only have happened, Derek Gregory (2011) has argued, by "enframing the city as target," by creating "a lethal calculus that abstracted, ensnared, and transformed living cities into dead ones." Strikingly, "these cities had been reduced to rubble – they were already 'dead cities' – *before any bombs were dropped*." One need not enter the ongoing debate about German war guilt, suffering, and the morality of the Allied air war to recognize the transformation of an affective place into a space of target locations and grid coordinates so that the bombers "simply dropped their load into this abstraction" (Gregory 2011). The view of these target locations and grid coordinates from the perspective of place – that it, people on the ground – was rather different (Figure 16.5).

Conclusion

Place has long been a commonsense word to describe the location of various phenomena, but, as this chapter has tried to make clear, in human geography it has been much more than that. Its various meanings – as locale, location, as sense of place, and social construction – endow it with significant range, if also definitional ambiguity. Like its more expansive epistemological referent, space, place is essential to understanding how the world looks, how it functions, and how it feels to an incredibly wide range of social groups and individuals. Some of those groups are human geographers, probably like you who are reading this book; others simply use the word because it makes sense to them. One of the most important functions of "place" is its ability to bridge the scholarly realm of the academic geographer and everyday terrain of ordinary people trying to understand the world and make it better. Without "place," geographers risk losing their most important audience:

those engaged in the struggle to carve something meaningful out of an impersonal, abstract world.

References

Adams, P.C. (2009) *Geographies of Media and Communication: a Critical Introduction*. Wiley-Blackwell, Malden.

Adams, P.C., Hoelscher S.D., and Till K.E. (2001) *Textures of Place: Exploring Humanist Geographies*. University of Minnesota Press, Minneapolis.

Agnew, J.A. (1989) The Devaluation of Place in Social Science. In J. Agnew and J. Duncan (eds), *The Power of Place: Bringing Together the Geographical and Sociological Imaginations*. Unwin Hyman, Boston, pp. 9–28.

Agnew, J.A. (1987) *Place and Politics: The Geographical Mediation of State and Society*. Allen and Unwin, Boston.

Agnew, J.A., Smith J.M. (2002) *American Space/American Place: Geographies of the Contemporary United States*. Routledge, New York.

Aiken, C.S. (1998) *The Cotton Plantation South since the Civil War*. Johns Hopkins University Press, Baltimore.

Augé, M. (1995) *Non-Places: Introduction to an Anthropology of Supermodernity*. Verso, New York.

DeBlij, H. (2009) *The Power of Place*. Oxford University Press, New York.

Buttimer, A., Seamon, D. (eds) (1980) *The Human Experience of Space and Place*. Croom Helm, London.

Carter, P. (2010) *The Road to Botany Bay: An Exploration of Landscape and History*. University of Minnesota Press, Minneapolis.

Casey, E.S. (1997) *The Fate of Place: a Philosophical History*. University of California Press, Berkeley.

Cresswell, T.(1996) *In Place/Out of Place: Geography, Ideology, and Transgression*. University of Minnesota Press, Minneapolis.

Cresswell, T. (2004). *Place: a Short Introduction*. Oxford: Blackwell.

Dwyer, O.J., Alderman, D.H. (2008) *Civil Rights Memorials and the Geography of Memory*. Center for American Places at Columbia College Chicago, Chicago.

Entrikin, J.N. (1991) *The Betweenness of Place: Towards a Geography of Modernity*. Johns Hopkins University Press, Baltimore.

Ethington, P.J. (2007) Placing the Past: Groundwork for a Spatial Theory of History. *Rethinking History* 11 (4), 465–493.

Florida, R.L. (2004) *The Rise of the Creative Class: and How it's Transforming Work, Leisure, Community and Everyday Life*. Basic Books, New York.

Friedland, R. (1992) Space, Place, and Modernity: The Geographical Moment. *Contemporary Sociology* 21 (1), 11–15.

Friedman, T.L. (2005) *The World is Flat: a Brief History of the Twenty-First Century*. Picador, New York.

Friedrich, J. (2006) *The Fire: the Bombing of Germany, 1940–1945*. Columbia University Press, New York.

Gilbert, D. (2009) Times to Remember, Places to Forget. *New York Times*, 31 December, 2009.

Gordon, L. (2009) *Dorothea Lange: a Life Beyond Limits*. W.W. Norton and Co., New York.

Gregory, D. (2011) 'Doors into Nowhere': Dead Cities and the Natural History of Destruction. In M. Heffernan, P. Meusburger, and E. Wunder (eds), *Cultural Memories: The Geographical Point of View*. Springer, Heidelberg.

Harvey, D. (1993) From Space to Place and Back Again: Reflections on the Condition of Postmodernity. In J. Bird, B. Curtis, and T. Putman (eds), *Mapping the Futures: Local Cultures, Global Change*. Routledge, London, pp. 3–29.

Harvey, D. (1996) *Justice, Nature, and the Geography of Difference*. Blackwell Publishers, Cambrige, MA.

Harvey, D. (2001) Militant Particularism and Global Ambition: the Conceptual Politics of Place, Space, and Environment in the Work of Raymond Williams. In *Spaces of Capital: Towards a Critical Geography*. Routledge, New York, pp. 158–187.

Hewitt, K. (1983) Place Annihilation: Area Bombing and the Fate of Urban Places. *Annals of the Association of American Geographers* 73 (2), 257–284.

Hoelscher, S. (2003) Making Place, Making Race: Performances of Whiteness in the Jim Crow South. *Annals of the Association of American Geographers* 93 (3), 657–686.

Hoelscher, S. and Alderman, D. (2004) Memory and Place: Geographies of a Critical Relationship. *Social and Cultural Geography* 5 (3), 347–355.

Kearns, G., Philo C. (eds) (1993) *Selling Places: The City as Cultural Capital, Past and Present*. Pergamon Press, Oxford.

Kunstler, J.H. (1993) *The Geography of Nowhere: the Rise and Decline of America's Man-Made Landscape*. Simon and Schuster, New York.

Leach, W. (1999) *Country of Exiles: The Destruction of Place in American Life*. Pantheon, New York.

Lefebvre, H. (1991) [1974] *The Production of Space*. Blackwell, Cambridge, MA.

Lippard, L.R. (1997) *The Lure of the Local: Senses of Place in a Multicentered Society*. New Press, New York.

Long, J. (2010) *Weird City: Sense of Place and Creative Resistance in Austin, Texas*. University of Texas Press, Austin.

Low, S.M., Lawrence-Zúñiga D. (2003) *The Anthropology of Space and Place: Locating Culture*. Blackwell, Malden, MA.

MacLeish, A. (1938) *Land of the Free*. Harcourt, New York.

Massey, D. (2000) The Conceptualization of Place. In D. Massey and P. Jess (eds), *A Place in the World? Places, Cultures, and Globalization*. Oxford University Press, Oxford, pp. 45–86.

Massey, D. (1994) *Space, Place, and Gender*. University of Minnesota Press, Minneapolis.

Massey, D. (2005) *For Space*. Sage, Thousand Oaks, CA.

Meyrowitz, J. (1985) *No Sense of Place: the Impact of Electronic Media on Social Behavior*. Oxford University Press, New York.

Mitchell, D. (2000) *Cultural Geography: a Critical Introduction*. Blackwell, Malden, MA.

Mumford, L. (1957) [1926] *The Golden Day*. Beacon, Boston.

Relph, E. (1976) *Place and Placelessness*. Pion, London.

Rose, G. (1993) *Feminism and Geography: the Limits to Geographical Knowledge*. University of Minnesota Press, Minneapolis.

Rybczynski, W. (1995) *City Life: Urban Expectations in a New World*. Scribner, New York.

Sack, R.D. (1997) *Homo Geographicus: A Framework for Action, Awareness, and Moral Concern*. Johns Hopkins University Press, Baltimore.

Said, E.W. (1978) *Orientalism*. Pantheon Books, New York.

Schrag, P. (1970) *Out of Place in America: Essays for the End of an Age*. Random House, New York.

Short, J.R. (2006) *Alabaster Cities: Urban U.S. since 1950*. Syracuse University Press, New York.

Soja, E. (1996) *Thirdspace: Journeys to Los Angeles and Other Real-and-Imagined Places*. Blackwell, Oxford.

Solnit R. (2003) *River of Shadows: Eadweard Muybridge and the Technological Wild West*. Viking, New York.
Taylor, F. (2004) *Dresden, Tuesday, February 13, 1945*. HarperCollins, New York.
Taylor, P.J. (1999) Places, Spaces and Macy's: Place-Space Tensions in the Political Geography of Modernities. *Progress in Human Geography* 23 (1), 7–26.
Tocqueville A.D. (2004) [1840] *Democracy in America*. Library of America, New York.
Tuan, Y.-F. (1977) *Space and Place: The Perspective of Experience*. University of Minnesota Press, Minneapolis.
Tuan, Y.-F. (1991) Language and Making of Place: A Narrative Descriptive Approach. *Annals of the Association of American Geographers* 81 (4), 684–696.
Tuan, Y.-F. (1992) Place and Culture: Analeptic for Individuality and the World's Indifference. In W. Franklin and M. Steiner (eds), *Mapping American Culture*. University of Iowa Press, Iowa City, pp. 27–49.
Walter, E.V. (1988) *Placeways: a Theory of the Human Environment*. University of North Carolina Press, Chapel Hill.
Williams, R. (1983) *Keywords*. Oxford University Press, New York.
Williams, R. (1973) *The Country and the City*. Oxford University Press, New York.
Withers, C.W.J. (2009) Place and the "Spatial Turn" in Geography and in History. *Journal of the History of Ideas* 70 (4), 637–658.
Zeisel, J. (2006) A Sense of Place. *New Scientist* 4, 50–51.

Further Reading

The geographic literature on "place" is voluminous, but arguably the ur-text in the field is Yi-Fu Tuan's *Space and Place: The Perspective of Experience* (1977). This book, together with his *Topophilia* (1974) and Edward Relph's *Place and Placelessness* (1976), established place as a key analytical concept in human geography as it considers how values, perceptions, and bodily experiences structure the human relationship to their environments. *Textures of Place: Exploring Humanist Geographies* (2001), edited by Paul Adams, Steven Hoelscher, and Karen Till, extended many of these interests by putting them in dialogue with the insights and political concerns of critical theory. Tim Cresswell's *In Place/Out of Place: Geography, Ideology, and Transgression* (1996) similarly introduced the wider fields of social theory and cultural studies to investigations of place; his recent *Place: a Short Introduction* (2004) succinctly describes these and other scholarly trends. Several books by Doreen Massey – such as *Space, Place, and Gender* (1994), *A Place in the World? Places, Cultures* (2000), edited with Pat Jess, and *For Space* (2005) – set forth an influential understanding of place as multidimensional and unbounded. Similarly, David Harvey – in *Justice, Nature, and the Geography of Difference* (1996) and *Spaces of Capital: Towards a Critical Geography* (2001) to name only two – provides a critical understanding of the relationship of place to global capital.

Finally, students should explore the writing on place by non-geographers, who often have much to say about a concept that so easily jumps disciplinary boundaries. This includes philosophers such as Edward S. Casey and his book *The Fate of Place: a Philosophical History* (1997) and Jeff Malpas, *Heidegger's Topology: Being, Place, World* (2008); social theorists like Henri Lefebvre, *The Production of Space* (1991); art critics such as Lucy Lippard, *Lure of the Local: Senses of Place in a Multicentered Society* (1997); urban planners like Dolores Hayden *The Power of Place: Urban Landscapes as Public History* (1995); and historians such as David Glassberg's *Sense of History: The Place of the Past in American Life* (2001). A useful book that summarizes the work of many of these and other scholars is *Key Thinkers on Space and Place (2010)*, edited by Phil Hubbard, Rob Kitchin, and Gill Valentine.

Chapter 17

Territory
Part I

Stuart Elden

Introduction

William Shakespeare, writing in the late 16th and early 17th centuries, only uses the word "territory" twice in his plays. The word "territories" is more common, appearing in six plays in eleven separate instances.[1] Almost all these are places where "territories" means effectively the same thing as "lands." Richard II banishes the Duke of Hereford (the future Henry IV) from his "territories ... upon pain of life, Till twice five summers have enrich'd our fields."[2] Banishment from territories also occurs in *Henry VI, Part II*; and is threatened in *As You Like It* and *Two Gentlemen of Verona*.[3] In other places people are welcomed into the territories of a kingdom[4] and there is the constant threat of conquest or conflict.[5]

However two instances are worth a little more attention. In *Henry VI, Part II*, Lord Somerset reports on the situation in France: "That all your interest in those territories, Is utterly bereft you; all is lost."[6] While this may appear to be another use of "territories" in a sense of lands, or as a battlefield fought over and surrendered, the relation of interest shows that it is not simply property or a strategic sense, but the political control of and stake in those places. The same phrasing appears in *King Lear*, in the most intriguing reference to "territory" in his plays. Lear is discussing his plans for the inheritance of his kingdom between his three daughters:

> ... Tell me, my daughters,
> (Since now we shall divest us both of Rule,
> Interest of territory, cares of state)
> Which of you shall we say doth love us most?
> That we our largest bounty may extend
> Where nature doth with merit challenge ...[7]

The Wiley Blackwell Companion to Human Geography, First Edition.
Edited by John A. Agnew and James S. Duncan.
© 2011 John Wiley & Sons, Ltd. Published 2016 by John Wiley & Sons, Ltd.

King Lear is a play which quickly moves beyond this division of land, but this is the initial spur for the reactions of Lear's three daughters, including the break with Cordelia. While the elder daughters Goneril and Regan obsequiously profess their love of their father, receiving lands in return; Cordelia refuses to play along, stating that she loves her father "according to my bond; no more nor less."[8] Lear fails to realize that Cordelia has no wish to join her sisters in their cheap flattery, and that she alone probably loves him most. But Lear is not a foolish king in making such a division. Rather, as Harry Jaffa has convincingly argued, Lear is struggling with the question of succession and the unity of the kingdom he has created.[9] Goneril is married to the Duke of Albany, and Regan to the Duke of Cornwall. These were the extremities of the kingdom, Albany being the north including Scotland. Lear has clearly decided what lands these couples should receive, because they are given their gifts immediately after the speeches of the first two daughters, but before Cordelia's.[10] In other words, Lear is not really comparing the speeches in order to distribute the lands, but using this as pretence to buy off the two Dukes. Division into three does not mean each was equal, although Lear continues to suggest that this is open to question. He rewards Regan's speech with "this ample third of our fair kingdom/No less in space, validity, and pleasure,/Than that conferr'd on Goneril," but them immediately indicates to Cordelia that she could gain "A third more opulent than your sisters."[11]

Lear therefore gives Goneril and Albany some lands close to their existing ones; and the same to Regan and Cornwall, reserving the central portion for Cordelia. Cordelia is not yet married, being courted by the Duke of Burgundy and the King of France. Jaffa thus claims that Lear is being very strategic in terms of division: "it was an action predestined by the very means required to bring unity to the kingdom. Lear, it appears, delayed the division as long as possible, but he could not put it off indefinitely, any more than he could put off indefinitely his own demise."[12] The intention, he suggests, is that of "living on as king with Cordelia, with Albany and Cornwall acting as his deputies in regions which he could not control without their loyalty anyway." In sum, he asks, "does it seem that Lear was giving up anything that he could, in any case, have kept to himself much longer?"[13] Yet in not going with his plan, Cordelia receives nothing from Lear, and is spurned by Burgundy. She flees with the King of France, which provides a strategic advantage in the conflict to come.

Much more could of course be said of *King Lear*, one of Shakespeare's most geopolitically interesting plays. But it is significant that the word "territory" is not frequently found in his plays, suggesting a history to the word, the concept and the practice. In addition several things in terms of territory can be gleaned from this single scene. Territory clearly implies a range of political issues: it is controlled, fought over, distributed, divided, gifted, bought and sold. It is economically important, strategically crucial and legally significant. Territory is often straight-forwardly understood to be a bounded space under the control of a group. That understanding, particularly in terms of a state exercising exclusive sovereignty within clearly demarcated boundaries, has not always been held, and is being profoundly challenged today, so an understanding of the political, historical and geographical complexities around the term may be helpful. In this chapter, the emphasis is on how territory emerged as a category within Western political thought. This is a story that cannot be understood other than in relation to questions of land, terrain, sovereignty, space and the state. This means that territory is conceptually very difficult to grasp. While territory can be seen as operating at a range of spatial scales, from the locality marked by gang graffiti, to the attempts to constitute a supranational territory of Schengenland, here I want to try to offer an account of how the term itself took on a modern meaning within Western political thought; a sense which is extended up or down in other analyses.

The English word "territory," as well as related words in most Western European languages, derives from the Latin term *territorium*. While there has been some debate about the meaning of this word, focusing on its derivation from *terra* – land or terrain – or *terrere* – to terrify, to frighten – there has been less discussion about when the word actually meant something close to our contemporary usage.[14] *Territorium* in classical Latin did not mean the land over which a political unit extended its power. Rather, it was a simple extent of land, such as the surrounding agricultural lands belonging to a town or a religious order.[15] Like many of Shakespeare's uses, it was a synonym for land. Isidore of Seville, for instance, writing in the early seventh century in his *Etymologiae*, sets out his understanding of the classical tradition. He puts the notion of a *territorium* half way down his scalar understanding of units of measure. He begins with *Terra*, the earth; and then works down to *terrae*, single parts of land such as Africa and Italy; places [*loca*], which are expanses of land [*terrae spatia*], which themselves contain provinces, parts of which are regions which are colloquially called cantons. Territories are parts of regions.[16] Elsewhere he continues the theme:

> Measure is whatever limit is set in respect to weight, capacity, length, height and mind. And so the ancients divided the planet [*orbem*] into parts, the parts into provinces, the provinces into regions, the regions into places, the places into territories [*loca in territoriis*], the territories into fields, the fields into hectares [*centuriis*], hectares into acres, the acres into *climata* [sixty feet square], the *climata* into hides, perches, yards, grades, cubits, feet, spans, inches, and fingers. For so great was their ingenuity![17]

Territorium here clearly means an expanse of land, and not of especially great extent. It is a piece of land, somewhat larger than a single field, but predominantly agricultural. As he says, "a *territorium* is so called as if it were a *tauritorium*, that is "broken by a plow" [*tritum aratro*] and by a team of oxen (c.f. *taurus*, "bull") – for the ancients used to designate the borders of their possessions and *territoria* by cutting a furrow."[18] While the etymology is, like many of Isidore's, rather fanciful, the point is important: *territorium* did not have its current connotations.

The use of the term through most of the Middle Ages bears this out. Gregory of Tours's *Histories*, usually called *The Histories of the Franks*, regularly uses the term, but usually in the sense simply of surrounding lands,[19] although he sometimes uses the compound term *urbis territurio* to mean a city or town and the neighboring district.[20] The two are in some sense distinct: the town has a *territorium* under its rule, rather than the town itself being a *territorium*. He occasionally pairs *territorium* with *termini*, border or limit, to invoke a bounded area. For instance he says that someone "lived within the borders of the Trier lands [*intra Treverici termini territurio*]";[21] or that action took place "within the borders of the lands of Angers [*infra Andegavensis territorii terminum*]."[22] The border is, here, not the defining characteristic of the *territorium*, but a secondary attribute. It is essential to recognize that in all these uses, the *territorium* is at most the land owned or controlled by a political unit, a political-economic or political-strategic relation. The idea that the *territorium* was the very extent of political power is a much later sense of the term.

Much careful work remains to be done in tracing the history of the term, but the emergence of territory in a recognizably modern sense appears to be due to the combination of two things: the re-adoption of classical Greek terminology concerning the *polis*, especially from Aristotle; and the rediscovery and reworking of Roman law. Aristotle's political works had been almost completely unknown in the Latin West in the Middle Ages, both because of a lack of availability of the texts but also the very limited knowledge of Greek. Initially rediscovered through Arabic translations, by the thirteenth century workable versions of the *Politics*, the *Nicomachean Ethics* and the *Rhetoric* were available to thinkers such as Thomas Aquinas.[23] Greek terms were sometimes simply transliterated – *politeia* and *politicus* – and sometimes rendered as variants of *civis* – *civitas, civis* and *civilis* for *polis, polites*, and *politicos*.[24] The life of the city, citizenship and the civic – terms with a Roman heritage – become fused with the Greek notion of the *polis*. As Aquinas put it in his commentary on Aristotle's *Ethics*, the third part of moral philosophy concerns "the action of the civil community [*multitudinis civilis*] and is called political [*politica*].[25] Aquinas renders Aristotle's *zoon politikon* as *animal civile*, but also as *animale sociale* and *animale politicum*, used in the *Summa Theologiae* and other works.[26] The living being whose nature is to be in the *polis* becomes the civil animal, the social animal, and the political animal.

The sophisticated Greek terminology for understanding political rule was of great value to secular rulers in their assertion of independence from papal authority. At this time a range of theorists were trying to articulate the scope of kingly power, or to clarify what powers the Emperor had in relation to the Pope. Of papal origin, the articulation of eternal spiritual and temporal secular power as the "two swords" became the dominant terms of debate. Eternal or spiritual power was over souls and their salvation; temporal or secular power was over human's actions on this earth. The "two swords" model derives from a reading of Luke's gospel, when Jesus is readying the disciples for the conflicts and persecution to come, and he tells them to sell their goods to buy swords.[27] They tell him "Lord, behold, here *are* two swords," to which Jesus replies "it is enough."[28] It was significant, according to the papacy, that Jesus said "it is enough" rather than "it is too many" or "too few." They drew further lessons from the encounter between the disciples and the high priest and his entourage. One of the disciples cuts off the ear of a servant. Jesus tells him to "put up again thy sword into his place: for all they that take the sword shall perish with the sword."[29] Both swords – that is spiritual power and temporal power – belong to the church, but while the former is to be both possessed and used, the second is to command, rather than directly use. The church should therefore empower the secular arm to do its bidding, such as it did most directly with its crowning of the Holy Roman Emperor, or the use of Kings to pursue the crusades.

Yet the political situation in Europe was considerably more complicated in practice. There were kingdoms outside of the Empire, notably England and France, and so the Emperor's temporal power could not claim to be universal, even if the Pope did claim a monopoly of spiritual power. Indeed it was Pope Innocent III in 1202 who declared that the French king "recognized no superior in temporal matters."[30] This put a clear limit on the power of the Emperor: his power did not extend beyond the bounds of the Empire. It was then a short step for the King's jurists to phrase his power as functionally equivalent to the Emperor: within his kingdom, the King had the same powers as the Emperor in his Empire.[31] These two formulations were of different lineage, but taken together they asserted supremacy of temporal power within the bounds of the kingdom, where the spatial extent is not merely the possession of the ruler, but the very limit of their power. The struggles that continued between the French King Philip the Fair and Pope Boniface VIII hinged on these issues. On behalf of the King, the most eloquent exponent was John of Paris, who argued that while it was possible to have a universal Church with supreme authority; it was impossible to conceive of universal or world government. Temporal power requires the use of the sword, and since this cannot be done over large distances, there are limits to temporal power.[32] Giles of Rome, working on behalf of the Pope, argued that even if there were different temporal powers, all were subordinate to the spiritual power of the Pope, and "kingdoms under the Vicar of Christ."[33]

Various writers then tried to articulate the scope and powers of various secular polities. Dante used this as an opportunity to argue for the importance of a revived Empire, or *Monarchia*; Marsilius of Padua to stress the importance of the independence of cities within the Italian peninsula; and William of Ockham claimed that the church should, like the disciples, be poor, by which he meant not simply lacking in wealth but also unengaged in worldly matters.[34] All of these writers, albeit in very different ways, wanted to remove the power of the papacy from political concerns, but crucially recognized that scope of political power was limited, not simply in terms of what it could do, but in where it operated. Yet none of them had the conceptual terminology to articulate this clearly. The papacy had made the distinction between the two powers, looking to reserve both for itself, but opening up the way in which temporal power could be taken as separate. And the Emperor and Kings who argued against papal involvement in their own affairs also made possible later arguments for non-involvement in the affairs of smaller political units. Yet while the Greek political vocabulary took such theorists so far, and recognizably modern arguments are being made, there was, as yet, only an inchoate sense of what that political power was actually over.

It is only with the rediscovery of Roman law in the Italian city-states in the later Middle Ages that this question began to be properly answered. It was in the works of the post-glossators or commentators, working with the text of Justinian's *Corpus Iuris Civilis* that the notion of *territorium* became explicitly tied to that of jurisdiction. Justinian was a Byzantine Emperor in the sixth century who had codified the Roman law up to his time. *Corpus Iuris Civilis* means the body of civil law, and comprised imperial pronouncements of the law, a large selection of commentaries on them, a primer for students, and the new pronouncements of Justinian's own time.[35] This text was not widely known in the Latin west for several centuries, but a complete manuscript was discovered in Pisa in 1077. While it provided an almost ready made legal system, many of its claims were unclear, being five hundred years since Justinian's codification and several more since some of the parts had been written. The work of the first generations of scholars was that of philology and hermeneutics – reconstructing the text and providing explanations and interpretations. They wrote notes or glosses in and around the text, and were known as the glossators. Not everyone appreciated their labors, with the novelist Rabelais seeing them tarnishing the law books, which he described as a "fine cloth-of-gold robe, marvelously grand and costly but trimmed with dung."[36]

Nonetheless, the lawyers following them were able to build on their labors, interpreting and reworking them in the context of their time. But while the Roman law had originally been written to apply to an empire and its constituent parts, these laws were now being read in the context of popes, emperors, kings and independent cities. The question was whether these kingdoms were *imperium*, or whether they were closer to the Aristotelian *civitas* or *regnum*, the terms used in the medieval translations. France could clearly not be understood simply as a *provincia*, nor could a free city simply be thought of as a *municipium*.[37] An answer to this question came from the post-glossator Bartolus of Sassoferrato, who argued that the independent polity had two origins: an Aristotelian *polis* and an Empire on a reduced scale.[38] This fusion of Greek political thought and Roman law is crucial, since it brought together two strands of ancient thought in a modern context. As Bartolus suggests:

> *Dominium* is something that inheres in the person of the owner [*domini*], but it applies to the thing owned. Similarly jurisdiction inheres in an office [*officio*] and in the person who holds the office, but it applies to a *territorium*, and is thus not a quality of the *territorium*, but rather of the person.[39]

Bartolus's use of *territorium* here is significant. He is taking the notion of land, or land belonging to an entity, as the thing to which jurisdiction applies, thus providing the extent of rule. The *territorium* then is not simply a property of a ruler; nor is jurisdiction simply a quality of the *territorium*. Rather the *territorium* is the object of rule itself. This runs through Bartolus's work, where he contends that the actions of an individual merchant or trader were bound by the laws of the place he was, rather than by the city to which he belonged. This was a crucial shift from the personality of law to the territoriality of law.[40] Bartolus also coined the phrase "*civitas sibi princeps*" to explain the status of the cities: the cities were a prince, a leader, unto themselves, rather than having to show deference to some higher power. Like the idea of the king being supreme within his kingdom, just as the emperor was within the empire, the idea of a sovereign city shows that the law, jurisdiction, is territorially defined.

This is still some way from separate independent states with discrete territories and clearly defined boundaries, which was something that emerged slowly, unevenly and unequally over the next several centuries. But it does mean that attempts to date the emergence of the modern state, its territorial control or the international system of states to the middle of the seventeenth century are misleading.[41] The religious wars of that time, culminating in the settlement of the Peace of Westphalia in 1648, are continuations of the debates concerning the relation between the papacy, the Emperor and the constituent parts of the empire and external polities.

The Westphalia treaties give the *jus territoralis* to the polities, a territorial right, but this was an application rather than the beginning of the principle. The equivalent German term was *Landeshoheit*, supremacy over the land.[42]

The danger with the notion of territory is that a rather particular, historically and geographically limited, sense of the term is taken to be the definition as a whole. The idea of a bounded space under the control of a group, perhaps a state, is one that has several discrete elements which need to be interrogated. Equally the idea that a ruler had a monopoly of power – legitimate physical violence, in Weber's phrase – within a territory long predates the idea that those boundaries were in any way fixed.[43] Rulers believed that conquest, purchase, marriage or concession could increase the size of the lands under their control. Territorial redistributions at the end of conflicts were common until the twentieth century. And of course colonialism was predicated on the idea that certain lands were open to conquest by European powers.[44] As John Agnew has convincingly argued, much work on international relations and geopolitics remains tied to an unproblematic assumed sense of territory, what he calls "the territorial trap."[45] What we do when we fall into this trap is to buy-into a state-centered narrative that naturalizes and normalizes this way of thinking.[46] A historical investigation is one way to begin to go beyond those assumptions.

Territory needs to be interrogated in a range of ways. While it cannot be reduced to land, there are a range of political-economic elements to the way in which territory is conceived, fought over, and distributed. The historical emergence of the concept is of course related to the practices of feudalism and the emergence of capitalism. Globalization has reconfigured sovereignty-territory relations in ways that are still poorly understood, with a certain strand of the literature contending that the remaking of spatial relations has meant the end of the importance of territory.[47] Similarly, territory can be interrogated through its relation to political-strategic concerns. Conflict over land is peculiar in that it is both the stake and site of struggle: what might be called the question of terrain. Yet, just as with land, territory cannot be seen simply as terrain. Alongside the importance of developments in the law and categories such as authority, supremacy and sovereignty, and most especially what these forms of power are exercised *over*, territory is dependent on the availability and advance of a range of techniques. Cartography and land-surveying, among developments in statistics, accounting and the military, make possible the knowledge and control of much larger expanses from a central point. It is not coincidental that states put a large amount of resource into the use of such practices, but also, more crucially, their development in the period of the fifteenth to seventeenth centuries.[48] Territory then should not be understood as a static product or object, but rather as part of a rationality, dependent on calculation as much as control and conflict, what Michel Foucault called a "political technology."

To assert the importance of the question of territory is not to privilege it above other spatial questions. Rather it is to recognize that alongside other terms such as place, scale, network and region, territory is part of the conceptual vocabulary of geography, especially political geography.[49] As the German philosopher Peter Sloterdijk puts it, "the political is the product of collective madness and territory."[50] Yet territory is only one form of state space, and only a historically and geographically limited element within the wider domain of political space. But it remains a crucially important one. It is precisely because territory is a partial, historically specific, and non-exclusive way of spatial ordering that it needs to be interrogated more thoroughly. Yet while it has received some excellent analysis in terms of specific territorial conflicts, arrangements and settlements, there has been much less interrogation of the term conceptually or historically.[51] Such work would enable geographers to much better account for the profound changes taking place in the post-Cold War period concerning the relation between territory and sovereignty; and the challenges globalization and climate change make to any unproblematic thinking that relies on a fixed notion of territory as exclusive control within hard, impermeable borders.[52]

Notes

1   Alexander Schmidt, *Shakespeare-Lexicon: A Complete Dictionary of all the English Words, Phrases and Constructions in the Works of the Poet*, Third Edition revised by Gregor Sarrazin, Berlin: Georg Reimer, Two Volumes, 1902, Vol II, p. 1193.
2   *Richard II*, Act I, scene iii.
3   *Henry VI, Part II*, Act III, scene ii; *As You Like It*, Act III, scene I; and *Two Gentlemen of Verona*, Act III, scene i.
4   *Henry VI, Part I*, Act V, scene iv.
5   *King John*, Act I, scene I; Act V, scene ii; *Coriolanus*, Act IV, scene v; Act IV, scene vi; Act IV, vi; *Henry VI, Part I*, Act V, scene v.
6   *Henry VI, Part II*, Act III, scene i.
7   *King Lear*, Act I, scene i. I have used the Arden Edition, edited by Kenneth Muir, London: Routledge, 1972. The line in parentheses was introduced only for the Folio edition; they do not appear in the Quarto. See Mark Jay Mirsky, *The Absent Shakespeare*, Fairleigh Dickinson Univ Press, 1994, p. 33. The story also appears in Geoffrey of Monmouth, *The History of the Kings of Britain*, translated by Lewis Thorpe, Harmondsworth: Penguin, 1966, II, 11, but there the King simply says his intent is to divide the kingdom. On the links and differences between the two texts, see Mark Allen McDonald, *Shakespeare's* King Lear *with* The Tempest: *The Discovery of Nature and the Recovery of Classical Natural Right*, Lanham: University Press of America, 2004, p. 221.
8   *King Lear*, Act I, scene i.
9   Harry V. Jaffa, "The Limits of Politics: *King Lear*, Act I, Scene I," in Allan Bloom with Harry V. Jaffa, *Shakespeare's Politics*, New York: Basic Books, 1964, pp. 113–45, p. 113.
10 Jaffa, "The Limits of Politics," p. 127.
11 *King Lear*, Act I, scene i.
12 Jaffa, "The Limits of Politics," p. 122.
13 Jaffa, "The Limits of Politics," pp. 123–124.
14 For the relation to *terrere*, see William E. Connolly, *The Ethos of Pluralization*, Minneapolis: University of Minnesota Press, 1995; Mark Neocleous, "Off the Map: On Violence and Cartography," *European Journal of Social Theory*, Vol 6, 2003, pp. 409–25; and Barry Hindess, "Terrortory," *Alternatives*, Vol 31, 2006, pp. 243–257. For a longer discussion which draws on the etymological arguments, see Stuart Elden, *Terror*

and Territory: The Spatial Extent of Sovereignty, Minneapolis: University of Minnesota Press, 2009, pp. xxviii–xxx.
15 See, for example, Cicero, *Orationes*, with a commentary by G. Long, London: Whittaker and Co., Four Volumes, 1858, Vol IV, p. 522; *Bede's Ecclesiastical History of the English People*, edited by Bertram Colgrave and R.A.B. Mynors, Latin-English edition, Oxford: Clarendon Press, 1969, chapter V, 24.
16 Isidore of Seville, *Etymologiae*, edited by W.M. Lindsay, Oxford University Press, Oxford, 1911; *The Etymologies of Isidore of Seville*, translated by Steven A. Barney, W.J. Lewis, J.A. Beach and Oliver Berghof, Cambridge: Cambridge University Press, 2006, chapter XIV, v, 20–21.
17 Isidore of Seville, *Etymologiae*, chapter XV, xv, 1. My account here is indebted to John Henderson, *The Medieval World of Isidore of Seville: Truth from Words*, Cambridge: Cambridge University Press, 2007, pp. 178–180.
18 Isidore of Seville, *Etymologiae*, chapter XVI, v, 22.
19 For example Gregory of Tours, *Historia Francorum*, *Libri Historiarum X*, http://www.thelatinlibrary.com/gregorytours.html; translated by Lewis Thorpe as *The History of the Franks*, Penguin: Harmondsworth, 1974, chapter III, 35; IV, 42; IV, 44.
20 Gregory of Tours, *Historia Francorum*, chapter VIII, 45; see II, 35; X, 3.
21 Gregory of Tours, *Historia Francorum*, chapter III, 15.
22 Gregory of Tours, *Historia Francorum*, chapter IX, 18; see also VIII, 43; IX, 19.
23 See, among other works, Bernard G. Dod, "Aristoteles Latinus," in Norman Kretzmann, Anthony Kenny and Jan Pinborg (eds.), *The Cambridge History of Later Medieval Philosophy*, Cambridge: Cambridge University Press, 1982, pp. 45–79.
24 Joseph Canning, *The Political Thought of Baldus de Ubaldis*, Cambridge: Cambridge University Press, 1987, p. 161. For a very helpful discussion see Nicolai Rubenstein, "The History of the Word *Politicus* in Early-Modern Europe," in Antony Pagden (ed.), *The Languages of Political Theory in Early Modern Europe*, Cambridge: Cambridge University Press, 1987, pp. 41–56, especially pp. 41–48.
25 Thomas Aquinas, *In Decem Libros Ethicorum Aristotelis ad Nicomachum Expositio*, edited by Raymundi M. Spiazzi, Turin: Marietti, 1949, Chapter I, 1.
26 See, for example, Thomas Aquinas, *Summa Theologiæ*, Latin-English Edition, London: Blackfriars and Eyre & Spottiswoode, Sixty Volumes, 1963–76, Ia 96.4; *In Decem Libros Ethicorum Aristotelis*, Chapter I, 1. See also the brief comment by Hannah Arendt, *The Human Condition*, Chicago: University of Chicago Press, 1958, p. 23.
27 Luke 22: 36.
28 Luke 22: 38.
29 Matthew 26: 52; see Mark 14: 47.
30 Innocent III, "Per Venerabilem," in Brian Tierney, *The Crisis of Church and State 1050–1300*, Toronto: University of Toronto Press, 1988, pp. 136–138.
31 See, for instance the anonymous texts in R.W. Dyson (ed.), *Quaestio de Potestate Papae (Rex Pacificus)/An Enquiry into the Power of the Pope: A Critical Edition and Translation*, Lewiston: Edwin Mellon, 1999; and "A Dispute between a Priest and a Knight," Latin and English text, edited and translated by Norma N. Erickson, *Proceedings of the American Philosophical Society*, Vol 111 No 5, 1967, pp. 288–309.
32 John of Paris, *On Royal and Papal Power*, translated by Arthur P. Monaghan, New York: Columbia University Press, 1974, Chapter 3.
33 *Giles of Rome's On Ecclesiastical Power: A Medieval Theory of World Government*, Latin-English edition, edited and translated by R.W. Dyson, New York: Columbia University Press, 2004, Chapter I, iv.
34 See Dante Aligheri, *Monarchia*, translated and edited by Prue Shaw, Cambridge: Cambridge University Press, 1995; Marsilius of Padua, *The Defender of the Peace*,

translated by Annabel Brett, Cambridge: Cambridge University Press, 2005; *Writings on the Empire: Defensor Minor and De translatione Imperii*, edited by Cary J. Nederman, Cambridge: Cambridge University Press, 1993; and for a sampling of Ockham's voluminous political writings, *A Short Discourse on the Tyrannical Government*, edited by Arthur Stephen McGrade, translated by John Kilcullen, Cambridge: Cambridge University Press, 1992; *A Letter to the Friars Minor and Other Writings*, edited by Arthur Stephen McGrade and John Kilcullen, translated by John Kilcullen, Cambridge: Cambridge University Press, 1995.

35 The most important part is the second: *The Digest of Justinian*, edited by Theodor Mommsen with Paul Krueger, translation edited by Alan Watson, Latin-English Edition, Philadelphia: University of Pennsylvania Press, Four Volumes, 1985.

36 François Rabelais, *The Histories of Gargantua and Pantagruel*, translated by J.M. Cohen, Harmondsworth: Penguin, 1955, p. 183 (Book 2, Chapter 5).

37 Cecil N. Sidney Woolf, *Bartolus of Sassoferrato: His Position in the History of Medieval Thought*, Cambridge: Cambridge University Press, 1913, p. 113.

38 Woolf, *Bartolus of Sassoferrato*, p. 267. On Bartolus, see also Francesco Maiolo, *Medieval Sovereignty: Marsilius of Padua and Bartolus of Saxoferrato*, Delft: Eburon, 2007.

39 Bartolus, commentary on *Digest* II.1.1, in *Opera quae nunc extant omnia*, Basileae: Ex Officina Episcopiana, 11 Volumes, 1588–89, Vol I, p. 160.

40 "Territoriality" here, of course, means a condition of territory, rather than the more active connotation that has increasingly replaced that older meaning. The best book on territoriality is Robert D. Sack, *Human Territoriality: Its Theory and History*, Cambridge: Cambridge University Press, 1986.

41 For a recent assertion of this commonplace of IR, see Daniel Philpott, *Revolutions in Sovereignty: How Ideas Shaped Modern International Relations*, Princeton: Princeton University Press, 2001. A comprehensive analysis and debunking can be found in Benno Teschke, *The Myth of 1648: Class, Geopolitics and the Making of Modern International Relations*, London: Verso, 2003.

42 See Andreas Osiander, "Sovereignty, international relations, and the Westphalian myth," *International Organization*, Vol 55, 2001, pp. 251–287.

43 Max Weber's famous definition can be found in "The Profession and Vocation of Politics," in *Political Writings*, edited by Peter Lassman and Ronald Speirs, Cambridge: Cambridge University Press, 1994, pp. 309–69, p. 311. For helpful discussions, see Michael Mann, "The Autonomous Power of the State: Its Origins, Mechanisms and Results," *Archives Européennes de Sociologie*, Tome XXV No 2, 1985, pp. 185–213; and Arjun Appadurai, "The Grounds of the Nation State: Identity, Violence and Territory," in Kjell Goldmann, Ulf Hannerz and Chaler Westin (eds.), *Nationalism and Internationalism in the Post-Cold War Era*, London: Routledge, 2000, pp. 129–142.

44 Among many references, particularly good on the territorial aspect is Bertrand Badie, *The Imported State: The Westernization of the Political Order*, translated by Claudia Royal, Stanford: Stanford University Press, 2000.

45 John Agnew, "The Territorial Trap: The Geographical Assumptions of International Relations Theory," *Review of International Political Economy*, Vol 1, 1994, pp. 53–80.

46 This is an argument that Neil Brenner and I have made at length in "Henri Lefebvre on State, Space and Territory," *International Political Sociology*, Vol 3 No 4, 2009, pp. 353–377. A very valuable analysis of how the modern state system emerged, and how it almost did not, is provided by Hendrik Spruyt, *The Sovereign State and Its Competitors: An Analysis of Systems Change*, Princeton: Princeton University Press, 1995.

47 For a discussion and critique, see Stuart Elden, "Missing the Point: Globalisation, Deterritorialisation and the Space of the World," *Transactions of the Institute of British Geographers*, Vol 30, 2005, pp. 8–19.
48 This argument is made in more detail in Stuart Elden, "Governmentality, Calculation, Territory," *Environment and Planning D: Society and Space* Vol 25 No 5, 2007, pp. 562–80; and "Land, Terrain, Territory," *Progress in Human Geography*, Vol 34 No 1, 2010, pp. 799–817.
49 See Bob Jessop, Neil Brenner and Martin Jones, "Theorizing Sociospatial Relations," *Environment and Planning D: Society and Space*, Vol 26 No 3, 2008, pp. 389–401; Joe Painter, "Rethinking Territory," *Antipode: A Radical Journal of Geography*. Vol 42, 2010, pp. 1090–1118.
50 Peter Sloterdijk, *Sphären I Blasen: Mikrosphärologie*, Frankfurt am Main: Suhrkamp, 1998, p. 84.
51 The best work on territory, to my mind, remains Jean Gottmann, *The Significance of Territory*, Charlottesville: University Press of Virginia, 1973. There are two recent helpful textbooks: David Storey, *Territory: The Claiming of Space*, Harlow: Prentice Hall, 2001; David Delaney, *Territory: A Short Introduction*, Oxford: Blackwell, 2005. I have also learned a great deal from two unfortunately untranslated books: Paul Alliès, *L'invention du territoire*, Grenoble: Presses Universitaires de Grenoble, 1980; and Claude Raffestin, *Pour une géographie du pouvoir*, Paris: Libraires Techniques, 1980. Of recent works see particularly Linda M. Bishai, *Forgetting Ourselves: Secession and the (Im)possibility of Territorial Identity*, Lanham: Lexington Books, 2004; Rhys Jones, *Peoples/States/Territories: The Political Geographies of British State Transformation*, Oxford, Blackwell, 2007.
52 See, for example, Elden, *Terror and Territory*; Thom Kuehls, *Beyond Sovereign Territory: The Space of Ecopolitics*, Minneapolis: University of Minnesota Press, 1996; John Agnew, *Globalization and Sovereignty*, Lanham: Rowman and Littlefield, 2009.

Chapter 18

Territory
Part II

Jacques Lévy

Introduction

In Molière's famous 17th century play, *Le Bourgeois Gentilhomme*,[1] the central character, Mr. Jourdain, discovers with delight that he has been producing for years, by his simple speech and without even being aware of it, quantities of pieces of a literary style which he had foreseen up to then as unattainable: prose. Like Mr. Jourdain, geographers have been "producing" something, in this case conceptions of territory, without being aware of it. To become aware of such a fact has implied on their part, and more generally on that of the community of social researchers at large, making two efforts – firstly, identifying the various categories of space that constitute their object of study and, secondly, establishing the best way to classify them including where "territory" fits in.

When taking a look at the genealogy of concepts, it appears that the linguistic fields within which the concepts emerge play an important role in determining meaning. It turns out that the equivalent of the English word "*territory*" is currently found in the common glossary of Romance languages, in particular that of French (*territoire*), Italian (*territorio*), Spanish (*territorio*) and Portuguese (*território*). It is often employed as a less formal equivalent of the word *space*, when designating an inhabited spatial unit, the words *espace*, *spazio*, *espacio* or *espácio* preserving, as does sometimes *space*, the evocation of a void, of room. It is particularly the case in French, for which the equivalent of the English word *area* (*aire*) – whose similar forms come by as common words in several languages – appears less adequate and pertains to a more formal register. On the contrary, the German word *Territorium* is rarely used and very technical while the term designating space in general (*Raum*) is commonplace. The latter term was most frequently used in the German geopolitics theorized first by Friedrich Ratzel and later pursued by Karl Haushofer. The notion of *Lebensraum*, at first sight an ordinary "living space," becomes within their works

The Wiley Blackwell Companion to Human Geography, First Edition.
Edited by John A. Agnew and James S. Duncan.
© 2011 John Wiley & Sons, Ltd. Published 2016 by John Wiley & Sons, Ltd.

a concept of both naturalistic and confrontational inspiration (the "living space" of the *Volk*).

In English, the opposition between the general idea of spatial organization – which the word *space* underlies – and the concrete realities of partitioned spaces leads to the creation of words such as *area*, *region* or *place*. In English, *territory* is often restricted to the space occupied by a state or other political entity such as an empire. In German, besides *Ort* (place, in the sense of *location*), *Gebiet* or *Region*, one can encounter the words *Landschaft* (in its primary meaning of "landscape"), which for a long time was in fact rather close to the English word *region*. In light of this, it appears that within European languages, the word *territory* covers a very wide range of usage in French and becomes very specific in German and English. Within French-speaking geography in the nineteen eighties and nineties (Le Berre, 1982), this word has also been used as an effective notion in order to deal with the matter of spatial identity, through a process totally similar to the use of the word *place* within the English-speaking world.

These specificities must be kept in mind in order to understand the recent history of the concept of *territory* in human geography. The latter is in fact a double history: either it involves the analysis of a particular type of space which one wants to emphasize (as in the territory of a state), and in which case it is a transnational history, or it involves a more general reflection on the relations human beings have with space, on their *geographicity*, so to speak, and in which case it is above all a French history, that has then been "translated" in various ways into other linguistic domains but primarily by implicit adoption from French-language authors.

Since the 1980s, then, usages and meanings have multiplied, confusing communication and exchange between researchers. We can disentangle the polysemy of the word *territory* into nine distinct significations. I shall outline the first eight in a critical light in order to finally suggest a ninth approach as more satisfactory overall.

Eight Significations

1. No particular special signification due to nor limited use of the word

Such a choice has been prevalent during the modernist phase of geography's renewal since the 1960s. Compared to territory, "space" has been seen as having a more mathematical and analytical tone, and thus was supposedly more scientific, even if "territory" could have been, to the contrary, a manner of embodying in one word the prior eagerness for regional exceptionalism, the difficult comparison and evaluation of different geographical situations. Such a tendency remains that of those who preferentially use the word "space" and who from time to time dispose of the word "territory" as a synonym for space with no particular signification of its own (Haggett 1965).

2. A synonym for "space"

What we have here consists in the opposite choice taken at the time: some researchers, especially the French-speaking ones, distrusted the abstract connotations borne by the word "space" and its disconnection from History. Consequently, they often preferred "territory," which they considered conveyed a sense of realities that were not solely geographic, and used "space," from time to time, as a substitute.

3. A synonym for the term "local space" or for, more generally, any space of an intermediate scale, situated between that of a district and that of a region

This signification or meaning is fairly recent and most frequently used in the Romance languages, would it be in geography, but more especially in economics and in political science. Among these academic disciplines, the word "territory" comes spontaneously to mind to designate the specificity of various spatial objects – such as cities or regions – that fit within a wider whole, whether the latter are national, continental or worldwide. Architects also gladly use this term to contrast with the more local scale at which they feel the most qualified to intervene, whether it be that of the building or that of micro-local "urban design." In a traditionally centralized state such as France, the denomination "territorial authority" (*collectivité territoriale*) is used when designating any political authority of an infra-national level – which the current decentralization process under way in France tends to promote. The word "territory" then replaces the word "local," bearing the advantage of considering relationships of various geographical dimensions including linkages beyond the local – an advantage that is less successfully carried out in a dialogue with non-specialists when using the word *place*. To the contrary of the word "space," which has a strong technocratic connotation, "territory" may so characterize a space whose historic foundations and identity together create a specificity which can be mobilized as a resource for local economic development. In the United States, however, the word "community" is often used in this context, within a specialized (and "spatialized!") approach, when considering this category of objects.

4. A synonym for the term "inhabited space"

One tries here to distinguish between a concept as used within the social sciences from a concept as a philosophical category. In this regard, the concept of *territory* corresponds simultaneously to a socialized or socially constructed space, to the *geographical* space, as well as to the intellectual construction that enables us to reflect upon a geographical space as an object. The purpose here is both to assert the social character of the object and to avoid confusing an external reality with the concept of a study attempting to build a comprehensive knowledge out of it (Ferrier 2003). The term and what it putatively referred to becomes the primary focus: an abstract theorizing about the nature of "inhabited space."

5. A limited and controlled space

Such a definition takes us back to the oldest and most commonly used meaning of the term: that of a space that fits into the logic of the state, the latter marrying an internal political space on the one hand with strict external borders on the other.

This signification is most commonly used in political science and international relations. Robert D. Sack (1986) magnified the idea by transforming it into the concept of territoriality as a political strategy available to many organizations. To him, territory is characterized by the achieved topology of its limits, to know its borders, so to speak, and by the degree of self-sufficiency delineating the control assumed by whoever masters the given territory (Badie 1995; Delaney 2005).

6. A metaphor from animal studies applied to human organization of space

Following on from research carried out in ethological or animal-behavior studies, a concept of territory that was originally borrowed from usage in the social world and that had then entered the field of biology was in turn given a new signification in the field of the human sciences. In this construction, territory becomes a space of exclusive control, a space typically acquired using non-violent means to contribute to the survival of a given animal or species. It is in fact an understanding very close to the previous one, but, when applied to the social world, it is often presented as the manifestation of a general law of the living world, of which human beings would offer only a specific manifestation. Concerning this matter, let us observe that – as Jared Diamond (1997) reminds us – mammals can be classified into two categories when considering the logic relating to their physical security: they are either "gregarious," protected by the density of the membership group, or they are "territorial," secured by the control of a space assuming precise limits. The latter "method" is utilized above all by, for example, felines and not at all by the primates, the biological group to which humans belong. There is thus no biological continuum leading to a universal "territoriality" so defined.

7. An "appropriated" space

Basing themselves on the previous signification, which is fairly specific, a number of French geographers believed it was legitimate to generalize the term using the idea of "appropriation." Following such an approach, "territory" would designate a space beholden, in one way or another, to an attribution of either *ownership* or *identification* – two notions which are in fact quite different from one another, but that the French signification of the word "appropriation" can lead to mixing up. In the core of this approach, territory is understood as the element of identity, or say representation, of a space. Such a tendency, typically "Latin," is equivalent of the use of the word "place" among certain trends in English-speaking geography, of either a culturalist or phenomenological inspiration (e.g. Tuan 1974). Finally, this approach has been much influenced by the use Gilles Deleuze and Félix Guattari (1987 [1980]) have made of the word "deterritorialization" – a term both literal and metaphorical. Following their lead, the dialectic between "deterritorialization" and "reterritorialization" movements has been explored: what is then at stake is the analysis of place dynamics, the latter losing their former singular attributes – which supposed a macrocosm of separate and isolated spatial units – and finding, in an interlinked and interdependent World [monde], a new singularity (Haesbaert da Costa 2003; Debarbieux 2003).

8. A moment in the history of ideas

A convenient classification consists in isolating three "moments" within the history of modern geography: that of *environment*, embedded in Lamarck's naturalism coming to fruition in the early twentieth century; that of *space*, ending the influence of Vidal's regional "exceptionalism" (and related traditions outside of France), referring to a mainly geometric Cartesian spatialism of 1960s-era spatial analysis; and finally that of *"territory"* (in French) or of *"place"* (in English), where the geographical effects of individual and societal identities enter into prime consideration. Contrary to the previous signification, "territory" is no longer simply a subcategory within that of "space," but an intellectual alternative to it, corresponding to different school of thought and to another interpretative approach within geography.

A Necessary Critique

These eight significations all have their specific utilities. They sometimes fit the general conceptions of geography's supposed purpose. Such would be the case with number 4. They sometimes fit specific problems and theories. Such would be the case with numbers 5 and 6. Each of them possesses a certain form of coherence. They all, however, have their flaws. The first four are similar in their entrapment of the term, whether the latter occurs by completely rejecting its use, by making it swap significations with another term, or by granting it an excessively general signification. It is also the case with the seventh signification, which *seems* specific but which, once confronted with practical situations, reveals itself as in fact defining any social space: what social object is not, in a way – if only through the association between a place and a name (toponym) – "appropriated?" It is tautological to say that you have explained anything simply by stating that humans and their societies use space and thereby defines territories and that these can be made and unmade. The conceptual dimension of territory is undoubtedly present everywhere in space: concrete things do have meanings and words have their importance in how we navigate around, all of which happens in a manner that many of us can admit is both interlinked with material reality and often deprived of any hierarchical political basis. Unless one believes in a very "materialistic" materialism and considers all representations as simple "superstructures," then the seventh signification, in various manifestations, reveals itself an interesting way of thinking in the sense that it widens the range of reflections, but questionable in practice because of its lack of any real empirical scope. Excessively precise definitions indeed bear the inconvenience of confining the term "territory" to a narrow meaning. But the alternative need not be to trivialize it by covering such a wide spectrum of meanings that thereby make it comparable to the range already included in much usage of the word *space*.

Much the same impetus to define subjective spaces and spatial identities as territories in French has lain behind English-speaking geography's adoption of the word place ("lieu") with much the same result. It is open to question for much the same reason that has made the entrapment of the term "territory" in terms of any appropriated space questionable. Such a tendency is clearly absurd when one is led to translating "*territoire*" as "place" or "place" as "*territoire*," two terms both elementary and fundamental that no practicing geographer could consider as synonymous.

Such a difficulty underlines the problem spawned by the transformation of the names issuing from research and scientific trends into terms pertaining to a standard international vocabulary. It is in no way bothering to assert that there is a real interest in defining the role of conceptual spaces as expressed through the emphasis put on the words *territory* or *place*. Nevertheless, it becomes embarrassing when one comes, with an almost "savage" behavior and without any wide range of vision, to recreate an entire lexical basis for a "new" geography – corresponding to the establishment of the latest trend as suggested in point number 8 above.

As a matter of fact, this "predatory" approach, consisting in creating a new semantic enclave rather than proceeding to a vast reconstruction of terminology, is not solely restricted to geography. It is a typical reaction coming from theoretical innovation that has not yet entirely made its way into a scientific paradigm. If "territory" were indeed simply the opposite of "space," it would mean that one had opted for a "gentleman's agreement" within which the various domains would have been distributed among neighbors, in order to avoid having to speak with one another as disciplinary colleagues.

We would so have on the one hand the "space" concept, of a geometrical, a-social and a-historical nature, while on the other hand, we would find its symmetrical concept, of a more "humanist," say "phenomenological" and "literary" nature: that of "territory" or "place." But is not such an opposition the very epistemological disaster one would care to prevent?

Finally, despite the taxonomic advantage assumed by the historical approach in number 8, it also leads to difficulties. The fact that we decide to characterize the present days as those of the French "*territoires*," or the English "places," does not exempt us from proposing an approach as rigorous as possible in the justification it can offer of the latter notions within a broader and coherent system of classification.

Because they are linguistically so simple and clearly so spatial, the terms "territory" and "place" are undoubtedly fundamental. As a consequence, their elimination, just as much as an excessively restricted or specific utilization, seems excluded. And if we lack coming to a decision between an historical approach and the epistemological one, we risk finding ourselves trapped into Umberto Eco's world of "glispositions,"[2] "slippery" oppositions that would make his Cacopedists roar with laughter (1995): male/adult, local/nature, or blood related/hunter ... and so on.

Reconsidering the Problem by Introducing the Notion of Metrics

These various criticisms would bear lighter implications if we did not lack so many words to embody the notions recently developed in geography. The path is hard to find between the two paralyzing tendencies that are, on the one hand, an immoderate production of neologisms that gets in the way of scientific communication – whether the latter is internal or external to a discipline – and on the other hand, a use of terms both too vast and too vague that obstructs the terminological clarification of innovative concepts and notions. One has to admit that in the choice of such an in-between path lays a degree of arbitrary decision. When so choosing to use the word "territory" under a 9th signification, I do not contest the idea that any of the other options could have been, in itself, possible. It seems to me nevertheless more effective to employ the word "territory" in order to designate a large ensemble of spaces, that encompasses those concerned by definitions 5 and 6, generalizing somewhat the latter's extension.

To go beyond such difficulties, it may be useful to stand back from the problem treated so far, stand back from the criticisms one can make of the various solutions and initiatives considered up till now, and come back to the very fundamental organization of space classification. The latter process makes one come immediately upon the notion of metrics, a notion that is essential to geography. The very idea of metrics as a tool of classification becomes obvious as soon as one admits that there is no single distance in itself, but only *a various number or types of distances*. Metrics constitute one of the three elementary determiners of a space, along with scale and substance – scale establishing the thresholds of discontinuities within the measuring of distances; substance covering the non-spatial constituents of a given phenomenon. The analysis of spaces in terms of metrics offers one the opportunity to connect two mathematical sectors that have remained for a long time separate, those known as geometry and topology.

If thus one takes as a starting point the idea that metrics are both the perception one has and the measure one makes of a specific type of distance, effective in a given spatial situation, one can give a definition of territory as a geometrical form: "a space with topographic metrics" (Lévy 2003). The territorial ensemble includes all the realities bearing continuous – but not necessarily uniform – metrics. It can be opposed to another large ensemble of metrics: that of topology or of networks. Contrary to the word "surface," pertaining solely to the world of geometry, "territory" belongs to a field of spaces relating to the social world. Same case but different world – here the medical one: the use of the term "areolar," in order to characterize spaces bearing topographic metrics, seems unsuitable because of its simple and clearly not belonging to the vocabulary of social life.

Since what is at stake here is an elementary distinction, one must not attempt to multiply the characteristics standing between the two objects. Those that concern the limits for instance – that is to say *the border* when dealing with topology and *boundaries* when dealing with topography – are subject to another classification principle: one can find, both among territories as well as networks, spaces carrying either vague or clear limits. With this in mind, one can cross-over a set of criteria, as observed in the following table:

Table 18.1 An Elementary Classification of Metrics.

		Inner Metrics	
		Topographical: Territory	*Topological: Network*
Metrics of Limits	Topographical: Borderland	**Horizon** *Linguistic, cultural space; urban neighbourhood*	**Rhizome** *Relational space of an individual*
	Topological: Borderline	**Country** *Rural area; state*	**Grid** *TV network*

Such a table helps us understand which precise understanding of space has absorbed on its own almost exclusively all the attention of "classical" geography studies (1850–1950). *Country* is a term, which, in several languages (for example *Land* in German, or *pays* in French), designates both the countryside and the state's territory. This "state-agrarian" pattern of space construction as territory carries a double strength: on the one hand, it underlines the configuration of similarities between geopolitical states (states as we know them now) and rural countries, the sort of territorial unit out of which the former have been made; and on the other hand, it perfectly illustrates the necessity for states to establish a strong alliance with their rural populations or peasantries in order to ensure territorial control. Within the dominantly defensive geopolitical studies pertaining to the old European states that arose in the late nineteenth century, such a model of space became the only viable one, the only one therefore deserving to generate both observation and promotion. Enclosed in such a historical-geographical context, territories with fuzzy boundaries were considered dangerous chimeras and networks were only perceived as simple links in logistical chains that served the interests of the territory.

Yet numerous phenomena occurring at various scales from an individual's everyday life to the operations of transnational firms, as well as state-operated police surveillance, show that *networks* can be fully apprehended as *spaces* carrying a multitude of applications. One might even go further, assuming that if territory as an object remains a utopia, because of its infinity of points, network on the other hand is the most pragmatic and typical expression of the spatiality inherent in individual action. The latter can also be subject to a composition of limits, generating an even more general opposition between what is "topographic" and what is "topological." Understanding space as a network is particularly crucial to the apprehension of contemporary globalization. Indeed, the current process is not only constituted by a radical change of scale, but also by the perhaps temporary but nevertheless spectacular victory of networks over territories (Rosenau 2003).

The modern world is a gigantic evolving civil society, within which individuals, groups, organizations and companies continually get hold of "market shares" which had for long remained "riveted to the ground" in structures, such as geopolitical states. The development of a solid partnership between state and society, through the use of building a community, so as to experience a *nation*, has demonstrated its political power ever since 1792 – when the first massive gathering of a majority of male citizens to wage war was organized in France – to 1989, and the end of the Cold War. The combination of state and nation both enabled the world to freeze its incipient globalization process following the 1929 crisis and provoked at its climax the auto-extermination war that was World War II. But the link between nation and state is undoubtedly weakening (Antonsich 2009). The territorial state has clearly been thrown into crisis by the globalization of all that can be exchanged in a market or anywhere else (Flint and Taylor 2007).

Spatial capital – which is the capacity to control existing and emergent spatialities or ways of organizing space (both territorial or areal and networked) – can be converted into other types of capital, whether economic, social, or of another kind, but typically today is established through a combination of metrics (Lévy 2007).

Thus migrants do not simply "migrate" any more: they circulate (Tarrius 1995), constantly moving between their resource territories and their commitment networks, of a both risky and promising nature. At the same time, workers "entrenched" behind the sandcastle walls of national-welfare-states find themselves increasingly deprived materially and bitter politically when confronted by spatial evolutions of which they have no grasp.

Indeed, these days spaces bearing an exclusive access of control can be relatively easily identified (e.g. states, private spaces or "buffer zones") and constitute a fairly small share of the total range of types of spatial configurations. Thus one should not, in my opinion, give territories of an absolute type the sort of prominent position in taxonomies of space that we typically still do.

In fact, it is more useful to conceive of spaces as a more or less articulated overlapping or intersections of territories and networks. This is relatively clear with respect to urban space, in which *changeover locations* such as railway stations provide for articulation between a railroad network, on the one side, and the city territory, on the other. Also, the geography of languages, splendidly launched at the beginning of the 20th century by Ferdinand de Saussure, illustrates how territories within which states have tended to enforce an exhaustiveness of the official language using school, media and law, meets with networks constituted of communities, of travelers of all kinds, and of Internet consumers to define the effective reach of the language in question.

Along with strictly bordered territories and networks carrying precise limits – as in the *Grid* model of electrical services – one can also find territories deprived of any kind of clear border, such as cultural spaces like the German Mitteleuropa or sphere of influence, that stretches eastward without anyone being able to give it explicit edges – the German geographer Gehrard Sander (1987) even forged the notion of *Horizont* in order to understand such fuzzy territorial spaces. One can also consider such zones as the collection of rhizomes, objects reflecting the working of the botanical metaphor provided by the works of Deleuze and Guattari (1987 [1980]) and enriching the notion of network by transforming its limits into vague outskirts rather than definite endings.

Beyond Geopolitics: Rethinking Political Territory

The wars triggering Yugoslavia's dismantling (1990–1995) have shown to what extent the confrontation between obsessions about territorial borders, on the one hand, and a complex and intertwined ethnic-social world on the other, can produce horrors and disasters. The territoriality conceptualized in traditional geopolitics is in two respects actively antithetical to the life of societies: because firstly it dictates by force the arbitrary outlining of front lines and borders and because secondly it attempts, in order to succeed in mobilizing inhabitants' approval, to activate myths that also are at odds with the present realities animating the spaces in question. The contradictions arising from the application of classic territorial sovereignty underline the growing difficulties such a logic experiences when trying to impose itself upon a more fluid and fragmented social world and in relation to normative goals, particularly those bearing a universal ambition such as ensuring individual rights within an increasingly globalized society.

In the contemporary world, we can be said to experience a multitude of more or less stable "sovereignty regimes" (Agnew 2009). Within this context, the state-based territorial project is generally weakening and increasingly suffers a failure in legitimacy at the paradoxical moment when the commanding authorities in many of these states had the feeling that, thanks to the creation of powerful nationwide armed forces, schools systems, and media grids, they had achieved the utopia of a pervasive, ubiquitous control. However, twenty years after the fall of Berlin's "Wall of Shame," all the enclosures now preventing free circulation – whether they be in Jerusalem, in Nicosia, in Ceuta or on the Rio Grande – provoke a profound disillusionment in the minds of those who witness their existence, whether or not they are citizens of the states in question.

Every territorial project must therefore hold an increasing awareness of "its limits' respective limits" (Lévy 1994). Concurrently, every political project must concede that the territoriality within which it takes place provides one of its foundational components that cannot be transcended without the project itself disappearing. It is the territory that guarantees the presence for the state of an attribute of a both more abstract and longer term nature than that of the limited short-term space of state action. The territory's self-sufficiency – which of course has always been a spatial utopia – makes another utopia possible: that of time. Such an abstraction then becomes that of political action, encouraging citizens of a country to consider themselves in charge of a past and a future without any other limit than that of the chronological continuity proper to the territory labeled under the given name of the country.

As a "country," the political territory however also possesses limits that guarantee its "republican" character, in the sense theorized by Kant (1795). Tyranny, its opposite, so begins when "he who decides" does not pertain to the same territory as "they who suffer the consequences of the decision" (Lévy 1994). The classic case of such a distortion is that of the *empire*, in which the "metropolitan space" – using its state and even, possibly, its democracy – enforces its law in the colonial space, the latter having no influence whatsoever on its own fate. At the same time, and diametrically opposite to this transcendental situation, within which the bigger space can be said to carry out its influence over the smaller one, one can also see a sort of immanence at work in some cases, whereby the small spatial units "belonging" to a much vaster one are in possession of a sufficiently abounding power to prevent the latter from really controlling itself.

One comes upon such a case, for example, when observing the political action, in Europe or in North America, of small sub-or outer-urban municipalities, populated with wealthy residents, that refuse to be incorporated into an area regulated by a metropolitan government. These secessionist municipalities take advantage of their political autonomy to act as free riders: their inhabitants benefit from the urban concentration without having to support its cost. The struggle of geopolitical states against the constitution of democratic urban governments at the scale of functional metropolitan spaces demonstrates that the territorial issue is still fundamental as a question of political philosophy and practice.

To conclude, then, putting the notion of territory into a richer perspective of spatial vocabulary and considering the variety of metrics and ensembles of spaces which the metrics generate, does not thus result in eliminating "territory" from the field of concerns proper to geographers, but rather leads to the clearer specification and actualization of what role, in our multiple and intertwined spatialities, this specific way of being within the world has played and continues to play. It also encourages open-mindedness about other patterns of thought when having to consider the range of spatialities to be found in the social worlds we all inhabit. For instance, Peter Sloterdijk's works establish the cognitive power of spatial metaphors – such as those of "interlocked spheres," of "bubbles," or even of "foam" – in order to expose the overall complexity of human spatiality. A better understanding of geographicity (how the world is organized geographically) leads us then to give back to territory its righteous importance, not more, not less.

Notes

1 1670; known in English as *The Bourgeois Gentleman* or *The Middle-Class Gentleman*.
2 French contraction of *"glissant"* (slippery) and *"opposition."*

References

Agnew, J.A., (2009) *Globalization and Sovereignty*. Rowman and Littlefield, Lanham.
Antonsich, M. (2009) On territory, the nation-state and the crisis of the hyphen. *Progress in Human Geography* 33 (6), 789–806.
Badie, B. (1995) *La fin des territoires*. Fayard, Paris.
Debarbieux, B. (2003) Territoire. In J. Lévy, and M. Lussault (eds), *Dictionnaire de la géographie et de l'espace des sociétés*. Belin, Paris, pp. 910–912.
Delaney, D. (2005) *Territory: A Short Introduction*. John Wiley & Sons, Inc, Hoboken.
Diamond, J. (1997) *Guns, Germs, and Steel: The Fates of Human Societies*. Norton, New York.
Deleuze, G. and Guattari, F. (1987 [1980]), *A Thousand Plateaus*. The University of Minneota Press, Minneapolis.
Eco, U. (1995) *How to Travel with a Salmon and Other Essays*. Harvest Books, San Diego.
Ferrier, J-P. (2003) Territoire. In J. Lévy, and M. Lussault (eds) *Dictionnaire de la géographie et de l'espace des sociétés*. Belin, Paris, pp. 912–917.
Flint, C. and Taylor, P.J. (2007) *Political geography: world-economy, nation-state, and locality*. Pearson, Harlow.
Haesbaert da Costa, R. (2003) Déterritorialisation. In J. Lévy, and M. Lussault (eds), *Dictionnaire de la géographie et de l'espace des sociétés*. Belin, Paris, pp. 244–245.
Haggett, P. (1965) *Locational Analysis in Human Geography*. Arnold, London.
Kant, I. (1795) Perpetual Peace: A Philosophical Sketch. http://www.mtholyoke.edu/acad/intrel/kant/kant1.htm (accessed 15th October 2010).
Le Berre, M. (1982) Le territoire dans ses rapports avec l'espace géographique, concept ancien, utilisation nouvelle. In *Géopoint 82*, Groupe Dupont, Avignon.
Lévy, J. (1994) *L'espace légitime*. Presses de Sciences Po, Paris.
Lévy, J. (2003) Territoire. In J. Lévy, and M. Lussault (eds), *Dictionnaire de la géographie et de l'espace des sociétés*. Belin, Paris, pp. 907–911.
Lévy, J. (2007) Globalization as a Political Invention: Geographical Lenses. *Political Geography*, 26 (1), pp. 13–19.

Rosenau, J.N. (2003) *Distant Proximities: Dynamics beyond Globalization.* Princeton University Press, Princeton.

Sack, R.D. (1986) *Human Territoriality: Its Theory and History.* Cambridge University Press, Cambridge.

Sandner, G. (1987) Mitteleuropa als "Kulturlandschaft. In H-A. Steger and R. Morel (eds), *Ein Gespent gebt um...: Mitteleuropa.* Theo Eberhard Verlag, Munich, pp. 127–152.

Tarrius, A. (1995) *Les fournis de l'Europe. Migrants riches, migrants pauvres et nouvelles villes internationales.* L'Harmattan et Plan urbain, Paris.

Tuan, Y-F. (1974) *Topophilia: A Study of Environmental Perception, Attitudes, and Values.* Prentice-Hall, Englewood Cliffs.

Chapter 19

Globalization
Part I

Richard Florida

Introduction

When we think of "globalization," we usually think of the outward spreading or decentralization of companies, jobs and economic activity. "The World Is Flat" is the phrase New York Times columnist Thomas Friedman uses to describe globalization in his best-selling book on the subject (Friedman 2005). Thanks to advances in technology the global playing field has been leveled, the prizes are there for the taking, and all of us are players – no matter where on the surface of the earth we may reside. "When the world is flat," Friedman writes, "you can innovate without having to emigrate" (Friedman 2005: 216).

It's an old idea with a long history. Since the turn of the twentieth century, commentators have been writing about the leveling effects of trade and technology that make place unimportant. From the invention of the telegraph and the telephone, the automobile and the airplane, to the rise of the personal computer and the Internet – many have argued that technological progress has eroded the economic significance of physical location.

The same prophecies persist today and have for some time. In 1995, *The Economist* proclaimed the "Death of Distance" on its cover (Cairncross 1995). "Thanks to technology and competition in telecoms," journalist Frances Cairncross predicted, "distance will soon be no object." Some years later the same magazine proudly announced the "Conquest of Location": "The wireless revolution is ending the dictatorship of place in a more profound way" (Cairncross 1997). The new communications technologies were proving to be the "great levelers" in an increasingly globalized world. Place, we've been led to believe, is no longer relevant. We should feel free to live wherever we please.

By almost any measure, the international economic landscape is not at all flat. "There are many advantages that children can enter this world with – including Intelligence, physical power and agility, good looks and caring parents," wrote UCLA economist and global trade expert Edward Leamer in a review of *The World*

The Wiley Blackwell Companion to Human Geography, First Edition.
Edited by John A. Agnew and James S. Duncan.
© 2011 John Wiley & Sons, Ltd. Published 2016 by John Wiley & Sons, Ltd.

Is Flat: "It also matters where you live" (Leamer 2007: 144). And while theoretically we can choose to live virtually anywhere, the reality of the global economy is that certain places offer far more opportunity than others.

The most obvious challenge to the flat-world hypothesis is the explosive growth of cities and urban areas worldwide. More and more people are clustering in urban areas – and there's no evidence to suggest that they'll be stopping anytime soon. The share of the world's population living in urban areas increased from just 3 percent in 1800 to 14 percent in 1900. By 1950, it had reached 30 percent. Today, this number stands at more than 50 percent. In the advanced countries, three-quarters of people live in urban areas (World Population Prospects 2006).

Population growth isn't the only indicator that the world is anything but flat. In this chapter, I'll show detailed maps that illustrate the extreme concentrations of economic activity and innovation. In terms of both sheer economic horsepower and cutting-edge innovation, today's global economy is powered by a surprisingly small number of places. What's more, the playing field shows no sign of leveling. The tallest spikes – the cities and regions that drive the world economy – are growing ever higher, while the valleys – places that boast little, if any, economic activity – mostly languish.

Certainly, globalization is powerful. Places that never had a chance to participate in the world economy are now seeing some action. But not all of them are able to participate and benefit equally. Innovation and economic resources remain highly concentrated. As a result, the really significant locations in the world economy remain limited in number.

The reality is that globalization has two sides. The first and more obvious one is the geographic spread of routine economic functions such as simple manufacturing or service work (for example, making or answering telephone calls). The second, less obvious side to globalization is the tendency for higher-level economic activities such as innovation, design, finance, and media to cluster in a relatively small number of locations.

When thinkers like Friedman focus on how globalization spreads out economic activity they miss the reality of this clustering. Michael Porter, Harvard Business School professor and expert on competitive strategy, dubs this the "location paradox." Porter told *BusinessWeek*: "Location still matters," and "The more things are mobile, the more decisive location becomes." And "this point," he added, "has tripped up a lot of really smart people" (Engardio 2006). The mistake they make is to see globalization as an either-or proposition. It's not.

Spiky Globalization

Let's take a look at some maps of what I call spiky globalization. Based on traditional measures of population density and new measures of global economic production and innovation, these maps show the striking location-based spikiness of globalization (Florida 2005). There are roughly two or three dozen places that dominate the global economy.

Figure 19.1 charts population distribution across the globe. It is based on existing data that my team and I collected in order to identify the world's mega-regions. The most populous region is India's Dehli-Lahore, which is home to more than 120

Figure 19.1 Global Distribution of Population (Florida, 2005).

Figure 19.2 Global Distribution of Economic Activity (Florida, 2005).

million people. There are eight regions with more than 50 million people; another twelve are home to 25–50 million people; and thirty-three more have between 10–25 million people.

Of course, population density is a rudimentary measure of economic activity that does not fully convey the vast gulf separating the world's most productive regions from the rest. Sometimes, relatively small cities like Helsinki, Stockholm and Copenhagen can be immensely rich in per capita output. Conversely, some enormous urban settlements like those of the developing world do not generate a lot of economic output and remain quite poor. So it is important to identify mega-regions not just in terms of their population but also in terms of their economic output.

Unfortunately, there exists no single comprehensive information source for the economic production of the world's regions. A rough proxy is available, though. Our second map shows a variation on the widely circulated illustration of the world at night, with higher concentrations of light and thus higher energy use – and, presumably, stronger economic production – but in greater relief (see Figure 19.2).

As this map shows, the world economy takes shape around twenty-four mega-regions. Two of them produced more than $2 trillion in economic output – Greater Tokyo ($2.5 trillion) and the giant mega-region stretching from Boston through

New York to Washington, D.C. ($2.2 trillion). These two mega-regions would rank as the third and fourth largest economies in the world, about the same size as Germany: only the United States and Japan are larger. Four more mega-regions produce more than $1 trillion in output – the great mega that runs from Chicago to Pittsburgh ($1.6 trillion), Europe's Am-Brus-Twerp ($1.5 trillion), Japan's Osaka-Nagoya region ($1.4 trillion), and the Greater London region ($1.2 trillion). Each of them would place among the top ten national economies in the world; they are all bigger than Italy, Canada, India, South Korea, Russia, or Brazil. There are forty that produce more than $100 billion in economic output each. Not only are mega-regions becoming the economic powerhouses behind national economies; they're behind the global economy as well.

Although they do not yet rival those of the United States, Europe, or Japan, the economies of both India and China are also considerably spiky. In China, 68 percent of economic output is produced in places that house just 25 percent of its people. In India, places with 26 percent of the population produce more than half (54 percent) of the nation's total output (Florida 2008). Compare that to the United States, where regions produce economic output roughly in proportion to their population. The population and productive capacity of the United States, as spiky as it is, is spread over a relatively large number of places. China and India, which industrialized much later, have seen their resources and productive capability concentrate to a much greater degree. Our current round of globalization is making the world even spikier than before.

Population and economic activity are both spiky. But it is innovation – the engine of economic growth – that is most concentrated. It's here that the playing field is least level. The third map shows the world's innovation centers, as measured by patents granted worldwide (Figure 19.3). This map of global innovation clearly shows a world composed of innovative peaks and valleys. The leaders – the tallest spikes – are the metropolitan regions around Tokyo, Seoul, New York, and San Francisco. Boston, Seattle, Austin, Toronto, Vancouver, Berlin, Paris, Stockholm, Helsinki, Osaka, Seoul, Taipei, and Sydney also stand out. Innovation is also cropping up in certain locations in China and India, as their economies develop. Though they are not nearly as tall as the biggest spikes, a number of cities in these countries

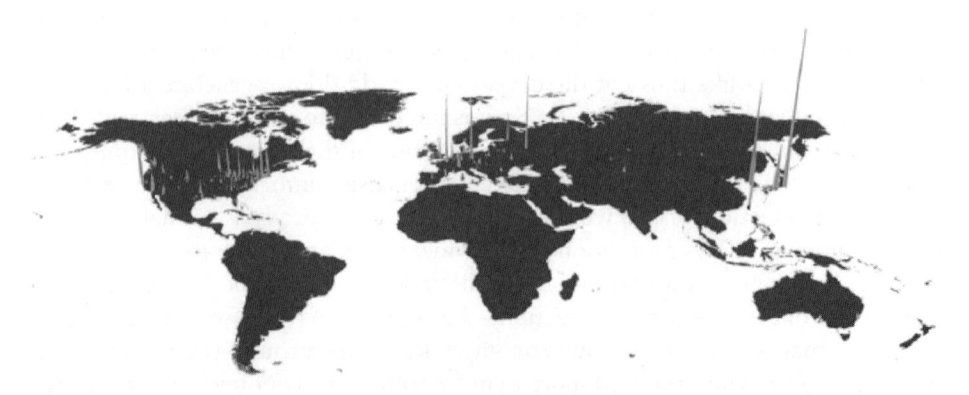

Figure 19.3 Global Distribution of Innovation (Florida, 2005).

are developing significant innovation capability. In India, Bangalore produces about as many patents as Syracuse, while Hyderabad is comparable to Nashville. In China, Beijing produces about as many patents as Seattle or Phoenix, while Shanghai produces about as many as Toronto or Salt Lake City. Our estimates show that innovation in these cities has increased fourfold between 1996 and 2001 and has likely grown at an even greater rate in recent years. Beijing and Shanghai appear poised to join the ranks of global innovators.

This trend may come at the expense of the United States, which has long depended on the innovative and entrepreneurial capabilities of Indian and Chinese immigrants. The detailed research of AnnaLee Saxenian, of the University of California, Berkeley, has shown that Indian and Chinese entrepreneurs ran roughly 25 percent of all Silicon Valley startups from 1980 to 1999, which generated $17 billion in annual revenue and about 58 000 jobs (Saxenian 1999; Dossani 2002; Wadhwa *et al.* 2007; Wu 2007). By 2005, that percentage had increased to 30 percent. But as the map shows, there are still at most two dozen places worldwide that generate significant innovation. These regions have ecosystems of leading-edge universities, high-powered companies, flexible labor markets, and venture capital that are attuned to the demands of commercial innovation – and there aren't many of them.

Scientific discovery – the source of much technological innovation – is also concentrated and spiky. Most significant discoveries occur not just in a handful of locations – primarily in the United States and Europe. The fourth map (see Figure 19.4) shows the residence of the 1 200 most heavily cited scientists in leading fields, note the similarities between the third and fourth maps. Commercial innovation and scientific advance are both highly concentrated – and there are places that enjoy both and do very well in the global economy.

Several cities in East Asia – particularly in Japan – are home to significant commercial innovation but still heavily depend on scientific breakthroughs made elsewhere. Similarly, other locations excel in scientific research but not in commercial adaptation.

When you look at the four maps together, an intriguing pattern appears. With each layer that is added – population density, economic activity, and innovation – the map becomes increasingly concentrated. At the base, population is already

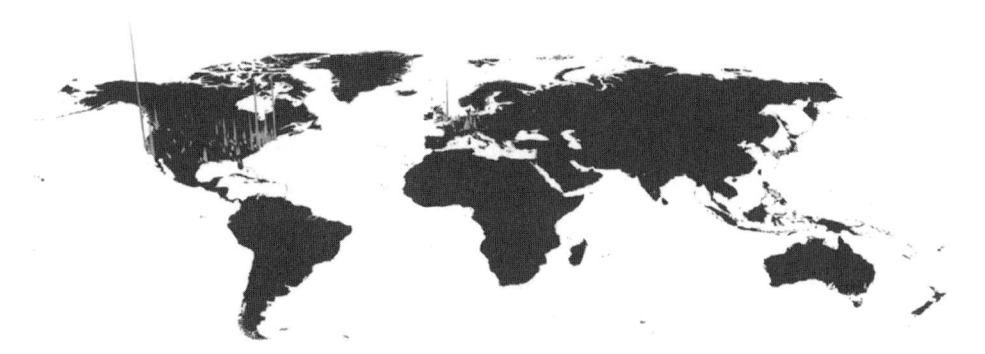

Figure 19.4 Global Distribution of Scientists (Florida, 2005).

highly concentrated: most of the world's people live in a relatively small number of big cities. The distribution of economic activity is even more skewed: Many locations, despite large populations, barely register. Innovation and star scientists come from fewer places still.

The world gets spikier and spikier the farther you climb up the ladder of economic development, from producing basic goods to undertaking significant new innovations.

Geographic concentration is particularly important for innovation. Ideas flow more freely, are honed more sharply, and can be put into practice more quickly when innovators, implementers, and financial backers are in constant contact with one another, in and outside of work. Creative people cluster not simply because they like to be around each other, or because they all happen to prefer cosmopolitan centers with lots of amenities, though both of those things tend to be true. Creative people and companies cluster because of the powerful productivity advantages, economies of scale, and knowledge spillovers such density brings.

So although one might not have to emigrate to innovate, geographic concentration remains a prerequisite for cutting-edge innovation. Innovation, economic growth, and prosperity continue to occur in places that attract a critical mass of top creative talent. Because globalization increases the returns on innovation – by allowing for fast rollouts of innovative products and services to consumers worldwide – it increases the lure of innovation centers for our planet's best and brightest. All this only reinforces the spikiness of economic activity across the globe.

The Rise of the Mega-Region

When we think about globalization, we usually think in terms of nation-states. David Ricardo long ago famously theorized, discretely defined countries have incentive to specialize in different kinds of industries, which would allow them to gain and maintain "comparative advantage" over others (Ricardo 2006).

The comparative advantage Ricardo identified still matters today, but national borders no longer define economies. Instead, the mega-region has emerged as the new natural economic unit (Florida, Gulden and Mellander 2008). It is not an artifact of artificial political boundaries, like the nation-state or its provinces, but the product of concentrations of centers of innovation, production, and consumer markets. Today's mega-regions, which are essentially agglomerations of contiguous cities and their suburbs, extend far beyond individual cities and their hinterlands. I sometimes describe a mega-region as somewhere you can walk all the way across, from one side to the other, carrying nothing but some money without ever getting thirsty or hungry.

In 1957, the economic geographer Jean Gottmann first used the term "megalopolis" to describe the emerging economic hub that was the Boston-to-Washington corridor (Gottmann 1961). Derived from the Greek and meaning "very large city," the term was later applied to a number of other regions: the great swath of California stretching from San Francisco to San Diego; the vast Midwestern megalopolis running from Chicago through Detroit and Cleveland and down to Pittsburgh; and the bustling Tokyo-Osaka region of Japan. In 1993, the Japanese management expert Kenichi Ohmae wrote an influential Foreign Affairs article which argued that the globe's natural economic zones, or "region states," had replaced nation-states as the organizing economic units of what he famously dubbed the "borderless world"(Ohmae 1993, 1995).

A number of experts have updated Gottmann's and Ohmae's work with empirical data, charting the scope and extent of mega-regions in the United States and elsewhere. Lang and Dhavale (2005) of the Metropolitan Institute at Virginia Tech found that the ten mega-regions that power the US economy are home to nearly 200 million Americans, more than two-thirds of the national population, and growing at considerably faster rates than the nation as a whole.

My research team used the satellite images of the world at night (described earlier) to identify mega-regions as contiguous lighted areas (Florida, Gulden and Mellander 2008). Based on that, we are able to distinguish those large areas of economic activity from smaller centers. I realized the power of these world-at-night images on a plane trip from South Carolina to Toronto late one evening in fall 2007. When we left South Carolina in the heart of the great Char-Lanta mega, one could see brilliant lights for at least forty-five minutes. Then the sky went dark for about an hour, until we approached Buffalo at the outskirts of the Tor-Buff-Chester mega. The light in the clouds on the horizon ahead looked as if day were breaking, even though we were traveling in the dead of night.

A mega-region must meet two key criteria. First, it must be a contiguous lighted area with more than one major city or metropolitan region. Second, it must produce more than $100 billion in economic output, what we call light-based regional product (LRP). By that definition, there are exactly forty mega-regions in the world. The next three maps show the mega-regions of the US, Europe and Asia. Mega-regions are the key economic orienting force of the global economy.

If we take the largest mega's in terms of population:

- The ten biggest are home to 666 million people, or 10 percent of world population;
- The top twenty comprise 1.1 billion people, 17 percent of the world total; and
- The top forty are home to 1.5 billion people, 23 percent of global population.

When we look at economic activity, the figures are even more striking:

- The world's ten largest mega-regions in terms of economic activity (or LRP), which house approximately 416 million people or 6.5 percent of the world's population, account for 43 percent of economic activity ($13.4 trillion), 57 percent of patented innovations, and 53 percent of the most-cited scientists.
- The top twenty mega-regions in terms of economic activity account for 10 percent of population, 57 percent of economic activity, 76 percent of patented innovations, and 76 percent of the most-cited scientists.
- The top forty mega-regions in economic activity, which make up about 18 percent of the world's population, produce 66 percent of economic activity, 86 percent of patented innovations, and house 83 percent of the most-cited scientists.

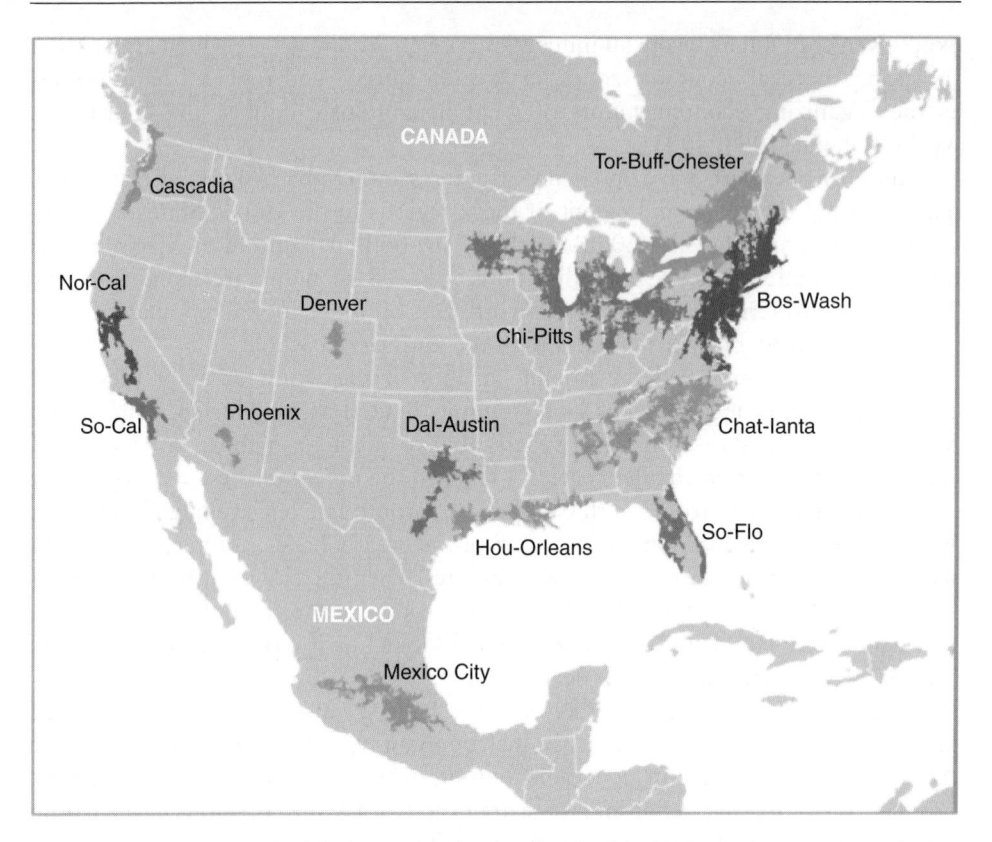

Figure 19.5 The Mega-Regions of North America (Florida, Gulden and Mellander, 2008).

The Clustering Force

There is a powerful geographic flip-side to globalization. At the same time that some, more standard kinds of economic activity – like manufacturing or call centers – becomes spread more widely across the globe, other more higher-end economic activities – like high-tech industry or music scenes – cluster more closely together. You can think of this clustering force as the flip side to globalization. Ever since Alfred Marshall's seminal writings, economists and geographers have thought of cities as clusters, or "agglomerations," of firms, factories and industries (Marshall 1890).

"If we postulate only the usual list of economic forces," the Nobel Prize–winning economist Robert Lucas wrote in 1988, "cities should fly apart" (2002: 59). After all, Lucas reminds us, land "is always far cheaper outside cities than inside." Why, then, didn't businesses and people move en masse out to where costs are substantially lower? Lucas answered his question with another, equally simple observation: "What can people be paying Manhattan or downtown Chicago rents for, if not to be around other people?"

To answer that question he drew on the pioneering work of the urbanist Jane Jacobs, writing that: "I will be following very closely the lead of Jane Jacobs, whose

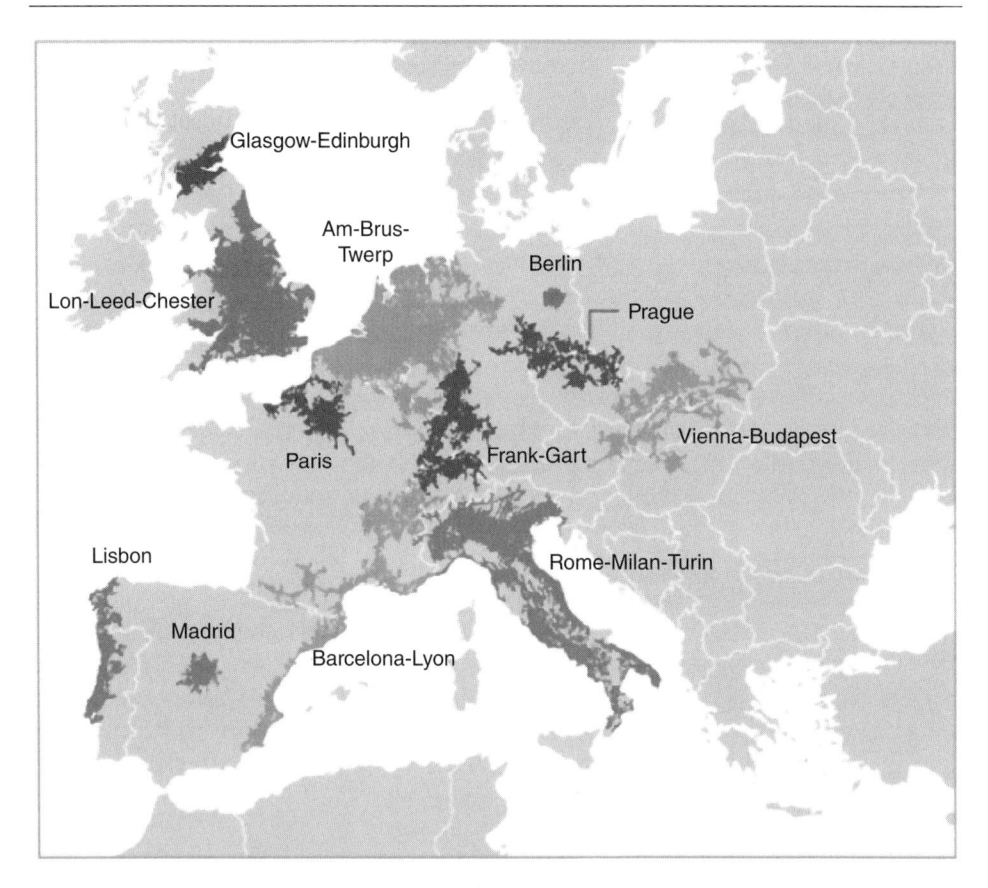

Figure 19.6 The Mega-Regions of Europe (Florida, Gulden and Mellander, 2008).

remarkable book, *The Economy of Cities*, seems to me mainly and convincingly concerned (although she does not use this terminology) with the external effects of human capital" (Jacobs 1970). Although she did not have a PhD and never taught at university, Jacobs was perhaps the most important urban thinker of the 20th century. Jacobs added substantially to our understanding of the forces of agglomeration, arguing that the true power of cities comes from the clustering of people, rather than the clustering of firms.

Building on Jacobs' fundamental contribution, Lucas declared the multiplier effects that stem from such talent clustering to be the primary determinant of economic growth. Labor, capital and technical knowledge are all well and good, he conceded, but none of those would amount to anything significant if people could not combine their talents, ideas, and energy in real places. When people – especially talented and creative ones – come together, ideas flow more freely, and as a result individual and aggregate talents increase exponentially: the end result amounts to much more than the sum of the parts. This clustering makes each of us more productive, which in turn makes the place we inhabit even more so – and our collective creativity and economic wealth grow accordingly. This in a nutshell is the clustering force. One consequence of the clustering force is a sorting of regions into an

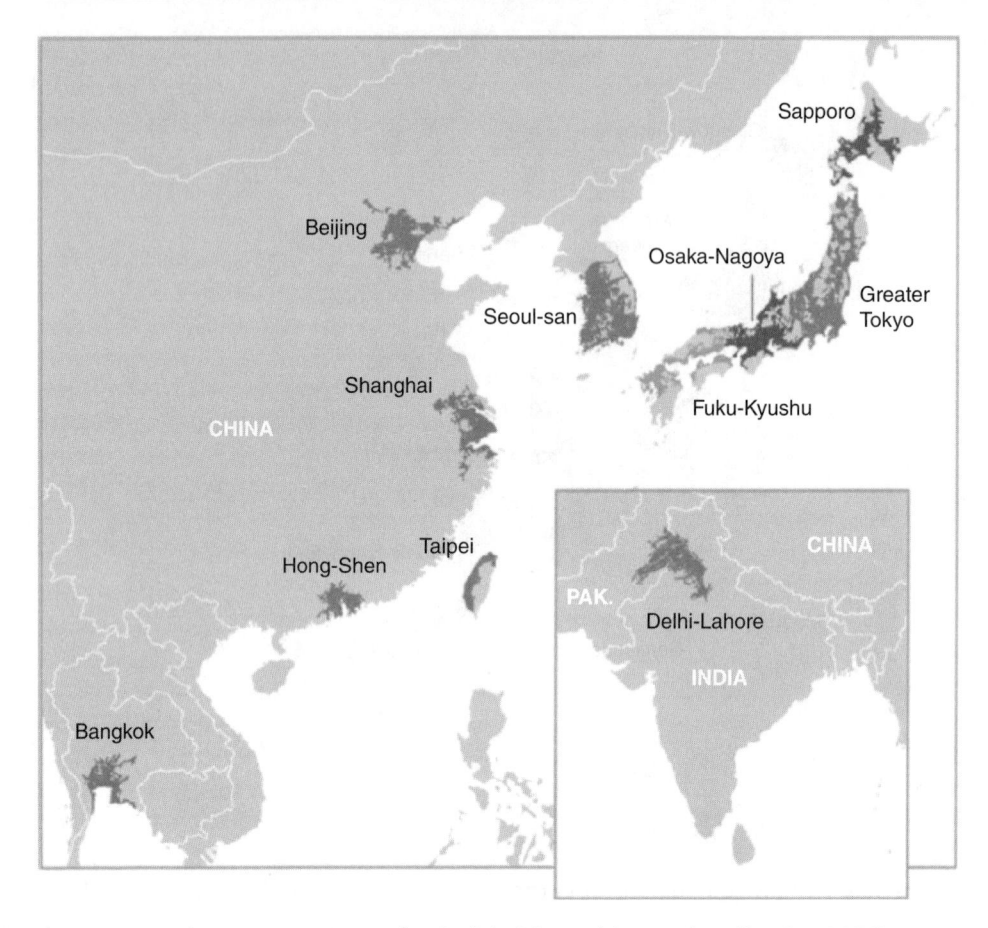

Figure 19.7 The Mega-Regions of Asia (Florida, Gulden and Mellander, 2008).

economic hierarchy. And as talented and highly educated people cluster together in certain regions, the location of work becomes more concentrated and specialized as well. According to the theory, when people cluster together in cities, they will produce more and thus the cost of living in those places will inexorably rise, generating those "Chicago rents" Lucas mentions. Eventually, communities and people will sort themselves into an economic pecking order.

Peaks and Valleys of the Global Economy

The landscape of spiky globalization can be characterized by four kinds of places.

- The first group comprises the relatively small number of locations that generate innovations. Those are the tallest spikes. They have the capacity to attract global talent, generate new knowledge, and produce the lion's share of global innovation. Thanks to the ever-increasing efficiency of long-distance communication and transportation, ideas circulate among these places easily and constantly.

- The second group includes regions that use established innovation and creativity – often imported from other places – to produce goods and services. Those are the world's emerging peaks. Some of them, such as Dublin, Seoul, and perhaps Singapore and Taipei, are transitioning into places that not only use knowledge but generate it. Most of them, though, function primarily as the manufacturing and service centers of the twenty-first-century global economy. From Guadalajara and Tijuana to Shanghai and the Philippines, they produce the world's goods, take its calls, and support its innovation engines.
- The third group is composed of the mega-cities of the developing world – with large population concentrations but insufficient economic activity to support their people. Many of these mega-cities are ravaged by large-scale "global slums" with dense concentrations of homelessness, poverty, and deprivation, high levels of social and political unrest, and little meaningful economic activity (Davis 2006). These places, increasingly disconnected from the global economy, make it difficult to celebrate what appears to be a level world for only a fortunate few.
- Finally, there are the huge valleys of the spiky world – rural areas and far-flung places that have little concentration of population or economic activity, and little connection to the global economy.

The main difference between now and even a couple of decades ago is not that the whole world has become flatter but that the world's spikes have become more dispersed, and that the world's hills or emerging peaks – the industrial and service centers – have proliferated and shifted. For the better part of the twentieth century, the United States claimed the lion's share of the world's economic and innovative peaks, with a few outposts in Europe and Japan. But the United States has since lost many of those peaks, as industrial-age powerhouses such as Pittsburgh, St. Louis, and Cleveland have fallen back from the global front lines. At the same time, a number of regions in Europe, Scandinavia, Canada, and the Pacific Rim have stepped up.

For some, the world today looks flat because the economic and social distances between the peaks have gotten smaller. People in spiky places are often more connected to each other, even from half a world away, than they are to people and places in their own backyards. This peak-to-peak connectivity is accelerated by the highly mobile creative class worldwide. They participate in a global technology system and a global labor market, both of which allow them to migrate more freely among the world's leading cities. While the world itself is far from flat, the dense network of interconnections among its peaks can make it appear that way to a privileged minority.

Conceiving the world as spiky has very different geopolitical and economic implications than seeing it as essentially flat. The flat world theory says that emerging areas can easily plug in to the rest of the world. Emerging economies like India and China certainly combine cost advantages, high-tech skills, and entrepreneurial energy, which allow them to compete effectively for manufacturing and standardized service industries. In the flat world view, the tensions set in motion by the increasingly leveled playing field afflict mainly the advanced countries, which see not only manufacturing work but also higher-end jobs, in fields like software development and financial services, moving off-shore.

That theory blinds us to far more insidious problems building in the world economy and, worse yet, leaves policymakers with little leverage over them. It's no longer sufficient to think of the world in traditional binaries: rich and poor, advanced and developing. For the foreseeable future, global politics will hinge on the growing tensions among the world's growing peaks, sinking valleys, and shifting hills. Through that lens, we can see growing divides and tensions on several overlapping fronts: between the innovative, talent-attracting "have" regions and the talent-exporting "have-not" regions; in the escalating and potentially devastating competition among second-tier cities from Detroit to Nagoya to Bangalore for jobs, people, and investment; and in rapidly worsening inequality across the world and even within its most successful and innovative regional centers.

This is a noxious brew – far more harrowing than the flat world Friedman describes and a good deal more treacherous than the old rich-poor divide. Contrary to Samuel Huntington's famous thesis, which pits so-called modern Judeo-Christian values against "backward" Muslim ones, what we face is not a clash of civilizations but a deepening economic divide among the world's spikes and valleys (Huntington 1993, 1996). Most of the world's conflicts – even those seemingly unrelated to economics – stem from the underlying forces of a spiky world.

More than a decade ago, the political theorist Benjamin Barber presciently wrote that the rise of the global economy, which he called "McWorld," was so powerful and all-encompassing that it was reinforcing an enormous backlash (Barber 1992, 1995). That tendency – what he dubbed "Jihad" – has its roots in the anxiety and fear felt by millions upon millions of people in regions whose factions or "tribes" are being threatened by the impersonal force of globalization. Lacking the education, skill, or mobility to connect to the global economy, these people are stuck in places that are falling further and further behind.

Not surprisingly, spiky globalization is wreaking havoc on the transitional and emerging economies. China's rapid growth in the past decade has brought it to the front lines of the global economy. It is increasingly seen as the "world's factory," the manufacturing center and outsourcing destination for the world's leading companies. Experts note that China is quickly moving up the creative ladder by expanding its science workforce, improving its universities, and attracting the world's top technological workers.

But China's remarkable growth is a result of only a handful of propulsive regions, which are attracting the majority of its talented people, generating the great bulk of its innovations, and producing most of its impressive wealth. Talent is concentrated in a few spiky centers such as Shanghai, Shenzhen, and Beijing, each of which is a virtual world apart from its vast impoverished rural areas. The top ten Chinese regions account for just 16 percent of the nation's population, yet they house nearly 45 percent of its talent-producing universities and 60 percent of its technological innovations (Li and Florida 2006).

China exemplifies the growing class divide affecting rapidly developing economies. Its major cities are home to some 560 million people who reside in increasingly innovative, energetic, and cosmopolitan places. Left in their wake are their countrymen – 750 million Chinese who inhabit the rest of the mostly rural country. According to detailed polling by the Gallup Organization in 2006, average household incomes in urban China were two and a half times those in rural areas, and have nearly doubled since 1999. According to our own calculations, residents of China's leading mega-regions are three and half times wealthier than those in the rest of the country. A Chinese student of mine summed it up succinctly: "In Shanghai, regular middle-class people live better than those in the United States, while in the countryside, just outside the city, people live in what can only be described as pre-civilized conditions." His impressions are borne out in statistics: 17 percent of China's population lives on less than a dollar a day, almost half lives on less than 2 dollars a day, and 800 million farmers cannot afford to see a doctor. This spiky and uneven nature of China's economy is rearing its head in the country's politics. In 2005, the Chinese countryside was the scene of an estimated 87 000 riots and demonstrations, up 50 percent from 2003 (Watts 2007). As China's internationally connected peaks grow closer to their global counterparts, rural areas and their populations are sure to be left behind.

But all that pales in comparison with the growing pains felt by India's poor. India's growing economic spikes – city-regions such as Bangalore, Hyderabad, Mumbai, and parts of New Delhi – are also pulling away from the rest of that crowded country.

The backlash to the spiky world extends beyond emerging economies. At the heart of the rejection of the European Union constitution by the populations of France and The Netherlands in 2005 were lower-skilled suburban and rural workers who understandably fear globalization and integration. They may live in the advanced world, but they are also being left behind.

Spiky globalization is also behind political and cultural polarization in the United States, where economic and social rifts between innovative and globally connected metropolitan regions and the rest of the country are ever increasing. As my own calculations show, the spikiest, most innovative centers in the United States – Silicon Valley, Boston, and North Carolina's Research Triangle, for example – also boast the nation's highest levels of inequality. It can be seen by rising anxiety, anger and populism which have registered itself in American politics.

Left unaddressed, the festering anxiety caused by spiky globalization has already spurred a potentially devastating populist political backlash against the global engines of innovation. Across the world, there is fear, insecurity, anger, and resentment emanating from those falling farther and farther below the world's peaks. On top of that, countries are witnessing the departure (or intended departure) of their best and brightest. And there is no shortage of narcissistic political zealots out there – whether in rural Pennsylvania, the French countryside, Eastern Europe, or the Middle East – willing to stoke these mounting fears simply for political gain.

If this resembles a Hobbesian world, it's because globalization, poverty, and affluence have all given rise to a new sorting process that geographically separates economic and social classes both domestically and globally. In today's spiky world, social cohesion is eroding within countries and across them. Little wonder we find ourselves living in an increasingly fractured global society, in which growing numbers are ready to vote – or tear – down what they perceive to be the economic elite of the world.

The flat-world theory is not completely misguided. The world is clearly becoming more interconnected. More goods are being produced than ever before, and wealth is growing in the aggregate. Overall, people around the world have more opportunity to participate in the global economy. But most people don't care about aggregate effects; justifiably, they care about their own well-being. While emerging economies do stand to gain the most from spiky globalization, they will not be immune to its negative effects. And because modern communication makes the world smaller at the same time that globalization makes it spikier, those trapped in the valleys are looking directly up at the peaks, the growing disparities in wealth, opportunity, and lifestyle staring them right in the face.

We are thus confronted with the greatest dilemma of our time. Economic progress requires that the peaks grow stronger and taller. But such growth simply exacerbates economic and social disparity, fomenting political reactions that further threaten innovation and economic progress. By maintaining that the world is flat, that the playing field is level, and that anyone and everyone has a shot, we make it impossible to confront the problems of globalization that afflict so much of the world. Only by understanding that the spiky nature of our world's economy is one beset by growing disparities and tensions can we begin to address them. Managing the disparities between peaks and valleys worldwide – raising the valleys without sacrificing the peaks – is surely the greatest political challenge of our time.

References

Barber, B. (1992) Jihad vs. McWorld. *Atlantic Monthly* 269, 53–63.
Barber, B. (1995) *Jihad vs. McWorld: How the Planet Is Both Falling Apart and Coming.* Crown, New York and Toronto.
Cairncross, F. (1995) The Death of Distance. *The Economist* 336 (7934), 1–28.
Cairncross, F. (1997) *The Death of Distance.* Harvard Business School Press, Massachusetts.
Davis, M. (2006) *Planet of Slums.* Verso Press, Brooklyn.
Dossani, R. (2002) *Chinese and Indian Entrepreneurs and Their Networks in Silicon Valley.* Stanford University, Shorenstein APARC, California.
Engardio, P. (2006) Q&A with Michael Porter [Harvard professor and popular author]. BusinessWeek. Retrieved from http://www.businessweek.com/magazine/content/06_34/b3998460.htm (accessed 15th October 2010).
Florida, R. (2005) The World is Spiky. *Atlantic Monthly* 3 (10), 48–50.
Florida, R. (2008) *Who's Your City? How the Creative Economy is Making Where You Live the Most Important Decision of Your Life.* Random House, Toronto.
Florida, R., Gulden, T., and Mellander, C. (2008) The Rise of the Mega-region. Cambridge. *Journal of Regions, Economy and Society* 1, 459–476.
Friedman, T. (2005) *The World Is Flat.* Farrar, Straus and Giroux, New York.
Gottmann, J. (1961) *Megalopolis, The urbanized northereastern seaboard of the United States.* The Twentieth Century Fund, New York.
Huntington, S. (1993) The Clash of Civilizations? *Foreign Affairs* 72 (3), 22–49.
Huntington, S. (1996) *The Clash of Civilizations and the Remaking of World Order.* Simon and Schuster, New York.
Jacobs, J. (1970) *The Economy of cities*, 1st edn., 1969. Vintage, New York.
Lang, R. and Dhavale, D. (2005) *Beyond Megalopolis: Exploring America's New Megalapolitan Geography.* Brookings Institution, Metropolitan Policy Program, Washington D.C.
Leamer E. (2007) A Flat World, A Level Playing Field, a Small World After All or None of the Above? A Review of Thomas L. Friedman's The World Is Flat. *Journal of Economic Literature* 45 (1), 83–126.

Li, T. and Florida, R. (2006) Talent, Technological Innovation and Economic Growth in China. Retrieved from http://www.rotman.utoronto.ca/userfiles/prosperity/File/Talent_Technological_Innovation_and_Economic_Growth_in_China.w.cover.website.pdf (accessed 15th October 2010).

Lucas, R. (1988) On the Mechanics of Economic Development. *Journal of Monetary Economics* 22, 3–42.

Lucas, R. (2002) *Lectures on economic growth*. Harvard University Press, Massachusetts.

Marshall, A. (1890) *Principles of Economics*. Macmillan, London.

Ohmae, K. (1993) The Rise of the Region State. Foreign Affairs. Retrieved from http://www.foreignaffairs.com/articles/48759/kenichi-ohmae/the-rise-of-the-region-state (accessed 15th October 2010).

Ohmae, K. (1995) *The End of the Nation-State: the Rise of Regional Economies*. Simon and Schuster Inc., New York.

Ricardo, D. (2006) *Principles of Political Economy and Taxation*, 1st edn., 1817. Cosimo, Inc., New York.

Saxenian, A. (1999) *Silicon Valley's Immigrant Entrepreneurs San Francisco*. Public Policy Institute of California, San Francisco.

Wadhwa, V., Saxenian, A., Rissing, B., and Gereffi, G. (2007) *America's New Immigrant Entrepreneurs: Part 1. Social Science Research* (Working Paper Series No. 23). Duke University, Duke Science, Technology and Innovation, North Carolina.

Watts, J. (2007) Thousands of Villagers Riot as China Enforces Birth Limit. Guardian. Retrieved from http://chinaview.wordpress.com/2007/05/22/thousands-of-villagers-riot-as-china-enforces-birth-limit (accessed 15th October 2010).

World Population Prospects. (2006) Urbanization data are from "World Population Prospects: The 2006 Revision Population Database." Population Division, Department of Economic and Social Affairs, United Nations 2007. Retrieved from esa.un.org/unpp/ (accessed 15th October 2010).

Wu, T. (2007) Urban Rural Divide in China Continues to Widen. Gallup. Retrieved from http://www.gallup.com/poll/27028/urbanrural-divide-china-continues-widen.aspx (accessed 15th October 2010).

Chapter 20

Globalization
Part II

Emily Gilbert

Everything has been globalized except our consent.

(Monbiot 2003: 1)

Introduction

In the early 1960s, Marshall McLuhan proposed that the expansion of electronic media would "extend our central nervous system in a global embrace, abolishing both space and time as far as our planet is concerned" (1964: 3). New media would allow people to immediately and intensely connect with others around the world, and hence usher in a "global village." Satellite images of earth, such as those from the Apollo 8 in 1968, or the iconic Blue Marble image of 1972, further fostered a sense of world-wide connection. These images crystallized the globe as a knowable sphere in the popular imagination. Thus paradoxically, just as technology was bringing the global into view as an object to be studied, mapped and governed, narratives of the new technologies cast space as irrelevant. The loosening of place from its moorings persisted across the boom industry of globalization studies that emerged in the 1980s and 1990s. Euphoric narratives of technological success celebrated the transcendence of national borders. Works such as Kenichi Ohmae's *The Borderless World* (1990); Francis Fukuyama's *The End of History and the Last Man* (1992); Benjamin Barber's *Jihad vs McWorld* (1996); and Thomas Friedman's *Lexus and Olive Tree* (1999), and his more recent *The World is Flat* (2005), cast globalization as the inevitable future and, energized by the fall of Berlin Wall and the collapse of the Soviet Empire, as a vindication of western liberal democracy over other kinds of political formations.

The Wiley Blackwell Companion to Human Geography, First Edition.
Edited by John A. Agnew and James S. Duncan.
© 2011 John Wiley & Sons, Ltd. Published 2016 by John Wiley & Sons, Ltd.

In contrast with these bombastic projections, geographers have largely sought to provide more nuanced accounts of the events, processes, and imaginaries associated with globalization as different parts of the world are being drawn more intensively and extensively into one another's orbit. They have not only undermined the triumphalist inevitability of globalization discourses, but have attended to the very paradoxes thrown up by the above literatures. Geographers have provided more grounded understandings of global processes that can also help undercut the sense of powerlessness that is often associated with what Giddens has called this brave, new "runaway world," echoed in the quote by George Monbiot that opens this paper (Giddens 1999). Local studies have enabled geographers to challenge determinist, top-down approaches to globalization and disrupt the neat ordering of the world in terms of discrete global, national, regional and local spheres, or simplistic dualisms of local and global (Herod and Wright 2002). While it is important to consider global forces, as is clear when gazing at a three-dimensional model of the globe, only one surface comes clearly into view depending upon how the axes are rotated. Geographers have thus emphasized the importance of situated knowledge, especially feminist geographers who have sought to infuse the usually gender-neutral discourses of globalization with studies of intimate spaces at the scale of the body, household and community (Mountz and Hyndman 2006; Nagar et al. 2002). This has challenged and interrogated the masculinist thrust of globalization as a discourse of "penetrating" conquest that threatens the "small and relatively powerless" local (Gibson-Graham 2002: 27).

In what follows I will address these issues in more detail with respect to the ways that geographers have engaged with and critiqued globalization in light of three themes: firstly, global ontologies, secondly; global topographies; and thirdly; global mobilities. To begin, the section on global ontologies examines the ways that the debates on globalization have spun around questions regarding the existence of both the state, and of scale. These ontological questions signal the significant disruptions heralded by the globalization debates. I then turn to examine global topographies, that is, the ways that global processes are evoked in particular places. As will be made explicit, geographers have paid particular attention to the uneven landscapes thrown up by globalization, especially as they are infused with neoliberal and neo-imperial ambitions. A third section addresses global mobilities and interrogates contemporary patterns of human mobility. Who moves? Who is able to move? And who is forced to move? This section suggests that national borders are being reconfigured to make them more permeable for some, while for others they are becoming hardened and impassable.

Global Ontologies

Globalization is associated with a wide range of phenomena. Extensive economic transformations are reshaping the world, from the influence of the international reach of markets, to the stretching of production chains, the outsourcing of the service industry, rapid flows of capital and foreign direct investment, offshore financial centers, and developments around transportation, technological and communication networks (Dicken 2007). The rapid diffusion of media and culture through economic networks and information technologies has led to an internationalization of representation and consumption, and a fear that local cultures are being eroded (Washbourne 2005; Radcliffe 2006). Transnationalism and diaspora are loosening the bonds between people to any one single state so that it is no longer a key source of political identity (Nagel 2004). In the realm of politics, new forms of transnational and international alliances are undermining the role and responsibility of central governments, while sub-national regions and cities are also assuming more powers (Agnew 2009; Brenner 2004). At the same time, global cities are assuming a greater standardization, so that Neil Smith casts globalization as simply an internationalized gentrification (Smith 1997).

How to understand this multiplicity of transformations? Disproportionate attention has been directed to the flag-bearers of globalization – the "hyper-globalists" such as Ohmae, Barber, Fukuyama, and Friedman – and their celebration of inevitable global futures and the demise of the nation-state (Dicken 2007: 5). Yet questions as to whether or not the state exists have also been central to academic debate, although usually tackled from a less celebratory perspective. A more nuanced approach can be found in Bob Jessop's influential work which characterizes the state as "hollowed out" rather than obsolete, with power being shifted upwards, outwards and downwards (Jessop 2002). Poststructuralist critique has also been deployed to undermine the state as a foundational category of being by drawing attention to sub-national and regional constellations of power (Sparke 2005). Other works lament the demise of the nation-state precisely because it is the twentieth-century Keynesian *welfare* state that is under threat, with its aspiration to social provision and redistribution. Anti-globalizers also decry the end of the nation-state as an end to forms of public accountability, representation, responsibility and even transparency, even if these characteristics were more facts of principle, rather than practice.

One of the confusions around the changing role of the state arises from its tight tithing to neoliberal economics that promotes privatized and competitive free-markets (Tickell and Peck 2003). Both globalization and neoliberalism have risen to prominence in about the same period, and are associated with changes to the state and the market, and the shift to internationalized, export oriented economies, and a laissez-faire capitalism that depends on deregulation. Both, too, are invested with discourses of inevitability which not only seek to describe the processes at hand, but also provide the rationalization or legitimation for further economic integration (Gilbert 2005). But globalization is also disconnected from neoliberalism in many ways, for example, states such as Singapore, China, Kuwait, and Abu Dhabi have become successful precisely because they have retained control over their domestic economies and resources (Agnew 2009: 17). These examples are instructive. Not only are practices counter to neoliberalism enabling success under globalization, but clearly globalization has not eradicated states. Rather, globalization is constituted by and for states: some are made stronger and others weaker, with the US largely being able to enforce its will post WWII (Cox 1997: 104). Indeed, geographers have argued that the state is still the most important form of bounded territory even as its role and structure is being reconfigured (Dicken 2007: 18). As much as economies, cultures, and politics are enmeshed across national divides, there are still legal, regulatory, jurisdictional, institutional, cultural, and resource differences across place that lead to regional concentrations and disparities.

Questions regarding the existence of the state also have been pivotal to ontological reimaginings. Scale as nested and hierarchical categories of local, national, global etc, no longer appear to have the same coherence in a globalizing world. Eric Swyngedouw has popularized the term "glocalization" to capture the doubled rescaling of social reproduction both upwards to the transnational or global scale, and downwards to the local and the urban (Swyngedouw 1997). This neologism reinforces that scale is a social process, but also focuses on the spatial fixes that are put into play that draw upon the global, and reorient discussions of power away from the national scale. Others, however, have proposed a completely different reimagining of spatial relations. Ash Amin presents a model of "energized network space" that consists of nonlinear networks, understood through metaphors of folding and unfolding (Amin 2002: 395). Nigel Thrift has encouraged a decentered concept of globalization through the "skein of *networks*" not a predetermined ordering of local and global, or even understanding these as enmeshed, as with "glocalization" (Thrift 2002: 37; emphasis in the original). Drawing upon actor-network theory, Thrift suggests that there is no scale, but merely some forms of social relations that are more durable, that have emerged out of iterative relations across place. These approaches echo with a wide-ranging shift in spatial metaphors, whether McLuhan's "global village," the "networks" and "flows" of Manuel Castells's information society (1996), the "scapes" of Arjun Appadurai (1996), or the assemblages of Saskia Sassen (2006).

At the extreme, these new spatial metaphors have led to a call for the wholesale rejection of scale within human geography. Arguing that there is neither any agreement on the use of the term or its operalization, nor that it is possible to overcome an implicit nested hierarchization within the concept, Martson et al. have suggested adopting a new, flat ontology that does not contain within itself any horizontal or vertical predetermination (Marston et al. 2005: 422). A flat ontology, they argue, permits "new spatial concepts that linger upon the materialities and singularities of space" (Marston et al. 2005: 424). Such site-specific research, they suggest, is especially important given the weight and heft associated with the "juggernaut" of globalization discourses, which mystify "sites of ordering practices, as well as the possibilities for undoing them" (Marston et al 2005: 427).

The abandonment of scale has been hotly critiqued, not least because it is seen as drawing geographers too closely into orbit with the "flat" world narratives of the hyper-globalizers. Marston et al., however, flatly deny that their ontological remit has any commonalities with what they call the "origiastic capitalocentrism" of the hyper-globalizers (Martson et al. 2007: 51). Their follow-up article on the Nollywood film-industry in Laos, Nigeria, promotes a politics of site-specific research in all its singularities precisely in an effort to counter local-global binaries, or homogenizing globalization narratives. The site-specificity of a flat ontology may provide an impetus for providing more modest accounts that attend to new forms of connection as well as disconnection. Rather than exaggerated representations of globalization as overactive yet decidedly abstracted capitalist modernity, it echoes with the works of a wide cohort of geographers who advocate the study of the spatial nuances of the global and, also for many, a sensitivity to the vulnerabilities of globalization's contradictions (Conway and Heynen 2006; Nagar et al. 2002). Indeed, this attention to the unevenness of globalization's reach and its effects has been the subject of a significant amount of work in geography, and it is to what I turn in the following section.

Global Topographies

In the early 1990s, Doreen Massey wrote of a "global sense of place" to capture the ways that a single site comprises a complex hybrid of layered and interconnected relations (Massey 1991). She examined the ways that the global exists in place, while also attending to the "power geometry of time-space compression" in these sites, that is, the uneven constitution of identity that exist along axes such as race and gender in the organization of the global. Similarly, Cindi Katz has articulated a radical, topographical approach to globalization that engages with place by drawing upon a rich ethnography that moves beyond simple scalar categorizations, and reaches across global sites to identify the simultaneity of oppressions and opportunities (Katz 2001). These "counter-topographies" are presented as a political response to globalization that allow for an "oppositional politics" to open up new ways of forming alliances by way of a relational concept of place. Thus, while Massey and Katz approach space in ways that resonate with the language of flows, networks and assemblages described above, they differ from those works in that they very explicitly demand a political analysis of spatial transformation.

A political approach to globalization is also manifest in David Harvey's critique of the uneven accumulation that is intrinsic to global capitalism, whereby new "spatial fixes" are created through "accumulation by dispossession," and cycles of investment and disinvestment (Harvey 2006). Among the spatial fixes that geographers have examined is the rise of the region. New territorializations of power are emergent, along with forms of co-option and violence, that generate new geographies within globalization and new forms of governance (Larner and Walters 2004). The consolidation of the European Union and the economic integration engendered by the North American Free Trade Agreement are often held up as emblematic of these regional fixes. Other forms of regionalization are also arising, from the initiatives for the transnational organization of currencies that are emergent around the world (Gilbert 2008), to the sub-national cross-border alliances that are being consolidated in western Canada and the US, which are driven by economic interests but which also affect mobility and other issues (Sparke 2005). Some have posited that these regional reconfigurations are a stepping stone towards the consolidation of an international triad of regional blocs, and may even portend an eventual global government – but this eventuality is hotly debated. Where this literature concurs is that global processes have not flattened space, even within emergent regional systems, but have:

> increase[d] the complexity of territorial-spatial differentiation in the global political system and creating new territorial traps. (Albert and Reuber 2007: 550)

To better understand these territorial traps and the power geometries of globalization, geographers have reached back into the past to uncover and recover the contemporary legacies of colonialism and imperialism (Harvey 2003; Smith 2003;

Agnew 2009; Herod 2009). Within this history, the dominant and determinative role of the US, especially over the last century, has featured prominently (Smith 2003; Sparke 2003). The imperialism of the US has come into view even more clearly with the war on terror, with pundits such as Niall Ferguson and Michael Ignatieff recommending a strengthened US empire, backed by a global militarism, to benevolently administer international order. Harvey, by contrast, has signaled that the US acts only according to its own self-interests; the military occupation of Iraq is a culmination of a longstanding effort to control oil in the Middle East to ensure its dominance in the world economy (Harvey 2003). Similarly, Derek Gregory examines US strategy post 9/11 not to insist on its newness "but to show that it has a complex genealogy that reached back into the colonial past and, equally, to show how it was used by regimes in Washington, London and Tel Aviv to advance a grisly colonial present (and future)" (Gregory 2004: 13). The term "colonial present" is used precisely to undermine future-oriented narratives of globalization that are delinked from the past.

Cast inward, the militarizing impulse manifests itself in the expansion of the US prison system which has been offered up as the solution to the demise of the welfare state under neoliberalizing globalization, with disproportionate impact on racialized communities (Gilmore 2002). This landscape of incarceration speaks to the increasing inequalities of wealth and health that have erupted in industrialized nations over the past several decades. Yet these inequalities are perhaps even more persistent across First and Third Worlds (Dicken 2007: 441). Dick Peet examines the conditionalities and structural adjustment reforms that have been imposed by what he calls the "unholy trinity" of the International Monetary Fund (IMF), the World Bank and the World Trade Organization (WTO), which have been largely culpable for these inequities (Peet 2003). The excessive liberalization, deregulation and decentralization of developing economies orchestrated through these organizations have been blamed for economic problems, such as the Asian financial crisis of the late 1990s (Conway and Heynen 2006: 31). As Risa Whitson has detailed *vis-à-vis* Argentina, the imposition of structural adjustment programs has meant that work has become more informalized and hence more precarious; she examines the significant gender and class implications of these transformations, both within the workplace and at home – issues that are not always addressed in the literature (Whitson 2010).

Geographers have also sought to represent the global South not as a "mere recipient of globalization," but "as being able to act on and transform this global complex" (Nagar *et al.* 2002: 265). Philip Kelly's thorough analysis of globalization in the Philippines in the 1990s examines the landscapes of change at the national scale in the Philippines, but also the impact of export processing zones, such as that at Cavite, on local villages and changes to labor markets, lifestyles etc., as they shift away from agricultural activities. Kelly reveals, however, that the dramatic and uneven changes to landscape were not simply the result of the imposition of neoliberal policies by the west, but rather encouraged and legitimized through domestic politics which fully subscribed to this mandate. In another vein, Gillian Hart's rich ethnography of social and economic transformation in South Africa in the 1980s foregrounds the investment and mobility of Taiwanese entrepreneurs, and the impetus of neoliberal market reforms modeled on East and South East Asian "miracle" of liberalization (Hart 2002). Globalization is constituted by the practices and discourses that are deeply embedded in relations of power; spatial analysis, rooted in the everyday, brings these power relations into view and the historical geographies through which they are constituted (Hart 2002: 12).

In the South Pacific many islands are faring badly under globalization, bearing the brunt of the exploitation of their natural resources by international companies. Some forms of regional cooperation, such as the Pacific Plan of 2006, have emerged as a push-back against these globalizing forces (Roberts *et al.* 2007). Yet the impact of global climate change appears intractable, as rising sea levels are already destroying low-lying coastlands and communities. This is an issue not of their own design, but of a world suffering "from the hyper proliferation of global toxic waste, effluence and general contamination" (Heynen and Njeru 2006: 183). As geographers such as Simon Dalby have emphasized, efforts at global governance around greenhouse gas emissions, such as the Kyoto Protocol, wrestle with the divides across North and South which have different interests in and responsibilities for climate change (Dalby, 2002). So too with respect to the liberalization of agricultural policy. Food security vulnerability has increased in the global South, while Western nations experience rising epidemics of obesity and food-related illnesses such as diabetes because of the inequalities in the implementation of liberalization (Young 2004). These divides bifurcate North and South even as they are brought more closely into one another's ambit. The demand for consumption, like a cup of coffee in cosmopolitan urban centers can, for example, be directly linked to the ecological destruction in the tropical regions where coffee beans are grown (Heynen and Njeru 2006).

Uneven development around urbanization is an explicit outcome of globalization. New forms of urban governance emerge as state power has been rescaled downwards onto the urban, as Neil Brenner documents with respect to western states (Brennner 2004). This has involved the devolution of power to the urban; strategic urban investment; and the repositioning of cities in terms of global capital. Cities, particularly "global cities," have become strategic sites for managing and servicing corporate capital and finance, and hence important nodes for linking national economies to global networks (Sassen 1998). These processes can be seen in the east as much as the West; in newly industrializing economies of East and Southeast Asia, for example, it is common to find mega-urban developments in core regions to tap into global trade and capital networks (Kelly 2000). Moreover, in the Pacific Rim, foreign investment runs in multiple directions; Canadian cities have been reshaped by Chinese foreign investment, most notably in Vancouver where Hong Kong's largest property developers invested billions of dollars into redevelopment projects such as the downtown Pacific Place (Olds 2001). In detailed case studies of the gateway cities of Mumbai (India) and Accra (Ghana), Richard Grant and Jan Nijman (2002) provide a sustained analysis of the reorganization of the space-economies of these cities due to the changing international corporate presence there. There are clearly commonalities across these two sites that reflect some common colonial legacies, but there are also significant differences with what is taking place in cities of the West. The authors argue that contemporary transformations need to be understood in terms of their historical and geographical contexts to reveal both these commonalities and differences. They assert that far too much of the globalization literature is Western in its focus and replicates Western norms and ideals that are not applicable to sites elsewhere.

As cities become sites of the global agglomeration of capital and power, they also increasingly rely upon workers who are marginalized and made precarious (Sassen 1998). Women, immigrants and racialized workers have borne the brunt of urban restructuring as demands for flexible economies and flexible labor are realized through changes to labor conditions. But cities, as much as they have been a fulcrum of uneven geographies of globalization, have also been key sites of resistance. Just as work itself bears the imprint of global processes, so too have workers mobilized across international alliances and through the transnationalization of bargaining (Aguiar and Herod 2006; see also Featherstone 2008). It is in urban space that these politics of solidarity have become most visible, as with the anti-globalization protests in Seattle in 1999 or those in 2003 in Cancun that targeted the World Trade Organization ministerials. The sites themselves, however, are constitutive of the resistance and the forms that it takes, so that who and what are mobilized at the protests varies across place (Wainwright 2007). Thus, even the anti-globalization protests exemplify an uneven landscape in the ways that global networks touch down on the ground.

Global Mobilities

An endemic aspect of globalization is that people and cultures are on the move (Cresswell 2006). Narratives of seamless borders, of the free flow of people abound. But as geographers have sought to illustrate, as mobility becomes a permanent condition of the global economy, the trajectories of individuals and communities are much more complicated than such narratives of openness and opportunity would suggest. Critical work on tourism, for example, has foregrounded the variable opportunities open to people of different classes, gender, race and sexuality. There are also important implications for host countries. Beverley Mullings, for example, has examined the rise of sex tourism in Jamaica which has restructured its tourism industry to better capitalize on foreign exchange, and to overcome the problems brought about by liberalization, privatization, and devaluation of the economy (Mullings 1999). As she describes, women struggling to get by in the wake of structural readjustment, who have been shut-out of the booming commercialization of all-in-one touring packages, have had to turn to sex work for additional income. This is part of a growing international economy of the sex trade that relies on the commodification and exoticification of local subjects. Its reaches out to global subjects, but the impact resonates locally, and in intimate ways as local communities live with the public health consequences of outbreaks of sexually transmitted diseases. As this research suggests, understanding contemporary patterns of mobility demands research that is historically and geographically situated, attuned the politics of sending and receiving countries, sensitive to questions regarding identity formation, and aware of ongoing patterns of colonialism and imperialism.

Similar issues need also to be addressed with respect to migration. While only a small percentage of people live outside their country of birth, no state is unaffected as either a sending or receiving country (Munck 2008). Labor and education opportunities are strong motivators for migration, and remittances are becoming an increasingly important mechanism of global economic redistribution. Notably, however, there is perception that migration is North-South, from non-OECD countries to the OECD, but most migration is actually contained within the global South (Munck 2008). Moreover, much of the migration associated with globalization is actually within states, from rural to urban areas. As Philip Kelly details, global investment and reinvestment has generated rural to urban mobility as the economy has shifted away from agricultural activities towards urban-based globally oriented capitalist development (Kelly 2000). Similarly, Melissa Wright has compared and contrasted the experiences of women who are lured from their rural homes to work in the urban, multinational factories that have been set up in both Mexico and China (Wright 2006). These labor-intensive factories depend upon disposable but also heavily disciplined labor. With these characteristics in mind, women are hired as ideal workers, but are also made especially vulnerable in the process. This vulnerability seeps beyond the factory walls. In Chihuahua, Mexico, women have been targeted and murdered in the streets. Thus, while migration might offer multiple economic opportunities, it can bring about radical changes to communities, and to the migrant self-understanding.

This complexity is also a facet of international migration. For some, particularly the entrepreneurial classes, relocation offers an opportunity to maximize on economic and cultural capital across multiple sites. Aihwa Ong describes the neoliberalized "flexible citizenship" of Chinese entrepreneurs who acquire dual citizenship in "their quest to accumulate capital and social prestige in the global arena" and assume a subjectivity that iterates neoliberal ideals of mobility and flexibility (Ong 1999: 6). New migration policies in countries such as the US, Canada and Australia have, since the 1980s, made it possible for business migrants to gain expedited access to citizenship in their new countries. For these migrants, dual or flexible citizenship has increased exponentially. And yet, at the same time, there has also been increasing regulation over other categories of migrant groups. More hurdles have been placed in front of refugee claimants, while there has also been a wholesale increase in temporary labor mobility agreements. Agricultural worker programs, for example, are expanding in North America (Gilbert 2007), and have been the template for new programs introduced in New Zealand and Australia. These programs, however, are highly constrained: the duration of stay is limited, usually for less than a year; workers are tithed to contracts; and workers are obliged to return to their country of origin, with no possibility of acquiring more permanent status within the receiving country. The Canadian domestic worker program, which Geraldine Pratt has written about extensively, is somewhat different in that it does allow for employees to apply for citizenship status at the end of the contract (Pratt 2004). As Pratt indicates, however, during the contract, domestic workers live under a system of quasi-indentured labor whereby employees are tied to a specific employer. Under this contractual arrangement, some workers have been subject to significant abuse. Through her collaborative work with the Philippine Women Centre in Vancouver, Pratt has highlighted the ongoing struggles of these women to articulate their rights, particularly around the work place, given their marginal status. As this work reveals, these women not only endure the absence of their families back home, but experience a double-marginalization with respect to gender and race within the Canadian polity.

Interviews and ethnographic research have been used extensively to elaborate the ways that migrants straddle expansive geographies and negotiate complex identities around landscape and home, past and present on a daily basis (Tolia-Kelly 2004). Claire Dwyer's study of diasporic, young South Asian women in the UK draws attention to the paradoxes of multiple forms of belonging (Dwyer 1999). For the young Muslim women who adopt the veil it becomes a visible marker of difference that constitutes them as outsiders among mainstream British youth. Yet interviews also suggest that dress is used to negotiate alternative subjectivities by these women: their clothing is used to both challenge mainstream perceptions of Muslim women, but also to navigate their own positionality within their diasporic communities. Geographer Richa Nagar, in an eloquent and moving essay, outlines her own personal experiences of migration and their contribution to her research agenda (Nagar 2006). She describes moving across multiple international sites first for education and then to undertake research. She recounts the struggles she faced as she sought to make her work relevant on the ground in these multiple communities. Her solution has been to work in collaboration with NGO workers and activists to generate conversations and produce knowledge that reaches across these multiple points, especially outside the academy (Sangtin and Nagar 2006).

These personal stories emphasize that migration can be both enabling and constraining, but geographers have emphasized that the conditions under which people migrate needs to be addressed. As work in geography on asylum seekers and refugees insists, there are a great many people who are under pressure to move, or who endure forced mobility (Hyndman 2005; Mountz 2006). The implementation of off-shore processing zones, as in Australia, so that potential migrants are processed or detained in spaces outside of the country of application, reveal the way that geography itself is being used to regulate mobility and to curtail the claims of mobile subjects (Hyndman and Mountz 2007). In their host countries, asylum seekers are often stigmatized and criminalized, and in the contemporary context of heightened security in the "war on terror" analogies are frequently drawn between refugees, criminals and terrorists (Hyndman 2005). Migration is in fact often represented as the "dark side" of globalization in that human rights are disregarded in the name of security concerns (Hyndman and Mountz 2007: 80).

The "war on terror" has only magnified a fear of "the other" and legitimized a racialized nativism that has surged alongside globalization (Sivanandan 2006: 2). As Joseph Nevins has documented at the US-Mexico border, while the introduction of free trade policies in the 1990s eroded the border with respect to goods and capital, it was also when more and more physical barriers were erected at the border to foreclose the easy movement of people (Nevins 2002). As security concerns have intensified with the "war on terror" border security concerns have been more deeply interiorized within the nation-state (Coleman 2007). As a result, borders exude a complicated and often contradictory mix of security and economy mandates. This complex bifurcation of interests is not simply manifest in North America, but in places such as the emergent city-region of the Indonesia-Malaysia-Singapore Growth Triangle which is becoming increasingly enmeshed in economic terms, but which "is transected by all kinds of divides and disjunctures that represent a veritable efflorescence of boundary drawing" (Sparke *et al.* 2004: 496). Finally, geographers have illustrated that as borders are undergoing significant reconfiguration, attention needs to be addressed to the variable kinds of mobility experienced by different groups of people. In North America and in Europe, for example, preferential pre-clearance programs have proliferated which allow expedited access across the border for those who are enrolled as members, while those who are not are often the target of more stringent border controls (Gilbert 2007).

These striations in mobility and citizenship would not seem to bode well for the emergence of a globalized citizenship. And yet, there has been a certain amount of attention to this possibility. For some groups, transnationalism offers the hope of solidarity that transcends national conventions. New forms of organizing, consciousness and energy can transcend national conventions. This is particularly important for communities whose history is one of diaspora and dispersal. Katherine McKittrick and Clyde Woods argue, for example, that for those of African descent, black "diaspora geographies" will "bring into focus local concerns, alternative worldviews, and the stakes of being a global black subject" (McKittrick and Woods 2007: 8). In other words, global connections may help to address ongoing marginalization. Others, however, advise caution about the celebration of transnational communities, especially if they are based on delineating and policing authentic forms of identification and belonging (Binnie 2004). Yet whether or not new forms of transnational citizenship are emergent, work in this area clearly reveals that the globalized world has not resulted in a flat world, but an uneven landscape with respect to both the economy and to the mobility of peoples.

Conclusions

The financial crisis that exploded in 2009 revealed new fault lines in the geographies of globalization. In but one example, the failure of residential mortgage-backed securities by US-based Citigroup were deeply felt by the town of Narvik in the far north of Norway, which lost most of its $78 million investment that was slated for public investment (Aalbers 2009: 35–36). Different national and sub-national regulatory processes – and lack thereof – have resulted in a sketchy patchwork of oversight, alongside a "new geography of predatory lending and over inclusion" (Aalbers 2009: 38). The racial and ethnic composition of this patchwork geography has also been apparent, as in the US. "Areas that are over 80 per cent minority have more than five times as many foreclosures as areas that are less than 10 per cent minority" (Aalbers 2009: 38). These snapshots of the global financial crisis further reinforce the uneven landscapes that are intrinsic to globalization. Yet there may also be another, new feature of globalization on the horizon: a "reversed globalization" whereby emerging economies are coming to the rescue of the "developed" world (Aalbers 2009: 41). Is this the beginning of the end of globalization, or at least a kind of globalization that is fastened to neoliberalism? Walden Bello suggests that it is only through "deglobalization" that a more socially equitable future will be possible as economies are re-embedded into society (Bello 2009).

Addressing these kinds of questions will become more and more important as contemporary issues appear to be intractably global in their reach: terrorism, climate change, environmental disasters and response, resources, food security, pandemics, etc. As Andrew Herod has suggested, the effects of the global are so pervasive that it appears to be "the scale of social life from which there is no escape" (Herod 2009:

ix). Yet geographers, including Herod, argue that despite this totalizing narrative, space has become more, not less, important (see also Smith 1997). To come to terms with this spatial dimension requires analysis that is grounded in both space and time (Herod and Wright 2002: 1). Describing events, processes or imaginaries as global invests them with a particular kind of power (Herod and Wright 2002: 2). What or who gets to count as global? What or who gets relegated to the local? What does the term globalization make possible? What does it hide? How do the ways that globalization is defined affect our views and assessments of contemporary processes and their agendas? (Herod 2009: 222). These are questions that geographers have sought to address on the ground in their research and writing on global ontologies, global topographies and global mobilities.

References

Aalbers, M. (2009) Geographies of the financial crisis. *Area* 41 (1), 34–42.
Agnew, J. (2009) *Globalization & Sovereignty*; Rowman and Littlefield Publishers, Inc. Lanham.
Aguiar, L.M. and Herod A. (2006) *The Dirty Work of Neoliberalism: Cleaners in the Global Economy*. Basil Blackwell, Oxford.
Albert, M. and Reuber, P. (2007) Introduction: the production of regions in the emerging global order – perspectives on 'strategic regionalisation. *Geopolitics* 12 (4), 549–554.
Amin, A. (2002) Spatialities of globalization. *Environment and Planning A* 34 (3), 385–399.
Appadurai, A. (1996) *Modernity at Large: Cultural Dimensions of Globalization*. University of Minnesota Press, Minneapolis.
Barber, B. (1995) *Jihad vs. McWorld*. Ballantyne, New York.
Bello, W. (2009) The virtues of deglobalization. Foreign Policy in Focus http://www.fpif.org/articles/the_virtues_of_deglobalization (accessed 15th October 2010).
Binnie, J. (2004) *The Globalization of Sexuality*. Sage, London.
Brenner, N. (2004) *New State Spaces: Urban Governance and the Rescaling of Statehood*. Oxford University Press, Oxford and New York.
Castells, M. (1996) *The Network Society*. Blackwell, Oxford.
Coleman, M. (2007) A geopolitics of engagement: neoliberalism, the war on terrorism, and the reconfiguration of US immigration enforcement. *Geopolitics* 12 (4), 607–634.
Conway, D. and Heynen N. (eds) (2006) *Globalization's Contradictions: Geographies of Discipline, Destruction and Transformation*. Routledge, New York.
Cox, K. (ed.) (1997) *Spaces of Globalization: Reasserting the Power of the Local*. Guilford Press, New York.
Cresswell, T. (2006) *On the Move: Mobility in the Modern Western World*. Routledge, New York.
Dalby, S. (2002) Environmental governance. In RJ Johnston, P.J. Taylor, and M.J. Watts (eds), *Geographies of Global Change: Remapping the World*. Blackwell, Oxford, pp. 427–439.
Dicken, P. (2007) *Global Shift: Transforming the World Economy*. Sage, London.
Dwyer, C. (1999) Veiled meanings: young British Muslim women and the negotiation of differences. *Gender, Place and Culture* 6 (1), 5–26.
Featherstone, D. (2008) *Resistance, Space and Political Identities: The Making of Counter-Global Networks*. Wiley-Blackwell, Malden.
Friedman, T. (2005) *The World is Flat*. Farrar, Straus and Giroux.
Friedman, T. (1999) *Lexus and Olive Tree*. Farrar, Straus and Giroux.

Fukuyama, F. (1992) *The End of History, and the Last Man.* (trans. A. Blunden 1988[2005]). Penguin.
Gibson-Graham, J.K. (2002) Beyond global vs. local: economic politics outside the binary frame. In A. Herod and M. Wright M (eds), *Geographies of Power: Placing Scale.* Blackwell, Oxford, pp. 25–60.
Giddens, A. (1999) *Runaway World: How Globalization is Reshaping Our Lives.* Profile, London.
Gilbert, E. (2008) Banal neoimperialism and the territorial reconfiguration of money. *Political Geography* 27, 617–629.
Gilbert, E. (2007) Leaky borders and solid citizens: governing security, prosperity and quality of life in a North American partnership. *Antipode* 39 (1), 77–98.
Gilbert, E. (2005) The inevitability of integration? Neoliberal discourse and the proposals for a new North American economic space after September 11. *Annals of the Association of American Geographers* 95 (1), 202–222.
Gilmore, R.W. (2002) Race and globalization. In R. Johnston, P. Taylor, and M. Watts (eds), *Geographies of Global Change: Remapping the World.* Blackwell, Oxford, pp. 261–274.
Grant, R. and Nijman, J. (2002) Globalization and the corporate geography of cities in the less-developed world. *Annals of the Association of American Geographers* 92 (2), 320–340.
Gregory, D. (2004) *The Colonial Present: Afghanistan, Palestine, Iraq.* Blackwell, Oxford.
Hart, G. (2002) *Disabling Globalization.* University of California Press, Berkeley.
Harvey, D. (2006) *Spaces of Global Capitalism: Towards a Theory of Uneven Development.* Verso, London.
Harvey, D. (2003) *The New Imperialism.* Oxford University Press, Oxford.
Herod, A. (2009) *Geographies of Globalization.* Wiley-Blackwell, London.
Herod, A. and Wright, M. (eds) (2002) *Geographies of Power: Placing Scale.* Blackwell, Oxford.
Heynen, N. and Njeru, J. (2006) Neoliberalizing the global environment. In D. Conway and N. Heynen (eds), *Globalization's Contradictions: Geographies of Discipline, Destruction and Transformation.* Routledge, New York, pp. 181–195.
Hyndman, J. (2005) Migration wars: refuge or refusal? *Geoforum* 35, 3–6.
Hyndman, J. and Mountz, A. (2007) Refuge or refusal? The geography of exclusion. In D. Gregory and A. Pred (eds), *Violent Geographies: Fear, Terror, and Political Violence.* Routledge, London, pp. 77–92.
Jessop, B. (2002) *The Future of the Capitalist State.* Polity, Cambridge.
Katz, C. (2001) On the grounds of globalization: A topography for feminist political engagement. *Signs* 26 (4), 1213–1234.
Kelly, P.F. (2000) *Landscapes of Globalization: Human Geographies of Economic Change in the Philippines.* Routledge, London.
Larner, W. and Walters, W. (eds) (2004) *Global Governmentality: Governing International Spaces.* Routledge, London.
Marston, S., Woodward, K., and Jones, J.P. III (2007) Flattening ontologies of globalization: the Nollywood case. *Globalizations* 4 (1), 45–63.
Marston, S.A., Jones, J.P. III, and Woodward, K. (2005) Human geography without scale. *Transactions of the Institute of British Geographers* 30, 416–432.
Massey, D. (1991) A global sense of place. *Rethinking Marxism* 38.
McLuhan, M. (1964) *Understanding Media.* Mentor, New York.
McKittrick, K. and Woods, C. (eds) (2007) *Black Geographies and the Politics of Place.* Between the Lines, Toronto.
Monbiot, G. (2003) *The Age of Consent: A Manifesto for a New World Order.* Flamingo, London.

Mountz, A. (2006) Human smuggling and the Canadian state. *Canadian Foreign Policy* 13 (1): 59–80.

Mountz, A. and Hyndman J. (2006) Feminist approaches to the global intimate. *Women's Studies Quarterly* 34 (1&2), 446–463.

Mullings, B. (1999) Globalization, tourism and the international sex trade. In K. Kempadoo (ed.), *Sun, Sex and Gold: Tourism and Sex Work in the Caribbean*. Roman & Littlefield, London, pp. 55–80.

Munck, R. (2008) Globalization, governance and migration: an introduction. *Third World Quarterly* 29 (7), 1227–1246.

Nagar, R. (2006) Local and global. In S. Aitken and G. Valentine (ed.), *Approaches to Human Geography*. Sage, London.

Nagar, R., Lawson, V., McDowell, L., and Hanson, S. (2002) Locating globalization: feminist (re)readings of the subjects and spaces of globalization. *Economic Geography* 78 (3), 257–284.

Nagel, C. (2004) Questioning citizenship in an "age of migration." In J. O'Loughlin, L. Staeheli, and E. Greenberg (eds), *Globalization and Its Outcomes*. The Guilford Press, New York, pp. 231–252.

Nevins, J. (2002) *Operation Gatekeeper: The Rise of the "Illegal Alien" and the Remaking of the U.S.-Mexico Boundary*. Routledge, New York.

Olds, K. (2001) *Globalization and Urban Change*. Oxford University Press, Oxford.

Ohmae, K. (1990) *The Borderless World: Power and Strategy in The Interlinked Economy*. Harper Collins.

Ong, A. (1999) *Flexible Citizenship*. Duke University Press, Durham.

Peet, R. (2003) *Unholy Trinity: the IMF, World Bank and WTO*. Zed Books, London.

Pratt, G. (2004) *Working Feminism*. Edinburgh University Press, Edinburgh.

Radcliffe, S.A. (ed.) (2006) *Culture and Development in a Globalizing World; Geographies, Actors and Paradigms*. Routledge, London.

Roberts, S.M., Wright, S., and O'Neill, P. (2007) Good governance in the Pacific? Ambivalence and possibility. *Geoforum* 38, 967–984.

Sangtin, W. and Nagar, R. (2006) *Playing with fire: feminist thought and activism through seven lives in India. Foreword by Chandra Talpade Mohanty*. University of Minnesota Press, Minneapolis.

Sassen, S. (2006) *Territory, Authority, Rights: From Medieval to Global Assemblages*. Princeton University Press, Princeton.

Sassen, S. (1998) *Globalization and Its Discontents*. New Press, New York.

Sivanandan, A (2006) Race, terror and civil society. *Race & Class* 46 (1), 1–8.

Smith, N. (2003) *American Empire: Roosevelt's Geographer and the Prelude to Globalization*. University of California Press, Berkeley.

Smith, N. (1997) The satanic geographies of globalization: uneven development in the 1990s. *Public Culture* 10 (1), 169–189.

Sparke, M. (2005) *In the Space of Theory: Postfoundational Geographies of the Nation-State*. University of Minnesota Press, Minneapolis.

Sparke, M. (2003) American Empire and globalisation: postcolonial speculations on neocolonial enframing. *Singapore Journal of Tropical Geography* 24 (3), 373–389.

Sparke, M., Sidaway, J.D., Bunnell, T., and Grundy-Warr, C. (2004) Triangulating the borderless world: geographies of power in the Indonesia-Malaysia-Singapore Growth Triangle. *Transactions of the Institute of British Geographers* 29, 485–498.

Swyngedouw, E. (1997) Neither global, nor local: "glocalization" and the politics of scale. In K. Cox (ed.) *Spaces of Globalization: Perspectives on Economic Change*. Guilford, pp. 137–166.

Thrift, N. (2002) A hyperactive world. In R. Johnston, P. Taylor, and M. Watts (eds), *Geographies of Global Change: Remapping the World*. Blackwell, Oxford, pp. 29–42.

Tickell, A. and Peck, J. (2003) Making global rules: globalization or neoliberalization? In J. Peck, H. Wai-chung, and H. Yeung (eds), *Remaking the Global Economy: Economic-Geographical Perspectives*. Sage, London, pp. 163–181.

Tolia-Kelly, D. (2004) Materializing post-colonial geographies: examining the textural landscapes of migration in the South Asian home. *Geoforum* 35, 675–688.

Wainwright, J. (2007) Spaces of resistance in Seattle and Cancun. In H. Leitner, J. Peck, and E. Sheppard (eds), *Contesting Neoliberalism: Urban Frontiers*. Guilford, New York, pp. 179–203.

Washbourne, N. (2005) Globalisation/globality. In D. Atkinson, P. Jackson, D. Sibley, and N. Washbourne (eds), *Cultural Geography: A Critical Dictionary of Key Concepts*. IB Tauris, pp. 161–168.

Whitson, R. (2010) The reality of today has required us to change: negotiating gender through informal work in contemporary Argentina. *Annals of the Association of American Geographers* 100 (1), 159–181.

Wright, M. (2006) *Disposable Women and Other Myths of Global Capitalism*. Routledge, New York.

Young, E.M. (2004) Globalization and food security: novel questions in a novel context? *Development Studies* 4 (1), 1–21.

Chapter 21

World Cities
Part I

Carolyn Cartier

Introduction

Since its popularization in the 1980s, the idea of the world city has traveled widely through the literatures of urban geography, international planning and interdisciplinary urban studies into diverse public spheres, including urban governance and applied urban and regional planning. As a scholarly idea, the world city has generated both programmatic and innovative research, from the original formulation of the concept and a prescriptive research agenda, to contemporary scholarship that takes the world city idea in new theoretical directions. What is interesting about this sweep of literature is that the world city has been neither displaced nor fundamentally replaced by the idea of the global city or any other paradigm. The world city has continued to be infused with new ideas and approaches, the continuing focus of scholarly interest, investigation and intervention. This prevailing condition underscores the need to make intellectual sense of the large cities of the world, and to develop research approaches that allow understanding the differences among cities as well as general processes of urbanization. It also underscores a general trend in theoretical practice toward increasing complexity of ideas and interdisciplinary theorization.

The world city has also become a world phrase. It is often used interchangeably with "the global city" – as is "world economy" with "global economy" and in recognition of the processes of globalization – especially in the media and government and business arenas. The sheer ubiquity of the term would appear to signal widespread understanding and acceptance of its meanings, yet especially upon entering the public sphere, and not unlike globalization, the world city has also become a term that alternately transmits, brackets and elides different realities and values, and their cultural and political economic contexts. In the urban studies literature, world cities are not reliably the cities of the world. Rather than appraising all of the world's large cities, or reliably conveying the complexity of the world's largest cities, some uses of the world city offer snapshots or limited portrayals of urban realities and their economic conditions. To address the questions and problems that such different uses engender, this chapter considers the origins and development of the world city idea from three integrated perspectives: world cities as economic centers in historic perspective; definitions and changing approaches to research on world cities, including new theoretical formulations; and the idea of the world city in diverse public spheres, including cultural commentaries, governing discourses, and applied urban and regional planning. To illustrate, the discussion adopts a historical perspective that draws comparative attention to the Pacific and world cities in Asia.

Historic World Cities

In the evolution of the world economy, cities have played central roles in the emergence of the major regimes of accumulation: mercantilism, industrial capitalism and late or advanced capitalism (Knox et al. 2003). Many contemporary world cities trail long histories of local and regional accumulation with global reach, while others are relatively new on the scene. In the mercantile period of long-distance trade, from the 16th through the 18th centuries, port cities anchored international economic activity. Some mercantile cities continued to grow and restructure with the shifts to industrial capitalism to late capitalism. Among them, the settlement at London, with origins in the early medieval period, endured across the centuries. Tokyo originated in the 15th century, while the founding of New York City is bound up with the early European settlement in North America. By contrast, once key mercantile centers like Malacca and Venice are now better known as heritage cities. Modern ships demanded larger ports, and Malacca bequeathed its function as the major entrepôt on its eponymous strait to deepwater Singapore, which emerged in the early 19th century with the onset of the industrial period. China's great historic capitals and largest urban settlements, including Beijing, Hangzhou, Nanjing and Xi'an, are all inland cities; and while Hangzhou and Nanjing are commercial centers in the canal-laced water world of the Yangzi River delta, mercantile cities flourished relatively late on the Chinese maritime shore except for the far south China coast. The idea of a "global Shanghai," for example, owes to the rise of the 19th century trade between China and the West when Shanghai was opened as a result of the Opium War, and to the reopening of the People's Republic of China (PRC) to the world economy after 1978 (Wasserstrom 2009). Guangzhou, by contrast, in the south, was historically the main trading city "before European hegemony" (Abu-Lughod 1991), and even has monuments dating from Arabian trade with the Tang dynasty (618–907).

In the first general treatment of world cities, Peter Hall (1966) introduced the integrated functional conditions of eight leading world city-regions beginning with London and Paris, among six European city-regions, and ending with New York and Tokyo. His characterization defined the world city as an outstanding national center of economic activity and political, educational, and cultural institutions: "By what characteristics do we distinguish the world cities from other great centers of population and wealth? ... These cities are the national centers not merely of government but also of trade. Characteristically they are great ports, which distribute imported goods to all parts of their countries, and in return receive goods for export to the other nations of the world" (Hall 1966: 7). The city of mercantilism and industrial capitalism was a center of exchange, a place for the transfer of commodities as well as people and ideas whose migrations and diffusions in the early world economy necessarily circulated through port cities. The historic Asian port cities have been cosmopolitan ports, including Bombay, Hong Kong, Guangzhou, Macau, Malacca, Shanghai, Singapore and Tokyo, among others – while they were not region's primary centers of political rule. Historic Asian political capitals were often geographically distant from the port cities of diaspora and difference. Angkor, Beijing, Delhi and Kyoto were centers of commerce and cultural change while their overriding historical significance made them cities of political, religious and moral authority.

Before the concept of the world city, the literature of historic urbanism identified the "orthogenetic city" as "the place where religious, philosophical and literary specialists reflect, synthesize and create out of the traditional material new arrangements and developments that are felt by the people to be outgrowths of the old," by contrast to the "heterogenetic city," "a place of conflict of differing traditions, a center of heresy, heterodoxy and dissent, of interruption and destruction of ancient tradition, of rootlessness and anomie" (Redfield and Singer 1954: 58). From these views, Beijing and Kyoto were the political centers to Shanghai's and Tokyo's mercantile markets and their cultural mixing. Thus by comparison to the history of Western urbanization, in which the history of the city is inextricably bound up with the evolution of capitalism and liberalism, the history of the city in Asia is rooted in different trajectories of transformation. Tokyo became the political center of Japan only after the capital was moved from Kyoto in the 19th century. From the perspective of Beijing, the cities of Shanghai and Hong Kong – even as, together and alternately, they have served as international economic and financial centers of China across three centuries – are still brash commercial places that have no comparable claim on political authority and Chinese culture.

In the context of the shift to late capitalism associated with the world oil price shocks in 1973–1974, the eight city-regions at the focus of Hall's analysis entered a period of complex economic and geographical restructuring. Multinational corporations fundamentally reorganized their geographies of production: research and development and corporate headquarters concentrated in cities of the core, while manufacturing shifted offshore to lower cost locations in the semi-periphery and periphery. Services industries, including producer services, grew and diversified, supported by increased transport and telecommunications connectivity. With two exceptions, Rotterdam and Tokyo, Hall's original group of eight city-regions yielded seaport functions to specialized container ports, even as international trade and transport services industries, including insurance and logistics, continued to grow among producer services industries in world cities. In this process, the world city of the industrial era became the world city of late capitalism.

Local-global urban restructuring on the US West Coast demonstrates these shifts. Among contemporary world cities, Los Angeles has a major port adjacent to the Port of Long Beach, and the ports of Los Angeles and Long Beach are the busiest container ports in the US: based on 2007 data, together they would rank number five in the world (AAPA 2009). Yet the place of the Port of Los Angeles itself, annexed by the city in the early 20th century, forms a fist at the end of a narrow arm of territory along a freeway some 35 kilometers from the city. It was not an immigration port, and Los Angeles does not have coastal settlement origins. Los Angeles captured a port at a distance as an economic resource and, the youngest of major American cities, existed on a relatively small scale before the rise of the automobile. Indeed, the idea of Los Angeles as a coastal city is an imaginary geography in which the name of the city is conflated with the larger scale Los Angeles County mega-urban region: other municipalities (including Malibu and Santa Monica) occupy the Pacific shore along its range of latitude. The ports of Los Angeles and Long Beach grew with containerization, and the subsequent practice of double-stacking containers on rail cars (Erie 2004). The railroad system that serves Los Angeles and Long Beach funnels China's exports across the US to ports on the Gulf Coast and beyond. But Los Angeles and Long Beach import more than export and Southern California's once strong manufacturing economy has also diminished.

By contrast, the first major port of the West Coast, San Francisco, lost its role to containerization, which became established on the east side of the San Francisco Bay at the terminus of the transcontinental railroad in Oakland. But when double-stacking standardized in the 1980s, container handling at Oakland decreased because the tunnels through the Sierra Nevada, which separates central California from the nation, cannot accommodate the practice. The San Francisco Bay Area's continuing centrality in the world economy derives from the knowledge-based economy and the rise of Silicon Valley and the rounds of speculative capital that its local-global information and technology industries engender. Yet San Francisco's social and cultural conditions, including a tradition of liberal democratic values, trace to the history of the dockworkers' labor movement that made San Francisco a union town (Nelson 1988). Its large gay community also emerged in the male-gendered stevedoring culture of the historic port (Stryker and Van Buskirk 1996). Los Angeles never had a large union labor movement integrated with the life of the city. Its contemporary creative industries form a "gig economy," a project-to-project freelance workforce based in the global entertainment industry of Southern California, which is emblematic of urban entrepreneurialism under late capitalism (Harvey 1989). However, historical perspectives on cultural and social conditions have not been regularly incorporated in research on world cities.

Urban economic restructuring generated by the shift from industrial to late capitalism has resulted in the "global shift" of manufacturing and port facilities not only outside world cities, but also outside the trans-Atlantic core of the world economy. "In this sense," observes photographer/essayist Allan Sekula (1995: 134), "the port of Los Angeles was paradigmatic, both in its remoteness and in the artificiality of its construction. Unlike New York, Los Angeles never had to turn its back on the industrial waterfront. ... Developed from an inauspicious tidal estuary offering no natural shelter at the beginning of America's imperialist initiative in the Pacific ... here was a port that would be perpetually suspended between its hatred and fear of, and need for, the Asian continent on the other side of the Pacific." Indeed, at the global scale, manufacturing and container cargo trade has decisively shifted to the Asia Pacific. Based on container handling, only two among the 10 largest ports remain in Europe: Rotterdam and Hamburg (Containerisation International Yearbook 2009). If Dubai is included, eight of the top 10 ports are in Asia, of which four are in the PRC. Singapore and Shanghai are in the top two positions, followed by Hong Kong and Shenzhen in south China, Yingkou in north China, Busan of South Korea, and Kaohsiung, Taiwan. The cities of Tokyo and Yokohama, which form the world's largest conurbation (geographically conjoined, unlike Los Angeles and Long Beach), were also each among the world's most active ports while now together they do not rank among the top 15. Thus by contrast to the middle of the 20th century, when the Atlantic trade and western European cities dominated the world economy, the shift in the balance of international trade to the Asia Pacific points to the rise of different urbanizing regions in the world economy.

Changing Approaches to the World City

Research on world cities has widely incorporated insights from understanding the conditions of the world economy under late capitalism. The main research framework for world cities, the short "world city hypothesis," developed by John Friedmann (Friedmann and Wolff 1982; Friedmann 1986), outlined a networked hierarchy of major cities based on an adaptation of world systems theory (Wallerstein 1984). In its regionalization of the capitalist world economy, the world city hypothesis identified primary and secondary cities in the "core" and primary and secondary cities in the "semi-periphery." It defined world cities as centers of multinational corporations, international capital circulation and diversified services industries, and as destinations of international labor migration. Consequently, it also recognized uneven development in the context of the international division of labor and the intensification of urban problems under late capitalism, including increasing social inequality and spatial polarization of accumulation. Some treatments of the concept have examined a full range of issues faced by "world cities in a world system" (Knox and Taylor 1995), while the bulk of research increasingly focused on networks among multinational firms and the development of producer services industries.

The world city concept was extended by development of the idea of "the global city" (Sassen 1991), which distinguished the largest financial centers – London, New York and Tokyo – and their networked relations in the world economy. The global city concept differs in its focus on intensified concentration of producer services industries and diversification of services industry products that serve multinational corporations. In the literature, global cities are effectively a subset of world cities, while the sheer popularity of "global" leads to the two terms, world city and global city, being used interchangeably. Research on the world city system and the global city have commonly prioritized two cities, London and New York, as centralizing nodes where producer services industries concentrate and coordinate decision-making among networked firms, "the command and control centers" of the world economy (Taylor 2003). The global city is also defined by increasing polarization of the workforce, skewed between professionals in highly compensated producer services jobs and low-skilled workers and migrants in low-paying service jobs, which often serve the professional classes. Yet as Doreen Massey (1999: 120–121) points out, the global city also prioritizes defining cities primarily as centers of financial power. Other cities are as large as or larger than London and New York, and different networks characterize banking and financial services in Islamic regions. There are also other forms and conceptualizations of power, as well as non-hierarchical network configurations.

Thus one of the outstanding issues in the scholarship on world cities is the degree to which research has taken up the range of topics presented in the original framework. Has the scholarship addressed urban inequality? To what degree has it represented all major cities, or the worlds of all peoples in the city? Three conditions have structured most of the research. First, the world city framework, from its inception, excluded cities in the economic "periphery," no matter their size or national significance. The coverage blanked out Africa except Johannesburg, among other regions. In specifying cities by networks and levels of economic development, oriented to the top tier – in which "top" itself is a representation and acceptance of financial industry growth and power – research disproportionately focused on high growth and growth-oriented economic conditions. Second, the framework bracketed emerging capitalisms in post-socialist economies. It focused on capitalist market economies in the core and semi-periphery, thus pre-setting conditions for neglect of world city formation in China, which reopened to the world economy in 1978. Third, a consensus early emerged on what are the top cities in the hierarchy and other networked "growth cities" such that "the central facet of world cities literature has been to rank cities according to their disproportionate geo-economic power in the world-system ..." (Beaverstock *et al.* 1999: 445). As a consequence, the scholarship's wider readership has more often served normative economic interests than perspectives on equity and social justice, and has had the effect of reaffirming the notion of the greater importance of cities in the "capitalist West."

Because world systems theory provided a model of demonstrating inequalities between the core and the periphery, limitations of the research on world cities has become a concern. Based on rankings by "geo-economic power," one of the outcomes of the world cities research has been to effectively reconstruct the priority of former colonial metropolises that world systems theory sought to displace. The emphasis on the centrality of London and New York resonates as if an enduring paean to the capitals of trans-Atlantic capitalism. Even world/global cities studies that include Tokyo have regularly concluded that Tokyo is not comparable to London and New York by several measures, including its relatively low receipt of international capital, greater state-industry relations, larger degree of integration with the national economy, less extreme wealth polarization, and significantly less immigration (Douglass 2000; Hill and Kim 2000). Among differences in Chinese city-regions, including Hong Kong and the Pearl River delta and Shanghai and the Yangzi River delta, many manufacturing industries are moving inland rather than offshore, resulting in urban and regional production/consumption networks (Cartier 2009). Thus empirical realities outside the traditional "core" are pointing to some different conditions and questions about the dynamics of world cities.

Stepping back to analyze world cities research in the context of urban political economy allows a broader assessment of its changing directions. The empirical research on networked producer services – financial services, including accountancy, investment banking, law and insurance; the knowledge-based economy and creative industries, including advertising and software; and a transport industry, especially seaport and air transport logistics – especially engages normative urban planning and business interests. In the period of late capitalism, these industries are associated with positive economic growth. Late capitalism has also been characterized by restructuring of the role of the state at both national and urban scales with consequences for reduced state funding, which compels cities to seek and secure fiscal resources and jobs growth, compete for capital investment, and provide business-oriented urban infrastructure. This "neoliberalization" of the urban economy especially pressures governing interests to promote growth-oriented services industries and, in many countries, decrease social services (Harvey 2005; Hackworth 2007). But most of the world cities research does not consider the effects of neoliberalization on the urban economy (Brenner and Keil 2006). This neglect of the changing role of the state also hinders adequate comparison with cities in Asia, where the state remains comparatively strong in both economic and social spheres.

Focus on the contemporary economic power of major cities also distances the world city concept from engagement with historical processes of urban formation. For example, considerable research on gentrification in urban geography does not appear in association with research on world cities, even as the places at stake – major growth cities – are regularly the same. Within the range of important geographical scholarship on urbanization, research on the world city has also generally neglected the core Marxian analytics and associated processes of historic capital accumulation. By giving more attention to economic growth than problems engendered by uneven growth, studies of world cities reproduce language of competition and economic power, as well as promote its urban symbolic forms – often in spectacular urban redevelopment and "starchitecture". New skyscraper construction has also predominantly shifted to Asia, where the region's world cities compete to build the tallest high rises. Shanghai has built the Shanghai World Financial Center, at 492 meters, to symbolize its renewed position as the commercial center of China. The two tallest buildings in Hong Kong are the International Financial Center, at 414 meters, and the Hong International Commerce Center at 484 meters. The latter and the Shanghai World Financial Center are, at the end of the first decade of the 21st century, among the 10 tallest buildings in the world, of which six, if Taipei is included, are in China. Meanwhile, the world cities literature continues to return to London because the City of London itself promotes a London-centric view of the global business world (Massey 2007). Such discursive reification of the city contributes to understanding why the world cities research has tended to neglect the uneven landscape of development and the realities of uneven development for people living at the margins.

Partly as a consequence of these limitations, human geographers have developed different approaches to the world city. Among leading contributions, scholarship produced by the Open University group has established lines of inquiry that differentially query the idea of "world" and the recognition of different worlds or experiences within the city (e.g. Massey *et al.* 1999). These perspectives concern diverse major cities, not just ones that rank high on a global list of producer services. A related project is based on the idea of "ordinary cities", which reclaims the intellectual ground gained through post-structural and post-colonial theory. Jennifer Robinson explains how perspectives on "ordinary cities:"

> ... move beyond the divisive categories (such as Western, Third World, African, South American, South-East Asian, or post-socialist cities) and hierarchies (such as global, alpha or world cities) ... [to] challenge the colonial and neo-imperial power relations that remain deeply embedded in the assumptions and practices of contemporary urban theory. (Robinson 2006: 2)

The idea of the ordinary city upholds examining the social and economic differences that make all cities relevant, complicated and powerful, thus revealing their comparative potential irrespective of economic categorization. Among monographs on single cities, Massey's (2007) *World City* theoretically builds bridges between the world city literature, post-structural approaches and processes of neoliberalization, while demonstrating the elite project to produce London as the world's leading financial capital. Outside the world city rubric, Harvey's (2003) historical materialist account of Paris also grounds the city in the daily life of social and economic differences otherwise ignored in the normative literature.

Publics and the World City

The idea of the ordinary city challenges research on world cities to enliven the city and reintegrate experiences of urban citizens. One step toward this turn is to ask, who represents the city? Normative writings on world cities, and especially governing, media and planning discourses, often treat the city as a subject or agent itself (historically gendered female, i.e. referring to cities, like ships, as "she"). Such writings do not reliably recognize that the public for which the city stands regularly comprises diverse publics; that the population of a city does not constitute *the* public or one public sphere but diverse public interests contending to shape urban futures. However, the interests that ultimately prevail regularly reflect power relations brokered by urban elites who disproportionately repeat universalizing notions of the city, often in saleable terms. Urban institutions seek to promote themselves by inventing and repeating images of would-be city significance. Such discursive turns then emerge in incongruous promotional pitches, such as the notion of Los Angeles as "the capital of the Pacific Rim" (LAWAC 2008) even as regional conditions of the city's international division of labor are bound up with the US southern border and Mexico. Research on world cities generally endeavors to distinguish among ways of representing the city and what institutions represent or speak for the city, yet the normative empirical literature, and consumption of it by political economic elites, rarely adopts a post-structural analytic and thus risks reproducing unproblematized discourses of growth and power.

Public and media discourses representing the world city contribute to the formation of urban expectations about how cities should function, what they should offer, how they should be built, and how their environments should appear. More than elite boosterism, city governments now develop media-oriented profiles through entrepreneurial "branding" exercises as platforms for advancing urban competitiveness. Such urban growth strategies dovetail with planned economic development in Asian cities. Among them, the government of Hong Kong branded Hong Kong as "Asia's world city" (http://www.brandhk.gov.hk) in advance of

Hong Kong becoming a Special Administrative Region of China in 1997. More than discourse, the local state in Hong Kong actively promotes and regulates the economy, which belies its regular international ranking as the "freest economy in the world" (http://www.heritage.org/Index/). For example, in 2009, the Hong Kong Monetary Authority ordered local banks to compensate buyers of the collapsed Lehman Brothers' "minibonds" (HKSFC 2009), which were not disclosed as risky derivatives. But the normative literature on world cities tends not to problematize state-society relations, thereby working in thrall to the ups and downs of the financial industry rather than generating research that explains the complexity of urban economies or questions the sustainability of industries based on speculative capital.

The use of the world city as an urban planning model is the clearest indication of its transference to realms of applied policy interests. In China under reform, widespread redevelopment of existing cities and the building of new ones – urbanization itself – serves as the material basis of economic growth, and in the 1990s Chinese national planning prioritized the redevelopment of Beijing and Shanghai as leading world cities, especially through large scale, spectacular urban development projects – through the Olympics in Beijing, the Pudong New District in Shanghai and the 2010 Shanghai World Expo. The plan for Pudong, which was opened as a special economic zone in 1990, drew from a suite of urban design proposals from international consultants (Olds 2001). The Shanghai World Financial Center is located there in addition to the Shanghai Tower project, which is projected for completion at 632 meters and among a new class of super tall buildings. In south China on the Hong Kong border, the new city of Shenzhen was originally opened in 1980 as a special economic zone for export-oriented manufacturing – a semi-periphery for the restructuring core – while by the 1990s it restructured and planned a new city center as the basis for anchoring its developmental trajectory as a world city (Cartier 2002). The new Shenzhen city center at Futian hosts a suite of international-standard buildings, while its overall landscape represents the rectilinear form of historic Chinese imperial capitals – as if reaching to claim the cultural-political symbolism of ruling China. By the mid-2000s, Shenzhen's ambitious built environment led to the establishment of the Shenzhen-Hong Kong Bi-City Architecture Biennale in 2005. The Dutch architect Rem Koolhaus, whose firm OMA designed the instantly iconic Chinese Central Television headquarters in Beijing, presided over the 2009 Shenzhen-Hong Kong biennale as if the architect of a megacity, proposing once unthinkable dialogue about integrating Hong Kong and Shenzhen. Different Japanese interpretations of the world city have also been adapted into urban economic planning in Tokyo (Saito and Thornley 2003), which underscores how applied planning uses of the world city diverge from scholarly approaches to the global city.

Contemporary paradigms in planning and development for the world's largest cities are moving beyond the world city or global city to the perspective of the megacity and the mega-region (Jones and Douglass 2008; Ross 2009). Also termed mega-urban regions, polycentric urban regions and global city-regions, the mega-region has been adopted within international institutions including the United Nations as a basis for identifying, comparing and planning the development of the world's largest city-regions. The definitional basis for the megacity does not, like the global city, prioritize producer services, and differs from that of the world city in its fundamental recognition that contemporary large cities have developed functionally and territorially beyond their city limits through a multitude of networked processes that connect with their wider region as well as the world. The perspective also underscores the need for coordinating infrastructure between cities in a region, and the significance of complex metropolitan regions in the world economy as economic units (Storper 1997). The megacities perspective incorporates concerns about uneven development and social polarization, while its applied planning outlook prioritizes the regional scale and so may also overlook the realities of daily life for people on the margins. Defined by the United Nations as cities with over 10 million inhabitants, in 2005 the world had 20 megacities, of which 11 are in Asia, including Shanghai and Beijing (UN 2005). The Tokyo area remains the largest at 35 million, followed by New York-Newark and Mexico City. By 2015, Mumbai (Bombay) is predicted to take second place at nearly 22 million, when Guangzhou, at the heart of the Pearl River delta in south China, is projected to join the list. Beijing and Shanghai (numbers 18 and 7, respectively, on the 2005 list) are now under government mega-region planning. The population of the Pearl River delta, as a mega-urban region including Hong Kong, Macau and Shenzhen, is already estimated at over 35 million, which underscores its present, past and future as a different kind of globalizing city-region between China and the world.

References

AAPA (American Association of Port Authorities). (2009). Online: http://aapa.files.cms-plus.com/Statistics/WORLDPORTRANKINGS2007.xls (accessed 1st November, 2009).
Abu-Lughod, J. (1991) *Before European Hegemony*. Oxford University Press, Oxford.
Beaverstock, J.V., Smith, R. G., and Taylor, P.J. (1999) A roster of world cities. *Cities* 16 (6), 445–458.
Brenner, N. and Keil, R. (eds) (2006) *The Global Cities Reader*. Routledge, London.
Cartier, C. (2002) Transnational urbanism in the reform-era Chinese city. *Urban Studies* 39 (9), 1513–1532.
Cartier, C. (2009) Production/consumption and the Chinese city/region. *Urban Geography* 30 (4), 368–390.
Containerisation International Yearbook (2009) http://www.informacargo.com/ite/article.htm?articleId=20017599573 (accessed 15th October 2010).
Douglass, M. (2000) Mega-urban regions and world city formation. *Urban Studies* 37 (12), 2315–2335.
Erie, S.P. (2004) *Globalizing L.A.* Stanford University Press, Stanford.
Friedmann, J. and Wolff, G. (1982) World city formation. *International Journal of Urban and Regional Research* 6 (3), 309–344.
Friedmann, J. (1986) The world city hypothesis. *Development and Change* 17 (1), 69–83.
Hackworth, J. (2007) *The Neoliberal City*. Cornell University Press, Ithaca, New York.
Hall, P. (1966) *The World Cities*. McGraw-Hill, New York.
Harvey, D. (1989) From managerialism to entrepreneurialism. *Geografiska Annaler, Series B* 71, 3–17.
Harvey, D. (2005) *A Brief History of Neoliberalism*. Oxford University Press, Oxford.

Harvey, D. (2003) *Paris, Capital of Modernity*. Routledge, New York.
Hill, R.C. and Kim, J.W. (2000) Global cities and developmental states. *Urban Studies* 37 (12), 2167–2195.
HKSFC (Hong Kong Securities and Futures Commission) (2009) SFC, HKMA and 16 banks reach agreement on minibonds. Hong Kong. Online: http://www.sfc.hk/sfcPressRelease/EN/sfcOpenDocServlet?docno=09PR100 (accessed 15th October 2010).
Jones, G.W. and Douglass, M. (2008) *Mega-urban Regions in Pacific Asia*. NUS Press, Singapore.
Knox, P.L. and Taylor, P.J. (1995) (eds) *World Cities in a World System*. Cambridge University Press, Cambridge.
Knox, P.L., Agnew, J.A. and McCarthy, L. (2003) *The Geography of the World Economy*, 4th edn. Oxford University Press, Oxford.
LAWAC (Los Angeles World Affairs Council) (2008) S.B. Sample, *Los Angeles: The Capital of the Pacific Rim*. Los Angeles, November 10.
Massey, D. (2007) *World City*. Polity Press, Cambridge.
Massey, D., Allen, J. and Pile, S., (1999) (eds) *City Worlds*. Routledge, London.
Nelson, B. (1988) *Workers on the Waterfront*. University of Illinois Press, Urbana.
Olds, K. (2001) *Globalization and Urban Change*. Oxford University Press, Oxford.
Redfield, R. and Singer, M.B. (1954) The cultural role of cities. *Economic Development and Cultural Change* 3, 53–73.
Robinson, J. (2006) *Ordinary Cities*. Routledge, London.
Ross, C.L. (2009) *Megaregions: Planning for Global Competitiveness*. Island Press, Washington, D.C.
Saito, A. and Thornley, A. (2003) Shifts in Tokyo's world city status and the urban planning response. *Urban Studies* 40 (4) 665–685.
Sassen, S. (1991) *The Global City*. Princeton University Press, Princeton.
Sekula, A. (1995) *Fish Story*. Witte de With, Rotterdam, Richter Verlag, Düsseldorf.
Storper, M. (1997) *The Regional World*. Guilford Press, New York.
Stryker, S. and Van Buskirk, J. (1996) *Gay by the Bay*. San Francisco Chronicle Books, San Francisco.
Taylor, P.J. (2003) *World City Network*. Routledge, London.
UN (United Nations) (2005) World urbanization prospects: fact sheet 7, mega-cities. Online: www.un.org/esa/population/publications/.../2005WUP_FS7.pdf. Accessed 1 Nov. 2009.
Wallerstein, I. (1984) *The Politics of the World Economy*. Cambridge University Press, Cambridge.
Wasserstrom, J. (2009) *Global Shanghai*. Routledge, New York.

Further Reading

Arndt, G. and Chua, B.H. (eds) (2009) *Port Cities in Asia and Europe*. Routledge, London.
Basu, D.K. (ed.) (1985) *The Rise and Growth of the Colonial Port Cities in Asia*. University Press of America, Lanham.
Broeze F. (1997) *Gateways of Asia*. Kegan Paul International, New York.
Cartier, C. (2001) *Globalizing South China*. Blackwell, Oxford.
Cybriwsky, R. (1998) *Tokyo*. John Wiley & Sons, New York.
Ginsburg, N., Koppel, B., and McGee, T. G. (eds) (1991) *The Extended Metropolis*. University of Hawai'i Press, Honolulu.
Gugler, J. (ed.) (2004) *World Cities Beyond the West*. Cambridge University Press, Cambridge.
Haneda, M. (2009) *Asian Port Cities, 1600–1800*. National University of Singapore Press, Singapore.

Lo, C.P. (1992) *Hong Kong*. Bellhaven Press, London.
McGee, T.G. (1967) *The Southeast Asian City*. Frederick A. Praeger, New York.
Meyer, D. (2000) *Hong Kong as a Global Metropolis*. Cambridge University Press, New York.
Scott, A. (ed.) (2002) *Global City-Regions*. Oxford University Press, Oxford.
Wu, F. (2006) *Globalization and the Chinese City*. Routledge, London.
Wu, H. (2005) *Remaking Beijing*. University of Chicago Press, Chicago.

Chapter 22

World Cities
Part II

Paul L. Knox

Introduction

It might reasonably be claimed that few, if any, of the world's cities are "ordinary:" each has its own distinctive built environment, its special socio-cultural attributes, its distinctive economic base, its unique historic legacies and cultural identity, and its singular idiosyncrasies. But beyond these distinctive attributes (many of which can be accounted for by a particular combination of general processes and local responses), urban geographers have always recognized that the economic, cultural, political and social processes that lend distinctiveness to individual cities also operate between cities, so that urban geography must also be concerned with recognizing and understanding the interdependence among cities as they fill specialized roles in complex and ever-changing regional geographies.

In global context, some cities are *extra*ordinary because of the degree of their key roles in organizing influencing, and integrating space and society beyond their own national boundaries. The term "world cities" is often applied to these places. The term was first used almost a century ago by the pioneer thinker and writer on city and regional planning, Patrick Geddes (1915), in a chapter on "World Cities and City Regions." A half-century later, Peter Hall began his comparative study of *The World Cities* (1966) by observing that: "There are certain great cities, in which a quite disproportionate part of the world's most important business is conducted." Another half-century or so further on, and the term has become a routine – if sometimes loosely used and occasionally contested – term in the lexicon of urban studies. The fact that the term pre-dates contemporary globalization processes points to the changing nature of spatial interdependence. In the first stages of capitalism, the key roles of world cities involved the organization of trade and the execution of colonial, imperial, and geopolitical strategies. Among the world cities of the

The Wiley Blackwell Companion to Human Geography, First Edition.
Edited by John A. Agnew and James S. Duncan.
© 2011 John Wiley & Sons, Ltd. Published 2016 by John Wiley & Sons, Ltd.

seventeenth century were London, Amsterdam, Antwerp, Genoa, Lisbon, and Venice. In the eighteenth century, Paris, Rome, and Vienna also became world cities, while Antwerp and Genoa became less influential. With the onset of the Industrial Revolution, the likes of Berlin, Chicago, and Manchester became world cities, while Venice and Lisbon became less influential. Such changes fit broadly with the theoretical approach of economic historians like Braudel (1984), Arrighi (1994) and Wallerstein (1984), with the ascendance of certain cities associated with successive hegemonic nation-states.

Taylor *et al.* (2009a) have tested this association through an analysis of cities' explosive growth spurts (defined as an annual growth of 1 percent or more over a 50-year period) between 1500 C.E. and 2005. Altogether, over 200 cities experienced such a growth spurt, and the frequency and magnitude of the growth spurts were found to increase with the growth of the modern world-system. The overall pattern of urban demographic growth spurts broadly reflects three hegemonic cycles: a Dutch cycle in the fifteenth and sixteenth centuries and a British cycle in the eighteenth and nineteenth centuries overlapping with an American cycle in the nineteenth and twentieth centuries. Significantly, the pattern also showed that explosive city growth spurts tended to be front-loaded in hegemonic cycles, strongly suggesting that certain cities have been the drivers of economic and political hegemony. Taylor *et al.* take this as support for Jane Jacobs' insistence (1984) that cities are the fundamental context for economic innovation and growth: "cities are the engines of economic growth and therefore they are where hegemony can be and is created." There were, however, numerous cases of explosive demographic growth in the twentieth century that would not fit this interpretation. The explanation is "over-urbanization," a result of the timing of demographic transition relative to economic development such that large increases in population have been generated well in advance of any significant levels of rural economic development or urban economic growth. As more affluent core countries have put up barriers to immigration, the only option for the growing numbers of impoverished rural residents in many peripheral countries has been to move to towns and cities – out of desperation and hope rather than being drawn by jobs and opportunities. Because these migration streams have been composed disproportionately of teenagers and young adults, exceptionally high rates of natural population increase have led to explosive demographic growth and thus to the emergence of mega-cities, rather than world cities.

Meanwhile, the capitalist world-economy entered a new phase in the 1970s with the first wave of corporate globalization, led by manufacturing conglomerates whose global reach had the triple objectives of reducing labor costs, outflanking national labor unions, and increasing overseas market penetration. In the 1980s, as the globalization of manufacturing spread and the new information economy began to grow, the leading firms in advanced business services – accountancy, advertising, banking, and law – established global networks of their own in order to serve their most important clients. At the same time, the shift from Fordist mass production and mass consumption to the competitive consumption and the aestheticization of everyday life associated with "romantic capitalism," (Campbell 1987) the "dream economy," (Jordan 2007) and the "society of the spectacle" (Debord 1967) significantly increased the importance of design services – architecture, product design, graphic design, fashion, interior design, and design consultancies – in facilitating the circulation and accumulation of capital, helping to stimulate consumption through product differentiation aimed at particular market segments (Knox 2010). Design professionals, along with the employees of advanced business services, came to be key members of an influential new class fraction, the transnational capitalist class (Sklair 2005), people who operate transnationally (whether or not they actually travel) as a normal part of their working lives.

To some observers, the shifts involved in the rise of global capitalism – "super-capitalism," in Robert Reich's terminology (2007) – amount to an epochal change: what Ulrich Beck (2006; Beck and Lau, 2005) has argued as the onset of a second modernity, an emergent era of re-modernization, this time at the global scale and involving cosmopolitanism, transnationalism, and supranationalism. Interestingly, these trends are generally at odds with the top-down managed capitalism and planned modernization of the first modernity. More significantly from the perspective of world cities, whereas economic and urban development during the first modernity was framed by competitiveness within closed geographic systems (national states) that were, in turn, competing with one another, urban development at the beginning of the second modernity is subject to competitiveness at the global scale. Meanwhile, in attempts to recapture some control over the scale of the new economic logic and its social, cultural, and environmental implications, national governments have become increasingly collaborative, supranational entities have emerged, many institutions have extended their focus from a national to an international frame of reference, and many local and regional organizations have become involved in cross-border collaborative networks of one sort or another.

Since the mid-1970s, the key roles of world cities have been concerned less with the orchestration of trade and the deployment of imperial power and more with transnational corporate organization; international banking and finance; fashion, design and the media; and supranational government and the work of international agencies. World cities have become the sites of extraordinary concentrations of activities associated with organizing the finance and investment and creating and managing flows of information and cultural products that collectively underpin the economic and cultural globalization of the world, including processes of neocolonialism and postcolonialism. Meanwhile, as Allen Scott points out, one consequence of the growth and development of the new economy (or, as he suggests calling it, the new cognitive-cultural economy) has been the resurgence of a distinctive group of metropolitan areas that are now forging ahead on the basis of their command of knowledge-based and creative industries, their ability to exploit globalization to their own advantage, and the selective revitalization of their internal fabric of land use and built form. In these metropolises, "distinctive clusters of firms in this new economy congregate together in specialized industrial districts within the fabric of urban space where they typically also exist cheek by jowl in association with a range of allied service suppliers and dependent subcontractors" (Scott 2008: 554). These specialized districts act as "creative fields," distinctive settings rich with innovative energies, dense interpersonal contacts and informal information exchanges. As Scott observes, much of the information that circulates in this manner is little more than random noise. "Some of it, however, is occasionally of direct use, and discrete bits of it – both tacit and explicit – sometimes combine together in ways that provoke new insights and sensibilities about production processes, product design, markets and so on" (Scott 2008: 555). In this way, the creative-field effects within metropolises with concentrations of new-economy industries facilitate individually small-scale but cumulatively significant processes of learning and innovation, underpinning their resurgence within the global economy. Cities that have been most caught up in these processes have not only experienced profound changes in their economic and demographic profiles, but have also undergone dramatic transformations in their physical appearance. These include gentrification, branded neighborhoods, large-scale urban regeneration projects, iconic buildings, and "semiotic districts" specializing in goods and services with high semiotic content: flagship stores, megastores, shops-in-shops, high-end restaurants, cafés, art galleries, antique stores, and luxury retail shops.

World cities thus provide an interface between the global and the local. They contain the economic, cultural, and institutional apparatus that channels national and provincial resources into the global economy, and that transmits the impulses of globalization back to national and provincial centers.

World Cities as a Research Topic

Academic interest in world cities was ignited by John Friedmann (1986, 1995; Friedmann and Wolff 1982), who drew on traditional concepts of hierarchies of regional urban systems and introduced the idea of a global urban system in which a select hierarchy of cities had come to operate as the command and control centres of global corporations in their management of the new international division of labor. This notion of world cities had intuitive appeal and soon came to dominate the literature. Also inflential was Saskia Sassen's refinement of this approach, emphasizing the distinctiveness of "global" cities at the very top of the international hierarchy, where concentrations of financial, professional, and creative firms have led to extraordinary concentrations of corporate power and influence within the world economy (Sassen 1991, 1994, 1995). An extensive array of literature soon developed around world cities and their roles in globalization processes (for example, Beaverstock *et al.* 2000; Knox and Taylor 1995; Taylor 1997, 2001; Sassen 2002). For synoptic reviews of the world cities literature, see Brenner and Keil (2006); Short (2004); and Short and Kim (1999).

Research on the external relations of world cities has been facilitated by the Globalisation and World Cities (GaWC) research network, founded by Peter Taylor with a web portal (http://www.lboro.ac.uk/gawc/group.html) hosted by the Department of Geography at Loughborough University. Much of the work by Tayor and colleagues has been set within the framework of Wallerstein's world-systems theory. Sassen's concept of the "global city," meanwhile, has prompted a large amount of research on the internal attributes and dynamics of the cities at the top of the global urban system. Central to Sassen's argument are the agglomerative tendencies and dynamics of advanced business services and design services that result in the distinctive clusters and districts that are the locus of influence and innovation within global cities. In addition to the neo-Marshallian logic of external economies, these clusters are reinforced by some important aspects of sociality: personal interaction with clients, after-work drinking and dining in settings where key professionals can learn about new opportunities, review one another's products and practices, and keep abreast of the internal politics of one another's firms (Kennedy 2005). This aspect of global-city sociality tallies with research in economic sociology, which has emphasized the notion of "embedded firms" in networks of economic, social and cultural relations (Granovetter 1985; Crewe 1996). This perspective views economic activity as embedded in networks and institutions that are socially constructed and culturally defined and acknowledges the importance of "untraded interdependencies" among firms, emphasizing the various informal arrangements and practices and tacit knowledge that are not fully quantifiable but nonetheless enhance innovation and creativity through networks of firms and actors.

Another crucial socio-cultural dimension of global cities to have emerged from research concerns their symbolic cultural capital. Global cities derive a kind of monopoly rent as a result of the image they acquire from the particular concentrations of products, business services and firms they are associated with: advertising and finance in New York; architecture, insurance, and banking in London; media and entertainment in Los Angeles; haute couture in Paris; logistics in Singapore; design in Milan; and so on. Favorable images, reinforced and amplified by the media (Doel and Hubbard 2002; Krause and Petro 2003), create entry barriers for competing places, while the wealth generated in successful cities helps them to become thriving settings for high-end consumption, establishing them, in turn as global tastemakers, the "valorisation of milieu" extending to all sorts of products and activities through branding that simply invokes the city's name (Molotch 2002; Breward and Gilbert 2006). The positive images of global cities relate, of course, to their "front regions:" the financial districts, cultural quarters, design districts, entertainment districts, and semiotic districts that are the principal settings for activities with international connections. Less well publicized and documented are the "back regions" of global cities – their gentrified neighborhoods, neobohemias, and "ordinary" neighborhoods – and the associated issues of difference, diversity and inequality (Fainstein 2001; Hamnett 2002; Massey 2007).

Meanwhile, in an increasingly interconnected world, many "ordinary" cities have developed certain attributes of world- or global-cityness: settings for innovative production clusters in the fields of information and communications technology, medical engineering, biotechnology, the media industry, and for minor concentrations of transnational corporate organization; international banking and finance; fashion, design and the media; and supranational non-profit and governmental agencies. Amin and Graham (1997) suggest that the fundamental commonalities rest on the "multiplexity" of contemporary urban life, involving four main dimensions: the emergence of "relational proximity" (the combination of intense face-to-face interactions and mediated flows of communication and contact via technical media to the broader city and beyond); the development of dense clusters, quarters and districts of knowledge and knowledgeable people, within agglomerations of specialized firms, or within a critical mass of cultural creativity; the increasing heterogeneity and cultural hybridity of urban populations; and the increasing concentration and complexity of institutional assets in cities. Density and diversity are certainly key to the "creative buzz" associated with the social production of knowledge and diffusion of innovation in world- and global cities. As Jane Jacobs pointed out long ago (1961), density and diversity generate serendipity, unexpected encounters and "new combinations" that can lead to innovation. Peter Hall, in *Cities in Civilization* (1998) has written about the importance of a creative milieu to the "golden ages" of world cities. Such creative milieux, he observes, are quintessentially chaotic but culturally many-sided: rich in fundamental knowledge and competence, with good communications internally, through close physical proximity, and also externally. The synergy comes from variation and diversity among activities that are often small-scale (Hall 2000).

Conceptual and Empirical Problems

Framed around the seminal work of Friedmann and Sassen, the world city literature has been vulnerable to critique. The focus on finance, advanced business services and related command functions led to a relative neglect of other important economic processes and to an emphasis on control functions at the expense of interdependence and complexity. The focus on global cities and the big world cities of the "Global North," meanwhile, led to a relative neglect of the great majority of cities around the world. As a result, smaller cities' roles in globalization processes have been undertheorized (Bell and Jayne 2009). For Robinson (2002), the world cities literature pushed "ordinary" cities "off the map" and led to the idea of world cities as a "regulating fiction," a standard toward which other cities were tacitly assumed to aspire.

A more prosaic problem has been the lack of sound, comprehensive, comparable data with which to test and develop the hypotheses associated with world cities (Short *et al.* 1996). This problem has been compounded by conceptual confusion and uncertainty about just what constitutes a world city or a global city. In some studies, data are deployed to confirm world city status rather than a city's status being defined by criteria and then tested through data. Confusing permutations of proxy variables and a seemingly infinite number of rankings, typologies and hierarchical classifications entered the world cities literature. These rankings and classifications were grist to the mill of the urban entrepreneurialism (Harvey 1989) and city branding (Donald, Kofman and Kevin 2009) in the neoliberal political economy associated with globalization (Harvey 2007; Brenner and Theodore 2002). They were also rooted in the legacy of central place theory and the habitual thinking of systems of cities in terms of structured hierarchies (Alderson and Beckfield, 2004). As Stefan Krätke and Peter Taylor point out (2004), there is a geographical complexity to globalization that cannot be reduced to a simple "hierarchy" of world cities functioning as global business service providers. There are indeed multiple globalizations within the business service sector and, by implication, beyond this sector. It follows that the world city system is not just a collection of mini-Londons and little New Yorks: "All world cities will have mixtures of cutting edge economic functions but these need not just be advanced producer services. The key is to find economic niches but without being vulnerable to economic specialization" (Taylor *et al.* 2009b). The key to analyzing and understanding cities in this context is to use relational data to investigate patterns of interdependence within complex, fluid networks.

World Cities in Global Networks

The more recent literature on world cities has emphasized this approach, recognizing that a key point about contemporary globalization is that it is based upon trans-state processes, with firms, not cities, as the principal agents of change (Dicken *et al.* 2001; Friedmann 2001; Sassen 2002; Smith 2003; Taylor 2004). The seminal conceptual framework here derives from Manuel Castells' hugely influential *The Rise of the Network Society* (1996). Castells argues that the dominant spatial form before the onset of globalization was a space of places, a geography that is being overwritten as new enabling technologies – the combination of communication and computing industries – have led to a new, variable geometry within a global of space of flows of capital, information, and people. This leads to a search for connectivities and complementarities within networks of cities. As Taylor *et al.* (2009b) emphasize, cities exist in city networks and networks can only exist through collective complementarities; cities are both cooperative and competitive, growing through relations with one another but not by eliminating one another. They also emphasize that the networks are complex and multi-layered. One set of networks, for example, is constituted by the infrastructures – airline, telephonic, internet, etc. – that make Castells' Network Society possible. Another is constituted by the relations among and between firms conducting business with a global reach; and another still is constituted by the social as well as the economic relations within the clusters of activities in the cities that constitute the nodes and hubs through which Network Society is routinely organized.

This last dimension has prompted Taylor *et al.* (2009b) to invoke another seminal conceptual framework: Jane Jacobs' (1984) emphasis on cities as engines of economic development. Jacobs argued that economic growth resides principally in innovative urban settings, where new, creative work creates new export markets (the export multiplier effect) while imports are replaced through imitation and improvisation (the import-replacement multiplier effect). In sum, economic growth is generated *in* cities and expanded and diffused *through* cities, via interlocking networks of infrastructure, firms, and individual actors. Following this logic, Taylor and his associates treat network relations as generic to cities and hierarchical relations as contingent: city competitiveness varies in space and time with competitive relations being stronger locally and in cyclical downturns. Thus, rather than interpreting change as a matter of cities "rising" or "falling" in a global urban hierarchy, they view cities as changing connective configurations in transnational networks and flows of knowledge, capital, people, etc.

Operationalizing this approach, Taylor *et al.* make the assumption that the more important a firm's office, the more working flows it will generate. Aggregating all potential working flows for all firms located in a city then provides an estimate of its relations with other cities; when this is done for all cities, it reflects the lineaments of the world city network (Taylor, Catalano and Walker, 2002). Using data on the office networks of global service firms in accountancy, advertising, banking/finance, insurance, law, and management consultancy, Taylor *et al.* are able to identify break-points in cities' aggregate levels of integration within the world city network, resulting in taxonomy of alpha-, beta- and gamma-level world cities (Table 22.1). Of particular note in their analysis of the most recent data (Taylor

Table 22.1 Alpha-level world cities in 2008. *Source*: From Taylor *et al.*(2009b) Measuring the World City Network: New Developments and Results. GaWC Research Bulletin 300; http://www.lboro.ac.uk/gawc/rb/rb300.html.

Alpha ++	*Alpha +*	*Alpha*	*Alpha −*
London	Hong Kong	Milan	Warsaw
New York	Paris	Madrid	Jakarta
	Singapore	Seoul	Sao Paulo
	Sydney	Moscow	Zurich
	Tokyo	Brussels	Mexico City
	Shanghai	Toronto	Dublin
	Beijing	Mumbai	Amsterdam
		Buenos Aires	Bangkok
		Kuala Lumpur	Taipei
			Rome
			Istanbul
			Lisbon
			Chicago
			Frankfurt
			Stockholm
			Vienna
			Budapest
			Athens
			Prague
			Caracas
			Auckland
			Santiago

et al. 2009b; Derudder *et al.* 2009) are several points about levels and patterns of integration. First, London and New York are tightly inter-related with one another ("NYLON"; see McGuire and Chan, 2000; Jackson, Stevenson and Watkins 2006) and are both significantly more integrated in the overall world city network than any other city. Second, Hong Kong (not Tokyo) has emerged as the third most highly integrated city. Overall, the level of connectivity in the world city network rose steadily between 2000 and 2008. Cities in the United States and Sub-Saharan Africa, however, experienced a decline in global connectivity in the period (Los Angeles, San Francisco and Miami, in particular). Derudder *et al.* point out that US cities have always exhibited lower levels of integration than might be expected and suggest that this appears to be a result of the very large US domestic market for advanced business services. This means that foreign firms find it hard to penetrate the US market and tend to represent clients through just a New York office. It also means that US business service firms, with a big domestic market, have less reason to gamble on global expansion. The increased overall level of integration in the world city network is largely a result of the increased global connectivity of South Asian, Chinese and Eastern European cities (Shanghai, Beijing and Moscow, in particular), reflecting the importance of "emerging markets" in the dynamics of globalization.

As Taylor *et al.* (2009c) acknowledge, this pattern, along with overall levels of connectivity, will have been dented by the global financial meltdown of late 2008 and the subsequent economic recession. Nevertheless, the world cities listed in Table 22.1 remain extraordinary, not just for their connectivity with one another through the office networks of global service firms in accountancy, advertising, banking/finance, insurance, law, and management consultancy, but also because of their connectivity and complementarities in terms of publishing, design, theatre, governance, music, and popular culture.

References

Alderson, A.S. and Beckfield, J. (2004) Power and Position in the World City System. *American Journal of Sociology* 109 (4), 811–851.
Amin, A. and Graham, S. (1997) The Ordinary City. *Transactions of the Institute of British Geographers, New Series* 22, 411–429.
Arrighi, G. (1994) *The Long Twentieth Century*. Verso, London.
Beaverstock, J.V., Smith R.G., and Taylor P.J. (2000) World-City Network: A New Metageography? *Annals of the Association of American Geographers* 90 (1), 123–134.
Beck, U. (2006) *Power in the Global Age: A New Global Political Economy*. Polity, London.
Beck, U. and Lau C. (2005) Second modernity as a research agenda: theoretical and empirical explorations in the "meta-change" of modern society. *British Journal of Sociology* 56, 525–557.
Bell, D. and Jayne M. (2009) Small Cities? Towards a Research Agenda. *International Journal of Urban and Regional Research* 33 (3), 683–699.
Braudel, F. (1984) *The Perspective of the World*. Collins, London.
Brenner, N. and Keil, R. (eds) (2006) *The Global Cities Reader*. Routledge, London.
Brenner, N. and Theodore, N. (eds) (2002) Spaces of Neoliberalism. *Urban Restructuring in North America and Western Europe*. Blackwell, Oxford.
Breward, C. and Gilbert, D. (eds) (2006) *Fashion's World Cities*. Berg, London.
Campbell, C. (1987) *The Romantic Ethic and the Spirit of Modern Consumerism*. Blackwell, London.
Castells, M. (1996) *The rise of the network society*. Blackwell, London.
Crewe, L. (1996) Material Culture: Embedded Firms, Organizational Networks and the Local Economic Development of a Fashion Quarter. *Regional Studies* 30 (3), 257–272.
Debord, G. (1967) *La Société du Spectacle*. Buchet-Chastel, Paris.
Derudder, B., Taylor, P.J., Ni, P., *et al.* (2009) Pathways of Growth and Decline: Connectivity Changes in the World City Network, 2000–2008. GaWC Research Bulletin 310; http://www.lboro.ac.uk/gawc/rb/rb310.html (accessed 15th October 2010).
Dicken, P., Kelly, P.F, Olds, K., and Wai-Chung Yeung, H. (2001) Chains and Networks, territories and scales. Towards an analyical framework for the global economy. *Global Networks* 1, 89–112.
Doel, M. and Hubbard, P. (2002) Taking world cities literally: Marketing the city in a global space of Flows. *City* 6 (3), 351–368.
Donald, S.H., Kofman, E. and Kevin C. (eds) (2009) *Branding Cities: Cosmopolitanism, Parochialism, and Social Change*. Routledge, London.
Fainstein, S. (2001) Inequality in Global City-regions. In A. J. Scott (ed.), *Global City-Regions: Trends, Theory, Policy*. Oxford University Press, Oxford, pp. 285–298.
Friedmann, J. (1986) The world city hypothesis. *Development and Change* 17, 69–83.

Friedmann, J. (1995) Where we stand: a decade of world city research. In P. L. Knox and P.J. Taylor (eds), *World Cities in a World-System*. Cambridge University Press, Cambridge, pp. 21–47.

Friedmann, J. and Wolff, G. (1982) World city formation: an agenda for research and action. *International Journal of Urban and Regional Research* 6 (3), 309–344.

Friedmann, J. (2001) Intercity Networks in a Globalizing Era. In A. J. Scott (ed.), *Global City-regions: Trends, Theory, Policy*. Oxford University Press, Oxford pp. 119–138.

Geddes, P. (1915) *Cities in evolution*. Benn, London.

Granovetter, M. (1985) Economic action and social structure: the problem of embeddedness. *American Journal of Sociology* 91 (3), pp. 481–510.

Hall, P. (1966) *The World Cities*. Weidenfield and Nicolson, London.

Hall, P. (1998) *Cities in Civilization*. Weidenfeld and Nicolson, London.

Hall, P. (2000) Creative Cities and Economic Development. *Urban Studies* 37, 639–649.

Hamnett, C. (2002) *Unequal City. London in the Global Arena*. Routledge, New York.

Harvey, D. (1989) *The Condition of Postmodernity*, Blackwell, Oxford.

Harvey, D. (2007) *A Brief History of Neoliberalism*. Oxford University Press, Oxford.

Jacobs, J. (1961) *The Death and Life of Great American Cities*. Random House, New York.

Jacobs, J. (1984) *Cities and the Wealth of Nations*. Random House, New York.

Jackson, C., Stevenson, S., and Watkins C. (2006) NY-LON: Does a Single Cross-Continental Office Market Exist? Working paper, Centre for Real Estate Finance, Cass Business School, City University, London.

Jordan, P. W. (2007) The Dream Economy – designing for success in the 21st century. *CoDesign*, 3 (Supplement 1), 5–17.

Kennedy, P. (2005) Joining, constructing and benefiting from the global workplace: transnational professionals in the building-design industry. *Sociological Review* 53, 172–197.

Knox, P.L. (2010) *Cities and Design*. Routledge, London.

Knox, P.L. and P.J. Taylor (eds) (1995) *World Cities in a World-System*. Cambridge University Press, Cambridge.

Krause, L. and Petro, P. (eds) (2003) *Global Cities. Cinema, Architecture and Urbanism in a Global Age*. Rutgers University Press, New Brunswick.

Krätke, S. and Taylor, P.K. (2004) A world geography of global media cities. *European Planning Studies* 12 (4), 459–477.

Massey, D. (2007) *World City*. Polity Press, Cambridge.

McGuire, S. and Chan, M. (2000) The NY-LON life. *Newsweek*, 13 November, 40–47.

Molotch, H. (2002) Place in product. *International Journal of Urban and Regional Research* 26, 665–688.

Reich, R. (2007) *Supercapitalism: The Transformation of Business, Democracy, and Everyday Life*. Knopf, New York.

Robinson, J. (2002) Global and World Cities: A View from off the Map. *International Journal of Urban and Regional Research* 26 (3), 531–554.

Sassen, S. (1991) *The Global City*. Princeton University Press, Princeton.

Sassen, S. (1994) *Cities in a World Economy*. Pine Forge, Thousand Oaks.

Sassen, S. (1995) On concentration and centrality in the global city. In P. L. Knox and P. J. Taylor (eds), *World Cities in a World-system*. Cambridge University Press, Cambridge, pp. 63–78.

Sassen, S. (ed.) (2002) *Global Networks, Linked Cities*, Routledge, London.

Scott, A. (2008) Resurgent Metropolis: Economy, Society and Urbanization in an Interconnected World. *International Journal of Urban and Regional Research* 32 (3), 548–564.

Short, J.R. (2004) *Global Metropolitan. Globalizing Cities in a Capitalist World*, Routledge, London.

Short, J.R. and Kim, Y. (1999) *Globalization and the City*. Longman, London.

Short, J.R., Kim, Y., Kuus, M., and Wells, H. (1996) The dirty little secret of world cities research: data problems in comparative analysis. *International Journal of Urban and Regional Research* 20 (4), 697–719.

Sklair, L. (2005) The Transnational Capitalist Class and Contemporary Architecture in Globalizing Cities. *International Journal of Urban and Regional Research* 29 (3), 485–500.

Smith, R.G. (2003) World city actor-networks. *Progress in Human Geography* 27 (1), 25–44.

Taylor, P.J. (1997) Hierarchical tendencies amongst world cities: a global research proposal. *Cities* 14, 323–332.

Taylor, P.J. (2001) Specification of the world city network. *Geographical Analysis* 33, 181–194.

Taylor, P. J. (2004) *World City Network. A Global Urban Analysis*. Routledge, London.

Taylor, P.J., Catalano, G., and Walker D.R.F. (2002) Measurement of the world city network. *Urban Studies* 39, 2367–2376.

Taylor, P.J., Firth, A., Hoyler, M., and Smith, D. (2009a) Explosive City Growth in the Modern World-System: An Initial Inventory Derived from Urban Demographic Changes. GaWC Research Bulletin 316. http://www.lboro.ac.uk/gawc/rb/rb316.html (accessed 15th October 2010).

Taylor, P.J., Ni, P., Derudder, B., *et al.* (2009b) Measuring the World City Network: New Developments and Results. GaWC Research Bulletin 300; http://www.lboro.ac.uk/gawc/rb/rb300.html (accessed 15th October 2010).

Taylor, P.J., Ni, P., Derudder, B., et al. (2009c) The way we were: command-and-control centres in the global space-economy on the eve of the 2008 geo-economic transition. *Environment and Planning A*, 41, 7–12.

Wallerstein, I. (1984) *Politics of the World-Economy*. Cambridge University Press, Cambridge.

Chapter 23

Governance
Part I

Wendy Larner

Introduction

For the last three months the UK Border Agency has had my New Zealand passport, assessing whether or not I am eligible for permanent settlement in the United Kingdom. Surely this is an unambiguous example of state power in that a centralized government department is exercising its authority to decide who should become a member of a particular nation-state? But on closer inspection there are a very diverse range of immigration actors in the United Kingdom. I initially entered the country on a work permit overseen by my university, which is formally licensed to sponsor skilled workers under the new points-based system. Because I have now lived here for five years I am eligible to apply for settlement in the UK, which will also entitle me to live and work elsewhere in the European Community if I so choose. As part of my application I have to provide evidence that I had passed a mandatory "Life in the UK" test so I had duly bought the study guide from a local bookshop, and then made an appointment with the small multicultural community centre that holds the tender to deliver the tests in Bristol. Once I had passed the test and received my official certificate, my passport, application and a sizeable fee were mailed to a processing office in Liverpool. If I was wealthier I could have hired an immigration consultant to compile my file and smooth the overall process, but only if this consultant was formally registered with the Office of the Immigration Service Commission. And if I had not wanted to relinquish my passport for this long I could have paid the additional fee for "same day" processing offered by an immigration office based in Birmingham. Who, where and what is the "state" in this story?

It is precisely these kinds of complicated organizational arrangements, in which diverse actors have been actively enrolled into multi-level governmental processes,

The Wiley Blackwell Companion to Human Geography, First Edition.
Edited by John A. Agnew and James S. Duncan.
© 2011 John Wiley & Sons, Ltd. Published 2016 by John Wiley & Sons, Ltd.

that have underpinned the rise of the term "governance" in political and academic lexicons in recent years. At the most general level, the term governance is used to capture an apparent shift away from state-centric, top-down, monolithic forms of political power. A commonly used definition is that of Rhodes (1996: 652–653) who suggests that governance is "a change in the meaning of government, referring to a new process of governing; or a changed condition of ordered rule; or the new method by which society is governed." More specifically, the use of the term is an attempt to both describe and analyze the new polycentric multi-actor political networks that now operate within and beyond the conventional realms of state agency. It signals the increasing importance of supra-national and sub-national political authorities in governing processes, as well as the growing involvement of private and third sector actors in a diverse range of activities once conventionally associated with the state. For geographers it has opened up a series of new questions about the spatialities and temporalities of governing processes, and the very nature of political power.

Existing reviews of the literature on governance usefully underline how the term has become common in a wide range of practitioner and academic settings as a means of capturing both shifts in thinking and in ways of working (Stoker 1998; Walters 2004). These authors also stress that the term draws together a very disparate set of disciplinary and theoretical debates. In engaging with these debates this chapter will suggest that the rise of the term governance signals two broad interrelated shifts: first, a set of new substantive orientations in examinations of statecraft that identify and explore the changing actors and spatialities of political power; and second, a distinctive shift in theoretical approaches to social scientific and geographic accounts of political authority and rule. In the chapter I use the literature on neoliberalism to illustrate aspects of the broad dimensions of these empirical and analytic shifts, highlighting how diverse efforts to make sense of changes in the contemporary political order have underpinned the broader conceptual changes. I conclude by assessing the broader significance of the new tripartite political-geographic vocabulary of government, governance and governmentality, stressing that it is important not to read these three terms as a chronological narrative about political change, as each of these formulations asks different conceptual questions and gives rise to different accounts of governance itself.

Globalization and Governance

For many geographers, state theorists and other social scientists, the term governance is most immediately an attempt to make sense of the changing nature of political authority and rule in a globalizing, neoliberalizing world. Such accounts initially focused on the apparent erosion of the power of the nation-state, often captured in the phrase the "withering away" of the state or claims about "states against markets" (Boyer and Drache 1996). Once it was realized that it was not simply that market regulation had usurped the state, nor that "more globalization = less nation-state sovereignty = weaker states" (Sharma and Gupta 2006), governance emerged as a term associated with more nuanced and carefully documented accounts of changes in the role and nature of the state. That said, most often such accounts continued to reflect wider efforts to understand changes in the contemporary political economy of capitalism and the implications of these changes for the organization of the state. Rather than marking a new analytical approach, the adoption of the term governance was an attempt to broaden "government" beyond the strictly delineated world of nation-state action as both supra-national and sub-national institutions became more visible, and to engage with the efforts to harness a diverse range of non-state institutions and actors in both the making of policy and the delivery of services. Governance is, as Walters (2004: 28) points out, overall an attempt to engage with and describe a new policy style that is understood to reflect broader structural changes associated with both globalization and neoliberalism.

The influence of this empirical shift in politics and policy was profound. As geographers, amongst others, began carefully tracking the reconstitution of the spaces, processes, networks and mechanisms of power, they began to see more of the complex ways in which political rule was being differentially restructured. A wide range of substantive discussions and empirical foci fed into this re-orientation. At the most macro level, governance became linked to, and a way of referring to, the emergent architecture of global and supra-regional institutions marked by the growing prominence of organizations such as the WTO, World Bank, IMF and EU (Woods 2006). Explanations for the rise and growing influence of these international institutions varied. For some this was seen as a relatively benign political development, for others an attempt by capitalists to subvert nation-state authority (Peet 2007), or the generalized outcome of an "epochal shift" from a fixed world of sovereign states to a world "beyond" or "without" government (du Gay 2007). However this new institutional architecture was explained, the result was an increased interest in researching global processes as the new political-economic relationships between nation-state and supra-national institutions began to be identified and explored. Under the broad heading of "global governance" increased attention was paid to the changing roles, missions and activities of the institutions themselves as well as their relationships with transnational networks of authority made up of diverse forms of political, professional and technical expertise. Discussions of new forms of political authority and "soft power" also emerged.

During the same period as governance was adopted as a key descriptor of the new supra-national political terrain, there were cognate moves at the national level as neoliberal political projects and state sector restructuring became the focus of increased attention. In these discussions the shift from government to governance was seen primarily as a way of capturing a new role for private and third sector actors in both setting policy agendas and providing services. Consequently, analyses of governance were linked to diverse discussions, such as the introduction of new public management in to the core public sector, the increased emphasis on the outsourcing of government activities, as well as the growing recognition of the political claims of diverse stakeholders which gave rise to a new emphasis on networks, partnerships, and other novel forms of participatory engagement. One of the best known formulations of the newly disaggregated political terrain was that of state theorist Jessop (2002), who associated the shift from government to governance with the move from what he termed the Keynesian National Welfare State to the Schumpeterian Post-national Workfare Regime (KNWS to SPWR). Contesting claims that the state was simply becoming smaller because of a new emphasis on privatization and marketization, he argued that there were three sets of interconnected changes that need to be considered: de-nationalization (the restructuring of the state to both supra- and sub-national levels), de-statization (the incorporation of a wide range of non-state actors in political processes), and the internationalization of policy regimes. In geographic literatures, exploration of these new domains was closely associated with the use of "regulation theory" by British geographers who were examining changes in state forms and functions, and the use of "regime theory" by their American counterparts who were more likely to focus on analyzing local coalitions (Jones 1998). Also influential was the work of Brenner (2004), who brought together a diverse range of economic and political geography literatures to theorize the rescaling of statehood and the rise of "new state spaces" in the context of economic globalization.

Urban geographers also made important contributions to broader debates about governance. The focus of their discussions was initially the "new urban politics" in which political elites engaged in the courting of private investors. Efforts were made to identify the new class coalitions coming together around market-oriented strategies and spaces such as enterprise zones and public private partnerships, and the relationships between city officials and private sector actors that shaped the financing, construction and management of these new spaces. As with the global and national debates above, initially the increased involvement of the private sector in urban governance was understood as the "rolling back" of the local state, but increasingly it was recognized that the rise of the "entrepreneurial city" (Harvey 1989) was more usefully understood as involving political, institutional and geographical reorganization of urban politics. The result was a literature that showed how efforts to re-establish the conditions for economic growth gave rise to new clusters of political-economic activity, involving not only reconfigured relationships between local states and firms, but also between educational institutions and infrastructural providers. A parallel and related discussion developed around the role of social movements and not-for-profit organizations in urban governance. As budgetary pressures tightened, and local states increasingly contracted out services, a new role emerged for the community and voluntary sectors in social policy and provisioning. Wolch (1990) called this phenomenon the "shadow state" in her influential account of these emergent relationships. In the years since she made this observation the new relationships between government agencies and so-called "third sector" organizations have proliferated. Associations, advisory groups, forums, regeneration agencies, social enterprises and local partnerships have all emerged as new forums in which urban governance decisions are made. Goodwin and Painter (1996: 635) capture the overall shifts in this terrain in their discussion of local governance, "A fairly uniform system of local government has been transformed into a more complex one of local governance, involving agencies drawn from the public, private and voluntary sectors."

Most recently, a new focus on self-governance has become an integral part of geographical discussions of governance as accounts of diverse forms of subject formation have become more common. It was recognized relatively early on that governance was in part about government agencies fostering self-governing networks and actors that would allow the shared addressing of political concerns (Stoker 1998). In this context commentators began to explore how new forms of governance are both premised on, and actively constitute, distinctive understandings of collective and individual subjects (Dean 1999; Rose 1999). A new emphasis on autonomous, entrepreneurial subjects who were capable of self-managing and are responsible for their own destinies was identified as underpinning the new forms of governance. This new understanding helps explain why less well off communities and individuals are now increasingly seen as responsible for addressing their own misfortune and solving their own problems. Rather than poverty, ill-health or homelessness being a situation that any of us might find ourselves in, and thereby most effectively resolved by government agencies delivering collective social programs, the unemployed, homeless and poor are now more likely to be seen as individuals who should be encouraged and helped to improve their life chances through self-responsibility, choice, and empowerment (Cruikshank 1999). Moreover, these expectations are often made manifest through indirect, process oriented, approaches to the exercise of political rule and authority such as "facilitating," "steering" and, most recently, "nudging." In this context governance refers not only to a new politics of inclusion and exclusion, but also to distinctive forms of citizenship and ways of constituting political subjects based on assumptions about the desirability of self-governance.

Overall, the result of these diverse governance research agendas that relationships between public and private, state and society, global and local, government and freedom are all beginning to look very blurry. The "territorial trap" (Agnew 1994) that underpinned mainstream approaches to state theory has also now come firmly in view. Nation-states are no longer seen as self-evident and fixed containers of political power, relationships between supra-national institutions and domestic politics are becoming increasingly complex, and the assumption that states, markets and societies are coterminous has begun to look like an archaic formulation in the context of internationalized financial and production processes and the increased mobility associated with new forms of migration and citizenship. As the questions generated through sustained research into these new empirical domains became clearer, it also became obvious that rigorous analyses of these new forms of governance would require new conceptual approaches.

Government, Governance and Governmentality

The sustained focus on these new multi-scalar, multi-actor forms of governance was associated with a significant departure from the more traditional conceptions of state theory. For much of the post-war period there had been an assumption amongst social scientists that state, economy and society were relatively fixed conceptual categories. The state was understood to be the holder of centralized authority, and exercised power in top down exercises over territorially bounded economies and societies. Of course this is not to say that state theorists were agreed on the nature of the state, or on the relationships between political and economic processes. It was widely accepted that states were socially constructed and politically contested. Even amongst the Marxist accounts that have tended to dominate in the geographical literatures there were marked differences between, for example, between those who saw the state as a relatively straight forward expression of capitalist power and those more influenced by various neo-Marxisms that saw the state as a mode of regulation, or even as relatively autonomous. But it is to suggest that these accounts were premised on a "centered view of power" in which the state was seen as a unitary, and to a certain extent, singular, actor (Allen 2003). Moreover, whether state theorists were focused on cultural and representational frames, or structural and functional approaches, the post-war period was characterized by what is often described as "methodological nationalism," in which it was assumed that states were nation-states and that national economies and societies were their natural objects of intervention.

As the new geographies of state power became more visible so too was there a search for new analytical tools. The term governance is often associated with this conceptual shift in state theoretical debates, in which efforts were made to capture the reorganization of the national state, both in terms of territoriality and sovereignty. Initially this took the form of debates over how best to understand the multiple sites, scales and locations of political power. It was argued that the rise of international institutions such as the EU and WTO that sought to govern at supra-national levels couldn't just be analyzed as the rise of a "super-state" and theorized using the familiar tools of state theory. Rather these empirical changes demanded new analytical approaches that would capture the new terrain of "global governance" by being sensitive to new "indirect" expressions of power (for example, harmonization, benchmarking, standards, subsidiarity) and would trace the content of the new policy mobilities, epistemic communities and governance networks made up of politicians, technocrats, experts, NGOs, social movements and so on, operating across and beyond the traditional boundaries of nation-states. These shifts were also understood to have implications for spatial and temporal orders. For example, influential analyses such as those of Sassen (2006) suggest that territory, sovereignty and rights have all been "unbundled" and rearticulated as states themselves increasingly participate in the formation of a new organizing logic for international action and collaboration.

As similar discussions emerged at national and urban scales, these new political geographies fostered a shift from relatively monolithic conceptions of the state and political power to more heterogeneous conceptions of governance and political rule. In part, this was a consequence of the shift in emphasis from particular governmental projects to process-oriented accounts of governance. But in geographic literatures it was also a reflection of the growing prominence of debates about neoliberalism. Indeed, it is noteworthy that in his review article Sparke (2006) directly links the diverse reterritorializations of contemporary forms of governance with neoliberalism. In this literature the shift from project to process was captured by a shift in geographical terminology from neoliberalism to neoliberalization (Peck and Tickell 2002) and a growing recognition that "actually existing neoliberalism" took many and diverse forms, both temporally and spatially. As analysts became more interested in how different theories, policies and techniques came together to constitute neoliberalism in different forms in different places, so too did post-structuralist perspectives, including cultural economy, actor-network and governmentality literatures, emerge as increasingly important analytical approaches in this literature (Larner 2003; Mitchell 2002). Assemblage, topologies and networks began to challenge states, scales and institutions as the conceptual language of political-economic geography in general, and governance in particular.

Particularly influential amongst political and economic geographers has been the neo-Foucauldian governmentality literature (see Rose *et al*. 2006 for a useful review). This work is concerned to theorize political power as an assemblage of diverse knowledges and governing practices. There are three aspects to these discussions. First, this literature focuses on problematizations – an examination of the historically and geographically specific ways in which problems are defined and solutions imagined. These discussions have highlighted a new role for the state as a partner in government whose role is to facilitate and support the self governing of both organizations and individuals. Second, this literature has drawn attention to the specificity of the objects and subjects of governance identified and constituted through policies and programs. Of particular interest here has been the shift away from conceptions of governance premised on universalizing conceptions of society, towards multiple and heterogeneous conceptions of community, and the new emphasis on citizens as active, entrepreneurial subjects. Third, increasing attention has been paid to the strategies and techniques used in governance. Of particular interest are the relatively mundane techniques through which particular objects and subjects of governance are constituted. These analyses have identified the new emphasis on "governing at a distance," and it is argued there is a new relationship between expertise and politics as accountancy, audit, enumeration, calculating, monitoring and evaluation have taken centre stage in governing processes.

Two important bodies of work have emerged as a result of these new heterogeneous conceptions of governance. The first body of work consists of detailed ethnographies of particular "global assemblages" (Ong and Collier 2005). Li's (2007) work on community forestry management programs is an exemplary contribution to this discussion. Rather than seeing this as yet another example of the neoliberalization of nature, she shows how a diverse array of agents (villagers, laborers, entrepreneurs, officials, activists, aid donors, and scientists) and objectives (profit, pay, livelihoods, control, property, efficiency, sustainability, conservation) come together in such an assemblage. Similarly Sharma's (2008) recent book on women's empowerment projects in neoliberal India demonstrates how feminist, Freirian, and Gandhian approaches articulate with the market-oriented approaches advocated by the World Bank and international donors in positioning empowerment as a technology of government and development. The second body of work – and this is where geographers have been more involved – has seen a more careful tracing of the mobile actors, policies and techniques that have underpinned a renewed focus on the transnational networks of scientific and economic expertise. For example, in an article on New Zealander Mike Moore, I traced how this working class unionist came to be Director General of the WTO and what this meant for his understanding of global trade, markets and economic justice (Larner 2009). More generally a recent special issue of *Geoforum* has explored the mobilities and mutations that characterize policy transfer and the diverse and embodied actors involved (Peck and Theodore 2010).

Although there are important differences between these two sets of approaches, the literatures on global assemblages and policy mobilities both show that there are complex geographies and sociologies that need to be carefully examined if we are to conceptualize and research the new multi-actor, multi-scalar political formations that have become visible in the research on governance. Moreover, these accounts reveal that the actors involved in the new political formations captured by the term governance are even more diverse than initially assumed. New forms of governance cannot be explained by simply focusing on paradigmatic figures, for example, Friedrich Hayek, Margaret Thatcher and Ronald Reagan in accounts of neoliberalism. There are also "oppositional" figures that play key roles in governmental assemblages, as Li shows by highlighting the role of activists and academics in her research on community forestry management. Nor is governance politically aligned. There is now a significant body of work that reveals that techniques associated with "governing at a distance" have been taken up by both authoritarian and left leaning governments, as well as those more market oriented governments we might expect to be sympathetic to neoliberalism (Ferguson 2010). There are also examples where governance has used to strengthen the state or in projects of social welfare that are in part a response to neoliberalism (Collier 2009). Tracing carefully how actors and techniques move from one context to another, and the work that they do in different settings is thus revealing unexpected alliances. It is also helping us explain why political claims and key words formed in struggles against states – including empowerment, equality, participation, transparency and accountability – have become part of the accepted vocabulary of governance.

Conclusion

The term governance marks a re-orientation for both state theorists and political-economic geographers. It reflects both substantive and analytic shifts in the focus of political and geographic discussions (cf. Goodwin and Painter 1996). Most immediately, it has made visible many actors and mechanisms of governance that did not previously appear in accounts of political rule and authority. To return to the example of UK immigration processes that I opened with, it has allowed researchers to identify and examine the roles of the diverse actors that have been enrolled in "border control," including not only multiple government agencies located in different places and performing different aspects of the overall process of border control, but also organizations that would not have conventionally been associated with immigration such as universities, immigration consultants, book shops and community centers. It has highlighted the complex geographies of governance; exactly where is the border in this account? It also reveals the multi-scalar dimensions of citizenship and belonging; while "leave to remain" in the United Kingdom will also enable me to live and work elsewhere in Europe, I have no intention of eventually relinquishing my New Zealand passport. Consequently I will be a member of three state-like domains all at the same time. Finally, it has drawn attention to ways in which "acts of prosaic stateness" (Painter 2006) such as citizenship tests, application forms, and points systems shape governmental processes in distinctive ways.

These shifts have also fostered new kinds of conceptual approaches. Whereas government was a term closely tied to the conventional domains of the state, both governance and governmentality understand that political power works beyond the institutional domains of the mainstream conceptions of politics. In this context it is not surprising that the terms government, governance and governmentality have become closely intertwined, and that they now jostle for attention in contemporary geographical scholarship. However it is important to understand that there remains identifiable conceptual differences between these approaches. Whereas governance seeks to chart a relatively centred network of institutions and trace their effects on political objects and subjects, governmentality focuses on the heterogeneous assemblages of knowledge and practices that produce political objects and subjects in particular forms. In short, governance remains closely wedded to more conventional forms of state theory even while scholars of governance are working to avoid over valuing the state, whereas governmentality focuses on the heterogeneous practices that make subjects and objects governable thereby realizing Foucault's ambition to "cut the head off the king."

It is important, therefore, to avoid the growing tendency in geographic literatures to present government, governance and governmentality as blocks of abstract "governing styles" that are "allotted clear and unambiguous identities as they overtake and supersede one another in an onward march towards their dominant contemporary manifestation" (du Gay 2007: 165–167). It is not that we have moved from government to governance to governmentality over time. Nor are these three approaches "Russian dolls" that nestle within each other, allowing the analyst to move from discussions of macro-processes to micro-politics, from global institutions to calculative practices. As Allen (2003: 35) warns more generally, the story of governance too often remains linear or framed in terms of a descending order of spatial scales. Instead, we might begin by recognizing and examining the hard and heterogeneous work associated with contemporary attempts to governing and building our conceptual analyses from there. This would ensure that accounts of governance always centre the changing, unfinished and contested nature of political rule and authority.

References

Agnew, J. (1994) The territorial trap: The geographical assumptions of international relations theory. *Review of International Political Economy* 1 (1), 53–80.

Allen, J. (2003) *Lost Geographies of Power*. Blackwell, Oxford.

Boyer, R. and Drache, D. (1996) *States against Markets: the limits of globalisation*. Routledge, London.

Brenner, N. (2004) *New State Spaces: Urban governance and the rescaling of statehood*. Oxford University Press, London.

Collier, S. (2009) Topologies of Power: Foucault's analysis of political government beyond "governmentality". *Theory, Culture and Society* 26 (6), 78–108.

Cruikshank, B. (1999) *The Will to Empower: democratic citizens and other subjects*. Cornell University Press, Ithaca.

Dean, M. (1999) *Governmentality: Power and rule in modern society*. Sage, London.

du Gay, P. (2007) *Organising Identity: persons and organisations "after theory"*. Sage, London.

Ferguson, J. (2010) The Uses of Neoliberalism. In N. Castree, P. Chatterton, N. Heynen, W. Larner, M. Wright (eds), *The Point is to Change It: Geographies of hope and survival in an age of crisis*. Wiley-Blackwell, Oxford.

Goodwin, M. and Painter, J. (1996) Local Governance, the Crisis of Fordism and the Changing Geographies of Regulation. *Transactions of the Institute of British Geographers* 21 (4), 635–648.

Harvey, D. (1989) From Managerialism to Entrepreneurialism: The Transformation in Urban Governance in Late Capitalism. *Geografiska Annaler. Series B, Human Geography* 71 (1), 3–17.

Jessop, B. (2002) Liberalism, Neo-liberalism and Urban Governance: A state-theoretical perspective. *Antipode* 34 (3), 452–472.

Jones, M. (1998) Restructuring the Local States: Economic governance or social regulation? *Political Geography* 17 (8), 959–988.

Larner, W. (2003) Guest Editorial: Neoliberalism? *Environment and Planning D: Society and Space* 21 (5), 309–312.

Larner, W. (2009) Neoliberalism, Mike Moore and the WTO. *Environment and Planning A* 41 (7), 1576–1593.

Li, T. (2007) Practices of Assemblage and Community Forest Management. *Economy and Society* 36 (2), 263–293.

Mitchell, T. (2002) *Rule of Experts: Egypt, Techno-politics, Modernity.* University of California Press, Berkeley.

Ong, A. and Collier, S. (2005) *Global Assemblages: Technology, Politics and Ethics as Anthropological Problems.* Blackwell, Oxford.

Peck, J. and Tickell, A. (2002) Neoliberalising Space. *Antipode* 34, 380–404.

Peck, J. and Theodore, N. (2010) Mobilizing Policy: Models, methods and mutations. *Geoforum* 41 (3), 169–174.

Peet, R. (2007) *Geography of Power: The making of global economic policy.* Zed Books, London.

Rhodes, R. (1996) The New Governance: Governing without Government. *Political Studies* 44, 652–667.

Rose, N. (1999) *Powers of Freedom: Reframing Political Thought.* Cambridge University Press, Cambridge.

Rose, N., O'Malley, P., and Valverde, M. (2006) Governmentality. *Annual Review of Law and Society* 2, 83–104.

Sassen, S. (2006) *Territory, Authority, Rights: From medieval to global assemblages.* Princeton University Press, Princeton.

Sharma, A. (2008) *Logics of Empowerment: Development, gender and governance in neoliberal India.* University of Minnesota Press, Minneapolis.

Sharma, A. and Gupta, A. (2006) *The Anthropology of the State: A Reader.* Blackwell, London.

Sparke, M. (2006) Political geography: political geographies of globalization (2) – governance. *Progress in Human Geography* 30 (3), 357–372.

Stoker, G. (1998 [2002]) Governance as Theory: Five Propositions. *International Social Science Journal* 50 (155), 17–28.

Walters, W. (2004) Some Critical notes on "Governance." *Studies in Political Economy* 73, 27–46.

Wolch, J. (1990) *The Shadow State: The government and voluntary sector in transition.* The Foundation Centre, New York.

Woods, N. (2006) *The Globalizers: The IMF, The World Bank and Their Borrowers.* Cornell University Press, Ithaca.

Further Reading

Students interested in pursuing the subject of governance in greater depth are advised to engage with both theoretical works of state theory, and more recent studies of government, governance and governmentality in diverse geographical settings. Gerry Stoker's article

("Governance as Theory: five propositions") is now the classic introduction to the field. The work of state theorists such as Philip Abrahms ("Notes on the Difficulty of Studying the State"), Phillip Corrigan and Derek Sayer (*The Great Arch: English State formation as cultural revolution*), Bob Jessop (*State Theory: Putting the capitalist states in its places* and *The Future of the Capitalist State*), Neil Brenner (*New State Spaces*), Nancy Fraser (*Justice Interruptus*) and Wendy Brown (*States of Inquiry*) should be required reading for anyone concerned with the conceptual aspects of these debates. Distinctive geographic contributions include those of John Allen (*Lost Geographies of Power*), John Agnew (*Hegemony: the new shape of global power*) and Jamie Peck (*Workfare States*). Influential scholars tracing the new contours of governance include Ngaire Wood (*The Globalizers*), Dick Peet (*Geography of Power: The making of global economic policy*), Michael Powers (*The Audit Society*) and Janet Newman (*Modernising Governance*) amongst others. For a very useful sceptical account of governance see William Walter's article ("Some Critical Notes on 'Governance' "). The key introductions to governmentality are the books by Mitchell Dean (*Governmentality: Power and Rule in modern society*) and Nikolas Rose (*Powers of Freedom: Reframing political thought*). Particularly useful overviews of recent developments can be found in the introduction to Aradhana Sharma and Akhil Gupta's *The Anthropology of the State* and John Clarke's *Changing Welfare, Changing States*. Key geography journals for students of governance include *Political Geography* as well as mainstream human geography journals such as *Transactions of the Institute of British Geographers*, *Annals of the Association of American Geographers* and *Progress in Human Geography*. More widely in the social sciences, journals such as *Economy and Society*, *Review of International Political Economy* and *Policy and Politics* (to give just a few disparate examples) regularly publish articles on diverse aspects of governance.

Chapter 24

Governance
Part II

Stephen Legg

Introduction

"Government" is both an institutional practice and an analytical category. It describes the administrative capacities and aspirations of the state in its national, regional, and local manifestations. But it also describes the attempt to delineate a realm of power relations that is distinct from, but is mutually related to, categories including those of sovereignty, monarchy, democracy, development, and imperialism. Government, as conventionally conceived, can thus be thought of as an apparatus (*dispositif*); it usually seeks stability and order, striating and territorializing the ground of global nation-state systems, as much as ordering our conceptions of political space and its scalar divisions of responsibility and capacity. This conventional apparatus is, however, a relatively recent and now unraveling invention, bequeathed us by a liberal art of government and its associated social sciences (Foucault 2007).

One agent of this unraveling is the practical and analytical assemblage (or "agencement," Phillips 2006) of "governance." It describes the capacities of, and aspiration towards, organization, coordination and control that encompass the processes of government, but also exceeds the many boundaries of the state, to include businesses, charities, families and communities (Stoker 1998). While government is formed through its relationship to objects, subjects or other forms of power, governance can be said to exist solely through those relationships; to be the sum of conduct of conducts, not the trace they leave behind or the hand that desires their guidance. That is, a more de-territorializing and de-scaling relational practice and concept (Hardt and Negri 2009: 227). It is reshaping current appreciation of the duties, obligations and abilities of the state, as well as of the power relations that constitute the state, economy, civil society, population and territory.

The Wiley Blackwell Companion to Human Geography, First Edition.
Edited by John A. Agnew and James S. Duncan.
© 2011 John Wiley & Sons, Ltd. Published 2016 by John Wiley & Sons, Ltd.

Since the 1990s that reshaping has operated under the lodestar of neo-liberalism, in which government of the economy by the state has been discouraged, whilst governance of an entrepreneurial and securitized society has been encouraged, by the agents of capital accumulation. The "credit crunch" and global recession from 2008 into the century's second decade led to hopes for a re-governmentalization of neo-liberalism: targeting casino capitalism and protecting depositors from banking big-dicks; bolstering American health care and reconsidering Keynesian stimulus packages as antidotes to the ravishes of market crises; and securing funds for less wealthy countries in the face of recession and the costs of global warming. But the neo-liberal anti-politics machine (Ferguson, 1994) also has an uncanny ability to manufacture its own crises into opportunities to display its malleability and adaptive genius, and to reframe funding crises as opportunities for efficiency drives and the redistribution of responsibility and *œconomy*. Hence the cuts in UK University funding to bolster the case for increased tuition fees by students (*née* academic knowledge consumers) and the use of low-interest rate borrowing by banks to guarantee corporate bonuses, rather than to facilitate small loans or lower mortgage rates for the economic citizenry. At the heart of these debates will be the nature of governance and its future under post-crunch neo-liberalism, or whatever succeeds it.

Geographers have contributed to commentaries on the changing nature of the government-governance balance, just as they have reflected upon the changing power relations these patterns denote. Particular attention has been paid to the processes of social and economic coordination, management and steering (Painter 2009). In particular, attention has lingered on inter-organizational coordination that has not reproduced the logic of the market or the vertical chains of a hierarchical ontology, but has functioned more like a self-organizing network (Brenner 2004). This has particular implications for reconsidering the scalar importance of local and extra-national networks, supposedly at the expense of the state, although there has also been work on the geographical spread of governance beyond the urban (see Goodwin 1998, on rural governance). Geographers such as Stuart Corbridge have also worked to examine non-urban, non-western encounters with the agents of good-governance and how these practices are influencing the way rural populations "see the state" (Corbridge *et al.* 2005).

This is in exception to a literature that has, however, been marked by a socio-economic focus at the expense of other domains of practice and analysis, and has focused on governance in civil society at the expense of studying the governmentalization of the state. This review will attempt to widen out this work by reconsidering the state in the light of Foucault's recently translated lecture courses. It will then consider the question of governance and politics through dwelling on questions of exclusion: first through the anti-democratic lens of Carl Schmitt; and secondly through considering the constitutive exclusions of liberal governance itself. This will be used as a platform to briefly consider international governance and to question whether lessons learned at this scale can be transplanted to other scales or places. The example of moral conduct will be used as a test case, including the extreme exemplar of Gandhian self-discipline. In conclusion, some of the methodological consequences of assemblage theory for rethinking geographies of governance will be suggested.

The State

> The scholarly analysis of the state is liable to reproduce in its own analytical tidiness ... imaginary coherence and misrepresent the incoherence of state practice ... To be more precise, the phenomenon we call "the state" arises from techniques that enable mundane material practices to take on the appearance of an abstract, nonmaterial form.
> (Mitchell 1999 [2006]: 169)

In an influential review Stoker (1998: 17) suggested that "Governance is ultimately concerned with creating the conditions for ordered rule and collective action. The outputs of governance are not therefore different from those of government. It is rather a matter of a difference in process." The geographical significance of this difference was made immediately apparent in that the public/private distinction becomes blurred: governance mechanisms do not depend upon recourse to the authority and sanction of government; rather, governance depends upon the multiplicity of governing each other. Institutionally, this spatial shift is represented by altered relations between the state and civil society. Non-governmental organizations, voluntary associations, and privatized public utilities increasingly become involved in distributing the rights and responsibilities of citizenship. But this is necessarily dependent upon the imagination of the welfare state, which itself relies upon more abstract conceptualizations of political space and the art of liberal government. The "Ordo-liberalism" of post-war Germany, it has been suggested, accepted that the state would need to protect society from the market forces of economy, whilst American neo-liberalism imagined society as a section of economy, and thus exposed it more fully to the "veridictional" market logic of political economy (Foucault 2008).

Amongst the many inspirations for theorizing governance Stoker acknowledged institutional economics, international relations, development studies, political science, and Foucauldian theorists. The "governmentality studies" that have emerged from the work of the latter has been especially responsible for encouraging a theoretical turn away from the "cold monster" of the state to what are, in many respects, the techniques of governance (Foucault 2007: 109; Rose and Miller 2008). These studies were particularly dependent upon the translation of one of Foucault's (1978 [2001]) lectures and the published course summaries of his late 1970s work. The translation of these lectures in full (Foucault 2003, 2007, 2008) has done much to situate Foucault's call to study techniques of governmentality within the ongoing development of Reason of State, and the reflections of the state upon the development of what we can retrospectively term governance. It must still be acknowledged that governmentalities target individual conduct, and bring previously autonomous spaces (most famously the home) into the purview of governance (through, for instance the "policing of families," see Donzelot 1979). Disciplining abnormal minorities and regulating the security of the body politic is, as such, the work of capitalist economies, philanthropic organizations and social reformists as much as that of the state.

The state, however, must also be acknowledged to be the product of governmentalities; resting upon "local" techniques and being produced itself as an effect of governance work (Foucault 2008: 67). One of the foremost theorists of socio-economic governance has recently acknowledged the significance of Foucault's "state effect" in this light (Jessop, 2011). Intervening in, and emerging through, the historical evolution of power relations in the arts and sciences of governance, the state evolved from one of justice, to one of administration, to one of security (triangulating these former interests in place and period specific governmentalities). Thus, while governmentalities orchestrate geographical comprehensions of territory, and statistically survey their specific populations, they also have a scalar logic which creates impression of semi-autonomous domains (society, economy and population) and the spread of networks over increasing scopes of space, while they also exert nominalist powers of scale-naming (what is local, what is national, what is international etc.) (Jessop 2007; Legg 2009b). This gives the state powerful effects, but not a universal essence, through its capacities to vary and tailor its technologies, to select their deployment, and to retain those that prove useful (Jessop, 2011).

But how exactly does the governance literature relate to governmentality studies? Lemke (2007) suggests that the latter overcomes some of the limitations of the former, which is described as a strategy, process, procedure or program for controlling, regulating or managing problems on a global, national, local or organizational level. While both governance and governmentality analytics focus on "how" questions of practice, go beyond the state, and have a relational sense of power, Lemke suggests they also have three significant differences. Ontologically, the pre-existence of objects of governance is assumed, as against the more nominalist analytics of governmentality. Politically, governance tends to emphasize dialogue, participation and inclusion through consultation in the public sphere (what Schmitt would deride as discussion rather than decision, see below) rather than conflict or domination. While governmentality studies do not always succeed on this front either, they are more attuned to power relations and the constitutive, and possibly oppressive, outcomes of problematizations. And, technologically, governance theory reinforces the myth of the networked, decentralized, assimilative response to social change, rather than that which acknowledges the ongoing force of the state, of conflict, and of antagonism.

Emerging from these debates, therefore, are the problems of politics, and of the limits of the state. Eric Swyngedouw has addressed these issues in his geographical research into the shift from government-through to governance-beyond contemporary western states (that is, the externalization of state functions, and the up- and down-scaling of governance). He stresses how many practitioners and analysts of governance theory are oblivious to the contradictory tensions (between state, market and civil society) in which any governing must be embedded (Swyngedouw 2005). Recent tensions are associated with: the growth of the "multitude" and associated counter-hegemonic social movements within civil society; cultural divisions within capitalist production, markets and actors; and the restructuring geographies of the state mentioned above. Vitally, Swyngedouw links these processes to questions of democracy, political citizenship and the role of inclusion and exclusion in purportedly post-political/democratic times. Confirming this analysis, Hardt and Negri have recently followed up their work on *Empire* and *Multitude* with reflections on *Commonwealth* that discusses "imperial governance" after US hegemony.

The various notions of governance thus share an idea of the deconstitutionalization and the governmentalization of *dispositifs* of the production of law that takes command away from sovereignty, makes it adequate to the market, and distributes it among a variety of actors. No one should confuse this governance, however, with democracy. (Hardt and Negri 2009: 227)

Similar questions have been pursued from an historical perspective by Timothy Mitchell, who has explored colonial governmentalities within and beyond the Egyptian state (Mitchell 1988, 2002) as well as the theoretical conundrum of the state itself (Mitchell 1999 [2006]). In the latter he showed that debates over where the limit of the state *was* were misplaced; we should, rather, be historicizing and exploring the problem of when, where and how the state/society or state/economy distinction was produced. Such distinctions, it was argued, are produced *by* institutions of social and political order, but are then reified: "The ability to have an internal distinction appear as though it were the external boundary between separate objects is the distinctive technique of the modern political order" (Mitchell 1999 [2006]: 170). Whilst appearing separate to the economy and society, therefore, the state should be seen to be constitutively engaged with these domains, though their distinctions remain serious and real. But, turning to the political, Mitchell also stressed that the state does not just function as a "decision maker," but is made and functions through minute processes of spacetime organization, surveillance and arrangement. The question of the political, the "limit," and the exception is one of central importance to governance debates. One reading suggests that the foundational moment of the political is the ability to distinguish between friend and enemy, a decision that can place that latter in a state of exception beyond the protection of the liberal state and its inclusive norms of governance. But Neal (2008: 45–46) has suggested that such readings: "… reify, naturalize and transcendentalize exceptions and exceptionalism as latent structural inevitabilities: exceptions *will arise* because of the structural limits of liberal democracy, and the structural limits of liberal democracy *will produce* exceptions and practices of exceptionalism." How, then, might governance as a practice and as a theory comprehend the political significance of the limit?

The Political

The specific political distinction to which political actions and motives can be reduced is that between friend and enemy. This provides a definition in the sense of a criterion and not as an exhaustive definition or one indicative of substantial context. (Schmitt 1932 [1996]: 26)

Whilst the governance approach to politics puts it at odds with governmentality studies, it places it in diametric opposition to the political work of Carl Schmitt, which is currently undergoing a reappraisal (see Balakrishnan 2000; Kalyvas 2008; Kalyvas and Müller 2000; Rasch 2005). Schmitt has been denounced for his collaboration with the Nazi party in interwar Germany, and for providing justification for Hitler's placing the Jews and other minorities of the qualitatively totalitarian Third Reich into states of exception which exposed them to the ultimate manifestation of violence. But Schmitt also provided a critical reading of liberal constitutionalism more broadly, suggesting that it weakened sovereignty and disabled politics by removing the power of the state to decide upon the friend/enemy distinction. Liberal states substituted democratic discussion for authoritarian decisions, and brought the state into a stifling technological unison with the complex society it sought to govern. In this sense, Schmitt can be viewed as an early critic of "governance," as opposed to strong "government" (see McCormick 1997). His writings are, however, being reconsidered for their potential to re-invigorate western democracy through promoting *agonistic* debate (though not antagonism, see Mouffe 1999). But they also seem to offer insights into a post-9/11 world in which neo-conservative policies have divided the world into those "with" or "against" the remaining claimant to the dais of global sovereignty (Gregory 2007). Must governance, therefore, be considered non-political?

Foucault's writings propose a radically different approach to politics that suggest how governance could become aware of its own political implications. Some suggest that Schmitt's interests were delimited to "high politics" and foreign affairs, not the intricacies of governmentality and resistance that Foucault directed us to (Deuber-Mankowsky 2008). But this scalar division underplays the extent to which Schmitt remained committed to examining law as it was put into play in concrete situations; sensitive to "substantial context" (see the quote above). Schmitt's work could be attentive to "low politics," but its focus was always the decisions of sovereigns, petty or grand. The real distinction between the two was that Schmitt dismissed as the dissolution of politics the very process by which Foucault detected the emergence of a new, bio-, politics. Both, after all, were critics of liberal government; one because it undermined politics, the other because it defined a new politics that brought modern "man's" existence as a living being into question (Foucault 1979: 143).

This of course raises the question of what, for Foucault (and thus for governmentality, as opposed to governance), is political? Foucault did not provide a consistent definition of the "political," although through his 1975–1979 lectures some interlinked definitions of politics occurred: as war pursued by other means (Foucault 2003: 15); as mechanisms of security-population-government that open up the field called politics which made government so much more than sovereignty (Foucault 2007: 76); as the new pastoralism, a replacement for the guiding hand of God (Foucault 2007: 144); of how politics emerged from this to become "... a domain, a set of objects, a type of organization of power." (Foucault 2007: 247). Most explicitly, Foucault (2007: 217) suggested that: "The analysis of governmentality [...] implies that 'everything is political.' [...] Politics is nothing more and nothing less than that which is born with resistance to governmentality, the first revolt, the first confrontation." Unlike Schmitt, therefore, Foucault's politics does not require a decisionistic figure (Deuber-Mankowsky 2008: 153), though it does require a body.

Such an approach to politics could invigorate the governance literature which, Walters (2004) has persuasively argued, is comprehensively anti-political. While claiming to increase transparency, participation and stakeholdership in the name of democracy, Walters suggests that governance only prioritizes the problem-management and consensus building elements of democracy. Whilst various other traditions of political thought prioritize struggle and contestation; "Governance, on the other hand, marks the space of a liberal game of assimilation." (Walters 2004: 35) Although his most explicit promotion of the importance of resistance came late in his life (Foucault 1982), Foucault had earlier insisted on the excesses of the plebeian subject (Ransom 1997: 73) and of counter conducts (Foucault 2007: 194).

While this governmentality work may offer a useful corrective to governance neutrality, it is also important to recall the exclusions that are constitutive of liberalism itself. This is contrary to the popular view that associates liberalism with freedom: the free market; the freely voting individual; a society of economic subjects making free decisions on what to buy or sell; and the liberty of individuals to exist without impositions upon freedom by a police state or authoritarian government. Foucault stressed that whilst freedom was at the heart of the emergence of liberalism as an art of government, this did not equate to an *increase* in freedom. Nor is freedom a universal right or principle; rather, it is a *relation* between governors and governed. As such, liberalism *consumes* freedom, which means that it must also produce it and manage it; that it sees to it that one is free to be free (Foucault 2008: 63). This creates a tension in that this production of freedom could equally lead to its limitation and destruction; and adjudicating this tension is the central purpose of apparatuses of security. However, despite these brief comments, Foucault did not adequately investigate how liberalism excluded and penalized groups thought to threaten the body politic, whether because they posed a pernicious threat, or simply because they were unworthy of the responsibility of liberty.

Such questions have been critically examined in postcolonial literature through exploring different geographies of governance, and through considering 19th century liberal debates about imperialism. In terms of the former, governance beyond the state has taken the form of for instance, the necropolitics of private entrepreneurs on coffee plantations in colonial Ceylon (Duncan 2007). Historical geographers have also looked at the effects of philanthropists and campaigners on colonial states (Lambert and Lester, 2004). Phillips (2002), for instance, has shown how purity campaigners forced the colonial Indian state to abandon its registration and inspection of prostitutes, while Howell (2009) has explored the spatialities of repealists within the Empire the United Kingdom itself (see Legg 2010, for the continued fight in interwar colonial India).

The simultaneous strengthening of liberalism and colonialism in the 18th century ultimately laid foundations for the liberal but autocratic colonial states of the late 19th century (Mehta 1999: 7). These states embodied the confrontation between the universal claims of liberalism and the challenge of the unfamiliar, a problem encountered by the unemployed or the "insane" as much as by colonial subjects (Valverde 1996: 363). Yet certain categories of subject were permanently excluded from the capacity for development. J.S. Mill's *On Liberty*, in 1858, famously argued that liberal considerations would only be applied to mature adults, those societies not in a state of war or severe turmoil, and not to "backward societies" (cited in Mehta, 1999: 70). Referring to the latter, Mill also stated: "Despotism is a legitimate mode of government in dealing with barbarians, provided the end be their improvement" (cited in Valverde 1996: 360).

Rather than seeing this as an historically exceptional blip in the development of liberal government, Hindess (2005: 403) insists that liberal political reason only claims that there are certain important contexts in which free interaction (regulated through "governance") might be the most appropriate means of regulation; the rest of the population may have to be governed in other ways (including more authoritarian forms of "government"). Governance might, therefore, be analyzed politically through looking at its limitation, by which the capillary circulation of governance norms actually marks the space reserved for freedom within the state. But Hindess (2005: 405) also stresses that governance has been used to consider relations that cross the boundaries between states, and thus necessarily raises the question of scale.

The Scalar: International Relations and Self-Conduct

One of the foundational assumptions of governance theory and practice is that it is trans-scalar. This has been central to understanding its transcendence of previous theories of government, and of its ability to link, for instance, Europe-wide policies with regional regeneration, often at the presumed expense of the state. While much of the foregoing discussion has focused on the relevance or not of the state, and thus has implicitly been concerned with the geographical scale of the nation-state, governance is always attached both to more intimate and more global scales of ambition and achievement. The previous discussion of freedom highlights how individual liberty is central to the liberal project, as further discussed below. But in his lectures on liberalism Foucault provided one of his rare acknowledgments of the importance of the world-scale for European governmentalities. Next to the veridification of the market and the limitation of government, Foucault (2008: 61) listed the unlimited expansion of European capitalism in a world market as a defining feature of liberalism. Taken alongside his previous comments about the centrality of the diplomatic-military apparatus to the balance of power in Europe and the formation of modern governmentalities (Foucault 2007: 298), it is clear that the liberalism that so clearly allowed the emergence of governance as a political category and practice was heavily intertwined with the extra-European world.

Viewed in socio-economic terms, governance can be seen to be the logical result of the steady development of liberalism, from its 19th century manifestation, through its welfare state adaptation in the mid-20th century, to its neo-liberal flourishing in the 1990s. But viewed in geopolitical terms, governance also has to be seen as a reaction to the weakening of state socialism after the fall of the Berlin Wall in 1989 and the implosion of the USSR in 1991. Writing in the immediate aftermath of these events, Rosenau (1992) asked what the role of global governance would be in the absence of global government (or of its cold war dualistic forbearer). Global governance was thought to be especially suitable for a world politics without an overarching supreme governmental authority. This belief was confirmed over the following 15 years, in which "global governance" emerged as a central theme in post-cold war international affairs. Geographers commented extensively on this emergence of this "unruly world" between governance and geopolitics (Herod *et al.* 1998). The tensions emerging in this world have been examined through case studies of, for instance, global warming (Barnett 2007) and cross-border infrastructures (Yang 2006).

Standard accounts explain global governance, as Walters (2004) suggested, as a response to the demands of a globalized world, without which protectionism and conflict might increase. Whilst conforming to the latter view, Barnett and Duvall (2005: 2) also questioned the role of power relations in governance, defined as "... the rules, structures, and institutions that guide, regulate, and control social life, features that are fundamental elements of power."

International relations have traditionally focused on inter-state relations, in which power is defined in realist terms as the capacity to influence other nations. However, if power is understood broadly as "... the production, in and through social relations, of effects that shape the capacities of actors to determine their own circumstances and fate" (Barnett and Duvall 2005: 3) then different typologies of power emerge (such as compulsory, institutional, structural, and productive). Running throughout international relations are not just formal power structures, but also discourses and values that reinforce a liberal agenda and a normative consensus (Kiersey 2009). These can detract our attention from the continuing ways in which global life is organized, structured and regulated.

As Mitchell argued, the externalization of distinctions forged by states to create the appearance of separate and inviolable domains must be historicized. My own work on interwar India highlights how "globalization" was debated through terms such as internationalism or trafficking (Legg 2009c). But the international, as a domain, concept and form of power relations, was only just emerging into popular consciousness; the "imperial" was the more widely accepted framework for thinking about the structuring of global relations. This mentality divided the world into chains of states, orchestrated by European powers. These states were conceived of as containers of their own sovereignty, although colonial sovereignty was more malleable than the imagined sovereignties emerging from the 1648 Treaty of Westphalia (Strang 1996). While imperialism established lines of command and government between the core and periphery of imperial world systems, internationalism promised a different type of relationship between actors across state borders. While the League of Nations largely failed in its attempts to bind states by international law, it was much more successful at encouraging cooperation on technical and health issues (Weindling 1995). In ways that resonate much more strongly with capillary forms of normative governance than with any sort of international government, the League also worked alongside religious, charitable, voluntary and hygiene associations to tackle agreed-upon social problems.

Hygiene is a particularly apposite example of the scalar dimensions of governance. Particularly popular in interwar manuals and journals, "International Hygiene" (Hutt 1927) demanded attention in a world of increased trade and migration, in which diseases and epidemics would traverse the world ever more quickly without a coordinated response. Hygiene was also an imperial issue, integral to the strengthening of races, both those which coordinated empires and those which worked to make them profitable (Bashford 2004, Heath 2010). Yet hygiene was also, centrally, focused on the individual. Supplementing Victorian sanitary science, interest in urban infrastructure, or population level programs of vaccination, hygiene targeted individual conduct (Legg 2009a). This could take the form of "social hygiene," from a medical perspective, or "moral hygiene," which advocated risk-averse conduct. In this sense, hygiene perfectly epitomizes Foucault's (1979) insistence that management of the population cannot be dissociated from individual self-formation and subjectivization (see Macey 2009).

While state based government does, of course, have the power to interpolate subjects into being, it is at the level of individual conduct that the power of governance becomes clear. Hunt (1999) has examined one form of this governance, termed "moral regulation," which desires the control of problematic conducts, values, and other cultures. Like governance, this emerges from "below," linking the government of others to that of the self, and is not just orchestrated through law or the state, but also through plural authorities in civil society. Quoting Foucault, Hunt (1999: 4) suggested that this regulation be thought of as governing because of its attempt to structure the possible field of action of others, in the process creating moralized subjects and objects, knowledge's, normativities, practices and fears. Hubbard (2008), for instance, has examined the geographies of heteronormativity through which the ethical and corporeal desire for the opposite sex is structured into our cities, routines and aesthetics.

It was this individualized practice of ethical self-formation that Foucault went on to examine in his lecture courses after the governmentality lectures of 1978–1979. His existing publications have already had a massive impact on studies of self-surveillance and self-discipline, the intersection between human sciences and psychology, and the way discursive subject categories translate into an individuals subjection to these norms (Butler 1997). But Foucault's existing and forthcoming lecture translations promise to shed greater light on the interconnections between the government of self and others, drawn from the ancient world (Foucault 2005) or from early Christianity (*On the Government of the Living*, 1980). The latter lectures followed directly on from the *Birth of Biopolitics* analysis of liberalism and extended the theorization of:

> ... "government," this notion being understood in the broad sense of techniques and procedures for directing human behaviour. Government of children, government of souls and consciences, government of a household, of a state, or of oneself. Inside this very general framework, we studied the problem of self-examination and confession. (Foucault, 1994: 80)

These lectures linked the Church's command to confess to an early form of individualized governance: one could not now just obey; one must know thyself and make thyself Christian. Power and truth were, thus, bound together *before* the historic appearance of the modern state (Landry 2009). But what about alternative types of power and truth within the modern state system, or even *beyond* it?

Returning again to the place and period of interwar India, we find evidence of a comprehensive counter-governance. In its aspirations to statehood and political power it can also be read as a counter-government. But what is fascinating about this alternative is that it insisted that governance was the priority, and that government would follow. This was the agenda pursued by the Indian National Congress (INC) under the leadership of MK Gandhi. In it's reimagining of the geography of India the INC was nationalist; in its war against the Government of India it was anti-colonial; but in its quest for *swaraj* (self-rule) the INC, through the work of Gandhi, was fixated on governance. Gandhi tied the self-rule of the nation to individual rule-of-self. He demanded extreme bodily self-discipline, through regulating sex, diet and clothing (Alter 2000). He stressed that political power lay in the consent of all of the people, not in the hands of the elite. Seizing this power would require a de-orientalization of Indians' self conceptions, instituting self improvement through the uplift of widows or untouchables, which would allow a different view of civilization to emerge: "Civilization is that mode of conduct which points out to man the path of duty. Performance of duty and observance of morality are convertible terms. To observe morality is to attain mastery over our mind and our passions." (MK Gandhi, quoted in Leela Gandhi 1996). This was Gandhi's primary aim and set him apart from politicians such as Nehru, for whom government and the state were often the prime focus:

> Political power, in my opinion, cannot be our ultimate aim ... The power to control national life through national representatives is called political power. Representatives will become unnecessary if the national life becomes so perfect as to be self-controlled. It will then be a state of enlightened anarchy in which each person will become his own ruler. ... In the ideal State there will be no political institution and therefore no political power. That is why Thoreau said in his classic statement that that government is best which governs least. (MK Gandhi quoted in Leela Gandhi 1996: 137)

Here Gandhi turns the distinction of "governance without government" into an opposition, centralizing individual ethical self-formation and displacing the state from the heart of the question of sovereignty. Gandhi's governance was an assemblage of bodily comportment and discipline, individual reflection and commitment, economic production and abstinence, and periodic political mass mobilization. The radical heterogeneity of this assemblage pushes us to find a similarly unnerving and challenging methodology to study the amorphic geographies of governance, to complement the political sciences we have to examine the apparatuses of the state. This may push us from the social dynamics of state politics to the affective registers of neuro-politics (Connolly 2002), or from a comfortable archive to the confusion of a multi-methodological tracking of the arteries and capillaries of power. Such socio-economic routes have been tentatively mapped by existing work on governance. This review has attempted to suggest some of the ways in which thinking about the state, political limits, liberal exclusions, internationalism and ethical self-formation might provide further linkages between the governance of self and others.

References

Alter, J.S. (2000) *Gandhi's Body: Sex, Diet, and the Politics of Nationalism*. University of Pennsylvania Press, Philadelphia.
Balakrishnan, G. (2000) *The Enemy: An Intellectual Portrait of Carl Schmitt*. Verso, London; New York.
Barnett, J. (2007) The Geopolitics of Climate Change. *Geography Compass* 1, 1361–1375.
Barnett, M. and Duvall, R. (2005) Power in Global Governance. In M. Barnett and R. Duvall (eds), *Power in Global Governance*. Cambridge University Press, Cambridge, pp. 1–32.
Bashford, A. (2004) *Imperial Hygiene: A Critical History of Colonialism, Nationalism and Public Health*. Palgrave Macmillan, Basingstoke.
Brenner, N. (2004) *New State Spaces: Urban Governance and the Rescaling of Statehood*. Oxford University Press, Oxford.

Butler, J. (1997) *Psychic Life of Power: Theories in Subjection*. Stanford University Press, Stanford.

Connolly, W. (2002) *Neuropolitics: Thinking, Culture, Speed*. University of Minnesota Press, Minneapolis; London.

Corbridge, S., Williams, G., Srivastava, M., and Véron, R. (2005) *Seeing the State: Governance and Governmentality in Rural India*. Cambridge University Press, Cambridge.

Deuber-Mankowsky, A. (2008) Nothing Is Political, Everything Can Be Politicized: On the Concept of the Political in Michel Foucault and Carl Schmitt. *Telos* 142, 135–161.

Donzelot, J. (1979) *The Policing of Families*. Pantheon Books, New York.

Duncan, J.S. (2007) *In the Shadow of the Tropics: Struggles over Bio-Power in Nineteenth Century Ceylon*. Ashgate, Aldershot.

Ferguson, J. (1994) *The Anti-Politics Machine: "Development", Depoliticization, and Bureaucratic Power in Lesotho*. University of Minnesota Press, Minneapolis.

Foucault, M. (1978 [2001]) Governmentality. In J.D. Faubion (ed.), *Essential Works of Foucault, 1954–1984: Power*. Vol. 3. Penguin, London, pp. 201–222.

Foucault, M. (1979) *The History of Sexuality Volume 1: An Introduction*. Allen Lane, London.

Foucault, M. (1982) The Subject and Power. In H. Dreyfus and P. Rabinow (eds), *Michel Foucault: Beyond Structuralism and Hermeneutics*. University of Chicago Press, Chicago, pp. 208–226.

Foucault, M. (1980) On the Government of the Living. In P. Rabinow (ed.), *Essential Works of Foucault 1954–1984: Ethics; Subjectivity and Truth*. Penguin, London, pp. 80–85.

Foucault, M. (2003) *Society Must Be Defended: Lectures at the Collège De France 1975–1976*. Penguin, London.

Foucault, M. (2005) *The Hermeneutics of the Subject: Lectures at the College De France 1981–198*. Picador, New York.

Foucault, M. (2007) *Security, Territory, Population: Lectures at the Collège De France 1977–78*. Palgrave Macmillan, Basingstoke; New York.

Foucault, M. (2008) *The Birth of Biopolitics: Lectures at the Collège De France, 1978–79*. Palgrave Macmillan, Basingstoke.

Gandhi, L. (1996) Concerning Violence: The Limits and Circulations of Gandhian "Ahisma" Or Passive Resistance. *Cultural Critique* 35, 105–147.

Goodwin, M. (1998) The Governance of Rural Areas: Some Emerging Research Issues and Agendas. *Journal of Rural Studies* 14, 5–12.

Gregory, D. (2007) Vanishing Points: Law, Violence and Exception in the Global War Prison. In D. Gregory and A. Pred (eds), *Violent Geographies: Fear, Terror and Political Violence*. Routledge, London; New York, pp. 205–236.

Hardt, M. and Negri, A. (2009) *Commonwealth*. Harvard University Press, Cambridge.

Heath, D. (2010) *Purifying Empire: Obscenity and the Politics of Moral Regulation in Britain, India and Australia*. Cambridge University Press, Cambridge.

Herod, A., Ó Tuathail, G. and Roberts, S.M. (1998) *An Unruly World?: Globalization, Governance, and Geography*. Routledge, London.

Hindess, B. (2005) Politics as Government: Michel Foucault's Analysis of Political Reason. *Alternatives* 30, 389–413.

Howell, P. (2009) *Geographies of Regulation: Policing Prostitution in Nineteenth-Century Britain and the Empire*. Cambridge University Press, Cambridge.

Hubbard, P. (2008) Here, There, Everywhere: The Ubiquitous Geographies of Heteronormativity. *Geography Compass* 2, 640–658.

Hunt, A. (1999) *Governing Morals: A Social History of Moral Regulation*. Cambridge University Press, Cambridge.

Hutt, C. (1927) *International Hygiene*. Methuen & Co, Ltd, London.

Jessop, B. (2007) From Micro-Powers to Governmentality: Foucault's Work on Statehood, State Formation, Statecraft and State Power. *Political Geography* 26, 34–40.

Jessop, B. (2011) Constituting Another Foucault Effect? Foucault on States and Statecraft. In U. Bröckling, S. Krasman and T. Lemke (eds), *Governmentality: Current Issues and Future Challenges*. Routledge, New York, pp. 56–73.

Kalyvas, A. (2008) *Democracy and the Politics of the Extraordinary: Max Weber, Carl Schmitt, and Hannah Arendt*. Cambridge University Press, Cambridge.

Kalyvas, A. and Müller, J. (2000) Introduction: Carl Schmitt; Legacy and Prospects. *Cardozo Law Revie* 5–6, 1469–1472.

Kiersey, N. J. (2009) Neoliberal Political Economy and the Subjectivity Crisis: Why Governmentality Is Not Hollow. *Global Societ* 23, 363–386.

Lambert, D. and Lester, A. (2004) Geographies of Colonial Philanthropy. *Progress in Human Geography* 28, 320–341.

Landry, J.-M. (2009) Confession, Obedience, and Subjectivity: Michel Foucault's Unpublished Lectures on the Government of the Living. *Telos* 146, 111–123.

Legg, S. (2009a) Governing Prostitution in Colonial Delhi: From Cantonment Regulations to International Hygiene (1864–1939). *Social History* 34, 447–467.

Legg, S. (2009b) An "Indispensable Hypodermis"? The Role of Scale in the Birth of Biopolitics. *Journal of Cultural Economy* 2, 219–225.

Legg, S. (2009c) Of Scales, Networks and Assemblages: The League of Nations Apparatus and the Scalar Sovereignty of the Government of India. *Transactions of the Institute of British Geographers NS* 34, 234–253.

Legg, S. (2010) An Intimate and Imperial Feminism: Meliscent Shephard and the Regulation of Prostitution in Colonial India. *Environment and Planning D: Society and Space* 28, 68–94.

Lemke, T. (2007) An Indigestible Meal? Foucault, Governmentality and State Theory. *Distinktion: Scandinavian Journal of Social Theory* 15, 43–64.

Macey, D. (2009) Rethinking Biopolitics, Race and Power in the Wake of Foucault. *Theory Culture Society* 26, 186–205.

McCormick, J.P. (1997) *Carl Schmitt's Critique of Liberalism: Against Politics as Technology*. Cambridge University Press, Cambridge.

Mehta, U.S. (1999) *Liberalism and Empire: A Study in Nineteenth Century British Liberal Thought*. University of Chicago Press, Chicago.

Mitchell, T. (1988) *Colonising Egypt*. Cambridge University Press, Cambridge.

Mitchell, T. (1999 [2006]) Society, Economy, and the State Effect. In A. Sharma and A. Gupta (eds), *The Anthropology of the State: A Reader*. Blackwell, Oxford, pp. 169–186.

Mitchell, T. (2002) *Rule of Experts: Egypt, Techno-Politics, Modernity*. University of California Press: Berkeley; London.

Mouffe, C. (ed.) (1999) *The Challenge of Carl Schmitt*. Verso, London.

Neal, A.W. (2008) Goodbye War on Terror? Foucault and Butler on Discourses of Law, War and Exceptionalism. In M. Dillon and A. W. Neal (eds), *Foucault on Politics, Security and War*. Palgrave Macmillan, Basingstoke, pp. 43–64.

Painter, J. (2009) Governance. In D. Gregory, R. Johnston, G. Pratt, M.J. Watts, and S. Whatmore (eds), *The Dictionary of Human Geography (5th Edition)*. Wiley-Blackwell, Oxford, pp. 312–313.

Phillips, J. (2006) Agencement/Assemblage. *Theory, Culture & Society* 23, 108–109.

Phillips, R. (2002) Imperialism, Sexuality and Space: Purity Movements in the British Empire. In A. Blunt and C. McEwan (eds), *Postcolonial Geographies*. Continuum, London, pp. 46–63.

Ransom, J.S. (1997) *Foucault's Discipline: The Politics of Subjectivity*. Duke University Press, Durham; London.

Rasch, W. (2005) Introduction: Carl Schmitt and the New World Order. *South Atlantic Quarterly* 104, 177–183.
Rose, N. and Miller, P. (2008) *Governing the Present*. Polity Press, Cambridge.
Rosenau, J.N. (1992) Governance, Order and Change in World Politics. In J.N. Rosenau and E.-O. Czempiel (eds), *Governance without Government: Order and Change in World Politics*. Cambridge University Press, Cambridge, pp. 1–29.
Schmitt, C. (1932 [1996]) *The Concept of the Political*. University of Chicago Press, Chicago.
Stoker, G. (1998) Governance as Theory; Five Propositions. *International Social Science Journal* 50, 17–28.
Strang, D. (1996) Contested Sovereignty: The Social Construction of Colonial Imperialism. In T.J. Biersteker and C. Webber (eds), *State Sovereignty as Social Construct*. Cambridge University Press, Cambridge, pp. 22–49.
Swyngedouw, E. (2005) Governance Innovation and the Citizen: The Janus Face of Governance-Beyond-the-State. *Urban Stud* 42, 1991–2006.
Valverde, M. (1996) "Despotism" and Ethical Liberal Governance. *Economy and Society* 25, 357–372.
Walters, W. (2004) Some Critical Notes On "Governance." *Studies in Political Economy* 73, 27–46.
Weindling, P. (ed.) (1995) *International Health Organisations and Movements, 1918–39*. Cambridge University Press, Cambridge.
Yang, C. (2006) The Geopolitics of Cross-Boundary Governance in the Greater Pearl River Delta, China: A Case Study of the Proposed Hong Kong-Zhuhai-Macao Bridge. *Political Geography* 25, 817–835.

Chapter 25

Mobility
Part I

David Ley

Introduction

Some papers seemingly kick-start themselves as ideas sparked by external events rush together faster than they can be recorded. For others the scholarly muse is much more grudging, serving up only thin gruel to the hungry author. This paper was launched by a bountiful muse as I departed from Dulles Airport to return to Vancouver from the annual conference of the Association of American Geographers. Assuming an all-too common mobile identity in the air was notable for one reason only. As I flew west to Vancouver in April 2010 those wishing to fly east to Europe remained on the ground, marooned by the ash cloud circling over the continent from Iceland's Eyjafjallajökull volcano that immobilized European air space. In the following days, taken-for-granted routines and expectations were frustrated as planes were grounded, huge losses accumulated for airlines, business meetings were compromised, family reunions disappointed, and perishable air freight commodities rotted in hangers. A continent denied mobility in the sky was quickly in crisis.

But the muse, bless her, was even more *sympathique*, for no sooner were we up in the air from Dulles, then behold, there was *Up in the Air* (Paramount 2009) before me on the in-flight monitor. The film examines the life of a master of mobility who spends 320 days and nights a year in airplanes and indistinguishable airport hotels around the United States, in serial anonymous spaces as he conducts his unlovely job as a hired hand moving from city to city, firing managers from downsizing firms that do not have the wit or charity to do it themselves. In this recession-shaped morality tale, we are led to the strong suspicion that, though he does not realize it himself, our hero's hypermobile life is deficient, missing out on permanent relationships and effectual place-making. He is simultaneously both a master and a prisoner of mobility. But there is more. For our hero does not become reflexively

The Wiley Blackwell Companion to Human Geography, First Edition.
Edited by John A. Agnew and James S. Duncan.
© 2011 John Wiley & Sons, Ltd. Published 2016 by John Wiley & Sons, Ltd.

aware of any disability in his way of life until he meets another seemingly like himself, another denizen of late-night airport bars and expense-account hotels. When he meets her, questions of lasting relationships and rootedness are eventually awakened. But all to no avail for she is playing a different game with mobility. She is already rooted with a home and a family, and uses mobility to engage in an ephemeral identity of fleeting encounters. Impermanence, anonymity, life without a history or a future, allows for some games of chance; relationships too are up in the air.

The film is a morality tale about hypermobility that I shall re-tell from the experience of household heads of the so-called astronaut families among the overseas Chinese, whose lives ply across the Pacific air routes from revenue sources in East Asia to consumption destinations in Sydney, San Francisco or Vancouver, the present homes of their families. But before we meet these often wealthy aviators there is an important back story to consider about the historic contexts of mobility. We begin with the tight connections between mobility and modernity.

Mobility and Modernity

In his book, *On the Move: Mobility in the Modern Western World*, Tim Cresswell (2006), who has thought about mobile lives perhaps more than any other geographer, astutely historicizes mobility within the unfolding of modernity. The Enlightenment's haughty Eurocentrism was reproduced as Europeans travelled overseas and found other societies against which to measure themselves. As the inventors of the conceptual measuring sticks, the comparison was always complimentary for Europeans and invidious for the other (Anderson 2007). Of course, voyages of discovery and explanation did not simply permit the construction of unfavorable stereotypes of distant others, but also shaped tangible networks, including trading routes, missionary trails and the lineaments of empire.

Greater mobility of minds and bodies brought an abrupt end to the stasis of the pre-industrial world in Europe as well as parts of the overseas territories its nations colonized. What Peter Laslett (1965) called *The World We have Lost* was a European society of greater closure and self-sufficiency, where village units were organized around the central place of a market town. In human geography this constellation of society and environment constituted the celebrated *pays* studies of the French School under Vidal de la Blache, where people and place were bonded, in a felicitous phrase, like a snail and its shell (Wrigley 1965). Daily action was largely confined to the parish round and weekly visits to a market town, though war was always on the horizon to take young men away to foreign battle fields. But following such disruptions a seemingly timeless normality would return. The sunken lanes of rural north-western Europe are a landscape testimony to the generations of bounded movement of people, animals, and carts from the village to the fields, steadily wearing down the surface of the lane below adjacent fields, commons and copses, and thereby both reflecting and reproducing inherently local lives.

This semi-closed world of impeded mobility was fundamentally dislocated by the Industrial Revolution that depended on enhanced movement of labor and commodities over broader territories. As Wrigley (1965) observed, the Vidalian paradigm foundered as it encountered industrial eastern France, where local geographies were transcended and *circulation* through inter-regional roads, canals and later the railway up-scaled the dimensions of people and place. The new forces of geographical organization were less the reciprocal bonding of local societies and their immediate physical environment, and more the world of movement connecting regional, national and even global centers of comparative economic advantage. Railway schedules, steamship times and capacities, and the commute, the journey-to-work, which bound city centers with their new suburbs became some of the salient parameters of spatial organization. So by the 1930s, the geographer P.R. Crowe was demanding that the centrality of movement be recognized in geographical studies. "Is progressive geography," asked Crowe (1938), inhaling the bracing air of Enlightenment confidence, "to be solely concerned with the distribution of Homo Dormiens?" He had a better project in mind: "A dynamic view implies that stress is to be laid neither upon terminal facilities, nor on the pattern of the system, but upon men and things moving." And in this project there were enough precedents and contemporaries in both art and popular culture during the 1918–1939 period that later talk of a contemporary "new mobilities paradigm" (Sheller and Urry 2006; Urry 2007) seems to have been anticipated much earlier.

Vidal's *France de L'Est* was published in 1917, coinciding with an experimental era in a modern art that, like that industrial captain of movement Henry Ford, wished to banish historical precedents and glorify contemporary mobile technologies, including the car, the train, the ocean liner and the airplane. Futurist artists and architects in particular privileged themes of technology, the vehicles of mobility and the dynamic energy of speed (Whyte 2000). By the 1930s, airpainting had appeared as a new theme within Futurism, glorifying flight, aerial landscapes and the speed of the airplane (Zoccoli 2000). In popular culture the creation of Superman in 1932, master of speed, mobility, and aerial vision, was a counterpart to the aesthetic projects of the Futurists – and a creation with ambiguous relations with eugenics. Superman's base camp was Metropolis, the name taken from Fritz Lang's ominous 1927 film set in a dysfunctional city of the future. In Anglo-America a related inspiration was Moderne or Streamline style, a 1930s development of Art Deco, with aerodynamic lines, long horizontal contours and gentle curves emphasizing speed and motion (Hillier and Escrit 1997). These forms became the house style for the 1939 New York World's Fair, an optimistic paeon to science, technology and advanced transportation in "Building the World of Tomorrow." Among streamline Moderne's better-recognized buildings is Florin Court, London (built 1936), known to television audiences as Whitehaven Mansions, home of Agathie Christie's affable detective Hercule Poirot. This popular television series, highlighting Cubist and Futurist themes in its opening credits and selection of locational sets, is a testimony to an interwar aesthetic that enthusiastically celebrated modern mobilities.

The possibilities of speed and circulation in a world of mass production were intoxicating to modern architects and designers. Le Corbusier's *Towards a New Architecture* (1927) is filled with photographs of cars, airplanes and ocean liners; his famous sketch of a modern townscape of freeways and high rises in a park, viewed appropriately from the roof of a tower block, whimsically includes three bi-planes hovering over the city. Le Corbusier was one of the prophets of the machine age aesthetic, with his well-known definition of a street as a factory for producing traffic. His exaggerated desire to incorporate movement and speed into the fabric of the modern city was perfected – fortunately only in theory – in his extraordinary plan for Algiers in 1930 where the residential towers become a single horizontal unit in a sinuous linear city, with the inevitable freeway running as if on a viaduct across their fused roofline. While this fanciful project was never built, Le Corbusier's habitual desire to obliterate old landscapes facilitated the massive urban renewal and freeway construction that was to follow in western cities in the 1950s and 1960s (cf. Merriman 2007). In this era of high modernism his model of the freeway, high rise city – the semiotic equivalent of the factory assembly line and its stacked products awaiting shipping – became an influential prototype.

Mobility and Cosmopolitanism

Mobility, modernity and urbanity are easily reconciled with cosmopolitanism, the expansive disposition of those who transcend local rootedness. The concept has developed from its seminal use by Immanuel Kant, the Enlightenment philosopher whose utopian vision for international peace and understanding followed from the deepening flows of international trade that broke open the economic cell of the nation state (Wood 1998). So too the universal ambition of the modern project in architecture – or the international style as it became in the United States – necessitated expunging the partisan categories of class, nation, and history in favor of a brave new world that would owe no favors to any of these outmoded lower order attachments. The clinical eye of the detached urban designer or modern artist was readily compatible with the calculating attitude Simmel detected in the modern city, and both converged with the rational and blasé disposition of the well-travelled cosmopolitan. The cosmopolitan's mobility between multiple sites empowered a worldview of reasoned comparison and generalization, and freedom from the more proximate boundaries of local commitment.

The parochialism of the parish order, what Vidal called *le patriotisme de clocher*, local pride constrained spatially by the visibility of the steeple of the parish church, was summarily dismissed in the long view corridors of the modern world city. In early social science the dualism of rural folk and modern urban societies became a cardinal line of separation not only in Vidal's human geography but also in Robert Redfield's anthropology and the *gemeinschaft-gesellschaft* distinction of German and American sociology. Bounded horizons were blown open by ambitions that exploded the stable life patterns of centuries. Consciousness of roots was succeeded by a celebration of routes. The scale of the shift surprised even the detached view of contemporary social scientists. Profoundly and poignantly, Oscar Handlin (1951) described the great European migration to America from 1880–1930 as the movement of *The Uprooted*.

Tim Cresswell (2006) contrasts the dualism of sedentarist *versus* nomadic ideologies. Sedentarism is linked to rooted practices of people in place, and territorially-bounded identities. Freedom from local constraints and rural confinements with the coming of the Industrial Revolution did not prevent nineteenth and early twentieth century theorists like Marx, Durkheim, Weber and Simmel from challenging the alienation, anomie, disenchantment, individuality, and anonymity of life which they variously detected in the industrial city – in some cases inspiring their own alternative cosmopolitan utopias. For the Chicago School, while the city had progressive opportunities, nonetheless its abiding culture was one of social disorganization. Mobility was deeply implicated in this social malaise. Cresswell (2006: 37) quotes from an unpublished essay of Nels Anderson, a student of Ernest Burgess in Chicago in the 1920s and author of *The Hobo,* an early monograph on urban homelessness. "The mobility of the city," wrote Anderson, "detaches and undomesticates the urban man ... with this independence comes a loss of loyalty."

But others would see local domestic loyalty as an impediment to be jettisoned without regrets in the advance to a cosmopolitan society. Cresswell (2006) outlines a parallel and more recent literature that praises mobility, sometimes excessively, evoking the Futurist themes of "movement, speed and circulation" (Thrift 1994). Here sedentarism is replaced by a nomadist ideology that endorses the opportunities and consequences of movement. Cresswell cites Bernard Tschumi's *The Manhattan Transcripts* (1994) as an exemplary model of nomadic ideology in its emphasis on an architecture shaped by bodies in motion. *Manhattan Transcripts* is reminiscent of the older *Manhattan Transfer* (1925), John Dos Passos' innovative and acclaimed novel of daily life in New York, a life of ephemera and cubist fragments, of glimpses and glances, unfinished sentences and unnamed publics, of characters and language constantly in flux and movement (Brosseau 1995). A major difference is that Dos Passos saw alienation, not celebration, in these truncated mobile lives.

Cresswell notes that the advocates of nomadism employ strangely generic humans to populate their moving sidewalks. And they are cast with inherently cosmopolitan personalities, the capacity, like their creators, to move across borders both political and conceptual. The cosmopolitan-local dichotomy is another parallel to sedentarism and nomadism. For the cosmopolitan is the person on the move, and cosmopolitanism, as Craig Calhoun (2002), has famously declared, is the class-consciousness of the frequent traveler. Cosmopolitans are those with some dexterity, holders of cultural capital who are able to move seamlessly between both concepts and continents. A familiar *cadre* would be the transnational capitalists described by Leslie Sklair (2001), embedded in multinational corporations, and pressing for a neoliberal utopia of free trade, open borders, and the erosion of the intrusive nation state. But there is a similar cohort with a location on the political left. In an analysis of surveys of Australian political dispositions, Katharine Betts (2002) has found a stable set of intersecting cosmopolitan attitudes and socio-spatial attributes: "It is they who support the moral values of international cosmopolitanism, social justice, anti-racism, multiculturalism, closer ties with Asia, and Aboriginal self-determination. Most of this group are members of the new class of university-educated professionals, concentrated in inner urban areas." The gentrified inner city with its exaggerated international options in cuisine, the arts, and political causes is often identified as the home of such social cosmopolitanism (Ley 2004; Binnie *et al.* 2006). The elite suburbs, in turn, are frequently the habitat of corporate capitalists whose estates convey a more patrician landscape of horses and rolling acreage. Westchester County outside New York provides this landscape for such members of the jet-setting capitalist class as Ralph Lauren and Martha Stewart, for whom rural Westchester is strategically located both for the railway commute to Manhattan and also the limousine ride to the New York airports (Duncan and Duncan 2004).

But closer examination challenges the neat relationship drawn between global mobility and cosmopolitan values. The Westchester elite, though contributing to global consumer identities, is extraordinarily protectionist on its home turf, and in the exclusion of socially incompatible others replays all of the prejudices of parish society (Duncan and Duncan 2004). Meanwhile the gentrifying inner cities of Sydney and Melbourne, like their counterparts all over the world, draw their provenance from the displacement of the typically lower-status groups who occupied the neighborhood before them (Ley 2004). In both cases, the cosmopolitan disposition of respect for otherness fails at the first hurdle of practical living. Cosmopolitan and perhaps inclusive at work, both groups are inherently localist and exclusionary at home. In this bipolar disposition they are in phase with their predecessor, Immanuel Kant. For despite Kant's celebrated treatise on cosmopolitanism, his own geographical categories were an embodiment of race, class and gender prejudice, "nothing short of an intellectual and political embarrassment" (Harvey 2009). Mentally global, he was materially local, never travelling more than 100 miles from his home town of Konigsberg in Prussia. In fact, mobility need not expedite more cosmopolitan life worlds even among today's global frequent fliers. As global capitalists move between high status enclaves in world cities they are engaging the same generic retinue of expensive hotels, up-market chain stores, high rise offices and low-rise nightclubs. Their privilege and worldview are likely to be reproduced by such restricted encounters. Neither socially inclusive, nor territorially varied, the social geography of the global capitalist may prove to be unexpectedly parochial.

Mobility and Migration

International migration is typically set out as a primary case of a new mobilities paradigm. The act of migration punctures a sedentarist lifeworld, and for some theorists this disruption of taken-for-granted routines and perspectives is sufficient justification to announce the presence of cosmopolitanism for migrants of different classes. The competencies and dexterities required to straddle languages and cultures by "middleman minorities," such as immigrant taxi-drivers or ethnic entrepreneurs, reveal the existence of a rather different cosmopolitanism "from below," an "ordinary cosmopolitanism" that from a position of economic necessity rather than elite power nonetheless permits navigation across cultural difference (Pécoud 2004; Binnie et al. 2006). Some theorists romanticize this subject position, the "migrant's-eye view of the world ... [that] celebrates hybridity, impurity, intermingling, and the transformation that comes of new and unexpected combinations ... It is the great possibility that mass migration gives the world, and I have tried to embrace it" (Rushdie 1991: 394).

But such a rendition seems some distance from the everyday realities of most immigrants, and critics have tended to deflate this rhetoric as the "hype of hybridity," an intellectual abstraction "increasingly disarticulated from history and political economy" (Mitchell 1997).

The character of the contemporary migrant is extraordinarily diverse. While we typically think of the major world cities as the sites of "superdiversity" (Vertovec 2006), and they are, the United Arab Emirates have the highest proportion of foreign-born, with the figure exceeding 80 percent in Dubai and almost 40 percent in Mecca (Saudi Arabia) compared with a quarter of the population in London and a third in New York (Samers 2010). Immigrant resources are also highly variable, including both the "human talents," an upper tier of sought-after skilled and business migrants, and also a lower tier of temporary contract workers, asylum seekers and the undocumented, who are merely tolerated or worse with limited or no citizenship entitlements. With migrants variously seeking security from persecution, poverty and war, economic prospects, family reunification, or higher education a plurality of motivations shapes their decision-making and their struggles *en route*. In this profuse variation it is impossible to define the average migrant, and any generalizations need to be contextually accountable.

One generalization that is readily defensible is the effect of the transport and communications revolutions on the movement of people, information and accompanying capital flows. Cheaper air travel facilitates the mobility of people, and the telephone and electronic communication aid families and friends to keep in contact with each other while apart. The important concept of transnationalism has been developed to describe the mobility and hypermobility of contemporary international migration facilitated by these technologies. Traditional ideas have been rethought. The conventional view of immigration has portrayed a linear process of departure from a homeland, followed by arrival, settlement, assimilation, citizenship and incorporation into a new nation state. But this tidy view of the peopling of settler societies has been disrupted in a transnational era where movement is often short-term, followed by return migration, and frequently by repeated rounds of departures and returns. So common has this model become that the UN's Global Commission on International Migration (2005: 31) has identified a paradigm shift, "where the old paradigm of permanent migrant settlement is giving way to temporary and circular migration."

It is not only advances in transportation and communication technology that lubricates movement, but also innovations in the state's view of citizenship. The novelty of dual citizenship permits the development of dual allegiances and the existence of more than a single national resource base. If one nation offers, for example, security, another may have better prospects for economic well-being, encouraging repeated movement between the two at different stages in the life cycle when one resource succeeds another in salience. Households are thereby able to act flexibly and strategically through migration as geographically differentiated opportunities rise and fall. Moreover, many states have suspended historic views of citizenship in favor of a neoliberal calculus of maximizing market benefits. If the search for the skilled worker, "human talent", exalts the status of the self-sufficient citizen, how much more valued is the business immigrant who brings not only human capital but also financial capital from an established record of entrepreneurial success in his home country. Not only self-sufficient, he bears the promise of multiplying economic value for himself and others in a new homeland. More than 30 nations have business immigration programs, competitively trawling for the attentions of the sought-after business immigrant. Among these, the Canadian version has proven most successful in landing the catch.

Mobility and the Astronaut Household

Many of the themes of this chapter converge around the millionaire migrants who ply the airline routes from Hong Kong, Taiwan and Mainland China to Pacific Rim cities that include Sydney, Auckland, San Francisco and Vancouver. They are attuned to what anthropologist Aihwa Ong (1999) calls an alternate Asian modernity, a society closely shaped by the market, with the state the enforcer of market freedoms and disciplines. This free for all is particularly evident in the property market, for land is a principal source of wealth and buying and selling property is an entirely dispassionate affair of pure calculation. Asia Pacific cities present landscapes of constant change, restless creative destruction, where large numbers of migrants in motion defy the presence of shared memories, and where newness is a cardinal virtue. In the late 1980s, when in pursuit of portfolio diversification East Asian capital made a dramatic landfall in Vancouver, new condominium projects in Vancouver were marketed in Hong Kong without any purchase opportunity in Canada at all (Ley 2010). Indignant protest led to the end of this commodifying practice, but the cult of modernity led to other conflicts as older homes in elite neighborhoods, with a sense of place revered by the native-born, were bought and demolished to permit the construction of a new building for wealthy immigrants. A cultural anthropology of property in East Asia leaves no room for sentimentality. Hong Kong's built environment, writes Ackbar Abbas, is committed to an unwavering march of profit and contemporaneity: "what are erased are cultural memories, what is rebuilt are more profitable buildings" (Abbas 1997: 80). This is the cultural meaning of property learned in Hong Kong and borne by the diaspora to overseas landscapes. In an Asian modernity fascination with the new, dismissal of the old, is both culturally progressive and good business practice.

Such members of the Chinese diaspora have been characterized by Gary Hamilton (1999) as "cosmopolitan capitalists." They are entrepreneurs *sans frontières*, establishing family networks across space, thereby maximizing access and information to new opportunities. True to the cosmopolitan ethos, they bear ambiguous relations to political territories and may evade local and national political commitments. A Vancouver survey (Hiebert and Ley 2006) showed that transnational business immigrants, disproportionately from East Asia, were much more likely than other immigrants to have a sense of Canadian identity only occasionally, or never; they were also less likely to have adopted Canadian citizenship. A second survey, in Toronto, revealed that high school youth from Hong Kong whose fathers were astronauts working primarily in Hong Kong had a weaker sense of belonging in Canada than other groups (Chow 2007). Regular trans-Pacific movement delays, and may even impede, an expressive and legal identification with Canada. In establishing a transnational outlook, there is the characteristic cosmopolitan neglect of locality. Trans-Pacific routes trump Canadian roots (Ley 2010). Aihwa Ong offers a stronger thesis that millionaire migrants in the Chinese diaspora actively circumvent the claims of different states upon them. "For many overseas Chinese," she observes, "there is no obvious continuity between family interests and political loyalty" (Ong 1999: 116). Consequently families have developed strategies "adept at subverting the political regimes of localization and control" (1999: 119). Political sedentarism is evaded in favor of cosmopolitan nomadism.

A *habitus* of mobility defines this population. Environmental scanning for new business opportunities, and short-term encounters with places and projects, what one respondent described to me as the "restless creativity" of the Chinese diaspora, does not co-exist comfortably with the containments of national citizenship. An example from my research among wealthy East Asian immigrants in Vancouver makes the point. The residency requirement within Canada for passage toward citizenship – part of the state's "regimes of localization and control" – has proven a frustrating hurdle to businessmen absent for most of the year managing a company in East Asia. The law prescribed that if a permanent resident did not maintain residency in Canada for at least 183 days in a 12-month period, there would be a danger under the Immigration Act of losing permanent residence status, and of an unwelcome interrogation by airport immigration officers with power of sanction. Businessmen on the trans-Pacific run are habitually out of Canada for longer than this period each year operating their enterprise in Asia, and would therefore be at risk of losing their permanent residency status. Predictably, this restriction is unpopular. The Taiwanese-Canadian readers of the *World Journal* daily newspaper were informed that an extension to the residency requirement would further infringe upon the mobility of business frequent fliers. As a result, opined an immigration lawyer, "they might not choose Canada" as a destination *(World Journal* 1999). A second story in another Chinese-language daily in Vancouver, *Ming Pao,* identified a solution to this dilemma (Cheung 1999). An end run around the barrier for some astronauts has been to enter the United States from Canada as a visitor and use an American airport as a point of trans-Pacific embarkation and re-entry, evading the watchful eye of Canadian immigration. *Ming Pao* reported that drivers would collect astronauts from the Seattle airport for $150–$200 and bring them across the border as short-term departees from Canada, thereby concealing a much longer absence.

"I can live anywhere in the world," declared a wealthy member of the overseas Chinese diaspora in California, "but it must be near an airport" (Ong 1999: 135). The geographical distribution of recent ethnic Chinese immigrants to Vancouver does indeed show a residential concentration in an arc around the favored site of the international airport (Ley 2010). The sedentary representation of dots on a map conceals the urge to move among this population that is revealed by proximity to the airport, that institutional hub of contemporary mobility (Cresswell 2006; Adey 2010). So, as we began, we are again *Up in the Air.* The "astronaut" is a vernacular term in the overseas Chinese settlements around the Pacific Rim. It is a translation of a colloquial Cantonese pun playing off the phonetic similarity of "space" and "empty wife" (*tai kung*) referencing the simultaneous status of "spacemen" and "separated families" (Skeldon 1995). And therein hangs the final section of this chapter.

The Injuries of Hypermobility

The modern, cosmopolitan businessman evinces a sense of mastery over distance, control over space, the exemplar of a new mobilities paradigm. The world appears indeed to be the oyster of the astronaut commuting between East Asia and selected world cities around the Pacific Rim. He has it all, an advantageous revenue stream with low taxation from his production realm on the humid and polluted coastal plains of Asia Pacific, and the high quality of life and abundant public and private services for family reproduction from his consumption realm in the elite neighborhoods and suburbs of San Francisco, Vancouver, Sydney and Auckland. But if the language of the "spaceman" conveys these gratifications, what of the world of "separated families"? Is life *Up in the Air* also an experience not of surfeit but of deficiency, its occupant as much a prisoner as a master of space?

Clara Law's film, *Floating Life* (Southern Star Films 1996) is an ominous representation of such diasporic cosmopolitanism. The film corresponds with Law's own departure from Hong Kong to Australia, and is about the *un*settled nature of life across space and between cultures. While a family friend moves to Vancouver, the Chen family selects Australia, the earlier destination of a daughter, while a son remains in Hong Kong and a second daughter migrates to Germany. Scattered between three continents, the family exemplifies the "bamboo network" of the contemporary Chinese diaspora, where family fragmentation achieves the dispersal of economic risk and the maximizing of economic opportunity. But there is also disorientation, trauma and frequently economic peril in such displacements. Depression, the condition whose name cannot be uttered in overseas Chinese communities, is a common medical response to such social and economic stresses (Shen et al. 2006).

The anxieties and depression of fragmented families take up considerable counseling resources in NGOs and churches serving the diaspora. Asia Pacific is a region with many versions of the transnationally divided family: Filipino domestic workers are separated for years from their children and other close family members (Parreñas 2005); "study mothers" from China accompany their children to educational opportunities in Singapore (Huang and Yeoh 2005); and overseas Chinese businessmen sometimes maintain a "second family" on the Mainland while absent from their legal wife in the diaspora (Shen 2005). Each of these models of separation represents an uncomfortable combination of public opportunity and private suffering, endured for the good of the family or more specifically the advancement of the children.

Clearly, the astronaut household with the chief breadwinner working in Hong Kong, Taiwan, China or South Korea, and commuting for short periods to visit family members on the other side of the Pacific Ocean is a family form with a distinctive emotional geography (Ley 2010). It became evident from my first interviews in Vancouver that the astronaut household was a common organizational model, and rife with personal and social tensions: women are effectively lone parents and often stressed in Canada, children are at risk from predators and subject to behavior problems, while absent men may be drawn into extra-marital affairs in Asia. In the words of one head of household, briefly united with his family in Vancouver from his business life in Taiwan, "Don't tell me I have a big house. This is a house of tears." A life *Up in the Air* implies the collision of economic and social objectives, an experience materially rewarding but subjectively draining. The mobile masters of transnational space are simultaneously the prisoners of emotional separation.

References

Abbas, A. (1997) *Hong Kong: Culture and the Politics of Disappearance*. Hong Kong University Press, Hong Kong.
Adey, P. (2010) *Mobility*. Routledge, New York.
Anderson, K. (2007) *Race and the Crisis of Humanism*. Routledge, New York.

Betts, K. (2002) Boat people and the 2001 election. *People and Place* 10 (3), 36–54.
Binnie, J., Holloway, J., Millington, S., and Young, C. (2006) Introduction: grounding cosmopolitan urbanism. In J. Binnie, J. Holloway, S. Millington, and C. Young (eds), *Cosmopolitan Urbanism*. Routledge, Abingdon, pp. 1–34.
Brosseau, M. (1995) The city in textual form: *Manhattan Transfer*'s. New York, *Ecumene* 2, 89–114.
Calhoun, C. (2002) The class consciousness of frequent travellers: towards a critique of actually existing cosmopolitanism. In S. Vertovec and R. Cohen (eds), *Conceiving Cosmopolitanism*. Oxford University Press, Oxford, pp. 86–109.
Cheung, L.C. (1999) Self-employment: transporting astronauts. *Ming Pao Daily News*, 8 (3), p. A1.
Chow, H. (2007) Sense of belonging and life satisfaction among Hong Kong adolescent immigrants in Canada. *Journal of Ethnic and Migration Studies* 33, 511–520.
Cresswell, T. (2006) *On the Move: Mobility in the Modern Western World*. Routledge, London.
Crowe, P.R. (1938) On progress in geography. *Scottish Geographical Magazine* 54, 1–19.
Dos Passos, J. (1925) *Manhattan Transfer*. Somerset Books, New York.
Duncan, J and Duncan, N. (2004) *Landscapes of Privilege*. Routledge, New York.
Global Commission on International Migration. (2005) Migration in an Interconnected World: New Directions for Action. (Geneva: Report of the UN Global Commission on International Migration.
Hamilton, G. (ed.) (1999) *Cosmopolitan Capitalists: Hong Kong and the Chinese Diaspora at the end of the Twentieth Century*. University of Washington Press, Seattle.
Handlin, O. (1951) *The Uprooted: The Epic Story of the Great Migrations that made the American People*. Little, Brown, Boston.
Harvey, D. (2009) *Cosmopolitanism and the Geographies of Freedom*. Columbia University Press, New York.
Hiebert, D. and Ley, D. (2006) Characteristics of immigrant transnationalism in Vancouver. In V. Satzewich and L. Wong (eds), *Transnational Identities and Practices in Canada*. UBC Press, Vancouver, pp. 71–90.
Hillier, B. and Escritt, S. (1997) *Art Deco Style*. Phaidon, London.
Huang, S. and Yeoh, B. (2005) Transnational families and their children's education: China's "study mothers" in Singapore. *Global Networks* 5, 379–400.
Laslett, P. (1965) *The World We Have Lost*. Methuen, London.
Le Corbusier. (1927) *Towards a New Architecture*. Brewer, Warner & Putnam, New York.
Ley, D. (2004) Transnational spaces and everyday lives. *Transactions of the Institute of British Geographers* 29, 151–164.
Ley, D. (2010) *Millionaire Migrants: Trans-Pacific Life Lines*. Blackwell-Wiley, Oxford.
Merriman, P. (2007) *Driving Spaces: A Cultural-Historical Geography of England's M1 Motorway*. Blackwell. Oxford.
Mitchell, K. (1997) Different diasporas and the hype of hybridity. *Society and Space* 15, 533–553.
Ong, A. (1999) *Flexible Citizenship; The Cultural Logics of Transnationality*. Duke University Press, Durham.
Parreñas, R. (2005) Long distance intimacy: class, gender and intergenerational relations between mothers and children in Filipino transnational families. *Global Networks* 5, 317–336.
Pécoud, A. (2004) Entrepreneurship and identity: cosmopolitanism and cultural competences among German-Turkish businesspeople in Berlin. *Journal of Ethnic and Migration Studies* 30, 3–20.
Rushdie, S. (1991) In good faith. In *Imaginary Homelands*. Granta, London, pp. 393–414.

Samers, M. (2010) *Migration*. Routledge, New York.
Sheller, M. and Urry, J. (2006) The new mobilities paradigm. *Environment and Planning A* 38, 207–226.
Shen, E., Alden, L., Sochting, I., and Tsang, P. (2006) Clinical observations of a Cantonese cognitive-behavioral treatment program for Chinese immigrants. In F.T Leong and S. Lopez (eds), *Psychotherapy: Theory, Research, Practice, Training* 43, 518–530.
Shen, H.H. (2005) The first Taiwanese wives and the Chinese mistresses: the international division of labour in familial and intimate relations across the Taiwan Strait. *Global Networks* 5, 419–437.
Skeldon, R. (1995) Emigration from Hong Kong, 1945–1994: the demographic lead-up to 1997. In R. Skeldon (ed.), *Emigration from Hong Kong: Tendencies and Impacts*. Chinese University Press, Hong Kong, pp. 51–77.
Sklair, L. (2001) *The Transnational Capitalist Class*. Blackwell, Oxford.
Thrift, N. (1994) In human geographies: landscapes of speed, light and power. In P. Cloke (ed.), *Writing the Rural: Five Cultural Geographies*. Paul Chapman, London, pp. 191–250.
Tschumi, B. and Young, R. (1994) *The Manhattan Transcripts*. Academy Editions, London.
Urry, J. (2007) *Mobilities*. Polity Press, Cambridge.
Vertovec, S. (2006) *The Emergence of Super-Diversity in Britain*. COMPAS Working Paper, Oxford, pp. 6–25.
Whyte, I.B. (2000) Futurist architecture. In G. Berghaus (ed), *International Futurism in Arts and Architecture*. de Gruyter, New York, pp. 353–372.
Wood, A. (1998) Kant's project for perpetual peace. In P. Cheah and B. Robbins (eds), *Cosmopolitics: Thinking and Feeling Beyond the Nation*. University of Minnesota Press, Minneapolis, pp. 59–76.
World Journal. (1999) Business immigrants would be affected most. *World Journal Daily News* 26 November, p. A4.
Wrigley, E. (1965) Changes in the philosophy of geography. In R.J. Chorley and P. Haggett (eds), *Frontiers in Geographical Teaching*. Methuen, London, pp. 3–20.
Zoccoli, F. (2000) Futurist women painters in Italy. In G. Berghaus (ed.), *International Futurism in Arts and Architecture*. de Gruyter, New York, pp. 373–397.

Chapter 26

Mobility
Part II

George Revill

Introduction

Since the publication in 2000 of John Urry's *Sociology Beyond Societies: Mobilities for the twenty-first century,* movement and mobility have taken an increasingly important place within the study of societies and social action. The rapid growth of mobilities research is reflected in the publication of a new journal *Mobilities* in 2006. (Hannem *et al.* 2006: 9; Blunt 2007: 684). Within cultural geography, Cresswell's pioneering work (2001a, 2006; Cresswell and Verstraete 2002) set an agenda for mobilities studies which is sensitive to historical and geographical specificity and placed within its distinctive political and cultural political contexts. This approach has been supported by work such as that by Merriman (2003, 2004, 2005a, 2005b, 2008) on motorways and driving and Adey (2004, 2010a) on airports and air travel setting the specificities of movement within particular technosocial arrangements, spatialities and conceptions of place (see also Divall and Revill 2005; Adey 2006, 2010b; Revill 2007, 2011; Merriman *et al.* 2008). Yet the role for cultural geography as part of what Cresswell terms the "mobilities turn," seems to be increasingly problematic, challenged by both the subject matter and the mode of investigation. The location of mobilities within specific techno-social networks, formations and assemblages challenge conceptions of what constitutes culture, how and to what extent notions of meaning and value can be extended beyond established conceptions of image, text and symbol. Whilst attempts to address the experience of mobility, the sensations of speed, flow, and effort, its moments of intensity and restraint, expose the limits of cultural representation as a means of understanding lived experience. New mobile methodologies for example, are often specifically designed to overcome what are believed to be the distancing and stabilizing effects of cultural representations, whose mediating effects appear to work counter to the

The Wiley Blackwell Companion to Human Geography, First Edition.
Edited by John A. Agnew and James S. Duncan.
© 2011 John Wiley & Sons, Ltd. Published 2016 by John Wiley & Sons, Ltd.

lived immediacy of mobile encounters (Hein *et al.* 2008; Fincham *et al.* 2010). This essay is concerned with the fate of culture in this context, how it might be formulated in a cultural geography faced by these issues.

Fixing Culture, Mobility Studies and Embodied Movement

Mobilities studies intersect with a broad range of academic interests including for example, histories and geographies of travel, transport and empire, sociologies of infrastructure, the politics of commodity circulation and sustainable transport policy (Urry 2007). However, in spite of these multiple intersections, the focus of mobilities studies is very clearly defined as the body in motion. Relatively early in the history of mobilities studies, John Urry placed the emphasis in his new mobilities paradigm "on how mobile subjects maintain connection with stationary locations while moving from point to point in ever increasing and expanding movement" (Urry 2000). Within geography for those taking up these ideas, this has increasingly become a territory for working with ideas of affect and non-representational theory. Studies of walking (Wylie 2005), cycling (Jones 2005; Spinney 2006), train travel (Bissell 2009a, 2009b, 2009c), or airports (Adey 2008, 2009) move relationships between humans, and landscapes, places and infrastructures towards a concern with practice and performance, the fleeting and transitory, the affective experience of movement and motion, or indeed stillness and quietue (Binnie *et al.* 2007). Mobility it is argued, is an inevitable and ubiquitous fact of human life regardless of gender, economic status, nationality, etc. (Binnie *et al.* 2007: 167–168; also Urry 2000; Cresswell 2006; Adey 2010b). Thus Thrift develops his nonrepresentational theory explicitly around the "leitmotif of movement in its many forms" (2008: 5). From this perspective mobility is foundational to the biological vitality of human existence:

> ... it would be possible to argue that human life is based on and in movement. Indeed, it might be argued that it is the human capacity for such complex movements and the accompanying evolution of movement as an enhanced attractor that has produced the reason for much of our rhizomatic, acentered brain. (Thrift 2008)

For Thrift movement captures the joy of "living as a succession of luminous or mundane instants" (2008: 5). Thus mobility articulates the points of intersection between humans and technologies suggesting the creative potential of human existence in all the contingencies of its elaborating and extrapolating techno-social complexity.

Central to such moves within geography and the social sciences more generally is a sustained criticism of representation as a focus for cultural analysis for example by authors such as Eve Sedgewick (2003) and Brian Massumi (1996, 2002). The conceptual centrality of language within theoretical approaches on which the "cultural turn" was built forms the focus for much of this criticism. It is certainly true that it has been all too easy for approaches to culture which adopted a "world as text" approach to become solidified and circumscribed into an approach in which the world was and could only be interpreted as language. Purvis and Hunt (1993: 486) characterized this as a move from "word as text" to "world is text." Thus what came to be known as "world as text" approaches are charged with collapsing meaningful social life into arbitrarily fixed, closed structures of signification. Critics argue that this forecloses the possibility of alternative meanings, of worlds beyond text and establishing disabling conceptual limits on individual freedom both to imagine such worlds and make them happen. In this context, Massumi characterizes critical thinking centered on semiotics in terms of fixed geometries, a process of "identifying points on a stable map of the always already known" (Massumi 2002: 12; Hemmings 2005: 554).

Within geography criticism of representation as fixed, fixing and totalizing merge with criticisms of place as stable, static and conservative as a key precept informing the move towards practice based and experiential approaches to travel and mobility. In this context it is easy to understand how the critique of representation and the valorization of affect and the nonrepresentational fit into the historiography of mobility within geography and the social sciences more generally. As Cresswell has shown work on mobilities within geography has historically drawn on two contrasting approaches which juxtapose stability and fixity. Firstly a sedentarist metaphysics, privileging fixed, bounded and rooted conceptions of place which interprets movement and mobility as abnormal and exceptional (Cresswell 2006: 26–27). In turn these are linked to particular ways of thinking which are themselves sedentarist, reaffirming and enabling the commonsense segmentation of the world into fixed representations and categorizations, things like nations, states, countries and places. In contrast, the nomad metaphysics identified by Cresswell builds on ways of thinking in which mobility is valued positively as progress, freedom, change and choice. Ways of thinking that emphasize mobility and flow over stasis and attachment have recently come to the fore. Cresswell identifies this current conceptual focus with an affective, nonrepresentational or even anti-representational world of practice, action and immediate experience (Cresswell 2006: 46).

Increasingly central to contemporary formulations of the mobilities turn within geography is the concept of affect as the basis for a nonrepresentational theory which problematizes the notion of culture. Affects might be characterized as unreflected states of feeling and though theorized in a number of ways, it is widely agreed that they are in some way pre-social; in excess of, beyond, behind, or autonomous from socially and culturally situated meanings (Hemmings 2005: 557; Barnett 2008; Pile 2010). Thus for Thrift the affective grounds of non-representational theory encourage a radical empiricism which values the pre-cognitive as something more than "an addendum to the cognitive and which is resolutely anti-biographical and pre-individual" (Thrift 2008: 7). This formulation certainly challenges those conventional conceptions of culture familiar in cultural geography since the 1980s in which culture is defined around socially constructed meanings embodied in symbolic patterns, objects and practices and the relatively consistent systems of signification in which they cohere.

Culture and the Politics of Mobility

In spite of these challenges to culture as a means of understanding mobilities, Cresswell (2001b), Kaplan (2000), Wolf (1992) and others have persuasively demonstrated that culture is fundamental to an understanding of mobilities as historically and geographically located. Cresswell has summarized these arguments, quoting Janet Wolff on the gendering of travel and the range of terms generated by so-called "travelling theory." The problem with terms like "nomad," "maps" and "travel" says Wolf, is that they are not usually located thus quite deliberately they suggest ungrounded and unbounded movement. Cresswell concludes that the consequent implication of free and equal mobility is itself a deception since "we don't all have the same access to the road" (Cresswell 2001b:13). These sentiments find eloquent restatement in Solnit's (2001) cultural history of walking where she too criticizes universalizing tendencies in the language of mobility. For Solnit, descriptions of the "postmodern body" shuttled around by airplanes and hurtling cars, or even moving around by no apparent means, "render the body nothing more than a parcel in transit, a chess piece dropped on another square." These she says, are problems arising from the level of abstraction in contemporary theory. Directly echoing Wolf, and Cresswell, she argues that much of the terminology of location and mobility – words like nomad, decentered, marginalized, deterritorialized, border, migrant, and exile – are not attached to specific places and people. Instead, they represent ideas of rootlessness and flux that seem as much the result of ungrounded theory as its presumed subject" (Solnit 2001: 28). It is clear that there are strong arguments to suggest that taken out of its historical and cultural context the language of mobility decontextualizes and flattens out difference, universalizing and naturalizing inequalities in the process. In this context the cultural politics enabled by theorizations of representation which bring to life questions concerning who or what gets to define, describe, speak for and on behalf of particular peoples, places and landscapes remains both relevant and important. Here Cresswell asks us to remember that indiscriminate valorization of a nomadic metaphysics may itself act as a point of fixing affording a reactionary politics in which the less mobile remain unrepresented, hidden behind those with the resources to move.

From the perspective of politics, there is clearly much to be gained from mobilities studies which are sensitive to the geographical specificities of culture. Yet we clearly also need to recognize, and take into account, the embodied experience of movement and motion. On the one hand culture seems to have supplied us with the means to engage with the historically specific consequences of mobility such as imperialism, migration or the development of scientific knowledge. On the other hand the experience of mobility itself seems to render the conventions of cultural representation obsolete apparently unable to grasp the substance of its study. Most recently Cresswell (2010: 18) has characterized mobility as "a fragile entanglement of physical movement, representations, and practices." For Cresswell such "constellations of mobility" are formed from three elements, in turn these are: particular patterns of movement, representations of movement and ways of practicing movement. In concert they constitute entities or systems which "make sense together." In this way Cresswell seeks to bring together a sensitivity to the affective experience of movement with a critical politics of cultural representations. By bringing movement as physical trajectory together with reflection and representation on mobility, simultaneously with the embodied action of movement, Cresswell's tripartite formulation suggests a Lefebvrian perspective on the production of movement within space. However necessary such analytical separation may be, it also runs the risk of missing the enveloping nature of mobility as a simultaneously social, technological and physical practice, unless there is an equally strong conceptual means for recognizing that which links these realms together. This is something which nonrepresentational theory seeks to do by asserting the primacy of an affective pre-social world as a unifying experiential force. In this way for example, Thrift argues that the non-representational may help us understand how technology can be engineered to act as a coercive power shaping and controlling wants, desires and expectations (Pile 2010). Yet, culture itself may provide clues towards the points of connection between apparently separate realms of existence. This is not because culture is a unified or universalizing dimension of experience, but because tracing it in action may shed light on the ways in which experience is made meaningful and understandable within specific circumstances. In this context, few have matched the subtlety of the historian and philosopher Michael Foucault as he mused on the "extraordinary" nature of the railway as a cultural product and producer of modern mobile life. The train, he said:

> ... is something through which one goes, it is also something by means of which one can go from one point to another, and then it is also something that goes by. (Foucault 1986: 23–24)

To a certain extent Foucault is merely reflecting ideas developed by media and communications theorists during the 1960s encapsulated in Marshal Mcluhan's (1964) slogan "the medium is the message." However there is arguably much more to his comment than this apparent simplicity might suggest. As simultaneously subject, object, representation and practice, the cultural experience of mechanized travel challenges the model of passive consumption developed by early theorists concerned with radio, TV and film and fuses its metaphor of mediation with one of envelopment and immersion. Framed in terms of entanglements rather than a set of isolatable or subtractable theoretical dimensions, Cresswell's formulation has much in common with Urry's "mobility systems." Thinking of mobility in terms of the technological, institutional, political, economic social and cultural systems in which movement is embedded has become an important way of recognizing both the politics and broader situations of mobilities as embodied practices. The focus on "automobility" particularly within sociology, but also cultural studies and social studies of technology literatures, illustrates the ways in which studies of mobility and travel have begun to forge an engagement between the embodied experience of mobility, its cultural representation and the structuring and organization of transport technologies. As Sheller and Urry put it (2000: 739) automobility is "a complex amalgam of interlocking machines, social practices and ways of dwelling" (Urry 1999, 2007; Featherstone *et al.* 2004). Automobilization "creates independence and liberates its subject from spatiotemporal constraints, it also formulates new dependencies reembedding its users (and nonusers) into another, highly mobile, yet equally structured way of life (Beckman 2001: 600–601). Thus Beckman echoes Foucault's train metaphor when he claims:

> As a result, the subject of automobilisation becomes its object. Rather than a self-determined subject, the car – driver is subjected to the expert systems framing this hybrid, which gradually turn him or her into the object of this very mobility paradigm. (Beckman 2001: 602)

The complex entanglements suggested by automobility indicate the importance of culture to broadly drawn politics of mobility. Yet the questions concerning culture and mobility raised earlier remain unresolved. As set out by Don Mitchell some years ago, conventional notions of culture are problematic for cultural geography. Conceptions of culture as simply fine art fail to allow us to engage with the meanings of everyday artefacts, objects, practices and technologies which make mobility possible. Definitions of culture as a whole way of life which engage with the experience of movement and travel are insufficiently discriminating to provide a useful analytical category. Major conceptual problems seem to occur however when one tries to define culture (Mitchell 1995; Eagleton 2000). However where Eagleton is concerned to define culture, Mitchell (1995: 113) argues that we should switch our focus to how culture functions. In this context mobility systems provide a distinctively anti-foundational means to examine the ways in which culture is both made and participates in the making of apparently distinct realms of economic, technological, biotic, geological, scientific, social and political life. As suggested both by Foucault's train metaphor and the problematic posed by automobility, from this perspective culture is not any one set of objects, images or practices. Rather it is an aspect or dimension of all socially meaningful objects and practices. In this context the major question is not: what is culture? But how does something called culture get to be defined? What work does it do? And how does it operate on the world and in society?

Communication, Text and Mobile Meanings

Perhaps one key to this problem is the relationship between representation and meaning in debates around the embodied experience of mobility. Though for example Thrift insists that his nonrepresentational theory remains centrally concerned with difference, the means by which difference is made meaningful and is translated into specific, desires, dispositions, attitudes and drives, or is transmitted from body to body, location to location, generality to specificity or abstract to substantial is unclear. Indeed as Pile (2010) has argued whilst affect is figured as a form of truth whose primary characteristic is that it lies beyond comprehension this is likely to remain the case. The issue is equally pressing in terms of the technologies, infrastructures, architectures and artifacts intrinsic to systems of mobility. As Michael has shown, culture plays a central role for many relevant theorists including Haraway and Latour even though it has rarely been placed under the kind of scrutiny to which it has been subjected by Mitchell, Eagleton and others. Thus if mobility is a purposive act rather than pure abstracted motion then what remains substantially under theorized given the current discomfort with representation as a core concept within theories of mobility, is the nature, making, transmission and understanding of meanings themselves. Though for example actor-network-theory paid little attention to the cultural *per se* it drew heavily on a version of culture as the richly semiotized medium in which social life is conducted. In this sense it reflects the well-known inclusive versions of culture put forward by cultural anthropologists like Clifford Geertz (1983) and cultural historians such as Raymond Williams (1981: 13; Eagleton 2000: 33). Akrich and Latour (1992) addressed the heterogeneous interactions and exchanges of actor-networks in terms of a broadly defined version of semiotics which resonates with these earlier formulations. Thus semiotics becomes:

> The study of how meaning is built, [where] the word "meaning" is taken in its original nontextual and non-linguistic interpretation: how a privileged trajectory is built, out if an indefinite number of possibilities; in that sense, semiotics is the study of order building or path building and may be applied to settings, machines bodies and programming languages as well as texts ... (Akrich and Latour 1992: 59; see also Michael 2000: 22)

Thus Arkrich and Latour draw on inclusive definitions of semiotics, in which "semiotics is concerned with everything that can be taken as a sign," drawn from key writers such as Umberto Eco (1976: 7). However they do not go on to explore and expand on how mobile meanings are built through contingently assembled paths of communication.

In the context of a geographical politics of inhabitation which has much relevance to the study of mobilities, Hinchliffe (2003: 215) argues in favor of similarly broadly defined semiotics and against the vogue for privileging the non-representational. Rather than arguing for less text, he suggests that textualities can actually be pursued for the work they do in producing a world which is simultaneously inhabitable and affective. Here Hinchliffe cites Whatmore's plea for a material semiotics which extends "the register of semiotics beyond its traditional concern with signification as linguistic ordering, to all kinds of unspeakable "message bearers" and material processes, such as technical devices, instruments and graphics, and bodily capacities, habits and skills" (Whatmore 1999: 29). As Hinchliffe argues the making of connections is always a process of ordering and reordering the world and this necessarily results in differentiation and redefinition. By this means practice, however unreflexive in its experiential moment, is always semiotic and always in a certain sense textual. It enables a recognition of human *and* non-human times and spaces and their roles in the co-constitution of worlds Hinchliffe (2003: 217). Thus it:

> Recognizes chains of translation of varying kinds and lengths which weave sound, vision, gesture and scent through all manner of bodies, elements, instruments and artefacts – so that the distinction between being present and being represented no longer exhausts, or makes sense of, the compass and possibility of social conduct. (Whatmore 1999: 30)

The implications of this for mobilities studies are that we start to open out a geography of movement through the pathways of contingently networked relations, as one able to trace the making, motion and remaking of meaning through a complex of heterogeneously constituted appropriations, fusions, amalgamations, agglomerations, accommodations, translations and transformations. In this context de Certeau's well-known playful invocation of the transport as communication metaphor has greater purchase than simply valorizing a topography of narrative. In modern Athens he says:

> The vehicles of mass transportation are called *metaphorai*. To go to work or to come home, one takes a "Metaphor" – a bus or a train. Stories could also take this noble

name: everyday, they traverse and organize places; they select and link them together; they make sentences and itineraries out of them. They are spatial trajectories. (De Certeau 1984: 115)

Key to an expanded concept of semiotics drawn from the literature on socio-material hybridity is the idea of the intermediary as an always already differentiated and semiotized property of artefacts, practices and entities which compose, order and form the medium of connection and communication within the networks they describe. They simultaneously define and distribute roles to humans and non-humans alike (Callon 1991: 137). Such a notion may be useful for understanding the processes of making, transmitting, receiving, interpreting, reflecting and remaking meanings at once elaborating meaning through poiesis (intentionally encouraged elaboration) and autopoiesis (unpremeditated self-organization) alike. The philosopher Michael Serres has become a principal theorist in this regard and expresses his thinking in a series of mythopoetic metaphors. His starting point is the claim that "our universe is organized around message-bearing systems." Serres' problematic is usefully articulated by Michael (2000: 26) thus: "How does one think of the contact and communication between disparate entities and endeavors? How is it possible that the same motifs appear in science and myth? How does a message move from the realm of the natural into that of the social?" For Serres, the figure of Hermes, the sometimes spurious messenger of the gods who gave his name to hermeneutics, provides a metaphor conveying the connectedness of thought across different, disparate domains. Most importantly, according to Michael, this figure also embodies the ways in which "messages" move from the material to the cultural and back. In the process, these messages are themselves transformed – they shift from being energies, matters, objects, into thoughts, ideas, cultural artefacts and vice versa (see, for example, Serres 1991). In Serres' view (Serres and Latour 1995; Serres 1995) what is needed is a philosophy of prepositions – "to," "from," "beneath," and "between" (Michael 2000: 27). Serres (1995) has found the figure of Hermes no longer adequate for the accelerating multiplicity of messages and movements enabled by modern technology. Thus he has replaced the singularity of Hermes with the figure of a host of Angels as his chosen metaphor to enable understanding of the circulations and connections of multifarious, heterogeneous entities: humans, knowledge's, languages, objects, processes. Such a formulation may suggest a means of understanding how the affective "raw feels" of movement are translated into socialized, reflective experience of travel as part of an iterative and creative process (Rorty 1979). At the same time it might also help to elucidate how the material infrastructures of transport and communication, its automobiles, pipelines, ports and airports, become freighted with social meaning as objects of consumer desire, civilized progress or national identity.

Creative Spaces of Connection

Whether couched as Greek gods or Christian angels, Serres' metaphors for the communication of meaning across heterogeneous spaces are problematic because of the way they impose a European history, culture and mythology on a set of processes which are not framed as time and place specific. Whether in terms of Serres' mythopoetic metaphors, "travelling theory" in cultural studies, "non-representational theory" or indeed earlier formulations in social physics or transport economics, there seems to be something about mobilities studies which encourages theoretical universalism. Yet in spite of this, Serres' work does itself carry an important message. For Serres and others, such messages are the stuff of culture and, therefore by implication, to study the conduits and channels of communication, its mobility systems, is to study the means by which social life is made meaningful, held together and remade. For Serres social life is made substantial and stable by the process of mediation in which hybrid quasi-objects link the heterogeneous confusion of matter and motion into socially meaningful structures and practices. In order to ground his poesy, Serres adopts a language simultaneously of transport, mobility and communication in order to ground his train of thought:

> *Metaphor*, in fact, means "transport." That's Hermes's very method: he exports and imports; thus he traverses. He invents and can be mistaken – because analogies which are dangerous and even forbidden – but we know of no other route to invention. The messenger's impression of foreignness comes from this contribution: that transport is the best and worst thing, the clearest and the most obscure, the craziest and the most certain. (Serres and Latour 1995: 66)

Focus on the messenger engaged in processes of connection, moving back and forth shuttling between entities, objects and practices, begins the process of asking questions about the forms, qualities and outcomes these connections might take. Thus it might be possible to combine some of the insights both from the literatures on socio-material hybridity and affect with more dynamic approaches to representation derived from post-colonial studies within a reformulated theory of communication. This requires close attention to an active, mobile sense of mediation and meaning. Thus the hypodermic needle model of cultural transmission (producer – message/ transmission – audience) familiar from communications studies dating back to the 1960s was widely and rightly criticized for its failure to recognize the participation of audiences and indeed the medium of communication itself in the production of meanings. Whilst infection, the model of dissemination adopted in nonrepresentational theory suggests a similar form of passive receptivity (Pile 2010). Elsewhere, biological theories of hybridity have also come under criticism for their focus on the new entity created by hybridization rather than the process of hybridization itself. Critiqued from post-colonial studies these merely justify and replicate discredited concepts such as acculturation and assimilation (Papastergiadis 1997; Brah and Coombes 2000). In contrast authors such as Hall (1988, 1991), Gilroy (1993), and Bhabha (1994) have stressed relationships of dialogue and difference in the processes of cultural translation. In this regard they echo Serres' call for a philosophy of prepositions, a study of that which operationalizes and directs movement and meaning. In one of the most useful formulations, Homi Bhabha (1994, 1996) argued that the core of cultural hybridity is the creative space which accompanies the act of translation. If one to one translation between languages or cultures is never possible then translation necessarily involves a point of improvisation rendering any translation always more than the sum of its parts. For Bhabha, the hybrid, therefore, is formed not out of an excavation and transferral of foreignness into the familiar, but out of an awareness of the untranslatable bits that linger on *in* translation. In this respect Bhabha is critical of approaches which allow the possibility of a simple appropriation or amalgamation of cultures (Papastergiadis 1997: 278). From this position, and speaking from the broader perspective of a material semiotics (see Law 2007, 2009), message bearers are themselves both creative spaces and catalysts for new engagements and newly opened points of intersection. They are points of ordering and chaos, construction and deconstruction, production and dissemination, a series of wholes and an elaborating fragment of parts. Thus according to Hinchliffe, the work of a material semiotics is not a zero sum game, or a process of linguistic capture. Rather bodies, things and words all have the potential to become more than they were before the articulations began (Hinchliffe 2003: 216). Thus:

> the pair human-nonhuman does not involve a tug-of-war between two opposite forces. On the contrary, the more activity there is from one, the more activity there is from the other. (Latour, 1999: 147)

Consequently and most importantly, the always already semiotized nature of mobile practice does not result in an "arid formalism" caricatured in criticisms of "the world as text." Instead more careful attention to the historical and geographical specificity of meaning in mobility, the communication, transmission and translation of meanings moves this kind of account "away from texts as static representatives and towards a sense of texts as habits, and as means to make connections" (Hinchliffe 2003: 215–216). Thought of in this way and understood through Cresswell's (2007) characterization of sedentary and nomadic metaphysics, the divide between the affective and the representational like that between place and mobility might be similarly overcome with the recognition that both fixity and fluidity are always partial and contingent.

In the context of meanings which are always conditional, contested and provisional the question "what is culture?" Is only answerable within specific historical and geographical contexts. Rather than defining culture a priori we might take a lead from Latour and follow the ways in which culture is built, defined and differentiated within the systems, patterns and conduits which carry meaning. Such an iterative and socio-material sense of meaning made through intersection and experience might also suggest that it is possible to embrace some of the liveliness of practical consciousness suggested by affective and nonrepresentational approaches to embodied mobility. At the same time it would be able to retain an engagement with the reflexivity which locates and animates mobilities in their sensuously situated vitality. Thus for example we might think for instance of railway stations and airports not so much as non places of sensory and cultural poverty (Augé 1995) but as "terminals" in the sense used by architectural critic Martin Pawley (1998). This term links mediums and messages and derives both from the transport hub and the computer. With this term the spaces and places of mobility become nodal points for the differential and contested access and exchange of a heterogeneous mix of information, flows and services. At the terminal, flows and circulations engage and exchange in the act of translation or transhipment from one register or circulation to another, cultural or economic, material and imaginable. Objects entities and practices are both brought into culture and disseminated to other realms, denoting and defining cultural location and social significance. In such sites and by such spatio-temporally specific message bearers are desires, wants, needs and expectations both generated and fulfilled.

References

Adey, P. (2004) Surveillance at the airport: surveilling mobility/mobilizing surveillance. *Environment and Planning A* 36, 1365–1380.
Adey, P. (2006) If mobility is everything then it is nothing: towards a relational politics of (im)mobilities. *Mobilities* 1, 75–95.
Adey, P. (2008) Airports, mobility and the calculative architecture of affective control. *Geoforum* 39, 439–451.
Adey, P. (2009) Facing airport security: affect, biopolitics, and the preemptive securitisation of the mobile body. *Environment and Planning D: Society and Space* 27, 274–95.
Adey, P. (2010a) *Ariel Life: spaces, mobilities, affects*. Wiley-Blackwell, Oxford.
Adey, P. (2010b) *Mobility*. Routledge, London.
Akrich, M. and Latour, B. (1992) A summary of a convenient vocabulary for the semiotics of human and non-human assemblies. In W.E. Bijker and J. Law (eds), *Shaping Technology/ Building Society*. MIT Press, Cambridge, Massachusetts, pp. 259–264.
Barnett, C. (2008) Political affects in public space normative blind-spots in non-representational ontologies. *Transactions of British Geographers* 33, 307–317.
Augé, M. (1995) *Non-places*. Verso, London.
Bhabha, H. (1994) *The Location of Culture*. Routledge, London.
Bhabha, H. (1996) Culture's In-Between. In S. Hall and P. du Gay (eds), *Questions of Cultural Identity*. Sage, London.
Beckmann, J. (2001) Automobility – a social problem and theoretical concept. *Environment and Planning D: Society and Space* 19 (5), 602.
Binnie, J., Edensor, T., Holloway, J., Millington, S., and Young, C. (2007) Mundane mobilities, banal travels. *Social and Cultural Geography* 8 (2), 165–174.
Bissell, D. (2009a) Travelling vulnerabilities: mobile timespaces of quiescence. *Cultural Geographies* 427–445.
Bissell, D. (2009b) Visualising everyday geographies practices of vision through travel-time. *Transactions of the Institute of British Geographers* 34, 42–60.
Bissell, D. (2009c) Conceptualising differently-mobile passengers: geographies of everyday encumbrance in the railway station. *Social and Cultural Geography* 10, 173–195.
Blunt, A. (2007) Cultural geographies of migration, mobility, transnationality and diaspora. *Progress in Human Geography* 31 (5), 684–694.
Brah, A. and Coombes, A.E. (2000) *Hybridity and its Discontents: politics, science, culture*. Routledge, London.
Callon, M. (1991) Techno-economic networks and irreversibility. In J. Law (ed.), *A Sociology of Monsters*. Routledge, London, 132–160.
Cresswell, T. (2001a) *The Tramp in America*. Reaktion, London.
Cresswell, T. (2001b) The production of mobilities. *New Formations* 43, 11–25.
Cresswell, T. (2006) *On the move: mobility in the modern Western World*. Routledge, New York.
Cresswell, T. (2010) Towards a politics of mobility. *Environment and Planning D: Society and Space* 28 (1), 17–31.
Cresswell, T. and Verstraete, G. (eds) (2002) *Mobilizing place, placing mobility: the politics of representation in a globalized world*. Rodopi, Amsterdam.

De Certeau, M. (1984) *The practice of Everyday Life*. University of California Press, Berkeley, California.

Divall, C. and Revill, G. (2005) Cultures of transport: representation, practice and technology. *Transport History* 26 (1), 99–111.

Eagleton, T. (2000) *The Idea of Culture*. Blackwell, Oxford.

Eco, U. (1976) *A Theory of Semiotics*. Indiana University Press, Bloomington.

Featherstone, M., Thrift, N., and Urry, J. (2004) *Automobilities*. Theory, Culture and Society series, London.

Fincham, B., McGuiness, M., and Murray, L. (2010) *Mobile methodologies*. Palgrave Macmillan, Hants.

Foucault, M. (1986) Of other spaces. *Diacritics* 1, 22–27.

Geertz, C. (1983) *Local Knowledge: further essays in interpretative anthropology*. Basic Books, New York.

Gilroy, P. (1993) *The black Atlantic: modernity and double consciousness*. Verso, London.

Hall, S. (1988) New Ethnicities. In K. Mercer (ed.), *Black Film, British Cinema*. Institute of Contemporary Arts, London.

Hall, S. (1991) Old and New Identities, Old and New Ethnicities. In A. King (ed.), *Culture, Globalization and the World-System*. Macmillan, London.

Hannem, K., Sheller, M., and Urry, J. (2006) Editorial: mobilities, immobilities and moorings. *Mobilities* 1 (1), 1–12.

Hein, J.R., Evans, J., and Jones, P. (2008) Mobile methodologies: theory, technology and practice. *Geography Compass* 2 (5), 1266–1285.

Hemmings, C. (2005) Invoking Affect: Cultural theory and the ontological turn. *Cultural Studies* 19 (5), 548–567.

Hinchliffe, S. (2003) Inhabiting – Landscape and Natures. In K. Anderson, M. Domosh, and N. Thrift (eds), *Handbook of Cultural Geography*. Sage, London, pp. 207–226.

Jones, P. (2005) Performing the city: a body and a bicycle take on Birmingham, UK. *Social and Cultural Geography* 6 (6), 813–830.

Kaplan, C. (2000) *Questions of Travel*. Duke University Press, Durhan, North Carolina.

Law, J. (2007) Actor Network Theory and Material Semiotics, version of 25th April 2007, available at http://www.heterogeneities/net/publications/Law2007ANTandMaterialSemiotics.pdf (downloaded on 18th May, 2007).

Law, J. (2009) Actor Network Theory and Material Semiotics. *Backwell Companion to Social Theory*. Blackwell, Oxford, pp. 141–158.

Latour, B.: (1999) *Pandora's Hope: Essays on the Reality of Science Studies*. Harvard University Press, Cambridge, Massachusetts.

Massumi, B. (1996) The autonomy of affect. In P. Patton (ed.), *Deleuze a Critical Reader*. Blackwell, Oxford, pp. 217–239.

Massumi, B. (2002) *Parables for the Virtual: movement, affect, sensation*. Duke University Press, Durham.

Mcluhan, M. (1964) *Understanding Media*. Routledge, London.

Merriman, P. (2003) A power for food or evil: geographies of the M1 in late-fifties Britain. In D. Gilbert, D. Matless, and B. Short (eds), *Geographies of British Modernity*. Blackwell, Oxford, pp. 115–131.

Merriman, P. (2004) Driving places: Marc Augé, non-places and the geographies of England's M1 motorway. *Theory, Culture and Society* 21 (5), 145–167.

Merriman, P. (2005a) Operation motorway: landscapes of construction on England's M1 motorway. *Journal of Historical Geography* 31, 113–133.

Merriman, P. (2005b) Materiality, subjectification and government: the geographies of Britain's Motorway Code. *Environment and Planning D; Society and Space* 23, 235–250.

Merriman, P. (2008) *Driving Spaces*. Blackwell, Oxford.

Merriman, P., Revill, G., Cresswell, T., et al. (2008) Landscape, mobility and practice. *Social and Cultural Geography* 9 (2), 191–212.

Michael, M. (2000) *Reconnecting Culture, Technology and Nature: From Society to Heterogeneity*. Routledge, London.

Mitchell, D. (1995) There's No Such Thing as Culture: Towards a Reconceptualization of the Idea of Culture in Geography. *Transactions of the Institute of British Geographers* 20 (1), 102–116.

Papastergiadis, N. (1997) Tracing Hybridity in Theory. In P. Werbner and T. Modood (eds), *Debating Cultural Hybridity*. Zed Books, London, pp. 257–281.

Pawley, M. (1998) *Terminal Architecture*. Reaktion, London.

Pile, S. (2010) Emotions and affect in recent human geography. *Transactions of the Institute of British Geographers* 35, 5–20.

Purvis, T. and Hunt, A. (1993) Discourse, ideology, discourse, ideology, discourse, ideology. *British Journal of Sociology* 44, 473–499.

Revill, G. (2007) William Jessop and the River Trent: mobility, engineering and the landscape of eighteenth century "improvement." *Transactions Institute of British Geographers* 32, 201–216.

Revill, G. (2011) *Railway*. Reaktion, London.

Rorty, R. (1979) *Philosophy and the Mirror of Nature*. Princeton University Press, Princeton.

Sedgewick, E. K. (2003) *Touching Feeling: affect, pedagogy, performativity*. University of California Press, Berkeley, California.

Serres, M. (1991) *Rome. The book of foundations*. Stanford University Press, Stanford, California.

Serres, M. (1995) *The Natural Contract*. University of Michigan Press, Ann Arbor.

Serres, M. and Latour, B. (1995) *Conversations on Science, Culture and Time*. University of Michigan Press, Ann Arbor.

Sheller, M. and Urry, J. (2000) The city and the car. *International Journal of Urban and Regional Research*, 24: 737–757.

Solnit, R. (2001) *Wanderlust: a history of walking*. Verso, London.

Spinney, J. (2006) A place of sense: a kinaesthetic ethnography of cyclists on Mont Ventoux. *Environment and Planning D: Society and Space* 24, 709–732.

Thrift, N. (2008) *Non-Representational Theory: space/politics/affect*. Routledge, London.

Urry, J. (2000) *Sociology Beyond Societies: Mobilities for the Twenty-First Century*. Routledge, London.

Urry. J. (2007) *Mobilities*. Polity, Cambridge.

Urry, J. (1999) Globalization and Citizenship. *Journal of World Systems Research*. 5 (2).

Whatmore, S. (1999) Hybrid Geographies: Rethinking the "Human" in Human Geography. In D. Massey, J. Allen, and P. Sarre (eds), *Human Geography Today*. Polity Press, Cambridge.

Williams, R. (1981) *Culture*. Fontana New Sociology, London.

Wolf, J. (1992) On the Road Again: Metaphors of Travel in Cultural Criticism. *Cultural Studies* 7, 224–239.

Further Reading

Now well established within social science, those interested mobilities studies have a substantial range of current, lively and challenging literature ranging from introductory surveys, through methodology to research monographs. The best general guides are found in the work of John Urry, *Mobilities* (2007) provides a wide ranging overview setting out both the conceptual and empirical scope of the burgeoning mobilities literature which is both thorough and accessible. Urry is sensitive to the wide range of work concerning mobilities; however it is Peter Adey's recent very useful introduction (2010) *Mobility* which makes the most explicit call for mobilities studies as an interdisciplinary endeavour. Within Geography, Tim Cresswell's work is centrally important. His book *On the move: mobility in the modern western world* is a major statement outlining an approach to mobilities which is centrally focused on the historical and geographical specificity of mobilities. His (2010) paper "Towards a politics of mobility," is also essential reading, it provides a very useful conceptual framework for the important task of examining the politics of mobility. Elsewhere in geography there are a growing number of book length studies of mobility systems which work with ideas of embodiment, and socio-material hybridity within specific historical formations, these include Merriman (2008), Adey (2010) and Revill (2011). The issue of culture, meaning, affect and representation is more difficult to follow. The major statement of nonrepresentational theory within geography is Thrift (2008). Don Mitchell's (1995) still offer's as a lively critique of the idea of culture within geography. The still somewhat nebulous field of material semiotics has been discussed in a highly accessible style by John Law (2007, 2009). Brah and Coombes (2000) usefully critique ideas of hybridity founded in cultural and science studies, from a geographical perspective, Whatmore (1999) is most useful.

Chapter 27

Scale and Networks
Part I

Andrew E.G. Jonas

Scale: The relation between the size of an object on a map and its size in the real world.
(Haggett 2001: 795)

The world is flat.
(Friedman 2005)

In several ways … the hierarchical model of scale is found deficient … and cannot be resolved by integrating [it] with network formulations. We elect to expurgate scale from the geographic vocabulary.
(Marston *et al.* 2005: 422)

Introduction

Human geography can be defined as the study of the diverse ways in which individuals and societies make use of, and in doing so transform, the landscape and the natural environment. Such a definition puts emphasis on seeing spatial organization as the result of materially purposeful and socially meaningful human activity without imposing *a priori* boundaries or territorial limits around such activity. Nevertheless in producing and transforming natural and cultural landscapes to satisfy basic material and social needs, people organize themselves and their activities around territorial structures that can – and often do – assume quasi-fixed spatial forms. Examples of these structures include cities, shopping malls, multinational corporations, school catchment areas, rooms, local government jurisdictions, communications networks, physical infrastructures, special economic zones, city-regions, nation states, and so forth. As these structures (and their associated powers and liabilities) stretch out across the landscape, they appear to form territorial hierarchies of different sizes

---

The Wiley Blackwell Companion to Human Geography, First Edition.
Edited by John A. Agnew and James S. Duncan.
© 2011 John Wiley & Sons, Ltd. Published 2016 by John Wiley & Sons, Ltd.

and spatial extents. Geographers frequently refer to such hierarchies as "scales." Typical scales that have been discussed at length by human geographers are the "global," "national," "regional," "urban," "local," "neighborhood" and "body" (Herod and Wright 2002).

Of late it has become a matter of some debate in the sub-discipline as to whether or not "scale" in fact means one or other of two seemingly contrasting ideas. On the one hand, there are those who think of scale in terms of fixed territorial hierarchies within which each scale – local, regional, national, etc. – occupies a discrete role or "level" in the overall hierarchy. We might call this perspective the *scale-as-hierarchy* viewpoint, and it is nicely illustrated by the above definition from Peter Haggett. On the other hand, there are those who think about scale as principally constituted not so much by formal geographic space as by the relations between human and physical entities distributed across the landscape. These relations often take the form of networks – or what Latour (1987) and others (see Latham 2002) have called "actor-networks" – that stretch across the landscape, connecting up sites into complex assemblages, topologies and entanglements of power. In this latter *scale-as-network* viewpoint, any given scale (e.g. the body) is examined not as a fixed hierarchy of territorial structures but instead as a network of overlapping and intermeshing patterns of association, the scale effects of which cannot be known *a priori* (Latham 2002: 131). The key difference between the two approaches to scale is that in the latter case there is no attempt to assign scalar networks to a pre-defined spatial hierarchy. Instead inter-scalar relations are flattened out across the landscape and priority is given to the analysis of power and authority relations as these unfold at specific sites or through actor-networks (Marston, Jones III and Woodward 2005).

The purpose of this chapter is to offer some brief insights into the variety of ways in which human geographers have come to think about scale from the vantage of, respectively, the hierarchical and network viewpoints; but most importantly to think of these perspectives as not so much different or opposed but as fundamentally interlinked. Whilst both viewpoints have a great deal of merit, there has been a tendency to conflate scale with areal *size* rather than geographic *scope*, a tendency which is in turn a legacy of the Kantian or spatial science tradition in human geography. I will argue that in the post-spatial science era "scale" is best approached as a way of thinking and writing about how "far" (i.e. stretched out) or "near" (i.e. co-present) particular social relations occur in space, and how seemingly discrete territories interconnect via socially meaningful relationships. To refer to a particular scale such as the "global" in this manner is not to presume its (elevated) position or level in a fixed territorial hierarchy but rather it is to use this scale as a starting point for investigating a range of different processes, meanings and interconnections (e.g. local *and* global; national *and* global; global *and* city-regional; etc.), and to do this without presuming an hierarchical spatial order at the outset.

I shall further suggest that scale is not just relational but also is political; it is always contested in place. This idea that scale is political, or what is increasingly referred to as a *politics of scale* (Cox 2002), is becoming very fashionable in human geography. This is partly because the analysis of scalar politics lends to the study of space, place and spatiality a sense of power dynamics and of its social construction, which contrasts with the somewhat static and asocial view of spatial science.

Nevertheless, it is important not to ignore how some scales – not least the national scale – can achieve a certain degree of permanence, fixity and stasis. Such stasis is itself a function of extant power relations and the flow of resources. Therefore one of the tasks of human geographical narrative should be to tease out the tensions and interconnections between what are otherwise often thought of as fixed or discrete scales, and in doing so expose the (often hidden) power structures and social networks through which certain "scales" (i.e. networks, territories, flows, etc.) can assume quasi-fixed territorial forms and meanings.

Scale and the Ordering of the Human Landscape: Scale-as-Hierarchy

In his classic text, *Geography: A Global Synthesis*, Peter Haggett (2001: 30, 795) is unequivocal in presenting the viewpoint that scale equates to the size of a specific geographical area. Moreover, each scale occupies an area or size of a particular order of magnitude. Seen through the lens of spatial science in this manner, scales can vary from the very small or microscopic to the extremely large, perhaps even the entire universe. Haggett goes further and suggests that geographers are mainly interested in a limited range of scales. These scales exist somewhere between the equatorial circumference of the Earth and an area not much smaller than Central Park in Manhattan. For Haggett, then, scale is a fixed measure of areal size within different orders of scalar magnitude (Figure 27.1).

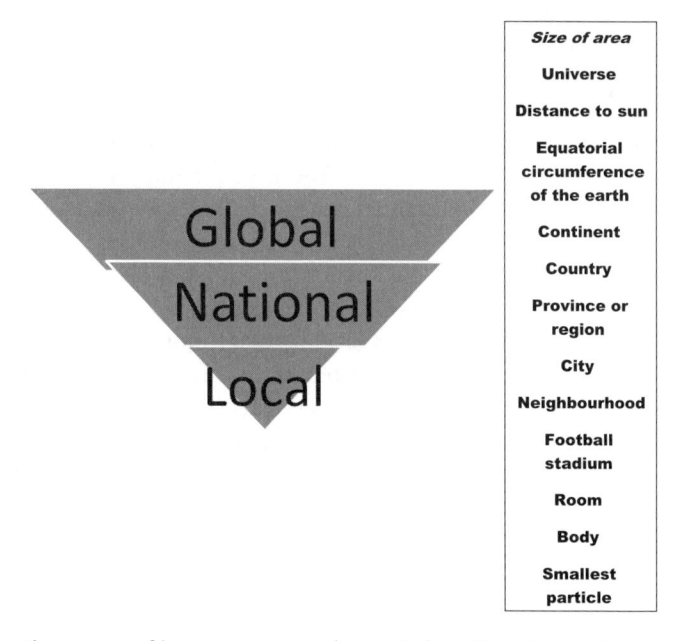

Figure 27.1 The scope of human geography as defined by hierarchical scales of analysis (after Haggett 2001: 21). According to Peter Haggett, geographers study a continuum of spaces of varying size between the circumference of the earth and an area roughly the size of central Park in Manhattan, New York. The scope of human geography is shown by the pyramid, which represents scale as a hierarchy of progressively larger or smaller spatial units.

Most contemporary discussions of scale in human geography still make reference to matters of size, spatial extent and orders of magnitude. However, it is generally the case that human geographers no longer reduce the analysis of scale to a spatial measurement exercise; nor do they limit themselves to the analysis of any one scale in isolation from others. Take, for instance, the scale of the city-region. Spatial analysts today often engage in the exercise of drawing boundaries around commuter zones and labor market areas in order to determine the size and shape of functional city-regions. This activity is of increasing importance for national policy makers and economic development practitioners who, recognizing that city-regions are important drivers of wealth creation across a national territory, want to know how to determine the size and extent of city-region boundaries in order to improve city-regional connectivity and hence national economic growth. Figure 27.2 illustrates one such interpretation of the geography of the English city-regions and, in this respect, isolates the city-region as a particular scale of policy analysis and state intervention, and separates it out from other scales, notably the national and global.

Knowing where city-region boundaries occur can be a useful starting point for identifying the city-region as a scale, thereby allowing state officials to channel public resources and expenditures more equitably and efficiently across the national territory. However, city-regions are inherently complex territorial structures and shaped by local, regional, national, and increasingly, global social, economic, political and environmental processes, all of which makes it difficult to reduce such complexity to the measurement of functional spatial-economic relationships at a specific scale. Indeed, some city-regions are dysfunctional, especially when considered not so much from a competitive economy point of view as from environmental or social vantage points (Jonas and Ward 2007). Moreover, whilst it might be useful for policymakers in the UK to focus exclusively on the *English* city-regions, there is a strong case to be made that the influence of one city-region in particular – Greater London, (or, at a wider scale, the South East region of England) – extends well beyond its immediate hinterland to a much larger scale, and arguably well beyond the UK altogether (Allen *et al.* 1998). For these reasons, cities like London, New York, Sydney, Tokyo and Los Angeles are often thought of as *global city-regions* (or at least would like to aspire to be so considered) because, in terms of flows of investment and other economic and social indicators, they have a much wider influence than their host national territories and occupy an elevated status the global hierarchy of urban places (Scott *et al.* 2001).

This discussion of city-regions illustrates the importance of investigating the *inter-scalar relations of power and politics* through which any given scale is socially constructed. We now turn to a discussion of the politics of scale, which represents an important extension and fine-tuning of the hierarchical approach to scale.

Inter-Scalar Relations and the Politics of Scale

When used in the hierarchical sense, "scale" usually refers to a self-contained territory and its constituent powers and structures. Thus activities described as "national" generally refer to processes taking place within, or having an impact upon, a nation-state but not necessarily at other, larger or smaller territorial scales. A national election, for example, gives voters the opportunity to elect representatives

Greater London

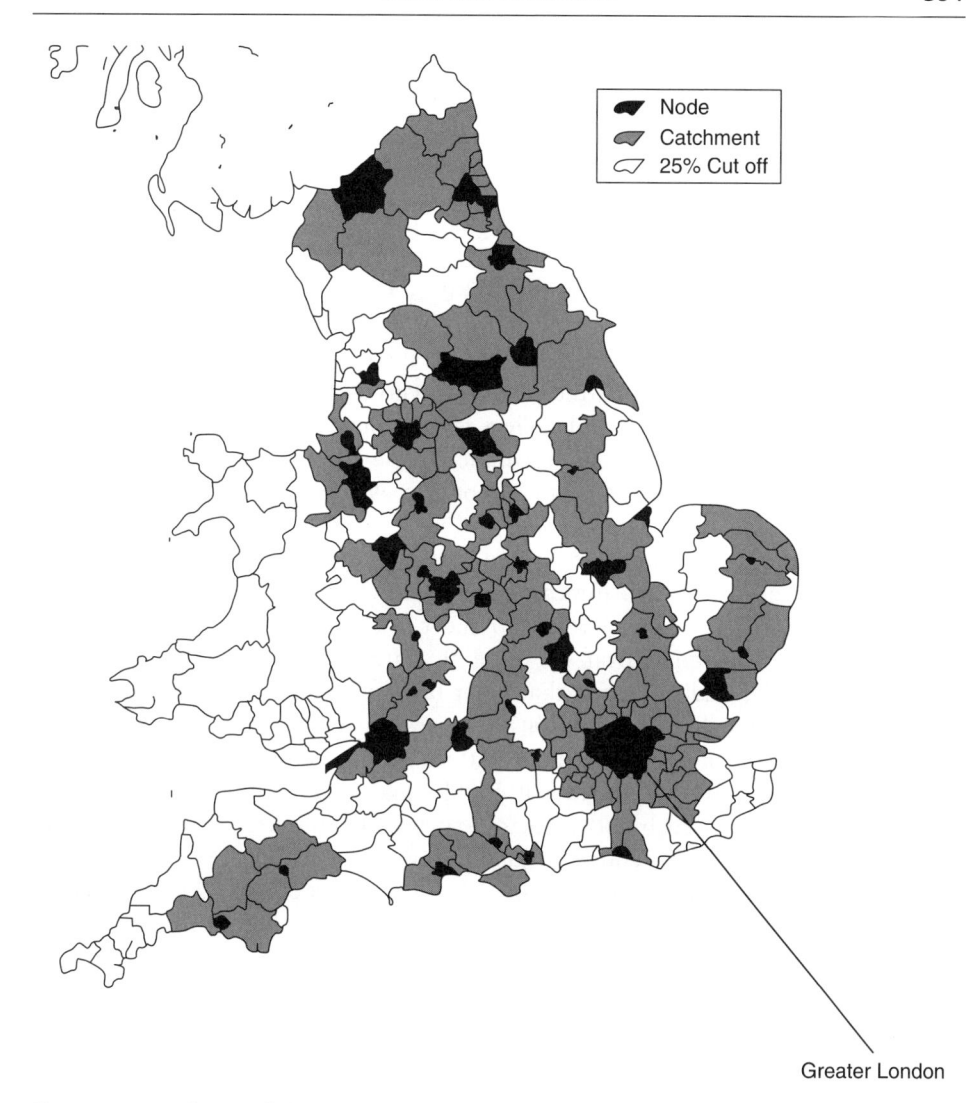

Figure 27.2 The English city-regions as a discrete scale of analysis (Source: adapted from ODPM 2006, http://www.communities.gov.uk/documents/citiesandregions/pdf/143846.pdf Map 5, p. 60; © Crown Copyright 2006). This map shows the English city-regions as defined by "nodes" and "catchment areas" for different types of labor market. Note that London is shown as the largest English city-region according to size of its catchment area, albeit clearly its influence extends well beyond the boundary shown on this map. Arguably, London qualifies for the status of "global city-region" but this "scale" would be difficult to represent on a map such as this. Doreen Massey (2007) looks at London from an alternative "global" perspective – as an intersecting network of both near and far off relationships.

to govern their country of citizenship; people who reside outside the country and even many inside, who are not citizens and registered to vote, cannot vote in national elections. Yet in most cases the outcome of a national election depends on how *local* votes are cast, and these might, or might not, aggregate up to the larger scale of the nation state to obtain a winning margin.

National voting outcomes are often no guide to local electoral behavior, or vice-versa, as presidential candidate Al Gore found out in the 2000 elections in the United States. The decision about who becomes US President is not decided by who wins the most number of aggregate votes nationally. Rather local votes are allocated State-by-State to the national level according to the system known as the Electoral College. One effect of this is that the candidate who wins the most individual votes but fails to carry sufficient Electoral College votes is not the candidate who is elected President. Al Gore won the popular vote nationally in 2000 but failed to win enough votes in the Electoral College when all 25 votes in Florida went to George W. Bush, the other presidential candidate.

The discrepancy between the effects and outcomes of similar processes operating at different spatial scales is sometimes examined as evidence of the *ecological fallacy* at work. The ecological fallacy refers to the practice of making (inappropriate) inferences about individuals from the general characteristics of the population at large. For example, studies suggest that voter turnout in national elections is influenced by the marginality of local constituencies; hence individual voter turnout could be a function of a more general pattern or perception of marginality (see Pattie and Johnston 2005). However it could equally be the case that local voter participation is influenced by other factors such as inability to cast a vote rather than a conscious act of abstention. Arguably this happened in the US elections of 2000 when it appeared that votes cast in some of the most contested Congressional districts were deemed "tainted" by the US Supreme Court, thereby influencing the eventual result of the national election.

For our present purposes, it is useful to recast this "individual versus the aggregate" effect as the problem of *scalar non-correspondence*. This problem refers to how similar processes operating at one scale may combine to produce a totally different outcome at another scale. When treated as a measurement problem like this, scale can possess causal properties, which result in different spatial effects, depending on the scale of analysis. The problem of scalar non-correspondence can be illustrated by the credit union movement in the United Kingdom, which has grown in importance nationally in the context of the restructuring of UK banking and finance over the past 20 years or so (Fuller and Jonas 2002). The number of UK residents joining credit unions as an alternative to mainstream banks and building societies has more than doubled in that time, as has the number of credit unions. Yet in comparison to the international scene, the British credit union movement is weakly developed. Figure 27.3 shows that when examined at the international scale, the credit union movement is far more developed in North America, the South Pacific and the Caribbean than in Europe (including the UK). On this basis, it can be inferred that the worldwide credit union movement has membership strongholds in some regions but not in others.

So scale does seem to make a difference to the analytical judgments we are able to make about the properties of different kinds of economic, political and social organizations.

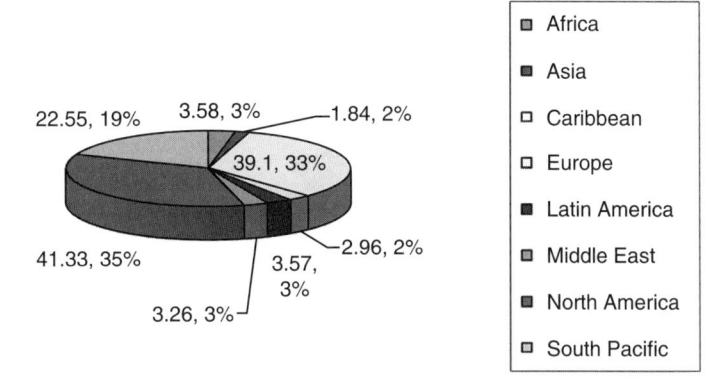

Figure 27.3 The international geography of the credit union movement in 2004 (data source: World Council of Credit Unions, 2004 Statistical Report, http://www.woccu.org/, first accessed June 2005). The numbers refer to the penetration rate, which is the total number of credit union members in each region divided by the economically active population. The percentages refer to the regional proportion of total worldwide credit union activity. North America accounted for 35% of worldwide credit union membership rates in 2004; whereas Europe only accounted for 2%. On this basis, it can be inferred that the worldwide credit union movement has membership strongholds in some regions but not in others.

Another way of thinking about inter-scalar relations and effects is to refer to what is known as the *politics of scale*. This concept draws attention to the possibility that organized political action often occurs at a different level in the hierarchy of territorial structures than that at which the desired change is brought into effect. Drawing on various analogies and examples, such as the "global" homeless vehicle, Neil Smith (1993) considers how the political meaning and influence of an object or actor can extend well beyond the physical geographic space it occupies. He calls this the act of *scale jumping*. However, I will use another example to illustrate the role of scale jumping. This comes from an analysis of the "regional question" in Italy.

The Northern League is a relatively young political party interested in promoting the regional interests of northern industrial cities in the Italian state. Over the years, the Northern League has increased its presence in national elections, often winning a majority in northern Italian communes and using this as a basis to increase its voice nationally (Agnew 1995). This could be used as an example of the growing importance of *regionalist* political processes in the nation-state, and hence how "regional" interests can, in effect, jump up and capture power at the "national" scale. But the Northern League has also been associated with a movement for greater *regional* autonomy, the ultimate goal of which would be to establish an independent nation known as Padania (Figure 27.4), in which case regionalism could be seen as a way of drawing political power downwards and away from the central Italian state. The processes by which powers shift up and down the state hierarchy are sometimes described as the politics of *state rescaling* (Brenner 1998; Swyngedouw 2000).

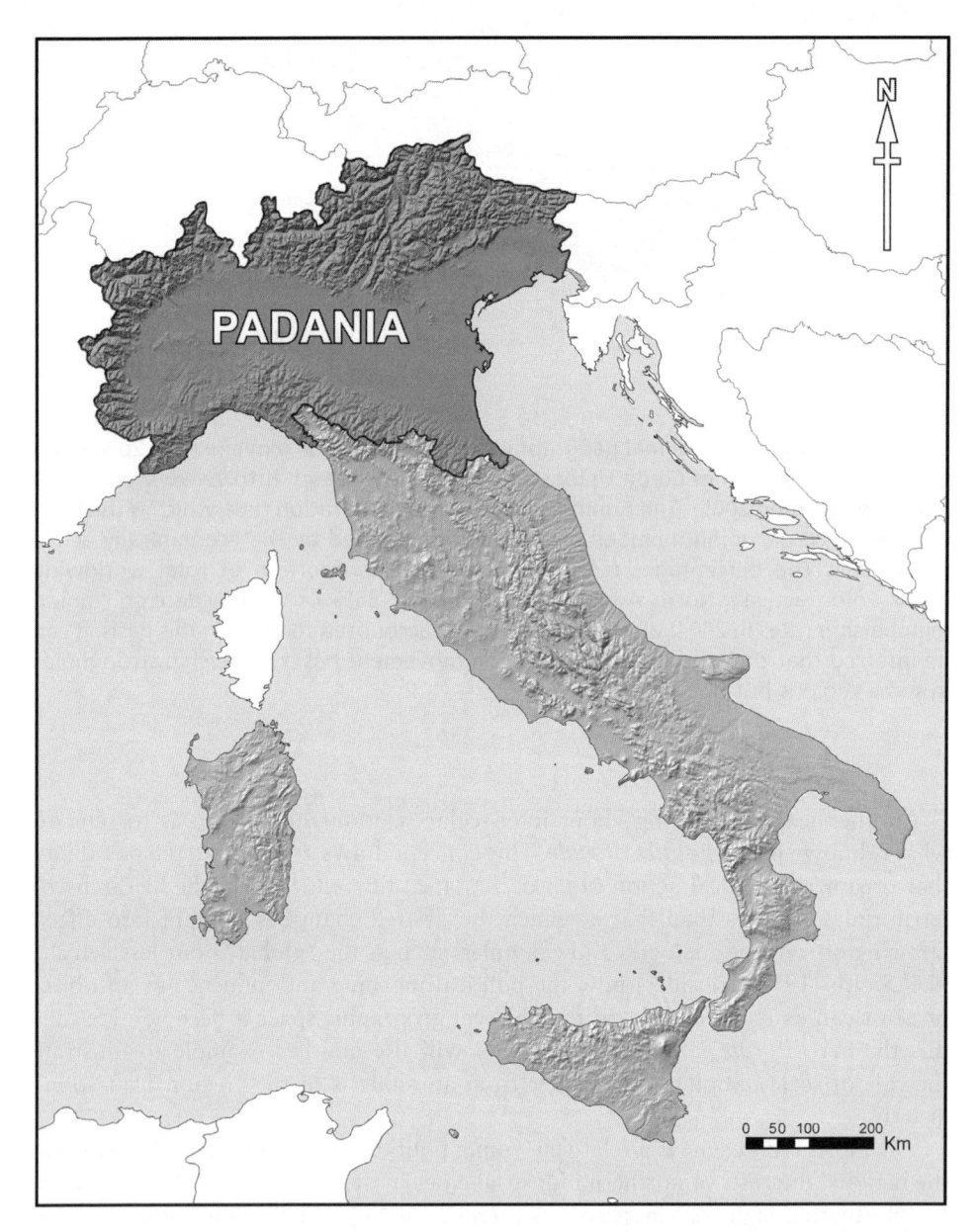

Figure 27.4 The imagined territory of Padania in northern Italy. The creation of the independent state of Padania could be marshaled as evidence for either the growing role of regional separatist tendencies or the strengthening of local interest group representation in national government. More theoretically, it serves as an example of the politics of state rescaling.

Such rescaling processes alert us to the possibility that geographical interests organized at one scale frequently combine, interact with, and influence, those at another scale. The analysis of scalar politics exposes the strategic interplay between territorial structures and identities distributed across the landscape, with each scale offering different *political opportunity structures* for mobilizations at different levels and points in time (Miller 1994). Extending these ideas to the realm of material relations other than exclusively those of the state, Kevin Cox (1998) usefully draws a distinction between the scales at which concrete material interests occur – what he refers to as *spaces of dependence* – and the scales of political engagement. These latter *spaces of engagement* are those where political actors and economic organizations draw down powers and resources in support of their spaces of dependence. If there has been an emphasis in the state rescaling literature on how power and politics works downwards in the scalar hierarchy, then empirical knowledge of spaces of dependence and spaces of engagement, respectively, can shed light on how social movement actors and interests actively engage with a range of scales "up," "down" or "across" space in order to harness strategic resources.

The "scale-as-hierarchy" approach continues to influence how geographers discuss ongoing changes in the political and economic landscapes of capitalism. The writings of Neil Smith (1984, 1993), Peter Taylor (1982), Erik Swyngedouw (1997, 2000) and Neil Brenner (1998, 2001), amongst others, have been especially important in sensitizing geographers to the production of scale, and how the apparent ordering of the world into discrete scalar hierarchies (e.g. world economy, nation-state, locality, etc.) should not be taken for granted insofar as each apparently discrete territorial scale represents a particular combination of processes of accumulation and uneven development, which work through all scales to differentiate the landscape into spatial patterns of interest to geographers. Thus in this respect there is a growing recognition both of the ways in which particular scales are produced and of how the relations among them are politically contested. In the process, certain scales, such as the body, the regional and the global, once deemed by Haggett to be of no great interest to geographers, have become materially and politically significant.

Relational Scale: the Network Approach and the Flattening of Space

Until quite recently, the hierarchical viewpoint was almost unchallenged as the accepted way that geographers should approach scale. Of course, there was some divergence of viewpoints on the relative importance of particular scales in the global hierarchy. While some geographers continue to assert that the global – or at least globalization processes – should always be at the heart of geographical analysis (Dicken 2004), and that other scales like the national are withering away or *hollowing out* (Jessop 1990), others have argued the case for the importance of the local or *locality*. Those who examine capitalism through a locality lens have suggested that the "local" (in the form of, e.g. localities, local labor markets, local economic development networks, etc.) offers a useful entry point for exploring wider questions of globalization and economic restructuring (Cooke 1987; Massey 1991). Locality studies have alerted us to the underlying tension between mobility and spatial fixity in the geography of capital accumulation and investment (Cox and Mair 1988). Here the "local" is examined in terms of the concrete geographic forms in which "global" capital embeds in particular places (Yeung 1998), whether these be localized transactions, networks, clusters, labor control regimes, infrastructural support mechanisms, or other aspects of the local industrial and political milieu.

If lately emphasis in social theory has been placed on thinking about capitalism as a *global space of flows* (Castells 1996; Latham 2002), there is a growing interest on the part of some human geographers in examining social, political and environmental processes outside the *local-global binary*. One influential critique of global "capital-centric" reasoning comes from the writings of J.K. Gibson-Graham. For Gibson-Graham (2002), those discussions about the economy that are framed in terms of the binary language of scale and its privileging of globalization and capital flows come at the expense of knowledge of more localized exchanges and trading systems. Accordingly, globalization discourses have disempowered those who want to voice the possibility that alternative economic systems might exist alongside or even outside the otherwise dominant discourses of globalization and neoliberal capitalism (Gibson-Graham 2006). Even when radical political-economic geographers have examined different geographies within global capitalism, "other" scales have all-too-frequently been represented as subordinate sub-systems rather than as "alternative" to the dominant global economic and political scale. Gibson-Graham (2002) proposes a rethinking of the economy that is less preoccupied with teasing out the inter-scalar relations operating *within* global capitalism and is more attuned to the creation of alternatives *to* capitalism at all scales.

Recent writing and thinking in human geography has been heavily influenced by post-structuralist thought in respect of space and place. Post-structuralists argue that the language of hierarchical scale has leant itself to a particular way of thinking about power relations and politics in which the role of human agency has seemingly played second fiddle to knowledge of wider political-economic (territorial) structures of capitalism. Since capitalist social relations are increasingly organized on a global scale, whereas human activities and interventions tend to be localized around specific sites, it is inferred that the language of scale has allowed functional-structural views of scale to creep into discussions of political-economic change. Post-structuralist thinking has inspired an emerging group of critics who are not bothered whether or not there is such a thing as "scale."

These critics point to the legacy of the Kantian or spatial science tradition; a legacy which has meant that discussions of scale in human geography often conflate or confuse *vertical* thinking about scale with the idea that the world is becoming more interconnected *horizontally* across space. As evidence of this slippage between the hierarchical and network views of scale, Marston, Jones III and Woodward (2005: 418) offer the following quote from Neil Brenner:

> *Scales evolve relationally within tangled hierarchies and dispersed interscalar networks.* The meaning, function, history and dynamics of any one geographical scale can only be grasped relationally, in terms of upwards, downwards and sidewards links to other geographical scales situated within tangled scalar hierarchies and dispersed interscalar networks. Each geographical scale is constituted through its historically evolving

positionality within a larger relations grid of vertically "stretched" and horizontally "dispersed" sociospatial processes, relations and interdependencies. (Brenner 2001: 605–606, emphases in original)

Marston *et al.* are concerned about the ambiguity contained in such statements: is scale vertical, horizontal or both? And where exactly is the locus of power in the scalar hierarchy?

Post-structuralists have recommended that usage of the word "scale" is abandoned in preference for language that resorts to "flatter" spatial concepts such as site and network; the point being that it is politically naïve to impose rigid "scale" boundaries around human agency and imagination. People and their institutions simply do not conform to neat scalar hierarchies, not least those constructed in the imaginations of political-economic geographers. Marston, Jones III and Woodward (2005: 426) offer instead an alternative "site-based" ontology, wherein "… a social site is not roped off, but rather that it inhabits a 'neighborhood' of practices, events and orders that are folded into variously other unfolding sites".

Such *non-scalists* (or "scale-as-networkers") are inclined to the view that scale is not a useful representation of space and time; for them, the world ontologically-speaking is flat. But this viewpoint should not be confused with what became popularized in Thomas L. Friedman's book, published in 2005, *The World is Flat* (Friedman is neither a proponent of scale nor a critical theorist; he is a journalist). Taken to such an extreme, a network or relational perspective on scale lends credence to certain claims that all places are beginning to assume similar characteristics, or share in common certain characteristics of the most globally important economic places, and that therefore the world is indeed "flat." The danger with flattening out the world in this way is that all prior knowledge of power hierarchies and place differences is eviscerated from critical spatial analysis.

Unlike Friedman, the *flat ontology* (network) perspective puts emphasis on seeing scale not as a fixed spatial entity or "level" in a vertical hierarchy but as a relational entity, which is co-produced by complex entanglements of actor-networks, resource flows and power relations. The precise geography of these entangled networks is hard to map but nevertheless is "visible" in the landscape, most especially when it produces locally-distinctive or site-specific emergent processes and effects. An example of the scale-as-network view would be the mapping of globalization not by measuring global trade flows but instead by observing how any given place (body, site, community, etc.) is infused with ideas, cultural signifiers and languages from far off places (Figure 27.5). The challenge in this case is to investigate empirically and in some depth a place without isolating or separating it from the wider networks and flows (or "scales") that given form and character to that place.

Since all sites in the human landscape are connected to other sites, including some that are far away, it can be difficult to determine *a priori* or even *ex post facto* which of any two connected sites – the "near" or the "far" – is the more powerful or causally influential. Nevertheless, a flat ontology does create some analytical challenges since it inevitably puts priority on studying the proximate ("local") at the expense of the distant ("global") (Jonas 2006). In terms of its methods, human geographical research has to start from some*where* and usually this involves looking at the world through the lens of geographic scale – either implicitly or explicitly.

Figure 27.5 Multilingual restaurant sign in the Barri Gotic district of Barcelona in northeastern Spain (photo taken by Andy Jonas in 2006). A popular destination for tourists and recent migrants, this vibrant district located in the centre of Barcelona is a hybrid of languages, cultures, political ideas and identities drawn from different corners of the globe and assembled together in one place.

The challenge is to decide at the outset which approach to scale, hierarchy or network, can be marshaled to best effect and shed light on different sorts of processes. Despite the inherent challenges and limitations of the scale-as-hierarchy perspective, abandoning scale altogether would in all likelihood prove to be very difficult.

Scales, Networks and Changing Perceptions of Time and Space

One interesting issue for critical human geography is to consider how changing perceptions of scale have intensified our experiences of time and space and, in doing so, has altered the sense of place (be this locality, region or nation). When considered in this way, the "local" is more than just a material scale or a social construct; it is also something that is experienced in relation to forces that might unsettle our sense of time and space. For example, the local or proximate can offer what seems a certain degree of *ontological security* against events that seem beyond our control or "out of scale" with our daily existence (Cox and Mair 1988).

Consider now the development of capitalism in the eighteenth and nineteenth centuries. Once commodities began to circulate more widely, previously isolated places became closely interconnected. In the process, places began to lose their individuality and assumed some of the characteristics of far off places – the places from which the changes were emanating. The classic example is the advent of industrialism in Europe, which eroded rural peasant life and its attendant material cultures and the accompanying sense of place, a theme examined in some depth by nineteenth century and early twentieth century scholars such as Paul Vidal de la Blache. In a similar way, if with different political and ecological consequences in the Americas, long-distance trade associated with colonialism disrupted local material cultures and ways of life of "native" Americans. It resulted in the dissolution of not just local material cultures but also local ecologies, belief systems and extant time-space relations (Harvey 1996: 222).

Furthermore, these above forces of *time-space compression* contributed to the growing tendency to distinguish the "local" from the "global." Whereas the local always tended to be seen as inward looking, passive or resistant to change, the global came to be represented as dynamic, place-shaping or even to some extent placeless. So a slightly different way of thinking about the "global" is to see how its scalar construction depends in turn upon the internal differentiation of space and time (Smith 1984). The important point is that what emerges is not a pre-ordained hierarchy of scales organized around static economies, ecosystems or political jurisdictions but rather a landscape in which the very nature of time-space relations across different scales is dynamically constructed, reconstructed and contested (Harvey 1996). Hitherto disconnected places (and scales) can suddenly be linked by processes that create larger territories in absolute space but at the same time foreshorten relative space around greatly reduced timescales of interaction between those places.

A related idea, and yet one that is also quite difficult to grasp, involves the role of metaphors of scale in creating *imagined communities* (which itself is an interesting scalar metaphor) (Anderson 1991). Imagined scales are formed out of those networks of solidarity that bind people together who otherwise share little in common with respect to a particular territory, be it the globe, a nation, a region, a part of the city, a local community, a stadium, a room in a house or a specific piece of land. Let us consider the case of global banking. When a multi-national corporation like HSBC bank brands itself as the "world's local bank", this refers neither to local or regional variations in banking-customer preferences, nor to the size of HSBC's operations and markets. Rather the particular meaning ascribed to the "local" in this instance refers to HSBC's sensitivity to *national* cultural differences and its attempts to capture diverse markets (Figure 27.6). The "local knowledge" mentioned here is an imagined scale, the meaning of which becomes apparent only when it is recognized that HSBC's global corporate network currently comprises some 8 500 offices stretching across 86 countries and territories around the world (see http://www.hsbc.com. Accessed January 2010).

Conclusions

Scale occupies an important place in the wider chronological development of socio-spatial thought, extending from conceptualizations of place, region and territory to those of scale and network (Jessop, Brenner and Jones 2008). This chapter has explored some of the contrasting ways in which scale itself has been incorporated into the lexicon of human geography. Specifically, it has focused on two major representations of scale, namely, the hierarchical and the network viewpoint.

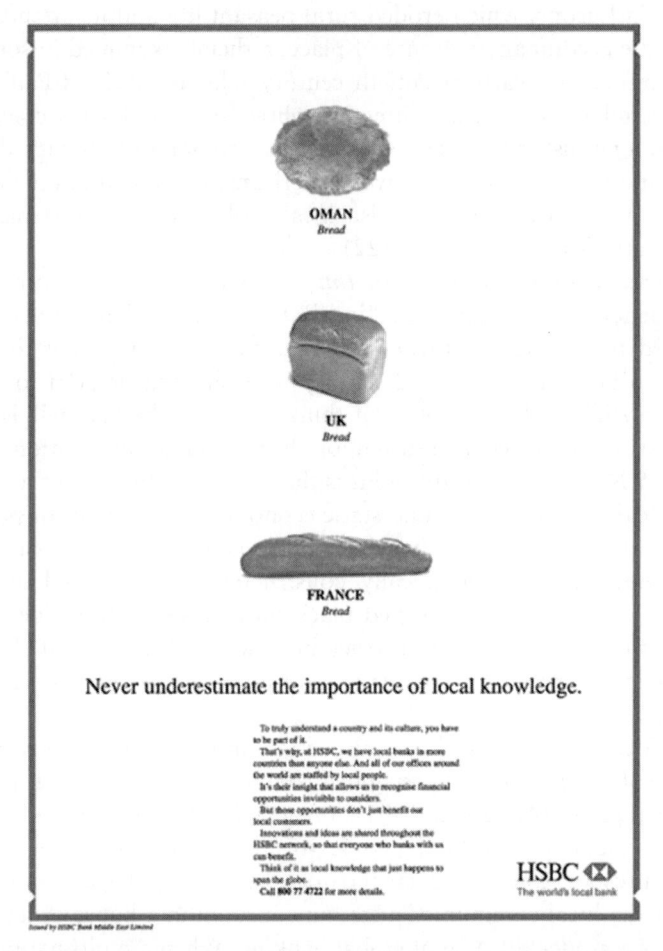

Figure 27.6 An ad campaign showing how HSBC has skillfully played on the ambiguity of scalar metaphor and branded itself as "the world's local bank" (Source: HSBC; reproduced with permission of HSBC). Ironically, both the baguette and the flatter pita bread featured in this marketing campaign are increasingly popular items baked and sold in British supermarkets, making it is hard to tell what the ad would mean to primarily a UK market.

Geographers have generally found the analysis of scale to be most amenable to the hierarchical viewpoint. Here scale has sensitized geographers to the production of new territorial structures in the landscape of capitalism, such as new spaces of the state, new regional governance arrangements, and variants of neoliberal globalization. But the language of territorial scale has also created some unique challenges, not least in terms of how to represent the politics of space as non-hierarchical yet nonetheless fraught with power relations and human possibility. Given the challenges of incorporating scale into narrative (Jonas 2006), some writers have found it useful to resort to metaphors of scale (Howitt 1998), whilst others suggest that scale needs to be banished from the lexicon of human geography altogether, believing that there is nothing to be gained from collapsing together hierarchical (territorial) and horizontal (network) representations of space (Marston *et al.* 2005).

One solution to an apparent impasse between territorial and network representations of space and scale is to avoid all references to these as examples of different *scalar typologies*. Whether or not scale refers to a hierarchy or a network, or perhaps both, is an empirical question, which varies with the strategic context. When human geographers refer to scale these days they usually signify the (spatial) extent to which social actors and their relations are stretched out, compressed and/or connected across territory, recognizing in turn that different "scales" can be organized around progressively smaller or larger territories. This reference to territory is crucial. Just as territory refers to a bounded and meaningful space (Delaney 2005), a given scale must be defined and given meaning by its constituent actors, agencies, power relations, resources and networks. Scale is not some pre-given or discrete "level" or size in a hierarchy of areal units of progressively smaller or larger size. Rather scale is always socially constructed and contested; its specific meaning arises from the contexts in which the language of scale is deployed by diverse social, political and economic organizations. Scale *can* be hierarchical, it *can* be networked and it also *can* be both.

Although the legacy of the "scale-as-hierarchy" perspective remains deeply entrenched in the sub-discipline of human geography, the incorporation of relational thinking about scale has provided a convenient basis for the sub-discipline to differentiate itself from spatial science and the physical "side" of the discipline. Scalar-attuned critical spatial synthesis has the potential to animate social scientific knowledge of economies, regions, nature, places, nations and globalization. Scalar categories can be marshaled to demonstrate how particular territorial structures become fixed in the landscape, are in the process of being destabilized, or serve to differentiate the world into semi-coherent scalar hierarchies and networks. Scale continues offer a powerful language for thinking about questions of hierarchy, power and spatial difference; it also remains a potent tool for thinking about networks, spatial interconnections and processes of political empowerment. Human geography cannot do without scale.

References

Agnew, J. (1995) The rhetoric of regionalism: the Northern League in Italian politics, 1983–1994. *Transactions, Institute of British Geographers* 20, 156–172.
Allen, J., Massey, D., Cochrane, A., et al. (1998), *Rethinking the Region*. Routledge, London.
Anderson, B. (1991) *Imagined Communities: Reflections on the Origins and Spread of Nationalism*. Verso, London.
Brenner, N. (1998) Between fixity and motion: space, territory and place in the social production of spatial scale. *Environment and Planning D: Society and Space* 16, 459–481.
Brenner, N. (2001) The limits to scale? Methodological reflections on scalar structuration. *Progress in Human Geography* 25, 591–614.
Castells, M. (1996) *The Rise of the Network Society*. Blackwell, Oxford.
Cooke, P. (1987) Clinical inference and geographic theory. *Antipode* 19, 407–416.
Cox, K.R. (1998) Spaces of dependence, scales of engagement and the politics of scale, or: looking for local politics. *Political Geography* 17, 1–23.

Cox, K.R. (2002) "Globalization" the "Regulation Approach" and the politics of scale. In A. Herod and M. Wright (eds), *Geographies of Power: Placing Scale*. Blackwell, Oxford, pp. 85–114.

Cox, K.R. and Mair, A. (1988) Locality and community in the politics of local economic development. *Annals of the Association of American Geographers* 78, 307–325.

Delaney, D. (2005) *Territory: A Short Introduction*. Blackwell, Oxford.

Dicken, P. (2004) Geographers and Globalization: (Yet) Another Missed Boat? *Transactions of the Institute of British Geographers* 29, 5–26.

Friedman, T.L. (2005) *The World is Flat: A Brief History of the Twenty-First Century*. Farrar, Straus and Giroux, New York.

Fuller, D. and Jonas, A.E.G. (2002) Institutionalising future geographies of financial inclusion: national legitimacy versus local autonomy in the British credit union movement. *Antipode* 34, 85–110.

Gibson-Graham, J.K. (2002) Beyond global vs. local: economic politics outside the binary frame. In A. Herod and M. Wright (eds), *Geographies of Power: Placing Scale*. Blackwell, Oxford, pp. 25–60.

Gibson-Graham, J.K. (2006) *A Postcapitalist Politics*. University of Minnesota Press, Minneapolis.

Haggett, P. (2001) *Geography: A Global Synthesis*. UK: Prentice Hall, Harlow, UK.

Harvey, D. (1996) *Justice, Nature and the Geography of Difference*. Blackwell, Oxford.

Herod A. and Wright M. (2002) (eds), *Geographies of Power: Placing Scale*. Blackwell, Oxford.

Howitt, R. (1998) Scale as relation: musical metaphors of scale. *Area* 30, 49–58.

Jessop B. (1990) *State Theory: Putting Capitalist States in their Place*. Polity Press, Cambridge.

Jessop, B., Brenner, N., and Jones, M. (2008) Theorizing sociospatial relations. *Environment and Planning D: Society and Space* 26, 389–401.

Jonas, A.E.G. (2006) Pro scale: further reflections on the "scale debate" in human geography. *Transactions of the Institute of British Geographers* 31, 399–406.

Jonas, A.E.G. and Ward, K. (2007) Introduction to a debate on city-regions: new geographies of governance, democracy and social reproduction. *International Journal of Urban and Regional Research* 31, 169–78.

Latham, A. (2002) Retheorizing the scale of globalization: topologies, actor-networks, and cosmopolitanism. In A. Herod, and M. Wright (eds), *Geographies of Power: Placing Scale*. Blackwell, Oxford, pp. 115–144.

Latour, B. (1987) *Science in Action: How to Follow Scientists and Engineers through Society*. Harvard University Press, Cambridge.

Marston, S.A., Jones III, J.P., and Woodward, K. (2005) Human geography without scale. *Transactions of the Institute of British Geographers* 30, 416–432.

Massey, D. (1991) The political place of locality studies. *Environment and Planning A* 23, 267–281.

Miller, B. (1994) Political empowerment, local-central state relations, and geographically shifting political opportunity structures: The Cambridge, Massachusetts, peace movement. *Political Geography* 13, 393–406.

Office of the Deputy Prime Minister (ODPM), (2006) *A Framework for City-Regions*. ODPM, London. Available at: http://www.communities.gov.uk/documents/citiesandregions/pdf/143846.pdf (accessed March 2010).

Pattie, C.J. and Johnston, R.J. (2005) Electoral participation and political context: the turnout-marginality paradox at the 2001 British General Election. *Environment and Planning A* 37, 1191–1206.

Scott, A.J., Agnew, J., Soja, E., and Storper, M. (2001) Global city-regions. In A.J. Scott (ed.), *Global City-Regions: Trends, Theory, Policy*. Oxford University Press, Oxford, pp. 11–30.

Smith, N. (1984) *Uneven Development*, Blackwell, London.

Smith, N. (1993) Homeless/global: scaling places. In J. Bird, B. Curtis, T. Putnam, G. Robertson, and L. Tickner (eds), *Mapping the Futures: Local Cultures, Gobal Change*. Routlege, London, pp. 87–119.

Swyngedouw, E. (1997) Neither global nor local: "Glocalisation" and the politics of scale. In K.R. Cox (ed.), *Spaces of Globalisation: Reasserting the Power of the Local*. Guilford, New York, pp. 137–166.

Swyngedouw, E. (2000) Authoritarian governance, power, and the politics of rescaling. *Environment and Planning D: Society and Space* 18, 63–76.

Taylor, P.J. (1982) A materialist framework for political geography. *Transactions of the Institute of British Geographers NS* 7, 15–34.

Yeung, H.W. (1998) Capital, state and space: contesting the borderless world. *Transactions of the Institute of British Geographers* 23, 291–310.

Chapter 28

Scales and Networks
Part II

John Paul Jones III, Sallie A. Marston, and Keith Woodward

Introduction

In this chapter we discuss geographic scales and networks. Depending on one's point of view, these are either: (a) actual things that exist in the real world or (b), concepts (analytic lenses) used to study geographic phenomena. The distinction between "thingified" and "conceptual" approaches to scales and networks pivots on whether one understands them to have an ontological status: Do they exist in the world, on a par with other seemingly bedrock aspects of spatiality such as place or landscape? And if so, what do we know about them and how can we best theorize how they work? Or are they better thought of as methodological tools, reflecting an epistemology that assists us in sorting through the chaos and complexity of an unruly world? And if the latter, then what are the benefits and limitations of using these concepts in understanding our geographies?

Such questions are important in light of the fact that scales and networks are now deployed in every branch of human geography, especially in economic geography, political geography, and political ecology. They also have reach beyond the discipline; indeed, it is hard for any scholar to describe the phenomena associated with "globalization" without relying on one or the other of them. Yet if scales and networks are concepts rather than concrete spatialities, then at least some of the *explanatory* weight they have been asked to carry, as both products and determinants, should be offloaded onto more secure geographic forms, such as region or connectivity. Finally, the ontological and epistemological status of scales and networks has proven to be central to ongoing efforts at theorizing social space more generally. Hence they have wide significance in our evaluation of the objects of human geographic analysis.

The Wiley Blackwell Companion to Human Geography, First Edition.
Edited by John A. Agnew and James S. Duncan.
© 2011 John Wiley & Sons, Ltd. Published 2016 by John Wiley & Sons, Ltd.

Scale

Scale has such varied meaning in geography that it sometimes seems as if most of the distinctions drawn about it are merely definitional. McMaster and Sheppard (2004) offer a helpful categorization based on scale's use in cartography, biophysical geography and human geography. From cartography we have a well known use of scale based on the "representative fraction" (where RF 1:24000 indicates that one distance unit on the map equates with 24000 such units on the earth's surface). Within this cartographic designation, McMaster and Sheppard find another distinction between the size of a geographical area studied – its spatial extent or "scale" – and the resolution or "granularity" of the data to be collected. On this point it is important to keep in mind that that there is no necessary relationship between spatial extensiveness and spatial resolution. The typical national census, for example, is conducted extensively, but at a high resolution (i.e. at a "small scale"); likewise a regression analysis using averaged data for states, provinces or other large areal units can have a large spatial extent but the data can hardly be said to reflect a high level of resolution. Still another confusion is introduced by the fact that small extents of space, when mapped (e.g. at RF 1:1000), are referred to as "large scale" (because the actual ratio is relatively larger than, for instance, maps based on RF 1:100000, which are referred to as "small scale"). And not lastly, when mapping is done in a digital environment of pan and zoom technology (as in GIS or Google Earth), there is no meaningful scale in terms of representative fraction (Goodchild 2004).

The problem of scale in the biophysical sciences has received a great deal of attention, but these discussions have been conducted separately from the debates in human geography. This is unfortunate, since in some respects the problems faced by physical geographers are similar and, especially in human-environment study (Manson 2008), relevant. Physical geographers have shown a keen interest in "operational" scale: the areal reach or extensiveness of environmental processes (see Bauer, Veblen and Winkler 1999; Manson 2008; Phillips 1997, 1999; Summerfield 2005). The primary problem with the operational approach arises from the fact that physical geographers deal in scales from the molecular to the planetary (Phillips 2004), at the same time that the appropriate scales of data collection and analysis shift with different objects of analysis, research questions, and methodologies. Sorting these complexities out has been a chore unto itself, but an even larger challenge is how to make linkages from one scale to another. In some process-response relationships, for example, variables that are independent at one scale become dependent at another (Phillips 2004: 90). In addition, crucial assumptions about processes and mathematical models necessary at one scale can be irrelevant at another. And finally, some concepts – such as equilibrium, complexity, and contingency – appear to be relevant only at specific scales. In a helpful review, Jonathan Phillips (2004: 97) points to "an inability to transfer representations at any given scale across the entire hierarchy of interest to physical geography," noting that methods and principles may be scale-restricted; at the same time, while seamless representation across a whole range of scales is impossible, interpreting results at one scale may in fact require embedding them within the contexts of broader or more detailed scales.

Though the connections are seldom recognized in the geography literature, there are parallels in some of the discussions about operational scale in both physical and human geography. For example, a relevant question in both subfields is: at what scale do certain processes become (ir)relevant, and what are the implications for explanation that accompany these shifts? Peter Taylor (1982) famously broached this question in human geography, wherein he concluded that political economic processes exist at three distinct "vertical" scales: (a) the global, at which resides the world-economy; (b) the nation, where the ideology of the state apparatus unfolds; and (c) the urban, the scale of daily experience. A couple of years later Neil Smith offered a landmark theoretical analysis of the production of scales under capitalism in his book, *Uneven Development* (Smith 1984). Greatly extending Taylor, Smith's assessment of capitalism's contradictory and disjointed character unhinged any simplistic reading of processes from scalar levels. In subsequent work (Smith 1992, 1993, 1996, 2000, 2004), Smith widened his discussions of scale to levels not previously considered, such as the body and the home (Marston and Smith 2001), as well as to other socio-cultural markers of difference (gender, race, sexuality). Another prominent scale theorist is Erik Swyngedouw (1997, 2000, and 2004). His work is noteworthy for including ecological processes alongside social ones, and for relying on ever more complex notions of interweaving, nesting, and shifting scales: "Scale configurations change as power shifts, both in terms of their nesting and interrelations and in terms of their spatial extent. In the process, new significant social and ecological scales become constructed, [while] others disappear or become transformed" (Swyngedouw 2004: 132). Finally, the research of Neil Brenner constitutes still another step forward in the move away from Taylor's initial model. Brenner coined the term "scalar structuration" to indicate "relations of hierarchization and rehierarchization among vertically differentiated spatial units" (1998: 603; also Brenner 2001), while his later writing dovetails into network theorizing by arguing that: "Each geographical scale is constituted through its historically evolving positionality within a larger relations grid of vertically "stretched" and horizontally "dispersed" sociospatial processes, relations and interdependencies" (2001: 605–606; also Brenner 2005; Leitner 2004).

While they may differ on specifics, these and many other theorists of the social production and construction of scale (e.g. Agnew 1993; Cox 1998; Cox and Wood 1997; Delaney and Leitner 1997; Harvey 1998; Herod 1991; Herod and Wright 2002; Howitt 1998, 2002; Jonas 1994; Mamadough, Kramsch and Van der Velde 2004; Marston 2000; Silvern 1999; Staeheli 1994) are united in their affirmation of the "thingness" of scale: that is, regardless of the complexity of spatial processes, there is an assertion, often implicit rather than explicit, that scale "exists" and, in the tradition of socio-spatial dialectics (Lefebvre 1991), is both produced by social activity and a powerful "platform" (Smith 2000) for it. This view does not, however, exhaust the range of scale theories, for a number of writers have asserted the conceptual view – that is, while scale may be an analytic device for thought, or even a perspective on the world, it is nothing more than that. As Katherine Jones put it in an early critique focusing on the discursive deployment of scale, "we may be best served by approaching scale not as an ontological structure which "exists," but as an epistemological one – a way of knowing or apprehending" (Jones 1998: 28). In an article titled "Human geography without scale," we pursued and built upon

Jones's line of argument (Marston, Jones and Woodward 2005). That paper, along with extensive commentary (Collinge 2006; Escobar 2007; Hoefle 2006; Jonas 2006; Leitner and Miller 2007) and our rejoinder (Jones, Woodward and Marston 2007), became known as the "scale debates" – a conversation that, in the words of Trevor Barnes (2008: 655), "never seems to end."

What are the coordinates of this debate? In brief, our argument (Marston, Jones and Woodward 2005: 422) was that scales – as levels or hierarchies of space – do not exist as such; they are the product of a particular epistemology, a "God's Eye view leveraged on the Archimedean point of the global from which the world is surveyed" (see also Haraway 1988). With Jones (1998), we did not reject the epistemological (or discursive) power of scalar thought. Instead, we approached the question ontologically, arguing that whenever processes are conceptualized according to vertical/scalar imaginaries, they become unhinged from their domain of actual practice (also Gibson-Graham 2002; Ley 2004; Massey 2004). We believe that scale thinking invariably slots processes into structured spatialities (e.g. global, national, regional, local) that are out of reach of everyday spatial life, and moreover it short circuits our ability to mobilize political forces capable of confronting inequality, exploitation, and oppression. This is not to say that some processes do not have more "reach" than others (although in emphasizing everyday doings and sayings over jumbo social formations such as "capitalist globalization" or "neoliberalism" we are less inclined to imagine them as floating over the actors that enact them). It is to say, however, that when conceptualized as a "nested hierarchical ordering of space" (Howitt 2002: 305) or as a "hierarchical scaffolding of nested territorial units stretching from the global, the supranational, and the national downwards to the regional, the metropolitan, the urban, the local, and the body" (Brenner 2005: 9), we are likely to "lose touch" with the concrete practices that form the bedrock of everyday life.

Numerous criticisms have been levied against our argument. Along with Leitner and Miller (2007), there are many (e.g. Hoefle 2006; Jones 2009; Jessop *et al.* 2008; Leitner *et al.* 2008; Neumann 2009; Rangan and Kull 2009) who continue to support the idea that scale is an actual thing existing in the world, not atypically through an affirmation of the "differences in powers and capacities, opportunities and constraints, among nested spaces" (Leitner and Miller 2007: 119; see Jones, Woodward and Marston 2007 for a reply to critics). At the same time, there are others who, like us, reject claims regarding scale's ontological status, but who see value in further assessments of its epistemological points of orientation and the discursive-practical work these enable (e.g. Kaiser and Nikiforova 2008; Legg 2009; Moore 2008). Still others support developing alternative ontologies that do not rely on scalar approaches (Ansell 2009; Escobar 2007; Hiller 2008; Isin 2007; McFarlane 2009; Pain 2009). One such approach revolves around networks.

Networks

Unlike discussions of scale – which have largely taken place within a truncated field populated by geographers – theoretical treatments of networks (and flows) have long been dominated by sociologists, especially under the banner of social network analysis (Wasserman and Faust 1994). With the emergence of globalization discourses in the 1990s, however, network approaches to spatiality also became prominent. At the forefront among political economists was the work of Manuel Castells. His "Information Age" trilogy (Castells 1996, 1997, 1998) was premised on the concept of "spaces of flows," a combination of technology, places, and people that "dissolves time by disordering the sequence of events and making them simultaneous, thus installing society in an eternal ephemerality" (1996: 467). This understanding of a "networked society" does not quite reach the status of spatial ontology, but it is certainly aimed at identifying material shifts in late capitalism that resonate broadly with David Harvey's (1989) notion of "space-time compression" and Doreen Massey's (1993) "power geometries."

As the network concept began to significantly shape geographers' spatial imaginaries over the past decade, it also began to inform studies focused on the dynamism and complexity of society-space relations (Coe and Bunnell 2003; Smith 2003a, 2003b). Today, the network frequently figures along side "relational ontologies" and "non-representational," approaches (Amin 2002) as a tool for negotiating the challenges to describing worlds "made up of billions of ... encounters ... consisting of multitudinous paths which intersect" (Thrift 1999: 302). Whatmore, for example, observes that the network "betokens a shift in analytical emphasis from reiterating fixed surfaces to tracing points of connection and lines of flow" (Whatmore 1999: 31). Still, characterizations of capital flows as total, singular and pervasive sometimes risks reducing critique and mobilization to hapless amazement in the face of a supposedly inevitable "global capitalism." Confronted with such omni-potent and omni-fluidic visions, it is worth recalling Massey's early reminder: "... different social groups and different individuals are placed in very distinct ways in relation to these flows and interconnections. ... some are more in charge of it than others; some initiate flows and movement, others don't; some are more on the receiving end of it than others; some are effectively imprisoned by it" (Massey 1993: 62).

Many of the orientations toward networks have been propelled by the cross-disciplinary popularity of actor-network theory (ANT), which has been widely adopted by human geographers interested in specifying the complexity of global economic and political relations. The theorists of ANT such as Bruno Latour (1993, 2005), Michel Callon (1991, 1998), and John Law (1999; 2004), examine single networks, or networks within networks, of material and semiotic relations between people, things and concepts. As a challenge to the rigidity of critical theory's earlier distinctions between structure-agency, this work re-envisions human/non-human relations as complicated, local inter-actions that give rise to complex global networks (Law 1999). From this perspective, agency appears less the exclusive regime of human choice and action, and more the broad workings of many aggregates of different things (Robbins and Marks 2010). Despite its enthusiastic employment of local-global frameworks, the extent of ANT's contribution to new forms of spatial theorizing is less obvious. In one sense, space is sometimes reduced to a self-evident trace in the continuum of networked relations, as in, for example, telecommunication and transport systems, where global reach is viewed as the outcome of relations that are "local at all points" (Latour 1993: 117). In a slightly different, though not unrelated sense, space is also invoked as the location across which many relations unfold: for example, the laboratory or the field site as the place where scientific objects and explanations get constructed (Latour 1999). Following a period of engagement with geographers in the early 2000s – and in the midst of a broader spatial turn within the humanities and social sciences – networked space was granted a more nuanced explanatory role (see Hetherington and Law, 2000 and related essays in the same issue of *Environment and Planning D*, Volume 18). At the same time, this was accompanied by something of a retrenchment of scalar logics. Latour's recent discussions of the sociality of networks, for example, while more attentive to space, nevertheless repeatedly equates them with abstract and "sizist" scalar imaginaries (Latour 2005: 203–204).

Today we find that networks are as pervasive as scale in offering descriptions of the spatialities of global institutions and actors. In economic geography, network approaches are used to explore how social actors, operating in dense and geographically extensive webs of social relations, produce and reproduce networks (wherein intrafirm, interfirm and extrafirm connections sometimes substitute for, or even drive, relations that are local, regional and transnational) (Berndt and Boeckler 2009; Yeung 1998, 2005; Henderson *et al.* 2002; Dicken *et al.* 2001; Dicken and Malmberg 2001). In further developing a global production network approach, some authors have sought to append scales to networks in order to sort some of the territorial and jurisdictional contexts of actor and institutional embeddedness (Kim 2006; Feagan 2007; Hall 2007). The conjoining of scale to networks is intended to introduce an element of causality to the latter by indicating how power struggles among differently situated actors/actants organized in a scalar hierarchy are able to shape behaviors within the network in significant ways. An emerging response to the "scalar networks" formulation (akin to Brenner's (2005) horizontal and vertical relations), however, has been to rally around an anti-scalar imaginary that recognizes networks as extensive bonds (specified as either flows or linkages) among geographically grounded associations that connect mobile actors (e.g. scientists, business managers), firms/institutions (e.g. transnational corporations, the state), and objects (e.g. technology, money) across regional and global space in a decisively grounded, horizontal emergence that challenges notions of materialized verticality (Amin 2002). Finally, it is not only economic geographers and political ecologists who have come to increasingly embrace network conceptualizations; political geographers too are employing network approaches, most often orienting their work around resistance projects (Bosco 2001; Ettlinger and Bosco 2004; Routledge 2008). It is also important to point out, however, that a substantive critique of the political limits of using networks to apprehend the contemporary global economy – including their constitutive inequalities, asymmetries and democratic deficits – has also been launched (Hadjimichalis and Hudson 2006).

Conclusion

What unites many of the perspectives we have discussed is a driving concern with the pervasive unevenness and exploitation that continues to unfold across the world today. Our recent work on site ontology has been presented as an alternative to many of these scalar and networked spatial theories because we share these same concerns while arguing for the recognition of new ontological spaces (Jones, Woodward and Marston 2007; Marston, Woodward and Jones 2007; Woodward, Jones and Marston 2010; also Shaw 2010). One thing that underwrites this work is the possibility that, while it is undeniable that globalized neoliberalism is in many senses performative (in the sense of discursively practiced: Butler 1990), many critical encounters with scales and networks unwittingly institute the very performativity they seek to discipline. Thus while critical spatial theory is typically launched against structural processes, it can nonetheless also enable capitalistic strategies that naturalize scalar hierarchies and reify global power relations. Accordingly, it is no longer sufficient, when faced with the question of radical politics, to mutter the old mantra that "space matters." We grant that it is difficult to over-estimate the importance of this observation for social theory in the 1980s and 1990s. Today, however, everyone knows that space matters: from structure-adjusting capitalists to landless anti-capitalists, all are mobilizing around a recognition that space is at the center of new forms of accumulation and exploitation as well as resistance. The questions for today are, rather: (a) how might we come to better understand the spatial complexities that daily enfold us and *enable the systematization of exploitation*; (b) how might geography be complicit in – and how might it again extract itself from – the production of knowledges that rationalize, teach, and disseminate the production of exploitative spatialities; and (c) how might we learn to enable – and learn from – new forms of situated political practice that refuse systemic oppression and produce egalitarian alternatives?

Acknowledgements

The authors thank Morgan Apicella for research assistance in the preparation of this chapter.

References

Agnew, J. (1993) Representing space: space, scale and culture in social science. In J. Duncan and D. Ley (eds), *Place/culture/representation*. Routledge, London, pp. 251–271.

Amin, A. (2002) Spatialities of globalization. *Environment and Planning A* 34 (3), 385–399.

Ansell, N. (2009) Childhood and the politics of scale: descaling children's geographies? *Progress in Human Geography* 33 (2). 190–209.

Barnes, T.J. (2008) History and philosophy of geography: life and death 2005–2007. *Progress in Human Geography* 32 (5), 650–658.

Bauer, B.O., Veblen, T.T., and Winkler, J.A. (1999) Old methodological sneakers: fashion and function in a cross-training era. *Annals of the Association of American Geographers* 89 (4), 679–687.

Berndt, C. and Boeckler, M. (2009) Geographies of circulation and exchange: constructions of market. *Progress in Human Geography* 33 (4), 535–551.

Bosco, F. (2001) Place, space, networks, and the sustainability of collective action: the Madres de Plaza de Mayo. *Global Networks* 1 (4), 307–329.

Brenner, N. (1998) Between fixity and motion: accumulation, territorial organization and the historical geography of spatial scales. *Environment and Planning D: Society and Space* 16 (4), 459–481.

Brenner, N. (2001) The limits to scale? Methodological reflections on scalar structuration. *Progress in Human Geography* 15 (4), 525–548.

Brenner, N. (2005) *New state spaces: urban governance and the rescaling of statehood.* Oxford University Press, New York.

Butler, J. (1990) *Gender trouble: feminism and the subversion of identity.* Routledge, London.

Callon, M. (1991) Techno-economic networks and irreversibility. In J. Law (ed), *A Sociology of Monsters: Essays on Power, Technology and Domination.* Routledge, London, pp. 132–165.

Callon, M. (1998) Actor-network theory: the market test. *Sociological Review* 46 (5), 181–195.

Castells, M. (1996) *The rise of the network society.* Blackwell, Oxford.

Castells, M. (1997) *The Power of Identity.* Blackwell, Oxford.

Castells, M. (1998) *End of Millennium.* Blackwell, Oxford.

Coe, N.M. and Bunnell, T.G. (2003) "Spatializing" knowledge communities: towards a conceptualization of transnational innovation networks. *Global Networks* 3 (4), 437–556.

Collinge, C. (2006) Flat ontology and the deconstruction of scale: a response to Marston, Jones and Woodward. *Transactions of the Institute of British Geographers* 31 (2), 244–251.

Cox, K. (1998) Spaces of dependence, spaces of engagement and the politics of scale, or: looking for local politics. *Political Geography* 17 (1), 1–23.

Cox, K. and Wood, A. (1997) Competition and cooperation in mediating the global: the case of local economic development. *Competition and Change* 2 (1), 65–94.

Delaney, D. and Leitner, H. (1997) The political construction of scale. *Political Geography* 16 (2), 93–97.

Dicken, P., Kelly, P.F., Olds, K., and Yeung, H.W.-C. (2001) Chains and networks, territories and scales: towards a relational framework for analyzing the global economy. *Global Networks* 1 (2), 89–112.

Dicken, P. and Malmberg, A. (2001) Firms in territories: a relational perspective. *Economic Geography* 77 (4), 345–363.

Escobar, A. (2007) The ontological turn in social theory: commentary on "Human Geography without Scale" by Sallie Marston, John Paul Jones III, and Keith Woodward. *Transactions of the Institute of British Geographers* 32 (1), 106–111.

Ettlinger, N. and Boscoe, F. (2004) Thinking through networks and their spatiality: a critique of the US (public) war on terrorism and its geographic discourse. *Antipode* 36 (2), 249–271.

Feagan, R. (2007) The place of food: mapping out the "local" in local food systems. *Progress in Human Geography* 31 (1), 23–42.

Gibson-Graham, J.K. (2002) Beyond global vs. local: economic politics outside the binary frame. In A. Herod and M. Wright (eds), *Geographies of power: placing scale.* Blackwell, Oxford, pp. 25–60.

Goodchild, M. (2004) Scales of cybergeography. In E. Sheppard and R.B. McMaster (eds), *Scale and geographic inquiry.* Blackwell, Oxford, pp. 154–169.

Hadjimachalis, C. and Hudson, R. (2006) Networks, regional development, and democratic control. *International Journal of Urban and Regional Research* 30 (4), 858–872.

Hall, S. (2007) Knowledge makes the money go round: conflicts of interest and corporate finance in London's financial district. *Geoforum* 38 (4), 710–719.

Haraway, D. (1988) Situated knowledges: the science question in feminism and the privilege of partial perspective. *Feminist Studies* 14 (3), 575–599.

Harvey, D. (1998) The body as an accumulation strategy. *Environment and Planning D: Society and Space* 16 (4), 401–421.

Harvey, D. (1989) *The condition of postmodernity.* Blackwell, Oxford.

Henderson, J., Dicken, P., Hess, M., Coe, N., and Yeung, H.W.-C. (2002) Global production networks and the analysis of economic development. *Review of International Political Economy* 9 (3), 436–464.

Herod, A. (1991) The production of scale in United States labor relations. *Area* 23 (1), 82–88.

Herod, A. and Wright, M. (2002) Placing scale: an introduction. In A. Herod and M. Wright (eds), *Geographies of power: placing scale*. Blackwell, Oxford, pp. 1–14.

Hetherinton, K. and Law, J. (2000) After networks. *Environment and Planning D: Society and Space* 18 (2), 127–132.

Hiller, J. 2008: Plan(e) speaking: a multiplanar theory of spatial planning. *Planning Theory* 7 (1), 25–50.

Hoefle, S.W. (2006) Eliminating scale and killing the goose that laid the golden egg? *Transactions of the Institute of British Geographers* 31 (2), 238–243.

Howitt, R. (1998) Scale as relation: musical metaphors of geographical scale. *Area* 30 (1), 49–58.

Howitt, R. (2002) Scale and the other: Levinas and geography. *Geoforum* 33 (3), 299–313.

Isin, E.F. (2007) City.state: critique of scalar thought. *Citizenship Studies* 11 (2), 211–228.

Jessop, B., Brenner, N., and Jones, M. (2008) Theorizing sociospatial relations. *Environment and Planning D: Society and Space* 26 (3), 398–401.

Jonas, A.E.G. (1994) The scale politics of spatiality. *Environment and Planning D: Society and Space* 12 (3), 257–264.

Jonas, A.E.G. (2006) Pro scale: further reflections on the "scale debate" in human geography. *Transactions of the Institute of British Geographers* 31 (3), 399–406.

Jones III, J.P., Woodward, K., and Marston, S.A. (2007) Situating flatness. *Transactions of the Institute of British Geographers* 34 (2), 264–276.

Jones, K.T. (1998) Scale as epistemology. *Political Geography* 17 (1), 25–28.

Jones, M. (2009) Phase space: geography, relational thinking, and beyond. *Progress in Human Geography* 33 (4), 487–506.

Kaiser, R. and Nikiforova, E. (2008) The performativity of scale: the social construction of scale effects in Narva, Estonia. *Environment and Planning D: Society and Space* 26 (3), 537–562.

Kim, S.-J. (2006) Networks, scale, and transnational corporations: the case of the South Korean seed industry. *Economic Geography* 82 (3), 317–338.

Latour, B. (1993) *We have never been modern*. (Transclation by C. Porter) Harvard University Press, Cambridge.

Latour, B. 1999: *Pandora's hope: essays on the reality of science studies*. Harvard University Press, Cambridge.

Latour, B. 2005 *Reassembling the social*. Oxford University Press, New York.

Law, J. (1999) After ANT: complexity, naming and topology. In J. Law and J. Hassard (eds), *Actor network theory and after*. Blackwell, Oxford, pp. 1–14.

Law, J. (2004) And if the global were small and noncoherent? Method, complexity, and the baroque. *Environment and Planning D: Society and Space* 22 (1), 13–26.

Legg, S. (2009) Of scales, networks and assemblages: the League of Nations and the scalar sovereignty of the government of India. *Transactions of the Institute of British Geographers* 34 (2), 234–253.

Leitner, H. (2004) The politics of scale and networks of spatial connectivity: transnational interurban networks and the rescaling of political governance in Europe. In E. Sheppard and R.B. McMaster (eds), *Scale and geographic inquiry*. Blackwell, Oxford, pp. 236–255.

Leitner, H. and Miller, B. (2007) Scale and the limitations of ontological debate: a commentary on Marston, Jones and Woodward. *Transactions of the Institute of British Geographers* 32 (1), 116–125.

Leitner, H., Sheppard, E., and Sziarto, K.M. (2008) The spatialities of contentious politics. *Transactions of the Institute of British Geographers* 33 (2), 157–172.

Ley, D. (2004) Transnational spaces and everyday lives. *Transactions of the Institute of British Geographers* 29 (2), 151–164.

Lefebvre, H. (1991) *The production of space* (Trans. D. Nicholson-Smith). Blackwell, Oxford.

Mamadough, V., Kramsch, O., and Van der Velde, M. (2004) Articulating local and global scales. *Tijdschrift voor Economische en Sociale Geografie* 95 (5), 455–466.

Manson, S.M. (2008) Does scale exist? An epistemological scale continuum for complex human-environment systems. *Geoforum* 39 (2), 776–788.

Marston, S.A. (2000) The social construction of scale. *Progress in Human Geography* 24 (2), 219–242.

Marston, S.A., Jones III, J.P., and Woodward, K. (2005) Human geography without scale. *Transactions of the Institute of British Geographers* 30 (4), 416–432.

Marston, S.A. and Smith, N. (2001) States, scales and households: limits to scale thinking? A response to Brenner. *Progress in Human Geography* 25 (4), 615–619.

Marston, S.A., Woodward, K., and Jones III, J.P. (2007) Flattening ontologies of globalization: the Nollywood case. *Globalizations* 4 (1), 45–63.

Massey, D. (1993) Power geometries and a progressive sense of place. In J. Bird, B. Curtis, T. Putnam, G. Robertson, and L. Tickner (eds), *Mapping the futures: local cultures, global change*. Routledge, London, pp. 60–70.

Massey, D. (2004) Geographies of responsibility. *Geografiska Annaler* B, 86 (1), 5–18.

McFarlane, C. (2009) Translocal assemblages: space, power and social movements. *Geoforum* 40 (4), 561–567.

McMaster, R.B. and Sheppard, E. (2004) Introduction: scale and geographic inquiry. In E. Sheppard and R.B. McMaster (eds), *Scale and Geographic Inquiry*. Oxford, Blackwell, pp. 1–22.

Moore, A. (2008) Rethinking scale as a geographical category: from analysis to practice. *Progress in Human Geography* 32 (2), 203–225.

Neumann, R. (2009) Political ecology: theorizing scale. *Progress in Human Geography* 33 (3), 398–406.

Pain, R. (2009) Globalized fear: towards an emotional geopolitics. *Progress in Human Geography* 33 (4), 466–486.

Phillips, J.D. (1997) Humans as geological agents and the question of scale. *American Journal of Science* 297 (1), 98–115.

Phillips, J.D. (1999) *Earth surface systems: complexity, order and scale*. Blackwell, Oxford.

Phillips, J.D. (2004) Independence, contingency, and scale linkage in physical geography. In E. Sheppard and R.B. McMaster (eds), *Scale and geographic inquiry*. Blackwell, Oxford, pp. 86–100.

Rangan, H. and Kull, C.A. (2009) What makes ecology political? Rethinking scale in political ecology. *Progress in Human Geography* 33 (1), 28–45.

Robbins, P. and Marks, B. (2010) Assemblage geographies. In S.J. Smith, R. Pain, S.A. Marston, and J.P. Jones III (eds), *The Sage Handbook of Social Geographies*. Sage, London, pp. 176–194.

Routledge, P. (2008) Acting in the network: ANT and the politics of generating associations. *Environment and Planning D* 26 (2), 197–217.

Shaw, I.G.R. (2010) Sites, truths, and the logics of worlds: Alain Badiou and human geography. *Transactions of the Institute of British Geographers* 35 (3), 431–422.

Silvern, S.E. (1999) Scales of justice: law, American Indian treaty rights and the political construction of scale. *Political Geography* 18 (6), 639–668.

Smith, N. (1984) *Uneven development: nature, capital and the production of space*. Blackwell, Oxford.

Smith, N. (1992) Contours of a spatialized politics: homeless vehicles and the production of geographical space. *Social Text* 33, 54–81.

Smith, N. (1993) Homeless/global: scaling places. In J. Bird, B. Curtis, T. Putnam, G. Robertson, and L. Tickner (eds), *Mapping the futures: local cultures, global change*. Routledge, London, pp. 87–119.

Smith, N. (1996) Spaces of vulnerability: the space of flows and the politics of scale. *Critique of Anthropology* 16 (1), 63–77.

Smith, N. (2000) Scale. In R.J. Johnston, D. Gregory, G. Pratt, and M. Watts (eds), *The dictionary of human geography*, 4th edn. Blackwell, Oxford, pp. 724–727.

Smith, N. (2004) Scale bending and the fate of the national. In E. Sheppard and R.B. McMaster (eds), *Scale and geographic inquiry*. Blackwell, Oxford, pp. 192–212.

Smith, R.G. (2003a) World city actor-networks. *Progress in Human Geography* 27 (1), 25–44.

Smith, R.G. (2003b) World city topologies. *Progress in Human Geography* 27 (5), 561–582.

Staeheli, L. (1994) Empowering political struggle: spaces and scales of resistance. *Political Geography* 13 (5), 387–391.

Summerfield, M. (2005) A tale of two scales, or the two geomorphologies. *Transactions of the Institute of British Geographers* 30 (4), 402–415.

Swyngedouw, E. (1997) Neither global nor local: "glocalization" and the politics of scale. In K. Cox (ed.), *Spaces of globalization: reasserting the power of the local*. Guilford, New York, 137–166.

Swyngedouw, E. (2000) Authoritarian governance, power and the politics of rescaling. *Environment and Planning D: Society and Space* 18 (1), 63–76.

Swyngedouw, E. (2004) Scaled geographies: nature, place and the politics of scale. In E. Sheppard, and R.B. McMaster (eds), *Scale and geographic inquiry*. Blackwell, Oxford, pp. 129–153.

Taylor, P. (1982) A materialist framework for political geography. *Transactions of the Institute of British Geographers* NS 7 (1), 15–34.

Thrift N. (1999) Steps to an ecology of place. In D. Massey, J. Allen, and P. Sarre (eds), *Human geography today*. Polity Press, Cambridge, pp. 295–322.

Wasserman, S. and Faust, K. (1994) *Social network analysis: methods and applications*. Cambridge University Press, Cambridge.

Whatmore, S. (1999) Hybrid geographies: rethinking the "human" in human geography. In D. Massey, J. Allen, and P. Sarre (eds), *Human geography today* Cambridge, Polity Press, pp. 22–40.

Woodward, K., Jones III, J.P., and Marston, S.A. (2010) Of eagles and flies: orientations toward the site. *Area* 42 (3), 271–280.

Yeung, H.W. (1998) *Transnational corporations and business networks: Hong Kong firms in the ASEAN region*. Routledge, London.

Yeung, H.W. (2005) Rethinking relational economic geography. *Transactions of the Institute of British Geographers* 30 (1), 37–51.

Chapter 29

Class
Part I

Andrew Herod

Introduction

"Class" is a term used to distinguish groups of individuals who are socially and economically stratified within various societies. For instance, whereas it has been common to describe individuals in feudal societies as being members of the peasantry or of the nobility, within capitalist societies individuals are often described as belonging to the "working class," the "middle class," the "upper class," or even the "ruling class." Although geographers have long recognized that all societies have classes, prior to the late 1960s there was relatively little explicit theorizing of class within capitalist societies, perhaps because the terminology of "class analysis" – how do people become stratified and with what consequences? – was considered to be too "subversive" within a fairly conservative academic discipline, especially within the context, at least in the United States, of the McCarthyism of the 1950s. However, the social upheavals of the 1960s encouraged many human geographers to try to make their studies more "relevant" to the problems of the day by addressing things such as the geography of poverty and of environmental destruction, with the result that many began to focus upon issues of class stratification and how such stratification has geographical elements to it – why, for instance, are working class people often more exposed to environmental toxins than are upper-class people and how is that related to the capitalist production process?

In this chapter, I discuss the concept of socio-economic class and how geographers have employed class analysis in their work. The first part of the chapter considers how three social theorists – Karl Marx, Max Weber, and Émile Durkheim – theorized class. I focus on these three specifically because they are generally considered by social scientists across a wide spectrum of disciplines to have been the three most influential theorizers of class and class relations. The second part of the chapter explores a number of contributions to thinking about class made by geographers, particularly claims that class is spatially constituted and constituting. This latter section focuses especially upon Marxist conceptions of class, for it is Marx's view of class that has dominated geographic theorizing during the past four decades or so.

Marx, Weber, and Durkheim on Class

Arguably, the three most important theorizers of class in the social sciences during the past century or so have been Karl Marx (1818–1883), Max Weber (1864–1920), and Émile Durkheim (1858–1917). Indeed, collectively these three have often been considered the principal foundational scholars of modern social science: in many ways, Marx is considered the father of modern political economy, whilst Weber and Durkheim are viewed as the co-fathers of Sociology. Although all three wrote about class, it is important to note that they did so from very different perspectives. Nevertheless, because Marx lived earlier, Weber (and to a lesser extent Durkheim) are often said to be in conversation with his ghost.

Marx's View of Class

Marx viewed class principally in economic terms, with a person's class position resulting from their relationship to the means of production; that is to say, the items (like factories or tools) that are necessary to produce the food and commodities that people use. Specifically, whereas many of his contemporaries and predecessors saw class arising out of, for instance, differences in individuals' religious affiliations, which might lead to a caste-like society, Marx saw class as having emerged out of the differential ownership of the means of production. This differential ownership, he argued, had itself developed over a long period of time, beginning in hunter/gatherer societies, as some human beings and their descendants gradually lost access to the means necessary for their own independent social and biological reproduction and had to go to work for others in order to survive. Hence, in the feudal era peasants worked on their lords' lands, producing a crop for the lord in exchange for protection from rival lords, whilst in the era of industrial capitalism workers have had to work for factory owners producing various commodities in exchange for a wage. In both eras, then, and with rare exception, the peasants and the workers have not owned the land or factories on/in which they have worked, nor have they owned the product of their labor (the food they grew and the commodities they have manufactured). Marx called the process wherein workers gradually lost control over the product of their labor and became little more than cogs in the production process that of their "alienation." For Marx, therefore, class was a relational phenomenon rather than a categorical one, something defined by social relationships between different groups (those who do and who do not own the means of production) rather than by statistical categories (wherein those who earn less than, say, $30 000 a year are considered to be in one class and those who earn more than $100 000 are in another). Although he argued that individuals might move between classes, he also argued that this should not be seen to negate the existence of classes themselves. Rather, he suggested, only collective public (rather than individualistic private) ownership of the means of production (and therefore the product of people's labor) would abolish classes and hence workers' alienation.

Within capitalism, Marx identified two major classes: those who own the means of production (capitalists, sometimes referred to as the "bourgeoisie") and those who must sell their labor for a wage in order to survive (the working class, sometimes referred to as the "proletariat"). He also identified a number of other "class fractions," including: a "petit bourgeoisie" (who might employ workers but who also themselves have to work, as with, for instance, shopkeepers); a "lumpenproletariat" (often vagabonds and beggars, people who are not really tied into the formalized economy and who do not regularly sell their labor in exchange for a wage); "landlords" (who make their income from charging rent on land rather than through directly employing waged laborers); and the "peasantry," who are generally subsistence farmers but who may produce commodities like cotton, which become the raw materials for industry. In developing his analysis, Marx relied upon a "historical materialist" approach, arguing that classes emerged out of struggles by some groups (like landlords or capitalists) to control the product of other groups' labor. For Marx, class struggle is the motor that drives history and the material development of societies. Consequently, he averred, all history has been the history of class struggle.

Marx's view of class, however, contained several other important elements. First, he distinguished between what he called a "class-in-itself" (*an sich*), by which he meant how groups of individuals objectively share a similar social and economic situation, and a "class-for-itself" (*für sich*), by which he meant how groups of individuals develop consciousness of their own existence (as when peasants or workers recognize their class position as peasants or workers, relative to landlords or capitalists).

Second, he argued that the economic relations of a society provide the foundations for its political and social infrastructure. This has often been referred to as the "base-superstructure" model of society. However, in different writings Marx theorized the relationship between the economic base and political and cultural superstructure in slightly different ways: in his earlier writings he was more inclined to see economic relations as shaping how civil and political life is conducted, whereas in his later writings he had a slightly more autonomist view of culture and politics. Hence, in the preface to his *A Contribution to the Critique of Political Economy* (Marx 1859: 20–21) he argued that "[t]he totality of these relations of production constitutes the economic structure of society, the real foundation, on which arises a legal and political superstructure and to which correspond definite forms of social consciousness. The mode of production of material life conditions the general process of social, political, and intellectual life. It is not the consciousness of men that determines their existence, but their social existence that determines their consciousness." However, in a later formulation, he suggested that "[t]he political, legal, philosophical, literary and artistic development rests on the economic. But they all react upon one another and upon the economic base. It is not the case that the economic situation is the *sole active cause* and that everything else is merely a passive effect. There is, rather, reciprocity within a field of economic necessity which *in the last instance* always asserts itself" (quoted in Coser 1971: 45). This shift in Marx's view, from a more dogmatic insistence on the priority of economic factors to a less deterministic view, has led to differing interpretations concerning whether he meant to suggest that the base *governed* how the superstructure developed in a kind of unidirectional manner or whether the superstructure was merely *conditioned* by the economic relations within society at any particular time.

Third, Marx viewed class in dialectical terms, with each class developing its historical form in relation to other classes in society; the working class develops, for instance, as a result of its relationship to the bourgeoisie. In such dialectical terms, both parties are inherently connected to one another – the working class cannot exist as a class without the bourgeoisie, and *vice versa* – but there are inherent contradictions between them: the bourgeoisie extracts surplus labor from the working class for which the latter is not paid, with this being, for Marx, the origin of profit (see Wolff and Resnick [1987] for more details on the Marxist notion of profit and how it differs from that of neo-classical economists' notions). For Marx, then, there is a unity between the proletariat and the bourgeoisie – they each exist in relation to one another – but there is also a contradiction/ tension between them, as they are fundamentally in conflict: the more surplus labor that the bourgeoisie extracts from the proletariat, the worse off is the latter. It is this contradiction within the unity that serves as the driving force of history.

Weber's View of Class

Whereas Marx understood class as emerging out of struggles in the realm of production over the appropriation of the surplus labor of one group by another, both Weber and Durkheim focused more upon class in the distributive/ consumptive realm. For Weber ([1922] 1978: 927), it was possible to "speak of a 'class' when (1) a number of people have in common a specific causal component of their life chances, insofar as (2) this component is represented exclusively by economic interests in the possession of goods and opportunities for income, and (3) is represented under the conditions of the commodity or labor markets." This, he suggested, "is 'class situation'." As a result of such a definition, for Weber people's class position is defined by their "life chances." These, in turn, are derived from two sources: the ownership of property, and the acquisition and possession of various skills. In the case of the first of these, Weber believed that differential ownership of land and the means of production largely explain the class situation as it existed during the industrial age of the early 19th century. In the case of the second, however, it is individuals' abilities to sell their skills in the marketplace, rather than (*à la* Marx) their relationship to the means of production, which Weber saw as playing the dominant role in shaping their life chances. This second situation Weber viewed as having largely arisen in the late 19th/early 20th century, when educational credentials and work skills increasingly replaced the outright ownership of property as the principal shaper of life chances (and thus class position). In other words, as capitalist society has developed, individuals' life chances have increasingly been shaped by the kinds of services they can offer, rather than whether or not they own property.

Whilst Marx was interested in understanding how class struggles drive history over the long term, Weber was more concerned with how societies are organized into hierarchical systems of domination and subordination and how this affects the distribution of power in society. To do this he saw "class" as interacting significantly with two other social attributes, what he called "status" and "party." Hence, whereas Weber defined "class" in terms of the unequal access to life chances in the market, he viewed "status" as resulting from different individuals' membership of various groupings based upon their consumption patterns and life style. He viewed this as being quite separate from individuals' class situation, for their status situation relates to the decisions individuals make about what kinds of goods they may choose to buy (a poor person may save up to purchase an expensive good; a wealthy person may buy cheap products) and what kinds of attributes they seek to cultivate in themselves and display to the outside world; Prussian army officers, for instance, might not have been rich but nevertheless often sought to develop a sense of social honor they considered superior to that of the wealthier landed aristocracy.

Finally, Weber argued that "party" refers to how political power is secured and marshaled, with individuals associating with various political parties (whether formally constituted or functioning more simply as interest groupings operating within the state) because of these latter's ability to allow such individuals to realize their own goals and aspirations. Whilst for Marx, then, economic class largely drove other social divisions, for Weber, although an individual's class, status, and party might overlap, these different dimensions of life – representing its economic, social, and political spheres – are not reducible to one another. However, Weber understood all three as playing a role in shaping an individual's ability to exercise power in society and so to realize their own will against someone else's. At the same time, though, despite their differences, both Marx and Weber argued that conflict between and amongst groups was a fundamental part of all societies and that, consequently, all social orders developed in the context of various social actors seeking to further their own interests at the expense of others. In this regard they are both typically referred to as "conflict theorists." By way of contrast, Durkheim believed that what defined societies was not the conflict within them but the harmony.

Durkheim's View of Class

For Durkheim, classes essentially emerge out of a society's division of labor and are collections of individuals who have shared interests and a sense of collective identity based upon the kind of work they do, whilst the division of labor itself results from the ways in which individuals divide up their labor and coordinate with each other to carry out various economic tasks (Durkheim [1893]1947). Durkheim was particularly interested in how the emergence of industrialization in the 19th century had led to significant social upheavals in the relationships between individuals, as traditional associations based upon tribal, kinship, or local geographic affiliations had been undermined. Whereas Marx and Weber were primarily concerned with social conflict, Durkheim focused on what keeps individuals together in certain social institutions, even as the disruption of traditional organizations brought about by, for instance, industrialization wracks them. He was, then, concerned with the role played by particular actors and institutions in either bringing about or impeding social cohesion. As a result, he has often been labeled a "functionalist."

In his exploration of social cohesion, Durkheim focused upon two principal forms of social integration: *mechanical* and *organic*. Of these, "mechanical integration" refers to social integration that derives from shared beliefs, identities, or sentiments. Thus, various individuals are connected through, for instance, common religious beliefs or ethnic identities. "Organic integration," on the other hand, emerges out of the specialization and need for interdependence that comes from the development of increasingly complex production systems (such as the shift from feudalism to industrial capitalism). Whereas early societies tended to be held together by forms of mechanical integration because there was little differentiation in the types of work each member did and each member tended to produce themselves much (if not all) of what they needed to survive, the diversity of types of work in industrialized societies, Durkheim averred, means that they have increasingly been held together through forms of organic integration, as people have become mutually dependent upon one another. Within the Durkheimian schema, then, it is the various occupations – rather than the broader class fragments, in Marxian terms – which principally shape people's identities and outlooks on life. However, despite perhaps gaining a sense of joy in their work through mastering particular skills, there is also the possibility that workers in industrial societies may experience what Durkheim called *anomie*, wherein they feel a sense of alienation due to how work may become increasingly routine and repetitive as tasks are progressively more standardized. He also believed that an excessive individualism (*egoism*) may occur in industrial societies as the communal ties of traditional life are broken down by industrialization. These two conditions – *anomie* and *egoism* – might result in social tensions. Consequently, he suggested, over time societies will establish institutions and frameworks, such as industrial laws, to minimize the potential for such tensions to emerge into full-blown conflicts. Thus, although he was no fan of capitalism, Durkheim believed that it would be transcended not through a revolutionary overthrowing of the system as a result of class warfare (Marx's hypothesized approach) but, rather, gradually through the unfolding of such institutions and frameworks.

Geographers Theorize Class

Within Geography, it is the Marxian and Weberian versions of class that have dominated analysis, perhaps because their focus upon issues of conflict between classes matched the political commitments of their advocates (to transform society) and/or because there was tremendous social upheaval occurring when geographers began to address issues of class analysis in their writings. Certainly, in the case of David Harvey, whose 1973 *Social Justice and the City* was one of the earliest geographical works to develop a sustained class analysis (he argued that the form of the built environment is shaped by capital's accumulation practices), the turn to Marxist class analysis was related to his feeling that the positivist approaches then dominating Geography did not speak to the realities of urban life in the 1960s. Having made the shift from positivist spatial science to Marxism, Harvey continued to explore how class struggles shape the built environment in a series of papers published in the 1970s (e.g. Harvey 1976, 1978). Other Marxist works focusing on class were also important, including those by writers like Manuel Castells (1977 and 1978) on urbanization under capitalism, Richard Peet (1983) on how class struggle shaped the evolution of the US's industrial geography, Richard Walker (1981) on how the encouragement of suburbanization was part of an effort to undermine working class militancy whilst simultaneously solving problems of low rates of capital accumulation in the post-WWII economy, and Neil Smith (1979) on gentrification as an element of class conflict.

These Marxist works were complemented and challenged, however, by those drawing upon Weberian ideas. In particular, a number of writers explored how various "housing classes" had emerged within different capitalist societies. Drawing upon the works of urban sociologists like Robert Moore, John Rex, and Sally Tomlinson, who explored how people's access to housing is shaped not only by economic class but also by, for instance, their ethnicity (e.g. Rex and Moore 1967; Rex and Tomlinson 1979), urban geographers investigated the roles played by various "gatekeepers" in shaping such housing classes' development. For instance, Ford (1975) explored how building society managers play important roles in stratifying urban housing markets (and hence classes), whereas Boddy (1976), Duncan (1976), and Williams (1978) looked at how housing markets are shaped by various urban decision makers, like mortgage brokers. For his part, sociologist Peter Saunders (1978) argued that home ownership can cut across class cleavages which emerge in the realm of production (i.e. workers and their bosses might come to share common political outlooks based upon their shared tenure as homeowners) and thus may play a significant role in determining class stratification. However, he later modified his ideas to contend that class stratification is only constituted within the realm of production but that such production-sphere divisions are not necessarily the primary determinants of many social cleavages in contemporary societies (Saunders 1984: 206) – as he put it, any "attempt to integrate housing tenure divisions into class analysis … is fundamentally flawed [because] it elides the analytically distinct spheres of consumption and production. [Instead,] we need to recognize that class is not the only major basis of social cleavage in contemporary capitalist societies, for increasingly people find themselves involved in political struggles which emanate not from their class location but from their location in … terms of 'consumption sectors'." In this light, he maintained that "home ownership does not alter people's class interests, but it is a major factor which helps to define their consumption sector interests."

Arguably, the differences in approach between those adopting a Weberian understanding of class and those adopting a Marxist one were most clearly illustrated in debates over gentrification. Hence, in a series of interventions Ley (1986, 1987, 1994) argued that what was driving gentrification in various North American cities was a back-to-the-city movement of educated elites and cultural producers who formed an *avant-garde* group of urban pioneers who had a cultural preference for urban residence. Smith (1979), on the other hand, saw gentrification as tied into the necessities of capitalist accumulation. Thus, he argued, it was a back-to-the-city movement of capital, not people, and was related to what he termed the "rent gap" (the difference between a property's current value and its potential future value should it be "renovated"). For Smith (1982), then, gentrification is connected to wider dynamics of class struggle over the accumulation process under capitalism and has been merely one aspect of a broader restructuring of urban space in the late 20th century connected to falls in capital's profit rate across the economy as a whole. Despite the gusto of these debates between neo-Weberians and Marxists in the 1980s, though, more recently such neo-Weberian approaches have somewhat fallen out of favor with Geographers because their argument that classes emerge out of both employment and housing situations has been seen as too broad to be useful analytically (Hall 2001: 28).

If Marxist versions of class have tended to dominate Geographical theorizing, this does not mean, however, that there have not been conceptual issues with such versions. One of the earliest critiques centered upon whether the Marxism adopted by geographers was too structuralist. This issue related to the so-called "structure-agency" debate that occurred in the 1980s and which was itself derived from the two different versions of the relationship between the economic base and the political and cultural superstructure outlined by Marx (see above). The opening salvo came from Duncan and Ley (1982). Specifically, they suggested that Marxist geographers' analyses of capitalism's class dynamics and the accumulation process relied too heavily on a reading of Marx which was itself derived from French structuralist Marxist Louis Althusser (1969). For his part, Althusser had drawn much of his understanding from Marx's earlier writings, which argued that the economic base determined the ideological superstructure. The problem, Duncan and Ley averred, was that such an approach basically tended to view humans as automatons blindly responding to the structural imperatives of capitalist accumulation. Chouinard and Fincher (1983), though, argued that Duncan and Ley had fundamentally misread extant Marxist geographical theorizing, failing to recognize, for instance, how post-structuralist debates had shaped Marxist theory in the 1970s. Equally, they suggested that Marx's ([1852] 1907) famous maxim that people make their own history but not under the conditions of their own choosing highlighted both the structure and agency in Marx's own thinking that allowed him to think of humans as neither automatons blindly driven by structures but, also, not as completely voluntaristic social actors who operate with no constraints placed upon them by social structures.

Within Geography, such debates had two important consequences. First, they encouraged the further development of a post-structuralist view of class, one less economistic. For instance, Gibson-Graham (1996) argued that there had been a tendency within Marxist circles to view capitalist economies as containing only capitalist economic relationships, as well as to privilege class as *the* way of understanding the world. By way of contrast, they suggested, capitalist economies may contain many different types of economic relationships, some capitalist and some not (e.g. worker collectives), and that individuals' lives under capitalism are shaped by a myriad of class and non-class processes and practices. Adopting an explicitly feminist position on the question of class, Acker (2006: 5) contended that both mainstream Marxist and Weberian understandings of class had:

i) generally conceptualized class and capitalism as gender- and race-neutral by failing to recognize that models of class understanding had usually been based upon an implicit view that workers and capitalists are white men;
ii) defined the capitalist economy, which at its heart is structured by class relations, in terms only of waged work and so had tended to ignore other types of social relations emerging from the extraction of surplus value by one class from another, even if not through the nexus of a monetary relationship; and
iii) had failed to acknowledge how masculinity and white privilege have historically shaped the development and functioning of class relations (see also Mann

[2007] on how the wage rate under capitalism has not simply been the result of market forces playing out between workers and capitalists but has also incorporated racial and gender aspects).

The second set of debates revolved around the relationship between class and space. Most specifically, in Marxist geographers' earliest considerations of class they had tended to view it as a social relationship which develops out of capitalism's economic relationships and then is played out geographically; in other words, class was viewed somewhat aspatially and as pre-existing space, onto which it is then simply projected. In such a view, class and space are ontologically separate. However, various geographers increasingly came to argue that class is inherently spatial: class practices and formations, they maintained, develop differently in different places whilst space is constitutive of class. For instance, in an analysis of the politics surrounding a manufacturing plant shutdown in the United States, in which a pro-business Governor sued the plant's owners yet the union urged workers not to be militant (positions quite contrary to what an aspatial analysis might have presumed), Herod (1991) showed that the positions of these two sets of class actors were deeply shaped by geographical considerations; the workers' geographical immobility in space and the Governor's defense of his state's economic territory. For their part, Sheppard and Barnes (1990) maintained that viewing class as geographically constituted makes a difference to how class relations are theorized (see also Herod et al. [2007] and Rainnie et al. [2007]). From a theoretical and political point of view, then, such Marxist-inspired geographers and others were seeking to amend Marx's famous dictum by suggesting that, in addition to making their own histories, people make their own geographies, though likewise not under the conditions of their own choosing. Analysis of class formation, structures, and relations, they argued, should therefore rely upon historical-geographical materialism.

Summary

Various different theoretical perspectives on class have been adopted by geographers over the years, including those drawing from Marxist, Weberian, and post-structuralist traditions. Each has viewed class in different ways, though within Geography it has tended to be Marxist understandings that have prevailed, even as these have been criticized more recently for failing to recognize the gendered and racialized nature of class formation. Arguably, though, whereas geographers have adopted ideas about class from other disciplines like Sociology, their most significant contribution to understandings of class has been to show how class is both geographically constituting and constituted, that class and space are not ontologically separate things but are intimately imbricated, the one with the other.

References

Acker, J. (2006) *Class Questions – Feminist Answers*. Rowman and Littlefield, Lanham.
Althusser, L. (1969) *For Marx*. Penguin, Harmondsworth.

Boddy, M.J. (1976) The structure of mortgage finance: Building societies and the British social formation. *Transactions of the Institute of British Geographers*, New Series 1 (1), 58–71.
Castells, M. (1977) *The Urban Question: A Marxist Approach*. MIT Press, Cambridge.
Castells, M. (1978) *City, Class and Power*. Macmillan, Basingstoke.
Chouinard, V. and Fincher, R. (1983) A critique of 'structural Marxism and human geography.' *Annals of the Association of American Geographers* 73 (1), 137–146.
Coser, L.A. (1971) *Masters of Sociological Thought: Ideas in Historical and Social Context*. Harcourt Brace Jovanovich, New York.
Duncan, J. and Ley, D. (1982) Structural Marxism and human geography: A critical assessment. *Annals of the Association of American Geographers* 72 (1), 30–59.
Duncan, S.S. (1976) Self-help: The allocation of mortgages and the formation of housing sub-markets. *Area* 8 (4), 307–316.
Durkheim, É. ([1893] 1947) *The Division of Labor in Society*, translated from French by George Simpson. Free Press, Glencoe.
Ford, J. (1975) The role of the building society manager in the urban stratification system; Autonomy versus constraint. *Urban Studies* 12 (3), 295–302.
Gibson-Graham, J.K. (1996) *The End of Capitalism (As We Knew it): A Feminist Critique of Political Economy*. Blackwell, Oxford.
Hall, T. (2001) *Urban Geography*, 2nd edn. Routledge, London.
Harvey, D. (1973) *Social Justice and the City*. Edward Arnold, London.
Harvey, D. (1976) Labor, capital, and class struggle around the built environment in advanced capitalist societies. *Politics and Society* 6 (3), 265–295.
Harvey, D. (1978) The urban process under capitalism: A framework for analysis. *International Journal of Urban and Regional Research* 2 (1), 101–131.
Herod, A. (1991) Local political practice in response to a manufacturing plant closure: How geography complicates class analysis. *Antipode* 23 (4), 385–402.
Herod, A., Rainnie, A., and McGrath-Champ, S. (2007) Working space: Why incorporating the geographical is central to theorizing work and employment practices. *Work, Employment and Society* 21 (2), 247–264.
Ley, D. (1986) Alternative explanations for inner-city gentrification: A Canadian assessment. *Annals of the Association of American Geographers* 76 (4), 521–535.
Ley, D. (1987) Reply: The rent gap revisited. *Annals of the Association of American Geographers* 77 (3), 465–468.
Ley, D. (1994) Gentrification and the politics of the new middle class. *Environment and Planning D: Society and Space* 12 (1), 53–74.
Mann, G. (2007) *Our Daily Bread: Wages, Workers and the Political Economy of the American West*. University of North Carolina Press, Chapel Hill.
Marx, K. ([1852] 1907) *The Eighteenth Brumaire of Louis Bonaparte*. Kerr and Co., Chicago.
Marx, K. ([1859] 1970) *A Contribution to the Critique of Political Economy*. International Publishers, New York.
Peet, R. (1983) Relations of production and the relocation of United States manufacturing industry since 1960. *Economic Geography* 59 (2), 112–143.
Rainnie, A., Herod, A., and McGrath-Champ, S. (2007) Spatialising industrial relations. *Industrial Relations Journal (Britain)* 38 (2), 102–118.
Rex, J. and Moore, R. (1967) *Race, Community and Conflict: A Study of Sparkbrook*. Oxford University Press, Oxford.
Rex, J. and Tomlinson, S. (1979) *Colonial Immigrants in a British City: A Class Analysis*. Routledge and Kegan Paul, Boston.

Saunders, P. (1978) Domestic property and social class. *International Journal of Urban and Regional Research* 2 (2), 233–251.

Saunders, P. (1984) Beyond housing classes: The sociological significance of private property rights in means of consumption. *International Journal of Urban and Regional Research* 8 (2), 202–227.

Sheppard, E. and Barnes, T.J. (1990) *The Capitalist Space Economy: Geographical Analysis after Ricardo, Marx and Sraffa*. Unwin Hyman, Cambridge.

Smith, N. (1979) Toward a theory of gentrification: A back to the city movement by capital, not people. *Journal of the American Planning Association* 45 (4), 538–548.

Smith, N. (1982) Gentrification and uneven development. *Economic Geography* 58 (2), 139–155.

Smith, N. (1987) Gentrification and the rent gap. *Annals of the Association of American Geographers* 77 (3), 462–465.

Walker, R. (1981) A theory of suburbanization: Capitalism and the construction of urban space in the United States. In M. Dear and A.J. Scott (eds), *Urbanization and Urban Planning in Capitalist Society*. Methuen, London, pp. 383–429.

Weber, M. ([1922] 1978) *Economy and Society: An Outline of Interpretive Sociology, Volume 2*. University of California Press, Berkeley and Los Angeles.

Williams, P. (1978) Building societies and the inner city. *Transactions of the Institute of British Geographers, New Series* 3 (1), 23–34.

Wolff, R.D. and Resnick, S.A. (1987) *Economics: Marxian Versus Neoclassical*. Johns Hopkins Press, Baltimore.

Chapter 30

Class
Part II

Clive Barnett

What Questions is "Class" the Answer to?

Lamenting the apparent decline of class analysis in geography, Neil Smith (2000) asks "What happened to class?" The answer turns out to be that class has been displaced in favor of identity-based, culturalist approaches to understanding inequality and power. Smith calls for a revival of class as a focus of unifying analysis in an era when "neoliberalism" is restoring class power with a vengeance. Smith's argument belongs to a broader genre of left-criticism which opposes "Class," understood as a material, objectively economic vector of social power, to "Identity," understood as more subjective, and based on non-economic forms of power. For example, David Harvey criticizes political philosophies of cosmopolitanism because they focus on all sorts of diversities and differences "except the central difference that really matters: class power and its associated social inequalities" (Harvey 2009: 115). This critical genre acknowledges that there are plural sources of harm, inequality, and injustice in the world. It just presumes in advance that some of these are more fundamental than others, analytically and politically.

In geography the question "what happened to class?" really means "whatever happened to Marxism?" And *class* was never quite as central to geography's radical trajectory in the 1970s and 1980s as Smith's lament would have everyone believe. For a long time in geography "the key analytic has tended to be capital rather than labor, a focus which has often bypassed a broader interpretation of class, its subjectivities and materialities, and its lived experiences" (Stenning 2008: 9). The

The Wiley Blackwell Companion to Human Geography, First Edition.
Edited by John A. Agnew and James S. Duncan.
© 2011 John Wiley & Sons, Ltd. Published 2016 by John Wiley & Sons, Ltd.

prevalence of capital-logic styles of conceptualization in geography's canonical Marxism is indicative of a division between different ways of ordering concepts. Some approaches theorize "vertically," deriving orders of temporal, causal, or normative priority from layered architectures of abstraction and concretization. This style of theory has generated some of the most important geographical work on "the urbanization of capital" and "the production of space." But you can also theorize horizontally, as it were, in terms of the articulation of different processes alongside one another. In this respect, it is notable that in the work of Doreen Massey (1984), *class-formation* rather than *capital* remains a more fundamental category of explanation than in other styles of Marxist geography, and for that very reason this work has been able to integrate other social relations and dimensions of inequality into a conjunctural conceptualization of the spatiality of politics in a genuinely pluralistic way.

Class is certainly a flourishing topic of research in geography (e.g. McDowell 2006, Dowling 2009). This is because ways have been found of investigating those processes that geography's canonical Marxism has always struggled with: class as a lived, experiential dimension of everyday life, often studied ethnographically in contexts of housing, education, political organization, or employment, (e.g. Bridge 2006, Jeffrey 2010, McDowell 2009), and always with an understanding of the ways in which class intersects with (e.g. Valentine 2007) or "articulates" with other processes of racial formation, gender divisions of labor, or state formation (e.g. Chari 2004, Hart 2007), and situated historically in the politics of collective action and the geographies of labor (e.g. Griffin 2009, Revill 2005). At the same time, class is a central concern of quantitative spatial science, focused as it is on enduring patterns of inequality and whether or not these help to explain behaviors such as voting or relative life chances (e.g. Dorling 2008).

Rather than asking "whatever happened to class" as if there is only one thing to which class as a concept can refer to, Wright (2005) suggests that the way to proceed is to ask: "If 'class' is the answer, what is the question?" He identities six "anchoring" questions to which "class" might emerge as an important part of the answer:

- How are people objectively located in distributions of material inequality?
- What explains how people, individually and collectively, subjectively locate themselves and others within a structure of inequality?
- What explains inequalities in life chances and material standards of living?
- What social cleavages systematically shape overt conflicts?
- How should we characterize and explain the variations across history in the social organization of inequalities?
- What sorts of transformations are needed to eliminate oppression and exploitation within capitalist societies?

In geography, quite a lot of research is anchored by variations of the first three questions. But the headline debates in which "class" is invoked or dismissed most forcefully revolve around different versions of the last three questions. Debates about "class" matter in geography because they have been central to contested visions of where inequality and injustice come from, and how they are and should be politicized.

Making "Class" the Answer to an Obsolete Question

In order to develop the sort of analysis suggested by Wright's focus on the questions to which "class" is meant to be the answer, it is worth focusing in on the work of David Harvey. Harvey's reconstruction of Marxism as *historical-geographical materialism* has been focused on transforming explanations of the variability of inequality and injustice over time and space – based on the assumption that the capital/labor relation is the central antagonism driving social conflict and deducing a privileged pathway to emancipation from this assumption. Harvey's emphasis has been on tracking reconfigurations in the production and appropriation of surplus, the distinguishing conceptual focus of Marxist class analysis. Harvey's work helps to disrupt and displace a classical Marxist teleology in which more and more inequality is generated by the appropriation of the labor power of property-less workers through capital's control over the labor process. The process of *exploitation*, rooted in an understanding of Marx's labor theory of value, certainly remains the core dynamic of capitalist development in Harvey's work. But Harvey's Marxism is concerned with how this core social relation of class is both dependent upon and displaced across various spatial-temporal practices beyond the labor process as such. The names and concepts for this process of displacement have been elaborated over time – from a theory of capitalist crisis cycled through secondary and tertiary *circuits of capital* (Harvey 1982) to the *urbanization of capital* (Harvey 1985), from *postmodern flexibilization* (Harvey 1989) to neoliberalized *accumulation through dispossession* (Harvey 2005). In Harvey's historical geography of the capitalist present, inequality is generated across a distributed system for the production, appropriation, exchange and distribution of surplus. The flip-side of Harvey's *displacement* of the logics of capital accumulation into spatially and temporally distributed networks of relative mobility and fixity, is that class as a potential focal point for cultural and political identification is consistently disrupted and fragmented. The stories Harvey tells about the urbanization of consciousness, about postmodernism as a form of generalized cognitive dissonance, and about the politically disorienting and fetishizing effects of neoliberal financialization are all shaped by a phenomenological sensitivity to the changing spatial and temporal rhythms through which "experience" itself is configured.

If Harvey's analysis of accumulation has emphasized the multiple dynamics through which surplus is extracted and appropriated, and if his cultural theory has always emphasized the multiple dimensions of identification generated by living under capitalist social relations, then the framing presumption of these analyses has remained a search for a single principle of universalization. The presumption that contentious politics can and should converge on a single, unified focus of global struggle, and that the principle of this universalization (i.e. "Class") can be decided upon through the abstract theoretical deductions of Marxist theories of capital accumulation and the production of space, is indicative of an imbalance between diagnostic critique and normative reconstruction that characterizes radical geography (Sayer 1995). This imbalance is related to the difficulty that capital-logic styles of Marxism have with thinking about politics in a strongly constitutive sense, a problem that bedevils Marxist class theory more generally. This is best illustrated by the inadequate attention given by this tradition of thought to conceptualizing the political agency of "capital." For example, in Harvey's influential narrative of neoliberalism as a political project aimed at restoring "class power," capital's internal imperatives of accumulation are assumed to be directly voiced by "the state." This reflects a longer habit of thought in which the state has only ever been theorized as a functional adjunct to collective-action problems which capital faces in securing the conditions of extended accumulation (e.g. Harvey 2001).

The elision of the analysis of class-formation "from above" is the condition of the assumption in this style of Marxism that the generality of capitalist social relations reflects a coherent strategy of universalization. This in turn leads to the insistence on finding a universalizing principle of equivalence across all social struggles which can match the apparent "universal" scope and reach of capital's singular capacity for self-expression. There is therefore a pivotal ambivalence between Harvey's systematic analysis of the displacements of capital accumulation through urbanized, financialized, monetized infrastructures, and his own gloss on these conceptualizations when it comes to programmatic statements about possibilities of political action. The spatialized analysis of capitalist development seems to challenge fundamental assumptions about class-formation in the Marxist heritage. For example, Harvey (2005) conceptualizes neoliberalism with reference to the concept of accumulation by dispossession, referring to practices of privatization, deregulation, and the financialization of debt which transfer publicly or commonly held assets and resources into private property. This analysis reiterates the lesson that the accumulation of capital is not always and everywhere teleologically oriented towards the extraction of relative surplus value anchored in the deepening of the wage-relation and transformations of the labor process. There here are diverse strategies of surplus extraction and appropriation which can and do co-exist in space and time. In Harvey's narrative, nevertheless, accumulation by dispossession is presented as a coherent strategy that has the effect of fragmenting and particularizing social conflicts which could in principle be unified around a class-based identification.

In short, Harvey's analysis indicates that social cleavages should not be expected always and everywhere to form around the central antagonism of exploitation in the labor process, that is, in terms of "class" as it is understood in classical Marxism. But more fundamentally, the silences and elisions in this account indicate that there is no good reason for supposing that these dynamics of conflict should be conceptualized as *diverging* from that classical problematic either. Harvey's invocation of "class" as a universalizing focal point of political identification runs against the force of the very argument presented. And anyway, it turns out that "materialist" class analysis has itself undermined assumptions that would lead one to suppose that a singular term such as "Class" must always be provided in answer to the question "what sorts of transformations are needed to eliminate oppression and exploitation within capitalist societies?"

Class Isn't What It Used To Be (and It Never Was)

In the history of Marxist social theory, there has developed a whole conceptual vocabulary of fetishism and reification and false consciousness and repressive desublimation and ideological interpellation to account for the "voluntary servitude" by which capitalist exploitation has been *legitimized* through the active consent of those whose labor is the source of profit and who are also the primary victims of injustice. Complex vocabularies of space and spatiality emerge from this same theoretical problematic of the reproduction of capitalist social relations despite their contradictory effects. Issues of space and urbanization first enter the lexicon of Western Marxism to help account for "the survival of capitalism" (Lefebvre 1976), and a prevalent model of critique in human geography depends on the assumption that the reason that "thinking spatially" matters so much is because particular spatial ontologies (flat, bounded, territorialized ones) function *ideologically* – they "legitimize" existing power relations by essentializing and naturalizing contingent relationships of inequality, exploitation and oppression.

In contrast to this ideological problematic that defined so much Western Marxism in the twentieth-century is a historical tradition of thought in which "culture" has been understood as a field for the self-expression of working class experiences, grievances and aspirations – as "a whole way of struggle" or "whole way of conflict," in E.P. Thompson's (1961) Marxist "correction" of what became a more famous formulation by Raymond Williams (1961). Thompson helped inaugurate a startlingly assertive view of working-class formation as a process of pro-active "making" that seemed at least to escape the classical scheme in which the working class could only become a self-conscious subject "for-itself" once it been objectively constituted as a "class-in-itself" through the development of industrial capitalism. One of the most important recent contributions and challenges to the expressive paradigm of working-class history, at which Thompson stands at the apex, is the recent work of Carolyn Steedman on domestic service in late eighteenth and early nineteenth century England. Not only were the vast majority of the workforce in the period normally thought so central to the emergence and consolidation of industrial capitalism involved in non-industrial service work, but the intimate relationships with servants were pivotal to the ways in which ideals of self-hood, labor, and rights were conceived in this period (Steedman 2003). Steedman (2007: 41–42) argues that the elision of domestic servants is in fact a central condition of the development of the labor theory of value from Adam Smith through to Marx. This theory depends upon the banishment of types of work which do not lead to the production of commodities separable from the laborer from the realm of properly "productive" labor, in the sense of being directly consumed in the course of production for the valorization of capital.

Steedman challenges a whole set of inherited conceptual problems around the relationships between work, culture, and politics. Crucially, she locates the lived sense of grievance that arose from everyday experiences of intimate, caring service work for others (and their children) as central to the emergence of working-class self-hood in this period. Steedman argues that her own work on domestic service and recent work on the historiography of the "Black Atlantic" systems of slave labor challenge the centrality accorded to industrial production as the norm around which class formation is theorized in the Marxist tradition. In short, class formation – even if still understood as rooted in practices of deploying labor for the production and appropriation of surplus – turns out to have a markedly different history from the one that has served as the conceptual framework for the analysis of the class formation and class-based politics in the Marxist tradition. This argument is bolstered by analysis of the restructuring of labor and employment in "post-Fordist" and "neoliberalized" economies, which are dominated by low-paid insecure employment across sectors. This two-pronged revisionary movement in thinking about the material organization of the central process identified by Marxist class analysis – surplus extraction – shows how "incredibly partial and potentially distortive" the normative model of social formation based on industrial capitalism and waged work in manufacturing has been (Eley 2007: 168). And opening up understandings of class-formation to a much wider array of practices of surplus extraction and labor coercion beyond the restriction to wage labor in the industrial labor process means that "Class" need not be thought of as the necessary universalizing principle around which "class politics" might emerge. What might still be thought of as the "hidden injuries of class" turn out to have been historically expressed through claims for "the right to be human" (Gilroy 2009), which have been rooted in experiences of oppressive labor systems that never conformed to a model of the real subsumption of the wage-laborer to the control of capital in the industrialized labor process.

These revisions in how class-formation is conceptualized matter beyond those fields in geography where class itself is an explicit object of research because they point to a fundamental fault line across the field of critical social theory. Geography's canonical Marxism remains one of the few fields of critical social theory where the epistemological, empirical, and normative image of revolutionary political agency – where the proletariat is the bearer of universal values by virtue of its inherent interest in overthrowing capitalism – remains intact. Axel Honneth (Fraser and Honneth 2003: 239) suggests that recent social theory takes different routes out of this "production paradigm," shaped by a shared concern with relocating the sources for the possibility of transformative political agency. First, in "normatively charged" accounts of the human psyche, drives, or the vitalism of the bodies, transformative energies are relocated to deeper ontological levels of one sort or other. Second, emancipatory and transformative potentials are relocated to different sorts of action, other than labor, the form of action privileged in Marxist social theory; here, the main reference point is Jürgen Habermas' reconstruction of critical social theory around an action-theoretic model of communicatively mediated interaction. Honneth's account of the relocation of the sources of critical social theory's normative force resonates with the argument of Luc Boltanski and Eve Chiapello (2005: xxiv–xxv) regarding two distinctive metaphysics of the social world that underwrite contemporary critical social theory. In one of these, characteristic of Marxist structuralism of the 1970s and Deleuzian inflected theories, the focus is on diverse relations of force that shape institutions and practices. From this perspective, the social is understood to exist on a single plane of immanence, and so the normative dimensions of social life are of little concern to it. A second strand, again associated with Habermas, does integrate the determinative role of normative practices – of law and morality – into its view of the social field.

Of the two trajectories of critical social theory identified above, critical human geography has cleaved more closely to the immanentist tradition. The ontological register of this tradition lends itself to geography's existing conventions of constructing alternative spatial ontologies. The action-theoretic strand has had a subordinate role in the discipline's recent theoretical adventures. This relative imbalance in attention is illustrated by the influence of styles of post-Marxist thought still haunted by the epistemological and political hang-ups of the tradition of class reductionism they appear to depart from.

Ontology is Not An Answer to Political Questions

The most influential style of post-Marxist thought in human geography is indebted to the reconceptualization of hegemony developed by Laclau and Mouffe (1985). This is one source of a broader flowering of interest in concepts of "the political" as a distinctive ontological seam or layer, defined by relations of struggle, conflict, dissensus and agonism. Emerging from the breakdown of previous paradigms of class analysis which attempted to salvage a sense of the determination in the last instance by economic relations while making room for the constitutive role for politics and ideology in shaping class struggle, concepts of "the political" in this post-Marxist vein of thought end up granting politics an absolute, as distinct from merely relative, degree of autonomy from other practices. Laclau and Mouffe laid the basis for a distinctive conceptualization of the political field as entirely shaped by the contingent relations held together in discourse, where discourse is understood as a semiotic field for the articulation of meanings. Words such as "freedom," "the people," or "democracy" function as "empty signifiers," as the contingent-universals around which disparate struggles are linked into temporary chains of equivalence. This is actually not a theory of discourse at all; it is a theory of politics as a practice of *naming*. In this tradition of political theory, the social field is freed from the strictures of class reductionism only to be reduced to an effect of political strategy, a reduction only further enhanced by geography's embrace of theories of governmentality indebted to Foucault's analysis of modern political rationalities.

Where does this sort of post-Marxism leave the concept of "class" then? In the anti-essentialist class analysis developed by Resnick and Wolff (1987: 25), class is reduced to an arbitrary conceptual *entry-point*, which is not at any cost to be to be confused with a causal essence. This understanding of the epistemological pitfalls and potentials of Marxist class analysis (stalked by the ghost of Louis Althusser) has been developed in geography by Gibson-Graham (1996), who pluralize the points of identification around which the intersections of economic and non-economic practices generate political mobilization. But this strand of thought is marked by the conflation of different senses of "essentialism:" it is assumed that various harms associated with essentialized views of race, or sexuality, or gender, are legitimized by epistemological essentialisms rooted in notions of explanatory causality. And this conflation reiterates a long-standing inflation of the importance of having the correct epistemology to ensure good politics, only now the proper epistemology is one of contingency and "over-determination."

Post-Marxist accounts of "the political," hegemony, and over-determination certainly represent a genuine pluralization of conceptualizations of the sources of inequality and injustice. While sometimes choosing class as an entry point, these approaches neither suppose that class is a necessary point of political identification and nor do they suppose other sources of inequality are derivative of or subordinate to class-based forms. They do however, retain the long-standing "ideological" emphasis on thinking of social formations as sutured together through the constitution of political subjectivities at the level of meaning and, more recently, of "affect."

There is a second strand of post-Marxist theory associated with a tradition of European political thought that develops a critique of the classical Marxist privileging of the industrial proletariat as the universal subject of emancipation. Rooted in a tradition of Italian *autonomista* thought and most fully developed by Antonio Negri, it focuses on a concept of "immaterial labor" and a provocative interpretation of Marx's *Grundrisse*, sifted through the lens of Spinoza and Deleuze. A key concept to emerge from this field of work is that of "precarity." Precarity is a concept that links empirically observable transformations of work (Castree *et al.* 2003, McDowell and Christopherson 2009, Ross 2009), into a revisionist history of the present as marking a decisive new stage in the development of capitalism, characterized by the emergence of new forms of political subjectivity such as the "precariat" and "the multitude" (Gill and Pratt 2009). Arguing that capitalism is now characterized by the dominance of knowledge and information, this tradition of political analysis underscores the sense that industrial capitalism and Fordist social formations are neither typical nor a *telos* of capitalist development (Neilsen and Rossiter 2009).

Behind the stated commitments to the multiple dimensions of political subjectivity, there remains in this tradition a resolutely monist imagination linking economic processes to cultural and political practices. It belongs to a long-standing lineage of Marxist thought in which it is not laborers themselves but the structure of socialized labor in general which assures the immanent possibility of the overcoming of capitalism. The argument that the informational, knowing, cognitive dimensions of labor are more and more important to the dynamics of capital accumulation (Thrift 2005) is worked-up by this distinctive strand of still-quite-Marxist thought into an argument about the deepening and extension of the "real subsumption" of labor to capital to include the whole field of social reproduction, education, and popular culture. It therefore retains a privileged focus on the analysis of logics of surplus extraction and appropriation. The distinctive concern with re-theorizing subjectivity in affective terms, rather than discursively, remains rooted to the idea that social formations are sutured all the way down by "getting at" people's beliefs, desires, and feelings. From this perspective, neoliberalism is as a process by which the state facilitates the emergence of a new form of marketized, financialized capitalism *and* the generation new type of individual appropriate to this new form (Lazzarato 2009).

What is most distinctive about this capacious account of the condition of political transformation "after the end of work" (see Grantner 2009, Vandenberghe 2002) is the optimistic interpretation of the political significance of contemporary transformations of capitalism. Writers such as Hardt and Negri (2000), Virno (2004), and Gorz (2010) discern in the dynamics of immaterial labor, precarity, and knowledge capitalism the already present possibilities of fundamental transformation. But not in the image in which it has previously been pictured by the Marxist revolutionary tradition. The gravediggers generated by the immanent logics of capitalist development are no longer the proletariat; the new political subject generated by this phase of capitalist development turns out to be a revivified version of Spinoza's image of "the multitude," a figure for a mode of dispersed collective action which retains its constitutive diversity while managing to address affairs in "common." So it turns out that the way out of the impasses of Marxist analyses of class politics is to displace the animating questions of this tradition to an ontological level in which both the dynamics of capitalism and the resistance to capitalism emerge immanently from the same type of action. Which means that not a lot of thought has to be put in to thinking about the hard-work that goes into political organization in fast changing political-economic conditions (cf. Wills 2008).

Political theories of "hegemony" and of "the multitude" squeeze normativity out of the social and political fields, under the weight of ontologies of abundance, immanence, and lack; or of purely strategic understandings of political identification. But this ontologization of politics is really an evasion: "There is no transitivity between ontology and politics" (Critchley 2007: 105). But to register the full implications of this thought, we need to shift theoretical terrain.

Why "Class" Isn't the Only Answer to Questions about Emancipation

Geographers' have contributed to projects which multiply the modes of surplus extraction and appropriation through which inequalities and injustices are understood to be structured. Geography's debates about these matters since the late 1980s have been framed in terms of a series of overlapping binary oppositions: class versus identity, economy versus culture, materiality versus discourse. But there are other routes through these same issues, routes which invite a more thorough overhaul of the social-theoretic assumptions inherited from Marxist theory. What defines these traditions, returning to Wright's anchoring questions, is a focus on the variable combination of *plural* sources of inequality and injustice, rather than restricting themselves to identifying multiple variations on a single dynamic of surplus extraction which continues to define a Marxist "entry-point" into these issues. We have seen that some strands of post-Marxist analysis also open themselves up to this sense of plural sources of inequality. But they remain wedded to a reproduction problematic in which functionalist concepts of subjectivity continue to exert powerful influence. In contrast, the broad family of social theory I have in mind – it would include thinkers such as Luc Boltanski, Pierre Bourdieu, Nancy Fraser, Axel Honneth, Hans Joas, Michael Mann, Charles Tilly, Loic Wacquant – is defined by a concern with understanding the rationalities of different forms of action through which the social field is coordinated (see Joas and Knöbl 2009).

The difference between cultural theories centered on concepts of subjectivity and social theories centered on concepts of action has largely been overlooked in geography's debates about the significance or otherwise of Marxist theory. This is indicative of the sidelining of the second of the two routes out of the "production paradigm" discussed above; the route which pluralizes forms of action beyond a privileging of labor to include communication (Fraser and Honneth 2003: 246–247). Axel Honneth's own project to reconstruct the normative foundations of critical social theory synthesizes the emphasis on affective dimensions of subjectivity developed by theorists of immanence with the Habermasian emphasis on the rationalization of different forms of action. Honneth retains from Habermas the emphasis on the normative expectations built into communicative relationships through which social life is coordinated. He departs from Habermas in arguing that we should not equate "the normative potential of social interaction with the linguistic conditions of reaching understanding free from domination" (Honneth 2007: 70).

He re-centers the normative core of critical social theory on the dynamics of *recognition*, which has affective, embodied aspects which the Habermasian emphasis on the cognitive dimensions of communication fails to credit. There is "a core of expectations of recognition that all subjects bring to social interaction" (Fraser and Honneth 2003: 247). Social conflicts emerge when these expectations are systematically undermined and flouted. The central claim of this approach is that felt experiences of *disrespect* animate transformative political agency, experiences which draw on "intuitive notions of justice violated" (Honneth 2007: 11).

The concept of recognition which Honneth develops is rooted in the history of class analysis, namely; Hegel's account of labor as the scene for recognition and misrecognition. Honneth pluralizes this struggle for recognition beyond the social relations of labor to which it has been classically contained by Marxist theory, to include plural forms of disrespect. In the shift from a linguistically-oriented theory of communicative action to a philosophical anthropology of recognition, he also rejects the economism of Marxism which frames recognition in epistemological terms of grasping objectively shared common interests. Honneth (1995: 160–170) argues that there are three analytically distinct dimensions of recognition which are essential to identity-formation: emotional concerns; rights-based concerns; and social esteem. This framework informs a diagnosis of the multiple social pathologies generated by contemporary capitalist modernity, which revolve around multiple forms of disrespect: violations of the body, denials of rights, and denigrations of ways of life (Honneth 1995: 131–139).

While Honneth emphasizes the affective dimensions of recognition and disrespect, this analysis does not remain on a single plane of immanence. The affective dimensions of disrespect have "cognitive potential:" "the injustice of disrespect does not inevitably *have to* reveal itself but merely *can*" (Honneth 2005: 138). This argument points in the direction of an analysis of the role of political movements in articulating "intuitive senses of justice violated," one which departs markedly from the idea of the contingent suturing together of identities around empty signifiers. Honneth's point is that analysis of mobilization and movement formation needs to be attentive to the "dynamics of moral experiences" animating social conflicts. This "experiential" framing of the communicative dynamics of movement formation has been developed also by other thinkers working a Habermasian vein of thought, such as James Bohman, John Dryzek, Nancy Fraser, and Iris Marion Young, all of whom investigate the ways in which the "cognitive potentials" of the dynamics of disrespect are *geographically* articulated in and through movement politics (see Scheuerman 2006). Honneth's project also has affinities with Andrew Sayer's (2005) account of the "moral significance of class." Sayer argues that recognition "is thoroughly materialized in the distribution of material goods" A key implication of this linking of recognition and distribution cuts to the heart of the issue most at stake in different perspectives on how class matters in social theory. Sayer argues that social scientists must take seriously "lay normativity," by which he means the ordinary sense of "what matters" to people; what goods and valued ways of life they strive towards and for which they seek recognition. This injunction requires us to break with the understanding of social power that informs one-tier ontologies of pure immanence, for as Sayer (2005: 6) argues, the struggles of the social field are not only about habitual actions or the pursuit of power – they are crucially shaped by the disputes over the things which matter to people (e.g. Skeggs 2004; Tilly 2008).

The pluralization of power and justice is also a feature of the style of "pragmatist" French social theory pioneered by Luc Boltanski and "the conventions school" of economic sociology. This tradition reinserts a concern with ordinary normative action into the overwhelmingly strategic, even cynical, view of power developed by social theorists such as Bourdieu and Foucault. It seeks "to take seriously the imperative to justify that underlies the possibility of coordinating human behavior" (Boltanski and Thévenot 2006: 37). For Boltanski and Thévenot, this commitment leads to an empirical program of investigating different "orders of worth" through which practices are coordinated, challenged, and criticized (cf. Stark 2009). Boltanski and Chiapello (2005a) develop this theoretical framework of situated practices of justification and "orders of worth" into a fully-fledged retheorization of the dynamics of capitalist modernity, in which capitalism is not so much *crisis-dependent* as it is *critique-dependent*: "In obliging capitalism to justify itself, critique compels it to strengthen the mechanisms of justice it contains, and to refer to certain kinds of common good in whose service it claims to be placed." Practices of justification are understood not as mere ideological superstructures, but as constitutive coordinating devices which exert constraints on accumulation processes.

A crucial feature of this conceptualization is the distinction between two senses of "legitimate" that runs through modern social theory, going back to Max Weber. In one sense, *legitimation* is understood as a process of "retrospective concealment," an understanding quite compatible with Marxist theories of ideology. This understanding of legitimation remains remarkably resilient in critical human geography, lending itself to the academic vocation of unmasking the real interests beneath mere appearances. In a second sense, *legitimacy* is the key concept, one which acknowledges the communicative, coordinating relevance of normative arguments. Boltanski and Chiapello's orientation to issues of legitimacy rather than legitimation re-opens a route to understanding what Marxism and post-Marxism think of as "hegemony" – the power-infused coordination of social action in space and time – as a process in which actors orient themselves to structured fields of choices (cf. Przeworski 1985). Taking justificatory practices seriously means that it is possible to acknowledge that different "spirits" of capitalism legitimize particular patterns of accumulation, but in so doing they also make possible the mobilization against certain forms of accumulation which are presumptively less just, less legitimate (Boltanski and Chiapello 2005b).

Paralleling Honneth's phenomenology of the multiples harms of misrecognition, Boltanski and Chiapello (2005a: 36–43) identify four different and irreconcilable "sources of indignation" that provoke criticism: capitalism as a source of disenchantment and inauthenticity; as a source of oppression; as a source of poverty and inequality; and as a source of opportunism and egoism. Each of these normative reference points provides a critical fulcrum which generates demands for justification. Boltanski and Chiapello argue that since the possibility of critique is internally related to the demand for justification, capitalism adjusts by responding unevenly to irreconcilable forms of criticism. These four types of criticism coalesce into two broad strands of critique, developed by coalitions of different social actors: an *artistic critique* combines the criticism of disenchantment and inauthenticity with the criticism of oppression, which emphasizes alienation, loss of meaning, the destruction of creativity; and a *social critique* which combines the critique of the egoism of private interests with the critique of the impoverishment. In Boltanski and Chiapello's reinterpretation of capitalist mutations since the 1960s, capitalism mutates by responding to the artistic critique. But the key point of their argument is that "evading a certain type of critique often occurs at the cost of satisfying criticisms of a different kind," which means that the processes of critique, justification and adjustment is never total nor complete; in their analysis, the social critique of capitalism is reconfigured and reasserted in response to the adjustments made to satisfy the artistic critique.

Conclusion

This chapter has tracked the ways in which various shifts in social theory – towards ontology, to theories of action, to practice-based concepts, to ethnographic styles of research, to culture, to conceptualizing "the political" – follow from attempts to escape the social-theoretical straightjacket imposed by a tradition of Marxist class analysis. In geography, it is certainly true that a great deal of conceptual innovation has been shaped by a perceived need to escape from what Thrift (2007: 23) calls "remorselessly monopolistic accounts of capitalism that act as a kind of intellectual and political bulldozer." But when geographers have focused on the limitations of Marxist concepts of accumulation or class politics, it has often been in an ontologized register of culture, the political, and materiality which leaves in place some of the most problematic assumptions of Marxist theory about how the social field is coordinated and transformed. Proponents of "class" as the universal principle of equivalence with the potential to unify otherwise disparate struggles, as well as the prevalent approaches that seek a way out of the totalizing ambitions on this particular Marxist shibboleth, hold to epistemic understandings of the dynamics of human agency which always lead back to the belief that the social field hangs together, and must be transformed, by "getting at" people's beliefs, desires and feelings without them knowing it. This is a legacy of theorizing about *subjectivity* rather than *action*, a trace of one particular trajectory out of Marxist analyses of politics. The reason these issues still matter, then, is because different ways of settling accounts with this heritage inform different understandings of the public spaces of critique: accounts which proclaim contingency and multiplicity are easily embodied in an ethos of revelatory education and aesthetic disruption; while those concerned with plural rationalities of action inform a more modest position in which academic knowledge is one voice in an open space of plural disputes about what matters.

References

Boltanski, L. and Chiapello, E. (2005a) *The New Spirit of Capitalism*. Verso, London.
Boltanski, L. and Chiapello, E. (2005b) The role of criticism in the dynamics of capitalism. In M. Miller (ed.), *Worlds of capitalism: Institutions, Economics, Performance and Governance in the Era of Globalisation*. Routledge, London.

Boltanski, L. and Thévenot, L. (2006) *On Justification*. Princeton University Press, Princeton.
Bridge, G. (2006) It's not just a question of taste: Gentrification, the neighborhood and cultural capital. *Environment and Planning A* 38, 1965–1978.
Castree, N., Coe, N., Ward, K., and Samers, M. (2003) *Spaces of Work*. Sage, London.
Chari, S. (2004) *Fraternal Capitalism*. Stanford University Press, Stanford.
Critchley, S. (2007) *Infinitely Demanding*. Verso, London.
Dorling, D. (2008) Cash and the not so classless society. *Fabian Review* 120 (2).
Dowling, R. (2009) Geographies of identity: landscapes of class. *Progress in Human Geography* 33, 833–839.
Eley, G. (2007) Historicizing the global, politicizing capital. *History Workshop Journal* 63, 163–188.
Fraser, N. and Honneth, A. (2003) *Redistribution or Recognition? A Political-Philosophical Exchange*. Verso, London.
Fraser, N. (2008) *Scales of Justice*. Polity Press, Cambridge.
Gibson-Graham, J-K. (1996) *The End of Capitalism (as we knew it)*. Blackwell, Oxford.
Gill, R. and Pratt, A. (2007) In the Social Factory? Immaterial labour, precariousness and cultural work. *Theory, Culture and Society* 25, 1–30.
Gilroy, P. (2009) *Race and the Right to be Human*. Treaty of Utrecht Chair Inaugural Lecture. University of Utrecht, Utrecht. http://www2.hum.uu.nl/onderzoek/lezingenreeks/pdf/Gilroy_Paul_oratie.pdf.
Gorz, A. (2010) The exit from capitalism has already begun. *Cultural Politics* 6, 5–14.
Grantner, E. (2009) *Critical Social Theory and the End of Work*. Ashgate, Aldershot.
Griffin, C. (2009) Placing political economy: organising opposition to free trade before the abolition of the Corn Laws. *Transactions of the Institute of British Geographers* 41 (4), 489–505.
Hardt, M. and Negri, T. (2000) *Empire*. Harvard University Press, Cambridge.
Hart, G. (2007) Changing concepts of articulation: Political stakes in South Africa today. *Review of African Political Economy* 111, 85–101.
Harvey, D. (1982) *The Limits to Capital*. Blackwell, Oxford.
Harvey, D. (1985) *The Urbanization of Capital*. Blackwell, Oxford.
Harvey, D. (1989) *The Condition of Postmodernity*. Blackwell, Oxford.
Harvey, D. (2001) [1976] The Marxian theory of the state. In *Space of Capital*. Edinburgh University Press, Edinburgh, pp. 267–283.
Harvey, D. (2005) *A Brief History of Neoliberalism*. Oxford University Press, Oxford.
Harvey, D. (2009) *Cosmopolitanism and the Geographies of Freedom*. Columbia University Press, New York.
Honneth, A. (1995) *The Struggle for Recognition*. Polity Press, Cambridge.
Honneth, A. (2007) *Disrespect*. Polity Press, Cambridge.
Jeffrey, C. (2010) *Timepass*. Stanford University Press, Stanford.
Joas, H. and Knöbl. W. (2009) *Social Theory*. Cambridge University Press, Cambridge.
Laclau, E. and Mouffe, C. (1995) *Hegemony and Socialist Strategy*. Verso, London.
Lazzarato, M. (2009) Neoliberalism in action: inequality, insecurity and the reconstitution of the social. *Theory, Culture and Society* 26, 109–133.
Lefebvre, H. (1976) *The Survival of Capitalism*. St Martin's Press, New York.
Massey, D. (1984) *Spatial Divisions of Labour*. Macmillan, London.
McDowell, L. (2006) Reconfigurations of gender and class relations. *Antipode* 38, 825–850.
McDowell, L. (2009) *Working Bodies*. Blackwell, Oxford.
McDowell, L. and Christopherson, S. (2009) Transforming work: new forms of employment and their regulation. *Cambridge Journal of Regions, Economy and Society* 2, 335–342.
Neilsen, B. and Rossiter, N. (2007) Precarity as a political concept, or, Fordism as Exception. *Theory, Culture and Society* 25, 51–72.

Przeworski, A. (1985) *Capitalism and Social Democracy*. Cambridge University Press, Cambridge.
Resnick, S.A. and Wolff, R.D. (1987) *Knowledge and Class*. University of Chicago Press, Chicago.
Revill, G. (2005) Railway labour and the geography of collective bargaining: the Midland Railway strikes of 1879 and 1887. *Journal of Historical Geography* 31, 7–40.
Ross, A. (2009) *Nice Work If You Can Get It*. New York University Press, New York.
Sayer, A. (1995) *Radical Political Economy: A Critique*. Routledge, London.
Sayer, A. (2005) *The Moral Significance of Class*. Cambridge University Press, Cambridge.
Scheuerman, W. (2006) Critical theory beyond Habermas. In J.S. Dryzek, B. Honig, and A. Phillips (eds), *The Oxford Handbook of Political Theory*. Oxford University Press, Oxford, pp. 84–105.
Skeggs, B. (2004) Exchange, value, and affect: Bourdieu and "the self". *Sociological Review* 52, 75–95.
Smith, N. (2000) What happened to class? *Environment and Planning A* 32, 2011–2032.
Smith, S.J. (2009) Everyday Morality: Where Radical Geography Meets Normative Theory. *Antipode* 41, 206–209.
Stark, D. (2009) *The Sense of Dissonance*. Princeton University Press, Princeton.
Steedman, C. (2003) Servants and their relationship to the unconscious. *Journal of British Studies* 42, 316–350.
Steedman, C. (2007) A boiling copper and some arsenic: servants, childcare, and class consciousness in Late Eighteenth-Century England. *Critical Inquiry* 34, 36–77.
Stenning, A. (2008) For working class geographies. *Antipode* 40, 9–14.
Tilly, C. (2008) *Credit and Blame*. Princeton University Press, Princeton.
Thompson E.P. (1961) The Long Revolution. *New Left Review* 9, 24–33.
Thrift, N. (2005) *Knowing Capitalism*. Sage, London.
Thrift, N. (2007) *Nonrepresentational Theory*. Routledge, London.
Valentine, G. (2007) Theorizing and Researching Intersectionality: A Challenge for Feminist Geography. *Professional Geographer* 59, 10–21.
Vandenberghe, F. (2002) Working out Marx: Marxism and the end of the work society. *Thesis Eleven* 69, 21–46.
Virno, P. (2004) *A Grammar of the Multitude*. Semiotext(e), New York.
Wills, J. (2008) Making class politics possible: organizing contract cleaners in London. *International Journal of Urban and Regional Research* 32, 305–323.
Williams R. (1961) *The Long Revolution*. Chatto and Windus, London.
Wright, E.O. (2005) Conclusion: If "class" is the answer, what is the question? In E.O. Wright (ed.) *Approaches to Class Analysis*. Cambridge University Press, Cambridge, pp. 180–192.

Chapter 31

Race
Part I

Kay Anderson

Part One

Conventionally, race has been approached in Geography and other social sciences in terms that maintain a firm boundary around "the human." In whichever way race is conceived, racial designation and discrimination have been understood within the confines of an essentially human domain of sociality. This is unsurprising. As Bruno Latour (2004) has pointed out, the social itself is usually considered as a more or less exclusively human arrangement; where, if they figure at all, its "non-human" members appear as just the "constructs" of human dispositions and relations that themselves remain explicable in their own – purely human – terms (Latour 2005: 39). This idea of the social has, however, been increasingly and variously, called into question in Geography and elsewhere (e.g. Braun and Castree 2001; Smith *et al.* 2009: 13–17; Panelli 2000; Sofoulis 2009). Not only has the boundary separating the human and the non-human – and culture from nature – become less and less secure, it has itself come to be understood as an artifice.

Latour traces this artifice to modernity (1993, 2004), while the two linked assumptions that (a) people are separate from other beings and (b) enjoy a uniquely privileged status among them, tend to be tracked to a much older Christian provenance (Latour 2008; see also Peterson 2001). Whatever the intellectual origins, however, such assumptions are under intensifying pressure amidst today's environmental call to arms. Most popularly, John Gray (2003) and Felipe Fernandez-Armesto (2005), among others, have questioned the claim that human beings

The Wiley Blackwell Companion to Human Geography, First Edition.
Edited by John A. Agnew and James S. Duncan.
© 2011 John Wiley & Sons, Ltd. Published 2016 by John Wiley & Sons, Ltd.

occupy a special place and have a special destiny on earth. More popularly still, it is not just the conceit, but the violence attached to this raising up, and valuing, of the human above all other life-forms that has come under widespread challenge in the name of ecology, and particularly "deep ecology" (see Dregson and Inoue 1996).

Intellectually, this critique of "human exceptionalism" has received considerable inspiration from Latour, whose questioning of the ontological distinction between humans and non-humans has impacted significantly on the discipline of Geography; a discipline traditionally separated according to its human and physical elements (Spenser and Whatmore 2002; Massey 2004). This critique has opened up an entirely new concern – in "naturecultures" geography, as well as certain quarters within the humanities (e.g. Hinchliffe 2008; Head 2007; the "ecohumanities corner" of *Australian Humanities Review*; Sandilands 2009; Whatmore 2002) with what the anthropologist Arjun Appadurai once referred to as "the social life of things" (1988). As Latour points out, "things" are not just the products of or vehicles for human interaction: they too are agents (2005: 39). As such, the social itself has to be re-conceptualised in what David Abram (1996) called "more-than-human" terms, and with an attention to the variety of ways in which humans and non-humans are entangled and co-exist.

There is, then, something of a methodological as well as an ethico-political decentering of the human taking place in Geography that is discernible in challenges to the legacy of ontological separation between humans and their non-human environment. Societies or cultures are coming to be recognized as collections or "assemblages" (DeLanda 2006; in Geography, see Robbins and Marks 2009), not just of people, but always also of "things" that are now recognized as playing a constitutive role in how people understand, organize and relate to others, as well as to themselves.

There is no doubt much exciting work being done, and still to do, in documenting the formerly neglected social lives of a range of non-human agencies in a "post-dualist" world (e.g. Bingham 2006; Braun 2008; Cerulo 2009). But, drawing upon work in a different vein, I want to show here that this critical interrogation of human exceptionalism also offers – even demands – a rethinking of "the human" itself; and so also a rethinking of those explanations of human behavior, relations, identity and so on, that have themselves remained confined to a humanist paradigm. To be pursued here, then, is the possibility that race might be understood beyond the confines of the human; and as such beyond the self/other framework of *identity politics* which has characterized so much work across numerous disciplines in the field of race and racism since the 1980s.

Earlier geographical work on race in the 1960s and 1970s had tended to pursue an *explicit* sociological approach in its focus on issues of inequality, discrimination, segregation and structural racism. Although somewhat narrow (even) within the terms of that approach, it is by no means discredited today and contributes a still useful documentation of the arrangements of racialized relations and inequality (e.g. Forrest and Dunn 2007; Ellis *et al.* 2007). It was, however, Peter Jackson's (1987) collection of essays *Race and Racism: Essays in Social Geography* among others (Anderson 1987), that signaled "a shift from more quantitative studies of social geographies of "ethnic segregation" to a more politicized theoretically grounded approach" (Dwyer and Bressey 2008: 2).

Jackson himself noted how geographical work on race relations had lagged behind the more radical critical approaches of the other social sciences (Jackson 1987: 5). Advocating an alternative way forward, he invoked Robert Miles (1984) to argue "we shall speak of the idea of 'race,' distancing ourselves from those who accord the concept explanatory status and focusing instead on its ideological effects in various domains" (Jackson 1987: 6). "We begin," he continues, "by recognizing that race is fundamentally a social construction rather than a natural division of humankind" (Jackson 1987: 6). In this respect, Jackson refers to Stuart Hall and, through him, to the influential work that followed the publication of Edward Said's *Orientalism* (1979) and its utilization of Michel Foucault's theorization of discourse (classically, see 1972). Subsequently, then, race came to be understood as the social and political construction of some humans by others, with nature – aligned (as it was) to an essentialization of difference and a naturalization of prejudice – kept resolutely outside of a purely human and interpretive framework.

The familiar, if not by now over-familiar, claim has been that race is "constructed" in the sense that it is a cultural and not a natural category. This is indicated by the fact that it is only some physical differences (skin color, hair type etc.), and not others, that have tended to provide a basis for racial classification and discrimination. Precisely *why* some differences and not others came to constitute the markers of racial categorization is – perhaps oddly – a question that has rarely been raised. I will come back to it. The main reason for this, though, has to do with the very character of the constructionist critique of race: on Arun Saldanha's (2006: 22) succinct formulation, the claim that "it's arbitrary! it's arbitrary!" which is to say that with no essential basis in nature or biology, race is considered "an arbitrary classification system [that is] imposed *upon* bodies" (Saldanha 2006: 10).

On the constructionist account, a racial meaning is considered as being added to or inscribed upon physical differences that are not in themselves significant. Discernible here is the structuralist influence of Ferdinand de Saussure's claim that language comprises an arbitrary system of differences. The social construction of race has thus usually been pursued – in an uncovering of the power invested in racial representation – as the critique of a linguistic or linguistically based discursive process (Spencer 2006). As Jackson (1987: 6) himself points out, "the urge to classify people into a finite number of 'races' ... should not be understood as having its roots in an unalterable 'human nature'."

For Nancy Stepan (1982: xii), in another important early intervention in this critical vein, race is "a primary form of self and group identification." This relationship between race and identity has, however, come to be configured in quite particular terms – that again owe something to the influence of Saussure, and the post-structuralism that he inspired. As Saldanha (2006: 11) notes: "After the "linguistic turn" ... society has been widely considered to operate in the same way that Saussurian signs do," such that, familiarly enough, "[i]n a social system of differences, dominance is achieved through the fearful discursive exclusion of 'the Other.' " As David Theo Goldberg (1993: 51) notes, "[r]acial differentiation – the mere discrimination between races and their purported members – is not as such necessarily racist." But, he continues, precisely when it "prompts identification ... racial differentiation begins to define otherness, and discrimination against the racially defined other becomes at once an exclusion of the different." The now standard argument is that because "subjects recognize themselves for the most part only in contrast to others," so these others are defined reductively (Goldberg 1993: 59–60). The racial classification of variations in human physical appearance is thus understood as the reflection of this drive to establish self-identity, and so to differentiate or denigrate those who look different (Goldberg 1993: 60; Mosse 1978). Race, in short, is considered as an inferiorizing mythology.

Goldberg (1993) himself links this dynamic to specifically modern forms of subjectivity. Jackson too, invoking, in the British context, colonialism, slavery and immigration, maintains that "the social construction of 'race' must … be understood historically" (Jackson 1987: 6; see also Anderson 1991). To this end, numerous studies in Geography and other social sciences documented the construction over time and space of racialized identities, including white identities, as constitutive of processes of boundary marking and exclusion. Perhaps more than other social scientists influenced by the post-structural turn, geographers have been keenly attentive to the contingent, located and specific terms of race's social and institutional construction and reconstruction within the dynamics of colonial capitalism (for useful recent reviews of this important literature, including on whiteness and white normativity, race's intersection with class, gender and sexuality, "mixed race" identities, and these concerns in non-western contexts, see e.g. Winders 2009, Price 2010, Sundberg 2008; also the forthcoming volume by Baldwin, Cameron and Kobayashi).

Despite the ongoing significance and innovation of anti-essentialist work that elicits the nuanced, complex, contradictory, and unstable nature of racialized identities (including work after Bhabha 1994 on postcolonial identities), the general applicability of the constructionist account of race is rarely itself put into fundamental question. Likely this is for sound political reasons given the undeniable liberatory value of the critical race paradigm for redressing racialized domination in all its abundantly current forms and guises (on the contemporary "remainders of race," see Amin 2010). As Price recently argues, there is a case for even stronger dialogue between geography and critical race theory to "make something happen" beyond intellectual critique (2010: 150). Indeed for this reason alone, an identity critique of race, racism and anti-racism that stays within the parameters of social evaluation will (and should) continue to occupy a central platform in contemporary geographic projects of resistance to what Delaney (2002:6) (after Morrison 1992) calls our "wholly racialized world."

There are, however, compelling theoretical reasons for trying to *also* think race beyond its social or discursive construction, especially where this holds the potential to arouse a different kind of political – in the case of this chapter, ecologically tuned – sensibility. Among the various critiques of social constructionism, both generally (Hacking 2000) and in the race field (e.g. Nayak 2006), Saldanha has perhaps engaged most fully with this neo-Saussurian understanding of race. He has done so, moreover, from a perspective that is at least partly informed by Latour's problematization of human exceptionalism.

Latour himself offers a forceful methodological critique of social constructionism, as he challenges the assumption that "things" – including here, bodies – constitute some kind of inert matter to which a human or cultural meaning might be simply attached (Latour 2005: 39). For Latour, things are constructed. But this proposition must be taken literally, for him, and beyond the limited semiotic concern with meaning, even as it becomes politically motivated and institutionally inscribed. Indeed "[i]t is only because semioticians studied texts – and literary ones at that – instead of things, that they felt obliged to limit themselves to "meaning." In effect they scientistically believed in the existence of things in addition to meaning (not mentioning their belief in the existence of a good old social context whenever it suited them). But a semiotics of things is easy, one simply has to drop the meaning bit from semiotics ..." (Latour 1998).

It is in the more literal and concrete sense that Latour describes as a process of "fabrication" involving the mobilization, engagement and assembly of a variety of conceptual and material elements (Latour 2005: 91; also 2009), that the construction of "things" is to be understood. For Manuel DeLanda, it is to be conceived as a "building or assembling from parts" (DeLanda 2006: 10). And it is something of this understanding that Saldanha takes up, in his own subjection of the claim that race is a social construction to the more recent "material turn" in Geography and the social sciences (see e.g. Whatmore 2006; a recent book series seeking to re-materialize Cultural Geography, also on racialized geographies and bodies, see Tolia-Kelly 2010; Bennett and Joyce 2010).

Saldanha writes against those – such as Paul Gilroy (2000) – who see the reference to racial differences as inevitably pernicious. For Saldanha, the refusal to admit the material fact of such differences is itself problematic; since, as Latour himself points out (1998 above), the claim that race is a social construction maintains a naive as well as inaccessible conception of "nature" before or outside of discourse. It thus "remains complicit with ... the metaphysical positing of an inert exteriority to language" (Saldanha 2006: 12), when it is nature itself that needs to be rethought. "Bodies," Saldanha argues, "need to be appreciated as productive in their own right, just like words, money or architecture."

The material fact of phenotypical variation does not, therefore, have to be disavowed in the name of some "postracial humanism." Rather, this variation only has to be taken seriously beyond the (flawed) assumption that "nature and biology, just like the body and matter in general," are "static and deterministic" (Saldanha 2006: 15). In this respect, Saldanha sees in the possibility of an empirical understanding of race – of "a thousand tiny races" – the possibility of an altogether different cosmopolitanism from Gilroy's post-racial version: one which rejects the self-other scheme of post-structuralism, not by annihilating nature from culture, but by immersing itself in "nature's lines of flight" (2006: 23).

Precisely in thinking across the nature-culture divide, Saldanha's argument displaces the terms in which race has been thought in social constructionist discourse. Similarly, it is in attempting to cross this divide that I have also sought to approach race from within a more Latourian frame, albeit with a different focus and orientation.

Part Two

Latour's critique of the separation between nature and culture – along with the privileging of "the human" that underpins it – has informed my recent explorations of race and the ontology of human exceptionalism. In this respect *Race and the Crisis of Humanism* (Anderson, 2007) focuses on the relationship between race and "the indigenous question." Substantively, it tracks the disturbance that was Australia – its people and the place – to a Christian Enlightenment notion of the human as a nature-transcending being. It documents the perplexity induced by a place that bore no apparent trace of what was optimistically assumed in Enlightenment thought to be the capacity of all people everywhere to separate from nature (see Meek 1967, for a discussion of social contract and stadial theory). This capacity, although thought to be constrained for some people in some places by environmental factors (like climate and soil), was nonetheless presumed to be a potential for all people the world over to cultivate crops, domesticate animals and settle collectively into social communities.

The book's narrative plot thus centers around the colonial confusion that the Australian "state of nature" presented to prevailing ideas of what it meant to be human: namely, to be exceptional in the sense of being above or beyond "nature," with nature conceived as (a) an external non-human world of environment, and (b) an internal animal-like corporeality over which people have imagined themselves to rise. Yet unlike other hunter-gatherer people encountered in Africa and the Americas, the Australian appeared *not* to have taken even the slightest distance from nature conceived in those terms (Williams and Frost 1988).

Within the context of a more general bewilderment with which the Great South Land confronted British voyagers and early colonists – in which, for example, the local flora and fauna defied metropolitan taxonomies (e.g. Smith 1985) – the apparently unimproved condition of the Australian Aborigines engendered deep confusion. Indeed more than that, the apparent inability of Aboriginal people to improve and settle, engendered no less than a *crisis* in the Christian Enlightenment notion of the human.

It is not only, then, that the Australian Aborigine was represented and regarded as a "savage" as so many have argued since Said (1979), for example, Attwood (1992, 1996) and Ryan (1996). Rather, it was the prevailing notion of savagery as a surpassable stage of human development that the Australian Aborigine put into question (see also Anderson and Perrin 2008). It follows that race – in its mid 19th century innatist or polygenist formulation – can be understood as a response to this crisis, and specifically, as an attempt to make sense of the Australian anomaly. For if Aboriginal people were not appearing to move out of nature, and despite the best colonial efforts to entice them to do so, then perhaps – so the speculation went – they inherently could not and would not ever. In this way, the book makes strange and shocking again the intellectual and affective turn to racial determinism in the mid-19th century. It was a "turn" that did indeed *take place*, the book argues, not through some over-general and aspatial will to colonize a generic New World other (see Harris 2004), but rather out of a specifically Southern crisis of confidence. Theorizing the rise of race in this way, *Race and the Crisis of Humanism* goes on to track the increasingly deterministic character of the race idea in select American and European texts over the 19th century.

Lying at the back of that story has been a still deeper (and, as yet, largely unaddressed) question of racial thought's relationship to European ideas of human autonomy from nature. In particular, the "clash of civilizations" described above prompts curiosity about its entanglement with a western logic of categorical separation from those beings gathered together under the label of "animals." At stake here

– we shall see in what follows in a necessarily highly condensed account – is the implication of a particular idea of "mind" in the very constitution of the ontologies of difference of interest to this chapter. For it was in the scientific project of craniometry that a quite specific formulation of mind as "intelligence" emerged and, later in the century, come Darwinism, of "mind as mental evolution"; both formulations of which drew constitutively on the idea of race.

As a number of post-humanist theorists have reminded us in acknowledging that people as a species are indeed unique, this is no "unique sort of uniqueness" (Fernandez-Armesto 2005). The humanist claim for peoples' categorically distinct difference from other beings has, however, been a notoriously persistent one (Ritvo 2009). As Glendinning (2000: 4) puts it, the long-standing presumption is that: "Man is only man in so far as he is essentially more than a human animal: only in so far as he possesses a unique, non-natural trait (the capacity to reason, the possession of self-consciousness, understanding or whatever) which distinguishes him from purely animal life." The query that follows this observation, then, is not with the difference of people as a species *per se*; this is self-evident and non-controversial. Rather it is with the sense in which human difference is typically conceived as a *qualitatively distinct* kind of difference. Phrased in other words: post-humanists (who are now a very disparate set of scholars) like to trouble the familiar premise that people are somehow above nature, and not just a (different) part *of* it. And my recent concern, as stated above, has been with precisely how the formulation of this uniqueness intersected with the elaboration of a biological conception of race in the 19th century.

It is well known that the head provided the key focus for the development of a biological conception of race. As John Carson (2007: 83) has put it, "[a]lthough skin and hair differences constituted the most obvious markers of racial distinctness ... virtually all parties ultimately accorded skull characteristics the greatest significance." Notoriously, it was through a variety of cranial measurements, that racial variations in head size and shape came to be correlated with a notion of intelligence that was itself seen as an innate, but variable, faculty for "civilizability" or "perfectibility" (Williams 1986: 263).

Conventionally, craniometry tends to be regarded as a racist practice that was contrived to give scientific credibility to longstanding racial prejudices or power impulses (e.g. Fryer 1984: 170; Turnbull 1982: 17; and Fabian 2002: 28, among many others). In this respect, the head has been taken to have constituted just another – even if privileged – focus for a racism that came to fasten upon it, in much the same way as it fastened upon those more obvious "markers of racial distinctness," skin and hair differences (e.g. Stepan 1982: xii; Goldberg 1993: 50). But, drawing upon Latour, my current work in this area pursues an alternative account in which the head is a constitutive player in the project of craniometry more so than a prop for racist representation.

Classically, Christian and Enlightenment ideas about the exceptional status of the human were identified with the soul or the mind. Against those metaphysical claims, Linneaus' (1758) assertion in the late 18th century – that the human was part of the "order of nature" and could be understood as a purely physical being – posed a significant challenge. As we shall see, however, this did not signal the end of the idea of the human's exceptional status. Far from it. Indeed not even Darwin's claim some 100 years later for human continuity with apes would unseat this idea, such was – and continues to be – its cherished status.

After Willis and Descartes, but more immediately after the phrenologists of the late 18th century, the mind had come to be equated with the brain and physically located in the head (Finger 2000). As Clarke and Jacyna (1987) point out, however, the materialist claim that "the mind was situated in the brain" generated "a great deal of contention"; as did the "intimate association" being posited by comparative anatomists such as Georges Cuvier between the nervous system and "the phenomenon of mind." During the first half of the 19th century, controversy raged around the argument that "there was not anything more to the soul than the simple functioning of the brain" (Jorion 1982: 10). To consider how the head assumed such significance for racial discourse is, therefore, to consider an object that acquired enormous ontological importance during the period of the late eighteenth and early nineteenth centuries. It was during that time period, after all, that the head concentrated intense debate around the claim that the human was "more" than just another animal.

Ordinarily the privilege accorded to the head by 19th century race scientists is not in itself considered contentious. The head is usually folded, as indicated earlier, into an apparently inexhaustible trajectory of racialized othering in the power-differentiated regimes of colonialism and slavery. This is to gloss over, however, not only the head's specificity as a racialized object, but also a time period that repays more attention if the conventional analytical optic on race is *reset to a wider horizon*: and, here, to that massive subject of the human. For, as stated above, this period – of the late 18th and early 19th centuries – is precisely one in which the identification of the human's exceptional status with a metaphysical defining characteristic became problematized. A new materialist "science of man" – led by comparative anatomists such as Cuvier – sought to determine the character of the human in physical, rather than metaphysical, terms (Cuvier 1802: 2-6). A great 19th century obsession ensued, measuring the skulls of the world's peoples, including so-called mad, degenerate, criminal, and also some female skulls (mostly male skulls were used, see Fee 1979; Schiebinger 2004). It was a project directed, above all, towards establishing the material existence of a distinctly human form of mind.

It is usually contended by race historiographers that the craniometrists of the early to mid 19th century took for granted the racial hierarchies that their own efforts served only to naturalize. In this respect, Gould's discussion of Samuel Morton's "finagling" of the results of his cranial measurements is well known (Gould 1996); as is the more general claim that craniometry may be understood as biologizing what "for nineteenth century investigators" was the "obvious and undeniable inferiority of certain peoples" (Carson 2007: 83). On these accounts, it seems impossible to avoid characterizing craniometry as anything other than the articulation of a racism, apparently compelled to repeat itself according to some "drive for domination" (Mosse 1995: 167). But, situating and approaching the practice of head measuring within the post-Linneaun context and Latourian methodology indicated above, raises another possibility (Anderson and Perrin 2009).

No doubt, "which groups were superior … and which inferior" was already "known" to craniometrists, as consistent with the various levels of development that certain peoples were understood to have achieved (Carson 2007: 83). In the terms of social contract and stadial theory, such levels of development had already been taken as a gauge of how much, or how little, the world's people had exercised a distinctly human capacity to transcend nature. The measurement of racial variations in head size and shape, and their correlation with variations in these levels of development, thus offered a way to pursue the hypothesis that the exceptional status of the human could indeed be established in physical or material terms.

The possibility raised, therefore, is that the racialization of the head was not just or only the product of the racist interests of nineteenth century craniometry (which bear no need of restatement here). This practice was also symptomatic of what Derrida (2003) has described as a "fundamental humanism" in western philosophy and theology, according to which the potentiality of the human is said to be realized in its taking distance from nature. Within this intellectual context, it becomes possible to argue that physical differences between people came to be regarded as "racial" differences in the very attempt to determine the human's unique and exceptional status among other forms of life on earth. Later in the 19th century, for example, and in the context of evolutionary theory, race was again postulated in support of the claim that "mind" was the agent of a distinctively human or cultural form of evolutionary development (see the discussion in Anderson 2007: 152–157).

The history of craniometry was that of various new, repeated, desperate, and failed attempts to develop an adequate index and method for correlating a faculty of mind, with variations in head size and shape. And the madness of this frantic – but, of course, futile – search for some accurate correlation between physical features and some score of intelligence, becomes clear in the sheer variety of measures, indices, ratios and instruments that craniometrists proposed as the 19th century progressed: including the facial goniometer, the cephalometer, the craniometer, the cranioscope, the craniophore, the craniostat, and so on. Indeed in the very fact that the practice of head measuring was such an intensive phenomenon, it is possible to identify an obsession that was related – not only to some drive for self-identity or domination over certain other people – but also a distinctively humanist anxiety. The practice of craniometry may then be understood, not as a resolved expression of racism, but as a fundamentally unresolved struggle to assert a cherished notion of the human.

As such, racial discourse itself might be considered beyond its usual explanation as an intersubjective dynamic of identity politics. More specifically, it might be considered as a *discourse on the human* in which the very question of the distinctively human was at stake. This is not meant here in the usual sense of racist invocations of the "more or less" human (and also of the "more or less" intelligent), where such stereotypes are reduced to conduits for the articulation of racial prejudices and discourses. Rather, if race can be traced to struggles surrounding the attempt to distinguish people among the world's life-forms, then these may be considered as the very terms in which race was formulated: in a precarious and unstable effort to establish the status and privilege of the human over all other beings.

This understanding of race would invite – if not demand – a substantial refiguring of race and racial violence. Pulling race out of the sometimes stifling and reductive domain of identity politics and into the framework of a broader ecological concern with the multiplicity of relationships in which human beings are embedded, it would, moreover, draw race fully into the ambit of a contemporary critical interrogation of our assumptions about what it means, and what it might yet mean, to be human among other beings. The pressing needs of the planet demand such reflection and not only from environmental geographers, on the very instability of our cultural dissociation from it. Indeed finally, here, it is from the disciplinary platform of a more unified Geography that a truly secular ethics of the human – shorn of what Latour refers to as some "supplement of the soul" (2008) – might find its more committed advocates and audiences.

References

Abram, D. (1996) *The Spell of the Sensuous: Perception and Smell in a More-Than-Human World*. Pantheon, New York.

Amin, A. (2010) The remainders of race. *Theory, Culture and Society* 27 (1), 1–23.

Anderson, K. (1987) The idea of Chinatown: the Power of Place and Institutional Practice in the Making of a Racial Category. *Annals Association of American Geographers* 77 (4), 580–598.

Anderson, K. (1991) *Vancouver's Chinatown: Racial Discourse in Canada, 1875–1980*. McGill Queen's University Press, Montreal.

Anderson, K. (2007) *Race and the Crisis of Humanism*. Routledge, London and New York.

Anderson, K. and Perrin, C. (2008) Beyond savagery: the limits of Australian "Aboriginalism." *Cultural Studies Review* 14 (2), 147–169.

Anderson, K. and Perrin, C. (2009) Thinking *with* the head: race, craniometry, humanism. *Journal of Cultural Economy* 2 (1), 83–98.

Appadurai. A. (1988) *The Social Life of Things: Commodities in Cultural Perspective*. Cambridge University Press, Cambridge.

Attwood, B. (1992) Introduction: Power, knowledge and Aborigines. *Journal of Australian Studies* 35, i–xvi.

Attwood, B. (1996) Introduction: The past as future: Aborigines, Australia and the (dis) course of history. In B. Attwood (ed.), *Age of Mabo*. Allen & Unwin, Sydney, pp. vii–xxxviii.

Baldwin, A., Cameron, L., and Kobayashi, A. (eds) (forthcoming) *Rethinking the Great White North*. UBC Press, Vancouver.

Bhabha, H. (1994) *The Location of Culture*. Routledge, London.

Bennett, T. and Joyce, P. (eds) (2010) *Material Powers: Culture, History and the Material Turn*. Routledge, London.

Bingham, N. (2006) Bees, butterflies, and bacteria: Biotechnology and the politics of nonhuman friendship. *Environment and Planning A* 38, 483–498.

Bonnett, A. (2000) *White Identities: An Historical and International Introduction*. Longman, London.

Braun, B. (2008) Environmental issues: Inventive life. *Progress in Human Geography* 32 (5), 667–679.

Braun, B. and Castree, N. (2001) *Social Nature: Theory, Practice and Politics*. Blackwell, Malden.

Carson, J. (2007) *The Measure of Merit: Talents, Intelligence, and Inequality*. Princeton University Press, Princeton.

Cerulo, K. (2009) Nonhumans in social interaction. *Annual Review of Sociology* 35, 531–552.

Clarke, E. and Jacnya, L.S. (1987) *Nineteenth Century Origins of Neuroscientific Concepts.* University of California Press, Berkeley.
Cuvier, G. (1802) *Lectures on Comparative Anatomy.* Longman and Rees, London.
DeLanda, M. (2006) *Assemblage Theory: A New Philosophy of Society.* Continuum, London.
Delaney, D. (2002) The space that race makes. *The Professional Geographer* 54, 6–14.
Derrida, J. (2003) And say the animal responded? Zoontologies. In C. Wolfe (ed.), *The Question of the Animal.* University of Minnesota Press, Minneapolis, pp. 121–146.
Dregson, A. and Inoue, Y. (eds) (1996) *The Deep Ecology Movement: An Introductory Anthology.* North Atlantic Books, Berkeley.
Dwyer, C. and Bressey, C. (2008) *New Geographies of Race and Racism.* Ashgate, Aldershot.
Ellis, M., Holloway, S.R., Wright, R., and East, M. (2007) The effects of mixed-race households on residential segregation. *Urban Geography* 28 (6), 554–577.
Fabian, J. (2002) *Time and the Other: How Anthropology Makes its Object.* Columbia University Press, New York.
Fee, E. (1979) Nineteenth-century craniology: The study of the female skull. *Bulletin of the History of Medicine* 53, 415–433.
Fernandez-Armesto, F. (2005) *So You Think You're Human: A Brief History of Humankind.* Oxford University Press, Oxford.
Finger, S. (2000) *Minds Behind the Brain: A History of the Pioneers and their Discoveries.* Oxford University Press, Oxford.
Forrest, J. and Dunn, K.M. (2007) Constructing racism in Sydney, Australia's largest ethni city. *Urban Studies* 44 (4), 699–721.
Foucault, M. (1972) *Archaeology of Knowledge.* Routledge, London.
Fryer, P. (1984) *Staying Power: The History of Black People in Britain.* Pluto Press, London.
Gilroy, P. (2000) *Against Race: Imagining Political Culture Beyond the Color Line* Harvard University Press, Cambridge.
Glendinning, S. (2000) From animal life to city life. *Angelaki: Journal of the Theoretical Humanities* 5, 19–30.
Goldberg, D.T. (1993) *Racist Culture: Philosophy and the Politics of Meaning.* Blackwell, Oxford.
Gould, S.J. (1996) *The Mismeasure of Man* (revised edition). W.W. Norton, New York.
Gray, J. (2003) *Straw Dogs.* Granta, London.
Hacking, I. (2000) *The Social Construction of What?* Harvard University Press, Cambridge.
Harris, C. (2004) How did colonialism dispossess? Comments from an edge of empire. *Annals of the Association of American Geographers* 94 (1), 165–182.
Head, L. (2007) Cultural ecology: the problematic human and the terms of engagement. *Progress in Human Geography* 31, 837–846.
Hinchliffe, S. (2008) *Geographies of Nature: Societies, Environments, Ecologies.* Sage, London.
Jackson, P. (1987) *Race and Racism: Essays in Social Geography.* Routledge, London.
Jorion, P. (1982) The downfall of the skull. *RAIN*, 48, 8–11.
Latour, B. (1993) *We Have Never Been Modern.* Harvard University Press, Cambridge.
Latour, B.(2004) *Politics of Nature: How to Bring the Sciences into Democracy.* Harvard University Press, Cambridge.
Latour, B. (2005) *Reassembling the Social.* Oxford University Press, Oxford.
Latour, B. (2008) Will non-humans be saved? An argument in ecotheology. *Journal of the Royal Anthropological Institute* 15, 459–475.
Latour, B. (2009) *The Making of Law: An Ethnography of the Conseil d'Etat.* Polity, Oxford.
Linneaus, C. (1758) *Systema Naturae.* Holmiae (Laurentii Salvi, 10th Edition) (in Latin). Updated and Expanded (in English) *A General System Of Nature, Through The Three*

Grand Kingdoms Of Animals, Vegetables, and Minerals (1806) (Ed. and trans. W. Turton), Allen Lackington, London.

Massey, D. (2004) Space-time, 'science' and the relationship between physical geography and human geography. *Transactions: Institute of British Geographers* 24 (3), 261–276.

Meek, R. (1967) *Social Science and the Ignoble Savage*. Cambridge University Press, Cambridge.

Miles, Robert. (1984) Marxism versus the 'Sociology of Race Relations? *Ethnic and Racial Studies* 7 (2), 217–237.

Morrison, T. (1992) Playing *In The Dark: Whiteness And The Literary Imagination*. Harvard University Press, Cambridge.

Mosse, G. (1978) *Toward the Final Solution: A History of European Racism*. J.M. Dent, London.

Mosse, G. (1995) Racism and nationalism. *Nations and Nationalism I* 2, 163–173.

Nayak, A. (2006) After race: Ethnography, race and post-race theory. *Ethnic and Racial Studies* 29 (3), 411–430.

Panelli, R. (2010) More-than-human social geographies: posthuman and other possibilities. *Progress in Human Geography* 34 (1), 79–87.

Peterson, A. (2001) *Being Human: Ethics, Environment and our Place in the World*. California University Press, Cambridge.

Price, P. (2010) At the crossroads: critical race theory and critical geographies of race" *Progress in Human Geography* 34 (2), 147–174.

Ritvo, H. (2009) Humans and humanists. *Daedelus*, 68–78.

Robbins, P. and Marks, B. (2009) Assemblage Geographies. In S.J. Smith, R. Pain, S. Marston, and J.P Jones (eds), *The Sage Handbook of Social Geography*. Sage, London, pp. 176–194.

Ryan, S. (1996) *The Cartographic Eye: How Explorers Saw Australia*. Cambridge University Press, Cambridge.

Said, E. (1979) *Orientalism*. Penguin, London.

Saldanha, A. (2006) Re-ontologizing race: The machinic geography of phenotype. *Environment and Planning D: Society and Space* 24, 9–24.

Sandilands, C-M. (ed.) (2009) Topia: Canadian Journal of Cultural Studies. *Special Issue: Nature Matters*, 21.

Schiebinger, L. (2004) *Nature's Body: Sexual Politics and the Making of Modern Science*. Pandora, London.

Smith, B. (1985) *European Vision and the South Pacific*. Yale University Press, New Haven and London.

Smith, S.J., Pain, R., Marston, S., and Jones, J.P. (2009) *Sage Handbook of Social Geography*. Sage, London.

Sofoulis, Z. (2009) Social construction for the 21st Century: A co-evolutionary make-over. *Australian Humanities Review* 46.

Spencer, S. (2006) *Race and Ethnicity: Culture, Identity and Representation*. Routledge, London.

Spenser, T. and Whatmore, S. (2002) Editorial: Bio-geographies: Putting life back into the discipline. *Transactions: Institute of British Geographers* 26 (2), 139–141.

Sundberg, J. (2008) Placing Race in Environmental Justice Research in Latin America. *Society and Natural Resources: An International Journal* 21 (7), 569–582.

Stepan, N. (1982) *The Idea of Race in Science: Great Britain 1800–1960*. Macmillan, London.

Tolia-Kelly, D. (2010) The geographies of cultural geography I: identities, bodies and race. *Progress in Human Geography* 34 (3), 358–367.

Turnbull, D. (1982) *Phrenology*. Deakin University Press, Melbourne.
Whatmore, S. (2002) *Hybrid Geographies: Natures, Cultures, Spaces*. Sage, London.
Whatmore, S. (2006) Materialist returns: Practicing cultural geography in and for a more-than-human world. *Cultural Geographies* 13 (4), 600–609.
Williams, E. (1986) *The Physical and the Moral: Anthropology, Physiology, and Philosophical Medicine in France, 1750–1850*. Cambridge University Press, Cambridge.
Williams, G. and Frost, A. (eds) (1988) *From Terra Australis to Australia*. Oxford University Press, Melbourne.
Winders, J. (2009) Race. In R. Kitchin, N. Thrift, N. Castree, *et al.* (eds), *International Encyclopedia of Human Geography*. Elsevier, London.

Further Reading

Bonnett, A. (2000) *White Identities: An Historical and International Introduction*. Longman, London.
Latour, B. (1988) *On actor network theory: A few clarifications*. Available at: http://www.nettime.org/Lists-Archives/nettime-l-9801/msg00019.html (accessed 14th October 2010).

Chapter 32

Race
Part II

Arun Saldanha

Feelings pulsate, and the face of the world is changed: ideas have hands and feet and force nature to do their will.

(Sellars 1916a: 214)

Introduction

How does geography build up knowledge that is not just about the world but is *critical* of it and suggests possible trajectories for amendment? Taking a clear side in an age-old philosophical debate, about how we know the world, this chapter will argue that geography has to be a *realist* science if it is to be critical of racism. Epistemological realism distinguishes itself traditionally from idealism and nominalism by granting a full reality to things and physical processes independent from human minds. This chapter hypothesizes that race has for some six decades increasingly been approached through epistemological idealism. To the traditional and still-hegemonic statement "there are races and they are unequal," antiracism replies "humans are equal and race is only an idea." Racism's belief that human worth can be read immediately from bodily differences is countered by the antiracist view that human worth has nothing to do with inherited characteristics of the body.

In its weaker and earlier version, antiracism in science holds that phenotypic differences within the human species do "exist" but tell us nothing about innate mental or physical capacities. Racist cultures invent categories where biologically speaking there are continuities and many exceptions (Benedict 1983). The later and

The Wiley Blackwell Companion to Human Geography, First Edition.
Edited by John A. Agnew and James S. Duncan.
© 2011 John Wiley & Sons, Ltd. Published 2016 by John Wiley & Sons, Ltd.

stronger version of theoretical antiracism is found in social constructionism and poststructuralism, which hold that phenotypic differences cannot be known immediately, since they are irrevocably mediated by power relations. On the whole, today's social sciences either are agnostic about the "reality" of phenotypic difference when talking about race, or critique the ways their predecessors and scientific colleagues represent race ideologically as natural and immutable.

After discussing the reasons behind the antirealism of antiracism, touching on the current popularity of science studies, I will appeal to a *critical realism* that has some affinities to the earlier, anthropological form of antiracism. Critical realism is capable of treating race as at once biological (phenotypic differentiation in biophysical environments) and ideological (science itself demonstrates that those differences are distorted and mystified in racist knowledge). The critical-realist approach to the racializing effects of globalization is compared with the "naive realism" in the well-known human biogeography of Jared Diamond. This leads to some final considerations on what realism can do for antiracism.

Is Race Real?

With every philosophical generation the debate about "what reality is" flares up anew. Currently the question is what the epistemology is of "postmodern theory," or more accurately, French philosophy departing from phenomenology and psychoanalysis. The biological explanations of race that dominated the social sciences before the Second World War have in the mainstream social sciences all but disappeared (Blaut 1992). This chapter seeks to first determine why this has been the case, and second to suggest racism can be better countered by addressing the biology it invokes.

Most scientists at the height of European imperialism (Francis Galton, Friedrich Ratzel) held that the reality of the nation's racial degeneracy requires unsentimental state intervention. The naive realism and objectivism driving the social sciences were therefore already invested in some form of eugenic politics. This scientific justification of racism led quite directly to Nazi biopolitics (Pichot 2009). Cultural anthropologists such as Ashley Montagu (1997) declared biology almost, but not quite, irrelevant to studying human variation. For pre-war realism the social sciences substituted an ingenuously culturalized version of *idealism*: race is real only *as* idea, myth, and prejudice. Physical variation was still knowable, especially through the new methods of population genetics, which, however, undermined the essentialism of erstwhile racial science. Hence "race" became nothing but an ideological rather than biological reality, a flawed, dangerous folk conception of human diversity (Hannaford 1996). Racial difference exists only insofar as it is conjured by the demands of European and Western power. Instead of positing and studying a reality of innate hierarchical capacities legible from bodily measurements, the social-scientific epistemology of race became overwhelmingly antirealist.

Poststructuralism went further than this "first wave" of antiracism (note the analogy in the history of feminism), denying that cultural and biological variation can be known in any unmotivated, transparent way at all. The ideas we have of bodily differences, and hence the identities we "construct" while participating in society, are themselves forever obstacles to knowing what those differences *really* are. Where the first wave was still hopeful for a progressive biology, poststructuralism's influence on the Anglophone study of racism rendered all biology, especially human genetics, inherently (by virtue of its epistemic aims) suspicious. What is posited as reality is an arena of conflicting discourses or reiterations with no knowable causal link to alleged biophysical or environmental differences. Moreover, racial discourses are endured rather than consciously directed by subjects. It is not that discourses operate randomly, or nihilistically, as humanists and Marxist scientists like Jean Bricmont instantly feared (Sokal and Bricmont 1999). Since idealities are all we have access to, progressive politics becomes a question of collectively discerning which ones can emancipate and which ones, like science, entrench subjects in eternal essences precisely through its authoritative claim to represent reality as it is.

It is worth noting that antirealism in philosophy and the social sciences has invited the racist scientists that still exist, especially in the US, to cling on to a shaky scientific realism (Sarich and Miele 2004). These claims to a reality of innate racial difference are easily exposed as nonsensical or at the least hysterically defensive, but their increasing circulation requires frontal confrontation on exactly what/whose "reality" the debate is about. Conservatives in the US and reactionary populists in Europe still think that the truth about racial difference is lodged securely in the materiality of bodies, in inherited physical and mental characteristics. According to James Blaut (1992) "cultural racism" still requires phenotypic recognition. However subtle it has become, in recent decades in comparison with the colonial era, the hegemonic Western understanding of race in media, medicine, criminology and the division of labor remains reductionist (phenotype equals race), essentialist (there are "races," though now usually called "cultures" or "communities") and surreptitiously supremacist (the white race is superior, and threatened). In short, the antirealist denunciation of race *has not worked*.

To meet the challenge of racist science and common sense requires drawing an Althusserian distinction between science and ideology. Sharing many tenets with poststructuralism, including a derision for realism and positivism, Althusser differs from the likes of Foucault and Derrida on account of his Marxist commitment to accumulating truths on the world (developed in a different way by his student Alain Badiou, 2005). True science demystifies structures of oppression such as racism, while ideology (in law, education, media, religion, and scientific practice itself) cements these structures on a mostly unconscious level (Althusser 1971). Like my call for realism, Althusser's distinction may seem rather old-fashioned, but I will argue that it is necessary for the extremely tricky exchange between critical geography and biology that the theme of race requires. Science is not opposed to or outside ideology in any simple way, but *extricates* itself carefully, and never fully, from dominant ideas in society:

> a "pure" science only exists on condition that it continually frees itself from the ideology which occupies it, haunts it, or lies in wait for it. The inevitable price of this purification and liberation is a continuous struggle against ideology itself, that is, against idealism. (Althusser, 1969: 170)

As it has been mostly conservative, even reactionary, realism has to be urgently rewritten in a critical vein capable of dismantling the claims of racial (pseudo) science. The next section will argue that realism is not just amenable but necessary to antiracism. Though Althusser is not a realist himself, his defense of the scientific project against what conservative forces appropriate it for can complement realism. The idealist attacks on racist science by liberal humanists, cultural anthropologists and poststructuralists have hardly diminished its continued virulence under biopolitical capitalism. The question is now whether a renewed attack from realism can be more effective.

Critical Realism

In the wake of cultural relativism in anthropology and American social phenomenology, it is common in sociology, law, media studies and geography to argue that race is a "social construction," real insofar as it reproduces power relations (e.g. Anderson 1991; Frankenberg 1993; Haney-López 1996; Jackson and Penrose 1994). The consolidation of social constructionist epistemology over the 1990s led Ian Hacking (1999) to write his sympathetic critique *The Social Construction of What?* Noting race is a crucial site for epistemological contentions about essentiality, Hacking's book leaves open the possibility that methodologically sound science can uncover socially relevant aspects of human biology. Inspired by Foucault, Hacking is a realist of sorts, insisting that the reality of individuals (the madman, the terrorist) and things (the quark, the Internet) is synonymous with their relevance; that is it is bestowed by human practice.

Such realism about knowledge-effects has become *de rigueur* when it comes to race. It is undeniable that though a product of social interactions, race makes people suffer, kill and avoid places. The reality of these *effects* is what social constructionists in fact insist on. But effect-realism is not a realism in the more fundamental sense, since it is realist about practices, discourses and technologies, and does not inquire into how exactly the world of things impinges upon and sabotages this humanly constructed reality. So anthropologists carve out racial classifications from an infinitely messier background that exceeds those classifications, but *how* that excess occurs is not a topic for the epistemologist.

An important starting point for developing a fuller realist framework is Roy Wood Sellars. His *Critical Realism* (1916a) inspects both the "natural realism" found in common sense and the "scientific realism" of scientists. These nonphilosophical forms of realism believe uncritically that things (tools, microbes, atoms) are actually present to experience, as if reality can be brought directly into the brain. Though naive realism is not exactly wrong – everyday and scientific practices require it – Sellars takes issue with the subject/object dualism and the *resemblance* between mental image and physical thing that it presumes. The philosophical precursor to these modern assumptions Sellars (1922) correctly finds in Descartes.

Sellars' anti-Cartesian, anti-Kantian, "genetic" conception of space (1922) is close to contemporary geography's. Space is not an empty container for bodies but a universal aspect *of* bodies insofar as they are *related to* and affect other bodies (Sellars 1909). "Things have size, shape, position; they are at certain distances and in certain directions from one another. Space is not a thing, rather is it the complex of these characters" (Sellars 1922: 88). Sellars' naturalistic position dictates that conceptions of space emerge dynamically from bodily interaction with the environment, and are gradually abstracted, first in scientific knowledge, then in philosophy. So the "mental maps" that the inhabitants of racially segregated cities accrue are not simply brain-copies of urban space. They are products (and ingredients) of activities literally bumping into barriers and markers of race: dereliction, trash, police sirens, darker bodies loitering and highway smog in one area, flowerbeds, coffee shops and SUVs in another. In addition to *representations of* racialized places such as Chinatowns (Anderson 1991), realism investigates a place's physical, sensuous arrangements "on the ground."

A more recent program of critical realism is championed by Roy Bhaskar (Bhaskar *et al.* 1988). Applying this program to sociology and geography, Andrew Sayer (2000) takes issue with social constructionism's division of reality into an ostensibly unchanging biological level and the sphere of meanings and politics. Social scientists cannot simply ignore genetic and anatomical factors, but like anything social, race is *emergent* in relation to those factors and others. However, Sayer is mostly silent about how geophysics, evolutionary biology or computer modeling could contribute to critical realism. To understand the material complexity of race, questions of evolution and the place of the human within the universe cannot be avoided; as science has itself persistently staged those questions. While Sellars' critical realism is closer to the physical sciences, drawing epistemological lessons from the likes of Whitehead and Bergson, Bhaskar (1993) resorts to Hegelian conceptions of subject/object and emancipation. The resulting "dialectical critical realism" is difficult to reconcile with the emergentist physicalism of Sellars' ontology.

In Sellars, ontology – how organisms live amid other things – strongly tends to precede his epistemology – how humans know things. This precedence of ontology can be compared with a better known realist today, Bruno Latour (1999). The reality of Latour's "realistic realism" is coproduced by humans. It remains fundamentally unclear what happens to reality before and after humans stir it. Moreover, Latour mainly talks about specialist knowledge, not the preconceptual knowing humans naturally engage in to stay alive. Latour's reality is, as the subtitle of *Pandora's Hope* has it, a reality *of* science studies, a possession, a territory claimed. Although Sellars would agree with Latour that scientists actively transform "external reality" in order to present it, reality for him stands very much on its own.

Against the splitting of reality into mind and matter, Sellars sees the self, social interaction, the material environment and all other objects of knowledge as components of *one continuous reality*:

> The not-self is not necessarily the physical; indeed, it is even more frequently, under the conditions of modern civilization, the social, another person or group of persons, a law, an obnoxious convention. I may seek to adapt *my* plans to the prejudices of the community or to the wishes of a friend. For our present problem the essential to realize is the coequal reality of these objects, be they physical things, wishes, the moral tone of the community, or my own plans. (Sellars 1916a: 214)

While Latour also likes to claim "coequality" for objects, he speaks as a modern *sociologist* who has hit on the embeddedness of human sociality amid physical constellations. For the Darwinian, Galilean naturalism that Sellars follows, this embedding is not even an issue. Sellars in fact takes another step that I don't find readily in Latour. Against both (Kantian and Hegelian) idealism and (Anglo-American) empiricism, Sellars asserts that the world in itself always "transcends" the mind, which in its turn is nonetheless only sparkled into existence by the world it participates in:

> Things in reality, although in dynamic continuity, exclude one another, but consciousness, the flow of experiencing, is not a stuff nor a thing alongside other things. It is a *variant* in the changes occurring in that part of reality we call the brain. In it alone are we on the inside of reality and participators in its process. It is a light that guides, but a light kindled by reality as friction kindles a flame. (Sellars 1909: 622)

Reality always exceeds what we know of it, but know it we must.

Sellars was on the whole too entrenched in the more specialized debates about philosophical psychology and metaphysics to engage with anthropology, biology and geography, which were still busy demarcating "races" in the first half of the twentieth century. We can nonetheless attempt to see what a critical realism of race could look like. Following a broadly Latourian framework, Geoffrey C. Bowker and Susan Leigh Star (1999) argue that racial classification in apartheid South Africa frantically attempted to tame a mass of shades into a limited number of legal categories. The anxieties about the slippage of racial classification are far from unique to the apartheid regime, of course, as they fed from earlier and other colonial regimes (the British Raj, the southern US, Dutch Indonesia, Rhodesia, etc.; Bowker and Star do not develop this wider historical geography). Given miscegenation, contradictory legal criteria, changing definitions, and the many ambivalent cases, this attempt could only prove in vain, and all the more brutally unjust for it.

Such an analysis of classification is an important step in the critique of racism, but the material realities of segregation come ontologically first. These materialities of *racism* have long been exposed by social geographers and environmental activists, of course, but they have on the whole shied away from theorizing *race* as something materially real (Jackson 1987; Massey and Denton 1993; Pulido 2000; Shrader-Frechette 2002). If considered more than an idea, race in South Africa plays out in disparities of housing, health, domestic and gang violence, imprisonment, education, access to transport and safe water, etc. (Hart 2002). Some of these are aggravated by classification schemes (whether legal or, more subtly, in post-apartheid neoliberal employment practices), but they are far from explicable by classification alone. What Bowker and Star are realist about is the consequences of legal names like "black," "white," "colored," etc. They are *nominal* realists seemingly indifferent about flows of sensuous experience, capital flows, sewage flows and gene flows, which to a realist *make up* people's lives much more than the census does. Science studies and students of "racial discourse" supply a small piece in the puzzle of how race works, but the puzzle is, unfortunately, much larger.

The question for realism after poststructuralism is twofold: what does our best knowledge of reality – including but not only science – tell us about what reality *really* consists of; and what is reality like despite this knowledge, that is to say *almost* unthinkably outside any provincialist human knowledge (Saldanha 2009a)? Even if explicitly opposed to social constructionism, Latour's so-called realism is predicated on the *study of* science. It serves to remind us that knowledge-objects

– in the case of racist science, aggregates of bodies, genes, affects, etc. – impinge upon scientific representation. It is true you cannot name and classify things as you wish. But may we not ask why you are preoccupied with other people's knowledge at all? Don't you want to know things for yourself?

Critical Biogeography

A realist geography of human variation has to engage with the physical sciences as more than discourses. As mentioned there is a lot of scientific research that is blatantly ideological. But there is more that is implicitly or explicitly antiracist, which *pace* Althusser, does not mean ideology cannot still be discerned. The most popular geography text in a long time, Jared Diamond's *Guns, Germs, and Steel* (1997) is an excellent example. The importance of this book for reconceiving race in a global and scientific setting is understood when placing it in a longer history of writings on European dominance (Blaut 1992, 1999). A starting point is to radically de-essentialize phenotype *on the biological level*. Diamond argues that phenotypic plasticity (rather "typically" celebrated in the book's photographs) is understood through a many-layered tapestry of genetic flows and biophysical circumstances. Admitting he reproduces a stereotypical division of the species into "blacks," "whites," etc. (Diamond 1997: 378–379), Diamond exhibits the bourgeois naiveté that an Althusserian critical realism departs from. While drawing some boundaries is unavoidable to discuss subspecies variation, a more topological approach – not a world map but a world diagram, a network of genetic vectors – can avoid essentialism more rigorously, with phenotypic differences imagined as multi-axial, fuzzy, unpredictable and, epistemologically speaking, self-obscuring.

More fundamentally, the critical imperative demands that we can never be certain that the complex reality of variation is grasped in our measurements or maps. Any grouping of physical characteristics (blood group, height, language) is only *arrived at* from mediate observation. It is provisional, probabilistic and, crucially, only relevant for a certain problem. Many groupings that have obsessed European science and public opinion are irrelevant to predicting achievement: skin color, nose shape, cephalic index, the "thrifty gene." Irrelevant racial groupings should be understood as *ideological* efforts to obscure the role of capitalism and colonialism in forming the inequalities between phenotypic clusters. When today's naive realists, including Diamond (2003), readily locate explanations at the genetic level, a critical realist points out that genes only become activated within socio-economic disparities.

There is nonetheless something to be gained from the biogeographical history of the species. Against residual racist science and (largely covert) public opinion, it shows there is no innate superiority leading northwestern Europeans to conquer the world. There is instead (and this is Darwin's original antiracist idea) a universal creativity in dealing with environmental constraints. Reviving the notorious environmental determinism of geography from Strabo to Ratzel, Diamond understands a population's capacities towards centralization and mobility as embedded in the biophysical environments wherein it first emerged, and only faintly in the physiology of the bodies of that population. Climate, available plants and animals for domestication, and ultimately, the very shape of Eurasia, is what explains white supremacy to Diamond, not hard work, let alone divine election. Alfred Crosby (1986) argues Europeans succeeded in subordinating landscapes and indigenous peoples through the numerous species they transported with them. Of course, like Diamond, Crosby neglects the colonial massacres and divisions of labor (compare Duncan 2007). The naturalist-realist point here is that "Neo-Europes" were constructed from coastline contours, climatic gradients, seeds, trade, violence, desires, diseases and deforestation before they were constructed from words.

Diamond (2005) goes one step further. Given the agriculture, stratification and decadence of large societies, they tend inherently towards self-destruction. Industrial climate change is no mere "example" of this tendency: for the foreseeable future it is the final demonstration that human reality is irrevocably at the mercy of its biophysical mooring. Now, we have to emphasize how climate change has profound *racializing* effects. Through the spread of capitalism and the nation-state form, one society – the European – has taken humanity hostage to a degree even the most racist ideologue could not have deemed possible. No society, indeed no species, ever created the conditions for its own demise on a planetary scale (and in a few centuries too). The biogeographical fact that populations are affected differently by climate change causes racial, class and other injustices to deepen. Europe, the European diasporas and new capitalist elites will have the resources to deal with climate change; most others will not; this will exacerbate the migrations already causing racist exclusion in the rich areas of the world.

So science – geomorphology, climatology, botany – does show that white domination derives from far more than culture and technology. But critical realism never accepts science unproblematically. *Science* becomes discernible from *ideology* when we define the thickness, the causal extent, of the embeddedness of the human in the biophysical. It needs no reminding Diamond's environmental determinism encounters strong resistance in historical geography (for example, Blaut 1999) and political ecology (Robbins 2003). His claims to geography are easily unmasked, as he does not engage the geographies of exchange, capital and food production. The Malthusian legacy to which Diamond (2005) professes he belongs presupposes that populations start equally, overcoming local shortages by sheer technical ingenuity. From a geographical perspective this omits the simple historical fact that states become powerful chiefly by trade and internal and external oppression (Harvey 2001). Even before colonial exploitation, Western Europe was banking on the spice and gold trade, drawing from Arab science, expelling Jews and the sick, uniting against Islam, and so forth. Any "advantage" lay only remotely in the biophysical environment, and much more obviously, in Europe's inter-state competition and self-entitlement to world dominion. A critical biogeography has to break sharply with the free market ideology underpinning biogeography and study networks and scales of societal interactions as *necessarily* uneven.

This brief critique of Diamond starts to demonstrate the distinction between critical science of phenotypic and ecosystemic variation and its much more influential ideological counterparts. We can combine simple rules of critical realism with political commitment. First, true science starts out from a full conception of spatial interconnection, which in the modern period obviously involves capitalist exploitation. Second, science understands its limitations, its propensity to become ideological glue for the realities it studies. Althusser's distinction between science and ideology is not descriptive but performative, future-oriented, anchored in the hope for equality. Through such an anti-positivist defense of science, a critical *bio*geography emerges that does not fear engaging biology, climatology or even geophysics. These sciences can show how nonhuman factors have allowed for a global Eurocentric system of exploitation to emerge, provided they do not pretend there is ever a level playing field for competing human populations.

Antiracist Realism

This chapter has argued that race is a complex assemblage of phenotypes and environments rearranged by colonialism and capitalism. Race is therefore as real as racism is. But while racism cannot logically exist without race, *race is more than racism*. The first reason is historical. The superiority of European Christian identity was from at least the Crusades postulated by educated men, but not in a very different way than in other chauvinisms, like the Chinese or Islamic. As Kay Anderson (2007) has shown, racism as *universal* process, elevating White Man to the chosen subject of history while anxiously dividing all humans into neat groups, came into force only over the nineteenth century. In contrast, race in early modernity was characterized by considerable ambivalence (Saldanha 2009b; Hannaford 1996). The splendid wealth of Asia, the Jews, the Arab dominance in maritime trade, the slave trade and indigenous suffering under the Spanish were not yet seen along consistently racist lines. Until the late eighteenth century racist violence was exceeded by messy everyday intercourse, especially between poor European men and native women, which was racialized but not always *racist* in a systematic way.

A second reason why "race" does not equal "racism" is political. If race is the material and mental division of bodies into groups according to shifting criteria, racism is the economic and moral *valuation* of those groups as naturally inferior and superior. Hence black power belongs to "race," but not racism. In very different ways, Malcolm X, hiphop and Oprah Winfrey revalorize black identity, so keep the division into "races" intact. Antiracist politics demands careful investigation of where and why identity, tradition, multiculturalism, exoticism and the culture industry end up reinforcing *race*, on which *racism* can easily take hold (Saldanha 2007). The universalizing tendency of race cannot be countered by racial, ethnic or national revalorization, but only by *another universality*, a Kantian-Marxian scientific universality that forever works to sidestep its ideological congealment into particularity.

So realism has to be "critical" in the Kantian sense of the term. In militating against dogma, antiracist critical realism is not after a unification of the sciences; does not see physics and mathematics as the standard against which all knowledge is to be measured; and always asserts the emancipatory above the utilitarian potentials of knowledge. The primer of critical theory, Adorno and Horkheimer's *Dialectic of Enlightenment* (2002) was written when the horrors of the racist potentials of science were becoming apparent. It is easy to see why critical theory has very much tended to define itself against science and its realist, objectivist, utilitarian epistemology. This is *a fortiori* the case with what is called "critical race theory," which unfortunately tends to limit itself to legal and pedagogical counterstrategy (Delgado

1999). Unlike these understandings of the term "critical," this chapter has argued there can be no intrinsic antimony between the physical sciences and Marxist and antiracist legacies.

It is evident that critical realism can in our discipline be elaborated into a "critical geography," but there is some debate about what this term consists of. Being the first widely read politically engaged geographer, David Harvey (2001) managed to identify "critical" with "Marxist." Many tacitly accept this identification, even geographers from "uncritical," conservative, or apolitical quarters. Some have tried to claim a subdiscipline of "critical geography," committed to analyzing not just the class dynamics of and alternatives to capitalism, but racial, sexual, ableist, and all other kinds of discrimination in "reality" as well as in "discourse." This no-longer-just-Marxist impetus is attempted in the plural form in the subtitle of *Acme*, the online journal for "critical geographies." Especially to British geographers, it seems, critical geography does not and cannot equal Marxist geography.

Relying on Sellars and biogeography in addition to Althusser, my position on race is clearly not simply Marxist. Nonetheless, just as critical theory commenced its transformative encounters with psychoanalysis, phenomenology, deconstruction, etc. *from within* an initially Marxist standpoint, so critical (bio)geography is irrevocably (umbilically?) linked to a spatialized Marxism. This linkage is only recognizable as such because geography embarks on theoretical adventures *not* foreseen by Marx, while continuing to be inspired by his scientific break with ideological forebears and contemporaries. For a phenomenon as multifaceted and ever-shifting as race, sticking with political economy and ideology critique is almost defeatist, as if manifest complexity can ever be subdued with familiar categories and slogans. Despite its fundamental call for radical change, Marxism is a theoretical orthodoxy if there ever was one (as Badiou [2005: 58] says, "*Marxism doesn't exist*,"; it has to be forever reinvented). Critical realism as I see it requires that we never submit to orthodoxy.

To conclude, the realism sought after here is more explicitly political than dominant forms of realism precisely because of the latter's continuing ideological dominance in the sciences of human variation. Sellars (1916b) was a social democrat and avowed humanist, not a radical, and oblivious to the various forms of racism American democracy was built upon. Bhaskar is conversant with Marxist thought but mostly on epistemological and ontological not political grounds. Critical realism has therefore been rather vague on the power structures that require critique and intervention, with Bhaskar venturing into increasingly arcane theosophical realms. Meanwhile newer forms of realism such as Latour's prove quite inept for intervening in unjust realities like segregation or climate change. By self-consciously turning away from the critical tradition Latour suppresses imaginations about what could be done. When he more recently avows to revive that tradition, he again shows his penchant for sardonic depolicitization: "The critic is not the one who debunks, but the one who assembles. The critic is not the one who lifts the rugs from under the feet of the naive believers, but the one who offers the participants arenas in which to gather" (Latour 2004: 246). A critical-realist's take on knowledge, as I see it, requires that it is realistic about its own groundedness (as Kant certainly was, and Latour demands), but more so, about its own power to debunk the state of things because it is unjust.

The failure of the United Nations summit on climate change in Copenhagen of December 2009 has crucial repercussions for the future of critical universalism. The question whether or not we "know" that climates are rapidly changing and disproportionately harming the world's poor has become moot (Oxfam International, 2009). What matters is that the West does not take up responsibility for having unleashed planetary environmental injustice over a couple of centuries, and that new capitalist classes now follow suit. Ecological and geophysical processes which have been going on for millions of years have brought the human species to a deeply racist predicament it has barely begun to address. From a realist perspective, confining antiracism to the critique of science (or a Latourian "assembling of participants") would be quite disastrous.

References

Adorno, T. and Horkheimer, M. (2002) *Dialectic of Enlightenment: Philosophical Fragments*. Translated by Edmund Jephcott (orig. 1944). Stanford University Press, Stanford.
Althusser, L. (1969) *For Marx*. Translated by Ben Brewster (orig. 1965). Verso, London.
Althusser, L. (1971) Ideology and ideological state apparatuses (notes towards an investigation). In *Lenin and Philosophy and Other Essays*. Translated by Bren Brewster. Monthly Review Press, New York.
Anderson, K. (1991) *Vancouver's Chinatown: Racial Discourse in Canada, 1875–1980*. Queen–McGill University Press, Montreal.
Anderson, K. (2007) *Race and the Crisis of Humanism*. Routledge, London.
Badiou, A. (2005) *Metapolitics*. Translated by Jason Barker (orig. 1998). Verso, London.
Benedict, R. (1983) *Race and Racism*, 1st Edn 1942. Routledge and Kegan Paul, London.
Bhashar, R. (1993) *Dialectic: The Pulse of Freedom*. Routledge, London.
Bhaskar, R., Archer M., Collier, A., Lawson, T., and Norrie, A. (eds) (1988) *Critical Realism: Essential Readings*. Routledge, London.
Bowker, G.C. and Star, S.L. (1999) *Sorting Things Out: Classification and Its Consequences*. MIT Press, Cambridge, Minneapolis.
Blaut, J.M. (1992) The theory of cultural racism. *Antipode*, 24 (4), 289–299.
Blaut, J.M. (1999) Environmentalism and Eurocentrism. *The Geographical Review*, 89 (3), 391–409.
Crosby, A. (1986) *Ecological Imperialism: The Biological Expansion of Europe, 900–1900*. Cambridge University Press, Cambridge.
Delgado, R. (ed.) (1999) *Critical Race Theory: The Cutting Edge*. Temple University Press, Philadelphia.
Diamond, J. (1997) *Guns, Germs, and Steel: The Fates of Human Societies*. Norton, New York.
Diamond, J. (2005) *Collapse: How Societies Choose to Fail or to Succeed*. Viking, New York.
Diamond, J. (2003) The double puzzle of diabetes. *Nature* (5), 599–602.
Duncan, J.S. (2007) *In the Shadows of the Tropics: Climate, Race and Biopower in Nineteenth Century Ceylon*. Ashgate, Aldershot.
Frankenberg, R. (1993) *White Women, Race Matters: The Social Construction of Whiteness*. University of Minnesota Press, Minneapolis.
Hacking, I. (1999) *The Social Construction of What?* Harvard University Press, Cambridge.
Haney-López, I. (1996) *White By Law: The Legal Construction of Race*. New York University Press, New York.
Hannaford, I. (1996) *Race: The History of an Idea in the West*. Johns Hopkins University Press, Baltimore.

Hart, G. (2002) *Dis-abling Globalization: Places of Power in Post – Apartheid South Africa*. University of California Press, Berkeley.
Harvey, D. (2001) *Spaces of Capital: Towards a Critical Geography*. Routledge, New York.
Jackson, P. (ed.) (1987) *Race and Racism: Essays in Social Geography*. Unwin Hyman, Hemel Hemstead.
Jackson, P. and Penrose, J. (eds) (1994) *Constructions of Race, Place, and Nation*. University of Minnesota Press, Minneapolis.
Latour, B. (1993) *We Have Never Been Modern*. Translated by Catherine Porter (1991). Harvard University Press, Cambridge.
Latour, B. (1999) *Pandora's Hope: Essays on the Reality of Science Studies*. Harvard University Press, Cambridge.
Latour, B. (2004) Why has critique run out of steam? From matters of fact to matters of concern. *Critical Inquiry* 30 (2), 25–248.
Massey, D., and Denton, N. (1993) *American Apartheid: Segregation and the Making of the Underclass*. Harvard University Press, Cambridge, MA.
Montagu, A. (1997) *Man's Most Dangerous Myth: The Fallacy of Race*, 5th edn. Rowman & Littlefield, Lanham.
Oxfam International (2009) Climate shame: get back to the table, briefing. 21 December 2009, http://www.oxfam.org/en/policy/climate-shame-get-back-table (accessed on 15th October 2010).
Pichot, A. (2009) *The Pure Society: From Darwin to Hitler*. Translated by David Fernbach (orig. 2001). Verso, London.
Pulido, L. (2000) Rethinking environmental racism: white privilege and urban development in Southern California. *Annals of the Association of American Geographers* 90 (1), 12–40.
Robbins, P. (2003) Networks and knowledge systems: an alternative to "race or place" *Antipode* 35 (4), 818–822.
Saldanha, A. (2007) *Psychedelic White: Goa Trance and the Viscosity of Race*. University of Minnesota Press, Minneapolis.
Saldanha, A. (2009a) Back to the great outdoors: speculative realism as philosophy of science. *Cosmos and History: The Journal of Social and Natural History* 5 (2), 304–321.
Saldanha, A. (2009b) So what *is* race? *Insights*, online journal of the Institute of Advanced Study, Durham University, http://www.dur.ac.uk/ias/insights/volume2/article12/.
Sarich, V. and Miele, F. (2004) *Race: The Reality of Human Difference*. Westview Press, Boulder.
Sayer, A. (2000) *Realism and Social Science*. Sage, London.
Shrader-Frechette, K. (2002) *Environmental Justice: Creating Equality, Reclaiming Democracy*. Oxford University Press, New York.
Sellars, R.W. (1909) Space. *Journal of Philosophy, Psychology and Scientific Methods* 6 (23), 617–623.
Sellars, R.W. (1916a) *Critical Realism: A Study of the Nature and the Conditions of Knowledge*. McNally, Chicago.
Sellars, R.W. (1916b) *The Next Step in Democracy*. Macmillan, New York.
Sellars, R.W. (1922) *Evolutionary Naturalism*. Open Court, Chicago.
Sokal, A. and Bricmont, J. (1999) *Fashionable Nonsense: Postmodern Intellectuals' Abuse of Science*. Picador, New York.

Chapter 33

Sexuality
Part I

Natalie Oswin

Introduction

The sexual is spatial and the spatial is sexual. These insights have yielded an incredibly rich and diverse body of geographical work over the last thirty years and the once marginal field of sexuality and space studies now has a firm place within the discipline. Evidence of this fact includes the publication of several journal special issues (Browne 2007; Browne *et al.* 2010; Nast 2002; Oswin and Olund 2010; Puar *et al.* 2003), undergraduate oriented texts (Hubbard [in press]; Johnston and Longhurst 2009) and the edited volume *Geographies of Sexualities* (Browne *et al.* 2007), as well as the incorporation of numerous survey articles in disciplinary compendiums Brown and Knopp 2003; Peake 2009; Phillips 2004; Valentine 2003) and journals (Brown 2008; Hubbard 2008; Knopp 2007; Oswin 2008).

Within these already existing works, elaborations of the history of sexuality and space studies within geography are plentiful. They generally describe its lineage as follows: scattered scholarly efforts of the late 1970s and early 1980s sought to put the experiences of sexual minorities on the disciplinary map with studies of gay residential and commercial spaces leading the way (Weightman 1980; Ketteringham 1983; Lauria and Knopp 1985) and work on lesbian geographies ensuing later (Rothenberg 1995; Valentine 1993). The field began to truly consolidate with the publication of *Mapping Desire* (Bell and Valentine 1995), which was not only the first major edited collection in sexuality and space studies, but also the publication that put geographers into concerted conversation with queer theory. Poststructural, politicized and anti-assimilationist, the new queer geography both contributed to and found a place within the discipline's "cultural turn." Taking on board the anti-essentialist understandings of sexual identity put forward by social theorists such as Judith Butler (1990) and Michel Foucault (1978), geographers became less preoccupied with locating gay and lesbian spaces and instead turned their attention to the ways in which sexual identities and spaces are performatively and discursively produced. Explorations of the coincidence of bodies, desires and

The Wiley Blackwell Companion to Human Geography, First Edition.
Edited by John A. Agnew and James S. Duncan.
© 2011 John Wiley & Sons, Ltd. Published 2016 by John Wiley & Sons, Ltd.

spaces have since proliferated in an exciting range of ways across various scales and sites. There is a wealth of sexuality and space work in the subdisciplines of urban, feminist and social/ cultural geography and it also has a noticeable presence in political and economic geography. Gentrification, citizenship, the closet, and the performance of queer subjectivities are particularly well studied while smaller literatures tackle areas such as rural or non-metropolitan issues, globalization, domesticity and migration. Finally, though the queer geographies literature to date has placed more emphasis on understanding homosexualities, the literature on heterosexualities is rapidly expanding such that geographers are now exploring not only "dissident sexualities" but also the instabilities of the heteronorm that they are cast against.

On the basis of this history, various commentators have pointed out the very many processes of sexualization that are in need of further excavation or, indeed, have yet to come under the purview of sexuality and space studies. For instance, Lim, Brown and Browne (2007: 218) call for attention to the sexual geographies of women and transgendered persons and to "the full range of non-hegemonic performances of masculinity." They want to see attention paid to a greater range of work on heteronormative and homonormative formations, to alternative queer spaces and practices and to the affective and emotional dimensions of desire. Binnie (2007: 30) has recently reiterated a call he first made in his 1997 article entitled "Coming out of geography" for geography to reflect on its "squeamishness" and truly grapple with "relationships between erotics, communities and identities." Hubbard (2008: 2) contends that it is "vital that geographers acknowledge the existence of many different heterosexualities" just as they recognize the existence of multiple "queer" subjectivities. Finally, Brown and Knopp (2003: 318) "ask all cultural geographers to recognize the centrality of sexuality to all aspects of culture," and specifically point to the areas of communication, transportation, trade, colonial/ postcolonial relations and nature-society as ripe for examination. Queer geographies, these scholars suggest, have come a long way but have much more to offer. They, and many others, want to see the field pushed in directions that will make even more significant and integral contributions to the discipline.

Adopting this forward-looking, expansive perspective, in what follows I join these calls to expand queer geography's reach. Whereas the dominant focus of the literature to date has been the interrogation of sexual identities (or, in other words, on the geographies of gays/ lesbians/ "queers" and heterosexuals), I argue for the productive potential of a queer geographical critique without a literal sexual referent. In other words, I argue that while it is of course necessary and politically important to examine the deployment of "queer" as an identity category, queer theory's poststructuralist critique of the notion of sexual identity pushes us to examine how certain subjects come to be seen as abnormal or "queer" while others are considered "proper." It calls our attention not just to the embrace of "queer" as an identity category but to the process of "queering" as a facet of governance. In what follows, I elaborate this queer theoretical critique and argue that de-privileging the heterosexual-homosexual binary to interrogate heteronormativity (as distinct from heterosexuality) expands the potential uses of queer theory to critical geography. For heteronormative social formations entail not just sexual norms, but are also mutually constituted by racial, gendered, class and other norms. Thus gays, lesbians and other "sexual dissidents" are not the only subjects who are rendered queer and queer theory might be deployed within geography to understand a wide range of sites, issues and subjectivities.

Queer as Critique

As a theoretical approach, queer offers a potent critique of identity politics. Whereas its predecessor gay and lesbian studies understood sexual identities to be natural, fixed and biologically determined, queer theory emerged to assert that sexual identities are social constructions that do not pre-exist their worldly (for example, cultural and linguistic) deployments. Attesting that sexualities are performed, that they are something we *do* rather than something we *have*, queer theory understands sexual identity as unfixed and constantly changing such that:

> ... gay is to straight *not* as copy is to original, but, rather, as copy is to copy. (Butler 1990: 41)

As such, hegemonic heterosexuality is socially, historically and geographically contingent and the critical task at hand is to challenge the myriad processes through which it becomes naturalized. But although sexual identities are fictions, they are fictions that are regulatory and constraining and they take on material force in our lives. Identity politics can by no means be forsaken and the term queer has taken on meaning in a great variety of cultural, political and scholarly contexts as a label for sexual minorities.

Queer is thus both an identity and a critique of identity and geographers have embraced each of these uses of the term. They study sexual dissidents, or "queers," using the tools of queer theory. Where earlier work sought to locate gays and lesbians in space, queer geographies question the fixity of these identities and interrogate their performance in context. Queer geographies also acknowledge a range of non-normative or "queer" subjectivities and have expanded the field's purview from a sole focus on gays and lesbians to studies of bisexuality (Hemmings 2002), trans issues (Browne *et al.* 2010), and "perverse" practices such as bestiality (Brown and Rasmussen 2010). Further, heterosexuality has been recognized as not simply a monolithic norm but as a multitude of performances and work in this area has proliferated to encompass both normative and non-normative expressions of heterosexualities (Besio and Moss 2006; Hubbard 1998). In light of this work, it is clear that geographers' engagements with queer theory have transformed, deepened and extended the challenge to homophobia and heterosexism that gay and lesbian geographies began to advance in the 1970s and 1980s.

It has become commonplace within social and cultural geographies (at least) to point out the hegemony of heterosexuality and the marginalization of gays, lesbians and other sexual dissidents. This is a significant accomplishment. But while geographers have developed a provocative and politically important literature interrogating sexual identities, I suggest that we have not yet fully expanded on the geographical possibilities of queer as a critical approach that can shed light on issues aside from sexual identity politics. Though queer geography (and queer theory generally) emerged out of a concern for the plight of sexual minorities, and is tied to identity politics in ways that cannot and ought not be severed as long as homophobia and heterosexism persists, it might also make other contributions to a broader array of disciplinary debates.

I am by no means the only geographer to suggest that there might be additional trajectories for queer geographies. Browne, for instance, implores us to explore "queer and its potentials beyond its deployment as an overarching term to describe multiple sexual dissidents (including lesbian, gay and bisexual)" (2006: 885–888). She "locate[s] 'queer' in the radical requirement to question normativities and orthodoxies, in part now by rendering categories of sexualities, genders and spaces fluid" and seeks "queer geographies that offer radical contestations and transgressions of 'normality.'" Yet how queer critique might help us interrogate normality broadly conceived is left unelaborated. In another example, Knopp compares the fields of feminist and queer geographies and finds that:

> Still, there is much more that queer geographies, in conversation and alliance with feminist geographies, could do. Such work could have the important effect of queering the geographical imagination itself, something that would open up a world of possibilities, in virtually every realm of geography. (Knopp 2007: 49)

Yet, again, he does not spell out precisely what this this particular queer geography would entail nor what its critical possibilities include. But Browne, Knopp and others who suggest that a queer approach can be more broadly integrated in geographical analyses are onto something important here, something that is worth pursuing more fully.

I contend that one of the (likely many) ways of re-articulating queer geographies to send the field in new directions lies in recognizing the limitations of placing the heterosexual/ non-heterosexual (or, in other words, heterosexual/ "queer") binary at the centre of our analyses. As Cathy Cohen (1997: 438) argues, the distinction between hetero*sexuality* and hetero*normatiivty* is an important one that far too frequently goes unacknowledged in queer scholarship and activism. She states; "In many instances, instead of destabilizing the assumed categories and binaries of sexual identity, queer politics has served to reinforce simple dichotomies between heterosexual and everything 'queer.'" Thus the fact that heterosexual privilege is not equally available to all heterosexuals is often missed. Phil Hubbard (2008: 645) argues along somewhat similar lines. He points out the importance of recognizing the existence of multiple heterosexualities and suggests that we ought to queer heteronormality, "exposing this not just as a regulatory fiction that represses non-heterosexuals, but as one that imposes a *particular* heterosexual norm that also marginalizes many heterosexual identities and practices." He implores geographers to attend not just to homosexuality's exclusion but to the ways that certain expressions of heterosexuality – for example, prostitution, promiscuity, bigamy – are also cast as "immoral" or "perverse." Heteronormativity, as deployed within much geographical scholarship, has been understood quite rightly as a cultural logic that makes heterosexuality seem natural or right and marks homosexuality as its deviant other. Hubbard expands the reach of queer geographies by offering the corrective that because heterosexualities are multiple it is necessary to interrogate the divide between a particular hegemonic heterosexuality and a range of sexual subjectivities that are cast as "queer." Building on this useful intervention, I argue that we can and ought to go even further by challenging the narrow sexual referent for such work. For, as Michael Warner notes, "sexuality isn't always or only about sexuality ... it is not an autonomous dimension of experience" (Warner 1995: 368). The fact that particular forms of heterosexuality seem natural or right cannot be fully understood by interrogating sexual norms alone. We ought to also grapple with the ways in which sexual norms are mutually constituted by ideologies relating to race, class, gender, nationality and more. To illustrate such an analysis of heteronormativity and substantiate why I argue that we might usefully go beyond the heterosexual/ "queer" binary to instead interrogate the multiple ways in which subjects are "queered", I now turn to an example from my research on colonial and postcolonial Singapore. In what follows, I seek to understand the persistence of a colonial era anti-homosexual law and find a heteronormative logic that does far more than produce a heterosexual-homosexual binary.

Sexual Tensions in Singapore

In the Southeast Asian city-state of Singapore, there have been unprecedented debates on the topic of homosexuality over the last decade. Attempting to shed an authoritarian image and foster a "creative economy," the government of this island nation has taken on board Richard Florida's (2002) contention that creative cities tend to exhibit tolerance towards gay and lesbian communities. As a result, gay and lesbian commercial establishments have been allowed to operate visibly, police raids that were not uncommon in past decades have largely ceased and gay and lesbian cultural production has flourished. But legislative and policy changes to counter pervasive heterosexual bias have proven stubbornly out of reach. Most significantly, a 2007 lobbying effort to repeal Section 377A of the Penal Code, a colonial era statute that criminalizes "gross indecency" between men, was dismissed. As Singapore's Prime Minister Lee Hsien Loong stated in a speech explaining why the law would stand, "the overall society ... remains conventional, it remains straight." He thus affirmed that while some limited space is available for expressions of gay and lesbian sexualities, the city-state is predominantly hetero*sexual*. As justification for this state of affairs, he offered the following:

> The family is the basic building block of our society. It has been so and, by policy, we have reinforced this and we want to keep it so. And by "family" in Singapore, we mean one man one woman, marrying, having children and bringing up children within that framework of a stable family unit. (Lee 2007)

So the city-state would remain predominantly heterosexual to protect this heter*onormative* state of affairs. As a critical response to this illiberal sexual politics, my research has focused on interrogating how this heteronormative logic was put into place in Singapore's past in order to better understand what is at stake in its maintenance in its present. By going back into the archives, it becomes apparent that what appears on the surface to be a contest between homosexuality and heterosexuality is in fact about much more.

According to the latest census data for Singapore, 82.1% of all households are categorized as "one family nucleus," another 5.6% are described as "two or more family nuclei" and only 12.3% fall under the "no family nucleus" distinction (Leow 2000). These statistics indicate remarkable demographic transformations since the period of colonial rule (from 1819 to the late 1950s) during which Singapore's majority population consisted of single male migrant laborers. Since gaining independence, the city-state's government has vigorously promoted a family ideal through a range of initiatives. These include policies that tie public housing allotments and subsidies to marriage and a willingness to live in close proximity to one's parents, institutionalization of a national matchmaking agency, aggressive anti-natalist measures that worked all too well and have been followed by pro-natalist initiatives, and constant exhortations to marry and (then) procreate via the state-controlled media, various government ministries and a battery of state-supported organizations. Within both state and popular discourse, the modernization of the family is recognized as an essential element in the city-state's propulsion from "third world to first" (Lee 2000). But this postcolonial development has important colonial precursors. While the colonial administration did not concern itself with transforming the intimate lives of the Straits Settlements' inhabitants for most of its rule, shifts in colonial policies that moved away from a narrow emphasis on production and toward a broad approach to social reproduction are evident from around 1910. Over the remainder of the colonial period, infant and maternal health was prioritized, immigration policies were reconfigured in order to balance the sex ratio and encourage family formation and reunification, the family planning association was founded, the Department of Social Welfare was established, and so on.

Thus heteronormativity in Singapore began to take shape during the colonial period. As discussed above, in the geographical literature heteronormativity tends to be understood as the valorization of heterosexuality over homosexuality/ deviant sexuality. So to understand this shift in colonial policy, I looked for evidence along these lines. I found, however, that explicit references to the threat of homosexuality are rare and perfunctory in Singapore's colonial archive. Some historians have found evidence that female prostitution was advocated by colonial officials to prevent the male population from turning to same-sex sexual activity and coroner reports of anal syphilis attest to the latter's existence nonetheless. But records of public attention to the issue are scarce. Three Straits Settlements Annual Reports contain brief references to efforts to stamp out male prostitution and, in the Legislative Council Proceedings, the Attorney General commented on the addition of Section 377A to the Penal Code by stating only that, "it is unfortunately the case that acts of the nature described have been brought to notice" (Straits Settlements 1938, B49). The positioning of homosexuality as a primary threat to the nuclear family is, it seems, a relatively recent narrative. In other words, it was not the primary impetus for the widespread efforts to transform this colonial entrepot comprised of single male migrant workers into a modern nation of families that began to take shape in the early part of the twentieth century. The family ideal that lay at the center of this heteronormative nation has always been about more than heterosexuality *per se*. To understand exactly what the postcolonial government seeks to protect by upholding Section 377A, we need to look beyond a narrow sexual referent to other colonial traces. Upon doing so, it becomes apparent that the set of initiatives that established heteronormality in Singapore's late colonial period were broadly aimed at correcting "abnormal" population dynamics and "backward" cultural practices.

One area in which we can find evidence of these colonial traces is that of housing policies and programs. Housing interventions have long been significant modes of social control in Singapore and currently more than eighty-five percent of its population lives in public housing, most as owners of their flats. The efforts of the governmental Housing Development Board (HDB) have been key to fostering socioeconomic development and governmental legitimacy in the postcolonial era. They have also, and concomitantly, been key to putting the nuclear family into place in Singapore's social and political landscape. This comes across clearly in its strictly enforced tenancy regulations. To purchase an HDB flat, applicants must be twenty-one years of age and "form a proper family nucleus" defined as: the applicant and fiancé(e); the applicant, spouse and children (if any); the applicant, the applicant's parents, and siblings (if any); if widowed/ divorced, the applicant and children under the applicant's legal custody; and, if orphaned, the applicant and unmarried siblings. In my archival research, I have sought to understand how this came to be. Looking back to the colonial era, initial public housing efforts by the Singapore Improvement Trust (formed in 1927, hereinafter referred to as SIT) were a central part of initiatives geared toward balancing the sex ratio and accommodating workers' families. But while the SIT, along with the rest of the colonial administration, was very interested in balancing the sex ratio and moving towards a nation full of families rather than single men, they did not take much interest in those families' compositions. In other words, they were not concerned about the size of families, about whether extended families lived together, about the number of wives that one man had, and so on. Tenancy was available to "five or more persons, including the applicant, who can be considered as forming a "family unit" having regard to the family customs of the community."

This changed drastically with the postcolonial successor of the SIT, the Housing and Development Board. From its founding in 1960, housing was available for those in nuclear family forms only. The tenancy restrictions then look virtually the same as the present ones. Though this policy change has certainly had repercussions for non-heterosexuals in Singapore, as in the broader colonial archive, there is no overt discussion of homosexuality as a threat to heterosexuality in the archives of the SIT or HDB. Rather, what drove this change was contestation over notions of traditional versus modern subjects. Though it valued its own monogamous form of marriage above all others, the British administration left negotiations over marriage customs in the colonized population up to its various communities. This was officially cast as a benevolent act but it served to perpetuate the secondary status of colonized communities; it ensured that they could never be modern subjects. But the postcolonial shift in emphasis did not come out of nowhere as a fully-fledged postcolonial development. Throughout the late 1940s and 1950s, a period during which self-rule was looking increasingly possible and thus the threat that imitation of colonial norms held for colonial rule was no longer a significant concern; both colonial representatives and selected members of the colonized elite conducted numerous studies on social and housing conditions. It is in these studies that we can see a shift in the conceptualization of the Singapore family. We can see the emergence of the married, monogamous, heterosexual, procreative couple.

For instance, in the *Social Survey of Singapore* (Singapore 1947), UK family composition patterns are offered for comparison and on this basis, it is argued that only those households that "have as their heads married men ... may be taken to represent the number of households which are organized on a normal family basis." Further, in the study *Urban Incomes and Housing* (Goh 1956), the normal family is more specifically characterized as "a kinship group of man, wife and children." Looking at these and numerous other archival documents, it becomes apparent that intimate possibilities were narrowed in order to achieve what the colonial administration never could; a nation of subjects. And the postcolonial city-state government, in pushing these reforms ever further with independence, has shown a desire "to be even *more consistently modern* than the former colonial masters were" (Wee 2007: 20). Thus postcolonial housing initiatives, and a battery of other initiatives intended to promote particular familial forms, are not simply about guarding against the threat of homosexuality. They are bound to a colonial impulse aimed at rooting out "backwardness" in the name of development and progress.

While the fact that Singapore's colonial-era sodomy law has been maintained in its postcolonial present has necessarily focused attention on the plight of gays and lesbians in the city-state, the heteronormative logic underpinning this law's perpetuation is not solely a gay issue. It encompasses not only the exclusion of homosexuals in Singapore but the stigma attached to being unmarried, the encouragement of the educated to have more children than other groups, the legal requirement that all migrant workers leave their families behind, the fear of male migrants as lascivious and therefore dangerous, the legal requirement that female migrant workers must be deported if they should become pregnant, and so on. Heteronormativity in Singapore thus works through the coincidence of race, class, gender, class and sexual norms. Prevailing notions of respectable domesticity and proper family play significant roles in rendering a wide range of subjects "queer."

Conclusion

Queer theory, as an anti-assimilationist, poststructuralist critique of the notion of sexual identity as a given, biological fact, has invigorated sexuality and space studies. Geographers have used its insights to challenge heterosexism, put the experiences of gays, lesbians and other sexual minorities on the discipline's agenda and reveal heterosexualities as performed. These are profoundly important contributions in both political and scholarly terms. But I agree with other geographers working in this area that queer perspectives can contribute even more to the broader field of critical geographies. The heterosexual-homosexual binary that has understandably been at the center of sexuality and space studies has perhaps overdetermined its priorities and limited the critical uses to which queer theory has been put within geography. For this sexual binary, like all binaries, can offer only a simplified view of inevitably more complex social and political relationships. It occludes understanding of the ways in which heternormative logics render a wide variety of bodies and practices abject/ abnormal/ queer. To understand how heternormativity becomes entrenched in place, we have to go beyond the establishment of dividing lines between the moral and the immoral/ perverse. We must attend to the subtle ways in which it works through family forms, reproductive practices, citizenship requirements and more.

Sexuality, as Foucault tells us, is a "dense transfer point for relations of power" (1978: 103). Expressions of individual desires are caught up, always and everywhere, in governmental processes that produce desirable subjects. Beyond "sexual identity," we can and ought to explore the politics of queering and the power of normalization. I ought to clarify here that I am not arguing that the fact that heteronormativity encompasses not just the sexual but also the racial, the classed, the gendered and more means that all those that are cast as illicit and improper subjects are therefore "queer" in the identarian sense of the term. I am instead arguing that they are "queered," that they are put on a different trajectory of life and death than those cast as licit and proper. Alongside the existing attention to self-consciously "queer" identity projects and activism, following these "queerings" will take us in new directions. It will lead to the advancement of a queer approach that goes beyond a literal sexual referent to consider the heteronormative politics of kinship, domesticity, family, reproduction, migration, nation, modernity and more. Thus offering new and different ways of seeing a range of existing areas of critical geographical enquiry, we might envision new and different ways of resisting.

References

Bell, D. and Valentine, G. (eds) (1995) *Mapping Desire: Geographies of Sexualities*. Routledge, London.
Besio, K. and Moss, P. (2006) Sexuality and Gender. Special issue of *ACME: An International E-Journal for Critical Geographies* 5 (2), 121–143.
Binnie, J. (2007) Sexuality, the erotic and Geography: Epistemology, methodology and pedagogy. In K. Browne, J. Lim, and G. Brown (eds), *Geographies of Sexualities: Theory, Practices and Politics*. Ashgate, Burlington, pp. 29–38.
Brown, G. (2008) Urban (Homo)Sexualities. Ordinary Cities and Ordinary Sexualities. *Geography Compass* 2 (4), 1215–1231.
Brown, M. and Knopp, L. (2003) Queer Cultural Geographies – We're Here! We're Queer! We're Over There, Too! In K. Anderson, M. Domosh, B, Thrift, and S. Pile, (eds), *Handbook of Cultural Geography*. Sage, London, pp. 313–324.
Brown, M. and Rasmussen, C. (2010) Bestiality and the queering of the human animal. *Environment and Planning D: Society and Space* 28 (1), 158–177.
Browne, K., Hines, S., and Nash, C. (eds) (2010) Towards Trans Geographies. Special issue of *Gender Place and Culture*.
Browne, K. (2006) Challenging queer geographies. *Antipode* 38 (5), 885–893.
Browne, K. (ed.) (2007) Lesbian Geographies Special issue of *Social and Cultural Geography* 8 (1), 1–7.
Browne, K., Lim, J., and Brown, G. (eds) (2007) *Geographies of Sexualities: Theory, Practices and Politics*. Ashgate, Burlington.
Butler, J. (1990) *Gender Trouble: Feminism and the Subversion of Identity*. Routledge, New York.
Foucault, M. (1978) *The history of Sexuality: An Introduction, Volume 1*. Vintage Books, New York.
Goh, K.S. (1956) *Urban Incomes and Housing: A Report on the Social Survey of Singapore, 1953–54*. Department of Social Welfare, Singapore.
Hemmings, C. (2002) *Bisexual spaces: A geography of sexuality and gender*. Routledge, New York.
Hubbard, P. (in press) *Cities and Sexualities*. Routledge, London.
Hubbard, P. (2008) Here, there, everywhere: The ubiquitous geographies of heteronormativity. *Geography Compass* 2 (3), 640–658.

Hubbard, P. (1998) Sexuality, Immorality and the City: Red-light Districts and the Marginalisation of Female Street Prostitutes. *Gender, Place and Culture* 5 (1), 55–76.

Johnston, L. and Longhurst, R. (2009) *Space, Place and Sex: Geographies of Sexualities.* Rowman and Littlefield, Lanham.

Ketteringham, W. (1983) The Broadway Corridor: gay businesses as agents of revitalization in Long Beach. Paper presented at the Annual Meeting of the Association of American Geographers, Denver.

Knopp, L. (2007) On the relationship between queer and feminist geographies. *The Professional Geographer* 59 (1), 47–55.

Lauria, M. and Knopp, L. (1985) Toward an analysis of the role of gay communities in the urban renaissance. *Urban Geography* 6, 152–169.

Lee, H.L. (2007) Speech to Parliament on reading of Penal Code (Amendment) Bill, 22 October 2007.

Lee, K.Y. (2000) *From Third World to First: The Singapore Story, 1965–2000.* Harper Collins, New York.

Leow, B.G. (2000) *Census of Population 2000: Households and Housing.* Department of Statistics, Singapore.

Lim, J., Brown, G., and Browne, K. (2007) Conclusions and future directions, or our hopes for geographies of sexualities (or queer geographies). In K. Browne, J. Lim, and G. Brown (eds), *Geographies of Sexualities: Theory, Practices and Politics.* Ashgate, Burlington, pp. 215–223.

Nast, H. (ed.) (2002) Queer Patriarchies, Queer Racisms, International. Special issue of *Antipode* 34 (5) 835–844.

Oswin, N. and Olund, E. (eds) (2010) Governing intimacy. Special issue of *Environment and Planning D: Society and Space* 28 (1), 60–67.

Oswin, N. (2008) Critical geographies and the uses of sexuality: Deconstructing queer Space. *Progress in Human Geography* 32 (1), 89–103.

Peake, L. (2009) Gender, race, sexuality. In S. Smith, R. Pain, S. Marston, and J.P. Jones III (eds), *Sage Handbook of Social Geographies.* Sage, London, pp. 55–77.

Phillips, R. (2004) Sexuality. In J. Duncan, N. Johnson, and R. Schien (eds), *A Companion to Cultural Geography.* Blackwell, Oxford, pp. 265–278.

Puar J.K., Rushbrook, D., and Schein, L. (eds) (2003) Sexuality and space: Queering geographies of globalization. Special issue of *Environment and Planning D: Society and Space* 21 (4), 383–387.

Rothenburg, T. (1995) And She Told Two Friends: Lesbians Creating Urban Social Space. In D. Bell, and G. Valentine (eds), *Mapping Desire: Geographies of Sexualities.* Routledge, London, pp. 165–181.

Singapore (1947) *A Social Survey of Singapore: A Preliminary Study of Some Aspects of Social Conditions in the Municipal Area of Singapore.* Department of Social Welfare, Singapore.

Straits Settlements (1938) *Proceedings of the Legislative Council of the Straits Settlements.* Government Printing Office, Singapore.

Valentine, G. (2003) Sexual politics. In J. Agnew, K. Mitchell, and G. Toal (eds), *A Companion to Political Geography.* Blackwell, Oxford, pp. 408–420.

Valentine, G. (1993) (Hetero)sexing Space: Lesbian Perceptions and Experiences of Everyday Spaces. *Environment and Planning D: Society and Space* 11 (4), 395–413.

Warner, M. (1995) Something queer about the nation-state. In C. Newfield and R. Strickland (eds), *After political correctness: The humanities and society in the 1990s.* Westview Press, Boulder, pp. 361–371.

Wee, C.J.W.-L. (2007) *The Asian modern: Culture, capitalist development, Singapore.* National University of Singapore Press, Singapore.

Weightman, B. (1980) Gay bars as private places. *Landscape* 24, 9–17.

Chapter 34

Sexuality
Part II

Mary E. Thomas

Introduction

When I teach geography undergraduates about sexuality and space, I typically ask them to imagine the open green space that marks center campus – what is known at my midwestern American university as "the Oval." During warm springtime after months of cold, gray days, coeds bare midriffs (or more!) in a public display of thousands of sun-starved bodies. I am sometimes afraid to walk through the Oval for fear of being decapitated by Frisbees, but in all honesty my greatest reaction to this springtime ritual is of dismay at the vast heterosexism that this common grounds illustrates. As a feminist, I worry whether my approaching middle age (well, let's face it, I am technically there now) makes me out of touch with the youth, and whether I am being conservative for thinking that the university is no place for the public exhibit of bikinied female bodies. Women's sexuality, after all, has so recently only been allowed a public acknowledgement, let alone an agential celebration. I worry that it might be misogynist to think that this public space should be primarily professional, not social. Or is the overdetermined heterosexism of the Oval so unwelcoming of fat, old, or disabled bodies to be wholly misogynist itself? I worry that the excessive heterosexual embodiment of the Oval will yet again reiterate the normative exclusion of queer students and their sexual expression. Thus, when I ask students to imagine a gay or lesbian couple walking down the main path, holding hands in the midst of the virtual heterosexual orgy, they find it pretty easy to understand the arguments I am making about everyday heteronormative spatiality. They can grasp my lessons about resistant practice and performative space, that the queer bodies in intimate clutch can expose and potentially shatter that assumed sexual hegemony because after all, it is a precarious social space and its foundations are pretty shaky to begin with.

But the harder lessons to teach students relate to the ways that the sexual space of everyday heterosexuality in the US is also a function of white privilege. Those lesbian, gay, or trans resistant bodies in the students' imaginations – those disruptive, political queers that can reoccupy straight campus – are all too obviously white to them. Admittedly, this is a function of the racial makeup of geography undergrads at my university, which is overwhelmingly white. It is also due to my own white body that asks them to imagine this disruptive scene, those sexualized bodies unmarked by race in my prompt. It is only too easy given the spatiality of discussion – both in class and in a supremacist America – to conjure heterosexuality and its resistors as white. But this ease is the very point I want to extend through this chapter: white privilege and positionality has allowed for race to be occluded in many theories of sexual space, and sexual subjectivity, that geographers posit. White privilege pervades more than the classroom, and it restricts potential theorizing of sexual subjectivity beyond the straight-queer binary. Thus, my argument is not merely a pedagogical challenge, but offers a critique of the priorities that urban, social, and cultural geographers have made over time concerning sexuality studies in the discipline. These priorities continually affect what literature is read and cited, what scholarship is developed, and what political interventions are posed and carried out.

I argue that the lack of theory about the racialization of sexuality means that whiteness is often the assumed embodiment of sexual subjectivity, which problematically prohibits close analysis of the ways that race, ethnicity, nationalism, and sexuality are continuously interarticulated in society and space. As Natalie Oswin (2008) remarks, when race is placed in intersection with sexuality, it is almost always non-white. Very often, it is also held in opposition to Western racializations (for example, work on transnational, immigrant, and mobile sexualities), so that non-white reads as non-Western. Thus, in this chapter I tackle the issue of white privilege in sexuality studies and in understandings of heteronormativity. I believe that this project is important because our theories and epistemologies of sexuality and subjectivity are impaired for not considering race and racialization. But I do not want this chapter to offer merely an intellectual contribution to sexuality and race studies; I also want to make a political injunctive: geographers must interrogate their positionalities of racial privilege and how these affect their understandings of heteronormativity, sexual identification, practice, and desire.

Unreflective Whiteness and the Limits of "Queer" Identity

In part, I understand the occlusion of race in sexuality studies to be an issue of positionality because the history of sexual studies in geography is marked by the bodies, identities, and priorities of those who have been able to *avoid* the minoritizing racialization of sexualities that whiteness permits (Bonnett 1997; Pulido 2002). There is a great potential in utilizing positionality to theorize white privilege that has not largely been done in sexuality studies, not to mention other fields (cf. Butz and Berg 2002; Holmes 2009). As has often been noted, positionality fails when it becomes a rote process of listing identities, of documenting one's social qualifiers. Such a procedure assumes that one can be reflexive about one's position in the world through assumed signifiers and static titles that give no sense of how they came to be, to operate, in and through the subject and self (Rose 1997).

Engaging in simplifying reflexive exercises as a mode of indicating one's positionality is an investment in a social-psychic ontology of the subject that insinuates a chartable subject; one who is capable of describing the historical geographies that gave social differences and practices their normative power. This subject is fully conscious, place-bound, and predictable (Pratt 2000). The exercise lacks an examination of the historicity and spatiality of social formations and how those formations are taken up only in the present time and space by academics – as much as those whom we research and about whom we theorize. In other words, identifying social difference as a factor only in the immediate neglects a consideration of why those identities or differences became salient and pressing, and how they continue to offer a contingency for imagining who the subject is. Further, Audrey Kobayashi writes that "indulgence in reflexivity is ironically the very act that sets us apart" from those whose lives and experiences we research. She continues:

> it can even work actively to construct a sense of the other, to deny the reflexivity of others, and to emphasise the condition of detached alterity. (Kobayashi 2003: 348)

The reflexive positionality act *itself* instantiates an identity of being somehow outside of ideology, rather than also constituted by its ongoing production, through and beyond subjectivity. Somehow, with reflexive positionality social difference need not matter to the theorist's or critical scholar's subjectivity because they have remarked on it.

To many readers, this may seem a dated argument. In our new decade, there may be a sense that "we" are well aware of the pitfalls of reflexivity and have developed more sophisticated language and methods of representation to avoid the simplifying of research, researched, and their relationality (Nagar and Geiger 2007). To the contrary, I think the new language of critique has displaced the effects of reflexive positionality on the ways we think of the social world. Scholars often rehearse their race, location, etc., in the service of a positionality that stops at this list. Such an exercise posits reflexivity in terms of a subjectivity that is capable of being self-evident; that is, a subject who is able to take itself as an object of inquiry (Butler 1997: 103) without attending to the ways that an "identity" functions as an exclusivity, as much as (or more than) it does as a conscious experience. Rather, I point to the words "reflexivity" and "positionality" in the spirit that Richa Nagar (2003: 360) does: as attempts at political and intellectual engagement with those "power hierarchies embedded in knowledge production." This should include the invisible privileges of whiteness. Thus, engaging positionality in sexuality studies is to think through how sexuality and sexual identity exist conceptually in scholarship through embedded power hierarchies of race, both in terms of our own development of research – what we think should be considered – and in terms of our research subjects' own social locations – how we theorize what "they" say, do, represent, stand for. Reflexivity is not just a process of methodology, but a way to think about who the subject is, and why some identifications and social meanings are highlighted over others, for example, why sexuality and not race/whiteness? Implying an insular identity neglects the ways that that identity only gets defined through the exclusions of other identities, and the politics and epistemology of that neglect.

There have been a number of explanations for how sexuality studies arose in Anglo geography through counter-political scholarship, driven by an epistemology of gay and lesbian scholarship and its arguments against hegemonic heteronormativity, and with a spirit of political intervention meant to disrupt the staid de-sexualized discipline (see previous chapter by Oswin for some examples of this history). To my knowledge, there has not been a likewise exploration of how these histories and trajectories have been accomplished through the ability to interject through normative racial inclusion. That is, being on the "outside of the [heterosexual] project" does not mean that one is similarly excluded racially. Economic difference within academic debates might matter less, given that those writing and attending conferences were largely working in the discipline or in the academy, even if not regularly; of course, one's own class privilege might also lead to easier omission of racial oppressions. Exercising white and class privilege means having an ability to *not* have to worry about and contend with racism and racial-ethnic exclusion, and to not engage with race theories because one is "seen" to be "doing sexuality." It means not having to theorize the complex subjectivity that cannot distinguish social categories of identity, or prioritize one identity or experience over another.

To be clear, I am not calling out an explicit racism here; as I stated above, this neglect is oftentimes invisible and unconscious. The work done by geographers bringing sexuality to an intellectual and pedagogic agenda has been remarkable, and I have benefitted from their research, presence, and struggles. Rather, my point is to ask what a trajectory of critique focusing on sexuality – and more recently, queerness – as an identity and subject-position means for the present moment of sexuality studies, in terms of what foundational concepts are taught, communicated, published, and ultimately advanced. Understanding the development of sexuality studies in geography helps us to identify how race was largely omitted from the outset, thus how white privilege never became a priority for theorizing heteronormativity.

White Hegemony and the Heterosexual Matrix

The concept of the heterosexual matrix has been an important one in the development of sexuality studies in geography. Simply, it is a phrase used to indicate that one's gender, normatively defined and evidenced along the hierarchical binary male-female, is naturalized via an accompanying heterosexual desire (Butler 1990, 1993, 1997). The articulation of binary gender therefore installs a corresponding "normal" heterosexuality in a cohesive social hegemony. A woman desires a man, a man a woman; men and women are heterosexuals. This heterosexual hegemony of sex-gender-sexuality forecloses same-sex desire, not to mention sexualities that do not organize around gender at all (Brown and Rasmussen 2010).

Feminist theories about compulsory heterosexuality (Rich 1980), the heterosexual matrix, and gender performativity, all focus important attention on the centrality of gender-sex binaries to the articulation of heteronormativity, and vice versa. Thus, gender-sex and sexuality are difficult if not impossible to disentangle in sexuality studies in geography after the heterosexual matrix, for example, see the chapters in the recent *Geographies of Sexualities*, edited by Browne, Lim and Brown 2007. Not so for race as you can see from the chapter by Haritawon of the same book title. This is not to say that there isn't a lot of work on sexuality and race (there is: see Oswin 2008), rather that heteronormativity and the heterosexual matrix are not thoroughly conceptualized through racial difference, economic privilege, or the particularized locations of their articulation (especially when those locations are not "outside" of the wealthy global north). Yet as David Eng (2001: 13–14) reminds us; "The assumption of a normative social identity requires a heterosexualizing imperative bound to a hegemonic structure of whiteness."

A "hegemonic structure of whiteness." The phrase is strongly worded; structure is not a term used lightly these days in theories of social difference and identification. I think it points especially toward a way of understanding what "identity" is, and is not. Identities are effects of historical, geographical, and political discourses, having no ontological existence separately from the modes through which they are represented, practiced, and materialized. As I hinted above, I prefer to think instead about identification and subjectivity, since "identities" as a term masks the social-spatial and psychic processes that emphasize rejection, abjection, refusal, closure, incorporation of the other – as much or more as they emphasize affinity or sameness. By neglecting to think about the processes of disidentification, scholars instead rely on a language of intersectionality to understand the ways that race, gender, sexuality, class, location, age, embodiment, etcetera, locate the subject in a range of social differences. In other words, the self's normative *identities* – consciously understood and self-recognized – are what matters most in intersectional analysis and is marked out in the intersectional framework. Ladelle McWhorter (2009: 15) points out that "… intersectional analyses tend to focus analytic attention primarily on identities rather than on institutions, discourses, and disciplinary regimes; but even when they do venture beyond accounts of identity construction, they still implicitly assume that racism, sexism, and heterosexism could and do operate sometimes in isolation from one another." Further, intersectionality problematically equates identity with oppression and inequality (Gimenez 2001), and with a corresponding investment in switching the binary to resistance. Thus as a conceptual tool, it situates power as oppressive or potentially liberatory via identities of resistant strength (e.g. queer subjects are written through with resistant connotations when "queer" is an adjective, see Winnubst 2006), without attending to how power both enables *and* constrains the subject all at once (i.e., subjectification, see Butler 1997). Identities are never simply oppressive *or* resistant (Cheng 2001).

Thus, while a queer liberatory identity might stress the resistant goals of anti-heteronormative politics, or the non-normative embodiment of same-sex desire or sexual practice, it does not *necessarily* interrogate how that identity operates through the possibilities afforded it through white hegemony and class privilege (there are certainly exceptions of each, and a few examples include Bell and Binnie 2004; Brown 2009; Brown *et al.* 2005; Hodge 2000; Nast 2000). Nor does queer, even as an "anti" identity, always work to undermine the autonomous subject who has agential power. An individual, as Shannon Winnubst puts is, "can clearly stake his or her own identity – psychologically, politically, and economically – in the chaotic world" (Winnubst 2006: 24). But staking an identity, she argues, is deeply ignorant of the historicity and spatiality of the ways that categories have developed. Staking even a resistant sexual identity like queer is to ignore the ways it has developed through whiteness and class privilege (particularly investments in property rights, as Winnubst shows).

Categories are also obviously the vehicles which drive exclusion. Thus, an identification is always also a disidentification. Saying "I am a woman" is the same as saying I am not a man, I am not a transvestite, I am not a cat. In geography, it is far past the time to ask how claiming sexual identity – regardless of whether this claim is meant to be progressive, since it is resistant to heteronormativity – is only possible through discourses beyond the heterosexual matrix. So while claiming that I am a woman involves the matrix, since woman is dominantly written as desirous of man in heteronormativity, the body – my body – is more than my sex-gender. As my opening example proves, its position invokes long, complex histories and spatialities of race, of age/authority (in the classroom, at least!), of Western liberalism, imperialism, and capitalism. Theorizing race and sexuality means analyzing contexts that enable identities to be both avowed *and* disavowed, and never in isolation.

Racializing "Boys are Stupid": a Brief Example

In my own research I am interested in understanding how feminist and popular identity politics of teenage girlhood in the US reduce girls' subjectivities to their sexuality-gender identity. "Girl power" is a resistant celebration of feminine heterosexuality that highlights girls' agency against misogyny. However, I argue that girl power fails to account for the ways that gender identity operates as much through misogyny as it does through empowerment. Thus, taking on "girl power" identities means emphasizing heteronormative and white femininity, and the development of this identity in the US has also placed it squarely within middle and upper class consumptive practices. Because I understand subjectivity to be more than articulated identities, I have tried to think about girls' narratives about school, family, friends, and urban spaces beyond what they explicitly say. What they don't say is just as important, as I hope this brief example will illustrate.

I interviewed girls in Los Angeles, California, after a "race" riot (that is, a large scale fight involving several hundred students) broke out at their high school between Latinos and Armenians. Because the fighters in that riot were almost exclusively boys, girls easily explained the fight as "just boys being stupid." The girls, who were primarily self-identified as Asian, Latina, and Armenian, and who were mostly first or second generation Americans, found it very easy to understand boys' violence through narratives about gender stereotypes like "testosterone," male anger, and through contrast to girls' fighting … which inevitably they saw as only arising from one-on-one, "catty" competition over boys. At the same time, they wanted their school to be a space of peaceful multiculturalism, where every student could "get along" regardless of race, ethnicity, income, or gender (Thomas 2008, 2009). Thus, their resistant voices were loudly evident: we resist male violence, we resist racism, and we want to have a happy school where all people can come together in peace.

Yet, as I talked with the girls in individual and group interviews, they went on to discuss boys' fighting in great detail, evaluating boys' strength, their sexiness and scariness, and hypothesizing about how masculine fighting developed through human evolution and history. Thus, one group of 15 and 16 year old Armenian-American girls had the following exchange about "why boys fight:"

Alexis: I think it started off from animals. When like monkeys try to dominate, and the best monkey gets the best female. I think that's what they're doing.
Grisselle: Talk about monkeys.
Alexis: Hey, remember we were doing research for science class last year. That's how I think it's turning out to be.
Grisselle: Yeah, they say that we evolved from monkeys.
Alexis: If you just look at the whole concept, that's exactly what they're doing.
Mary: So the women are the prizes. Do you feel like you're a prize?
Alexis: Well, you know [shrugging, nodding].
Mary: Do you like it when guys compete for you?
Alexis: No.
Grisselle: Yeah.
Anne: Yeah, like, you feel special. But I mean if they start hurting themselves, no, but if they're just like doing things, like showing off and like that, that's okay. But if they start hurting themselves, it's like never mind.
Mary: Then, that's not attractive.
Anne: Yeah, because then they'll have a bleeding lip and no eye.
Grisselle: And then you're going to feel guilty.
Anne: I won't feel guilty; I'd just feel like, "you guys are retarded."
Mary: Yeah, all of a sudden they're not as attractive, huh?
Anne: Yeah, they have cuts on their face.

My own understanding of "attractive" was taken up very differently by Anne – an unsurprising thing given that I was prompting a critique of boys' fighting that the girls did not follow or agree with. Their earlier insistence that "boys are stupid" for fighting, led me to think that that was where this story was heading as it unfolded (an "old" person's interpretation, no doubt in part! But also, related to different language nuances and vocabularies, different first languages, too). However, here and throughout the interview, the girls gave another version of boys' stupid fighting: they desire it. Alexis had a sole "no" which she did not further explain (and I do not remember if I even heard it at the time during the conversation; such is the risk of group interviews). That desire, in the context of the particular fighting at school, is writ through and through with racial difference. By analyzing this narrative as an example of the heterosexual matrix (boys fight, girls wait passively to be won), the racialization that frames it gets lost. The girls' heartfelt calls for multicultural understanding and inclusion at their school hits a wall when it comes to sexualizing the boys' racialized, group fighting. This crucial framing condition is key to any theory trying to understand the girls' reproduction of the heterosexual matrix and its gender-sex-sexuality framework.

There is a much longer story to tell than I have space for here, of course. However, the point to take away is that this interview excerpt is contextualized by a longer discussion and a broader time-space: girls explain their desire, which is bound with gender-heterosexuality, *in terms of the racial-ethnic violence at their school*. Gender and heterosexuality, therefore, are formative of racial difference; racism articulates itself as gender and sexual pleasure (Ferguson 2005). Further, girls provide idealized stories about what "life should be like" for teenagers in the US, and in LA, that are framed powerfully in white hegemonic discourses. These stories especially involve sexual freedom, dating, and teenage individuality given "traditional" ethnic familial expectations. (For example, girls also said that "American" girls are allowed to date, to have more freedom, than my "Armenian" or "Mexican" parents will allow me to have.)

In their complaints of boys' violence, the girls' simultaneous heterosexual valorizations of boys' strength indicate their desirous attachments to racial difference and racialized fighting. Binary hetero-gender and desire for boys' protection is foreground, precluding homosexuality or queer desire, even precluding misperformed gender roles. But at the core of this narrative lives the inextricable articulation of racial difference and gender-sexual difference; they are primary investments and result in the particular gendered, sexual, and racial practices of the girls. They get reproduced through conscious and unconscious attachments, disavowals, fantasies: social-spatial contexts of constraint into which the girls' place themselves through their categorization and identification. It may be performative, that is reproduced in every instant through girls' social practices, but they are reproducing meanings and discourses with long historicities/spatialities of which the girls have no or limited consciousness. This does not make them dupes to their social situations, but it does place a pause on the too-celebratory possibilities of their sexual-gendered agency. That agency must be tempered with an understanding of its accompanying investments in racial difference, white American hegemony and supremacy, and misogyny and racism.

Conclusion

I have always been inspired by Cathy Cohen (1997), who warns that queer critiques of heterosexuality risk assuming that all straight people occupy a sexually privileged position (similarly, I have asked whether heterosexual African-American youth occupy such privilege, Thomas 2004; also Hubbard 2008; Oswin on Cohen in this volume, and 2008, 2010; also the special issue *Governing Intimacy* edited by Oswin and Olund 2010). Without explicitly theorizing racial, economic, and gender privilege and oppression, sexuality studies might just be occluding where and how its ability to make arguments about heteronormativity and queer geographies developed – and thus, there is a risk in establishing an exclusionary vision for sexuality studies as a normatively queer, white project. This risk of bringing the "new homonormativity" (Duggan 2001, 2003) to geography is possible, that is, because of white privilege and the racialized positions of those who fail to theorize whiteness, its class and other privileges, race/ethnicity in its function, and its historical/geographical genealogies. Natalie Oswin (2008) warns that the use of queer too often is read as "resistant" in geography, which has meant that identities and spaces of non-straights get implied as singularly anti-heterosexual. The "heroic" gays and lesbians' racialized exclusions, class biases and spaces, and other social-spatial locations are largely omitted (Oswin 2008: 91). They are never normative themselves, only resistant, in the simplistic maneuver to locate them singularly along a sexual binary (straight/queer: normative/resistant). Again, I think that is partly true because of the invisibility of whiteness within heteronormativity's Anglo-American gendered subject.

Ladelle McWhorter, in her excellent *Racism and Sexual Oppression in Anglo-America: A Genealogy* (2009), traces the normalization of whiteness in the US with the current civil rights-based LGBT movements for formal, state recognition (legalization of gay marriage being the best known and advertised version of this). By doing so, she asks, what is the cost of such movements, and how do they advance on the backs of white privilege? McWhorter shows that the focus on the family (forgive the pun) of queers in new civil rights movements is a history embedded in the eugenics movement. Of course, both eugenics and its post-war, pro-family movement "were direct descendants of modern scientific racism" (McWhorter 2009: 291; see also Sommerville 2000). Abnormality was created through the biopower of scientific racism, and McWhorter writes:

> Given the persistence of the eugenic dream after World War II, oppressed groups apparently had only two options: convince the general (white, middle-class, heterosexual) public that your people actually are normal by their standards (despite rumors and prejudice to the contrary), or attempt to broaden the prevailing concept of normality to accommodate the differences characteristic of members of your group. Either way, a lot would depend on whether you could demonstrate a commitment to the Normal Family – meaning middle-class white masculinity and femininity as well as licensed monogamy – and a desire to conform to the dictates of a capitalist ethic of work and consumption. (McWhorter: 319)

Attempts to deconstruct heteronormativity in geography must factor in white hegemony and how racial difference imbues sexual difference through and through, else they risk reinscribing white privilege. Critique in sexuality studies then remains an exercise in the hegemony of a liberal subject, supposedly capable of liberating itself from constraint (also Winnubst 2006).

References

Bell, D. and Binnie, J. (2004) Authenticating queer space: citizenship, urbanism and governance. *Urban Studies* 41 (9), 1807–1820.
Bonnett, A. (1997) Geography, "race" and Whiteness: invisible traditions and current challenges. *Area* 29 (3), 193–199.
Brown, G. (2009) Thinking beyond homonormativity: performative explorations of diverse gay economies. *Environment and Planning A* 41 (6), 1496–1510.
Brown, K., Lim, J., and Brown, G. (2007) (eds) *Geographies of Sexualities: Theory, Practices, and Politics*. Ashgate, Aldershot.
Brown, M., Knopp, L., and Morrill, R. (2005) The culture wars and urban electoral politics: sexuality, race, and class in Tacoma, Washington. *Political Geography* 24 (3), 267–291.
Brown, M. and Rasmussen, C. (2010) Bestiality and the queering of the human animal. *Environment and Planning D: Society and Space* 28 (1), 151–177.

Butler, J. (1990) *Gender Trouble: Feminism and the Subversion of Identity*. Routledge, London and New York.

Butler, J. (1993) *Bodies that Matter: On the Discursive Limits of "Sex"*. Routledge, London and New York.

Butler, J. (1997) *The Psychic Life of Power: Theories in Subjection*. Stanford University Press, Stanford.

Butz, D. and Berg, L.D. (2002) Paradoxical space: geography, men, and duppy feminism. In P. Moss (ed.), *Feminist Geography in Practice: Research and Methods*. Blackwell Press, Oxford, pp. 87–102.

Cheng, A. (2001) *The Melancholy of Race: Psychoanalysis, Assimilation, and Hidden Grief*. Oxford University Press, Oxford.

Cohen, C. (1997) Punks, bulldaggers, and welfare queens: the radical potential of queer politics? *GLQ* 3, 437–465.

Duggan, L. (2001) The New Homonormativity: The Sexual Politics of Neoliberalism. In D. Nelson and R. Castronovo (eds), *Materializing Democracy*. Duke University Press, Durham, pp. 175–194.

Duggan, L. (2003) *The Twilight of Equality: Neoliberalism, Cultural Politics, and the Attack on Democracy*. Beacon Press, Boston.

Eng, D. (2001) *Racial Castration: Managing Masculinity in Asian America*. Duke University Press, Durham.

Ferguson, R. (2005) Of our normative strivings: African American studies and the histories of sexuality. *Social Text* 23 (3–4), 85–100.

Gimenez, M. 2001. Marxism, and class, gender, and race: rethinking the trilogy. *Race, Gender and Class* 8 (2), 23.

Haritawan, J. (2007) Queer mixed race? Interrogating homonormativity through Thai interraciality. In K. Browne, J. Lim, and G. Brown (eds), *Geographies of Sexualities: Theory, Practices, and Politics*. Ashgate, Aldershot, pp. 101–111.

Hodge, G.D. (2000) Retrenchment from a queer ideal: class privilege and the failure of identity politics in AIDS activism. *Environment and Planning D: Society and Space* 18, 355–376.

Holmes, C. (2009) Destabilizing homonormativity and the public/private dichotomy in North American lesbian domestic violence discourses. *Gender, Place & Culture: A Journal of Feminist Geography* 16 (1), 77–95.

Hubbard, P. (2008) Here, there, everywhere: the ubiquitous geographies of heteronormativity. *Geography Compass* 2 (3), 640–658.

Kobayashi, A. (2003) GPC ten years on: is self-reflexivity enough? *Gender, Place, and Culture* 10 (4), 345–349.

McWhorter, L. (2009) *Racism and Sexual Oppression in Anglo-America: A Genealogy*. Indiana University Press, Bloomington.

Nagar, R. (2003) Collaboration across borders: moving beyond positionality. *Singapore Journal of Tropical Geography* 24 (3), 356–372.

Nagar, R. and Geiger, S. (2007) Reflexivity and positionality in feminist fieldwork revisited. In A. Tickell, E. Sheppard, J. Peck, and T. Barnes (eds), *Politics and Practice in Economic Geography*. Sage, London, pp. 267–278.

Nast, H. (2000) Mapping the "unconscious": racism and the Oedipal family. *Annals of the Association of American Geographers* 90 (2), 215–255.

Oswin, N. (2008) Critical geographies and the uses of sexuality: deconstructing queer space. *Progress in Human Geography* 32 (1), 89–103.

Oswin, N. (2010) The modern model family at home in Singapore: a queer geography. *Transactions of the Institute of British Geographers* 35 (2), 256–268.

Oswin, N. and Olund, E. (eds) (2010) Theme issue: Governing intimacy. *Environment and Planning D: Society and Space* 28 (1) 60–67.

Pratt, G. (2000) Research performances. *Environment and Planning D: Society and Space* 18 (5), 639–651.

Pulido, L. (2002) Reflections on a white discipline. *The Professional Geographer* 54 (1), 42–49.

Rich, A. (1980) Compulsory heterosexuality and lesbian existence. *Signs* 5 (4), 631–660.

Rose, G. (1997) Situating knowledges: positionality, reflexivities and other tactics. *Progress in Human Geography* 21 (3), 305–320.

Sommerville, S. (2000) *Queering the Color Line: Race and the Invention of Homosexuality in American culture*. Duke University Press, Durham.

Thomas, M.E. (2004) Pleasure and propriety: teen girls and the practice of straight space. *Environment and Planning D: Society and Space* 22 (5), 773–789.

Thomas, M.E. (2008) The paradoxes of personhood: banal multiculturalism and racial-ethnic identification among Latina and Armenian girls at a Los Angeles high school. *Environment and Planning A* 40 (12): 2864–2878.

Thomas, M.E. (2009) The identity politics of school life: territoriality and the racial subjectivity of teenage girls in LA. *Children's Geographies* 7 (1), 7–19.

Winnubst, S. (2006) *Queering Freedom*. Indiana University Press, Bloomington.

Chapter 35

Gender
Part I

Michael Landzelius

Introduction

Back in 1995, David Bell and Gill Valentine (1995: 18) wrote, in their introduction to *Mapping Desire: Geographies of Sexualities*, that "the presence of queer bodies in particular locations forces people to realize … that the space around them, … the city streets, the malls and the motels, have been *produced* as (ambiently) heterosexual, heterosexist and heteronormative." Referring to Judith Butler's (1995: 19) notion of performativity, they continued: "Only through the repetition of hegemonic heterosexual scripts … does space (become and) remain straight." Recently commenting upon this conception of heteronormative space and its possible queering, Natalie Oswin finds that it has "caught on," "become dominant" and been "rehearsed in prominent reviews" and "recent readers" in geography (Oswin 2008: 90–91; Oswin particularly refers to Bell and Valentine 1995; Binnie 1997; Bondi and Davidson 2004; Domosh 1999; Hubbard 2000; Phillips 2004; Valentine 2003).

In the most recent work on the topic, *Geographies of Sexualities: Theories, Practices and Politics*, published in 2009, editors Gavin Brown, Kath Browne and Jason Lim introduce the volume with addressing "the mutually constitutive relationships between sexualities, spaces and places." I will begin this chapter with a brief examination of what this "mutuality" is understood to entail close to 15 years after the publication of *Mapping Desire* (Bell and Valentine 1995). I have chosen this up-to-date introduction by Brown, Browne, and Lim since they do claim to "provide an overview of the major strands of thought comprising the field" and to "explore the development of its most important concepts" (2009: 1). I will then proceed to discuss the understanding of this mutuality in relation to the ambiguous notions of space present in its conceptualization. This discussion will then be continued through a slightly more extensive engagement with a few recent articles selectively chosen to illustrate my points of criticism. This critique should not be read as a denial of "the possibilities of multiple ways of thinking about and doing geographies of sexualities" (Brown, Browne, and Lim 2009: 18), but as an argument that geographers need both to further articulate what space is all about in their work on sex, sexuality, and gender, and to engage with presently forgotten or taken-for-granted aspects of space.

Exactly what then, do the "mutually constitutive relationships between sexualities, spaces and places" boil down to according to Brown, Browne, and Lim? First, and in general, they state that "everyday spaces are produced through embodied social practices" (2009: 2). Thus the expressive presence of sexualized bodies produces accordingly sexualized spaces. Second, they note that such practices are supported by norms that range from "direct political and social injunctions" (2009: 3) to "unspoken understandings" enforced through informal means (2009: 2). Third, they identify other norms on "other scales of spatiality, including national, international and transnational spaces," giving heteronormative enactment of US migration legislation as an example (2009: 3). Fourth, they discuss a wider social "moral economy that becomes expressed as an imagined geography" which through legislation as well as practice comes to solidify as an "institutionalization" of "the power to define who belongs and to define what bodies are allowed to do, when and where" (2009: 4). Fifth, not forgetting the question of contestation and agency, Brown, Browne, and Lim note that "activities such as cottaging (that is public sex in toilet spaces) suggest that it is always possible to follow the desire to do something differently" (2009: 5). They sum up with writing that: "What we do makes the spaces and places we inhabit, just as the spaces we inhabit provide an active and constitutive context that shapes our actions, interactions and identities," and this counts equally much for "[a] home, a nation, a bathroom, a workplace" (2009: 4). Still in the present, through these forms and processes of mutuality and despite growing political dissent and contestations, heteronormativity is reproduced and "allows heterosexuality to go unmarked and unremarked upon" (2009: 8).

There is thus still after 15 years extensive overlap between *Mapping Desire* and *Geographies of Sexualities*. The shared basic notion is that spaces are produced through practices regulated by norms and scripts yet contested and reshaped by performances of doing things differently. Although I sympathize with this and with the Brown, Browne, and Lim-account of mutuality, I do have a number of reservations. I will not dwell on the problem related to the notion of scale, just note that Brown, Browne, and Lim contradictorily seem to conceive of scales as a number of differently sized boxes beginning with the everyday (or the body?), while simultaneously arguing that, for example, it is the heteronormative enactment in everyday situations that produce the national as well as international, which thus make also these "scales" into scales of the everyday. The debate in geography over the last decade suggests that 'scaling' is a more relevant concept, while it may well need to be understood as a process that also involves sexing, sexualizing, and gendering.

To introduce my following discussion, I here wish to note the ambiguity and polysemy of 'space' in the account by Brown, Browne, and Lim. They importantly stress norms of various kinds and degrees of institutionalization as regulating spaces; making spaces what they are through the practices they enable and constrain. Such norms range from meticulously explicated legislation to constitutive but unarticulated codes we did not know we held until confronted with misplaced abhorrent others. Yet what do they imply by 'space' when they talk about spaces such as "home," "nation," "bathroom," "workplace," "international," "transnational"? While all of these 'spaces' quite obviously (for someone influenced by years of scholarship in the field) are dependent upon discursive and other kinds of imaginary components related to sex, sexuality, and gender, what about the material? Both 'home' and 'bathroom' definitely seem to have material referents, but can, for example, the territoriality of a nation-state be understood in similar material terms? And what kind of space is a 'nation' in relation to a 'nation-state,' etc? Hence, do these terms refer to entities with qualitatively similar characteristics with regard to discursive, imaginary and material components or are they radically different from one another? What consequences would radical difference between them have for how the sexualizing (sexing, sexualizing, gendering) of these 'spaces' and the humans constituting as well as interacting within and across them can be understood and theorized?

Rather than further explore these questions based on the brief introduction by Brown, Browne, and Lim – which would be unfair given the short space of their introduction – I will continue with a discussion of some recent articles on geographies of sex, sexuality, and gender. I wish to stress that the examples discussed are chosen because I have found them important and rewarding, yet also ambiguous, polysemic, and ultimately unsatisfactory in their use and understanding of 'space,' and hence deeply problematic with regard to how the 'mutuality' between space, sex, sexuality, and gender is presented.

Sexualized Spaces in Geographies of Sexualities?

I wish to begin, however, with a slightly closer look at Bell and Valentine's notion of the sexual production of space. They explicitly distance themselves from "a commonsense notion that space is unencumbered," which would mean that "any sexual identity can assume space, and space can assume any sexual identity" (Bell and Valentine 1995: 18). When they state their position in positive terms, they write that the space around us, "the landscape ... , the city streets, the malls and the motels, have been *produced* as (ambiently) heterosexual, heterosexist and heteronormative" and "this heterosexing of space is a performative act naturalized through repetition – and destabilized by the mere presence of invisibilized sexualities" (1995: 18). So what we learn is that the sexualizing of space takes place through the practices and performances carried out there. Here, 'space' indeed refers to material entities: landscape (although its ontological status is a matter of long-term debate in cultural geography and may to some exist only in the eyes of the beholder), streets, malls, motels. To destabilize and effect changes of such spaces then becomes a matter of performing other sexual identities than those prescribed by heteronormativity. Yet while Bell and Valentine seemingly stress the "produced" character of urban spaces, I contend that they actually talk about performances, and not spaces, as "heterosexual, heterosexist and heteronormative." If the mere presence of performances of a different kind can change the sexuality of space (in this case: landscapes, streets, malls, motels), there is nothing about sexuality that adheres to space unless the implied notion of 'space' is 'human bodies'. Such a limited and confounded understanding is confirmed in their choice of qualifier: 'ambience' refers to the mood and atmosphere perceived in an environment, and thus refers back to the same 'human bodies' that perceive and perform. The question of the possibly sexualized characteristics and workings of those built forms they actually refer to is hence completely evaded, although it superficially appears to be addressed. Having "ambiently" added within parentheses may thus seem like a clarification, but is rather a qualifier that adds ambiguity and provides for an evasion of the question of any possible sexualizing of space beyond ambience-producing performances. So when they state that "space has both material and symbolic components" (Bell and Valentine 1995: 18), it remains unclear particularly how the sexualizing of the former component comes about.

Yet in the context of geography we may assume that the notion of "hegemonic heterosexual scripts," which Bell and Valentine (1995: 19) pick up from Butler (1993), includes; institutionalized norms and legislation that constrain destabilizing performances. Such scripts would contribute to produce spaces as heterosexual before performances take place there (because they would result from heteronormative performances elsewhere, such as in legislative bodies, etc.), and thus precede and enable the production of, for example, ambience in a particular space. These terms thus contextually refer to multiple dimensions of space (or in other words, to different complexly linked time-geographies). This is of course clear also from the literature on the manifold social and spatial struggles against heteronormativity and strategies involved in the production of non-heterosexual spaces, particularly gay neighborhoods (see Davis 1995; Lauria and Knopp 1985; Nash 2005, 2006). Yet these aspects are not theoretically disentangled and articulated but rather confounded in Bell and Valentine. They thus, I contend, basically end up with a container theory of space and some sort of performative voluntarism with regard to the effects they claim that bodies can have on the spaces they occupy. Spaces are, I contend, in a much stronger sense than the term 'ambiently' implies, produced according to a specific sexual normativity.

In his review of "the post-millennial literature on sexuality and space," Phil Hubbard summarizes that "questions of sex and desire infuse all manner of spaces" (2008: 641). He further states that heteronormative "expectations" are "inscribed" in spaces (2008: 643). Yet what he actually describes is that such expectations are held by those individuals or groups that dominate the spaces in question. And when he discusses performances that resist the heterosexual, he asserts that they "grate or gratify on the space in which they occur" (2008: 651), while the literature he refers to possibly show how such performances "grate" on those other humans co-present in space. Again when he contrasts heterosexual spaces with "the creation of increasingly visible gay spaces," the decisive difference assumed is simply one of occupation. In Hubbard's vocabulary, terms such as 'inscription,' 'creation,' and 'grating' are in relation to space ambiguous and either misleading metaphors or inverted synecdoches (the whole is claimed to be represented while only a part is addressed). The examples he gives have nothing to do with the production *of* space, but everything to do with the presence of particular groups *in* space understood as container. I would argue that it is only in passing, such as when Hubbard (2008: 646), talks about the reproduction of heteronormativity in relation to how "[o]vert policies of zoning and licensing hence exclude brothels, lap dancing, clubs and sex shops from the proximity of educational establishments," that he begins to come close to an embryonic spatial theorizing which includes a notion of mediation between bodies, norms, and material spaces.

Approaching his conclusion, Hubbard (2008: 653) states that "it is impossible to talk of heterosexual spaces *per se*, with such spaces being constituted through *practice*." What does 'practice' entail here? This is an important question because there is a series of practices involved in making "heterosexual spaces," many of which most people (seemingly including too many geographers) would not think of as (hetero)sexual but which nonetheless would definitely be heteronormative. The constitution of space through practice must hence be understood to include, not only "zoning and licensing" (which Hubbard touches upon but does not articulate), but also the normative acts of planning and design, as well as the final building of space as structured material configuration (see Dovey 1999; Landzelius 1999; Markus 1993; Rendell *et al.* 2000). Yet for Hubbard it seems that heterosexual space becomes just that when heterosexuals practice their sexuality in that particular space. That very same space would become homosexual if instead homosexuals practiced their sexuality in that same space. Et cetera: "After all, all manner of sexual practices are possible in different spaces" (Hubbard 2008: 653; note that this assertion equals the commonsense idea that Bell and Valentine verbally distance themselves from). In this view a space is an empty container waiting to be filled with sexuality by being occupied. A formative presence of sex, sexuality, and gender issues in other forms of space-constituting practices is nowhere touched upon in Hubbard's account of geographies of heteronormativity.

Queering Space in Geography?

Kath Browne, one of the editors of *Geographies of Sexualities*, has in a series of articles sought to queer geography and go beyond the "dominant" position, to use Oswin's term. In an article on the tensions between geographies of sexualities and queer geographies, Browne suggests that "queer enquiries ... entail radical (re)thinkings, (re)drawings, (re)conceptualizations, (re)mappings that could (re)make bodies, spaces and geographies" and thus push beyond established (and not only sexual) normativities. Queering space, she says, "would enable the radical reconstellation of spaces (the ways spaces do not have to come together to reform the dualism of man/woman, heterosexual/homosexual" (Browne 2006: 888). I quote this approvingly, yet what is 'space' in her notion of radical reconstellation? In her concluding comments on the "project" of queer geographies, Browne writes: "What comes to mind specifically are the queer transgressions, performative slippages and 'failures' that can be read in the betweeness (sic) of everyday spaces, places and lives" (2006: 891). It seems clear that Browne's notion of queering as well as that of space remains within the limits of performativity; queering takes place "*in* the *between*ness of everyday spaces." This notion of queering refers back to the human bodies involved in performances, while space is simply something these bodies are *in*; a container.

This is confirmed in an article by Browne on the heterosexualizing of everyday space and nonheterosexual women's experiences of being othered in restaurant spaces. Building on performativity theory, Browne stresses the "productiveness of practice beyond identity politics" (2007: 1004) and understands "the sexing of space as in a constant process of becoming" (2007: 1011). Thus she explicitly distances her own approach from a notion of spaces as "vessels within which performances occur" (2007: 1000). Again, I quote this approvingly. In discussing heteronormativity's impact upon the nonheterosexual women in her study, she notes that their restaurant experiences were dependent upon both their own age-dependent embodied time-geographies and the time-geographies of "mealtimes." Hence, "compulsory heterosexuality … is not as pronounced on weeknights" (2007: 1008), while on the other hand restaurant spaces are being produced as "hyperheterosexual" on Valentine's Day (2007: 1009). This can indeed be seen as "a constant process of becoming." Yet in what sense is what space here being sexualized? Browne does not want to "imply a lack of material manifestations of power" but rather stresses "the congealed materialities of power" (2007: 998); and contends that "power relations and networks (re)constitute materialities" (2007: 1000). She notes that "normative heterosexuality is (re)produced both materially and discursively"; and concludes that she "has sought to (re)place the spatial materialities and networks of power as persistent and congealing" (2007: 1012). As the last coupling "spatial materialities" makes clear Browne does link her notion of 'space' with one of 'materiality' as well as with the production of sexualized spaces with the materialities of power.

Yet nowhere is this notion of spatial materiality articulated, neither with regard to ways in which it is sexed, nor in terms of its components and how they take on normative powers in general, etc. The article by Browne does nowhere address differences between restaurant settings other than in terms of social and temporal differences and how those impact upon performances. How does a seemingly simple thing like available table-sizes affect, spatially distribute, and effect for example, heteronormative prescriptions of romantic love and hetero- as well as homo-normativities of sexual coupledom? Just as much as a human body, a table is an affective materialization, and these entities are in a restaurant forced to be conjoined with one another in an assemblage of, not a universal but an indeed particular kind. Given that performances are embodied, they are of course material, but restricting the notion of "spatial materialities" to bodies alone would be to trivialize the mediated relationality between bodies and spaces. Despite her introductory distancing from a notion of space as vessel, Browne treats spatial materialities as exactly that, unarticulated neutral containers "within which performances occur."

The same holds for an interesting article by Browne which addresses the question of women's separatist spaces in a discussion of the practices of and controversies around the Michigan Womyn's Music Festival (Michfest). Michfest is exclusively for "womyn-born womyn, that is, womyn who were born as and have lived their entire life experience as womyn," in the words of founder Lisa Vogel (quoted in Browne 2009: 548). Not surprisingly, the festival is "in trans studies and queer literatures … commonly used as an example of essentialist thinking … and trans oppression, because it does not recognize trans women as womyn" (Browne 2009:

542). Browne situates the controversies around Michfest in the context of "poststructural feminist enquiries" where "lesbian, radical and separatist feminisms ... are often caricatured as the "extreme" forms of "essentialist" feminism based on dubious fixed bodies/biologies that offer equally essentialist notions of women, patriarchy, men and male power" (Browne 2009: 542). In the midst of such controversies, Browne's article is about how spaces such as Michfest can have and indeed does have positive, reparative effects of both pleasure and amelioration on the womyn who attend, and ends "without proscribing and predicting" (Browne 2009: 552) what alternative spaces should look like. One might note that such a (non-)position fits well with Oswin's notion of "a queer approach that has no fixed political referent" (Oswin 2008: 96).

Browne writes that "thousands of womyn travel to the festival each year, creating a space (re)formed with reference to specific feminist separatist ideals" (2009: 544). This notion of "creating a space" is in her analysis limited to the social and performative. This is indeed legitimate in a heteropatriarchal world where, as one festival participant says "we have to wait for a whole year to be free and respected for one week" (Browne 2009: 546). Yet when Browne does refer to the materiality – rather than performativity – of Michfest space, it is only in passing: "designed, built, run and loved by women" (2009: 542); or in parenthesis: "(a 'long' crew builds and removes the festival over a period of three months ...)" (2009: 544); or with a hint of biased surprise that women can indeed trespass conventional boundaries of gendered skills: "The 'village' of Michfest materializes literally over the course of the summer and is maintained by womyn (from car maintenance and a fully functioning kitchen, to three stages built with sound and lighting)" (2009: 546). Given that Browne critically notes both that "paranoid ways of thinking about womyn's separatist spaces has limited the possibilities for considering these spaces," and that "geographical analyses of contemporary feminist separatist spaces have not developed," I find it surprising that her own 'geographical' analysis of Michfest space remains within the limits of social performativity. What is 'spatial' in her analysis? Simply noting the spatial fact of perimeter separatism, Browne again drops spatial questions once inside the perimeter.

In these geographies, the lack of attention to the multiple dimensions of the spatial, including space as structured material configuration, also makes it difficult to articulate the spatiality of those norms of various kinds that regulate spaces. The odd thing here is that such norms are identified as important by Brown, Browne, and Lim (2009). Hence, addressing sexing, sexualizing, and gendering, one needs to have a clearly articulated notion of various aspects and dimensions of space, including materiality, in order to theorize how different norms with different forms and degrees of institutionalization adhere to and constitute material spaces as well as human bodies and thus affect (and possibly effect) both heteronormative and oppositional performances. While it is obvious that Michfest spatially results from the controversial imposition of an exclusionary "womyn-born-womyn-norm," there is no discussion in Browne's text of the existence, or lack thereof, of norms within the perimeter that regulate the constitution of space in such a fashion as to make attending womyn perform differently (in distinction to separately). The problem remains, I contend, in another text by Browne which addresses nonheterosexual women's experiences of being "read as men in toilets" (Browne 2004: 331). The abuse of and reactions against these nonheterosexual women by other guests as well as bouncers in bars and clubs in her analysis tends to be reduced to individualized encounters between performers which through such encounters uphold and/or destabilize heteronormative space: "Genderism can be defined as the discriminatory encounters individuals experience when they are read as the opposite sex than the one they identify with or are 'read' as out of place in sites that are single sexed" (Browne 2004: 342–343). I suggest that genderism needs to be articulated as a more complex spatial issue that perhaps begins with the legislative and/or regulative imposition of norms, not "*in* sites that *are* single sexed," but in elsewhere situated practices (Pred 1990) that *produce* material sites *as*, that *make* them *become* already through their configuration, single sexed.

Sexing, Sexualizing, and Gendering of Bodies and Spaces

In 1974, long before geographies of sexualities became a field in Anglo-American academia, Henri Lefebvre (1991: 410) asked: "Is a final metamorphosis called for that will reverse all earlier ones, destroying phallic space and replacing it with a 'uterine' space?" In choosing the word 'destroy,' Lefebvre implies that phallic space is not replaced by uterine space by simply performing differently *in* space. In talking about a 'metamorphosis' of space, he does definitely not understand the shift from phallic to uterine as something related only to a queering of bodies, or to the replacement of one group or normativity with another ("Were such a movement to take the form of a feminine 'racism' which merely inverted the masculine version, it would be a pity" (1991: 410)). 'Metamorphosis' should in relation to space be understood in a stronger sense in terms of "a complete change of form, structure, or substance," to quote Webster's. For Lefebvre, what is now discussed in geography in terms of sex, sexuality, gender, and queer, is not first and foremost about non-heterosexual or queer performances *in* a space left untouched, but to engage entirely different sets of norms as well as different forms of sexed, sexualized, and gendered performances in the production *of* space including its dimension as structured material configuration. This complex configuration of spatiality, Lefebvre implies, is in need of being transformed from phallic to uterine.

In such a view, the question of sexing, sexualizing, and gendering space is not simply about those sexed, sexualized, and gendered practices/performances that take place in a particular space, but just as much about those practices in political, legislative, and planning bodies, architectural offices, etc., etc., that through the imposition of various kinds of norms and regulations constitute that space in a particular fashion. The metamorphosis Lefebvre imagines concerns all these dimensions of space. Taking Lefebvre seriously, this time-geographical layering of very different kinds of practices and performances needs to be researched as potentially sexed, sexualized, and gendered throughout its different stages, all including both imaginary and material components. This complexity is, I contend, unsatisfactorily considered and articulated in geographies of sexualities as well as in queer geographies. While Blum and Nast, in their discussion of the presumed heterosexualization of alterity in Lefebvre, claim that in his text "*structurally* female agency is foreclosed" and "*practically* such exclusion winds up rejecting everyday forms of nonmasculinist agency" (1996: 577), I would hold that Lefebvre's argument goes far beyond restricted notions of agency and needs to be taken seriously in any consideration of the sexing, sexualizing, and gendering of space.

In her notion of performativity, Butler stresses that heteronormative interpellations present even in grammar and beginning in childhood, come to shape an individual's sexuality and gender in ways that have deep both psychological and embodied impact: "a process of materialization that stabilizes over time to produce the effect of boundary, fixity, and surface we call matter" (Butler 1993: 9). For someone homosexual to come out of the closet or for someone straight to become queer are hence not simple issues, regardless of our positions with regard to the influence of the performative versus what is given by nature. Butler assures her reader that there are "sexually differentiated parts, activities, capacities, hormonal and chromosomal differences," yet stresses that "there is no reference to a pure body which is not at the same time a further formation of that body" (1993: 10). This rather complex notion of Butler's with regard to how long-term reiterated interpellations come to shape sex, sexuality, and gender with regard to the material, mental, and emotional realm of the body, or, in other terms, the actual material territorializations of the body through striation of intensities, prefigured sensitivities and reactions (Deleuze and Guattari 1987: 149–166; see also Lim 2009), are strangely wanting in sexual and queer geographies' treatment of space. As I have sought to show above, what we see is rather a voluntarist notion of spatiality where space as material entity supposedly immediately changes sex, sexuality, and gender simply because humans perform in non-heteronormative fashion, as if making, for example, queer into a verb in discourse and ascribing it to space would suddenly make hundreds of years of phallic norms and material layering's something entirely different.

In order to push the point I am seeking to make here about a homological (rather than analogical) relationship between bodies and spaces, and thus ways in which they may/should be theorized, it is necessary to slightly more extensively address the distinctions between sex, sexuality and gender. The conventional notion in patriarchy is that "[n]ature or sex is causally determinative of gender" (Chanter 2006: 16). This idea of causality has been extensively critiqued, and in his recent companion entry on sexuality in geographical studies, for example, Richard Phillips (2004: 263) notes that sexuality and gender are "complex and interrelated," but that "[p]ut simply, a person's sex is defined by their anatomy as male or female, whereas their gender is defined with reference to the social roles they learn and perform as men or women." This distinction is similar to Rosi Braidotti's in her important work on sexual difference in feminist theory:

> Sexual difference is ontological, not accidental, peripheral, or contingent upon socio-economic conditions; that one be socially constructed as a female is evident, that the recognition of the fact may take place in language is clear, but that the process of construction of femininity fastens and builds upon anatomical realities is equally true. (Braidotti 1994: 186–187)

From a queer position, one might note here that the constative claims of male/female and men/women in the Phillips-quote performatively reiterate and naturalize binarism in terms of both an ontology of nature (sex as the anatomy of either male or female), and an ontology of the social (gender as either man or woman). Braidotti, with regard to the particular quote here, stays free of such criticism since "sexual difference" can include any such difference, and since her focus on the "construction of femininity" does not exclude a focus on the construction of any other gender position.

However, sex and sexuality can not be equated with one another, and none of them have a simple relationship to gender. A heterosexual male person and a homosexual male person obviously share the same sex in the sense of being anatomically similar, yet just as obviously they differ with regard to sexuality (although e.g. psychoanalysis and queer theory may explain this difference in incommensurable terms). In addition, the difference from the role prescribed by heteronormativity is played out very differently for a homosexual man being in the 'right,' body and for a transsexual wo/man being in the 'wrong' body. Thus a heterosexual man and a homosexual man would share the same sex, may share gender, but would differ with regard to sexuality. Whereas a transsexual wo/man would have the same sex as a heterosexual man but differ with regard to both sexuality and gender; and would, for example, instead share sexuality with a heterosexual woman while his/her gender might be fluid. Et cetera. Some of these issues are illustrated in Browne's research on gender ambiguous bodies and the policing of sexed spaces (2004). I wish to stress here that these simplified examples are only intended to indicate the complexities involved in queer theorizations and to show that sex can not in any simple fashion be seen as having a causal or any other fixed relation to sexuality or gender (see apart from Butler, also Herdt 1994, Roughgarden 2004).

From a queer point of view, not only heteronormativity but any stable and specific coupling – in theory, practice, or both – between sex, sexuality, and gender may become an "orthodoxy" (Browne 2006: 889) or "normativity" (Oswin 2008: 92, 98), and thus an element of an oppressive sexual economy. That which is taken to be "queer" now "may not remain so queer," as Browne writes (2006: 889), and hence there is indeed a need of "turning attention to the advancement of a critical approach to the workings of sexual normativities and non-normativities" (Oswin 2008: 96). What I wish to proceed with, then, is to consider how such a queer deconstruction and disentanglement of patriarchal heteronormative causality with regard to the human body and the complex that we now conceive of as differentiated in terms of sex, gender, and sexuality (but which could well be thought of in other terms of differentiation), affects how one in a homological fashion might conceive of 'space.'

Spaces as Structured Material Configurations

I wish to suggest here that in attempts to queer geography, the ongoing deconstruction of patriarchal notions and rearticulation of the sex-gender-sexuality-complex has corresponded to a regrettable disarticulation of the spatial and a reduction of the spatial to a matter of vocabulary rather than theory (a problem observable also in other branches of human geography). One might think of Latour's critique of social science and the taken-for-granted collector 'society' and its, to simplify, simultaneous role as explanatory concept, name of an ontological domain, as well as cause and effect of so-called 'social' phenomena (Latour 2005). The black box of 'space' is just as elusive in much human geography.

Commenting on the work of Bell and Valentine, Richard Phillips writes:

> Material spaces become 'humanized' as spaces of community and identity in the course of individuals' and communities' encounters with and in them. More than simply material geographies, these places acquire meaning as they are reflected in the formation of personal and collective memories, bodily displays and performances, desires and fantasies. (Phillips 2004: 269)

Indeed much more than "simply material geographies" places are contrary to Phillips' assertion not passively 'reflected' in memories. I have myself always found material spaces to actively enable and constrain my life! How can material spaces 'become' humanized? Are they not *already* humanized since they are built by humans according to specific norms for particular human purposes? Was not that what Lefebvre articulated so well decades ago and which more recently has been rehearsed as "more-than-human-assemblages" in terms influenced by Latour as well as Deleuze and Guattari? However, Phillips does better further down in his piece where he actually does address the materiality of space in relation to sexualizing. With suburbia as example he writes:

> Yet these places are sexualized in important ways – they are identified with normalized heterosexuality. Heterosexual spaces may reproduce the hegemonic (dominant) sexual order, both ideologically by making this construction of sexuality and the power relations inherent in it appear natural; and materially by physically accommodating and therefore encouraging or enforcing certain heterosexual lifestyles. (Phillips 2004: 273)

While "identified with normalized heterosexuality" points to imaginary components of a sexualized spatiality, the coupling "physically ... enforcing" represents a norm-independent notion of material sexual causality. Yet to argue the latter point, Phillips would need to show that other sexualities or normativities could not give rise to the same material space. Is that possible? "In its apparent infinite versatility," Chanter notes, "capitalism functions in a way that adapts both to patriarchy and to racism" (2006: 33–34). Chanter restricts herself to argue that capitalism "reproduces itself at the material level by ensuring a continued supply of workers, and by relying on an unacknowledged source of labor in the form of [women's] housework" (2006: 38). But could one not argue that heteronormative, patriarchal, family-based capitalism is indeed inscribed in the design of houses and apartments as well as urban and regional planning schemes? (see for example Hayden 1981; Kohn 2003; Rendell *et al.* 2000; Wright 1981). That would support Phillips' claim. Hence, we find kitchens in every house/apartment (no idea of sharing meals outside of the family household); small bedrooms (machines for sleeping only); and a *master* bedroom with a *king*-size bed (where language speaks of heterosexual male power) for family-based procreation rather than mutual lust. Such spaces do indeed duplicate as structured material configurations the sexual and moral economy of heteronormativity and patriarchal capitalism. Commenting on US postwar development, professor of architecture Joan Ockman writes:

In a society that sought simultaneously to promote maximum productivity and maximum consumption, the public and private spheres had separate but complementary roles to play. Architecture served to reproduce and reinforce this gendered social division. (Ockman 1996: 204)

Take in this context a term such as 'housewife.' It is not only a patriarchal and heteronormative construct in discourse, but needs – in particular in human geography – to be understood literally as a more-than-human assemblage which indeed makes the house and the wife connected in space as a conjoined structured material configuration, an assemblage. Dolores Hayden notes that "capitalism and antifeminism fused in campaigns for homeownership and mass consumption" (2000: 267) that promoted "the construction of isolated, overprivatized, energy-consuming dwellings … which maximized appliance purchases" (2000: 268). This spatial material configuration of suburbia was in addition built around car dependency (Walker 1981) which facilitated gendered patterns of (non)mobility. Such accounts indicate that we face a situation where the more-than-human world we inhabit from its conception and erection (to use sexual metaphors) is sexed, sexualized and gendered from overarching material structures down to the smallest gadgets. Yet is Phillips' phrase "enforcing certain heterosexual lifestyles" a correct notion of material suburbia-causality?

Following Diane Richardson I would argue that this is a more complex affair. She makes a convincing argument in an article on neoliberal politics and forms of normalization of lesbians and gay men in relation to established practices of heteronormative society. Richardson argues that lesbians and gay men are accepted as long as they "adopt sexual practices … associated with a certain (heteronormative) lifestyle" by "demonstrating a specific form of 'domestic' sexual coupledom" (2005: 521). They are then offered a place within those new modes of (self-)governance in neoliberal society that emerge with the rolling back of the state and related shift towards citizens as consumers. That such "assimilationist politics" indeed have been favored by "many mainstream gay and lesbian organizations," is noted also by Oswin (2008: 92). The problem with this form of inclusion, writes Richardson, is that it interprets "equality through similitude" in relation to established heteronormativity and thus "that a particular version of what it is to be lesbian or gay (as well as heterosexual) is privileged" (Richardson 2005: 520). With regard to my argument here and the quote from Phillips above, what Richardson's discussion indicates is that a certain way of configuring built space – including both overarching urban planning patterns and individual housing units – may in a specific historical conjunction be simultaneously both outcome and generator of patriarchal heteronormativity, while in a later conjunction (in this case the present) the same spatial configurations may result from a sexual normativity where the borders between hetero and homo have been downplayed or even erased, while the norm of domestic sexual coupledom is retained and reinforced for (homo- as well as heterosexuals) as an instrument for both social and spatial inclusion/exclusion. It thus seems difficult to hold on even to a view that the spatial configuration of suburbia, up until the present a spatial icon of patriarchal heteronormativity, uniquely supports or results from a heterosexual lifestyle.

Although both Phillips' and Richardson's arguments have a bearing on the points I am trying to make here, I suggest that the above discussion supports the claim that neither geographies of sexualities nor queer geographies presently display any articulated notion of what is meant by 'space' in terms of its multiple dimensions and their interrelations, nor account for spaces as structured material configurations that – just like interpellated human bodies – in themselves need to be theorized and understood as sexed, gendered, and sexualized, and upon which, for example, queering should thus also have material effects.

Conclusion

Bodies and spaces importantly need to be understood as conjoined affective materializations. It seems that some old concepts and discussions in spatial science of how material space enables and constrains ought to be central – although theorized differently and hence not fetishized – for understanding how space affects what happens and can happen between sexed, sexualized, and gendered individuals, regardless of sexual preferences. Do not 'proximity' and 'distance' as well as 'friction of distance' and maybe a neologism such as 'lubrication of movement' sit well with conjoined affectivity? While institutionalized norms increase the friction of distance for "both homosexual and heterosexual new immigrants who exist outside the institution of marriage and the nuclear family" who seek entry to the US (Oswin 2008: 100; see also Brown, Browne, and Lim 2009: 3), other norms facilitate a lubrication of movement for other migrants such as sex workers, often illegal and often likewise outside of the institution of marriage, that satisfy needs shaped by heteronormativity. In both cases, corresponding material spaces emerge of, for example, repetitive migratory chains and marginal abodes of heteronormative oppression. Such chains and abodes are neither homes, nations, bathrooms or workplaces, to again refer to Brown, Browne, and Lim, yet do nonetheless "provide an active and constitutive context that shapes our actions, interactions and identities" (2009: 4). And while I have myself articulated differences neither between 'nation' and 'bathroom,' nor between 'space' and 'landscape,' in any comprehensive fashion in this chapter, I hope that my discussion has shown that queer geographies as well as geographies of sexualities need to develop an understanding of space in terms as complex as those deployed in, for example, disentangling patriarchal heteronormative notions of causality between sex, sexuality, and gender.

Hence if sex is about anatomy, would there not be a corresponding spatial term such as 'earthbound materiality' (cf. Merchant 1980); if gender concerns social roles, the corresponding term would reasonably be the already established 'social space,' or as some prefer, 'spatiality,' and if sexuality concerns the embodiment of desires, preferences, intensities and energies resulting from continuous interpellations, the corresponding spatial term would, I suggest, be 'structured material configuration.' Space particularly in the latter sense is surprisingly often treated as a 'black box' in geographical accounts, or reduced to a matter of aesthetics and symbolism (cf. my critique of Harvey in Landzelius 2009: 48–49). And with regard to interpellation and mediation between discourse, norms, other imaginary components and the material; what are spatial legislative measures, by-laws, urban planning proposals, planning regulations, neighborhood protests, briefs in architectural competitions, architectural designs, etc., etc., if not forms of interpellations that produce material space as simultaneously structured and structuring – sexed, sexualized, and gendered

– from its infancy to its ultimate death in face of capitalism's creative destruction? The concept of 'space' hence needs to be articulated much more fully, and, in short, queer theory needs to be transposed into a queer geography that relates the complex human embodiment of sex, sexuality, and gender, to a just as complexly understood and articulated production of space.

References

Bell, D. and Valentine, G. (eds) (1995) *Mapping Desire: Geographies of Sexualities*. Routledge, London.
Binnie, J. (1997) Coming out of geography: towards a queer epistemology. *Environment and Planning D: Society and Space* 15, 223–237.
Blum, V. and Nast, H. (1996) Where's the difference? The heterosexualization of alterity in Henri Lefebvre and Jacques Lacan, *Environment and Planning D: Society and Space* 14, 559–580.
Bondi, L. and Davidson, J. (2004) Situating gender. In L. Nelson and J. Seager (eds), *A Companion to Feminist Geography*. Blackwell, Oxford.
Braidotti, R. (1994) *Nomadic Subjects*. Columbia University Press, New York.
Brown, G., Browne, K., and Lim, J. (2009) Introduction, or Why have a book on geographies of sexualities. In G. Brown, K. Browne, and J. Lim (eds), *Geographies of Sexualities*. Ashgate, Aldershot, pp. 1–20.
Browne, K. (2004) Genderism and the bathroom problem: (re)materializing sexed sites, (re)creating sexed bodies. *Gender, Place and Culture* 11, 331–346.
Browne, K. (2006) Challenging queer geographies. *Antipode*, 38, 885–893.
Browne, K. (2007) (Re)making the other, heterosexualising everyday space. *Environment and Planning A* 39, 996–1014.
Browne, K. (2009) Womyn's separatist spaces: rethinking spaces of difference and exclusion. *Transactions of the Institute of British Geographers* 34, 541–556.
Butler, J. (1993) *Bodies that Matter. On the Discursive Limits of "Sex"*. Routledge, London.
Chanter, T. (2006) *Gender*. Continuum, London.
Davis, T. (1995) The diversity of queer politics and the redefinition of sexual identity and community in urban spaces. In D. Bell, and G. Valentine (eds), *Mapping Desire*. Routledge, London, pp. 284–303.
Deleuze, G. and Guattari, F. (1987) *A Thousand Plateaus: Capitalism and Schizophrenia*. University of Minnesota Press, Minneapolis.
Domosh, M. (1999) Sexing feminist geography. *Progress in Human Geography* 23, 429–436.
Dovey, K. (1999) *Framing Places: Mediating Power in Built Form*. Routledge, London.
Hayden, D. (1981) *The Grand Domestic Revolution: A History of Feminist Designs for American Homes, Neighborhoods, and Cities*. The MIT Press, Cambridge.
Hayden, D. (2000) What would a non-sexist city be like? Speculations on housing, urban design, and human work. In J. Rendell, B. Penner, and I. Borden (eds), *Gender, Space, Architecture: An Interdisciplinary Introduction*, Routledge, London, pp. 266–281. [Originally published in *Women and the American City*, Chicago University Press, 1981.]
Herdt, G. (ed.) (1994) *Third Sex, Third Gender: Beyond Sexual Dimorphism in Culture and History*. Zone Books, New York.
Hubbard, P. (2000) Desire/disgust: mapping the moral contours of heterosexuality. *Progress in Human Geography* 24, 191–217.

Hubbard, P. (2008) Here, there, everywhere: the ubiquitous geographies of heteronormativity. *Geography Compass* 2/3, 640–658.

Kohn, M. (2003) *Radical Space: Building the House of the People*. Cornell University Press, Ithaca, New York.

Landzelius, M. (1999) *Dis(re)membering Spaces: Swedish Modernism in Law Courts Controversy*. Gothenburg University, Gothenburg.

Landzelius, M. (2009) Spatial reification, or, collectively embodied amnesia, aphasia, and apraxia. *Semiotica* 175, 39–75.

Lauria, M. and Knopp, L. (1985) Toward an analysis of the role of gay communities in the urban renaissance. *Urban Geography* 6, 152–169.

Lefebvre, H. (1991) *The Production of Space*. Blackwell, Oxford.

Lim, J. (2009) Queer qritique and the politics of affect," *Geographies of Sexualities*. Ashgate, Aldershot, pp. 53–68.

Markus, T. (1993) *Buildings and Power: Freedom and Control in the Origin of Modern Building Types*. Routledge, London.

Merchant, C. (1980) *The Death of Nature: Women, Ecology, and the Scientific Revolution*. Harper and Row, San Francisco.

Nash, C.J. (2005) Contesting identity: politics of gays and lesbians in Toronto in the 1970s. *Gender, Place and Culture* 12, 113–135.

Nash, C.J. (2006) Toronto's gay village (1969–1982): plotting the politics of gay identity. *The Canadian Geographer* 50, 1–16.

Ockman, J. (1996) Mirror images: technology, consumption, and the representation of gender in American architecture since World War II. In D. Agrest, P. Conway, and L. Kanes Weisman (eds), *The Sex of Architecture*. Abrams Publishers, New York, pp. 191–210.

Oswin, N. (2008) Critical geographies and the uses of sexuality: deconstructing queer space. *Progress in Human Geography* 32, 89–103.

Phillips, R. (2004) Sexuality. In J. Duncan, N. Johnson, and S. Schein (eds), *A Companion to Cultural Geography*. Blackwell, Oxford, pp. 265–278.

Pred, A. (1990) *Making Histories and Constructing Human Geographies*. Westview Press, Boulder.

Rendell, J., Penner, B., and Borden, I. (eds) (2000) *Gender, Space, Architecture: An Interdisciplinary Introduction*. Routledge, London.

Richardson, D. (2005) Desiring sameness? The rise of a neoliberal politics of normalization. *Antipode* 37, 515–535.

Roughgarden, J. (2004) *Evolution's Rainbow: Diversity, Gender, and Sexuality in Nature and People*. University of California Press, Berkeley.

Valentine, G. (2003) Sexual politics. In J. Agnew, K. Mitchell, and G. Toal (eds), *A Companion to Political Geography*. Blackwell, Oxford, pp. 408–420.

Walker, R. (1981) A theory of suburbanization: capitalism and the construction of urban space in the United States. In M. Dear, and A. Scott (eds), *Urbanization and Urban Planning in Capitalist Societies*. Methuen, New York, pp. 383–430.

Wright, G. (1981) *Building the Dream: A Social History of Housing in America*. The MIT Press, Cambridge.

Chapter 36

Gender
Part II

Joanne P. Sharp

Introduction

Gender has been a concern of Geography for less than 40 years. Before that point, the subject of Geography was unreflexively male. As the Women in Geography Study Group (WGSG) of the Institute of British Geographers put it in 1984;

> Looking through a representative selection of geography books on a library or bookshop shelf, it appears as if most geography is concerned with 'man'. We are confronted by 'man and his physical environment,' 'man and culture,' or simply, 'man and environment'. The authors of such texts may not intend to portray humanity as being entirely *male* [but] … We might … be forgiven for thinking that *women* simply do not exist in the spatial world. (WGSG 1984: 19)

In the 1970s, the discipline's engagement with humanistic and radical approaches, drawn through Geographers' lived-experiences of the emerging women's movement, meant that gender came to the fore as a key descriptive and analytical concept and one, for feminists, also of central political importance. Forty years of engagement between feminism and geography have highlighted the centrality of space in the constitution and imaginings of gender, and the gendering of spatial form and process. The relationship between Geography and gender has been explored in a number of ways over this period. After a brief overview of the genealogy of gender in Geography, I will develop this around two themes; the place of gendered performance, and the scaling of gender.

The Wiley Blackwell Companion to Human Geography, First Edition.
Edited by John A. Agnew and James S. Duncan.
© 2011 John Wiley & Sons, Ltd. Published 2016 by John Wiley & Sons, Ltd.

A Brief History of Gender In Geography, and the Geography In Gender

Geography has traditionally been a very male subject, both in terms of the gendering of geographers themselves and the knowledges they produce. The foundation of the discipline – as an aid to statecraft at the height of empire – involved fieldwork in the far reaches of the world, an activity and a location both considered "unsuitable for ladies." Despite the pioneering voyages of women like Isabella Bird and Mary Kingsley, women were kept out of the discipline: presented as narrating personal trips rather than scientific expeditions, and barred from Royal Geographical Society membership until 1913. Even by the beginning of the 21st century, however, feminist geographers were still noting the marginalization of women in the discipline (WGSG 1984), the dismissing of feminist methods as too subjective and impressionistic (Thein 2005) and the persistent masculinism of the knowledge produced by Geography as a discipline (Rose 1993).

Until the 1970s, the subject of geography was unproblematically assumed to be "man," epitomized by discussions of the impact on man on his environment. A recognition of the difference that gender makes in the 1970s did force Geography to accept that men and women had different perceptions of the space, and differing abilities to access spatial resources, a situation explained by emerging feminist geographies in the 1970s and 1980s. Initially, work sought to describe the differences between male and female subjects in the world while feminist geography started to go beyond this, noticing the different geographies that women themselves might produce.

For these early works on the geography of women, gender was clearly located within the figure of "woman," and the effects on gender illustrated in their distinct geographies and use of space. The significance of gender as an analytical concept became important in the 1980s and signified a politically and philosophically feminist approach to Geography which believed that:

> Making women visible is simply not enough ... Hence we are concerned to introduce the idea of a feminist geography – a geography which explicitly takes into account the socially-constructed gender structure of society. (WGSG 1984:20–21)

Such approaches "considered the ways in which capitalist society as a whole, and individual men within it, appropriated women's domestic labor to ensure the daily reproduction of men as wage laborers, of children as future workers and of the system as a whole" (McDowell and Sharp 1997: 4).

The different roles and identities ascribed to men and women by gender norms are so deeply embedded within specific social and cultural context that they are often rendered invisible. In the West, women's biological role as mother has conventionally been extended to a gender norm, meaning they are seen as being good carers. This has been naturalized within the workforce so that "women's jobs" have traditionally grouped around caring professions such as nurses and teachers.

Gender norms in the West are based around a binary definition of gender. Conventional understandings of biological markers mean that each person is either male or female[1]. At the heart of Western Enlightenment thought are binaries, ordering the world into known and separate categories. Perhaps most important, is the binary which separate the mind and rationality from nature and the body. Women have been considered to be more given over to the body which is linked to a perceived lack of control over the senses that it was held was achieved through the mind: women have been regarded as closely aligned to natural patterns due to their role as mothers and through the cycles of menstruation, and through other womanly responses to situations, such as hysteria and fainting. This binary is reinforced by the existence of other structuring binaries running through Western thought (such as, reason-passion, culture-nature and production-reproduction), all placing women in the subordinate category.

Thus, masculinity and femininity, as the cultural traits associated with biological men and women, have been constructed as opposite but not as equal. The masculine side of the binary has traditionally been the characteristic which has been regarded as aspirational – rationality, reason, culture, production – whereas feelings, emotion, nature, reproduction have been traits to be removed from government, industry and academia, and kept in the home.

Feminism has as one of its central ambitions, the aim to denaturalize these binaries. To highlight their belief in the social construction of gender roles and identities (rather than accepting them as natural characteristics of each), feminists have conventionally differentiated sex from gender. This distinction was first articulated in the book *The Second Sex* 1949 by French theorist Simone de Beauvoir, who famously claimed that "One is not born but rather becomes a woman."

Feminist geographers have examined the ways in which the binary structure of gender identity and roles were spatialized. Women were excluded from the important spaces of political, economic and cultural decision-making in the public sphere; they were literally "out of place" in the spaces through which the public was articulated: spaces of politics and knowledge, of industry, of the city. Instead, social norms insisted that women's place was the home, the space of reproduction, of caring, and of the day to day. Feminist geographers showed how the form of the city reinforced these gender identities with suburbanization stretching out the gendered spaces of city center (masculine) and suburbs (feminine). McDowell (1983) took this further to argue that the spatial expression of modern western cities, with a spatial separation of work and home, in the city center and suburbs, reinforced the distinction between men and women, and made it all the more difficult for women to access resources and influence. Feminist geographers then had embraced the feminist cry of "the personal is political" to seek politics and power not only in the formal arena of political action, but diffused throughout social relations and thus saw the home and the domestic as political and powerful in the reproduction of society as much as the formal arenas of conventional political geography research. Feminists highlighted the central importance of the distinction between the public and the private in the control of women, and feminist geographers gave this spatial expression in their examination of the spatial distinction between public and private. The association of women with the domestic and the "skills" required therein (caring, mothering, cleaning, recreation) and men with the public (of work, money, ambition, progress and creativity) ensured a naturalization of differences in power.

However, just as the feminist movement has been criticized for adopting too simplistic a notion of gender, so too have attempts to create geographies of gender. Perhaps most notable have been critiques of Western feminists' projection of the idea of a shared experience of "womanhood" between women around the globe. Robin Morgan's "global sisterhood" was one attempt to look at the commonality which was the "result of a *common condition* which, despite variations in degree, is experienced by all human beings who are born female" (Morgan 1984:4). A number of Third World feminists have challenged Morgan's image of a global sisterhood arguing that it ignores all of the differences, inconsistencies and histories which make up the notion of womanhood in different places. For Mohanty (1997: 83) this automatic alliance erases the agency of women in particular historical struggles, and requires that "the categories of race and class have to become invisible for gender to become visible." For Third World feminists like Mohanty, the global sisterhood image silences the histories of colonialism, imperialism and racism from which Western feminists still benefit. As Rich (1986) put it so well, "a place on the map is also a place in history" so that none of us can escape the geographies of power that privilege or subjugate us. Others have also expressed geographies of gender. Feminists in post-socialist countries of Eastern Europe (Funk and Mueller 1993) critiqued the western feminist assumption that the home is a place of imprisonment for women, arguing instead that it had represented for them a place of political possibility (as black US feminists had also insisted [Hooks 1990]). Under communism, the public-private dichotomy described and critiqued by feminists in the West did not emerge. Instead the opposition was between the state and the family, a division "between public (mendacious, ideological) and private (dignified, truthful) discourses" (Einhorn 1993: 3).

Other groups of women have also started to be more vocal in their insistence that their experiences and identities be included into understandings of what it is to be female in different societies: lesbian and bisexual women have challenged the "compulsory heterosexuality" (Rich 1980) of much feminist politics, working class women have challenged the predominant idea in liberal notions of feminism that it is liberating to leave the house to find work (for them, this simply becomes yet another burden on their time), and disabled women critique the embodied assumptions underlying much feminist thought and politics (see Rich 1986; Nast 1999; Chouinard and Grant 1995).

This binary notion of gender was also challenged by "third wave" feminists for whom gender remained a central axis of power and identity, but one which could not be understood in isolation of other aspects of identity such as race, class, nationality and sexuality. Rather than regard gender identities being fixed around identities of male or female, this approach regarded them as constantly in change and negotiation. Indeed, this rejection of boundaries is, for some, epistemologically a feminist move. Continental European feminists in particular have been resistant to any attempts to define, capture and name the feminine, arguing that femininity is constructed as "that which disrupts the security of the boundaries separating spaces and must therefore be controlled by a masculine force" (Deutsche 1996: 301). Feminists such as Cixous (see Shurmer-Smith 1994) and Irigaray (1985) regard the establishment of boundaries as a fundamentally masculinist move, a will to power through the defining and delimiting of an essence into something known. Instead,

Cixous and Irigaray see feminism as always being in excess, always escaping categorization and limitation, always more than can be known and thus always subversive of accepted ways of knowing. Haraway (1991) took this refusal of capture by definitional boundaries a step further by embracing cyborgs and monsters – figures which embraced the impurity of beings which were not purely human but were connected to technologies and non-human natures – as heroines for her feminism.

This challenge to the coherence of "woman" has been accompanied by the development of the gender politics of masculinity which recognized the construction of social norms for men and the power relations that exist *within* definitions of masculinity. In his influential work on masculinities, Connell (1995) insisted that alongside analyses of power relations and the gender division of labor in theories of gender relations should be an examination of what he termed "cathexis," relations of desire and pleasure which, he suggested, could be coerced or consensual.

Placing Gender Performance

What these various challenges to the gendering of/in geography – and related disciplines – have highlighted is the multiplicity of "woman." Thus, more recently, the theorization of gender has moved away from a coherent and stable gendered agent towards an understanding of the formation of a gendered agent through every day practices and performances. The idea of performance is attractive to a feminist politics of gender because it requires the embodied presence of a subject. It refuses the possibility of abstract discussion and instead places at its core the lived body of the subject. This is not an innocent materialism, however, because the performing body is also performed on: it is "an inscriptive surface" (Grosz 1990), upon which societal expectations and norms are written and struggled over.

Many poststructural feminists take inspiration from the work of Michel Foucault (1977, 1978). Instead of "assuming a subject which has agency to think and act, poststructural accounts see the subject – and its subjectivity – as an epiphenomenon of discourse or performance: the discourse or act creates the sense of a knowing and capable actor" (Sharp 2009: 74). Queer theorist Judith Butler has drawn on Foucault's work to argue that the idea of a pre-existing defined subject performing sex and gender roles is a fiction. Instead, it is through the performance of gender identity that the notion of the pre-existing sexed subject is formed. The performance creates the sense of a separate, knowing being which is directing the action, so disguising the actual process. A culturally feminine performance by a female sexed body, then, is seen as normal and natural; it is not even noted as being a performance. The same performance by a body marked as male, however, is seen as transgression, drag, clearly a performance. Butler insists that *both* are performances, both reinforcing the idea that the "natural" distinction between male and female sexes pre-exists the cultural gender performances carried out through everyday life.

Butler's concerns are with sexuality but her ideas about "gender trouble" arising from performances of identity have been enthusiastically adopted by feminists. Butler argues that it is the repetition of performance that works to reinforce the norm of heterosexuality. The constant repetition of heterosexualized actions, she insists, ensures that the illusion of a heterosexual norm can emerge. Every day practices such as looking at advertising images, following soap opera storylines, placing pictures of families on office desks, unselfconsciously reproduce heterosexuality as the norm (see also Valentine 1993). Butler (1990) argues gay cultural politics simply reverse these performances (gay male bodies performing feminine roles, lesbian female bodies performing male roles). These performances – of "correct" heterosexual performance and "resistant" homosexual performance – produces a normalized conceptual map on which clear and distinct lines can be drawn dividing "straight" from "gay," "normal" from "deviant." However, for Butler, there is always the possibility of a range of resistances and transgressions in this model. Alternative practices – whether consciously or unconsciously performed – can destabilize and ultimately undermine these fragile assemblages (for instance, lipstick lesbians, gay skin heads, and the many other combinations of sex and gendered performances through which people articulate their identities). Feminist geographers have embraced Butler's ideas particularly the importance she gives to the historical and geographical specificity of each performance rather than viewing gender performance as being fixed and unchanging. As a result, feminist geographers have studied the role of performances and practices in both public and private spaces in the construction of gender and sexual identities. For example, McDowell (1997) has used the concept of performances to make sense of the presentation of gender identities in spaces of work, the manner in which these performances normalize the roles available to men and women, and the ways in which these norms are negotiated by women who seeking to get ahead in the organization.

The concept of gender thus becomes more fragmented and fluid, challenging inherited understandings of a clear binary mapping of male and female (whether considered to be an essential biological fact or the result of social construction). What is key to this performative model of gender is the specificity of where the performance takes place – a performance in one place or space might have the effect of reinforcing dominant identities, whereas elsewhere, it could produce subversive outcomes. Here we can see how some of the politics of gender continually play out through the most mundane of activities.

In her work looking at the ways in which gender identities and roles are maintained and challenged in different societies in sub-Saharan Africa and the Middle East, Denise Kandiyoti (1988) also challenges rigid and unchanging notions of gender identity through examining the practices of negotiating power, what she calls the "patriarchal bargain," between women and men, and between different groups of women. Kandiyoti (1988) argues that the "patriarchal bargain" explains that women always operate within a set of accepted constraints in their relationship with men. This idea of a "patriarchal bargain" represents an approach which attempts to view women as active agents who are nevertheless constrained by the effects of a patriarchal system (although Kandiyoti (1998) more recently argued that the concept needs to recognize more fully the context-dependency of women's positionality). Kandiyoti recognizes that women's gender performances are constrained by spatially and temporally specific contexts. In the context of North African Islamic societies, women's acceptance of constraints on their activity is "their half of this particular patriarchal bargain – protection in exchange for submissiveness and propriety" (Kandiyoti 1988: 283). With relative wealth, women are withdrawn from non-domestic work in keeping with more respectable domestic roles, even if this means that the household will decrease its potential income. For those who are forced into the marketplace by economic necessity, it is all the more important to intensify what Kandiyoti (1988: 283) calls "traditional modesty markers" (such as veiling or quiet and unassuming behavior in livestock markets [see Sharp *et al.* 2003]) in order to emulate as best as possible the roles expected of women in this patriarchal society. This situation is open to change, particularly with increasing market penetration to all aspects of productive life. Ironically, however, as has been explained elsewhere (Sharp *et al.* 2010), women themselves may be reluctant to take up these opportunities because of their perception of them as non-viable alternatives.

Thus, although women's roles and identities in any "patriarchal bargain" are shaped through conscious and quite strategic understandings of their potentials, due to the influence of socialization processes, women's own self-image is also constructed through these ideas of gender so shaping their unconscious actions too. The empowerment they receive from the "patriarchal bargain," and the sense of identity and security that this provides, offers – in some situations – more than any potential empowerment that more radical changes might offer. It will only be when the women themselves decide that the benefits of change outweigh the status quo, that any changes will represent empowerment rather than an act of last resort.

While not being based in the radical poststructural critique of Butler, like her, Kandiyoti challenges the notion of gender as unchanging and prior to action, instead regarding it as an identity, and set of capabilities, that are negotiated and compromised, working out differently in each context.

Some feminists are wary of accounts of gender and power that reject the central role of a knowing and thinking agent. Alcoff (1990: 73) insists that Foucault ignores the fact that "thinking of ourselves as subjects can have, and has had, positive effects contributing to our ability effectively to resist structures of domination." There are times when speaking "for women" in a united voice can be very powerful and transformative. Other feminists have reacted cynically to pronouncements of the "death of the subject" noting that this had occurred just when the male, white, subject might have had to share its status with those formerly excluded from subjectivity (Fox-Genovese 1986; Mascia-Lees *et al.* 1989).

In response, some have taken up Spivak's (1988) suggestion of a "strategic essentialism" from which women can forge a politics through which to fight patriarchal oppression. Here, rather than simply being a cultural identity, strategic essentialism is a political concept. It suggests that rather than a politics forged around shared identity, this should lead to coalition building. Mohanty (1988) argues that coalitions are formed not because they are necessarily enjoyable but because they are required for survival. This offers the possibility of retaining the idea of a "feminist politics" and the desire to make things better without the necessity of a belief in biological essentialism or any other claim to universalism.

Scaling Gender

While a feminist concern with the body and embodiment is key to the ways in which gender has been understood in Geography, a further concern about the focus on the embodied and specific nature of gendered performance is that it might draw feminist geographers away from theorizing at other scales. Indeed, feminist political geographers have drawn attention to the power relations involved in dividing space into the male-dominated political sphere and the women's space of the domestic, arguing that it is this division that has sought to marginalize women from the space of power.

Feminist political geography has sought to place gender relations at the heart of understanding the ways in which scales are connected and challenging the political effects of thinking of the world as divided into discrete scales. In economic and development geographies, feminists have produced compelling accounts of the entanglement of gender in the global workings of the economy (e.g. Nagar *et al*. 2002; Gibson-Graham 2006) challenging the "masculinist hypermobility" (Pratt and Yeoh 2003) that has characterized so many academic accounts of globalization. Massey (1993) has similarly noted the gendering of models of globalization, highlighting the ideas of a shrinking world where borders are fluid and space is no longer a barrier to movement, is true only for those who are appropriately embodied (white, well turned out), with the "correct" passport (western) and sufficient funds. For marginalized people (those whose bodies are marked as other, who do not have western citizenship and who do not have access to credit) movement has become more difficult, and rather than seeing the benefits of time-space distanciation, they are tied to place more than ever before.

Similarly, Nagar *et al*. (2002) examine the "double marginalization" of subjects and space characteristic of dominant accounts of globalization: "Women are sidelined, as is gender analysis more broadly, and southern countries are positioned as the feminized other to advanced economies". Their argument seeks to retheorize the global in a way that is attuned to the informal and casual connections that make up international flows; that provides a critical scalar politics that sees globalization as "multiple, intersecting, and socially and politically constructed" (Nagar *et al*. 2002: 266); and acknowledges the range of actors involved in globalization and to recognize the partial and contextual nature of these subjectivities.

Katz (2001) also prioritizes a feminist politics of connection over difference. Her work encourages politics of association not separation, promoting the idea of "topographes" (Katz 2001: 1232) to formulate a feminist politics that celebrates jumping scales, one that is both beyond place-based local politics and the forging of alliances because "[p]recisely because globalization is such an abstraction, albeit with varying forms, struggles against global capital have to mobilize equivalent, alternative abstractions":

> This grounded but translocal politics offers at the very least the possibility of countering the ways that the maneuvers of globalized capitalism exacerbate and build upon gendered, racialized, nationalist, and class axes of oppression and inequality in different historical geographies. What politics might work the contours connecting carceral California, sweatshop New York, maquiladora Mexico, and structurally adjusted Howa, and back again? These are the kinds of questions that topographies encourage us to ask. The prospects are tantalizing and the political stakes great. (Katz 2001: 1231; see also Mayer 2004)

The rewriting of international relations to include not only the experiences and views of those in the formal spaces of politics, as was conventionally the case in political geography, challenges the division of political-apolitical, and thus allows space for the experiences of women (and others) who have been silenced by this distinction. In her feminist re-readings of international relations, Cynthia Enloe (2004) has insisted on the fundamental role that women play in the making and remaking of the world, as economic migrants, refugees, sex workers and cleaners, roles normally excluded from narratives of global politics. Just as earlier feminists had argued that without women's domestic work capitalism could not function, so Enloe was arguing that without the everyday work of women servicing international capital, the military and other agents of globalization would also fail to operate. This rewriting of the actions of women (and other marginalized voices) into geopolitical thought represents a move towards recognizing the inherent and unavoidable embodiment of geographical processes and geopolitical relationships at different scales (Dowler and Sharp 2001). In order to rewrite the everyday experiences of individuals back into geopolitical events academics are relating the scale of their investigations from the global and national to that of the community, home and body. It is ever more clear since the attacks on the USA on September 11th, that geopolitics is not limited to formal political discourse but is always and everywhere embodied: in the protesters who are banned from shopping malls, the "Arab-looking" people who are watched and sometimes interrogated in the cities and airports of the west, and in the men, women and children who are at the receiving end of military strikes in Afghanistan and Iraq. It "has become clear that spatial divisions – whether in the home or in the workplace, at the level of the city or the nation-state – are also affected by and reflected in embodied practices and lived social relations" (McDowell, 1999: 35).

Conclusions

"Gender" has not been an unchanging presence in Geography. From its initial use as a marker of difference between female and male subjects, it has been destabilized over history, across space and scale, and through practice. Feminists' use of "gender" has allowed for challenge to objectifying labeling, resisting borders and other attempts to essentialize meaning.

However, it is undoubtedly the case that "geographies of gender" have gained currency over "feminist geography," particularly in recent years, perhaps *because* this escapes any possibility of essentialism. But, such a move is always in danger of emptying the *politics* of feminism into a *social* categorization. For feminists attempting to understand gender as a category is only the first step in a process which is always accompanied by a commitment to the politics of change.

Note

1   Contemporary biology, however, now explains that there are those who possess the biological characteristics of both men and women. Their existence has conventionally been explained away as "freaks of nature" rather than being allowed to challenge the logic of binary thinking.

References

Alcoff, L. (1990) Feminist politics and Foucault: the limits to a collaboration. In A. Dalley and C. Scott (eds), *Crises in Continental Philosophy*. SUNY Press, Albany.
Butler, J. (1990) *Gender trouble: feminism and the subversion of identity*. Routledge, London.
Chouinard, V. and Grant, A. (1995) On not being anywhere near "the project": revolutionary ways of putting ourselves in the picture. *Antipode* 21, 137–166.
Connell, R. (1995) *Masculinities*. Polity Press, Cambridge.
Deutsche, R. (1996) *Evictions*. MIT Press, Cambridge.
Dowler, L. and Sharp, J. (2001) A feminist geopolitics? *Space and Polity* 5 (3), 165–176.
Einhorn, B. (1993) *Cinderella Goes to Market: Citizenship, Gender and Women's Movements in East Central Europe*. Verso, New York.
Enloe, C. (2004) *The curious feminist: searching for women in a new age of empire*. University of California Press, California.
Foucault, M. (1977) *Discipline and punish: the birth of the prison*. Allen Lane, London.
Foucault, M. (1978) *The history of sexuality volume I: an introduction*. Allen Lane, London.
Fox-Genovese, E. (1986) The claims of a common culture: gender, race, class and the canon. *Salmagundi* 72, 119–132.
Funk, N. and Mueller, M. (eds) (1993) *Gender Politics and Post-Communism: Reflections From Eastern Europe and the Former Soviet Union*. Routledge, New York.
Grosz, E. (1990) Inscriptions and body-maps: representations and the corporeal. In T. Threadgold and A. Cranny-Francis (eds), *Feminine, masculine and representation*. Allen and Unwin, London.
Haraway, D. (1991) *Simians, Cyborgs and Women: the reinvention of nature*. Free Association Books, London.
Hooks, B. (1990) Marginality as a Site of Resistence. In R. Ferguson, *et al.* (eds), *Out there: Marginalization and Contemporary Cultures*. MIT Press, Cambridge, Massachusetts.
Irigaray, L. (1985) *Speculum of the other woman*. Cornell University Press, Ithaca.
Kandiyoti, D. (1988) Bargaining with patriarchy. *Gender and society* 2 (3), 274–290.
Katz, C. (2001) On the grounds of globalization: a topography for feminist political engagement. *Signs: Journal of women in culture and society* 26 (4), 1213–1234.
Mascia-Less, F., Sharp, P., and Cohen, C. (1989) The postmodern turn in anthropology: cautions from a feminist perspective. *Signs* 15, 7–33.
Massey, D. (1993) Power-geometry and a progressive sense of place. In J. Bird, B. Curtis, T. Putnam, G. Robertson, and L. Tickner (eds), *Mapping the Futures: local cultures, global change*. Routledge, London, pp. 59–69.
Mayer, T. (2004) Embodied nationalisms. In L. Staeheli, E. Kofman, and L. Peake (eds), *Mapping women, making politics: feminist perspectives on political geography*. Routledge, London and New York, pp. 153–167.
McDowell, L. (1983) Towards an understanding of the gender division of urban space. *Environment and planning D: Society and Space* 1, 59–72.
McDowell, L. (1997) *Capital culture: gender at work in the city*. Basil Blackwell, Oxford.
McDowell, L. (1999) *Gender, Identity and Place: understanding feminist geographies*. University of Minnesota Press, Minneapolis.
Mohanty, C.T. (1988) Under Western eyes: feminist scholarship and colonial discourses. *Feminist Review* 30, 61–88.
Mohanty, C.T. (1997) Feminist encounters: locating the politics of experience. In L. McDowell and J. Sharp (eds), *Space, Gender, Knowledge: feminist readings*. Arnold, London, pp. 82–97.
Morgan, R. (1984) *Sisterhood is global: the international women's movement anthology*. Anchor Press/Doubleday, New York.

Nagar, R., Lawson, V., McDowell, L., and Hanson, S. (2002) Locating globalization: feminist (re)readings of the subjects and spaces of globalization. *Economic Geography* 78 (3), 257–284.

Pratt, G. and Yeoh, B. (2003) Transnational (counter) topographies. *Gender, place and culture* 10 (2), 159–166.

Rich, A. (1980) Compulsory heterosexuality and Lesbian existence. *Signs: Journal of Women in Culture and Society* 5 (4), 631–690.

Rich, A. (1986) *Blood, bread and poetry: selected prose 1979–1985*. Norton, New York.

Rose, G. (1993) *Feminism and geography*. Blackwell, Oxford.

Sharp, J. (2009) Subjectivity. In R. Kitchen and N. Thrift (eds), *The international encyclopedia of geography*. Elsevier, Oxford, Volume 11, pp. 72–76.

Sharp, J., Briggs, J., Yacoub, H., and Hamed, N. (2010) Women's Empowerment: A Critical Re-evaluation of a GAD Poverty Alleviation Project in Southeast Egypt. In S. Chant (ed.), *The International Handbook on Gender and Poverty*. Edward Elgar Publishing, Cheltenham.

Shurmer-Smith, P. (1994) Cixous spaces: sensuous spaces in women's writing. *Ecumene* 1, 349–632.

Spivak, G. (1988) Can the subaltern speak? In C. Nelson and L. Grossberg (eds), *Marxism and the interpretation of culture*. Macmillan, Basingstoke.

Thien, D. (2005) After or beyond feeling? A consideration of affect and emotion in geography. *Area* 37, 450–456.

Valentine, G. (1993) (Hetero)sexing space: lesbian perceptions and experiences of everyday spaces. *Environment and planning D: Society and Space* 11, 395–413.

Women and Geography Study Group of the Institute of British Geographers (1984) *Geography and gender*. Harper Collins, London.

Chapter 37

Geopolitics
Part I

Phil Kelly

Introduction

Two essential ideas underlie the *classical* version of geopolitics: that relatively unbiased concepts and theories, based upon placement in geography, can be recognized, and that these can be applied to facilitate an understanding of international political events. Hence, such an approach is useful for academic study and as an aid to statecraft. In contrast, the post-modern *critical geopolitics* would argue that most generalization, spatial or otherwise, being tainted by Great Power hegemony, should be questioned, and that geopolitics is more a tool for establishing domination. I have argued (Kelly 2006) that the interest of the post-modern variety of geopolitics lies rather in exposing and then in transforming the current corrupt system into something better. The key words of difference between the two being *geography versus hegemony* respectively, frankly, I cannot image of any bridge that could easily span these wide differences between the classical and critical versions of geopolitics.

I must follow the classical perception, for my interest is to clarify the extant theory and to show its application to policy. I want my contribution to be in the clarification of theory, since to me this has been the most neglected area. Without a clear theory, the application falters, too. Indeed, the lack of a clear definition and description of traditional geopolitics has tarnished its reputation and, thus, has hindered its utility. I aim to help correct this. Accordingly, the purpose of this chapter is to refine for the reader several classical geopolitical concepts and theories and

The Wiley Blackwell Companion to Human Geography, First Edition.
Edited by John A. Agnew and James S. Duncan.
© 2011 John Wiley & Sons, Ltd. Published 2016 by John Wiley & Sons, Ltd.

then to apply these to two contrasting historical and regional structures: to the Peloponnesian war of ancient Greece (in Parts Two and Three) and to contemporary South America in the concluding part. But, first, I will share briefly with the reader some of the major influences in the development of my traditional approach.

I have gained mostly from the writings of Nicholas Spykman (1942), although he blended realist theory with his geopolitics. Thus, these two models need separating. Like most classicists, I also admire the original stimulation of Halford Mackinder (1919), despite my finding him less helpful than Spykman (Gerace 1991). Other influences come to mind also: Carlos de Meira Mattos (1975), Zbigniew Brzezinski (1997), Colin Gray (1977), and Saul Cohen (2003, 2009). But, none of these individuals touched much into theory, their approaches being more in application. Therefore, I have been almost alone in the theory sector. Consequently, my intent here is to conceptualize, then to apply the result to my two case examples.

Owing to what I believe to be the conceptual weaknesses of traditional geopolitics, the evolution of its study has waxed and waned over the past century as various movements have captured the concept, twisting the original neutral intent to their own ideological stamps. For instance, Mackinder's geopolitics became tied to the Nazi *geopolitik* and this link has damaged the term (unfairly I feel), particularly in North America. Later came a Cold War polemic of *power politics* that likewise became attached to the traditional term, blaming most international violence and instabilities on a further version of "geopolitics." Finally, the post-modernists have lent their mis-interpretations too, mostly negative and associated to hegemonic exploitation. Consequently, this evolution of geopolitics over recent times has been rather bumpy, to say the least, but perhaps my descriptions below might elevate the classical model to a higher level.

Part One: Theory As A Tool for Understanding

Theories enhance understanding. They help us to arrange facts and to compare situations and events so we can penetrate more deeply. We apply theory as a way to clarify, to explain, to predict, and to prescribe. This provides us with ideologically-neutral tools for delving more completely into national and international happenings. And, to me, theories are quite simple coming in rather short sentences, and linking some sort of an original stimulant to a probable outcome: "A" happening, this then leading to some likelihood of "B" resulting. For instance, "the more international borders countries possess, the higher their chances of involvement in war." Or, "greater distances weaken the attaining of states' foreign objectives." Or, "central positions of countries award certain advantages and certain disadvantages."

Such premises derive from logic, history, statistics, experience, or just common sense. But, they normally are quite sketchy and lack much detail, and their ability to assist us toward understanding is just a potential aid and not a guarantee of resolution, for theories can mislead as well as assist if we are not prudent in their application. However, despite the brevity and imprecision, this process of theory allows us an interpretative structure within which to envelope an event, or a theater of events, giving more depth for better understanding and comparison. We should not do without theory. And also, in our present situation, theory can help us with understanding the Peloponnesian war and contemporary South America.

But, there is more here than just theory, for we need also to consider *assumptions* and *concepts* within a still fuller package that I will label as a *model*. *Assumptions* underlie the complete landscape of theory, and one must accept these unconditionally despite the fact that they cannot be precisely proven. In geopolitics, we assume the geography of a region, for example, the spatial patterning of states and alliances such as in ancient Greece and in contemporary South America, will likely influence the diplomacy of those regions. Also, we study the impacts of the sea versus land-power dichotomy upon events, or the region's topography or resources affecting its military tactics. My point is that we simply must trust these assumed relationships to be true – features within geography affecting some of the processes of intra-state relationships and warfare – before we are able to proceed further toward examining the geopolitics of our interest areas. I tend to describe assumptions and theories inter-changeably, the exact divisor blurred, although the former represents the more abstract, the latter the more concrete.

In addition, *concepts* are the vocabulary or building blocks of theory; they describe the primary words and features that compose a theory. Again, in the realm of geopolitics, we speak about the phenomena of *shatterbelts, checkerboards, heartlands, choke points, spatial contagion*, and so forth within our geopolitical discussions. For instance, *shatterbelts* are regions where local conflicts intersect with strategic rivalries, whereas *checkerboards* show patterns of alliance and rivalry in which neighbors are opponents, but neighbors of neighbors are friends. Choke points are pivotal areas of strategic importance. Concepts are the more passive elements of the three, and often they lend themselves to eventual theory, but nonetheless they also are vital to our understanding of geopolitical relationships because assumptions and theories could not exist without such a vocabulary.

Finally, I wrap assumptions, concepts, and theories within a package or basket of a particular *model*, in our case, a model of geopolitics. What elements enter the geopolitical basket must conform to a specific definition of geopolitics, and those not conforming to this definition, accordingly are left out. Indeed, a model depends upon a defining of the topic that will bring all relevant elements together into this single compartment. Hence, a model is the structural container that holds and organizes the three parts – theories, assumptions, and concepts – each fitting a common premise. A model is passive, having no other function beyond containing its three parts.

As the outer skin or boundary or gate keeper of our model, I offer this definition of geopolitics:

> Geopolitics is the study of the impact or influence of certain geographical features – positions and locations of regions, states, and resources, plus topography, climate, distance, demography, and the like – upon states' foreign policies and actions, as an aid to statecraft. Accordingly, this study lends itself both to theory and to policy.

Again, those factors conforming to this definition would come into our geopolitical analysis, and, of course, those not conforming but diverting elsewhere would not fit our design but might be absorbed into another model.

An example of the "good fit" of geopolitical configurations both to contemporary South America and to the ancient Peloponnese is a similar *checkerboard* structure; *checkerboards* being the geopolitical trait of neighboring states as enemies but neighbors of neighbors as allies, a leap-frog patterning. In America, I can visualize Brazil, with Chile and Colombia, aligned against Argentina, with Peru and Venezuela. Similarly, in Greece, Persia, Boeotia, Corinth, Sparta, and Syracuse appeared to be configured against the Aegean cities, Athens, Argos, and Corcyra, each set within a contrasting alliance and opposition pattern. As we will see later, the outcomes of the two checkerboards took different directions, the contemporary American being quite benign, the ancient Greek being very hostile. But, I want to stress here the importance of this checkerboard configuration because it describes the primary geopolitical structure of the Greek foreign-affairs platform upon which the events of conflict did evolve. To me, we cannot analyze these geopolitical rivalries without relying upon this basic contrasting-places design.

One prominent geopolitical concept/theory, missing from ancient Greece but central to the contemporary strategic study of geopolitics, is that of the *heartland*, Halford Mackinder's thesis of the Eurasian pivot. The assumption here is that central position tends to yield advantages of protection, movement, and leverage, the possessor better able to probe opponents' weaknesses and to maneuver and reach the outer parts within a secure central pivot. Neither Athens nor Sparta could be seen as heartlands of Greece, and this absence was to exert an important impact upon the Peloponnesian war. The presence of such a pivotal region in South America, allegedly sought by Brazil, to an extent has pacified the American case.

Part Two: Applying Geopolitics to the Peloponnesian War

I want to outline the primary happenings of the second phase of the war (431–404 BCE). For this historical chronology, I have relied upon several academic accounts of the war in English as listed in my bibliography (Bagnall 2004; Hanson 2005; Kagan 1969, 1974). My interest here is that of a political scientist and not of a historian, that is, my purpose rests in applying a broader geopolitical model as an interpretation of the Greek struggle in contrast to discovering new facts about the war itself.

The first instances of the coming war began in 435 BCE with the Corinth-Corcyra intervention not the democrats' rebellion in Epidamnus, an Adriatic coastal colony of Corinth. Despite it being beyond the *spheres of influence* of both Athens and Sparta, the local struggle soon brought in the two hegemons or strategic cities, (1) Sparta offering mediation and military advice to Corinth, and (2) Athens agreeing to a defensive alliance with Corcyra. This geopolitical situation that helped turn Sparta against Athens I term a *shatterbelt*, or a two-level strategic/local rivalry (Kelly 1986) that culminated in the sea-battle victory of Corcyra over Corinth, the decisive factor being the involvement of an Athenian fleet in the Battle of Sybola (433 BCE). This event, typical of shatterbelts, began as a rather isolated local conflict that eventually drew the distant strategic city-states into an escalation of the turmoil that both had first wanted to avoid. To me, the beginnings of most wars come from the escalation probability within shatterbelts, the strife spreading from local into strategic.

Two additional events caused Sparta to enter war against Athens: (1) the Athenian "Megarian Decree" against Megara, a Spartan/Corinthian ally, that prohibited trade with Athens and its allies, probably as a punishment for Megara's assistance to Corinth in the Epidamnus revolt, and (2) the Athenian siege of rebellious Polidaea, again a Corinthian colony but within the *influence sphere* of Athens in the Aegean. Probably, both actions were miscalculations of Pericles, Athens's ruler, but many scholars attribute to these three happenings (Epidamnus, Megara, and Polidaea) the immediate stimulants to the second Peloponnesian war (especially Kagan 1969: 205).

Once the Spartan assembly had voted for war against Athens in 331 BCE, five Spartan land invasions of Attica, the territory surrounding Athens, ensued during the immediate years, but ended in 425, all bent upon ravishing the agricultural resources of Athens and thus tempting the city to enter into battle against the superior Peloponnesian army. Nonetheless, the Periclean strategy was to remain within the protective walls surrounding the city and its port at Piraeus and not to engage Sparta on land that would bring certain defeat. Instead, the Athenian fleet would harass the Peloponnese coast, seeking relief against the Attica invasions of Sparta, although neither of the tactics would render much of a strategic impact. The two leading and asymmetric capabilities – Spartan *land-power* and Athenian *sea-power* – were destined to stalemate for decades a resolution to the war because neither power could defeat the land/sea strengths of the other. Ultimately, and with Persian financial support, once Sparta could counter the *sea-power* advantage of Athens in the Aegean, the war's end soon became evident.

Unfortunately for Athens, confinement within the city's walls created conditions for a disastrous plague during the second year of the war that killed off a third of the population and thwarted the war effort for a decade. Perhaps the greatest disaster of the sickness was the death of Pericles, who was the ablest leader of Athens although his later-in-life diplomatic mistakes probably helped cause the war. Debate over his war strategy of attrition against Sparta continues still (Hanson 2005: 48). In creating the conditions for plague, the land-power superiority of Sparta, with its ability to force the concentration of Athenian forces within limited spaces behind walls, held geopolitical relevance. Additionally, Athens's reliance upon its sea-power strength brought on its confinement, and later its dependence upon resources secured via the Hellespont strategic *choke-point*.

The failed Athenian invasion of Sicily (415–413 BCE) proved to be a fatal mistake that contributed to the later Spartan victory. Here, a strong land and sea force from Athens attempted the subjugation of Syracuse but soon was annihilated due to *distance* and *difficult terrain*, poor Athenian leadership, adroit Spartan guidance to its Syracuse allies, and a confused Athenian strategy of expanding the theater of strife that did not correspond to the original prudent war interests. Pericles's earlier moderation was ignored, and Athens took a distant and reckless offensive on land and sea bent toward ridding its checkerboard encirclement. Its defeat seriously depleted its wealth and manpower, encouraging its colonies and tribute cities to revolt, and its opponents, importantly Persia, to become more aggressive. Again, in this Athenian Sicilian debacle the geopolitical patterns would include the several theories and concepts of *distance weakening, disadvantageous topography, influence spheres* (Athens intruding into that of Sparta), and a *contagion or spatial spread of conflict* against Athens that ensued within the Athenian empire and elsewhere because of the defeat at Syracuse. And once more, we observe the ubiquitous *shatterbelt* structure, the local strife in peripheral Sicily drawing in the outside strategic competitors, and the confining and dangerous encirclement of Athens brought on by the predominant *checkerboard* configuration of city-states.

To me, it is rather strange that the strategic Hellespont *choke-point* straits of the Northern Aegean, the food lifeline to Athens via the Black Sea and the Ukrainian grain fields, would not have been recognized as being important by Spartan and Persian strategists earlier in the war and, thus, defended more vigorously by Athens. Indeed, this Athenian vulnerability took the insight of the Spartan admiral, Lysander, to exploit, and earlier, the Persian rulers, to finance a Spartan fleet to neutralize the Athenian sea advantage in the Aegean. The Spartan sea-victory at Aegospotami (405 BCE) destroyed Athens's fleet, strangling the city and its sea port and, consequently, terminating the long struggle. Although most of the earlier events of the war happened distant from the Hellespont, the struggle ended abruptly once this *choke point* was lost by Athens.

Part Three: A More Specific Application of Geopolitical Themes

In this section I will apply several geopolitical theories toward giving a more structured and thus, a deeper, understanding of certain spatial aspects of the Peloponnesian war. Various other geopolitical applications existed as well that could satisfy, but these selections seemed most appropriate to me as examples for the war. As stated before, theory affords a further depth to an event and thus an insightful platform for explanation and comparison. Indeed, the geopolitical theatre of ancient Greece provides a good testing place for the geopolitical model.

Shatterbelts

These two-level conflict structures, the local intertwined with the strategic, appeared in at least five instances during the war, at Epidamnus, Megara, Potidaea, Plataea, and Syracuse, in each case a local conflict drawing the outside hegemons (Athens and Sparta) into the immediate strife but then the violence escalating well-beyond the immediate environs and into longer-term situations, and frequently against the hegemons' original strategic interests. These could be labeled in modern times "catalytic wars," the tail (local allies) wagging the dog (the strategic sponsors), showing that rigid perceptions and alliances can hamper the decision-making abilities of hegemons and draw them into destructive and unwanted confrontations.

Many wars emerge from the escalations of shatterbelts, and our war in Greece is no exception. But, certainly, wars-from-shatterbelts are not inevitable, for I suggest that allowances could have been established possibly to have prevented such happenings. For instance, the primary political leaders of both Sparta and Athens might have been more effective at resisting the war-passions of their governing assemblies and instead have insisted upon moderation, as Pericles and Archidamus had wisely advised. Or, the two cities might have better contained their weaker allies' pleas for support and intervention by erecting "fire-breaks" against unintended escalation. Ultimately, the opposing hegemonic-led leagues could have established means toward mediating conflict, especially in direct negotiations between Athens and Sparta, possibly reversing the perception of the war's inevitability and thus strengthening the peace factions in both cities.

A neutral *balancer* city or nation that might have intervened to prevent the conflict or decide the winner also was not present at first. Persia later played this latter role to the advantage of Sparta but not at the war's outbreak. Fear of Athens's supposed expansionism likewise stimulated distrust, a later fact that indeed bore some truth when the city's imperial actions took just this course. We could add as well the ubiquitous frontier disputes and the rigidities of the rival alliances, and similarly the lack of a dominant *heartland* in a position to temper the stalemate. But other factors, of course, helped start the war beyond geopolitical considerations – city loyalties, trade rivalries, ideological differences, poor leadership and short-sighted assemblies – all of these also contributed to the inevitability of the war.

Checkerboards

In contemporary South American geopolitics, the prevailing checkerboard structure there, in my judgment, has helped to bring a more stable peace, for reasons in part peculiar to the region's geopolitics, and these will be outlined later in this essay. But, it appears to me the opposite direction had occurred in the ancient Peloponnese. The five-city/nation checkerboard of Sparta with Persia, Boeotia, Corinth, and Syracuse arraigned against the four-member coalition of Athens with the Aegean colonies, Argos, and Corcyra proved to be detrimental to peace and quite susceptible to conflict escalation. So, in addition to the prevailing shatterbelts in these regions, the existing checkerboard structure also contributed to the war's outbreak and longevity, and both structures were to operate in tandem.

Consequently, why did this war-prone geopolitical structure in ancient Greece arise, for checkerboards need not always suffer conflict? I speculate here, but perhaps the absence both of long distances and of insurmountable terrain among most of the city-states enabled closer contact and thus greater frontier strife among the participants, as is characteristic of these "my-neighbor-my-enemy" configurations. Also, many frontiers seemed to have lacked clear demarcation, an absence of the partitioning roles of rivers or mountains, for example, and hence encouraged property disputes among immediate neighbors.

The presence of costly two-front wars did not appear to have retarded the struggle either, especially from the standpoint of Athens that suffered the most from encirclement, probably because she could depend upon her defensive walls and her authority upon the sea. The two alliances within the checkerboard, again being fairly equal in power, seemed relatively fixed in their opposition to the other side, lacking major defector cities, for instance, and these factors too contributed to stalemate, frustration, and an increasing rigidity and violence. Distant Persia played a "divide-and-conquer" game, wanting to break Athenian dominance over the Aegean in the later years of the conflict in the hopes of regaining its *sphere of influence* over the area. Whatever the causes, the checkerboard configuration appeared to have provided a rather natural setting toward encouraging the prolonged violence during the twenty-seven year war.

Land and Sea Power

The *land versus sea dichotomy* is an obvious geopolitical describer of the war, with Athens dependent upon sea-power and Sparta as much upon land-power, although some of the allies contrasted to these patterns; for example, the sea-power strength of Corinth. Again, the overall advantage seemed to lie with Sparta, because its army was largely invincible in battle and thus could not be seriously challenged throughout the conflict, at least in confronting an Athenian equivalent. Consequently, Athens would later lose its maritime supremacy when a newly-constructed Spartan armada began its war of attrition in the Aegean after Athens's defeat in Sicily and after Persia's substantial financing of the Spartan fleet. Here, the greater costs of naval warfare, in material and manpower, as contrasted to the less expensive land forces of Sparta, steadily depleted the resources of Athens, made the city more dependent upon tribute from its increasingly restive allies, and ultimately Athens could not match or attract the type of support for a dominant land- or sea-force as rendered to Sparta from the wealthy Persians.

Strategic Choke Points

The concept of *strategic choke points* to me signifies a particular locale that extends a strong impact over some greater expanse of space, a maritime strait or canal, an isthmus or mountain pass, or connecting routes within plains, for instance, thus indicating a place exerting pivotal importance to a possessor in struggles against rivals. In Greece, we see these features in the Corinthian isthmus through which the Spartan armies advanced toward Athens, and in the Corinthian Gulf through which the Athenian navies sought to control the central areas. But, as noted before, securing the strategic Hellespont proved in the end the survival or demise of Athens itself, for through these straits poured the strategic grain imports to the city drawn from the Black Sea ports of the Ukraine. Once this lifeline was closed by Spartan sea power, Athens suffered strangulation and the war quickly terminated. One might filter the further geopolitical considerations of *distance, sea versus land power, checkerboards*, and *contagion* into this mix.

Part Four: Conclusions

I contend that geopolitical concepts and theories do assist us toward a deeper understanding of the Peloponnesian war. The several shatterbelts appearing then brought inevitable conflict between the two alliances, and the checkerboard configuration further contributed to the conflict's outbreak and to the lengthy stalemate. The influence-spheres tended toward rigidity and thus augmented the strife and the land and sea-power patterns likewise drew out the fray without resolution until the Athenian debacle in Sicily encouraged Persian intervention. This contagion caused the final race for control of the Hellespont choke point that erased Athenian wealth and power.

From my standpoint, several aspects were missing from the geopolitical puzzle that might have prevented this Peloponnese *structure of conflict* and have shifted the region into a *zone of peace*. Below, I offer a brief outline of five pertinent themes, a listing of potential peace-contributors had they been present, again all from a geopolitical perspective. I have taken these five from my study of contemporary South America, a *zone of peace* (Kelly et al. 2002) in contrast to what I have observed for ancient Greece:

A power symmetry or balance existed among the Greek contestants, Athens, Sparta, and their allies, an equilibrium that brought stalemate via a structured checkmating between the rival alliances, lengthening the war and heightening the violence. Were there instead a dominant state or alliance within the region, the escalating violence might have become contained and the war shortened or prevented.

No *buffer states* appeared on the Greek stage, that is, neutral cities that would have cordoned off direct strategic confrontation, absorbed the violence exercised by the larger cities, and thus enhanced the isolation wrought by distance. Instead, without these buffers, the *checkerboard* rivalries tended to intensify border violence and encouraged *shatterbelt* escalation as well. Buffers were missing in part because neutrality simply was not permitted by the major antagonists, the tragedy of Melos being a prime example.

Frontier or march spaces were not wide enough to buffer local hostilities and to prevent the constant friction happening among the rival cities. Had a greater degree of separation and isolation been more evident, with greater distances among inhabitants, the tensions might have abated and the *checkerboard* and *shatterbelt* tendencies for escalation might have been reduced.

The asymmetry wrought by Athens's sea-power dependence and Sparta's land-power reliance tended to stalemate and prolong the war. In the initial years, Athens could not defeat Sparta's army, nor could Sparta challenge the Athenian marine. Eventually, Sparta's ability to construct a navy equal to Athens's decided the contest. Had a sea-power capability not been available to either side, Sparta would have won early on, its hoplites easily superior to the army of Athens. Or conversely, had a land-power strength been absent to Sparta, an Athenian victory would have been assured. Nonetheless, the geography of ancient Greece lent itself to both sources of military preponderance, sea- and land-power, and thus brought on a structure of stalemate.

A temptation to spread the conflict beyond Greece was present during the wars, with Athens earlier invading Egypt, then Sicily, and later facing the strength of Persia. Spartan involvement in some of these external actions transpired too. Consequently, lands external to Greece intensified the strife. Had the struggle been confined only to Greek lands, the extra-territorial adventures and alliances would not have been conceived so readily, and Greece, in isolation, might have become more united, or its major players might have recognized the coming stalemate and reconciled their aims.

Contemporary South America, I believe, exhibits different outcomes from the five geopolitical themes just outlined that I believe have stabilized its diplomacy. Today, the region exhibits a contrasting power asymmetry, the presence of a potentially dominant Brazil that, its neighbors fear, wants to extend its domains onto the continent's Pacific coast via the *Charcas triangle heartland* of Bolivia. This threat has prompted a Spanish-American encirclement that is poised to checkmate a potentially-aggressive Portuguese republic despite the predominant *checkerboard* configuration, thus reducing an escalation potential.

Further, the four interior *buffer states* of Ecuador, Bolivia, Paraguay, and Uruguay are positioned between the more powerful checkerboard actors (Brazil, Chile, Peru, Argentina), a northwest to southeast continental *corridor of conflict* that has brought most of the extant wars onto buffer territories and has seen the sacrifice of buffer lands as rewards to the larger victors. I believe the buffers' positions have contributed significantly to the existing stability.

Moreover, the South American republics do not exhibit a distinctive sea and land-power description, the American navies peripheral and the armies central to the checkerboard competitions, and this has tended to keep the countries more isolated from each other. Different from Greece, the extensive distances among population ecumens also has brought greater frontier isolation and thus calm. And finally, I label South America an "independent" or autonomous region in strategic world politics, its geopolitics kept within the continent, and other outlying areas including North America are peripheral to its political interests. Thus, outside disturbances in modern times, including any from the United States, have been very limited and not seriously disturbing to the republics' relationships. Consequently, no shatterbelts have appeared in South America for centuries.

These observations conclude my narrative – that the use of geopolitics for an interpretation of the Peloponnesian war may have given the reader some further insight into the distinctive features of that conflict. But, beyond the confines of the ancient Peloponnese and into present-day South America, I see in this essay too an even broader worth, that being an indication of the usefulness of applying a specific model of geopolitical traits to such happenings, as befits any such refining and fixing of theory to an international-relations event.

References

Bagnall, N. (2004) *The Peloponnesian War: Athens, Sparta, and the Struggle for Greece*. Thomas Dunne Book/St. Martin's Press, New York.

Brzezinski, Z. (1997) *The Grand Chessboard: American Primacy and Its Geostrategic Imperatives*. Basic Books, New York.

Cohen, S.B. (2009) *Geopolitics: The Geography of International Relations*, 2nd edn. Rowman & Littlefield Publishers, Lanham.

Cohen, S.B. (2003) *Geopolitics of the World System*. Rowman & Littlefield Publishers, Lanham.

Gerace, M. (1991) Between Mackinder and Spykman: Geopolitics, Containment, and After. *Comparative Strategy* 10 (4), 347–364.

Gray, C.A. (1977) *The Geopolitics of the Nuclear Era: Heartlands, Rimlands, and the Technological Revolution*. Crane, Russak, New York.

Hanson, V.D. (2005) *A War Like No Other: How the Athenians and Spartans Fought the Peloponnesian War*. Random House, New York.

Kagan, D. (1974) *The Archidamian War*. Cornell University Press, New York.

Kagan, D. (1969) *The Outbreak of the Peloponnesian War*. Cornell University Press, New York.

Kelly, P.L. (2006) A Critique of Critical Geopolitics. *Geopolitics* 11, 24–53.

Kelly, P.L. (1996) *Checkerboards and Shatterbelts: Geopolitics of South America*. University of Texas Press, Austin.

Kelly, P.L. (1986) Escalation of Regional Conflict: Testing the Shatterbelt Concept. *Political Geography Quarterly* 5, 161–180.

Kelly, P.L., de Hoyos, R., and Pérez L. (2002) Zonas Contextuales y en Disputa: Observaciones Generales y Modelo de la Cuenca del Rio de la Plata. *Argentina Global* 10, 1–10.

Mackinder, H. (1919) *Democratic Ideals and Reality: A Study in the Politics of Reconstruction*. Henry Holt, New York.

Meira Mattos, C. de (1975) *Geopolítico e Destino*. Livraria José Olympio Editora, Rio de Janeiro.

Spykman, N.J. (1942) *America's Strategies in World Politics: The United States and the Balance of Power*. Harcourt, Brace and Company, New York.

Chapter 38

Geopolitics
Part II

Merje Kuus

Introduction

Geopolitics is a controversial term invested with multiple meanings in political and intellectual debates. For some, it is attractive – a science that can authoritatively explain inter-state politics by properly anchoring it in stable geographical realities. For others, it is an ossified realm of state-centered, militaristic, and rigidly territorial understanding of the world – a trap to be avoided. In much of English-language geography today, geopolitics is neither to be coveted nor avoided; the term rather designates a critical analysis of the geographical assumptions and definitions that enter into the making of world politics (Agnew 2003: 2; O'Tuathail and Agnew 1992). To study geopolitics is to examine the ways in which political actors understand and practice international politics in spatial terms – through geographical and spatial conceptions of power, identity and justice. The geopolitical scholarship I discuss here does not content itself with stirring token "geographical variables" into analyses of world politics. To the contrary, it explicitly seeks to disrupt the mechanistic discourses that treat geographical space and geographical knowledge as variables. Its central focus is on the "politics of the geographical definition of politics" (Dalby 1991: 274). This strand of critical analysis has expanded rapidly over the last two decades.

This chapter highlights some key facets in current geopolitical scholarship and situates that work in broader intellectual developments within Anglo-American human geography. I approach the task in three steps. The following section will

The Wiley Blackwell Companion to Human Geography, First Edition.
Edited by John A. Agnew and James S. Duncan.
© 2011 John Wiley & Sons, Ltd. Published 2016 by John Wiley & Sons, Ltd.

briefly chart the path of the self-consciously critical scholarship from its emergence as a response to Cold War strategic analysis to its current diversity and internal debate. The subsequent section will give some sense of the key debates by looking at the field through the lens of one question: who are the agents or actors of geopolitics? I focus on that question because a number of current debates revolve around the role of different political institutions and social groups in everyday geopolitical practices. The concluding section will tentatively assess the influence of the field in geography and beyond. Throughout, my goal is to delineate one line of scholarship in contemporary human geography and situate this body of work in its wider social context. I attempt neither a neat definition nor a comprehensive review of the field.

Revival and Redefinition of Geopolitics

Throughout its history – the term was coined at the end of the 19th century – geopolitics has been associated with inter-state and nationalist violence. Because of its close ties to the military and intelligence apparatuses of states and empires, especially during World War II, the study of geopolitics was for decades after the war an intellectually stagnant field segregated from theoretical debates in the social sciences. Human geographers of the post-war years tended to stay away from the field; so much so that most geopolitical writing in these years had little to do with academic geography. Geographers did contest the dominant geopolitical discourses, but they by and large did not frame their arguments as geopolitical (Agnew 2009b).

The end of the Cold War spelled decline to the bipolar superpower rivalry that had framed world politics for 40 years. Much effort was quickly channeled into finding new explanatory models as politicians, academics, and pundits all started looking for explanatory fixes for the new world (dis)order. More geopolitical simplifications followed. As had been the case during the Cold War, the prominent texts came largely from outside geography. They were not necessarily framed in geopolitical terms because of the same image problems that the term had in geography. Neither did these writers explicitly advocate state expansion or inter-state conflict. However, the animating assumptions of these "new" models owed a great deal to classical geopolitics and Cold War strategic analysis from which they sprang. They were concerned with finding the best (i.e. the simplest) spatial fix to balance the presumed "objective" interests of territorially defined actors, chiefly states, and they were trapped in rigidly territorial binaries like Us versus Them, inside versus outside, or West versus East. Early blockbusters include Robert Kaplan's (1994) work on the "coming anarchy" of environmentally induced dystopia and Samuel Huntington's (1993) thesis of "civilizational clash" as an inevitable conflict among cultural blocks. Thomas Barnett's (2003) argument about the "non-integrating gap" – essentially the global South – as the principal source location of terrorism illustrates the same quest for clear models from the subsequent decade. In the 1990s, however, geography and other social sciences responded with direct critiques of the clichés sold as strategic insight in these packages (Kuus 2010).

This critical geographic work starts from the position that geographical knowledge claims are not neutral or objective. They do not simply describe but also produce political space (O'Tuathail 1996: 7). From this it follows that geography does not precede geopolitics as its natural basis. Rather, claims about the geographical bases of politics are themselves geopolitical practices. One could say that geographical claims are necessarily geopolitical as they inscribe places as particular types of places to be dealt with in a particular manner. Conversely, all politics is also geo-politics as it necessarily involves geographical assumptions about territories and borders. These assumptions are not abstract images floating above material interests but form an integral part of how interests and identities come into being. It furthermore follows that classical geopolitics' key claim – that it understands "objective" geographical determinants of power – holds no water. Such claims, the critics point out, in fact disengage from geographical complexities in favor of simplistic territorial demarcations of inside and outside, Us and Them. The mainstream geopolitical explanations are then not the hard-nosed objective descriptions of how the world "really" works that they claim to be. Instead, they are deeply political and ideological prescriptions how the world ought to work (Agnew 2003; Dalby 1991; O'Tuathail 1996).

As a body of work, this emerging scholarship came to be called critical geopolitics – "critical" because of its explicit departure from classical geopolitics. Much of this work is concerned with the social production of truth claims. For example, it does not ask how rivers or oil reserves as such shape international politics, which is the kind of question pondered in classical geopolitics. It rather asks how the primitive if widely held beliefs that these things "naturally" shape politics independently of human actions emerged historically, how it functions in contemporary political processes, and with what effects. The critical work brings into focus the ways in which complex political issues come to be framed as particular kinds of issues to be approached in a particular manner. Its goal is to offer richer accounts of space and power than those allowed within mainstream geopolitical analysis. In so doing, critical geopolitics seeks to destabilize such simplifications so that new space for debate and action could be established. Whereas traditional geopolitical writings try to make complex social realities seem familiar by molding them into various models, critical geopolitics seeks the opposite. It takes the familiar common-sense frameworks, such as the state system, and renders them unfamiliar by analyzing them as complex, contradictory, and contested historical and spatial processes (Agnew 2009b).

This may seem a rather straightforward shift from one dominant approach to another. It is not. The story of geopolitical writing in geography is not one of a linear expansion of one body of work, but of multiple dialogues and debates within and without geography. The core concern of these debates is not with the sources and structures of power in some general or universal sense; they rather seek to untangle the everyday operation of power relations in specific geographical contexts. The scholarship is therefore necessarily fractured. In an effort to make sense of the maze of interrelated arguments, I concentrate on one question: who are the subjects or agents of geopolitics? Put differently, who are the writers of geopolitics and how their interests and identities shape their daily work? How are we to study them without overlooking the social contexts and structures in which they operate? This question allows me to sketch some important arguments about the scope, method, and impact of geopolitical scholarship in human geography.

Who are the Subjects Of Geopolitics?

As geopolitics traditionally designates the realm of international politics, it is customarily if tacitly conceived as a high-brow matter best handled by specialized elites. Yet that same aura of power and secrecy also feeds popular fascination with geopolitics. Although explicitly geopolitical arguments evoke exclusive expertise, the categories of security and danger, community and enmity, Us and Them, on which these claims rely are formed at the popular level. There is a duality at play here whereby security and geopolitics excite popular fascination and play on popular beliefs and yet the authority to speak on them is relatively limited. This duality is a necessary part of geopolitical arguments. Their aura depends on it.

Traditional or classical geopolitics is crystal-clear about who are the subjects of geopolitics-as-statecraft: states and nations. The identities and interests of these subjects or actors are in this line of argument determined by their constant competitive struggle for primacy. Once this premise is destabilized, as it has been in geography and other social sciences, the path is open to ask who precisely make geopolitical concepts. Critical geopolitics has paid considerable attention to that question. The field's focus is not some putative pre-given actors (e.g. states) operating in pre-given places (e.g. state territories); it is rather on the spatial *processes* by which political subjects and their identities are formed. This attention to processes prompts discussion about geopolitical actors other than nation-states and spatialities other than state territoriality. The two facets of inquiry are linked. Once we open up the field of geopolitics to actors other than nation-states, we have to consider spatial frames other than the familiar patchwork of states. The reverse is true as well; once we give up the assumption that world politics is a game of territorial entities called states, we need to consider actors above and below nation-states; from international and supranational institutions like the United Nations or the European Union to non-governmental organization (NGOs) and transnational advocacy networks to everyday people in everyday places.

This interest in subject and identity formation is a part and parcel of the substantial work on culture and identity in geopolitics and international relations after the end of the Cold War. It is now widely accepted that geopolitical practices are intimately intertwined with the cultural concepts of community and identity. All states have geopolitical cultures, that is, traditions and customs of conceptualizing the state's interests and identity in global affairs. International sphere is not the realm of states expressing objective interests that pre-exist identity politics; rather the international sphere is a part and parcel of identity politics on multiple scales (Campbell 1998).

Empirically, the work on geopolitical cultures often focuses on statesmen (and until recent decades they were almost exclusively men), academics, and appointed advisors and bureaucrats who articulate putative state interests. They are intellectuals of statecraft – the academics, politicians, government officials and various commentators who regularly participate and comment on the activities of statecraft (O'Tuathail and Agnew 1992: 193). They are the agents of geopolitics that many people still have in mind – professionals like George Kennan (a key influence on the US's Cold War containment policy toward the Soviet Union), Henry Kissinger (former US government official and an influential commentator of international affairs), or Samuel Huntington (the author of the thesis of civilizational clash). Geography now includes a rich body of analysis of the conceptual frameworks of these US intellectuals of statecraft (Crampton and O'Tuathail 1996; Dalby 1990; O'Tuathail 1996; O'Tuathail and Agnew 1992). Geographers have also re-examined the key texts of classical geopolitics to illuminate the role of geographical knowledge in legitimizing the balance-of-power politics of the 19th and 20th centuries (Dodds and Atkinson 2000; Barnes and Farish 2006). The current period of warfare in Afganistan, Iraq, and elsewhere has drawn attention to the military-industrial complex and the spectacularly simplistic geopolitical models it propagates (Dalby 2008; Dodds and Ingram 2009; Gregory and Pred 2006; Roberts et al. 2003). A nuance to keep in mind is that the core concern of critical geopolitics is not with the specific content of what is said; it is rather with the assumptions and rules that make particular political practices seem legible and legitimate while making other practices appear illogical, unfeasible or illegitimate.

Although intellectuals of statecraft are closely linked to state institutions, we cannot assume that they merely voice some pre-given state interest. Their geopolitical practices need to be carefully contextualized in their specific societal settings. For example, we cannot understand American geopolitics of the Cold War era without considering the personal anti-communism of some of the leading writers (Crampton and O'Tuathail 1996). We likewise cannot comprehend the culturalist flavor Central European geopolitics without considering the arts and humanities backgrounds of many of the region's leading politicians (Kuus 2007). In that example, humanities backgrounds give these individuals special legitimacy to speak in the name of culture and identity.

Recent scholarship has also broadened analysis from top-level elected officials and their appointed advisors (like Kissinger) to career bureaucrats in multiple places in the state apparatus, as well as professionals in international organizations, corporations, NGOs and other non-state actors. This is linked to growing interest in policy processes not as straightforward expressions of state interest but as more unpredictable and open-ended processes. Intellectuals of statecraft do often further state interest, but they are not simply faceless unthinking minions of the state apparatus. As they occupy strategic positions in foreign policy institutions, they are also (relatively) well placed to resist and transform dominant geopolitical discourses. A better understanding of their role in the practice of geopolitics requires that we study the practices that have to do not only with the interests of particular players, but also with daily routines of bureaucratic coordination and social interaction. Iver Neumann (2007) points out that one major speech by the Norwegian Foreign Minister involves 120 hours of work by various officials in the ministry – or, more precisely – 120 hours "plus canteen talk." These 120 plus hours cannot be deduced from the end product, such as a speech by the Minister, but must be studied as an object of analysis in its own right. This would allow us to better discern the contingent and contested character of geopolitical practice.

This closer attention to daily policy processes is easier said than done of course. Foreign and security policies can still be remarkably insular and hierarchical affairs, more so than other realms of state policy. Because of the requirements of protecting "state secrets," foreign policy professionals are highly sequestered in terms of their access to information as well as physical space. As a result, much of foreign policy processes, especially discussions at higher levels of state institutions, are accessible solely through formal written documents. Although political geographers have taken noticeable interest in ethnographic methods in recent years in order to develop close-up accounts of the everyday processes of policy-making, empirical work is still scant (Jeffrey 2008; Megoran 2006).

Moreover, policy-making bureaucracies, whether state-based or not, are only one slice of geopolitical practice. As noted above, the allure and success of geopolitical reasoning depends on its seemingly common-sense character. Geopolitics appears at once an esoteric stuff of exclusive back-room deals in high places *as well as* a natural and self-evident matter of laws as visible as mountain-ranges. This points to the need to study how geopolitical practices operate in the sphere of popular culture. There is now indeed significant research on popular media, from newspapers and magazines through cartoons, graphic novels, films, and pop music, to computer games and blogs (Dittmer 2007; Dittmer and Sturm 2010; Dodds 2006; Dodds and Atkinson 2000; O'Tuathail and Dalby 1998; Power 2007; Sharp 2000). In particular, the current period of militarization and political violence has fuelled substantial geopolitics scholarship on the "war on terror" and its related practices of surveillance and control (Dodds and Ingram 2009; Falah *et al.* 2006; Gregory 2006; Gregory and Pred 2006; Kuus 2009; Pain and Smith 2008; Sidaway 2008). These studies analyze both the production and the consumption of geopolitical claims. They foreground the elite and popular legitimacy of geopolitical concepts like balance of power or buffer zone and they highlight the pivotal role of popular culture in both reproducing and contesting elite geopolitical practices.

Popular culture and everyday life are vast and diverse realms, and so is the scholarship on it. One key strand in this work is feminist geopolitics. This research explicitly shifts the focus from the operations of elite agents to the constructions of political subjects in everyday political practice. It thereby seeks to illuminate the institutional structure through which the illusory division between the recognizably political and putatively non-political spheres is constructed (Hyndman 2004; Secor 2001). For example, it argues, even critical scholars sometimes lapse into the assumption that the international sphere is the principal theatre of geopolitics, thereby treating "domestic" issues such as struggles over citizenship, military recruitment, or gender roles as non-geopolitical matters (Hyndman 2004; Gilmartin and Kofman 2004). Another burgeoning strand of this interest in actors other than elites is the scholarship on resistance geopolitics of resistance. This work shows that resistance involves not only heroic acts of opposition to overt repression but also a myriad of unremarkable subversive practices within hegemonic spaces that subvert dominant understandings of world politics without open protest (Kuus 2008; Pain and Smith 2008; Sharp *et al.* 2000). It stresses the close entanglements of power and resistance and the impracticality of searching for some romanticized analytical territory of the obviously good. As an example, one only needs to consider that resistance to dominant geopolitical discourses comes not only from various progressive groups (as is sometimes conveniently assumed), but also from fundamentalists of various stripes (Dittmer and Sturm 2010).

There has also been considerable effort to broaden the study of geopolitics out of the key centers of western power. As critical geopolitics emphasizes the particularities of geographical context, it logically seeks to understand how geopolitical claims are produced and consumed in different places. This is all the more important as many of the simplifications offered as global strategic insight are in fact highly parochial: they are developed in specific societal contexts – often the US – and then projected out as universal principles of how the world works. One of the tasks then is to show that these concepts arise from specific societal and historical context. Given the global impact of US foreign policy, much of critical geopolitics likewise focuses on the US. However, the appeal of geopolitics, with all its analytical traps, is not confined to the global North. The US and its closest allies are furthermore not the only actors with political agency in the world. As John Agnew (2003: 175) reminds us: "bad ideas are not an American or western monopoly." Concepts travel: good and bad ideas are adopted and appropriated in different places and are transformed in the process. There are now substantial literatures on powerful states like Britain, Germany, France, and Russia (Hepple 2000; Dodds 2002; Bassin 2003; O'Loughlin *et al.* 2005). In addition to these obvious cases, and perhaps more interestingly, there are also numerous studies of geopolitical traditions of smaller and historically more peripheral states (O'Tuathail and Dalby 1998; Dodds and Atkinson 2000; Megoran 2005; Sidaway and Power 2005; Kuus 2007). This work amply demonstrates both the consistency and diversity of geopolitical thought. In terms of consistency, claims of national exceptionalism or external threat are extraordinarily stable throughout the 20th century. As for diversity, geopolitical practices are deeply rooted in the specific political circumstances of particular countries. Some claims are indeed repeated, but their political functions and effects vary considerably.

This nudges us to analyze geopolitics beyond the "usual suspects" core states like the United States. The task is to counter geopolitical simplifications everywhere, whether they come from the corridors of the Pentagon or a village in Russia. There is no single tradition of geopolitical thought or practice; there are rather different geopolitical cultures owing to specific geographical contexts and intellectual traditions. These traditions involve not only the predictable right-wing tradition of geopolitical analyses but also a critical and radical tradition of geopolitics, as for example, on the pages of the French journal *Herodote* (Hepple 2000).

As indicated earlier, once we bypass the idea that states are the only important actors of world politics, we have to rethink the spatial frames of politics. Contemporary geographic scholarship shows that international politics does not conform to territorial forms: the familiar patchwork of states with clearly defined borders. It thereby advances the drift away from rigidly territorialized understandings of politics toward more nuanced understanding of the multiple overlapping spatialities at work. For example, we now have voluminous work on borders not as pre-given lines on the ground but as complex and contested practices of bordering at international as well as subnational scales (Newman 2006; Paasi 2005; Sparke 2006). This work does not deny or neglect the key role of the state – this would be clearly naïve. It rather decenters the state from its hitherto presumed monopoly position so that other spatial configurations can be analyzed. The key questions are not about the "real" sources, meanings or limits of state territoriality in some general or universal sense, but, more specifically, about *how* state power operates in territorial and non-territorial forms (Agnew 2009a; Coleman 2005; Cox *et al.* 2008).

All of these strands of inquiry draw attention to actors other than core states and their official representatives. The point they make is not simply that we should be considering more geopolitical actors, such as international organizations, non-profits, ethnic or religious groups, ordinary citizens, and so on and so forth. The task rather is to unpack geopolitical discourses without reifying social groups and the spatial effects of their practices. It is to more closely consider the daily production geopolitical knowledge in seemingly banal bureaucratic and everyday settings. This would help us to illuminate the *multiple* structures of authority and legitimacy through which geopolitical arguments work.

Conclusion: Geopolitics as Multiple Critiques

In one sense, then, geopolitics is quite a clear term in today's Anglo-American geography. It is a body of self-consciously critical analysis of the dominant practices of international politics. In another way, it is also ambiguous in that within this broad agreement, the lines of (re)examining the spatiality of politics have proliferated. When considering the significance of this multiplication and diffusion of critiques, it is not helpful to look for the "state of the art" or find out cumulative achievement. The field is too diverse for such an exercise. It is likewise overly simplistic to think of geopolitical work in negative terms as a monolithic critique of some equally monolithic traditional approach. It is rather a set of interrelated inquiries, drawing from broader critiques of positivist and state-centered conceptions of politics, into the multiple processes by which political space is produced.

This raises the question of whether change has been so profound that we can drop the adjective "critical" when describing this work. As Anglo-American human geography has debunked the myth about the natural workings of international politics, has the label critical become redundant? Does it imply – incorrectly – that work not branded as "critical" necessarily lacks such an analytical edge? Does it tacitly claim a monopoly of insight and thereby lead to a collective navel-gazing? Could excessive criticism moreover constitute an unhelpful negative program of undermining what exists rather than a positive effort of creating something new? One could argue that in today's context of violence and warfare, global environmental degradation, and staggering inequalities, scholarship needs to move beyond criticism and propose clear alternatives. These are questions worth pondering if critical geopolitical scholarship is to have impact beyond academia.

True, critical approaches to geopolitics have become mainstream in Anglo-American human geography. Work not labeled critical geopolitics is more often than not also informed by critical analytical stance from intellectual traditions like Marxism and feminism (Flint 2005; Cowen and Gilbert 2007; Pain and Smith 2008). However, it would be unhelpful to toss out the term "critical" altogether. This is because the impact of critical geopolitics on mainstream analyses of international affairs has been modest. The use of the term outside academic geography – the kinds of things that come up when one types "geopolitics" into various search engines or attends geopolitical discussions outside geography – still owes a great deal to classical geopolitics. Perhaps this goes with the territory: geopolitics has always been intimately tied to the exercise of state power and still is today. Anchoring militaristic and expansionary political strategies in seemingly self-evident geographical realities is still attractive. The last decade of military activities and high-profile security debates in many countries have indeed resulted in greater use of explicitly geopolitical language even in the circles – the European Union, for example – where it used to be frowned upon (Bialasiewicz *et al.* 2009). This comeback of geopolitics outside geography is all too often explicitly militaristic and mostly uninformed by calls for greater reflexivity. There is no lack of unexamined geographical assumptions to unpack as critical geopolitical analyses have mostly not reached the ears or minds of the many self assured geopoliticians outside academia. The project in critical geopolitics is moreover not one of criticism for its own sake – just to assert the field's intellectual distinction. It is rather to offer better accounts of how power operates spatially – better in the sense of more nuanced than those allowed within mainstream geopolitical analysis. Geopolitics in geography is ultimately a positive intellectual and political program of inquiry into the complex spatialities of politics.

References

Agnew, J.A. (2009a) *Globalization and Sovereignty*. Rowman & Littlefield Publishers, Lanham.

Agnew, J.A. (2009b) Making the strange familiar: geographical analogy in global geopolitics. *The Geographical Review*, 99 (3), 426–443.

Agnew, J.A. (2003) *Geopolitics: Re-visioning World Politics*. Routledge, London.

Barnett, T.P.M. (2003) Pentagon's new map: war and peace in the twenty-first century. *Esquire* 3, 174–179; 227–228.

Barnes, T.J. and Farish, M. (2006) Between regions: science, militarism, and American geography from World War to Cold War. *Annals of the Association of American Geographers* 96 (4), 807–826.

Bassin, M. (2003) Between realism and the "new right": geopolitics in Germany in the 1990s. *Transactions of the Institute of British Geographers* 28 (3), 350–366.

Bialasiewicz, L., Dahlman, C., Apuzzo G.M., *et al.* (2009) Interventions in the new political geographies of the European "neighbourhood". *Political Geography* 28 (2), 79–89.

Campbell, D. (1998) *Writing Security: United States Foreign Policy and the Politics of Identity*. University of Minnesota Press, Minneapolis.

Coleman, M. (2005) U.S. statecraft and the U.S.-Mexico border as security/economy nexus. *Political Geography*. 24 (2), 185–209.

Cowen, D. and Gilbert, E. (2007) Introduction. In D. Cowen and E. Gilbert (eds), *War, Citizenship, Territory*. Routledge, New York, pp. 1–30.

Cox, K., Robinson, J., Low, M. (2008) *The Handbook of Political Geography*. Sage Publications, London.

Crampton, A. and O'Tuathail, G. (1996) Intellectuals, institutions and ideology: the case of Robert Strausz-Hupe and "American geopolitics". *Political Geography* 15 (6/7), 533–555.

Dalby, S. (2008) Imperialism, domination, culture: the continued relevance of critical geopolitics. *Geopolitics* 13 (3), 413–436.

Dalby, S. (1991) Critical geopolitics: discourse, difference, and dissent. *Environment and Planning D: Society and Space* 9 (3), 261–283.

Dalby, S. (1990) *Creating the Second Cold War: The Discourse of Politics*. Guilford, New York.

Dittmer, J. and Sturm, T. (2010) *Mapping the End Times*. Ashgate, Aldershot.

Dittmer, J. (2007) The tyranny of the serial: popular geopolitics, the nation, and comic book discourse. *Antipode* 39 (2), 247–268.

Dodds, K. (2006) Popular geopolitics and audience dispositions: James Bond and the Internet Movie Database (IMDb). *Transactions of the Institute of British Geographers* 31 (2), 116–130.

Dodds, K. (2005) *Global Geopolitics: A Critical Introduction*. Pearson, Essex.

Dodds, K. (2002) *Pink Ice: Britain and the South Atlantic Empire*. Tauris Publishers, London and New York.

Dodds, K. and Atkinson, D. (2000) *Geopolitical Traditions: A Century of geopolitical Thought*. Routledge, London.

Dodds, K. and Ingram, A. (2009) *Spaces of Security and Insecurity: Geographies of the War on Terror*. Ashgate, Aldershot.

Falah, G.W., Flint, C., and Mamadouh, V. (2006) Just war and extraterritoriality: the popular geopolitics of the United States' war on Iraq as reflected in newspapers of the Arab world. *Annals of the Association of American Geographers* 96 (1), 142–164.

Flint, C. (2005) *The Geography of War and Peace: From Death Camps to Diplomats*. Oxford University Press, Oxford.

Gilmartin, M. and Kofman, E. (2004) Critically feminist geopolitics. In L.A. Staeheli, E. Kofman, and L.J. Peake (eds), *Mapping Women, Making Politics*. Routledge, London, pp.113–126.

Gregory, D. (2006) The black flag: Guantánamo Bay and the space of exception. *Geografiska Annaler* 88B (4), 405–427.

Gregory, D. and Pred, A. (2006) *Violent Geographies: Fear, Terror and Political Violence*. Routledge, New York.

Hepple, L.W. (2000) Geopolitiques de Gauche: Yves Lacoste, *Herodote* and French radical geopolitics. In D. Klaus and D. Atkinson (eds), *Geopolitical Traditions: A Century of Geopolitical Thought*. Routledge, London, pp. 268–301.

Huntington, S.P. (1993) The Clash of Civilizations? *Foreign Affairs* 72 (3), 22–49.

Hyndman, J. (2004) Mind the gap: bridging feminist and political geography through geopolitics. *Political Geography* 23 (3), 307–322.

Jeffrey, A. (2008) Contesting Europe: the politics of Bosnian integration into European structures. *Environment and Planning D: Society and Space* 26, 448–463.

Kaplan, R.D. (1994) The coming anarchy. *Atlantic Monthly* February, 44–76.

Kuus, M. (2010) Critical geopolitics. In R. Denemark (ed.), *Compendium of International Studies*. Blackwell, New York and London, pp 683–701.

Kuus, M. (2008) Švejkian geopolitics: subversive obedience in Central Europe. *Geopolitics* 13 (2), 257–277.

Kuus, M. (2009) Cosmopolitan militarism?: spaces of NATO expansion. *Environment and Planning* A41, 545–562.

Kuus, M. (2007) *Geopolitics Reframed: Security and Identity in Europe's Eastern Enlargement*. Palgrave Macmillan, New York.

Megoran, N. (2006) For ethnography in political geography: experiencing and re-imagining Ferghana Valley boundary closures. *Political Geography* 25, 622–640.

Megoran, N. (2005) The critical geopolitics of danger in Uzbekistan and Kyrgyzstan. *Environment and Planning D: Society and Space* 23, 555–580.

Neumann, I.B. (2007) A speech that the entire ministry may stand for. *International Political Sociology* 1, 183–200.

Newman, D. (2006) The lines that continue to separate us: borders in our "borderless" world. *Progress in Human Geography* 30 (2), 143–161.

O'Loughlin, J., O'Tuathail, G., and Kolossov, V. (2005) Russian geopolitical culture and public opinion: the masks of Proteus revisited. *Transactions of the Institute of British Geographers* 30 (3), 322–335.

O'Tuathail, G. (1996) *Critical Geopolitics: The Politics of Writing Global Space*. University of Minnesota Press, Minneapolis.

O'Tuathail, G. and Agnew, J. (1992) Geopolitics and discourse: practical geopolitical reasoning in American foreign policy. *Political Geography* 11 (2), 190–204.

O'Tuathail, G. and Dalby, S. (1998) *Rethinking Geopolitics*. Routledge, New York.

Paasi, A. (2005) Generations and the "development" of border studies. *Geopolitics* 10, 663–671.

Pain, R. and Smith, S. (eds) (2008) *Fear: Critical Geopolitics and Everyday Life*. Ashgate, Aldershot.

Power, M. (2007) Digitized virtuosity: video war games and post-9/11 cyber-deterrence. *Security Dialogue* 38 (2), 271–288.

Roberts, S., Secor, A., and Sparke, M. (2003) Neoliberal geopolitics. *Antipode* 35 (5), 886–896.

Secor, A.J. (2001) Toward a feminist counter-geopolitics: gender, space and Islamist politics in Istanbul. *Space and Polity* 5 (3), 199–219.

Sharp, J. (2000) *Condensing the Cold War: Reader's Digest and American Identity*. University of Minnesota Press, Minneapolis.

Sharp, J., Routledge, P., Philo, C. and Paddison, R. (eds) (2000) *Entanglements of Power: Geographies of Domination/Resistance*. Routledge, London.

Sidaway, J. (2008) The dissemination of banal geopolitics: webs of extremism and insecurity. *Antipode* 40 (1), 1–8.

Sidaway, J.D. and Power, M. (2005) The tears of Portugal: empire, identity, race, and destiny in Portuguese geopolitical narratives. *Environment and Planning D: Society and Space* 23, 527–544.

Sparke, M. (2006) A neoliberal nexus: economy, security and the biopolitics of citizenship on the border. *Political Geography* 25 (2), 151–180.

Further Reading

Textbooks that trace the history of geopolitics and offer engaging introductions to key concepts include Agnew 2003 and Dodds 2005. See also O'Tuathail and Agnew 1992 for a clear explanation of the tricky concept of geopolitical discourse. For a reader that includes excerpts from original geopolitical writings of the past hundred years, combined with short introductions to various aspects of the critical scholarship, see O'Tuathail, Dalby and Routledge 2006. In addition, edited volumes, such as O'Tuathail and Dalby 1996, Dodds and Atkinson 2000, Dodds and Ingram 2009, Gregory and Pred 2007; and Pain and Smith 2008 offer a range of essays on the history and contemporary practice of geopolitics. *Geopolitics* and *Political Geography* are the best geographic journals for geopolitical scholarship on a wide range of topics.

Chapter 39

Segregation
Part I

Larry S. Bourne and R. Alan Walks

Introduction

Segregation is a surprisingly old concept that in its modern form comes with both excess baggage and attitude. The literature on the subject is also vast and the history of academic interest in, and use of, the term is very long – from its medieval roots in natural science to its origins in contemporary social science, including the social reform movement of the late 19th century and human ecology in the early 20th century, to more recent studies of enclaves, citadels and ghettos.

There are at least two related meanings attached to the term. The first and broadest meaning is to differentiate, distinguish, or isolate, usually in a non-spatial way, one or more natural or social groups from the population from which it is taken, as one would do in a science experiment, in educational streaming, or in an attempt to prevent the spread of infectious disease. Under the second meaning, segregation refers to the spatial separation of specific social groups from the wider population within urban space, and this application is the subject of this commentary. Generally, a social group is considered "segregated" if the spatial distribution of its members (typically measured in terms of place of residence, either at the neighborhood or district scale) differs significantly from that of the larger population; the greater the difference in spatial distributions the higher the degree or level of segregation. This basic definition is more-or-less universally accepted, but it raises questions about application and interpretation that warrant further discussion and a critical reassessment. Beyond the fact that it is based on abstract notions of spatial evenness,

The Wiley Blackwell Companion to Human Geography, First Edition.
Edited by John A. Agnew and James S. Duncan.
© 2011 John Wiley & Sons, Ltd. Published 2016 by John Wiley & Sons, Ltd.

clustering, and integration, it also raises the question of whether more analytically precise terms would be more appropriate in certain circumstances.

There is, under this second geographical meaning, a strong negative connotation attached to the term "segregation," which to most readers implies some combination of induced or forced separation, isolation, and social deprivation. When ethnic or racial groups are segregated, the mechanism producing spatial unevenness is often assumed to be racial discrimination in the housing market. At its extreme, this is associated with processes of ghettoisation whereby an ethnic or racial group is compelled to concentrate in certain neighborhoods and marginalized from the social world of the "host" community, as has often been the case of blacks in the United States (Wacquant 2008). However, there is also an extensive literature on immigrant enclaves, in which newcomers to cities use local neighborhood community resources as stepping stones toward assimilation and potentially geographic dispersal. Under transnational globalization, concentrated "ethnic communities" and "ethnoburbs" are increasingly seen as the desired end-point, as neighborhoods of choice on the part of middle-class members of certain ethnic and racial communities (Li 2009; Qadeer 2005). There can therefore be both "good" and "bad" forms of ethnic concentration, and both voluntary and involuntary (discriminatory) forms of segregation can, and usually do, exist within the same city (though the neighborhoods relevant to each may differ) (Peach 1996, 2005).

The segregation of poor or low-income residents is conceptually distinct from racial and ethnic segregation, although in many places (such as the United States) the poorest class and the most marginalized race may be the same social group. But this is not always the case, and the mechanisms producing concentrated poverty are not necessarily the same as those producing racial segregation. A slum is not the same thing as a ghetto, even if they do appear in the same places in many cities. Instead, the segregation of the poor (and rich) is the combined result of unequal access to a differentiated housing market and significant inequality in income and wealth stemming from the operation of the capitalist labor market. It is thus neither voluntary nor involuntary in the same sense as ethnic and racial segregation, but induced by market inequalities. Unfortunately, a number of scholars make the mistake of equating class and racial segregation, for instance by referring to neighborhoods with poverty rates greater than 40 percent as "ghetto neighborhoods" (Jargowsky 1997; Kazemipur and Halli 2000). The distinction is important, because the policy responses required to alleviate concentrated poverty are different from those needed to address advanced racial marginalization (Wacquant 2008).

In this brief commentary we provide a critical review of the concept of segregation, and the emphasis placed on forms of urban residential segregation in the academic literature. The argument here is two-fold: that there has been an oversimplified emphasis on residential unevenness, and especially ethno-racial unevenness, in urban research at the expense of other equally important issues; and second, that the overwhelmingly negative interpretations attached to geographically concentrated residential communities inhibits careful assessments of important dimensions of urban daily life, including residents' aspirations for improved living conditions, and the specific problems they face. Before addressing these issues, however, we examine alternative measurement indices and outline a summary of different interpretations of the implications of segregation.

Dimensions and Measurement

Most researchers now agree that whatever definition of segregation is used it is not a uni-dimensional concept or the outcome of a singular process. Nor can it be accurately measured with a single index. Since the classic studies of Duncan and Duncan (1955), Peach (1975) and Massey and Denton (1988, 1993), the measurement of residential segregation is commonly recognized as requiring several components or dimensions. At least five different dimensions have been proposed: 1) evenness, 2) exposure, 3) clustering, 4) centralization and 5) concentration. The construction of these multivariate indices not only tells us something about the complexity of social segregation but also about the assumptions underlying the interpretation of those indices.

The first dimension, unevenness, as noted above, refers to the unequal distribution of social groups across spatial units within an urban area, and is typically measured by the dissimilarity index D. This index measures the residential location of one group in relation to the distribution of another reference group (usually the majority population), and is the most widely used measure of racial and ethnic segregation in the literature. A common alternative to D is the entropy index, which despite its interpretative complexity, has the distinct advantage of measuring separation between several groups on more than one variable at the same time, and thus provides the option of decomposing the spatial patterns and identifying the relative contribution of each variable to that pattern (Fischer 2003).

The second dimension is exposure, or its converse, isolation (various P* indices), defined as the probability that members of certain groups will be physically "exposed" to members of other groups through a sharing of urban residential space. This is a useful addition, but there is typically little or no reference to the actual spatial scales at which this exposure might take place, and little theoretical work to guide the developing of robust measures of true exposure. The other three dimensions are more explicitly spatial.

The third dimension, clustering, typically measured as spatial proximity (SP), refers to the extent that neighborhoods inhabited by ethnic or racial minority groups actually adjoin one another, based on the ratio of average distances within and between different groups.

The fourth dimension, defined as centralization (the ACE index), measures the degree to which the group in question is located close to the city centre, compared to the overall population distribution. In some cities, notably those with declining urban cores, this measure serves as a surrogate for sharp contrasts in the quality of living environments and accessibility to services and employment; in other cities this measure may be less informative.

The fifth dimension, a measure of concentration and dispersal (the C index), is based on the relative amount of space occupied by different groups, for example, by disadvantaged groups relative to the reference population. In this case space, and density, then act as indirect measures of both social isolation and potential interaction.

Each of these five, as Massey and Denton (1988; 1993) illustrate, have their own individual strengths and weaknesses, and each index measures a somewhat different expression of the residential segregation process. They argue that the most comprehensive view is provided when indices for all five dimensions are employed in combination. High scores on all five indices may indicate a condition of "hyper-segregation," a situation of extreme residential isolation, marginalization, and inequality. Although advances in measurement techniques continue to appear in the literature, including redefined neighborhood units and the use of more nuanced spatial statistics to overcome distortions due to the number or size of units, one does wonder whether the law of diminishing returns to effort has already set in for such indices.

An Assessment

Adding complexity to the measurement issue, and to any interpretation of causes and consequence, is the elementary point that localized segregation cannot be interpreted in isolation from the socio-economic and political contexts influencing the city and the broader society of which it is a part. Segregation – or what in more neutral terms might be labeled neighborhood or residential differentiation – is closely intertwined with (and embedded in) a myriad of other processes operating on and through the contemporary urban landscape. These include the changing geographies of poverty and unemployment, shifts in migration regimes and immigration flows, the nature of local systems of housing provision and mortgage finance, the myopic operation of real estate markets, changes in the distribution of public goods and services, disamenities such as crime and pollution, and the effects of unequal political representation and the skewed distribution of income and power, among other factors. These are all important expressions and processes that can and do lead to urban differentiation, and represent potential sources of social and spatial inequalities.

But the spatial patterns resulting from these processes are not necessarily strongly correlated within urban space. For example, not all areas of "concentrated" racial, ethnic or minority populations, not even all the classic ghettos in US inner cities, are low income; not all have homogeneous and politically marginalized populations; not all have poor public services, high crime rates or limited access to jobs. Indeed, the highest levels of ethnic residential concentration in many cities are often for some of the higher income groups, such as middle-class fractions of the Chinese or East Asian populations (Walks and Bourne 2006), and/or for groups that are not recent immigrants, such as the gay, Italian or Jewish populations. This place-of-living clustering occurs as a result of a myriad of processes, not all of which are related to discrimination at the neighborhood scale.

Moreover, residential location is only one point, albeit an important reference point, in the multiple prisms that constitute daily urban life. Is it justified to generalize from residential location patterns to social and living conditions writ large? Other relevant spheres of life include, but are not limited to, the composition of work-places and access to jobs, networks of social interaction, access to shopping, recreation, social services and the availability of health services. People radiate out from their home base to engage in these activities, or to consume services, and in doing so are involved in multiple spheres and communities of interest. Those communities may also have quite different characteristics, and entry conditions, than the neighborhood or districts from which the daily journey originated. Greater affluence and access to automobile transportation has brought higher levels of spatial mobility, resulting in a greater role for regional connections at the expense of local ones. A broader conceptualization of social differentiation, and a more precise definition of segregation, would thus have to include an individual's relative position in communities of interest beyond the immediate neighborhood, as well as the degree of personal mobility.

A related problem is that segregation indices, or at least high levels of observed residential concentration and unevenness, are often assumed to be equated with most or all of the varied dimensions through which urban life is organized. Residential location decisions, and levels of housing consumption, are clearly local manifestations of broader social, racial, gender, income, and political inequalities, but they are only part of the overall picture. The segregation label is often applied too widely and uncritically, and as a consequence it frequently conceals as much as it illuminates. The challenge for researchers is to separate, isolate, and disentangle the contribution of these various factors to residential differentiation and to identify their consequences in terms of the quality of life opportunities available within varying communities and at different spatial scales (e.g. from neighborhoods to the city at large).

Residential differentiation, aka segregation, is clearly a multi-dimensional process with a range of sources and multi-scalar outcomes. In current usage, however, segregation often implies motivation, the coordinated intention to isolate, dominate and control on the part of some group, usually the host (majority) population. It is often assumed to involve involuntary actions, based on limited choice, as the result of overt discrimination supported by an unequal distribution of power and/or outright social engineering by institutions and individual groups. In other words, structure prevails over agency. In some circumstances, such as the classic US ghetto, this interpretation is undeniably accurate, although even in this case the actual mechanisms driving concentration are frequently misidentified (Wacquant 1997, 2008) In many other cases the label is misleading or simply incorrect. Choice and preferences in residential selection are often not assigned a place of prominence in the discourse.

Most academic researchers are aware of these issues. A distinction is commonly made between voluntary separation, in which individuals chose to locate in close proximity to those with similar attributes in order to access a range of social supports, a critical mass of cultural infrastructure, ethnic institutions and businesses and religious services, etc.; and involuntary segregation, which is the result of being compelled to locate in particular districts (and/or discouraged/prevented from locating in other districts). But how do we distinguish between the two? Segregation indices certainly do not in themselves provide an answer, or even a means to an answer.

It is possible to argue – without evoking a Tiebout public choice paradigm – that in most circumstances, people do have choices, albeit often limited, and that after weighing the alternatives many chose to locate in communities dominated by people with shared origins and interests and similar service needs. The immigrant reception area is a classic and well-known example. These areas offer more hospitable and supportive environments especially for newcomers to the city and the host culture. The point is that own-group preferences and social networks may in fact play a very large role in residential location decisions (Clark 2002; Qadeer 2005; Peach 2005).

These critical comments are not, to be clear, intended to imply that segregation by race is not a serious issue in many cities, especially for black Americans and Hispanics in older US cities, or particular groups of immigrants in European and Canadian cities. Nor is it intended here to deflate the importance of discrimination against specific social groups, especially in the private housing market. Nor, on the other hand, is the above assessment meant to suggest that geographically concentrated poverty is not present in most western cities, or that concentrations of the most disadvantaged do not add significantly to the stresses of poverty in general. These issues, however, should be the target of further focused research (and public policy initiatives) and not assumed to be present whenever social clustering occurs. And, of course, even in the absence of induced or involuntary segregation, extreme levels of separation are undoubtedly costly in terms of social cohesion and market efficiency, for both society and the individuals involved (Carr and Kutty 2008).

There is a broader question as well of whether residential segregation has overly dominated research on the processes of growth and change in cities to an extent that is the detrimental to research on the actual processes of integration and on other crucial issues of social equity. This question is most obviously relevant in any review of the US literature in which segregation continues to be a dominant research paradigm, and in which the residential hyper-separation of black and white citizens is most apparent (Johnston, Paulsen and Forrest 2007; Wacquant, 2008). Indeed, the black/white cleavage remains the foundation and the frame for a large portion of American urban geography. Is this emphasis appropriate for contemporary periods and in other national contexts? There is, for example, recent evidence suggesting that levels of racial segregation in US cities have been declining, while those based on differences in income and status are increasing (Massey, Rothwell and Domina 2009). We can assume that the severity of the economic transformation that began in the late 2000s will only add to income, housing, and neighborhood inequalities.

A number of other specific criticisms are relevant here. As argued above, mainstream segregation measures typically address only residential location patterns and primarily at one scale, typically the census tract, rather than at multiple scales. Moreover, the standard indices are overwhelmingly based on place of residence not, as argued above, on differences in the full spectrum of communities in which households are enveloped as part of their daily urban life. Relatively little work has been done, for example, on work-place or occupational segregation in a disaggregated spatial context (Charles and Grusky 2004). Nor is there much research available on variations in the quality of public urban goods and services between neighborhoods (except perhaps for the quality of local schools), and on how these variations link to levels of "real" household income levels and to inequalities in opportunities. How much of a difference does it make to the quality of life and local consumption if the quality of public goods is highly variable or more-or-less uniform across urban neighborhoods, and how do these in turn relate to differences in the income or ethnicity of the residents? Do public goods and services substitute for wage income?

Typically, analyses of spatial differentiation and segregation are also cross-sectional; comparing snapshots of social landscapes based on census years. Seldom do they address the dynamics of residential change and mobility, the flow-through of populations, and the specific mechanisms provoking, restricting or shaping such changes. For example, there is limited evidence that would allow us to identify the length of time that households are resident in the most disadvantaged areas. As we know, turnover rates are especially high in lower income and immigrant areas and only a certain proportion of households actually remain in those areas for long periods of time. Those with the most limited mobility have different vulnerabilities and needs than the transitional populations for whom greater exit options exist. Do disadvantaged individuals – from either low income or ethno-racial groups – tend to move to neighborhoods with similar problems and attributes, such that the equality deficit is simply relocated? Or do they move to other neighborhoods with lower concentrations of like individuals and perhaps fewer problems? Typically, very little data exists that would help researchers distinguish between such groups, the processes driving relocation decisions, and the geography of relocation. Finally, segregation indices themselves tend to be macro rather than micro in focus; and like similar indices they are subject to spatial extremes, boundary effects, and distortions resulting from even minor differences in scales of analysis (including the size of districts and social groups). Segregation indices are thus a rather blunt instrument for analysis and policy intervention.

Social Mix: How, Where and for Whom?

The flip side of residential segregation, in theory and practice, is diversity, or more precisely, social mix. The strongly negative connotations usually associated with high levels of residential differentiation, especially again for disadvantaged populations, are made to seem worse by the simple exercise of "labeling" various forms of spatial differentiation as the outcome of segregation. This, in turn, has contributed to a recent resurgence of interest – in scholarly research and public policy – on the merits of social mixing, at least at the local or neighborhood scale. Indeed, social mix is now one of the taken-for-granted pillars of social housing policy and physical planning in cities throughout developed countries. The assumption is that if the concentration of one ethnic, racial or minority group, or alternatively of low income populations, is negative, then social mixing by definition (and diversity by implication) must be positive. Who, other than racists and elitists, could be against social mixing? Concentrating large numbers of disadvantaged people together in individual projects, neighborhoods or municipalities is assumed to impact their quality-of-life, and to augment problematic neighborhood effects that limit future life chances and mobilities. Of course, geographical separation and dispersal is equally unlikely to encourage more social understanding, empathy and acceptance among society's different social strata and diverse cultural groups.

But is social mixing desirable for all? And, if so, at what geographic scale should it be defined and encouraged? Is the relative absence of social mix in residential space – for example at the census tract level – a problem, and if so, for whom? How fine-grained should mixing be: the building, the street, the neighborhood, the municipality? In which institutions should a priority be placed on social mixing: schools, communities, workplaces, or political communities? Are the benefits of racial mixing and diversity the same as those of mixing the poor with wealthy households? Despite the lack of evidence available to answer these questions, social mixing is now accepted public policy practice. Paradoxically, while ethnic and racial diversity are usually cited as one of the goals of such a policy, the actual policy tools used to achieve "social mix" almost always involve the mixing of *classes*, usually through tenure mixing (renters and owners), and by giving a portion of local housing in a poor neighborhood (such as a social housing project) to middle class or wealthy residents. Recent reviews of the application of this concept in urban policy illustrate the limitations: these include recent studies of efforts to achieve greater mix in new suburban neighborhoods (Galster 2007), in gentrified inner city neighborhoods (Rose 1996, 2004; Lees 2008), and in the renewal and redevelopment of older distressed public housing projects in Europe (Musterd and Ostendorf 2008) and North America (August 2008).

The benefits of social mix remain ambiguous and unverified, and are difficult to define and measure. Both the objectives and methods used for achieving social mix tend to be uni-directional and inherently class-biased. Mixing is recommended for certain ethno-racial and low-income communities but seldom for higher-income neighborhoods or host communities. Homogeneous high-status neighborhoods are seldom the objects of criticism (except perhaps in the case of gated communities) or of public policy interventions. Instead, the redistribution of middle income households becomes the vehicle for achieving social mixing under the tenuous assumption that such households will provide attractive role models for otherwise aimless members of low-income households. The latter households, however, are seldom asked whether (or not) they see benefits from such mixing. Perhaps if asked they would instead prefer better housing and schools, more jobs, improved social services and enhanced environmental amenities, and perhaps more sympathetic police? While some homogeneous and disadvantaged neighborhoods are characterized by accumulated problems and limited exit options; many other low-income communities in contrast are rich in local social interactions, organizational capital, and services and support systems. Does residential separation discourage integration, and if so, what forms of integration? Does social mix at the residential end of the prism of daily life thus encourage greater social interaction and facilitate cultural integration? What are the short term and long term effects of mixing? The evidence here is again decidedly mixed (Bolt *et al.* 2009). In the case of policies directed at redeveloping social housing projects as mixed-income communities, an important question that has not received sufficient attention is whether such redevelopment leads to the privatization of public space, the destruction of existing community and the loss of affordable housing.

Canadian Cities: Diverse and/or Divided Places?

Canadian cities provide interesting, and for international readers less well known, case studies of some of these issues. These cities are on average smaller and younger than their American counterparts, and on many indicator scales fall in between US and European cities. Thanks to high levels of immigration over the last three decades, the larger Canadian cities now count among the most diverse in the world. Their social landscapes, as a result, are also among the most highly differentiated, but deriving from different sources and with still uncertain long term consequences.

Consider the Toronto example. With over 5.6 million people, the Toronto region is one of the most ethnically diverse metropolitan areas in the world (Anisef and

Lanphier 2003). Through high levels of immigration, the region has undergone a dramatic – perhaps unprecedented – social transformation in just 50 years; roughly 50 percent of the regional population is now foreign-born, drawn from over 200 ethno-cultural and racial groups; and approximately 50 percent are self-classified in the census as visible minorities (i.e. non-white). The result has been the rapid evolution of a highly varied social landscape albeit with moderate levels of residential differentiation (aka segregation). Indices of dissimilarity are not high relative to larger US cities, in part because of the large number and diversity of immigrant groups, but are higher than in most European cities. The highest indices among visible minorities tend to be for groups such as Chinese and south Asians, populations which are large enough to offer institutionally complete communities, or for much smaller recent immigrant groups. In the Toronto case blacks have slightly lower indices of concentration, in large part because their populations are themselves highly diverse in their cultural origins. Using conventional ethno-cultural groups the highest indices of residential dissimilarity are for the Jewish and Italian populations, relatively few of whom are recent immigrants. Over the last two decades the level of ethnic residential unevenness, unlike income, has been declining for most groups individually, although interestingly not for visible minorities as a whole (Walks and Bourne 2006).

This dramatic social and ethno-cultural transformation has taken place with relatively few signs of serious conflict with respect to cultural accommodation and integration (Qadeer 2005). Having said that, new social problems are emerging and some of the older social divisions are deepening. There is, for example, solid evidence of increasing poverty, growing inequalities in income, and increasing socio-spatial polarization by income and social status at the neighborhood scale in most Canadian cities, but especially in the larger and more diverse places (Bourne 1993; Fong and Shibuya 2000; Kazemipur 2000; Walks 2001; Walks and Maaranen 2008). Smaller and more ethnically homogeneous places in Canada tend to have lower levels of residential dissimilarity by income.

Neither Toronto, nor for that matter any other Canadian city, exhibits racial ghettos of advanced racial marginalization as found in many US cities (Walks and Bourne 2006; Johnston *et al.* 2007; Wacquant 2008). However, the partitioning of the landscape into distinct status areas has grown apace. This trend can be attributed to numerous factors, but most notably to the widening of income inequalities at the national level, reductions in social assistance, an aging population and workforce, and most importantly the relative decline in average incomes of new immigrants, especially those arriving since the early 1990s (Mok 2009).

The most obvious expression of these growing divides is the growth of low-income neighborhoods, some of which contain concentrations of social/public housing, in the older suburbs where a number of indices of disadvantage intersect. These are increasingly the residential spheres of recent immigrants who have been less successful in the metropolitan labor market than previous cohorts. These areas are not necessarily deficient in public goods, but tend to have fewer services of the kind traditionally serving low-income populations in the inner city (Smith and Ley 2008). They also suffer from limited public transit and a declining base of manufacturing jobs. These are now the city's "priority" neighborhoods for coordinated service investment and crime reduction. However, the highest levels of ethnic and racial concentration are not found in these aging disadvantaged suburbs, but in newer and wealthier neighborhoods near the suburban fringe, many of which have above-average incomes (Walks and Bourne 2006). Unevenness in racial and ethnic settlement in Toronto is therefore related to both class/income polarization, which concentrates the poorest of each minority group (and the poorest whites) in the least desirable neighborhoods, and at the same time the formation by choice of middle-class "ethnic communities" and "ethnoburbs" in the newer suburbs (Li 2009).

The lesson here is that while Toronto is an increasingly differentiated residential landscape in ethno-cultural and racial terms, the mechanisms producing unevenness and concentration are not necessarily those highlighted in the literature as driving ghetto formation and immigrant segregation in the US context. This also means that the policy responses should not mimic those required to counter systems of discrimination in the US (Uitermark 2003; Wacquant 2008). Indeed, with residential space being painted in different colors and languages, ethno-cultural concentration is likely to remain an important coping mechanism for those who are new or disadvantaged. Of course this assumes that the labor market remains relatively open and fluid, that the barriers faced by very recent immigrants can be overcome, and that institutions (such as the public school system and the local health system) function on a more-or-less uniform basis across the city. It is not yet clear, however, how these systems will adapt to wide variations in cultures, social needs and community resources, as well as to growing income inequality and significant economic transformation and upheaval. Space is an important but not the principal source or expression of these inequalities. The application of the label "segregation" here is not sufficiently precise or analytically meaningful to aid our understanding of the processes involved, or in meeting the policy challenges that lie ahead. It also does not adequately inform debates about the right form, degree, and scale, of social mix that might be targeted by public policy.

Conclusion

This commentary has examined the concept of segregation and its varied meanings within the evolving contemporary city. We highlight the differing ways of defining and operationalizing segregation, and how these influence the interpretations and meanings associated with residential unevenness. We suggest that there has been an over-emphasis on universal indices of residential segregation, to the exclusion of other dimensions of neighborhood restructuring and urban life. This has the potential to inhibit progress in other areas of urban geographical research on equity and social justice. The concept of segregation on its own is insufficiently precise to act as an analytical tool and instrument of progressive public policy. It potentially leads policy makers to misdiagnose the mechanisms producing residential differentiation, and thus the problem to which a policy response is commissioned. One example concerns the mislabeling, particularly outside of the United States, of the concentration of low income households and poor minorities in social housing projects as a form of ghettoization, with its connotations of harmful neighborhood effects, racial discrimination, and victimization. This mislabeling may result in damaging policy responses, including deconcentration, dispersal, "social mixing," and the privatization of social housing, each of which has more potential to harm rather than help low-income households who really just need adequate housing, better schools and other services, and access to employment. There is a need for more in-depth and qualitative research on the needs and preferences of various marginalized and low-income households. Assumptions should not be made on the basis of static and blunt quantitative measures of segregation.

References

Anisef, P. and Lanphier, M. (eds) (2003) *The World in a City*. University of Toronto Press, Toronto.
August, M. (2008) Social Mix and Canadian Urban Public Housing Redevelopment: Experiences in Toronto. *Canadian Journal of Urban Research* 17 (1), 82–100.
Bolt, G., Ozuekren, D., and Phillips, D. (2009) Linking Integration and Residential Segregation. *Journal of Ethnic and Migration Studies* 36 (2), 169–186.
Bourne, L.S. (1993) Close Together and Worlds Apart: An Analysis of Changes in the Ecology of Income in Canadian Cities. *Urban Studies* 30 (8), 1294–1317.
Carr, J. and Kutty, N. (eds) (2008) *Segregation: The Rising Costs for America*. Routledge, New York.
Charles, M. and Grusky, D. (2004) *Occupational Ghettos: The Worldwide Segregation of Men and Women*. Stanford University Press, Stanford.
Clark, W.A.V. (2002) Ethnic Preferences and Ethnic Perceptions in Multi-ethnic Settings. *Urban Geography* 23 (3), 237.
Duncan, O.D. and Duncan, B. (1955) A Methodological Analysis of Segregation Indices. *American Sociological Review* 20, 210–217.
Fischer, M. (2003) The Relative Importance of Income and Race in Determining Residential Outcomes in US Urban Areas. *Urban Affairs Review* 38, 669–696.
Fong, E. and Shibuya, K. (2000) The Spatial Separation of the Poor in Canadian Cities. *Demography* 37 (4), 449–459.
Galster, G. (2007) Should Policy makers Strive for Neighborhood Social Mix? An Analysis of the Western European Evidence Base. *Housing Studies* 22 (4), 523–545.
Jargowsky, P. (1997) *Poverty and Place: Ghettos, Barrios and the American City*. Russell Sage, New York.
Johnston, R., Paulsen, M., and Forrest, J. (2007) The Geography of Ethnic Residential Segregation: A Comparative Study of Five Countries. *Annals AAG* 97 (4), 713–738.
Kazemipur, A. (2000) Ecology of Deprivation: Spatial Concentration of Poverty in Canada. *Canadian Journal of Regional Science* 23 (3) 403–426.
Kazemipur, A. and Halli, S.S. (2000) *The New Poverty in Canada: Ethnic Groups and Ghetto Neighbourhoods*. Thompson Educational Publishing, Toronto.
Lees, L. (2008) Gentrification and Social Mixing: Towards an Inclusive Urban Renaissance? *Urban Studies* 45 (12), 2449–2470.
Li, W. (2009) *Ethnoburb: The New Ethnic Community in Urban America*. University of Hawaii Press, Honolulu.
Massey, D. and Denton, N. (1988) The Dimensions of Residential Segregation. *Social Forces* 67 (3), 281–315.
Massey, D. and Denton, N. (1993) *American Apartheid: Segregation and the Making of the Underclass*. Harvard University Press, Cambridge.
Massey, D., Rothwell, J., and Domina, T. (2009) The Changing Bases of Segregation in the United States. *Annals of the American Academy of Political and Social Science* 626 (1), 74–90.

Mok, D. (2009) Cohort effects, incomes, and homeownership status among four cohorts of Canadian immigrants. *The Professional Geographer* 61 (4), 527–546.

Musterd, S. and Ostendorf, W. (2008) Integrated Urban renewal in the Netherlands: A Critical Appraisal. *Urban Research and Practice* 1 (1), 78–92.

Peach, C. (1975) *Urban Social Segregation*. Longman, London.

Peach, C. (1996) Good segregation, bad segregation. *Planning Perspectives* 11 (2), 379–398.

Peach, C. (2005) The ghetto and the ethnic enclave' In D.P. Varady (ed.), *Desegregating the City: Ghettos, Enclaves, and Inequality*. State University of New York Press, New York, pp. 31–48.

Qadeer, M. (2005) Ethnic segregation in a Multicultural city. In D.P. Varady (ed,), *Desegregating the City: Ghettos, Enclaves, and Inequality*. State University of New York Press, New York, pp. 49–61.

Rose, D. (2004) Discourses and Experiences of Social Mix in Gentrifying Neighbourhoods: A Montreal Case Study. *Canadian Journal of Urban Research* 13 (2), 278–316.

Rose, D. (1996) Economic restructuring and the diversification of gentrification in the 1980s: A view from a marginal metropolis. In J. Caulfield and L. Peake (eds), *City Lives and City Forms: Critical Research and Canadian Urbanism*. University of Toronto Press, Toronto, pp. 131–172.

Smith, H. and Ley, D. (2008) Even in Canada? The multiscalar construction and experience of concentrated immigrant poverty in gateway cities. *Annals of the Association of American Geographers* 98 (3), 686–713.

Uitermark, J. (2003) Social mixing and the management of disadvantaged neighbourhoods: The Dutch policy of urban restructuring revisited. *Urban Studies* 40 (3), 531–549.

Wacquant, L. (2008) *Urban Outcasts: A Comparative Sociology of Advanced Marginalization*. Polity Press, Cambridge.

Wacquant, L. (1997) Three pernicious premises in the study of the American ghetto. International. *Journal of Urban and Regional Research* 21 (2), 341–353.

Walks, R.A. (2001) The social ecology of the post-fordist/global city? Economic restructuring and socio-spatial polarization in the Toronto urban region. *Urban Studies* 38 (3), 407–447.

Walks, A. and Bourne, L.S. (2006) Ghettos in Canada's Cities? Racial Segregation, Ethnic Enclaves and Poverty Concentrations in Canadian Urban Areas. *The Canadian Geographer* 50 (3) 273–297.

Walks, A. and Maaranen, R. (2008) Gentrification, Social Mix, and Social Polarization: Testing the Links in Large Canadian Cities. *Urban Geography* 29 (4), 293–326.

Further Reading

Balakrishnan, T.R. (2001) Residential Segregation and Socio-economic Integration of Asians in Canadian Cities. *Canadian Ethnic Studies* 33 (1), 120–131.

Bauder, H. and Sharpe, B. (2002) Residential Segregation of Visible Minorities in Canada's Gateway Cities. *The Canadian Geographer* 46 (3), 204–222.

Bouma-Doff, W. (2007) Involuntary Isolation: Ethnic Preferences and Residential Segregation. *Journal of Urban Affairs* 29 (3), 289–309.

Bourne, L.S. (2004) Canadian Cities in Transition: New Sources of Urban Difference. In M. Pak (ed.), *Cities in Transition*. University of Ljubljana, Slovenia, Ljubljana, pp. 87–107.

Darden, J. (2003) Residential Segregation: The Causes and Social and Economic Consequences. In C. Stokes and T. Melendez (eds), *Racial Liberalism and the Politics of Urban America*. Michigan State University, East Lansing, pp. 321–344.

Hiebert, D. and Ley, D. (2003) Assimilation, Cultural Pluralism and Social Exclusion among Ethnocultural Groups in Vancouver. *Urban Geography* 24, (1) 16–44.

Joseph, M. (2000) Is Mixed-income Development an Antidote to Urban Poverty? *Housing Policy Debate* 17 (2), 209–234.

Kaplan, D. and Woodhouse, K. (2004) Research in Ethnic Segregation 1: Causal Factors. *Urban Geography* 25 (6), 579–585.

Wong, D.W.S. (1997) The Spatial Dependency of Segregation Indices. *The Canadian Geographer* 41 (2), 128–136.

Chapter 40

Segregation
Part II

Steve Herbert

Introduction: A World of Lines

It is early morning in Seattle when the police car pulls into the parking lot of a dilapidated motel. The two officers intend to check on a registered sex offender who lives there, but their attention is immediately captured by two men dashing from the parking lot. Like hunting dogs on a scent, the officers sprint after the men and eventually overtake them. One officer acquires the men's' IDs and runs a check on their names. What the officer discovers leads him to arrest them both. Each man, it turns out, was previously "trespass admonished" from the motel. Those admonishments were made possible by a contractual relationship between the motel owner and the Seattle Police Department. By virtue of the contract, any officer can bar any individual from the motel whom the officer believes is on the premises with "no legitimate purpose." If admonished, individuals cannot return to the motel for two years. To return is to run the risk of arrest.

About 150 miles from Seattle lies the Haro Strait, which runs between Washington's San Juan Island and Canada's Vancouver Island. The Strait serves as principal feeding grounds for a group of orca whales. Because the orcas' presence in the Strait is predictable, and because San Juan and Vancouver Islands are easily accessible to major metropolitan areas, the area now hosts several whale watching operations. In the peak summer months, more than 30 boats often follow in close proximity to the whales as they travel in search of food (Koski 2008). Because of a scarcity of the whales' main food source, chinook salmon, this search is increasingly challenging. This reality helps explain the recent listing of this group of whales as endangered by the United States government. Amidst concern that the presence and noise of the whale watching boats hinders the whales' ability to forage, the US government is proposing vessel regulations. These regulations would require boats to remain at least 200 yards away from the whales and to refrain from parking in the path of foraging whales. The rules would further prohibit all boats in a zone stretching one-half mile along the west coast of San Juan Island.

These examples of spatialized regulation are somewhat mundane. In the first instance, an everyday police-citizen encounter ends in an arrest for a low-level offense that will result in a punishment of a day or two in jail. Though quotidian, the arrest emerges from a creative implementation of trespass law. The criminal trespass admonishment program now in force in Seattle and other cities (Beckett and Herbert 2009) provides the police robust new power to deny individuals access to commercial establishments, public libraries, and other spaces. In this way, "undesirable" individuals are encouraged to find other places to be; they are meant to be segregated from "respectable" people in both social and physical space. This is an attractive option for the police in this particular section of Seattle, which is populated by open air markets for drugs and sexual services. The trespass program, it is hoped by many, can work to help "clean up" the area.

The second instance is simply one of thousands of potential federal regulations proposed every year in the United States. Yet these regulations too operate on a deeply-spatial logic. A federal obligation to protect the whales translates into the construction of a wall around them, albeit a floating and perpetually-moving one. Part of Haro Strait is zoned as a "no go" area, and the rest carries an implicit set of boundaries that encircles the whales as they move. This is one manifestation of a trend toward "maritime spatial planning" (Douvre 2008; Douvre *et al.* 2007). To regulate the sea, in other words, is increasingly to embrace the need for the creation and reinforcement of zones.

Certainly, lines abound in modern life. Social actors are kept separate from one another through manifold and ever-increasing formal and informal acts; social power is commonly exercised and legitimated in the name of preserving various boundaries. The spaces we occupy are demarcated in multiple ways by multiple agencies. These agencies are empowered to regulate in varying degrees, and together enact a regime of formal social control that is wide and tentacular (Cohen 1985). Just as powerfully, individuals and groups informally demarcate themselves from one another in large part through the allocation and use of space. One need only visit a secondary school lunchroom to see these practices in action. In short, we live in a heavily-zoned world. Any complete understanding of power must recognize its inextricable relationship with the creation and maintenance of lines.

The impulse to segregate is ancient. Societies of any complexity were always riven with an array of social divisions, many of which are emplaced in spatial arrangements. In this sense, the modern world is like any other. However, the extent to which the logic of zoning permeates our world is more pronounced than ever, and its consequences are significant. These practices deserve ongoing critical attention.

I use this chapter to provide some such attention. I review the vast literature on segregation to consider three principal questions: Why does it occur? How does it occur? And what are its consequences? Although uniform answers to these questions do not exist in the literature, there is a strong enough consensus to draw a range of solid conclusions. Certainly, segregation is real and consequential. Some of its manifestations are mundane but others so significant they demand ongoing investigation.

Why Segregate?

Segregation is an overdetermined social phenomenon; its wellsprings are deep and varied. It is thus difficult to provide a thorough catalog of its underlying dynamics. That said, three types of (necessarily overlapping) motivations for segregation seem of unquestioned significance – symbolic, political and economic.

Symbolic work helps to define and reinforce social distinctions of various types. Indeed, this is probably the most commonly-used understanding of segregation, that is, as a reference to processes that separate social groups along key criteria like race. In the US context certainly, the word, segregation, commonly references the isolation of African-Americans from other groups, most notably in urban areas (Massey and Denton 1991). Yet African-Americans are hardly the only groups who find themselves ostracized in both social and physical space. Members of non-hegemonic national groups encounter similar realities (Fortier 2007; Hubbard 2005; Phillips 2006; Phillips *et al.* 2007; Smith and Ley 2008; Sundburg 2008). In like fashion, social lines of economic class (Drier, Mollenkopf and Swanstrom 2004), gender (Browne 2009; de Koning 2009) sexual preference (Browne 2007) and acceptable behavior (Dixon *et al.* 2006; Papayanis 2000; Phillips and Smith 2006) are also frequently distinguished by spatial lines of inclusion and exclusion. Further, these practices are hardly confined to urban areas, but take place in rural ones, as well (Holloway 2005a, 2005b; Vanderbeck 2006).

The need for social groups to make symbolic distinctions and physical separations from one another is difficult to explain definitively. Part of the explanation likely lies within the realm of ontological security. Urban residents, for instance, clearly feel more comfortable in environments that they can predict and control (Herbert 2006; Lofland 1973). For that reason, they often prefer to surround themselves with others whose appearance and behavior sit within their realm of experience. Those who seem different generate concerns and anxieties. For example, work by Robert Sampson and Stephen Raudenbush (2004) shows that perceptions of neighborhood "disorder" correlate closely with people's awareness of the presence of young black men in public space. Indeed, the overweening concern with "disorder" in contemporary American cities (Kelling and Coles 1996) illustrates the common practice of connecting unlike others with conceptions of impurity that impel practices of ostracism (Douglas 1991; Sibley 1995).

These segregative practices often help underwrite political power. The birth of the modern nation state, for instance, is inextricably tied to the erection and maintenance of boundaries. These not only help establish national identities (Anderson 1991; Bigo 2002; Winichakul 1997) but also to legitimate various "internal pacification" processes, such as census-taking, conscription, and policing (Giddens 1987; Mann 1988). Boundaries are hence very handy political objects. They assist in the demarcation of a polity to be governed, and their maintenance inspires a wide range of state-making operations. At a more micro-level, the creation of boundaries can make the mechanics of governance easier. The vignettes that introduced this chapter each illustrate this. The trespass arrest was a simple one for the officers involved. They saw the men, they learned of the admonishment, and that was that. The probable cause standard necessary for an arrest in the United States could hardly be lower. The zoning logic of the vessel regulations is similarly functional. It is fairly easy for law enforcement officers to measure distances at sea, and hence it is the simplest means by which they can take action to protect the orcas.

Of course, the power generated by boundary maintenance is all too easily overstretched. Actors like police officers and border patrol agents who are the "front line" agents of territorial integrity operate in a poorly-supervised environment and can make judgment calls of dubious legitimacy. This is especially true in instances where enforcement agents are constructed as components in various "wars," such as those waged against crime and terrorism (Beckett and Herbert 2009; Coleman 2007b, 2008; Ericson 2007; Gamlen 2008; Jones 2009; Simon 2007). Indeed, the overzealousness with which these "wars" are often fought can mean that the boundaries that separate us can move well beyond their particular demarcations on the map (Hannah 2006; Mountz 2004). In the case of the US-Mexico border, for instance, Mat Coleman (2007a) documents how that line is now present at multiple locations. It travels further into Mexico, where US officials try to engage in operations to discourage undocumented migrants from attempting the trek north, and it migrates into rural America to ferret out some of those who manage to enter. In these ways, the border is a decidedly elastic concept, embodied in border guards and instantiated in fences, yet simultaneously often as mobile as the migrants it seeks to exclude (Wells 2004). Immigration agents and asylum judges thus find themselves with significant power to determine the future course of many people's lives (Coutin 2000; Dow 2004; Franke 2009; Gill 2009; Neumayer 2006; Sparke 2006).

One significant consequence of the powerlessness of undocumented migrants is their inability to resist economic exploitation (Nevins 2001). Indeed, segregative practices often work to enhance economic power. The most obvious instance of this are the lines that surround private property (Blomley 2004; Cooper 2007), the possession and improvement of which is a central lynchpin of capitalist accumulation. Differentiations within capitalist markets are also enabled by boundaries. Here, distinctions within real estate markets are illustrative. Zoning regimes enable residential areas to be distinguished by building and lot size. Areas with large lots and limited only to single family homes tend to attract only those with significant means. The lesser well off are essentially zoned out (Underwood-Bultmann 2010). Increasingly, residential areas are surrounded by gates, ostensibly to increase security but also to help create clear market niches within the world of real estate (Atun and Doratli 2009; Caldeira 2000; Lemanski and Oldfield 2009; Low 2003). Some such communities develop their own internal rules and regulations to structure the use of property, the better to preserve real estate values (McKenzie 1996).

A similar process of spatial demarcation occurs with the urban redevelopment process known as gentrification. Older structures that often house the less-advantaged are rehabilitated and remarketed to middle class residents interested in living proximate to downtown amenities. Those with limited means are pushed aside and forced to relocate. These market dynamics thus work to reinforce and recreate class-based social and spatial boundaries (Atkinson 2003; Hackworth 2007; Lees *et al.* 2006).

In short, segregation springs from multiple and overlapping causes, the most notable of which are symbolic, political and economic. Multiplicity also characterizes the mechanisms of segregation, to which I now turn.

How Segregate?

The motivations for segregation are many. The same is true for the processes by which segregation is accomplished. These processes can be usefully distinguished between the formal and the informal. Formal processes occur through codified rules and are enacted by agents of clearly-identifiable authority. Laws passed and enforced by state agents are the most obvious example of formal segregation. Informal processes are less obvious, and are enacted by every individual, albeit to varying degrees and with varying effectiveness. All social actors and social groups make decisions about whether and how they will associate with others. These demarcations often take spatialized form in an array of actions that reproduce segregation on an ongoing basis.

As noted, legal rules are perhaps the most obvious illustration of formalized segregation. Zoning law clearly works to distinguish uses of space and thus implicitly to sort groups and activities. The enforcement of criminal law accomplishes much the same purpose. There are fewer more drastic acts of segregation than arrest and incarceration (Herbert 1997). When actors in the criminal justice system are empowered to so capture and confine individuals, their ability to participate in segregation is enhanced. This is most dramatically evidenced in the contemporary United States, whose rate of incarceration has increased sevenfold since the early 1980s, a consequence of a series of laws that ensure that convicted criminals will do a significant sentence (Beckett 1997; Simon 2007; Western 2006). These policies translate into the forced migration of convicts from largely urban areas to rural ones rife with the construction of new prisons (Bonds 2009; Gilmore 2007). Segregation also intensifies within prisons themselves, as those inmates considered most dangerous are increasingly isolated in solitary confinement for all but a few hours a week (Rhodes 2004). The urge to ostracize is manifest as well in a range of municipal level laws which criminalize various behaviors commonly engaged in by the homeless and others who spend considerable time in public space (Blomley 2007; Blumenberg and Ehrenfeucht 2008; Coleman 2004; Millie 2008; Weber and Bowling 2009). Some of these laws actively work to bar individuals from particular urban spaces (Beckett and Herbert 2009; Garnet 2005; Sanchez 1997). Although the United States is home to the discourses of "zero tolerance" and "broken windows" upon which these regimes of control are legitimated, similar legal initiatives are now underway in a wide range of national contexts (Belina 2007; Crawford 2009; Flint and Nixon 2006; Hunt 2009; Swanson 2007). Although not as powerful as state agents like the police, private security officials also play an increasing role in marking and regulating urban space to help make some individuals feel unwelcome in some spaces (O'Dougherty 2006; Yarwood 2007). In short, segregation is significantly reproduced though formal rules and the agents of authority empowered to enforce them.

Yet it is just as important to understand the informal means by which spatial boundaries are constructed and maintained. The distribution of cliques across a secondary school lunchroom (Thomas 2005), the chosen paths of different groups through a farmers market (Slocum 2008), and the location of different groups on a dance floor (Veninga 2009) all illustrate the sorting processes by which we render some people in place and some out of place (Cresswell 1996). From the defense of claimed space on public beaches (Edgerton 1979) to the "civil inattention" we pay to others at a bus stop (Lofland 1998), we police boundaries between ourselves and others. Indeed, efforts to buttress informal social control underlie many current efforts to improve security in urban areas (Herbert and Brown 2006). One can debate whether informal measures are enough to thwart serious crime, but they do help inscribe social differences in space. Real estate agents have long been suspected of "steering" individuals to particular neighborhoods based upon racial characteristics (Massey and Denton 1991); employers frequently make hiring decisions in like manner (Pager 2007). Although social and spatial divisions are inevitable and often harmless, these latter examples exemplify their uglier underside. As Sundburg (2008) illustrates in her discussion of the common and harshly negative portrayal of the detritus left behind in the Arizona desert by Latin Americans seeking to migrate to the United States without detection, the marginalized are often disparaged with particular moral force. These dynamics suggest that segregation can have notable consequences.

Why Does it Matter?

Even if segregation is intransigent, its consequences bear consideration. In particular, segregation can deny opportunity and political voice to marginalized individuals to a degree that is difficult to defend morally. When lines separate, those on the outside can suffer considerable pain, up to and including death.

At the national level, for instance, lines between inside and outside are commonly connected to citizenship status. To be an insider means to possess various political and civil rights denied those who are outsiders. One can vote, one can exercise due process rights, one can experience oneself as a full and legitimate member of the polity. To be an outsider often means not just a lack of political voice, but a daily existence fraught with peril and exploitation (Mountz 2004). One lives in perpetual fear of detection and deportation, one is powerless to resist degrading treatment by an employer (Coutin 2000). The desire to immigrate may be strong enough to impel movements through space that are lethally dangerous, as frequent deaths in the Arizona desert all too poignantly demonstrate (Nevins 2007). The abstract process of cartographically-demarcating a national line between countries generates specific daily practices of monumental consequence. To be sure, the formal existence of citizenship hardly means that all members of the polity are fully included in political processes (Carr, Brown and Herbert 2009; Feldman 2004), but it is frequently a jarring experience for immigrants when their lack of voice becomes obvious (Ehrkamp 2006; Ehrkamp and Leitner 2003; Secor 2004).

In many instances, segregation is a self-imposed reality. Communities necessarily define themselves in opposition to others (Herbert 2006). Often, such distinctions enable marginalized groups to develop sufficient cohesion to become a political force.

Undocumented migrants, for instance, need to erect barriers against possible surveillance to organize politically (Staehli *et al.* 2009). In similar fashion, women often feel a need for sanctuaries away from the harsh judgment of a masculinist world, the better to solidify an independent political identity (Browne 2009; de Kooning 2009). Thus, just as boundaries can work to speed marginalization, they can sometimes work to enable processes through which that very marginalization can be contested.

That said, it remains the case that seeming self-segregation is often largely a consequence of limited opportunities to move, in either symbolic space or physical space or both (Phillips 2006). Although some barriers to entry to some communities may be legitimate, too many are not. Further, the consequences of segregation are borne not only by the ostracized. To deny ourselves opportunities to engage with those who are different is to lose chances to grow and develop (Sennett 1992; Minow 1990; Young 1990). Indeed, those whom we disparage, such as the urban homeless, reveal themselves on close inspection to be far more capable and creative than their common portrayal suggests (Duneier 2000; de Verteuil *et al.* 2009). Perhaps it is better to recognize them in all of their complexity rather than to try futilely to clear them out.

Even if segregation is commonplace it is ever incomplete. Humans require anchors to place, and cannot always be moved about at will (Beckett and Herbert 2009; Mitchell 2004; Smith and Winders 2007). Lines may try to fix social life but they never fully cabin it, either symbolically or in terms of people's movements. Segregation may well be inevitable but so is the reality that we regularly share space with unlike others. Given this, it is often sensible to find opportunities to welcome those whom we might otherwise disparage and shun. Fortunately, this is an impulse that also manifests itself daily. Some cities, for instance, create sanctuaries for undocumented migrants (Ridgley 2008), others generate policies to help homeless people feel welcome in such public spaces as libraries (Hodgetts *et al.* 2008). Maybe the best path forward is to follow Darling (2009) who touts the practice of hospitality, the simultaneously easy and complicated act of establishing a connection to those who are different.

To embrace difference is not necessarily to obscure it. We can connect to others without necessarily causing ourselves or others to lose their distinctiveness. This is the instructive lesson of the analysis of Valentine, Sporton and Neilsen (2009). They compare two Somali refugee groups, one in Britain, the other in Denmark. The British group felt little pressure to assimilate whereas the Danish group felt a significant amount of pressure to do so. Yet the British refugees expressed a much stronger sense of belonging to their new home. This, the authors assert, is "because at a local level they have a sense of security and emotional attachment that comes from having their own place, which gives them the space to define their own narratives of identity beyond narrow prescriptions of Britishness" (Valentine *et al.* 2009: 247). A degree of integration can thereby occur even while groups maintain their own sense of themselves.

Conclusion

Segregation is inevitable. Humans make social distinctions that regularly find expression in spatial arrangements. Such arrangements spring from symbolic, political and economic motivations, and are reinforced through both formal and informal processes. Segregation's consequences are sometimes benign, sometimes malignant. The scope and significance of many of these consequences should impel ongoing and critical attention to the means by which boundaries are created, reinforced and legitimated. Some lines deserve respect but others may deserve challenge. Much can be learned about a social group through an examination of how it emplaces power through the construction of zones, and much can often be gained by questioning just where, how and why the lines are drawn.

References

Anderson, B. (1991) *Imagined Communities: Reflections on the Origin and Spread of Nationalism*. Verso, London.

Atkinson, R. (2003) Domestication by cappuccino or a revenge on urban space? Control and empowerment in the management of urban spaces. *Urban Studies* 40, 1829–1843.

Atun, R. and Doratli, N. (2009) Walls in cities: a conceptual approach to the walls of Nicosia. *Geopolitics* 14, 108–134.

Beckett, K. (1997) *Making Crime Pay: Law and Order in Contemporary American Politics*. Oxford University Press, New York and Oxford.

Beckett, K. and Herbert, S. (2009) *Banished: The New Social Control in Urban America*. Oxford University Press, New York and Oxford.

Belina, B. (2007) From disciplining to dislocation: Area bans in recent urban policing in Germany. *European Urban and Regional Studies* 14, 321–336.

Bigo, D. (2002) Security and immigration: Toward a critique of the governmentality of unease. *Alternatives* 27, 63–92.

Blomley, N. (2004) *Unsettling the city: urban land and the politics of property*. Routledge, New York.

Blomley, N. (2007) How to turn a beggar into a bus stop: law, traffic and the "function of the place". *Urban Studies* 44, 1697–1712.

Blumenberg, E. and Ehrenfeucht, R. (2008) Civil liberties and the regulation of public space: the case of sidewalks in Las Vegas. *Environment and Planning A* 40, 303–322.

Bonds, A. (2009) Discipline and devolution: Constructions of poverty, race and criminality in the politics of rural prison development. *Antipode* 41, 416–438.

Browne, K. (2007) (Re)making the other, heterosexualising everyday space. *Environment and Planning A* 39, 996–1014.

Browne, K. (2009) Womyn's separatist spaces: rethinking spaces of difference and exclusion. *Transactions of the Institute of British Geographers* 34, 541–556.

Caldeira, T. (2000) *City of walls: Crime, segregation and citizenship in Sao Paulo*. University of California Press, Berkeley and Los Angeles.

Carr, J., Brown, E., and Herbert, S. (2009) Inclusion under the law as exclusion from the city: negotiating the spatial limitation of citizenship in Seattle. *Environment and Planning A* 41, 1962–1978.

Cohen, S. (1985) *Visions of social control*. Polity, Cambridge.

Coleman, M. (2007a) Immigration geopolitics beyond the U.S.-Mexico border. *Antipode* 38, 54–76.

Coleman, M. (2007b) A geopolitics of engagement: Neoliberalism, the war on terrorism, and the reconfiguration of US immigration enforcement. *Geopolitics* 12, 607–634.

Coleman, M. (2008) Between public policy and foreign policy: U.S. immigration law reform and the undocumented migrant. *Urban Geography* 29, 4–28.

Coleman, R. (2004) Images from a neoliberal city: the state, surveillance and social control. *Critical Criminology* 12, 21–42.

Cooper, D. (2007) Opening up ownership: community belonging, belongings and the productive life of property. *Law and Social Inquiry* 32, 625–664.

Coutin, S. (2000) *Legalizing moves: Salvadoran immigrants' struggle for U.S. residency.* University of Michigan Press, Ann Arbor.

Crawford, A. (2009) Governing through anti-social behaviour: regulatory challenges to criminal justice. *British Journal of Criminology* 49, 810–831.

Cresswell, T. (1996) *In Place/Out of Place: Geography, Ideology, and Transgression.* University of Minnesota Press, Minneapolis.

Darling, J. (2009) Becoming bare life: asylum, hospitality, and the politics of encampment. *Environment and Planning D: Society and Space* 27, 649–665.

de Koning, A. (2009) Gender, public space, and social segregation in Cairo: of taxi drivers, prostitutes, and professional women. *Antipode* 41, 533–566.

DeVerteuil, G., May, J., and von Mahs, J. (2009) Complexity not collapse: recasting the geographies of homelessness in a "punitive" age. *Progress in Human Geography* 33, 646–666.

Dixon, J., Levine, M., and McAuley, R. (2006) Locating impropriety: Street drinking, moral order, and the ideological dilemma of public space. *Political Psychology* 27, 187–206.

Douglas, M. (1991) *Purity and danger: An analysis of the concepts of pollution and taboo.* Routledge, London.

Douvre, F. (2008) The importance of marine spatial planning in advancing ecosystem-based sea use management. *Marine Policy* 32, 762–771.

Douvre, F., Maes, F, Vanhulle, A., and Schrijvers, J. (2007) The role of marine spatial planning in sea use management. *Marine Policy* 31, 181–191.

Dow, M. (2004) *American gulag: inside U.S. immigration prisons.* University of California Press, Berkeley.

Drier, P., Mollenkopf, J. and Swanstrom, T. (2004) *Place Matters: Metropolitics for the 21st Century.* University of Kansas Press, Lawrence.

Duneier, M. (2000) *Sidewalk.* Farrar, Strauss and Giroux, New York.

Edgerton, R. (1979) *Alone Together: Social Order on a Public Beach.* University of California Press, Berkeley and Los Angeles.

Ehrkamp, P. (2006) "We Turks are no Germans": assimilation discourses and the dialectical construction of identities in Germany. *Environment and Planning. A* 38, 1673–1692.

Ehrkamp, P. and Leitner, H. (2003) Beyond national citizenship: Turkish immigrants and the (re)construction of citizenship in Germany. *Urban Geography* 24, 127–146.

Ericson, R. (2007) *Crime in an insecure world.* Polity, Cambridge.

Feldman, L. (2004) *Citizens without shelter: homelessness, democracy, and political exclusion.* Cornell University Press, Ithaca, New York.

Flint, J. and Nixon, J. (2006) Governing neighbours: anti-social behaviour order and new forms of regulating conduct in the UK. *Urban Studies* 43, 939–955.

Fortier, A. (2007): Too close for comfort: Loving thy neighbour and the management of multicultural intimacies. *Environment and Planning D: Society and Space* 25, 104–119.

Franke, M. (2009) Refugee registration as foreclosure of the freedom to move: the virtualisation of refugees' rights within maps of international protection. *Environment and Planning D: Society and Space* 27, 352–369.

Gamlen, A. (2008) The emigration state and the modern geopolitical imagination. *Political Geography* 27, 840–856.

Garnet, N. (2005) Relocating disorder. *Virginia Law Review* 91, 1075–1134.

Giddens, A. (1987) *The Nation-State and Violence.* University of California Press, Berkeley and Los Angeles.

Gill, N. (2009) Governmental mobility: the power effects of the movement of detained asylum seekers around Britain's detention estate. *Political Geography* 28, 186–196.

Gilmore, R. (2007) *Golden gulag: prisons, surplus, crisis, and opposition in globalizing California*. University of California Press, Berkeley and Los Angeles.

Hackworth, J. (2007) *The neoliberal city: Governance, ideology and development in American urbanism*. Cornell University Press, Ithaca, New York.

Hannah, M. (2006) Torture and the ticking bomb: The war on terrorism as a geographical imagination of power/knowledge. *Annals of the Association of American Geographers* 96, 622–640.

Herbert, S. (1997) *Policing space: territoriality and the Los Angeles Police Department*. University of Minnesota Press, Minneapolis.

Herbert, S. (2006) *Citizens, cops and power: recognizing the limits to community*. University of Chicago Press, Chicago.

Herbert, S. and Brown, E. (2006) Conceptions of space and crime in the punitive neoliberal city. *Antipode* 38, 755–777.

Hodgetts, D., Stolte, O., Chamberlain, K., Radley, A., Nikora, L., Nabalarua, E., and Groot, S. (2008) A trip to the library: homelessness and social inclusion. *Social and Cultural Geography* 9, 933–953.

Holloway, S. (2005a) Articulating Otherness? White rural residents talk about Gypsy-Travellers. *Transactions, Institute of British Geographers* 30, 351–367.

Holloway, S. (2005b) Burning issues: Whiteness, rurality and the politics of difference. *Geoforum* 38, 7–20.

Hubbard, P. (2005) Accommodating Otherness: anti-asylum centre protest and the maintenance of white privilege. *Transactions, Institute of British Geographers* 30, 52–65.

Hunt, S. (2009) Citizenship's place: the state's creation of public space and street vendors' culture of informality in Bogota, Colombia. *Environment and Planning D: Society and Space* 27, 331–351.

Jones, R. (2009) Agents of exception: border security and the marginalization of Muslims in India. *Environment and Planning D: Society and Space* 27, 879–897.

Kelling, G. and Coles, C. (1996) *Fixing Broken Windows: Restoring Order and Reducing Crime in our Communities*. The Free Press, New York.

Koski, K. (2008) Soundwatch 2008 Final Report. Available at: http://www.whalemuseum.org/downloads/soundwatch/2008%20Soundwatch%20Vessel%20Trends%20Report.pdf (accessed 15th October 2010).

Lees, L., Slater, T., and Wyly, E. (2006) *Gentrification*. Routledge, New York.

Lemanski, C. and Oldfield, S. (2009) The parallel claims of gated communities and land invasions in a Southern city: polarised state responses. *Environment and Planning A* 41, 634–648.

Lofland, L. (1973) *A world of strangers: Order and action in urban public space*. Basic Books, New York.

Lofland, L. (1998) *The Public Realm: Exploring the City's Quintessential Public Territory*. Aldine de Gruyter, Hawthornem New York.

Low, S. (2003) *Behind the Gates: Life, security, and the pursuit of happiness in fortress America*. Routledge, New York.

Mann, M. (1988): *States, War and Capitalism*. Basil Blackwell, Oxford.

Massey, D. and Denton, N. (1991) *American Apartheid: Segregation and the Making of the Underclass*. Harvard University Press, Cambridge, Massachusetts.

McKenzie, E. (1996) *Privatopia: homeowner associations and the rise of residential private government*. Yale University Press, New Haven, Connecticut.

Millie, A. (2008) Anti-social behaviour, behavioural expectations and an urban aesthetic. *British Journal of Criminology* 48, 379–394.

Minow, M. (1990) *Making All the Difference: Inclusion, Exclusion and American Law.* Cornell University Press, Ithaca, New York.

Mitchell, K. (2004) *Crossing the neo-liberal line: Pacific Rim migration and the metropolis.* Temple University Press, Philadelphia.

Mountz, A. (2004) Embodying the nation-state: Canada's response to human smuggling. *Political Geography* 23, 323–345.

Neumayer, E. (2006) Unequal access to foreign spaces: How states use visa restrictions to regulate mobility in a globalised world. *Transactions of the British Institute of Geographers* 31, 72–84.

Nevins, J. (2001) *Operation Gatekeeper: The Rise of the "Illegal Alien" and the Remaking the U.S.-Mexico Border.* Routledge, New York.

Nevins, J. (2007) Dying for a cup of coffee? Migrant deaths in the US-Mexico border region in a neoliberal age. *Geopolitics* 12, 228–247.

O'Dougherty, M. (2006) Public relations, private security; managing youth and race at the Mall of America. *Environment and Planning D: Society and Space* 24, 131–154.

Pager, D. (2007) *Marked: Race, Crime and Finding Work in an Era of Mass Incarceration.* University of Chicago Press, Chicago.

Papayanis, M. (2000) Sex and the revanchist city: zoning out pornography in New York. *Environment and Planning D: Society and Space* 18, 341–353.

Phillips, D. (2006) Parallel lives? Challenging discourses of British Muslim self-segregation. *Environment and Planning D: Society and Space* 24, 25–40.

Phillips, D., Davis, C., and Ratcliffe, P. (2007) British Asian narratives of urban space. *Transactions, Institute of British Geographers* 32, 217–234.

Phillips, T. and Smith, P. (2006) Rethinking urban civility research: Strangers, bodies and circulations. *Urban Studies* 43, 879–901.

Rhodes, L. (2004) *Total Confinement: Madness and Reason in the Maximum Security Prison.* University of California Press, Berkeley and Los Angeles.

Ridgley, J. (2008) Cities of refuge: Immigration enforcement, police, and the insurgent genealogies of citizenship in U.S. sanctuary cities. *Urban Geography* 29, 53–77.

Sampson, R. and Raudenbush, S. (2004) Seeing disorder: neighborhood stigma and the social construction of "broken windows". *Social Psychology Quarterly* 67, 319–342.

Sanchez, L. (1997) Enclosure Acts and Exclusionary Practices: Neighborhood Associations, Community Police, and the Expulsion of the Sexual Outlaw. In D. Goldberg, Musheno, M., and Bower, L., (eds) *Between Law and Culture: Relocating Legal Studies.* University of Minnesota Press, Minneapolis, pp. 88–105.

Secor, A. (2004) "There is an Instanbul that belongs to me": Citizenship, space, and identity in the city. *Annals of the Association of American Geographers* 94, 352–368.

Sennett, R. (1992) *The Uses of Disorder: Personal Identity and City Life.* W.W. Norton and Company, New York.

Sibley, D. (1995) *Geographies of Exclusion.* Routledge, London.

Simon, J. (2007) *Governing through crime: how the war on crime transformed American democracy and created a culture of fear.* Oxford University Press, New York.

Slocum, R. (2008) Thinking race through corporeal feminist theory: divisions and intimacies at the Minneapolis Farmers' Market. *Social and Cultural Geography* 9, 849–869.

Smith, H. and Ley, D. (2008) Even in Canada? The multiscalar construction and experience of concentrated immigrant poverty in gateway cities. *Annals of the Association of American Geographers* 98, 686–713.

Smith, B. and Winders, J. (2007) "We're here to stay": economic restructuring, Latino migration and place-making in the US South. *Transactions, Institute of British Geographers* 33, 60–72.

Sparke, M. (2006) A neoliberal nexus: Economy, security and the biopolitics of citizenship on the border. *Political Geography* 25, 151–180.

Staehli, L., Mitchell, D., and Nagel, C. (2009) Making publics: immigrants, regimes of publicity and entry to "the public". *Environment and Planning D: Society and Space* 27, 633–648.

Sundburg, J. (2008) "Trash talk" and the production of quotidian geopolitical boundaries in the U.S.-Mexico borderlands. *Social and Cultural Geography* 9, 871–890.

Swanson, K. (2007) Revanchist urbanism heads south: the regulation of indigenous beggars and street vendors in Ecuador. *Antipode* 39: 708–728.

Thomas, M. (2005) "I think it's just natural": the spatiality of racial segregation at a US high school. *Environment and Planning A* 37, 1233–1248.

Underwood-Bultmann, E. (2010) Zoning. In B. Warf. (ed.), *Encyclopedia of Geography*. Sage Publications, Thousand Oaks, California.

Valentine, G., Sporton, D. and Neilsen, K. (2009) Identities and belonging: a study of Somali refugee and asylum seekers living in the UK and Denmark. *Environment and Planning D: Society and Space*. 27, 234–250.

Vanderbeck, R. (2006) Vermont and the imaginative geographies of American whiteness. *Annals of the Association of American Geographers* 96, 641–659.

Veninga, C. (2009) Fitting in: the embodied politics of race in Seattle's integrated schools. *Social and Cultural Geography* 10, 107–129.

Weber, L. and Bowling, B. (2009) Valiant beggars and global vagabonds: select, eject, immobilize. *Theoretical Criminology* 12, 355–375.

Wells, M. (2004) The grassroots reconfiguration of U.S. immigration policy. *International Migration Review* 33, 1308–1347.

Western, B. (2006) *Punishment and Inequality in America*. Russell Sage Foundation, New York.

Winichakul, T. (1997) *Siam Mapped: A History of the Geo-Body of a Nation*. University of Hawaii Press, Honolulu.

Yarwood, R. (2007) The geographies of policing. *Progress in Human Geography* 31, 447–465.

Young, I. (1990) *Justice and the Politics of Difference*. Princeton University Press, Princeton, New York.

Chapter 41

Development
Part I

Glyn Williams

Introduction

In this chapter, I will attempt to briefly outline three separate, but inter-linked histories. The first is that of an imagined object, the Developing World. This is an object which defies easy containment within borders or maps, and the very proliferation of terms it attracts – which include the Global South, the Third World, the Majority World – suggests that there is a degree of discomfort or uncertainty involved in the practice of naming it. Despite these difficulties of definition, location and terminology, this object continues to have a powerful hold over how the world is represented, and divided, within our imagination. My argument here is that these representations matter even though they are often based around outdated, oversimplified or highly selective understandings of the places and peoples of the Global South. The second is the history of a set of institutions, ideas and practices, those of international development, which have come together in various combinations with the express intention of transforming the Developing World. It is a history commonly dated back to the immediate aftermath of the Second World War, and one which is periodically disrupted by paradigm shifts and crises. It is also a history which is shaped by changes in and of the Global South, many of which – despite international development institutions' aspirations to the contrary – have little to do with development itself. Major geopolitical events, global financial crises, or simply more local and quieter forms of demographic, cultural or economic change within the Global South have significantly shifted the ground on which development

The Wiley Blackwell Companion to Human Geography, First Edition.
Edited by John A. Agnew and James S. Duncan.
© 2011 John Wiley & Sons, Ltd. Published 2016 by John Wiley & Sons, Ltd.

operates, and caused a reconsideration of its goals. Here, I present the view that these changes mean that development is (yet again) facing a challenge to reinvent itself at the end of the first decade of the 21st century, and that questions about its actors and agendas are being raised as a result. The third history is that of the sub-field of development geography, which has sought to engage with and explain the former two histories. Here I briefly trace its roots in tropical geography, and consider the role which geographers of the Global South are playing today. In doing so, I am making an argument for the discipline of Geography as a whole to take more notice of the contributions of geographers working in the Global South. Geography has a valuable history of critical engagement with the ideas and practices of the development industry, but the work of many geographers working in and from the Global South goes beyond this as a particular concern. As a result, development geography is too important to be pigeon-holed as a specialist sub-discipline in a world where the Global South is playing an ever greater part in all our lives.

International development and global divisions

> A great variety of social scientists and even journalists from several different nations, diverse ideological perspectives, and academic disciplines suddenly found the idea of a third world useful for organizing their thinking about the international order that had emerged from the settlements (and unsettlements) attending the conclusion of World War II. ... It seems to have been one of those terms that arises spontaneously to fill a conceptual void. (Pletsch 1981: 569)

International development – both as an area of scholarship, and as a set of institutions and practices – has always focused on a sub-section of the world's surface. The borders of this space are indistinct and shifting, and the names applied to it have changed over time. Nonetheless, it has retained a powerful hold over our collective geographical imaginations, particularly since the end of Second World War[1]. At some point in the 1950s, "the Third World" became common parlance for the diverse collection of territories which lay beyond the industrialized nations of the "advanced" capitalist and communist North. As Carl Pletsch noted, the term was useful in filling a conceptual void, and did so in three ways. First, it went some way towards capturing "the facts on the ground:" it described a geopolitical order at the moment of the birth of the Cold War, in which the position of the decolonizing world was ambiguous and uncertain. If the term held out a tenuous promise of a "third way" towards modernity, it also strongly encapsulated the idea of being a residual territory, the bits left out from the First and Second worlds, and over which their ambitions and rivalries would be played out. Second, it acted as a powerful euphemism. At a time of Independence struggles across the globe, colonial terminology of "backward peoples" and "immature" nations was clearly inappropriate, and the idea of the "third world" was a useful replacement. It maintained a sense of a space separate from the North, but glossed over the distinctions on which this division was based (backward/advanced, traditional/modern). Finally, and closely linked to this, Pletsch argues that the term helped to structure a division of labor within post-war social sciences between "mainstream" sociology, economics and economics, and "area studies." The former took "universal" theory-building, implicitly based on the experience of the First World, as their primary task: the latter was the repository of ideographic knowledge of "other" places, often remaining a poor cousin as a result.[2] The third world also defined a physical space in which the newly emergent field of development studies could locate itself, with the paradoxical task of investigating the ways in which the very divisions on which it was built could be transcended.

Since the 1950s, of course, the world has changed dramatically. Not only has the Second World disappeared, but also the neat division between "advanced" and "backward," "modern" and "traditional" spaces have become a fiction which is more difficult to maintain when parts of the erstwhile Third World such as South Korea or Singapore outstrip the GDP per capita of many parts of Europe, or have the geopolitical reach of China. Our terminology has also shifted: "third world" quickly took on pejorative connotations in common parlance, and in academia it has been largely replaced by a host of other terms (Rigg 2007: 3–4). Whether these terms are equally euphemistic – "the developing world" – or explicitly aim to politicize the (now binary) divisions to which they refer – "the Global South," "the global periphery," "the majority world" – they all aim to fill the same hazily-sketched spatial and conceptual void. With decolonization and political Independence receding further into individual countries' histories, and a whole generation being born and growing to adulthood since the collapse of the Soviet Union, a territorial division with its roots in the start of the Cold War is a bizarrely anachronistic way of ordering our view of the world. It is important therefore to ask why does an idea of the Third World – or its modern avatars, such as the Global South – still survive at all?

In part, this is because of a series of reinventions. First, and most optimistically, there are those which emerge from the Global South itself. The Bandung Conference of 1955 established the Non-Aligned Movement, which had the aim of ensuring that newly decolonized states were not immediately made subservient to the interests of the USA or USSR. In 1964, the G77 was formed when 77 developing countries signed up to a joint declaration at the end of the UN Conference on Trade and Development to protect their collective interests. Both organizations continue today as groupings of over 100 states from Africa, Asia and Latin America, and by providing a platform for developing common economic and political positions they aim to recapture one of the original senses of the Third World, that of an alternative force in international affairs.

Second, it is a division which has been repeatedly reinvented within the Global North. The 1980 Brandt Commission report, *North–South: A Program For Survival* was one important example: it identified uneven terms of trade as a causal factor in the different development experiences of the North and South, and graphically represented the division between the two (Figure 41.1). If the Brandt Commission clearly saw North/South divisions as structurally produced and their resolution as of mutual benefit, it is important to remember that other views of the Global South are far less even-handed. There is a long history of negative Northern representations of the South's "otherness," based around the exoticism of its traditions, its need to be saved (economically or morally) by the North, or in terms of the threats to global security – such as "overpopulation" or political instability – it might pose (Williams,

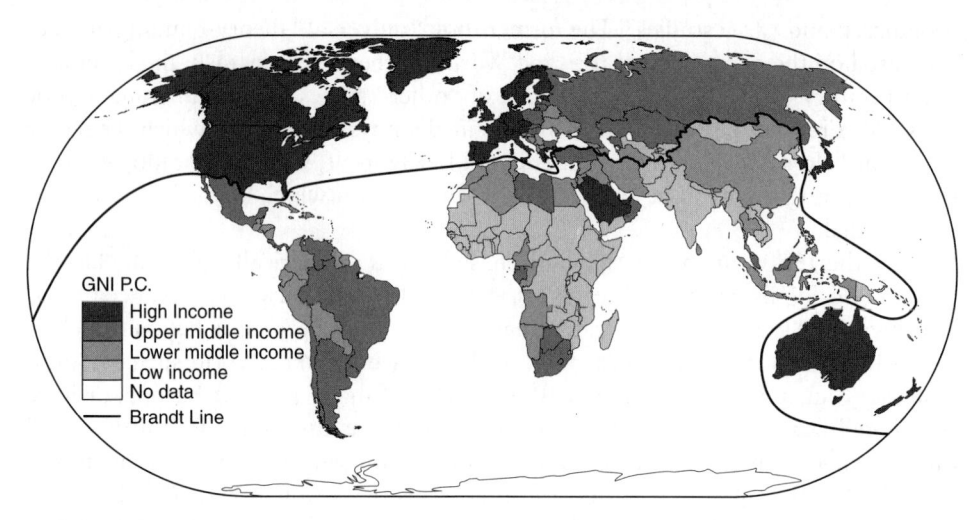

Figure 41.1 North-South Divisions, according to the Brandt Line. Source: Williams G., et al. 2009: 2.

Meth and Willis, 2009). This history matters, because elements of these representations remain very much with us today: some twenty-first century portrayals of the Global South (and Africa in particular) are entirely comfortable in labeling it as "problematic," blaming its lack of development on either "geographical facts" of climate and topography (Sachs and Gallup et al. 2001) or on deeply ingrained cultural traits (Landes 1999; for a critical commentary on both explanations, Watts 2003). At their most extreme, these contemporary views verge on the neo-colonial: more subtle, but no less problematic, is the reduction of the Global South (or its constitutive countries) to a set of seemingly objective statistics that place it apart from the rest of the world. What is being executed here is a process of "othering" – of reimagining and reinstating difference – through the lens of development, which brings into the present the post-War division of the world noted by Pletsch. Accordingly, we now turn to the ways in which the Global South is and constructed as a "problem" to be solved by an international development industry.

The Development of International Development

As with the "Third World," "International Development" is commonly presented as a set of institutions, ideas and practices that were born in the immediate aftermath of the Second World War. Some commentators are more precise, symbolically linking its invention to the inaugural address of US President Harry S Truman on 20th January, 1949, which promised to extend the benefits of advanced capitalism to peoples of the Global South (Esteva 1992; Escobar 1996: 3–4). What Escobar and others claim was being "invented" at this time was a particular vision of development, both in terms of its goals (an era of high economic consumption for all) and in terms of the mechanism through which it would be delivered, whereby direct intervention of a body of technical experts was deemed necessary to totally restructure the economies and societies of "underdeveloped" countries.

Three important qualifications are needed here at the outset. The first is that this idea of "development" as an intentional, active process (imminent development) is different from that within the works of Marx and others which would see "development" as a historical process which is continually unfolding without the will or direction of anyone (immanent development) (Ardnt 1981; Cowen and Shenton 1996). The second is that intentional, imminent development has a longer history than is sometimes recognized. For example, there are repeated references to the need to actively "develop" Australia as a territory from the mid-nineteenth century onwards, and the British Parliament passed a Colonial Development Act in 1929 drawing on what was already an extensive experience of planned intervention in its Empire (Ardnt 1981). The third is that both processes are closely interlinked, or as Sam Hickey and Giles Mohan note:

> Imminent development, led by a belief in the "makeability" of society, emerged over the past two centuries largely as a means of managing those "surplus populations" that have either been excluded from or "adversely incorporated" into processes of immanent development. (Hickey and Mohan 2004: 10)

This last point is doubly important – it points to both the faith in the possibility of planned change captured in Truman's address, but it also reminds us that the "development problems" which such change aims to address (whether they are malnutrition, lack of economic dynamism, or global poverty) should always be analyzed in the context of wider, and unplanned, development processes. This reflexive relationship between intentional intervention and broader economic and social change is important in driving forwards the "development of international development" as a dynamic set of intellectual concerns and policy agendas.

If their claims of the "invention" of development may be over-stated, what Escobar and others are certainly right in drawing attention to is the marked step-change in the ambition, prominence and institutional growth of international development which occurred in the post-1945 world. The World Bank has had a major influence over setting public agendas for international development ever since its first mission to produce a development strategy for Colombia in 1949, and although its policy emphases have changed over the intervening decades, ideas of development as modernization and market-led growth have dominated much of its work. The United Nations has also been a significant player, declaring the start of the first "development decade" in 1961, and setting up the United Nations Development Program in 1965. As noted by Leftwich, the presence of newly independent countries within the UN's General Assembly was important in placing a broader (and more redistributive) notion of development at heart of the UNDP, and its publication of annual Human Development Reports (from 1990) and Human Development Indicators have continued to challenge simplistic assumptions that economic growth equates to improving conditions for all (Leftwich 2000). Countries of the Global North have had their own international development departments, such as USAID (formed by Federal law in 1961), CIDA (Canada, 1968) and DfID (UK – originally the Overseas Development Ministry in the 1960s, and regaining Ministerial status from 1997), although their particular policy agendas and priorities have frequently been heavily entangled with their national self interests as donor countries (Mitchell

1995). The panoply of development NGOs, (Non-Government Organizations) which ranges from highly professionalized and truly global institutions such as Oxfam International to innumerable smaller grassroots organizations, has played an increasingly active role in development policy and research since the 1980s (Edwards and Hulme 1992; Lewis 2005), complicating the structure of "the development industry" still further.

A diversity of theoretical positions have competed for intellectual attention – and application within policy – in the field of development studies over this period, and detailed accounts of their evolution are available elsewhere (Toye 1987; Peet and Hartwick 1999; Kothari 2005; Willis 2005). A quick sketch of the evolution of ideas of international development since 1949 would perhaps look something like Table 41.1, but it is important to note that such a neat periodization can hide as much as it explains. Although it might be possible in retrospect to identify dominant ideas or key texts, this is a highly contested history, and it cannot be reduced to a series of "paradigm shifts" internal to academic debate. It is here that the interplay of imminent and immanent development becomes crucial, because "development" has always had to reinvent itself as a collection of both policy prescriptions and academic agendas in response to changes in the world; including those prompted by its own practical failings.

The new discipline of development economics and ideas of modernization may have dominated the field in the 1950s, but they were quickly challenged by alternative ideas and events. The Bandung conference, the formation of the G77 and the broader experience of the effects of the Cold War on the Global South all helped to underscore a radical critique of North-South power imbalances: in the work of Andre Gunder Frank and others, this crystallized as "underdevelopment" being an active process of exploitation. Less radical in approach, but of great practical importance was the spread of a "basic needs" agenda within development over the 1970s, which recognized that attempts to "modernize" economies of the Global South had done little to ensure that the benefits of growth had "trickle down" to many outside urban elites. Work of academics such as Dudley Seers was important in placing broad social improvement as a key development objective: under the presidency of Robert McNarmara (1968–1981), the World Bank response to this was increased spending on health, education and food security programs.

The symbolic start of development's neo-liberal "counter-revolution" may have been the 1982 debt crisis, but the critique of a dirigiste or rent-seeking state already had its antecedents in the work of Peter Bauer and Anne Krueger (Toye 1987). The harsh austerity measures it unleashed dominated the experience of many in the Global South, but an important counter-current in what was described as a "lost decade for development" was the emergence of "alternative" (or neo-populist) approaches. Calls for the development industry to reverse its existing biases – from urban to rural, from rich to poor, and from expert to lay knowledge – were encapsulated neatly in the work of Robert Chambers (1983), and strengthened further by the increasingly visible role played by NGOs over the decade. The 1990s saw the World Bank and others pull back from the extremes of neo-liberal development, with the "post-Washington consensus" recognizing that the state was necessary to secure market-led growth. The lexicon of development expanded accordingly, taking up ideas of good governance, civil society, participation and social capital. Sustainable

Table 41.1 The Development of International Development in the late 20th Century.

	Events	Paradigms and Concepts	Key Development Texts
1950s	1955 Warsaw Pact formed; Bandung Conference held 1956 Suez Crisis 1958 Cuban Revolution	*Stages of Economic Growth*: linear stages of development, mobilization of savings and technology transfer as drivers	1955 *The Theory of Economic Growth* A. Lewis
1960s	1961 Beginning of first UN "Development Decade" 1962 Cuban Missile Crisis 1964 UNCTAD Declaration and formation of G77 1969 Creation of OPEC	*Structural Change Model*: shift from subsistence to industrial economy through redeployment of agricultural "surplus labor"	1961 *The Stages of Economic Growth* W.W. Rostow 1967 *Capitalism and Underdevelopment in Latin America* A.G. Frank 1967 *The Wretched of the Earth* F. Fanon
1970s	1971 End of Gold Standard 1973 OPEC-led oil price escalation 1975 End of Portuguese rule in Angola and Mozambique 1979 Iranian Revolution and second oil crisis	*Dependency/Underdevelopment theory*: neo-colonial dependence, active underdevelopment of the South *Community development/ basic needs*: redistribution with growth, small scale enterprises, emphasis on equity	1974 *Small is Beautiful* E.F. Schumacher 1974 *Redistribution with Growth* H. Chenery 1977 *Why poor people stay poor* M. Lipton 1979 *Capitalist World Economy* I. Wallerstein

Table 41.1 Continued

	Events	Paradigms and Concepts	Key Development Texts
1980s	1982 Mexico's moratorium triggers "debt crisis" 1983 US invasion of Grenada 1984–1985 Famine in Ethiopia and Sudan 1989 Collapse of Communism in Eastern Europe; Tiananmen Square Massacre, China	*Neo-liberal counter revolution*: structural adjustment, "rolling-back" of the state, currency devaluation, and export-led growth *Neo-populism*: "reversal" of existing development priorities in favor of vulnerable groups and marginalized areas	1980 *North-South: A programme for survival* Brandt Commission 1981 *Poverty and Famines* A. Sen 1983 *Rural Development: Putting the Last First* R Chambers 1987 *Our Common Future* WCED ("The Brundtland Report")
1990s	1990 First Gulf War 1992 World Summit on Sustainable Development, Rio de Janeiro 1994 ANC gains power in first multi-racial elections, South Africa 1997 Asian Financial Crisis	*Post-Washington Consensus*: "good governance" as underpinning market-led growth, global poverty targets *Post-/Anti-Development*: development as a discourse of power, to be overcome by grassroots movements for political change	1990 *Governing the Market* R. Wade 1995 *Encountering Development* A Escobar 1996 *The Lie of the Land* M. Leach and R. Mearns 1999 *World Development Report 1999/2000: Attacking Poverty* The World Bank

Source: Abridged and updated from Thomas, A., *et al.* 1994.

development came to prominence at the Rio Earth Summit, representing the hope that long standing conflicts between environmental protection and the development aspirations of the Global South could be overcome, and "sustainable livelihoods" approaches linked these explicitly to the risks faced by the world's poor. The 1990s also saw the maturation of "post-developmental" critiques of the development project. The academic ideas drawn upon (particularly the work of Edward Said and Michel Foucault) were already well-rehearsed elsewhere in the social sciences: development studies arrived at the idea of "deconstructing" the relationships between representation, knowledge and power rather late, but it did so enthusiastically.

It is possible to read this as a history of relentless growth, in which ever more aspects of life in the Global South come to be governed under the rubric of "development." James Ferguson presents evidence of this happening in microcosm, portraying the development industry in Lesotho expanding not in spite of its own failings, but because of them (Ferguson 1994 [1990]). Where the cruder accounts of anti-developmentalism fall down is by seeing this as a global and singular history (Esteva 1992; Escobar 1996; for a critique, see Corbridge 2007), or one in which control over new elements of the discourse, such as participation is "masterminded" by malign and unspecified global forces (Rahnema 1992; for a response see Williams 2004). What we have, rather, is the emergence, and re-working by a range of diverse agents of many contrasting ideas and impulses, in which the conceptualization of development can be as varied as our imaginations of a better world.

Given the contested nature of this history, characterizing the current position of development at the end of the first decade of the 21st Century is a hazardous profession, but three elements appear to be significant. The first is that there has been a significant (re)centering of attention on the importance of poverty alleviation and governance in both "mainstream" and "radical" development alike. The Millennium Development Goals (MDGs) have been central not only to a war on poverty, but in trying to put forward "an incentive structure for pro-poor development, and a view of "development" in themselves" (Sumner and Melamed 2010: 1). David Hulme's work is useful in unpicking both the institutional politics that produced the particular content of the MDGs, and the broader ideas that underpin them. What they represent, he argues, is a re-emergence of a basic needs/human development approach, conceptually strengthened from its earlier incarnations by reference to the work of Amartya Sen on capabilities, which has been important in mobilizing a broad range of actors (including international NGOs) around the goals. At the same time, the MDGs' particular form as a set of goals, targets and indicators against which individual countries' performance is tracked, shows their dependence on ideas of results-based management currently in vogue within the World Bank and elsewhere. It is here, he argues, that the more radical content of a poverty agenda has been lost: the agreement of targets was dominated by the OECD, IMF and World Bank, which ensured that they embodied a view of poverty reduction that did not threaten their worldview[3], and institutional arrangements for their implementation have been too abstract and remote to link with real struggles for the improvement of livelihoods on the ground (Hulme 2010). If the focus on poverty has been something of a missed opportunity, so too, has the engagement with governance. "Governance" brings the state's role back to center-stage and encourages engagement with questions of power and politics that have long been central to critical development studies, but were declared off-limits by mainstream actors such as the World Bank because of its articles of agreement. This caused some shifts in thinking within the UK's Department for International Development, including recognition that improving governance requires significant change on the part of the Global North (DFID 2006). Elsewhere "good governance" has been seen more narrowly: as a set of idealized state structures and practices derived from the West's own experience of liberal democracy which the South must emulate (under the tutelage of the World Bank) in order to access development aid (Williams 2009). As ever, development is inseparable from wider political change here, and over the last decade "good governance" played an ambiguous role between development's "war on poverty" and George Bush's "war on terror."

The second is that despite the relative coherence this early 21st century development agenda, it has emerged at a point where the power of traditional development actors can no longer be assumed to be paramount. The 2008 financial crisis, which did little to dent the economic growth of either China or India, provides a convenient symbol of the growing frailty of the West, but the changes involved here are both more longer-term and potentially far-reaching. Although there are deep roots to South-South cooperation, what we are seeing now are changes in both immanent and imminent development in which a range of new Southern countries, headed by China, India, and Brazil but including regional actors such as South Africa, have become significant players in their own right. China's investment in Africa is particularly noteworthy here, extending as it does across a number of countries, and raising fears in US think-tanks and elsewhere about the dangers of China "capturing" strategic natural resources (Sudanese oil being one example) in a new "scramble for Africa" (Mawdsley 2007; Mohan and Power 2009). Such investments are not necessarily classed as "development interventions," but donations of foreign aid by a donor community that now includes a number of countries of the Global South generally are, and this disrupts conventional understandings of intentional development more directly. These are potentially significant geopolitical shifts, and ones which underscore the outdated nature of our geographical imagination of "the developing world." Northern aid conditionality, whether based on indicators of "good governance" or on agreement to poverty reduction targets can be challenged practically through the availability to (some) Southern countries of alternative partners in trade and investment (Mohan and Power 2008). It is also being challenged conceptually by a new language of development assistance as mutually beneficial which, for all its self-conscious deployment by "new" donor countries, does at least provide rhetorical alternatives to ideas of tutelage and inferiority which have continued to characterize asymmetric relationships between North and South (Mawdsley, unpublished).

Finally, this is a point at which development studies must take the intellectual criticisms of post-development seriously. While some initial formulations of post-development may have been as one-sided as they were thought-provoking, there are now a succession of studies that have taken the same theoretical starting points, and turned these into grounded and insightful studies of development as a form of governmentality (see, inter alia, Ferguson 1994 [1990]; Leach and Mearns 1996; Corbridge et al. 2005; Li 2007). Between them, these studies provide more than enough evidence to show that the framing of development problems is an exercise of power, and that development's own professional knowledge is often used to "render technical" the inherently political business of finding solutions. As Stuart Corbridge notes, although there can be no escape from governmentality, the response to this does not have to be either despair or practical disengagement (Corbridge 2007): equally, however, there can be no excuses for 21st century development failing to be a critically reflexive practice. In the light of these practical and intellectual challenges, "reimagining development" (to take the title of a current project at the UK's influential Institute of Development Studies) is perhaps as pressing a task as reimagining "the Third World." But there is still one further sense in which the post-war divisions identified by Pletsch might need to be re-thought, and that is in the disciplinary structuring of social science.

From 'Tropical Geography' to Geographies of the Global South

To recap, Pletsch saw post-1945 social science sharply and unproductively divided between "theoretical knowledge" produced through scholarship in and on the First World, a highly empirical "area studies" based elsewhere, and the newly emergent field of development studies which had the particular task of both theorizing and overcoming differences between "us" and "them" (Pletsch 1981; Corbridge 2007). Three decades on, his original oversight of geography in this division can be used as an opportunity to ask important questions about the position of "development geography" both within his schema and more broadly. How does development geography engage with the Global South, how is it positioned relative to the professional field of development, and what might its role be in challenging a nomothetic/ideographic division of labor?

In geography, debates around position of the discipline "in the service of empire," and in contesting its status as a theory-driven social science are well documented (Livingstone 1992; Driver 2001). As with anthropology, geography's role at the height of empire was important in providing knowledge about the condition (and ultimately the governability) of the colonies, and as such critical scholarship of the discipline's history has prefigured many of the post-colonial debates about the role and ethics of the development industry today. If the generation of knowledge about the Global South had once been central to the evolution of geography, by the post-war period what came to be known as "tropical geography" was in a rather more subservient position within the discipline. Jenny Robinson (2003) suggests that this is indicative of two wider trends, both recognized by Pletsch. The first is the marginalization of area studies relative to the production of theoretical knowledge, a trend magnified within geography given the battles the subject was fighting to retain its position relative to other social sciences at the time. The second is the "hegemonization of the field of regional studies by 'development'"(Robinson 2003: 278). It is this that Marcus Power and James Sidaway see as driving the "degeneration" of tropical geography from a rather uncritical ideographic regional geography (replete with unquestioned colonial metaphors of superiority) into development geography, which initially confined itself to the empirical application of modernization theory, mapping out development's impact as modernization surfaces and indices (Power and Sidaway 2004: 593). By the 1970s, development geography was engaging more directly with dependency theory but it also remained the repository of much "regional knowledge," defended by figures such as Bertram Farmer both directly (Farmer 1973) and through his career-long contribution to the scholarship of contemporary South Asia (Wise 1996).

If a sense of marginality has pervaded the sub-discipline of development geography since this period, it is perhaps not without reason. Jonathan Rigg highlights the continuing bias within geographical research, estimating that less than an eighth of the papers published in three top geography journals concerned themselves with the Global South, in what amounts to a dramatic show of parochialism towards some 80% of the world's population (Rigg 2007: 2). But in contrast to this rather depressing statistic, development geography has some very positive answers to each of the three questions about its (sub)disciplinary position posed above. Looking first at its location in relation to the professional field of development, it is clear that geographers continue to be active in critically engaging with the ideas and practices of the development industry. Issues around power/knowledge raised by the post-development critique are already hard-wired in to the consciousness of most geographers working on the Global South, where issues of positionality, and the ethical and practical difficulties of working "in the field" have long since been staple parts of the training of graduate students. Nor has this self-awareness led to a debilitating retreat to "armchair" studies, for development geography can legitimately claim to be making a significant contribution to the grounded evaluation of development practices in fields as diverse as slum displacement, participation, conservation management and the politics of aid.

In terms of geography's engagement with the Global South, however valuable its insights within the critical appraisal of development have been, it is vital that these do not become a straightjacket in terms of an agenda for teaching or research. Intentional development remains one way in which power is practiced in the erstwhile Third World, but in no way should it fix the parameters of "valid" geographical study. There are many other aspects of life in the Global South which raise important empirical and theoretical questions for contemporary geography, and the time to decenter "development" within the study of the Global South, either in the undergraduate curriculum (Williams, Meth and Willis 2009) or elsewhere, is long overdue. Part of the solution here is to ensure that geographers of the Global South state their credentials as researchers with a range of sub- and cross-disciplinary affiliations, rather than feeling forced to identify their field as "development geography" above all else: also important is the integration of aspects of political, economic or cultural geographies of the South as equal parts of the teaching and research of these sub-disciplines (Robinson 2003).

Such integration would also help geographies of the Global South play an important role in rebalancing a nomothetic/ideographic division of academic labor which remains as inappropriate and damaging today as it was when the Third World was first invented. As Jenny Robinson notes, rather than being a-theoretical, most geographers working in the Global South have to be adept at "cosmopolitan theorizing"; hybridizing local theoretical debates and empirical understandings of place, and placing this scholarship "within 'the' literature, which in most cases, is the authorized western canonical literature" (Robinson 2003: 277). These are skills which are needed throughout the discipline if it is to retain its relevance to the rapidly changing realities of the 21st century. It is here, perhaps, that "development geography" has the greatest role to play, not merely in telling interesting tales about far-away places, or in the important but ultimately insufficient act of deconstructing common tropes of representing the developing world. Rather, by holding a mirror up to the culturally-specific reference points on which "universal" social science theory is built, it can challenge Northern geographers to re-evaluate their own research practices, and push forwards a truly cosmopolitan agenda for the discipline as a whole.

Notes

1 Both international development, and the spaces with which it is concerned, have historical roots which go back far beyond 1945. I return to the spatial referents of earlier imaginations of development ("the colonies" and "the tropics"), and their relationship to the discipline of geography in the final section.
2 Geography is not mentioned by Pletsch, an oversight or disciplinary slight that is surprising given the active debates about nomothetic/idiographic approaches which characterized the discipline's history precisely during the period of his review.
3 As Hulme argues, "these organisations ensured that the MDGs fully recognised the centrality of income growth to poverty reduction and that the variant of human development the MDGs pursued was based on a basic needs approach and not human rights or reduced inequality." (Hulme 2010: 18). By contrast, the removal of goals on reproductive health came from more conservative members of the UN General Assembly largely within the Global South itself.

References

Ardnt, H.W. (1981) Economic Development: A Semantic History. *Economic Development and Cultural Change* 29 (3), 457–466.
Chambers, R. (1983) *Rural Development: Putting the Last First*. Pearson Education, Harlow.
Corbridge, S. (2007) The (im)possibility of development studies. *Economy and Society* 36 (2), 179–211.
Corbridge, S., Williams, G. et al. (2005) *Seeing the State: Governance and Governmentality in India*. Cambridge University Press, Cambridge.
Cowen, M. and Shenton R. (1996) *Doctrines of Development*. Routledge, London.
Crush, J. (ed.) (1995) *Power of Development*. Routledge, London.
DFID (1997) *Eliminating World Poverty: A Challenge for the 21st Century – a white Paper on International Development*. Department for International Development. HMSO, London.
DFID (2000) *Eliminating World Poverty: Making Globalisation Work for the Poor – a white Paper on International Development*. Department for International Development. HMSO, London.
DFID (2006) *Eliminating world poverty: making governance work for the poor – a white paper on international development*. Department for International Development. HMSO, London.
DFID (2009) *Eliminating World Poverty: Building Our Common Future – a white Paper on International Development*. Department for International Development. HMSO, London.
Driver, F. (2001) *Geography Militant: cultures of exploration and empire*. Blackwell, Oxford.
Edwards, M. and Hulme, D. (eds) (1992) *Making a Difference: NGOs and Development in a Changing World*. Earthscan Publications, London.

Escobar, A. (1996) *Encountering Development: The Making and Unmaking of the Third World*. Princeton University Press, Princeton, New Jersey.

Esteva, G. (1992) Development. In Sachs, W. (ed.), *The Development Dictionary: A guide to knowledge as power*. Zed, London, pp. 6–25.

Farmer, B.H. (1973) Geography, area studies and the study of area. *Transactions of the Institute of British Geographers* 60, 1–15.

Ferguson, J. (1994 [1990]) *The Anti-Politics Machine: 'Development', Depoliticisation and Bureaucratic Power in Lesotho*. Cambridge University Press, Cambridge.

Green, D. (2009) *From Poverty to Power: How Active Citizens and Effective States can Change the World*. Oxfam Publishing, Oxford.

Hickey S. and Mohan G. (2004) Towards participation as transformation: Critical Themes and Challenges. In S. Hickey and G. Mohan (eds), *Participation: from Tyranny to Transformation? Exploring new Approaches toParticipation in Development*. Zed Books, London New York, pp. 3–24.

Hulme, D. (2010) Lessons from the Making of the MDGs: Human Development Meets Results-based Management in an Unfair World. *IDS Bulletin* 41 (1), 15–25.

Kothari, U. (ed.) (2005) *A Radical History of Development Studies: individuals, institutions and ideologies*. Zed Books, London.

Landes, D. (1999) *The Wealth and Poverty of Nations: why some are so rich and others are so poor*. Knopf, New York.

Leach, M. and Mearns, R. (eds) (1996) *The Lie of the Land: Challenging Received Wisdom on the African Environment*. International African Institute, London.

Leftwich, A. (2000) *States of Development: on the primacy of politics in development*. Polity Press, Cambridge.

Lewis, D. (2005) Individuals, organizations and public action: trajectories of the non-governmental in development studies. *A Radical History of Development Studies: individuals, institutions and ideologies*. Zed Books, U. Kothari, London.

Li, T.M. (2007) *The Will to Improve: Governmentality, Development and the Practice of Politics*. Duke University Press, Durham, North Carolina.

Livingstone, D. (1992) *The Geographical Tradition: episodes in the history of a contested enterprise*. Blackwell, Oxford.

Mawdsley, E. (2007) China and Africa: emerging challenges to the geographies of power. *Geography Compass* 1 (3), 405–421.

Mawdsley, E. (in review) "Postcolonial Donors" and the changing landscape of foreign aid: contributions from gift theory. *Transactions of the Institute of British Geographers*.

Mawdsley, E. and Rigg, J. (2002) A survey of World Development Report I: discursive strategies. *Progress in Development Studies* 2 (2), 93–111.

Mawdsley, E. and Rigg, J. (2003) A survey of World Development Report II: continuity and change in development orthodoxies. *Progress in Development Studies* 3 (4), 271–286.

Mitchell, D. (1995) The Object of Development: America's Egypt. In J. Crush (ed.), *Power of Development*. Routledge, London, pp. 129–157.

Mohan, G. and Power, M. (2008) New African Choices? The politics of Chinese engagement. *Review of African Political Economy* 35 (115), 23–42.

Mohan, G. and Power, M. (2009) Africa, China and the "new" economic geography of development. *Singapore Journal of Tropical Geography* 30, 24–28.

Peet, R. and Hartwick, E. (1999) *Theories of Development*. The Guildford Press, New York.

Pletsch, C.E. (1981) The Three Worlds, or the Division of Social Scientific Labor, circa 1950–1975. *Comparative Studies in Society and History* 23 (4), 565–590.

Power, M. and Sidaway, J.D. (2004) The degeneration of tropical geography. *Annals of the Association of American Geographers* 94, 585–601.

Rahnema, M. (1992) Participation. In W. Sachs (ed.), *The Development Dictionary: a guide to knowledge as power*. Zed Books, London, pp. 116–131.

Rigg, J. (2007) *An Everyday Geography of the Global South*. Routledge, London.

Robinson, J. (2003) Postcolonialising Geography: Tactics and Pitfalls. *Singapore Journal of Tropical Geography* 24 (3), 273–289.

Robinson, J. (2006) *Ordinary Cities: between modernity and development*. Routledge, London.

Sachs, J., Gallup, J. et al. (2001) The Geography of Poverty. *Scientific American* (March), 70–75.

Sumner, A. and Melamed, C. (2010) Introduction – The MDGs and Beyond: Pro-Poor Policy in a Changing World. *IDS Bulletin* 41 (1), 1–6.

Toye, J. (1987) *Dilemmas of Development*. Blackwell, Oxford.

Watts, M. (2003) Development and Governmentality. *Singapore Journal of Tropical Geography* 24 (1), 6–34.

Williams, G. (2004) Evaluating Participatory Development: tyranny, power and (re)politicisation. *Third World Quarterly* 25 (3), 557–579.

Williams, G. (2009) Good Governance. In R. Kitchin and N. Thrift (eds) *International Encyclopaedia of Human Geography*. Elsevier, London, pp. 606–614.

Williams, G., Meth, P., and Willis, K. (2009) *Geographies of Developing Areas: the Global South in a Changing World*. Routledge, London.

Willis, K. (2005) *Theories and Practices of Development*. Routledge, London.

Wise, M.J. (1996) Obituary: Bertram Hughes Farmer, 1916–1996. *Transactions of the Institute of British Geographers* 21, 699–703.

Guide to Further Reading

Some of the arguments outlined here are explained in greater depth in (Williams, Meth and Willis, 2009), and an accessible introduction to development theory is provided by (Willis 2005). Table 41.1 highlights some of the "classics" of late twentieth century development studies, all of which were important markers of wider currents of work in the field. Current statements of "mainstream" development policy all bear the imprint (and interests) of the institutions producing them: the World Bank's annual *World Development Reports* (available online via http://www.worldbank.org/) (accessed 15th October 2010) are perhaps the best known, and are critically reviewed as a collection up to the early-2000s by Mawdsley and Rigg (2002; 2003). These could be usefully compared with the UNDP's *Human Development Reports* (available at http://hdr.undp.org/en/) (accessed 15th October 2010), or with the recent evolution of thinking within the UK government's Department for International Development traced through its four White Papers (DFID 1997, 2000, 2006 and 2009). *From Poverty to Power* (Green 2008) provides an alternative development agenda coming from a leading international NGO.

For academic debates which continue to be important within the discipline, *Power of Development* (Crush 1995) remains a useful collection on the links between development, power and representations of the Global South: Leach and Mearns (1996) address similar arguments in the field of environmental management in the Global South. The relationship between development and governmentality remains of great interest within critical development studies, and is explored through detailed, grounded studies of Lesotho, Indonesia and India by Ferguson (1990), Li (2007) and Corbridge et al. (2005) respectively. The historical links between geography and empire are explored briefly in Livingstone (1992), and in more depth in Driver (2001). Robinson (2006) is interesting as a piece of comparative urbanism, but also provides a practical example of the wider importance of geographical research on the Global South today in disrupting "universal" theory implicitly based around the experience of the North. Finally, Rigg (2007) provides an important and accessible reminder that life in the Global South isn't simply about "development."

Chapter 42

Development
Part II

Wendy Wolford

Introduction

Few concepts are as contradictory as "Development." For at least the past sixty years, the term has embodied a vague and unaccountable promise of improvement. It suggests continual upward movement along a given trajectory for countries that maximize returns through market production, the division of (wage) labor and specialization at multiple scales. And yet, for all the optimism that characterizes most common place definitions of Development, it could be argued (depending on how one reads the numbers) that as many countries are moving *out* of the exclusive league of "advanced economies" (as defined by the International Monetary Fund) as are moving in. Ultimately, Development is an internally contradictory concept because it is so improbable: it is highly unlikely that the earth could support the weight of global "high mass consumption" (Rostow 1960) by today's standards (see Cohen 1994 for an overview of the debate) and yet 143 countries are optimistically described by the IMF as in the process of developing (IMF 2010). A Herculean task made Sisyphean by the inexorable materialities of contemporary production and consumption. Yet even with regular high profile discussions about the dangers of finite resources and the need for attention to "sustainability" (Bond and Dada 2005), Development is still presented as a universal good. The various elements that constitute Development – a dignified standard of living, political freedom, education, health, property, etc. – are all considered Human Rights (the "economic, social and cultural rights" listed in Articles 22–28 of the International Declaration of Human Rights), and so this contradictory, improbable project is imbued with a moral urgency uncommon in an otherwise cynical age.

Faith in Development is complicated not just by its future but also by its past. After more than sixty years as a conscious project (some would say "industry," see

The Wiley Blackwell Companion to Human Geography, First Edition.
Edited by John A. Agnew and James S. Duncan.
© 2011 John Wiley & Sons, Ltd. Published 2016 by John Wiley & Sons, Ltd.

Ferguson 1994), with dedicated institutions, theories, policies, and considerable funding, it is not clear that Development has worked. On the one hand, average life expectancies across the world have risen, infant mortality is down and literacy levels are roughly fifteen percent higher in developing countries today than they were twenty years ago (UNESCO 2007: 7). On the other hand, the number of people considered "poor" (living on less than two dollars a day, in PPP) has increased significantly over the past twenty-five years (according to new data from the World Bank 2008: 20–21) and the income gap between rich and poor within and between nations is several times greater than it was at the beginning of the last century. In spite of technological and scientific advances in medicine, agriculture, communications and information processing, roughly two billion people live without regular access to clean water, sanitation services, or adequate housing.

This brief overview of Development thinking in Human Geography is not intended to be prescriptive, but it is influenced by one primary argument. For much of its history, and for most of the people concerned, Development has been treated as an object; an objective set of goods or characteristics that certain, identifiable subjects have or do not have. This perspective generates policies and programs that refashion the subject to perform better: with better medical care, access to education, treated mosquito nets, paved roads, etc. people in less developed countries will be able to generate the sustained economic growth and political openness that characterizes contemporary understandings of Development. In this chapter, I argue that while good medical care and education are necessary elements of a dignified living, sustaining them beyond the lifespan of a Development project requires refashioning our *perspective*, not the subject: Development is not just a thing, it is a relationship. At present, this relationship is dominated by dualisms: Developed and Underdeveloped, rich and poor, North and South, East and West, subject and object, past and future. Forged through time by various wars, particularly the Second World War and the Cold War, global trade, colonization and imperialism, social networks, flows of innovation, money and information, these relationships shape political, social, economic and even cultural life in ways that have significant consequences. Historically, there has never been Development without underdevelopment and, increasingly, overdevelopment, and yet the conventional (institutional) approach to Development in which aid is dispensed from one country or set of countries encompasses only one side of this relationship. Universals cannot, by definition, be dualisms. My argument is this: mounting evidence from contemporary environmental, economic and political crises suggests that we have exhausted the advances that can be made from thinking unilaterally: if lives are to be improved (and sustained), we must re-think not just Development policies and programs but the framework as a whole.

To get a sense for what a new framework would have to look like, imagine a global amnesty for the sins of the past, including colonization, debt and even the delineation of national borders. In a new borderless world, it is people who would participate not places (cf. Ferguson 2006), and the primary goal would be how to feed, clothe, house, educate, transport and govern everyone – not equally, but equivalently. Forget, for a moment, how unrealistic this suggestion may seem and simply try to imagine what a framework derived under those conditions would look like. The differences between the imagined framework and the conventional one highlight the problems with Development today.

The literature in Geography on Development is perhaps one of the most productive places to begin re-thinking the framework. Originally the handmaiden of imperialism (Smith 1984; Gregory 1994), the discipline took on a new radicalism in the 1960s and 70s (Harvey 1973, 1982; Smith 1984; Lefebvre 1991). A trenchant political economy exhumed writings by Karl Marx and Antonio Gramsci to argue that properly spatialized theories of capitalism were inherently theories of inequality, expansion and ecological imperialism (Watts 1983, 1993, 2001). Scholars in Development Studies draw on an interdisciplinary set of theories to examine the constitution of everyday life as well as the practices and meanings that inform the *work* that Development does rather than Development *per se*. Recent overviews by Gillian Hart (2001, 2002b, 2004) in *Progress in Human Geography* as well as *The Development Reader* compiled by Stuart Corbridge and Sharad Chari (2008) are invaluable guides to both the literature and the history of Development.

In keeping with their deeply historicized genealogical approach, this review attempts to situate key ideas of the English language literature on Development thinking in their particular historical and material context. The overview focuses not just on Development but also on alternatives to Development. Incorporating resistance throughout produces an account of Development that reflects its contingent specificity: as Giovanni Arrighi (1994) suggests in *The Long Twentieth Century*, the past was not inevitable and neither is the future.

Development in Theory and Practice: Origins and Expansion

The term Development reflects a concern with growth and expansion that has defined capitalism (Harvey 2003). As European merchants and mercenaries pushed the borders of their markets outwards in the 1600s and 1700s, philosophers celebrated the virtues of commerce, arguing that trade did not just create value, it created values, bringing civilization to the far corners of the globe. Montesquieu, a French philosopher of the Enlightenment, wrote in the early 1700s that, "it is almost a general rule that wherever manners are gentle, there is commerce" (quoted in Hirschman 1992: 107). In 1776, Adam Smith, considered by many to be the father of modern political economy, argued that production for the market required industriousness and thrift at odds with the slothful nobility of feudal Britain. And at the end of the 1700s, Condorcet suggested that, "the spirit of commerce and industry are enemies of the violence and turmoil which cause wealth to flee" (Condorcet 1795, quoted in Hirschman 1992: 107). In the late 1900s, this perspective would become popular again, with Milton Friedman (2002: 109) famously arguing that reliance on an increasingly expanded market would bring an end to racism and prejudice of all kinds because "the purchaser of bread does not know whether it was made from wheat grown by a white man or a Negro, by a Christian or a Jew."

By the 1800s, however, the ills of commodification and rapid capital accumulation were evident in the concentration of land ownership, rise of urban slums (the first tenements) and widespread use of child labor. In this context, the term Development came to signify not progress but a concern with the dark side of what would later be called the Industrial Revolution (Cowen and Shenton 1996; Watts 2000). The squalor and poverty of the "satanic mills" that provided Charles Dickens with the setting for his cutting social commentary also inspired a concern with fostering Development to counter the ills of economic progress. As Cowen and Shelton write in their influential overview, "Those who lived through the depressions of the first decades of the nineteenth century must have seen Malthus' grim predictions about the inevitability of crisis as borne out. ... The transience of capitalism could only be recognized by breaking with the early liberal view of progress as a "natural" process ungoverned by intention and erecting a theory of development, imbued with an overt sense of design, to take its place" (1996: 20). In the early 20th century, as the increasingly formalized field of Development Economics became more a tribute to industrial capitalism than a critique, its practitioners were still fundamentally concerned with stabilizing the vicious swings that seemed to be inherent to market economies.

The peculiar organization of Development thinking in the 1900s can be traced back to the wars and economic crises that haunted the first fifty years of the century. The faith in unfettered open markets that arguably characterized one hundred years of *Pax Britannica* (cf. Polanyi 2001 [1944]) was shattered by imperial resource wars and the Great Depression. As the second of the world wars drew to a close, politicians and scientists of various sorts debated proposals to guide economic recovery for the devastated countries of both Axis and Allies. If the Great Depression in Europe had facilitated Hitler's rise, then properly managed Development would play a role in re-producing geopolitical peace. This philosophy was justified by new economic theories, tools and data; the theories were influenced by John Maynard Keynes' demand-led macroeconomic approach (1936); the tools included the increasingly sophisticated economic models and mathematical reasoning that constituted the new field of econometrics (Mitchell 1998); and new data were available to provide indicators of relative international poverty and employment (cf. Clark 1957).

These new theories, tools and data were housed in the institutions that emerged from war-time discussions: the International Monetary Fund was created to monitor and stabilize international exchange rates and trade balances; the United Nations was created to provide a forum for international discussion and dispute resolution; the International Bank for Reconstruction and Development (IBRD) was created to oversee the Marshall Plan and Europe's economic recovery; and the General Agreement on Trade and Tariffs was put into place as a preliminary measure to manage international trade (McMichael 2003). By the late 1940s, this project of managed capitalism was extended globally as part of a broader strategic approach to (inter)national security and economic growth. Development was to replace the imperialism of the past, according to President Harry Truman who said in his inauguration speech on January 20, 1949: "We must embark on a bold new program for making the benefits of our scientific advances and industrial progress available for the improvement and growth of underdeveloped areas. The old imperialism – exploitation for foreign profit – has no place in our plans. What we envisage is a program of development based on the concepts of democratic fair dealing."

Whether or not Truman's speech marked the beginning of 20th century Development (the discursive weight of this moment is debated, Watts 2000), his speech illustrates a new approach to the global economy undergirded by faith in the ability of economic management to control market instability on an international level (Escobar 1995). Early Development Economics laid out clear blueprints for predominantly rural countries of the so-called Third World to build modern economic production systems (Gupta 1998). Influential economists such as Walt William Rostow and Arthur Lewis were trained in elite economic centers in the United States and England (Yale University and the London School of Economics, respectively) and argued that primitive economies dominated by traditional ideas and practices could become modern – or "Newtonian," defined by Rostow (1960) as "knowable" and run according to scientific rationality and the rule of law – with a concerted (in technical terms, "big") push fostered by the national state or an "external shock" introduced by outside aid (Rosenstein-Rodan 1944, 1961). Although these theories invoked Developed nations, they were not relational, they were *comparative*: early Development Economics relied on explicit comparisons between Developed (the West, or the First World, or the United States, Canada, and Europe) and Developing (the East, or the Third World, or the former colonies of the United States, Canada and Europe). The path to Development was that which had already been established by advanced industrial economies; others had only to imitate this economic, political and social organization to become Developed.

Modernization theories of Development from the early post-war period explicitly endorsed the idea that subsistence producers in the countryside of poor nations needed to be encouraged to leave their land and engage in wage labor in newly industrializing urban centers (Lewis 1954; Gupta 1998). This "big push" echoed classical concerns with primitive accumulation – what Adam Smith called "previous accumulation," – or the original accumulation necessary to foster capitalist investment for profit (Hart 2001; Perelman 2001; Polanyi 2001 [1944]; Harvey 2003). This period of primitive accumulation depends on the separation of a class of self-provisioners from the means of production such that they are forced (or allowed, depending on one's perspective) to participate in market production. Inequalities created through this process were justified by models such as the Harrod-Domar theory of growth that equates productive investment with savings and therefore encourages allocating resources in the hands of those who save (the wealthy). Geographers and others have since argued that primitive accumulation is an ongoing process of creating new markets and new laborers through dispossession of various kinds (Henderson 1999; Hart 2002a; Harvey 2003; McCarthy 2007; Perelman 2001; Prudham 2007).

As Development Economics moved on from the Second World War, it became increasingly entangled in a new geopolitical conflict: the Cold War. President Truman's early call for Development reflected the fear that global poverty and insecurity would provide dangerous breeding ground for anti-US sentiment;

> [Communism] adheres to a false philosophy which purports to offer freedom, security, and greater opportunity to mankind. Misled by that philosophy, many peoples have sacrificed their liberties only to learn to their sorrow that deceit and mockery, poverty and tyranny are their reward. (President Truman's Inaugural address; Thursday January 20, 1949)

Every country lost to socialism represented a loss of markets, resources and laborers for capitalism. This focus on national security explains why W.W. Rostow was awarded a Presidential Medal of Freedom (he was a national security advisor to both President Kennedy and Johnson) and why Norman Borlaug, a key architect of international agricultural modernization, was awarded a Nobel Peace Prize.

In the late 1940s and early 1950s, social scientists from developing countries, particularly in Latin America, were rethinking the terms of Development from their peripheral vantage point. The dominant theories belonged to the school of Structuralism and emerged from discontentment with the positioning of Latin America as a raw material exporting country after the Second World War. The Economic Commission for Latin America (ECLA, or CEPAL) was founded in 1948 in Chile under the auspices of the United Nations. From ECLA, Raul Prebisch, an Argentinean economist, developed what is referred to as the Prebisch-Singer thesis (due to work done simultaneously by Hans Singer). The main elements of the thesis were that the Industrial Revolution in England created a center-periphery duality in which poor countries were forced to import inappropriate technology that utilized capital rather than labor and thus generated structural unemployment. Over the long run, Prebisch (1950) argued, the center-periphery dynamic would be maintained because international demand for raw materials would never match the demand for manufactured goods. Raw materials faced competitive market conditions because of the number of developing countries engaged in production whereas industrial or manufactured goods essentially enjoyed monopolies and could both raise prices and reinvest profits or increase wages. The policy conclusions from the Structuralist school focused primarily on Import Substitution Industrialization (ISI) and land reform.

In theory, ISI meant importing the technology and tools for a given industry (automobiles in Brazil, for example) and then protecting local producers from international competition through a variety of subsidies and trade controls including tariffs, import quotas and exchange rate manipulation. The distribution of land to small farmers was intended to relieve the bottleneck created by unproductive large landowners; easy availability of cheap food would both lower wages and increase the domestic market. In the 1950s and 1960s, ISI was adopted by almost all Latin American countries as well as throughout Asia and Africa. Land reform was also carried out by authoritarian measure in US-controlled Axis nations such as South Korea and Japan as well as by democratic measure throughout Latin America. Throughout the 1960s and 70s, successful countries such as Brazil, Mexico, Chile, Korea and Taiwan grew at rates of 6 to 7 percent annually. In 1950, Volkswagen factories in Brazil imported all of their parts from Germany; by 1959 the cars were entirely produced on Brazilian soil.

Too much has been written on the shortcomings of ISI to summarize here (Baer 1972; Hirschman 1992), but by the early 1960s, problems were evident. Substitution was more effective in countries like Mexico and Brazil that had sufficient market size to allow producers to realize economies of scale and in 1964, the United Nations attempted to address market size issues by creating the Conference on Trade and Development (UNCTAD), with Raul Prebisch as the first Secretary General, and the "Group of 77" also formed as a loose political and economic coalition of developing nations. Initiatives to foster trade could not rectify the deeper problems: the choice of which industry to protect was too often circumstantial and based on traditional goods financed either through the parent industry or through debt and printing money. In addition, ISI as it was carried out in most countries was highly energy-dependent: for Latin America, oil as a percentage of total imports rose from 8 percent in 1960 to 27.4 percent in 1983. As the 1970s dawned, developing countries found themselves plagued with inefficient industries, high levels of unemployment, significant debt loads and political stalemates as elites negotiated the spoils of state-led development.

The unraveling of ISI generated opposite reactions. On the one hand, radical scholars argued that problems of poverty and inequality would not be solved by learning how to integrate more effectively into the World System, rather the problems created by the World System itself (Wallerstein 1974). Thus the solution was to focus inward, not to engage in international trade. Andre Gunder Frank (1966) argued famously in *The Development of Underdevelopment* that integration was not just incompatible with underdevelopment, it actually caused underdevelopment. In 1979, two well known Leftist sociologists, Fernando Henrique Cardoso and Enzo Faletto (from Brazil and Chile respectively), argued that integration did not necessarily preclude growth (because historically it had not) but that the growth possible for developing countries was a dependent one that required national elites to act for the domestic good rather than consuming and producing the luxury goods that perpetuated the dual economy characteristic of so many developing nations (Cardoso and Faletto 1979).

Dependency Theories were quite influential in the academic social sciences (and they would experience a revival in the 1990s), but the dominant work in Development was characterized by the piecemeal approaches of Basic Needs: micro-theories of reform based on immediate poverty delivering resources directly to the poor through tools such as Rapid Rural Appraisals and Participatory Rural Development. The focus on immediate poverty alleviation and the concentration on rural areas were both products of resistance in the international context. Wars and "uprisings" from Cuba to Vietnam, Cambodia, Nigeria and Maoist China were associated with rural or peasant unrest and Development work attempted (again) to counter the potentially revolutionary effects of isolation and poverty. In this, Robert McNamara, a veteran of World War Two and one of President Kennedy's original whiz kids, was influential. McNamara was Secretary of Defense from 1961 to 1968 and president of the World Bank for the next fourteen years. As Secretary of Defense he had coordinated the flow of resources into Vietnam to try and control the countryside where support for the communist North ran high (Goodman 2005). As president of the World Bank, he coordinated a flow of increases into the Bank to try and control the countryside. Inflows increased dramatically and money was spent on integrated rural development. The World Bank added the International Development Association (the IDA) as a soft-loan window that provided long term loans at low interest rates and allowed the bank to focus on rural development, poverty alleviation and services such as housing, nutrition, and infrastructure.

The concern for Basic Needs coincided with increasing instability in the international economy. The 1970s would be memorable for both high rates of growth and economic crisis. The largest economy in the world, the US economy, experienced stagnation, with two years of zero percent growth in 1974 and 1975, as well as increasing inflation as the country continued to back international currency exchanges by fixing the price of gold against dollars. As US trade deficits grew, countries that held balances converted dollars into gold, which increased the money supply in the United States and exacerbated inflation. In 1973, geopolitical disputes over international trade led President Nixon to dismantle the IMF convertibility clause and devalue the dollar as a way of discouraging imports and stimulating exports.

This devaluation had several immediate effects: oil producing nations received less for their oil exports and this combined with Western support for Israel in the ongoing Arab-Israeli war motivated the cartel to increase prices significantly in both 1973 and 1978; this in turn raised developing country expenditures because of the energy-dependent nature of post-war growth; explicit debt-growth decisions by many developing countries increases their vulnerability to international instability; and in 1978, the United States Federal Reserve doubles interest rates in an attempt to tighten the supply of money and reduce inflation. These actions culminated in what would come to be called the Debt Crisis. By the early 1980s, developing countries begin to default on their loans and the hierarchical and unequal palimpsest over which the international economy lay was exposed.

In this climate, the International Monetary Fund took on a new role as the "lender of last resort." The Fund created Structural Adjustment Programs (SAPs) that addressed fiscal imbalances by imposing stricter conditions for loan disbursals. These conditions emphasized austerity (the targeting or withdrawal of state spending), privatization (or de-nationalization of state property and rights, including mineral rights), and currency devaluation to foster exports. The constitution of SAPs reflected the new economic orthodoxy: a revival of classical liberalism in which trade, markets, property, labor and more were freed from state regulation (even if not free to move at will – migration and labor, for instance, became more tightly restricted even as they were increasingly "freed" from the intrusion of Fordist-era regulation). In spite of instant and fierce resistance to the new rules (riots broke out across Latin America, Africa and Asia), the SAPs heralded the end of an era of interventionist Development Economics and the rise of the so-called neo-liberal Washington Consensus. According to John Williamson (1990), the Consensus included the set of economic principles upon which all reasonable people could agree. For many observers, the fall of the Berlin Wall and end of Soviet Russia were both cause and effect of the superiority of neoliberal economic and political logic. As the Russian Foreign Minister Shevardnadze put it in 1988:

> The struggle between two opposing systems is no longer a determining tendency of the present-day era. On the modern stage, the ability to build up material wealth at an accelerated rate on the basis of front-ranking science and high-level techniques and technology, and to distribute it fairly, and through joint efforts to restore and protect the resources necessary for mankind's survival acquires decisive importance. (O'Tuathail, Dalby and Routledge 1998: 123)

Perhaps the cornerstone of the new global economy was to be trade liberalization (Mosley 2007). The General Agreement on Trade and Tariffs (GATT) finally came into its own as the World Trade Organization (on January 1, 1995) almost fifty years after it was originally drafted. The WTO was intended to arbitrate trade disputes and both establish and reflect the global consensus on trade. The principles of global trade embody the neoliberal consensus and nations that wish to join are impelled to conduct business accordingly (McCarthy 2007: 38–50). Through free trade agreements, the discourse of Globalization replaced the former focus on Development in the 1990s. Poverty became a product of self-imposed inefficiencies and inadequate attention to market dynamics.

The experiences of crisis during the 1980s generated a sense of inevitability that, as Gillian Hart (2004) writes, took two main forms for Development theory. The first was the belief in neoliberal globalization that characterized triumphal right wing pronouncements of the "end of history" (Fukuyama 1992; Lal 1985). The second was the progressive argument that Development discourse had functioned as a remarkably monolithic project of Western modernity that extended inexorably from the Enlightenment through colonization and post-war notions of progress (Escobar 1995; Esteva 1992; Sachs 1992). For very different reasons, both perspectives disavowed the enterprise of international economic Development.

Those who continued to study Development focused on the theoretical and empirical efficacy of various Development policies. Excellent work analyzed discourses of the "right" Development and proper subjects, particularly in relation to the distribution of material resources (Peluso and Watts 2001; Sundberg 2006). Development industry buzzwords were deconstructed; various analyses argued that participatory development tended to exclude the poorest (Agrawal and Gupta 2005; Agrawal 2005) and focused on households while ignoring gender-differentiated divisions of labor and care (Momsen 1991, 2004; Fisher, Reimer and Carr 2010); benefits from political decentralization were often captured by local elites (Mosse 2005; Ribot 2009); social capital was an oxymoron used to allow the World Bank to enter into social realms long considered extra-economic (Fox 1997; Woolcock 1998); community and civil society were often neither communitarian nor civil (Watts 2004); and non-governmental organizations tended to mimic state functions and employ neoliberal economic practices (Alvarez 1998). These were all important studies that excavated the practices of Development in rich detail.

Contemporary Conclusions: Development in the 21st Century

The 21st century introduced a new context for Development theory and practice. Just as the architects of neoliberalism ought to be reaping the rewards for their purported hegemony, there is increasing evidence of internal contradictions, resistance, and alternatives (Leitner, Peck and Sheppard 2007). Geographers, sociologists and anthropologists have been active in critiquing neoliberal models as well as documenting the work done by neoliberal discourse and the cultivation of new practices and meanings associated with Development (Goldman 2005; McCarthy 2007).

The new energy in Development thinking can be attributed to two very different challenges to the neoliberal hegemony of the 1990s. The first contemporary challenge is the war on international terrorisms that coalesced after the September 11, 2001 attacks on the World Trade Towers in the United States. These attacks unleashed a global discussion of international security that has reignited strategic interest in poverty, inequality, colonialism and military strength (all key facets of 20th century Development). In this context, there is renewed interest in the classic (but almost entirely ignored since the 1970s) question of "why are some nations so poor and others so rich" (Diamond 1997; Landes 1998; Sachs 2005). Most of the answers treat this question as a comparative one rather than a relational one: some countries are rich because they have better institutions, particularly property rights and the rule of law (Acemoglu, Johnson and Robinson 2001; de Soto 2000; North 1990; Rodik, Subramanian and Trebbi 2004), or are endowed with a favorable geographies from deeply historical geographies of land mass formation and orientation, quality and quantity of domestic plants and animals, and variety of weather patterns (Diamond 1997) whereas for others they are more contemporary geographics of access to navigable water, population density and proximity to markets (Gallup, Sachs and Mellinger 1999; Hausmann 2001), or are more "friendly" to global markets, for example, more open to international trade and investment (Bhagwati 2004; Friedman 2000).

At the same time, there is a second, less destructive, challenge to neoliberalism that comes from disparate locations across the globe. From the jungles of southern Mexico, on the streets from Argentina to New Delhi, and the fields of farmers from Brazil to South Africa and China (Escobar 2010), localized movements (the "new social movements" of twenty years ago, see Escobar and Alvarez 1992; Scherer-Warren and Krischke 1987) have come together in increasingly transnational networks over the past fifteen years to fight for alternatives to Globalization (and Development) that rely on local communities, non-capitalist production strategies, food sovereignty and alternative media. These solutions are inherently relational, not comparative; they highlight the interconnections between people, places and politics around the world. It is not clear where exactly the energy from these movements will lead but there is no question that over the past thirty years, they have helped to highlight the conditions of economic injustice. In so doing, they have re-shaped the future of a political-economic ideology that once seemed so hegemonic there could "be no alternative."

Acknowledgements

Much of my thinking on issues of Development comes from working with Gillian Hart (UC Berkeley Geography), and I would like to acknowledge my formidable intellectual debt; all errors are my own of course.

References

Acemoglu, D.S., Johnson, S., and Robinson, J.A. (2001) The Colonial Origins Of Comparative Development: An Empirical Investigation. *American Economic Review* 91 (5), 1369–1401.

Agrawal, A. (2005) *Environmentality*. Duke University Press, Durham.

Agrawal, A. and Gupta, K. (2005) Decentralization and Participation: The Governance of Common Pool Resources in Nepal's Terai. *World Development* 33 (7), 1101–1114.

Alvarez, S. (1998) Social movements and social relations. In S.E. Alvarez, E. Dagnino., and A. Escobar (eds), *Cultures of politics/Politics of culture: Re-visioning Latin American social movements*. Westview Press, Boulder, Colorado.

Alvarez, S. (2009) Beyond NGO-ization?: Reflections from Latin America. *Development* 52: 175–184.

Arrighi, G. (1994) *The Long Twentieth Century*. Verso, London.
Baer, W. (1972) Import Substitution and Industrialization in Latin America: Experiences and Interpretations. *Latin American Research Review* 7 (Spring), 95–122.
Bhagwati, J. (2004) *In Defense of Globalization*. Oxford University Press, Oxford.
Bond, P. and Dada, R. (2005) *Trouble in the Air: Global Warming and the Privatised Atmosphere*. TransNational Institute.
Cardoso, F.H. and Faletto, E. (1979) *Dependency and Underdevelopment in Latin America*. University of California Press, Berkeley.
Chari, S. and Corbridge, S. (2008) *The Development Reader*. Routledge, New York.
Clark, C. (1957) The conditions of economic progress. McMillian, London.
Cohen, J. (1994) *How Many People Can the Earth Support?* Johns Hopkins University Press, Baltimore.
Cowen, M. and Shenton, R. (1996) *Doctrines of Development*. Routledge, London.
Diamond, J. (1997) *Guns, Germs, and Steel: The Fate of Human Societies*. W.W. Norton & Co, New York.
De Soto, H (2000) *The Mystery of Capital: Why Capitalism Truimphs in the West and Fails everywhere else*. Basis Books, New York.
Esobar, A. and Alvarez, S.E. (eds) (1992). *The Making of Social Movements In Latin America: Identity, strategy and democracy*. Series in Policital Economy and Economic Development in Latin America. Westview Press, Boulder.
Escobar, A. (1995) *Encountering Development: The Making and Unmaking of the Third World*. Princeton University Press, Princeton, New Jersey.
Escobar, A. (2010) Latin America at a Crossroads: Alternative modernizations, post-liberalism, or post-development? *Cultural Studies* 24 (1), 1–65.
Esteva, G. (1992) Development. In W. Sacs (ed.), *The Development Dictionary: A Guide to Knowledge as Power*. Zed Books, London, pp. 6–25.
Ferguson, J. (1994) *The Anti-Politics Machine: Development, Depoliticization and Bureaucratic Power in Lesotho*. University of Minnesota Press, St. Louis.
Ferguson, J. (2006) *Global Shadows: Africa in the neoliberal world order*. Duke University Press, Durham.
Fisher, M., Reimer, J., and Carr, E. (2010) Who Should be Interviewed in Surveys of Household Income? *World Development* 38 (7), 966–973.
Fox, J. (1997) The World Bank and Social Capital: Contesting the Concept in Practice. UC Santa Cruz: Center for Global, International and Regional Studies. Retrieved from: http://escholarship.org/uc/item/6764j1h0 (accessed 20th October 2010).
Frank, A.G. (1966) The Development of Underdevelopment. *Monthly Review* 18.
Friedman, M. (2002) *Capitalism and Freedom*. University of Chicago Press, Chicago.
Friedman, T. (2000) *The Lexus and the Olive Tree: Understanding Globalization*, reprint edition. Anchor Books, New York.
Fukuyama, F. (1992) *The End of History and the Last Man*. Free Press, New York.
Gallup, J.L., Sachs, J.D., and Mellinger, A.D. (1999) Geography and Economic Development. *International Regional Science Review* 22 (2), 179–232.
Goodman, M. (2005) *Imperial Nature: The World Bank and Struggles for Social Justice in the Age of Globalization*. Yale University Press, New Haven.
Gregory, D. (1994) *Geographical Imaginations*. Blackwell, Cambridge.
Gupta, A. (1998) *Postcolonial Developments: Agriculture in the making of modern India*. Duke University Press, Durham.
Hart, G. (2001) Development critiques in the 1990s: culs de sac and promising paths. *Progress in Human Geography* 25 (4), 649–658.
Hart, G. (2002a) *Disabling Globalization: Places of power in post-apartheid South Africa*. University of California Press, Berkeley.

Hart, G. (2002b) Geography and Development: Development/s Beyond Neoliberalism? Power, Culture, Political Economy. *Progress in Human Geography* 26 (6), 812–822.

Hart, G. (2004) Geography and Development: Critical Ethnographies. *Progress in Human Geography* 28 (1), 91–100.

Harvey, D. (1973) *Social Justice and the City*. Johns Hopkins University Press, Baltimore.

Harvey, D. (1982) *The Limits to Capital*. Blackwell Publishers, Oxford.

Harvey, D. (2003) *The New Imperialism*. Oxford University Press, Oxford.

Harvey, D. (2005) *A Brief History of Neoliberalism*. Oxford University Press, Oxford.

Hausmann, R. (2001) Prisoners of Geography. *Foreign Policy* January/February, 44–53.

Henderson, G. (1999) *California and the Fictions of Capital*. Oxford University Press, Oxford.

Hirschman, A. (1992) *Rival Views of Market Society and Other Recent Essays*. Harvard University Press, Cambridge.

IMF (2010) *World Economic Outlook: Rebalancing Growth*. International Monetary Fund, Washington, DC.

Keynes, J.M. (1936) *The General Theory of Employment, Interest and Money*. Cambridge University Press, Cambridge.

Lal, D. (1985) *The Poverty of Development Economics*. Harvard University Press, Cambridge.

Landes, D. (1998) *The Wealth and Poverty of Nations: Why Some Are So Rich and Some So Poor*. W.W. Norton, New York.

Lefebvre, H. (1991) *The Production of Space*. Blackwell, Oxford.

Leitner, H., Peck, J., and Sheppard, E. (2007) *Contesting Neoliberalism: Urban Frontiers*. Guilford Press, New York.

Lewis, A (1995) Economic development with unlimited supplies of labour. Reprinted in A. Agarwala and S. Singh, (eds), *The Economics of Underdevelopment*. Oxford University Press, Oxford.

McCarthy, J. (2007) Privatizing Conditions of Production: Trade Agreements as Neoliberal Economic Governance. In N. Heynen, J. McCarthy, S. Prudham, P. Robbins (eds), *Neoliberal Environments: False Promises and Unnatural Consequences*. Routledge, London, 38–50.

McMichael, P. (2003) *Development and Social Change: A Global Perspective*. Pine Forge Press, New York.

Mitchell, T. (1998) Fixing the economy. *Cultural Studies* 12 (1), 82–101.

Momsen, J.H. (1991) *Women and Development in the Third World*. Routledge Press, New York.

Momsen, J.H. (2004) *Gender and Development*. Routledge Press, New York.

Mosley, L. (2007) The Political Economy of Globalization. In D. Held, and A. McGrew. (eds), *Globalization Theory*. Polity Press, Cambridge, pp. 106–126.

Mosse, D. (2005) *Cultivating Development: An Ethnography of Aid Policy and Practice*. Pluto Press, Ann Arbor, Michigan.

North, D.C. (1990) *Institutions, Institutional Change and Economic Performance*. Cambridge University Press, New York.

O'Tuathail, G., Dalby, S., and Routledge, P. (1998) *The Geopolitics Reader*. Routledge, New York.

Peluso, N., and Watts, M. (eds) (2001) *Violent Environments*. Cornell University Press, Ithaca, New York.

Perelman, M. (2001) The Secret History of Primitive Accumulation. *The Commoner* 2, 21.

Polanyi, K. (2001 [1944]) *The Great Transformation: The Political and Economic Origins of Our Time*. Beacon Press, Boston.

Prebisch, R. (1950) The Economic Development of Latin America and its Principal Problems. United Nations Dept. of Economic and Social Affairs.

Prudham, S. (2007) The Fictions of Autonomous Invention: Accumulation by dispossession, commodification, and life patents in Canada. *Antipode* 39 (3), 406–429.

Ribot, J. (2009) Authority over Forests: Empowerment and Subordination in Senegal's Democratic Decentralization. *Development and Change* 40 (1), 105–129.

Rodik, D., Subramanian, A., and Trebbi, F. (2004) Institutions Rule: The Primacy of Institutions Over Geography and INtegration in Economic Development. *Journal of Economic Growth* 2 (6), 131–165.

Rosenstein-Rodan, P.N. (1944) The International Development of Economically Backward Areas. *International Affairs* 20 (2), 157–165.

Rosenstein-Rodan, P.N. (1961) Notes on the Theory of the Big Push. In H. Ellis, and H.C. Wallich (eds), *Economic development for Latin America*. St. Martin's Press, New York.

Rostow, W.W. (1960) *The Stages of Economic Growth: A Non-Communist Manifesto*. Cambridge University Press, Cambridge.

Sachs, J. (2005) *The End of Poverty: Economic Possibilities for our Time*. Penguin Press, New York.

Sachs, W. (1992) *The Development Dictionary: A Guide to Knowledge as Power*. Zed Books, London.

Scherer-Warren, I. and Krischke, P.J. (1987) *Uma Revolução no Cotidiano?: Os novos movimentos sociais na América Latina*. Editora Brasiliense, São Paulo.

Smith, N. (1984) *Uneven Development: Nature, Capital and the Production of Space*. Basil Blackwell, New York.

Sundberg, J. (2006) Conservation, Globalization, and Democratization: Exploring the contradictions in the Maya Biosphere Reserve, Guatemala. In K. Zimmerer (ed.), *Globalization and the New Geographies of Conservation*. University of Chicago Press, Chicago, pp. 259–276.

UNESCO (2007) The Global Literacy Challenge. C. R. a. M. S.-I. Prepared and edited by Mark Richmond.

Wallerstein, I. (1974) *The Modern World System*. Academic Press, New York.

Watts, M. (1983) *Silent Violence: Food, Famine and Peasantry in Northern Nigeria*. University of California Press, Berkeley.

Watts, M. (1993) Development I: power, knowledge, discursive practice. *Progress in Human Geography* 17 (2), 257–272.

Watts, M. (2000) Development. In D. Gregory, R.J. Johnston, G. Pratt, M. Watts (eds), *Dictionary of Human Geography*. Wiley-Blackwell, New York.

Watts, M. (2001) 1968 and All That … *Progress in Human Geography* 25 (2), 157–188.

Watts, M. (2004) Antimonies of Community: Some thoughts on geography, resources and empire. *Transactions of the Institute of British Geographers* 29, 195–216.

Williamson, J. (1990) *Latin American Adjustment: How Much Has Happened?* Institute for International Economics, Washington.

Woolcock, M. (1998) Social Capital and Economic Development: Toward a theoretical synthesis and policy framework. *Theory and Society* 27 (2), 151–208.

World Bank (2007) World Development Report 2008: Agriculture for Development. Washington, DC, The International Bank for Reconstruction and Development / The World Bank.

Index

acclimatization 55
Acker, J 422
Ackerman, Edward 135–6, 172–3
   "The Inadequacy of the Regional Concept" 136
actor network theory 191–2, 198, 378, 388, 397, 408
Adam of Bremen 17–18, 20
Adorno, T and Horkheimer, M 461
   Dialectof Enlightenment 461
affect and experimentation 198, 200–1
Africa 12, 506, 568
   colonization 50, 56, 57, 60, 64
Agatharchides of Cnidus 12
Agnew, John 166, 235–6, 251, 266, 529
Agnew, John and Duncan, JS 173
airports 241–2
Akrich, M and Latour, B 378–9
Al-Biruni 16
Alexander the Great 12
alienated commodity landscape 212–13
Al-Jahiz 16
Al-Muqaddasi 16
Althusser, Louis 422, 432, 455–6, 459, 461, 462
Amazon 34, 146–7, 154, 194
American Geographical Society (AGS) 52, 56–7, 90–1, 93
American Indians 13
Amin, Ash 301
Anderson, Kay 461
   Race and the Crisis of Humanism 444
Anderson, Nels *The Hobo* 365
anthropocene 194, 197, 199
anthropogeography 76, 79, 94, 99
anthropomorphism 200–2
Anville, Jean Baptiste D' 41

apartheid 458
Appadurai, Arjun 301, 441
Arabs 12, 14, 15–17, 18, 19–20
Aristotle 13, 19, 29, 30, 32–3, 37
   Nicomachean Ethics 263
   Physics 250
   place 235–6, 238, 245, 250–1, 255
   Politics 13, 28, 263
   Rhetoric 263
   territory 263, 265
Arrighi, Giovanni 326, 577
   The Long Twentieth Century 577
arrogant rationalism 55
artists 133
assemblages 239–41, 341–2, 344, 347–8
Association of American Geographers (AAG) 57, 91, 105, 106, 130, 361
   Sauer 114, 117, 118, 120, 124–5, 138–9
   "The Personality of Mexico" 120
Association of Professional Geographers 91
assumptions in geopolitics 514
astronaut households 362, 367–9, 370
asylum seekers 307, 367
Austin, Texas 248–9
Australia 90, 252, 445, 562
   globalization 306, 307
   mobility 365, 370
Austria 54, 78, 150

Bacon, Francis 27–8, 30, 33, 40, 41
   Novum Organon 27, 33
Bakker, Karen *An uncooperative commodity* 187
Bale, John 31, 38
Bandung Conference 561, 564, 565
barbarism 12–17, 19, 53

The Wiley Blackwell Companion to Human Geography, First Edition.
Edited by John A. Agnew and James S. Duncan.
© 2011 John Wiley & Sons, Ltd. Published 2016 by John Wiley & Sons, Ltd.

Barber, Benjamin 294, 298, 300
　Jihad vs McWorld 294, 298
Barnes, Trevor 65, 168, 407
Barnes, T and Farish, M 132–3
Barthes, Roland 188
Bartolus of Sassoferrato 265
Battuta, Ibn 16–17
Beauvoir, Simone de *The Second Sex* 503
Beck, Ulrich 3, 327
Beckman, J 377
Bell, D and Valentine, G 486–90, 496
　Mapping Desire 465–6, 486, 487–9
Benton, Thomas Hart 133
Bergmann, Gustav 136
Bergson 199, 457
Berkeley School 83–4, 97
　landscape and region 114–19, 123, 125, 132, 134, 137, 139
Bhabha, Homi 381–2, 443
Bhaskar, Roy 457, 462
Bible 12, 24, 30, 32, 33, 263
Bingham, N 197, 200
biogeography 182, 454, 459–61, 462
Bird, Isabella 502
Blake, William 42
Blaut, James 120, 167–8, 455, 460
Blum, V and Nast, H 493–4
Boas, George 13, 115
Bodin, Jean 20
Boer War 64
Bohman, James 435
Boltanski, Luc 431, 434, 436–7
Boniface VIII, Pope 264
Bonpland, Aimé 25–6
Borlaug, Norman 580
Bourdieu, Pierre 116, 434, 436
Bowker, Geoffrey C and Star, Susan Leigh 458
Bowman, Isaiah 52, 53, 61–2, 63, 75, 82, 90
　The New World 61
Boyle, Robert 35, 40
Braidotti, Rosi 494–5
Brandt Commission 561–2
Brantlinger, Patrick 52–3
Braudel, F 85, 250, 326
Braun, Bruce 189–90, 200, 202
Brenner, Neil 304, 339, 395–7, 406, 309
Bricmont, Jean 455
Brigham, Albert 82
British Association for the Advancement of Science (BA) 50, 98–9
British Colonial Survey Committee 63–4

Brown, G, Browne, K and Lim, J 465–6, 468, 486–8, 492, 498
　Geographies of Sexualities 479, 486–8, 490
Browne, Kath 465, 468, 486–8, 490–2, 495
Brunhes, Jean 53, 62, 79, 82, 99–100
　La géographie humaine 82
Buddhism 16
Bunge, William 137–8
　Theoretical Geography 137, 168
Büsching, Anton 38
Bush, George W 392, 568
Butler, Judith 465–7, 486, 489, 494, 505–6, 507
Buttimer, Anne 236

Caesar, Julius 13, 14, 19–20
Cage, John 134
Cairncross, Frances 283
Camden, William *Britannia* 37
Canada 62, 90, 539, 541–3, 563, 579
　mobility 361, 367, 368–9, 370
Canary Islands 28
capitalism 156, 166, 248, 584
　class 415–17, 420–3, 427–31, 433–7
　development 562, 577, 578, 579
　gender 496–7, 499, 502, 509
　globalization 300, 301, 302
　governance 338, 340–1, 348
　mobility 365–6
　nature 185–8
　race 443, 456, 459, 460–3
　scale and networks 395–6, 398, 400, 406–8, 410
　segregation 550
　sexuality 480
　world cities 314–19, 325, 326–7
Cardoso, Fernando Henrique 581
cartography 4–5, 54, 75–6, 90–1, 405
Casey, Edward 246, 250
Cassini surveys of France 34, 36
Castells, Manuel 301, 408, 420
　The Rise of the Network Society 331
Celts 14, 18
Certeau, M de 379–80
Challenger expedition 51
Chanter, T 496
chaotic empiricism 28–33, 34, 37–42
checkerboards 54–17, 518, 519–21
Chiapello, Eve 431, 436–7
Chicago School 81, 95, 364–5
Chimborazo, Mount 25–6

China 12, 15–17, 18–19
  astronaut households 362, 367–9, 370
  development 561, 568, 581
  globalization 286–7, 292, 293–5, 306
  mega-regions 292
  segregation 537, 542
  world cities 314–15, 317–19, 321–2, 332
Chisholm, George 56, 95, 149–50
  Handbook of Commercial Geography 56, 96, 149
choke points 514, 516, 517, 519
chorography and chorology 29, 31–3, 35, 37, 39, 83, 90
  Germany 77, 83
  landscape versus region 115–18, 130–2, 134–7, 139–42
  place 250
  region to space 148–50, 155–6, 162, 164, 165, 167–8
Christaller, Walter 77, 167
Christianity 17, 27–8, 30, 40, 356
  Newtonian influence 33, 35, 37
  race 440, 445, 446, 461
  T-O maps 24, 25, 26
chronology 4–5
circles of affinity 75
citizenship 367, 368–9
city-regions 390–1
Cixous, Hélène 504–5
Clarke, William 36
class 415–23, 426–37, 504
  Durkheim 416, 419–20
  globalization 294–5, 303, 305
  Marx 416–18
  mobility 365–6
  segregation 535, 539, 540–4, 549, 550–1
  sexuality 478, 480, 482
  Weber 416, 418–19
Clayoquot Sound 189–90
Clifford, James 3
climate 13, 35, 55, 59, 61, 182
  globalization 304, 308
  race 460, 463
Cohen, Cathy 482, 468
Cold War 5–6, 132, 267, 278, 354
  development 560, 564, 576, 579
  geopolitics 513, 524, 526, 527
  region to space 147, 152
Colonial Development Act (1929) 563
colonialism and colonialization 4, 50–66, 353, 362, 583
  development 560–3, 569, 576
  gender 504

globalization 302–3, 305
  Greeks 12
  race 443, 445, 447, 455, 458–61
  Singapore 469–72
  world cities 320, 325, 327
Columbus, Christopher 11–12, 19–20, 26–33, 38
  Enlightenment change of philosophy 36, 37
communication 378–80, 381
Conant, James 131
concepts 514
Condorcet, Nicolas de 577
Confucius 15
connectivity 42–4
Conrad, Joseph 54, 56
  Heart of Darkness 52–3
containerization 316–17
conventialism 79
Cook, James 35–6, 38
Copland, Aaron 133
Corbridge, Stuart 348, 569, 577
Cosgrove, Denis 117, 141, 211, 212, 227
cosmologies and cosmography 26, 27–33, 37–40, 43
  Enlightenment 33–8, 42
  mechanical 33–7
cosmopolitanism 364–6
cosmopolitics 198, 201–3
Cox, Kevin 102, 395
craniometry 446–8
creative spaces of connections 380–3
credit union movement 392–3
Cresswell, Tim 246, 362, 364–5, 373, 375–7, 382
  On the Move 362
crime and segregation 551, 552
critical geopolitics 525, 526–31
critical realism 456–9, 460, 462
critical regions 171–2
Cronon, William 185, 186, 187
  Nature's Metropolis 186
Crowe, P R 121, 362
Crutzen, Paul 194
ctesias 12, 15
Cuba 28, 565, 581
Cultural Geographies 190
culture and cultural geography 95, 123–5, 245–6, 374–8
  class 417, 421–2, 426, 430, 433–4, 437
  gender 502–3, 505–6, 507
  genres de vie 83, 120, 149

geopolitics 526, 527, 528
globalization 3–4, 299–300, 305
landscape 83–4, 209–11, 221, 224–9, 231
landscape versus region 114–25, 132, 140
mobility 366–7, 368, 373, 374–8, 380–3
nature 188, 190, 192, 199
place 238, 245–6, 247–9, 252
race 441–2, 444, 449, 453–6, 461
region to space 149
scale and networks 397–8, 399–400
segregation 538, 540–1, 542–3
sexuality 465, 466, 469, 476
world cities 313–16, 325, 327–30, 333
Curry, John Steuart 133
Cuvier, Georges 447
cycle of erosion 59

Da Gama, Vasco 28, 33
Daniels, Stephen and Cosgrove, Denis 212, 222, 227
  The Iconography of Landscape 227
Dant, Tim 193
Dante 264
Darby, Clifford 95, 103, 135
Darwin, Charles and Darwinism 58–9, 76, 181
  Origin of Species 43, 56, 181
  race 446–7, 457, 459
Dasein 224–5
Davies, Gail 201, 202
Davis, William Morris 44, 53, 57–60, 94, 180
  French and German schools 81–3
Debt Crisis 582
DeLanda, Manuel 239–41, 444
Deleuze, Gilles 191, 199, 222, 239, 250, 496
  class 431, 433
  territory 274, 279
Demangeon, Albert 63
dependency theories 581
Derrida, Jacques 188, 189, 448
Descartes, Rene 33, 222–6, 447, 456
deterritorialization 240–1, 242, 274
development 559–71, 575–84
Diamond, Jared 274, 454, 459–60
  Guns, Germs, and Steel 459
Diaz, Bartholomew 28
Dickens, Charles 577
Dickinson, R *City Region and Regionalism* 102

Dilthey, Wilhelm 182
Diodorus of Sicily 12
discipline-centred regions 17102
Dos Passos, John *Manhattan Transfer* 365
Driver, Felix 52, 53, 60, 65
Dryzek, John 435
Dubois, Marcel 59
Dubow, J 222, 231
Duncan, James 118, 124, 212, 422
Duncan, SS 421, 422
Durkheim, Émile 167, 364, 416, 419–20
  class 415, 416, 418, 419–20
dwelling *see* housing

Early Modern era 37–42
Eco, Umberto 276, 378
École Normale Supérieure 59
ecological fallacy 392
Economic Commission for Latin America 580
economic activity 285
  globalization 284–90, 293, 296
  world cities 314, 317–18, 321, 326, 330–1
economic geography 56, 103–4, 105, 466, 508
  governance 342, 343
  region to space 146, 147, 149, 153, 156
  scale and networks 404, 409
Edney, Matthew 54
Egypt 13, 36
elections 390, 392
embodiment 225–6, 228–9, 374–5
Empire 14, 50–66, 263–5, 280, 563
  world cities 320, 325
empiricism 119–20, 121, 125
  chaotic 28–33, 34, 37–42
Enlightenment 33–7, 40–2, 53, 131–2, 503
  Development 577, 583
  mobility 362, 363, 364
  race 445, 446
Enloe, Cynthia 509
Entrikin, Nicholas 125, 251
environment 76, 146–7, 179–80, 190, 194–5
  effect on character 13–18, 20, 39, 51
environmental determinism 4, 51, 58–9, 61, 64, 81–3, 98
  culture 123
  race 459, 460
  regional geography 94
  region to space 149–50
epistemology 77–9, 81, 83, 84, 200–1

Eratosthenes of Cyrene 12, 19
Escobar, A 562, 563
Ethington, Philip 246
Euclid 29
European mega-region 289, 291
European Union (EU) 172, 338, 341, 526, 531
Evans, E Estyn 135
Evans, Walker 133
existential phenomenology 222–6
expressive role 240, 242
Eyjafjallajökull volcano 361

Faletto, Enzo 581
Faxian 16
feminism 105, 235, 299, 342, 528
  gender 492, 494, 497, 501–9
  sexuality 465, 469, 475, 478, 480
Finch, Vernor 118
Fitzsimmon, Margaret "The matter of nature" 179
fixed capital 213
flat ontology 397
Flavio, Biondo 33, 37
  Italia Illustrata 31–2
Fleure, Herbert 83, 95, 100, 135
Florida, Richard 248, 469
Ford, Larry 210, 211
forestry 187, 189–90, 341, 343
Foucault, Michel 188, 250, 266, 567
  class 432, 436
  gender 505, 507
  governance 344, 348–50, 352–6
  mobility 377, 378
  race 442, 456
  sexuality 466, 472
France 5, 73, 78–86, 94, 99, 132, 181
  Cassini surveys 34, 36
  colonization 12, 52, 54, 56–7, 59, 62–3
  landscape vs region 132, 135
  mobility 362–3
  region to space 149, 165, 173
  territory 264–5, 272–6, 278
  universities 78–9
Franco-Prussian War (1870–1871) 56, 76
Frank, Andre Gunder 564, 581
  The Development of Underdevelopment 581
Fraser, Nancy 434, 435
Friedland, Roger 246
Friedman, Milton 577

Friedman, Thomas 283–4, 294, 298, 300, 387, 397
  Lexus and Olive Tree 298
  The World is Flat 283–4, 298, 397
Friedmann, John 317, 328, 330
Friends of the Earth 183
Freshfield, Douglas 58, 64
Fukuyama, Francis 298, 300
  The End of History and the Last Man 298

Gandhi, Mahatma 342, 348, 356–7
Garrison, William 103, 134, 137, 153
  Studies of Highways Development and Geographic Change 153
gazetteers 39
Geddes, Patrick 56, 96, 325
gender 13, 40, 480–2, 486–99, 501–9
  admission of women to RGS 57
  class 422–3, 427, 432
  globalization 299, 302–3, 305–6
  segregation 549, 553
General Agreement on Trade and Tariffs (GATT) 578, 582
genres de vie 83, 120, 149
gentrification 421, 466, 550
Geoforum 190, 342
geographic information systems (GIS) 65, 104, 169, 172, 305
Geographical Association (GA) 91, 92, 98
Geographical Association in Britain 57
geographical impressionism 52–4
Geographical Magazine 93
geographical societies 56–7, 60
geographicity 272, 281
geomorphology 180, 182
geopolitics 5, 279–81, 325, 512–21, 523–31
  development 559, 560, 561, 578
  globalization 293
  Peloponnesian War 515–21
  Territory 266, 271, 276–8, 279–81
Geopolitik 77, 78, 84, 130
George III 40
Gerald of Wales 18, 20
Germany 5, 13, 73–84, 94, 95, 99, 102
  Empire 52, 64
  governance 349, 351
  landscape geography 114, 122, 132
  landscape vs region 114, 116–17, 121, 135–6, 138–41
  Landschaft 272
  mobility 364

nature 180
positioning geography 54, 58, 59
Raum 165, 167, 271
region to space 148–9, 150, 152, 162, 165, 167, 173
Tacitus 14, 19–20
territory 271–2, 279
universities 74–5, 76, 78, 81
vitalism 42–4
ghettos 534, 535, 538, 543
Gibson, Edmund 37
Gibson-Graham, JK 396, 422, 432
Giddens, Anthony 156, 299
Gilbert, David 98, 246–7, 254
Stumbling on Happiness 246
Gilbert, EW 98, 130
"Geography and Regionalism" 130
Giles of Rome 264
Gilroy, P 381, 444
Giovanni di Pian di Carpine, Fra *History of the Moguls* 18
Glacken, Clarence 38–9
global city-regions 390–1
global divisions 560–2
Global North 561–2, 563, 568, 571
Global South 569–71
development 559–62, 564, 567–71
Globalisation and World Cities Research Network 328, 332
globalization 1, 3–5, 7, 40, 85, 283–96, 298–309
clustering force 290–2
development 583, 584
gender 508–9
governance 337–40, 355
landscape vs region 142
mega-regions 288–92
mobilities 305–8
ontologies 299–302
peaks and valleys of economy 292–6
place 246–8
race 454
region to space 155–6
scale and networks 395–7, 400–1, 404, 407–8, 410
segregation 535
sexuality 466
spiky 284–8
territory 266, 267, 278, 280
topographies 302–5
world cities 313, 317, 325–8, 330, 331–3

glocalization 301
Goh, KC *Urban Incomes and Housing* 472
Goldberg, David Theo 442–3
Goodman, David *From Farming to Biotechnology* 187
Gore, Al 392
Gottmann, Jean 80, 84, 132, 288–9
Gough, Richard 37
Gould, Peter 115, 168, 169, 172
Gourou, Pierre 55, 62, 63
governance 302, 313, 336–44, 347–57
development 564, 566, 567–8
globalization 302, 337–40
government and governmentality 340–4, 347–50, 353, 354
grammars 39–40, 41
Gramsci, Antonio 188, 577
gravity 33
Great Trigonometrical Survey of India 36
Greeks 4, 11–15, 16–17, 19, 148, 263
Peloponnesian War 513–14, 515–20
T-O maps 24
Greenpeace 182–3
Gregory of Tours *The Histories of the Franks* 17, 262
Gregory, Derek 156, 169, 256, 303
Grosvenor, Gilbert 93
Group of 77 (G77) 561, 564, 565, 580
growth spurts of cities 326
Guattari, Félix 239, 250, 274, 279, 496
Guillemard, Francis 63
Guthrie, William *New Geographical, Historical and Commercial Grammar* 39–41

Habermas, Júrgen 431, 434–5
Hacking, Ian *The Social Construction of What?* 456
Hägerstrand, Torsten 156, 168
Innovation diffusion as a spatial process 168
Haggett, Peter 102, 146–7, 153–6, 168
Geography: A Global Synthesis 389
Locational Analysis in Human Geography 146–7, 153, 154
scale and networks 387, 388, 395
Hall, Joseph *Mundus Alter et Idem* 32
Hall, Peter 314, 315, 325
Cities in Civilization 330
The World Cities 325
Hall, Stuart 188, 381, 442
Handlin, Oscar *The Uprooted* 364

Haraway, Donna 132, 191, 201–2, 378, 505
Hardt, M and Negri, A 350–1, 433
Harrod–Domar theory 579
Hart, Gillian 303, 577, 583
Hartshorne, Richard 5, 44, 75, 84, 97, 101, 138–9
  nature 180
  OSS 151–2
  Perspective on the Nature of Geography 136–7
  regional geography 95–6, 97
  regional geography vs region 114–25, 130, 135–40
  region to space 150–2, 155, 165–6, 167–8
  The Nature of Geography 95, 97, 115, 117–18, 125, 135–6, 138–9, 150–1
Harvey, David 3, 186, 212, 320, 408, 462
  class 420, 426, 428–9
  Explanation in Geography 169
  globalization 302, 303
  place 237–8, 246, 249, 252
  region to space 155, 167, 169
  Social Justice and the City 169, 420
Haushofer, Karl 62, 271
Hayek, Friedrich 343
heartlands 514, 515, 518, 520
Hecateus of Miletos 12
  Histories 12
  Journey Round the World 12
Hegel, Georg 435, 457–8
Heidegger, Martin 221, 224–5, 227, 230, 237
Herbertson, Andrew 53, 97–8, 149, 181
Herod, Andrew 308–9, 423
Herodotus 11–12, 13, 14–16, 20
heterosexual matrix 478–80
Hettner, Alfred 5, 53, 78, 84, 95
  Länderkundliche Schema 148–9
  landscape vs region 116–17, 122, 130, 136, 140
  region to space 148–9, 150, 155, 165
Heylyn, Peter *Cosmographie in Foure Bookes* 38
Hills, Major EH 50–2, 57, 63–5
Hinchliffe, Steve 192, 197, 200, 379, 382
  Geographies of Nature 191
Hindus 16
Hippocrates 13, 19
  On Airs, Waters and Places 13
historicism 119, 125
Hitler, Adolf 351, 578

Hoare, Richard *Ancient History of Wiltshire* 37
Holdich, Col Sir Thomas 63–4
Holy Roman Empire 263–5
Homer *Iliad* 24
homophobia 467–8
Honneth, Axel 431, 434–5, 436
housing 225, 226–8, 368, 421–2
  segregation 535–44, 549, 550, 552
  Singapore 470–2
HSBC 399–400
Hubbard, Phil 466–8, 489–90
Hudson, Brian 53
human exceptionalism 441, 443
human–non-human relations 200, 203, 204, 408
human rights 575
humanism 169–70
Humboldt, Alexander von 25–6, 76, 131, 140–1, 148, 162
  Cosmos 43
  Essai sur la Geographie des Plantes 25
  Mount Chimborazo 25–6
Humboldt, Wilhelm von 74
Hume, David *A Treatise of Human Nature* 34
Huns 14–15, 17, 19
Huntington, Ellsworth 61, 62, 94, 96–7, 149–50
  Economic and Social Geography 96–7
Huntington, Samuel 294, 524, 527
Husserl, Edmund 182, 223–4
  Cartesian Mediations 223
hybrid geographers 191–2
hybridization 381–2
hydrology 182
hygiene 355
hypermobility 369–70

identities and sexuality 455–68, 472, 476–8, 479–80
idiographic approach 84, 136–7, 180
idiographic–nomothetic distinction 84, 137
Igor Pruitt public housing project 154
imagined communities 399
immigration and migration 336, 343, 366–7, 443
  gender 487, 498
  globalization 305–8
  segregation 535, 537–43, 550, 552–3
  world cities 315, 317, 326
imperial overstretch 50

imperialism 52–66, 90, 355, 454, 480, 504
  development 576–7
  globalization 302–3, 305
Import Substitution Industrialization (ISI) 580–1
impressionism 52–4
India 12, 15–17, 19, 36, 54, 94
  development 568
  globalization 284, 286–7, 292–3, 295, 304
  governance 342, 356
  mega-region 292
  world cities 315, 322, 332
Indian National Congress 356
Industrial Revolution 326, 362, 364, 577, 580
influence spheres 515–16, 518, 519
information overload 29
Ingold, Tim 184–5, 226–8, 230–1
  The Temporality of the Landscape 226–8
Innocent III, Pope 264
innovation 286–9, 291–5
Institute of British Geographers (IBG) 91, 98, 153, 501
instruments of consumption 213
instruments of production 213
International Bank for Reconstruction and Development (IBRD) 578
International Development Association (IDA) 581
International Geographical Congresses 57
International Geographical Union 92
International Monetary Fund (IMF) 303, 338
  development 567, 575, 578, 582
international relations 354–7
internationalism 173
Iraq 303, 509, 527
Irigaray, L 504–5
Isard, Walter 152–4
Isidore of Seville 23–9, 262
  Etymologies 23, 262
  T–O maps 23–5, 27
Islam 16, 307, 506–7
Italy 12, 32, 393–5, 537, 542
Ives, Charles 133

Jackson, JB 132, 209–11, 226, 229
  Landscape 210
Jackson, Peter 441–3
  Race and Racism 441
Jacobs, Jane 290–1, 326, 330, 331
  The Economy of Cities 291
James, Preston 115, 124, 130, 132

James, Preston and Jones, CF *American Geography* 131
Japan 52, 54, 285–6, 287, 288–9, 292–3
  mega-regions 288–9, 292
  world cities 314–15, 317, 321, 322, 332
Jencks, Charles 154
Jessop, Bob 172, 300, 338
Jews and Judaism 16, 18, 460, 461, 537, 542
John of Paris 264
Johnson's dictionary 38, 41
Johnson, President LB 580
Jones, Clarence F 131, 146–7, 150, 153–4
  Economic Geography 146
Jones, Emrys 100, 102
  Human Geography 100
Jones, Katherine 406–7
Jordanes 17
Justinian *Corpus Iuris Civilis* 264–5
Justus Perthes Geographic Institute 74

Kandiyoti, Denise 506–7
Kant, Immanuel 75–7, 79–81, 280
  landscape vs region 136, 138
  mobility 364, 366
  race 456, 458, 461, 462
  region to space 165, 167
  scale and networks 388, 396
Katz, Cindi 302, 508
Kelly, Philip 303, 306
Keltie, James Scott 58
Kendall, Henry 136
Kennan, George 526
Kennedy, President John F 580, 581
Keynes, John Maynard 152, 578
  The General Theory of Employment 152
keywords 164, 171–2, 245
  region to space 161–6, 170–3
Khaldun, Ibn 16–17, 20
  Muqaddimah 17
Khan, Kubilai 15, 18–19
Kimble, George 95, 136, 166
Kingsley, Mary 502
Kirk, William 153
Kissinger, Henry 526–7
Kloppenburg, Jack *First the Seed* 187
Kniffen, Fred 135, 139
Knopp, L 466, 468
Kooning, Willem de 133
Kuhn, Thomas 4
Kulturlandschaft 140
Kunstler, James 248
Kyoto Protocol 304

La Condamine, Charles de 34
labour theory 212–13
Lacan, Jacques 188
Lacoste, Yves 63
Lamarck, Jean Baptiste de 58, 80, 275
land-power 516, 519, 520–1
Landscape (journal) 132
landscape 83, 118–20, 138–41, 211–15, 221–31, 488
  Germany 77, 83
  learning 209–11
  memory and performance 229–30
  phenomenology 221–31
  region to space 164, 165
  scale and networks 387, 388, 389–90
  teaching 215–16
  vs region 5, 114–25, 130–42
Landschaft 77, 83, 138, 141, 165
Landschaftkunde 114, 116–17, 121, 130, 139–40
Lang, Fritz *Metropolis* 363
Lange, Dorothea 133, 253–4
language 12, 16, 430, 432, 442, 477
  mobility 374–5, 376, 379–80, 382
  place 252–3
  scale and networks 397–8, 400–1
  territory 271–2, 273–9, 280–1
Laslett, Peter *The World We Have Lost* 362
Latin America 393, 552, 561, 580–2
  geopolitics 513–15, 18, 520–1
Latour, Bruno 200, 201, 388, 408–9, 495–6
  mobility 378, 381, 382
  Pandora's Hope 457
  race 440–1, 443–4, 446–7, 457–8, 462–3
Lauren, Ralph 365
Law, Clara *Floating Life* 370
Le Corbusier 363–4
  Towards a New Architecture 363
Le Play, Fràdéric 85
Le Play Society 96
Leach, William 247, 254
League of Nations 355
Lee Hsien Loong, Prime Minister 469
Lefebvre, Henri 247–8, 252, 493–4, 496
Leibniz, Gottfried 42, 167
Leighly, John 114–15, 117–19, 139, 150
Leland, John 31–3, 37–8
Lewis, Meriwether 36
Lewis, Peirce 209–10, 211
Ley, D 421, 422
Li, T 342, 343

liberalism 353, 354, 356
light-based regional product (LBR) 289
Linneaus, C 446, 447
Lippard, Lucy 251
  The Lure of the Local 245
literature 134
Liu Yuxi 16
Livingstone, David (explorer) *Missionary Travels* 56
Livingstone, David 52, 55, 58, 61, 140, 116, 148
locale 235–6, 251, 256
location 235–7, 245, 251, 256, 284
Locke, John 40–1
logging 187, 189–90, 341, 343
Lorimer, Hayden 192, 228, 229
Lösch, August 167–8
Louis IX of France 18
Low, SM and Laurence-Zúñiga, D 246
Lowenthal, David 11, 125, 209, 215
Lucas, Robert 290–2
Lukermann, Fred 121, 123, 125
Lussault, Michael 1
Lyell, Charles *Principles of Geology* 34

Mackinder, Halford 43–4, 52–3, 56–8, 89, 95–6, 98–9
  "Geographical Pivot and History" 62
  geopolitics 513, 515
  nature 180
  "On the Scope and Methods of Geography" 98
  political geography 84
  practical use of geography 61–2, 63
MacKinnon, Danny 146, 157
MacLeish, Archibald *Land of the Free* 254
Macmillan, Harold 147
Magnus, Albertus 28
Majority World Development 559
Malaspina, Alejandro 36
Malcolm X 461
Malthus, Thomas 460, 578
  Essay on the Principle of Population 35
Mandeville, Sir John 11, 19
Mann, Michael 434
mappae mundi 25, 28
maps 23–5, 50–1, 54, 64
  Cook 36, 38
  Early Modern 38, 40–1
  Enlightenment 34–7
  Renaissance 29, 30–1
  T–O 23–6, 27, 28
  Ulm 23–6, 28

Marcellinus, Ammianus 13, 14–15
marketization 339
Markham, Sir Clements 93
Marsh, JP 82
Marshall, Alfred 290
  Principles of Economics 181
Marshall Plan 578
Marsilius of Padua 264
Marston, SA 301, 387
Marston, SA, Jones, John and Woodward, Keith 396–7, 406–7
Martonne, Emmanuel de 63
Marx, Karl 155, 169–70, 319, 340, 364
  A Contribution to the Critique of Political Economy 417
  capitalism 185–8
  class 415, 416–18, 419–23, 426–37
  development 562, 577
  landscape 212, 213
  nature 185–8, 190, 192
  race 455, 461, 462
Massagetai 14
Massey, Doreen 147, 302, 317, 391, 408
  class 427
  gender 508
  place 237–8, 241, 250, 251
  region to space 155–6, 169, 170
  Spatial Divisions of Labour 147
  World City 320
Massumi, Brian 374, 375
material role 240, 242
materiality/life 198–9
mathematical empiricism 33–7, 37–42
Mauro, Fra 28
McDowell, L 503, 506
McKibben, R 183–5
  Enough: Staying Human in an Engineered Age 183
  The End of Nature 183
McLuhan, Marshall 298, 301, 377
McNamara, Robert 564, 581
McWhorter, Ladelle 479, 483
  Racism and Sexual Oppression in Anglo-America 483
mechanical empiricism 40, 42
megacities 321–2, 326
mega-regions 284–6, 288–92, 321–2
Megasthenes *Indika* 12
Meinig, Don 209, 211
Mela, Pomponius 29
  De Situ Orbis 39
mercantilism 314–15

Mercator, Gerardus 30–2, 36, 37, 38, 40
  Atlas 30, 41
Merleau-Ponty, Maurice 221, 225–6, 229–30, 237
methodology 84
metrics 276–8, 280
Mexico 290, 306, 307, 508, 550
  development 566, 580, 584
  world cities 320, 322, 332
Michael, M 378, 380
Michigan Womyn's Music Festival (MichFest) 491–2
Midwestern School 114–15, 119, 124, 137
migration *see* immigration and migration
militarism 40, 303
Mill, Hugh Robert 56, 59, 61
Mill, JS *On Liberty* 353
Millennium Development Goals (MDGs) 567
Mitchell, Don 141, 378
Mitchell, T 349, 351, 355
mobility 3, 361–70, 373–83
  globalization 299, 305–8, 309
model of geopolitics 514
Mohanty, CT 504, 507
Molière *Le Bourgois Gentilhomme* 271
Monbiot, George 298, 299
Mongol Empire 18, 19
Montesquieu 20, 577
  Spirit of the Laws 35
More, Thomas *Utopia* 32, 38
more-than-human geography 197–8, 200, 201
Morgan, Robin 504
Morrill, Richard 153, 168
motel trespass admonishment 547–8, 550
multinational geographies 198, 199–200, 202, 203
Mumford, Lewis 132, 247
Münster, Sebastian 29–31, 35
  Cosmographia 29–31, 40, 41
Murchison, Roderick 56
music 133–4
Muslims and Islam 16, 307, 506–7

Nagar, Richa 307, 477, 508
Napoleon 36
Napoleonic wars 132
National Council for Geographical Education 91
National Geographic (magazine) 59, 93–4, 106
National Geographic Society 57, 91, 93

naturalism 119
nature 179–95, 197–204, 227, 231
   cultural construction 188–90
   meaning 183–5
   production 185–8
Nazis 77–8, 84, 135, 139, 150, 351
   geopolitics 513
   race 454
Nehru 357
neoliberalism 407, 410, 497
   class 426, 428–9, 431, 433
   development 564, 582, 583–4
   globalization 300, 303–4, 308
   governance 337–8, 341–3, 348–9, 354
   mobility 365, 367
   world cities 319, 320, 330
Nestor of Kent 18
networks 331–3, 407–9
   scale 387–401, 404–10
Newbigin, Marion 82, 99
Newton, Sir Isaac 33–7, 38–42, 166–7
   Principia 34
Nixon, President Richard 582
nomadism 14–17, 19–20, 364–5, 368, 375–6, 382
nomothetic approach 84, 136–7
Non-Aligned Movement 561
non-governmental organisations (NGOs) 307, 341, 370, 527
   international development 564, 567, 583
non-representational geography (NRG) 191–2
North American Free Trade Agreement (NAFTA) 302

Ockman, Joan 496–7
Odorica da Pordenone, Fra 18–19
   Description of the Land of the Infidel 18
OECD 172, 306, 567
Office of Strategic Services (OSS) 151–3
Ohmae, Kenichi 289, 298, 300
   The Borderless World 298
Olwig, KR 141, 172
Ong, Aihwa 306, 368
ontography 58
ontologies 299–302, 309, 432–4, 437, 457
OPEC 565
Ortelius, Abraham 30, 32, 40
Oswin, Natalie 476, 482
   gender 486, 490, 492, 497
Ottoman Empire 63
Oviedo 27
Oxfam 564

Pacific Plan (2006) 304
Park, Robert 81
Participatory Rural Development 581
Passarge, Siegfried 116, 122
patriarchal bargain 506–7
Paul the Deacon 17
Pausanias 31
Peace of Westphalia 265–6
Pearson, Mike 229
Peet, Richard 303, 420
Peloponnesian War 513–14, 515–17, 518–21
Penck, Albrecht 50–1
Penn, Mischa 121, 125
Persia 12–13, 16
Peschel, Oskar 76
phenomenology 221–31, 237
Philip the Fair, King 264
Philip II of Spain 29, 35, 40
Phillips, Richard 494, 496, 497
photography 133
physical geography 179–80, 182–3, 194–5
place 4, 170–1, 235–42, 245–57, 272–6
   globalization 246–8, 283, 298, 302
planning 80, 313–14, 319, 321–2, 325, 496–7
Plato 44, 251
Pletsch, Carl 560, 562, 569
Pliny the Elder 15, 29, 31
   Natural History 15, 28, 29, 32
pluralism 1–3, 201
politics and political geography 5–6, 84, 98, 351–4
   class 417, 422, 427–33, 435, 437
   effect of climate 35
   gender 503, 506, 507, 508–9
   globalization 295–6, 298, 300, 302
   governance 337–43, 348, 351–4, 356–7
   landscape vs region 122, 125
   mobility 375–8
   race 442
   region to space 147
   scale 388, 390, 392–5
   scale and networks 404, 409
   sexuality 466
   territory 262–7, 273–4, 275, 279–81
Polk, D 36
Pollock, Jackson 133
Polo, Marco 18–19, 20, 25, 27–8
   "Conversation about the World" 18–19
population 35, 186–7, 285
   globalization 284, 285, 287–9, 291, 293–5

Posidonius of Apamea 12, 14
positioning geography 54–61
positivism 6, 84, 164, 166–7, 169, 420
   France 79–82
   Germany 78
possibilism 79, 80, 82
post-phenomenology 230–1
post-structuralism 396–7, 466, 472
   class 422, 423
   gender 505, 507
   race 443, 444, 454–6, 458
poverty 567, 576–9, 581, 583
   segregation 535, 537, 539, 540, 542
Pratt, Geraldine 306
Prebisch–Singer thesis 580
precarity 433
Pred, Allan 156, 161, 168
pre-scientific regions 171
prison systems 303
privatization 339
problematization 342, 350, 375, 443
process philosophy 191
prospect 238–9
Prudham, Scott *Knock on Wood* 187
Prussia 54, 56, 74, 76, 78
Ptolemy 12, 27, 29–31, 38, 44
   Geography 23, 37
publics 320–2
Pytheas of Massalia 12

quarternary environmental change 182

Rabelais, François 265
race 4, 440–9, 453–63, 480–2, 577
   class 421, 422–3, 427, 432
   colonialism 54, 60, 64
   gender 504
   Germany 77, 78
   globalization 302, 305–8
   place 253–4
   segregation 535–43, 549, 552
   sexuality 476–8, 479–83
Rapid Rural Appraisals 581
Ratzel, Friedrich 44, 53, 59, 75–7, 84, 140
   anthropogeography 76, 79, 94, 99
   French school 79, 72
   race 454, 459
   territory 271
Reagan, President Ronald 343
Reclus, Emlisée 44, 55, 85
Rectangular Survey 36
refugees 307

region 121–2, 133–4
   to space 146–57, 161–73
   vs landscape 5, 114–25, 130–42
regional geography 82–3, 84, 94–7, 101, 104
Regional Studies Association (RSA) 153–4, 155
relational space 171
Relph, Edward 236, 248, 250
Renaissance 27–33, 34
research 92, 93, 171–2
reterritorialization 274
Rex, John 421
Ricardo, David 288
Richardson, Diane 497
Richthofen, Ferdinand von 76, 140
Rio Earth Summit 567
Ritter, Carl 43, 76, 79, 139, 140–1, 180
   Culturlandschaft 140
   Die Erdkunde 140, 148
   region to space 148–9, 162
Robbe-Grillet, Alain 231
Robinson, Jenny 319–20, 330, 569, 570
Romanillos, JL 231
Romans 12, 14, 16, 17, 24
Romanticism 131, 132
Roosevelt, President Franklin 62
Rorty, Richard 193
Rostow, Walt William 579–80
Rothko, Mark 133
Rowell, Theresa 201
Royal Geographical Society (RGS) 50, 90–3, 98, 105, 502
   Hints to Travellers 60, 90
   positional geography 56–8, 60–1
   practical use of geography 63–4
Russia 54, 62, 135
Russell, Richard 139
Rustichello da Pisa 19
Rutherford, Ernest 181

Sack, Robert 241, 246, 250, 274
Said, Edward 52, 55, 252, 442, 567
   Orientalism 442
Saldanha, Arun 442, 443, 444
Sander, Gehrard 279
Sassen, Saskia 301, 328, 330, 341
Sauer, Carl 4, 44, 75, 94, 97, 188, 190
   "Foreword to Historical Geography" 139
   landscape 83, 114–25, 132, 134–41, 210–11, 222, 226
   "The Morphology of Landscape" 118–19, 124, 139

Saunders, Peter 421
Saussure, Ferdinand de 279, 442, 443
Saxenian, AnnaLee 287
Sayer, A 435–6, 457
scale 35, 83, 252, 398–9, 405–7
   Early Modern 26, 37–8, 44
   gender 487, 501, 507–9
   globalization 3, 301
   governance 350, 354–7
   hierarchy 388, 389–90, 395–9, 401, 407
   networks 387–401, 404–10
   non-correspondence 392
   ordering human landscape 389–90
   politics 390, 392–5
   relational 388, 395–8
   territory 273, 277, 278
scale debates 407
scale jumping 393
Schaefer, Fred 136–8
Schlúter, Otto 77, 83, 116, 139, 140
   Kulturlndschaft 139
Schmitt, Carl 348, 350, 351–2
Schonberg, Arnold 134
Schrag, Peter *Out of Place in America* 247
Scott, Allen 154, 327–8
Scott, Sir Walter *The Antiquary* 37
Scythians 13, 14, 15, 19
scientific discovery 287–8, 289
Seamon, David 229, 236, 239
sea-power 516, 519, 520–1
Seers, Dudley 564
segregation 458, 534–44, 547–54
Sekula, Allan 316
Self, Peter 153–4
self-conduct 354–7
self-governance 339–40
semiotics 379–80, 382
Sellars, Roy Wood 453, 456–8, 462
   Critical Realism 456
Semple, Ellen Churchill 75, 82, 94, 149, 181
   colonization 58, 62
sense of place 235–6, 251, 256
Serres, Michael 380–1
sexuality 305, 316, 432, 465–73, 475–83
   gender 486–99, 504–6
   heterosexual matrix 478–80
   segregation 537, 549
   Singapore 469–72
Shadwell, Thomas *The Virtuoso* 37
Shahn, Ben 133
Shakespeare, William 260–2
   Henry VI 260
   King Lear 245, 247, 260–1

shatterbelts 514–15, 517–18, 519–21
Shevardnadze, Foreign Minister 582
Sima Qian 1–16, 20
Simmel, Georg 167, 364
Singapore 469–72
Singapore Improvement Trust (SIT) 471
slavery 56, 430, 443, 447, 461
Sloterdijk, Peter 266, 281
Smith, Adam 430, 577, 579
Smith, J Russell 149–50
   Industrial and Commercial Geography 149
Smith, Neil 58, 115–16, 121, 138, 185–7, 300
   class 421, 426
   scale and networks 393, 395, 406
   The Assassination of Landscape 138
   Uneven Development 185–6, 406
Snow, CP 182
social construction 251, 256
social mix 540–1, 543
social reproduction 213–14, 215
social sciences 103, 179, 180–2, 201, 374
   class 416, 435
   landscape vs region 117, 120
   race 440, 442, 443, 454–5, 457
   region to space 151–2
Société de Géographie de Paris 57
society–nature dualism 184, 191–2, 194
Soja, Edward 246, 250
Solnit, Rebecca 247, 376
Soper, Kate 185
South Africa 102, 303, 458, 565, 568, 584
South America *see* Latin America
space 154, 161–73, 398–9
   gender 487–99, 501–3, 506, 508–9
   geopolitics 523–6, 528
   place 251–2, 254–5
   race 456–7
   region and social practice 163–4, 169–71, 173
   segregation 534–8, 547–53
   sexuality 475–6
   territory 271–81
Spanish–American War (1898) 59
spatial analysis 163–4, 166–9
spatial contagion 514, 516–17, 519
spatial socialization 169
Spinoza 433
state 349–51, 355, 357
   governmentality 340–4, 347–51
state rescaling 393–5

Steedman, Carolyn 430
Steinbeck, John *The Grapes of Wrath* 134
Stengers, Isabelle 200, 201–2
Stewart, Martha 365
Stoker, G 349
Stone, Kirk 151
Strabo of Pontus 12–15, 20, 31, 40, 162, 459
   Geography 39
Structural Adjustment Programs (SAPs) 582
structure–agency dualism 105, 170, 171, 421
Swift, Jonathan 38
Swyngedouw, Erik 301, 350, 395, 406
systematic geography 84, 95, 100, 163–4, 166–9

Tacitus 13, 14, 16, 19–20
Taylor, Griffith 101
   Geography in the 20th Century 130
Taylor, Peter 251, 395, 406
   world cities 326, 328, 330, 331, 333
Tennyson, Alfred Lord *Ulysses* 93
territorialization 240, 242, 302
territory 171, 260–7, 271–81
terrorism 303, 307–8, 524, 528, 550, 568
   World Trade towers 509, 583
Thatcher, Margaret 343
Third World 6, 303, 320, 470, 504
   Development 559–62, 569, 570, 579
Thomas Aquinas 263
Thomas, William *Man's Role in Changing the Face of the Earth* 182
Thomson, Vigil 133
Thornhill, R and Palmer, C *A Natural History of Rape* 184
Thrift, Nigel 141, 156, 170, 192, 197, 301
   class 437
   mobility 374, 375, 377, 378
   Non-representational theory 192
time 398–9
Tocqueville, Alexis de 247
Tomlinson, Sally 421
topography 37–8, 277–8, 299, 302–5, 309
topology 167, 171, 277–8
tourism 306
TPSN Framework 172
transgendered persons 466, 495
transnationalism 367
Troll, Carl 135
tropical geography 560, 569–71
Truman, President Harry S 562–3, 578–9

Tschumi, Bernard *The Manhattan Transfer* 365
Tuan, Yi-Fu 125, 236–7, 246, 250, 251–2
   Space and Place 251

Ullman, Edward 103, 153
United Arab Emirates 366
United Kingdom (UK) 5, 6–7, 14, 36, 90–2, 94–9, 102–4
   chorography 31, 32
   class 430
   colonialization 36, 50–2, 54, 64–5, 90
   French school 81, 83
   globalization 286, 307
   governance 336, 339, 343, 348
   international development 563, 568–9, 577–9
   landscape phenomenology 230
   landscape vs region 130, 136
   migration 336, 343, 366
   nature 180–1
   non-representational geography 192
   political geography 84
   positioning geography 54, 56, 58, 60
   practical use of geography 61, 63
   race 443
   region to space 149, 153–4, 156, 165–6, 169–70
   regional geography 83
   scale and networks 390–1, 392
   segregation 553
   universities 5, 92, 95–6, 98, 102–4, 348
   world cities 314, 317–19, 326, 328–9, 332
United Nations 321–2, 367, 463, 526
   development 561, 563, 565, 578, 580
United States of America (USA) 5–6, 90–2, 95, 97, 100–2, 106
   class 415, 420, 423
   colonization 52, 54, 57, 64–5
   development 561, 563, 568, 579–83
   environmental determinism 82
   French school 82, 83–4
   geopolitics 526–7, 529–30
   Germany 81, 82, 83
   globalization 246–8, 285–90, 293, 295, 300, 302–3, 306–8
   governance 339, 349, 350
   landscape 83–4, 209–10
   landscape vs region 114–25, 130–6, 139
   mega-region 288, 289, 290
   mobility 364–6, 369
   nature 180–1

United States of America (USA) 5–6, 90–2, 95, 97, 100–2, 106 (*cont'd*)
   place 246–8, 252–5
   positioning geography 54, 57, 58, 59
   practical use of geography 61–3
   race 455, 462
   region to space 149–55, 165–7, 169, 172–3
   regional geography 83
   scale and networks 392, 399
   segregation 535, 537–9, 541–3, 547–52
   sexuality 475–6, 480–3
   territory 273
   universities 5, 92, 95, 102–3, 131–2, 134, 137, 139, 152–3
   world cities 314–18, 320, 322, 326, 329, 332
universities 5–6, 11, 40–1, 44, 52, 92–8, 101–6, 181
   France 78–9
   Germany 74–6, 78, 81
   positioning geography 54–9
   practical use of geography 63
   UK 5, 92, 95–6, 98, 102–4, 348
   USA 5, 92, 95, 102–3, 131–2, 134, 137, 139, 152–3
Up in the Air (film) 361–2, 369, 370
urbanization 280, 339
   class 420, 421, 427–30
   globalization 284, 304, 305, 306
   world cities 313, 315, 317, 319–22, 325–7, 330
Urry, John 374, 377
   Sociology Beyond Societies 373

Valkenburg, S van *Economics and Social Geography* 96–7
Varenius, Barnhard *Geographia Generalis* 38
Vidal de la Blache, Paul 44, 53, 59, 61–3, 75, 78–84, 99
   France de L'Est 363
   landscape vs region 119, 130, 139
   mobility 362–4
   nature 181
   regional geography 94–5
   scale and networks 399
   territory 275
   The Personality of France 149
vitalism 42–4
Vogel, Lisa 491

Wacquant, Loic 434
Walker, Richard 214, 420
Wallerstein, I 326, 328
Walters, W 338, 352, 354
Washington Consensus 582
water market 187
Weber, Max 266, 364, 416, 418–19
   class 415, 416, 418–23, 436
whales 547–8, 550
Whatmore, Sarah 191–2, 201–2, 379, 408
   Hybrid Geographies 191
Whitehead, AN 44, 199
Whittlesey, Derwent 117, 131–2, 135, 139, 150
   "Sequent Occupance" 117
   "The Regional Concept and the Regional Method" 131
William of Ockham 264
William of Rubruck, Brother 18, 28
Williams, FE *Economic and Social Geography* 96–7
Williams, Raymond 161, 163, 184–5, 187, 430
   culture 245–6
   Keywords 161, 184
   landscape 212, 215
   mobility 378
Wilson, President Woodrow 63, 90
Wimmer, Joseph *Historische Landschaftkunde* 140
Winfrey, Oprah 461
Wittgenstein, Ludwig 148
Wolf, Janet 375–6
Women in Geography Study Group (WGSG) 501–2
Wood, Grant 133
Woolridge, SW and East, WG 130
   The Spirit and Purpose of Geography 96, 97, 130
World Bank 303, 338, 342
   Development 563–4, 567–8, 576, 581, 583
world cities 313–22, 325–33
   alpha level 332
World System 581
World Trade Organization (WTO) 303, 305, 582
   governance 338, 341, 342
World War I 55, 63, 64, 90, 560–1
   Germany 77, 78, 80, 82
World War II 102, 179, 181, 255–6, 278, 300, 524
   Development 559–62, 576, 578–81
   Germany 77, 78, 84
   landscape vs region 132–3, 135, 137, 139
   region to space 151–2, 166, 169, 171

Wright, EO 427, 428, 434
Wright, Frank Lloyd 133
Wylie, John 192, 222

Xiongnu 15
Xuanzang 16

Young, Iris 435
Yugoslavia 279

Zeisel, John 246
Zhonghang Yue 15–16
zone of peace 19, 520